Crime, Justice, & Social Control

First Edition

Edited by Christine Curtis and Stuart Henry
San Diego State University

Bassim Hamadeh, CEO and Publisher
Christopher Foster, General Vice President
Michael Simpson, Vice President of Acquisitions
Jessica Knott, Managing Editor
Kevin Fahey, Cognella Marketing Manager
Jess Busch, Senior Graphic Designer
Seidy Cruz, Acquisitions Editor
Sarah Wheeler, Senior Project Editor
Stephanie Sandler, Licensing Associate

First published in the United States of America in 2013 by Cognella, Inc.

Trademark Notice: Product or corporate names may be trademarks or registered trademarks, and are used only for identification and explanation without intent to infringe.

Printed in the United States of America

ISBN: 978-1-62131-532-2 (pbk)/ 978-1-62131-533-9 (br)

www.cognella.com   800-200-3908

CONTENTS

PART III: READINGS ON POLICING AND INVESTIGATIONS

PART IV: READINGS ON CORRECTIONAL POLICIES AND ISSUES

PART V: READINGS ON JUVENILE JUSTICE

PREFACE

The focus of this text is crime, justice, and social control. Our purpose is to demonstrate that law and the criminal justice system are set in a wider context of social control. Thus, rather than the formal system of law, courts, and police being the only ways members of society are held together in a social order, we show that there is a plurality of systems that control our behavior.

This idea of a plurality of control systems is often taken for granted because we do not see the more subtle ways that groups and organizations police us, channel us, and even punish or correct our actions in everyday relationships. In fact, most social control comes through non-state systems such as the informal norms and sanctions of social groups and institutions like family, schools, and the church, but also through the formal rules and private justice systems of organizations and social institutions such as medicine, insurance companies, and workplaces. We deviate and violate the norms, rules, and laws in a variety of social settings and situations, and the system or subsystem of society that we are a part of takes action to curb our untoward behavior.

This broader view of informal and non-state systems of social control provides students with the context needed to understand how criminal justice fits with a comprehensive theory of social control. This is important because, not only is the vast scope of social control made clear, but also we can see better how informal mechanisms operate in formal criminal justice settings such as police discretion and plea bargaining. Rather than aberrations, these are integral mechanisms of social control that reflect the ways control is exercised in the wider society.

This book, therefore, starts with an introductory overview that explores the origins and different types of social control through sections on informal social control and medical social control, before focusing in more depth on formal social control. It reviews the social context and origins of law, models of the courts and sentencing, the system of law enforcement, and the philosophies behind the system of corrections. It concludes by looking at the importance of criminal justice policy issues and alternatives in each area of the justice system.

Following the introductory overview we include a selection of articles that provide a sociological analysis of criminal justice and social control, and articles focused more specifically on the different areas of the formal system discussed in the introduction. The articles raise key questions being discussed by criminal justice academics, policy makers, and elected officials today. The articles allow students to understand the complexity and range of challenges faced by all those involved in the criminal justice process, give them an opportunity to think critically about the alternatives, and formulate their views about social control, taking into consideration research and policy analyses presented by experts in the field.

Christine Curtis and Stuart Henry,
September 30, 2012

INTRODUCTION

What Is Social Control?

> All social groups make rules and attempt, at some times under some circumstances, to enforce them. Social rules define situations and the kinds of behavior appropriate to them, specifying some actions as "right" and forbidding others as "wrong". When a rule is enforced, the person who is supposed to have broken it may be seen as a special kind of person, one who cannot be trusted to live by the rules agreed upon by the group. He is regarded as an *outsider*.
>
> But the person who is thus labeled an outsider may have a different view of the matter. He may not accept the rule by which he is being judged and may not regard those who judge him as either competent or legitimately entitled to do so. Hence a second meaning of the term emerges: the rule breaker may feel his judges are *outsiders*. (Becker 1963: 1–2)

Sociologist Howard Becker (1963) explains that rules may be formal, codified as laws, or informal based on social norms, customs, or traditions. In effect, rules are cultural imperatives for how people should act. Becker observes that all rules are founded on some level of consensus within a social group. Laws are a special kind of rule, ones that are sanctioned by the state through a specific governmental process of legislation and explicitly written, with consequences specified for their violation. Social norms are standards expected by social groups but are not explicitly written and are not formulated by persons approved by governments to establish them.

For the most part, in criminal justice we are concerned with enforcement of laws and the sanctions imposed by the state, which we will see are called formal social control. But the need for laws is partially based on the failure of other, more informal mechanisms of social control. Donald Black (1976) posits that the amount of law and formal justice in a society depends on the amount of informal social control and its effectiveness, suggesting that when informal control mechanisms break down or become ineffective, more formal law is needed (see also, Friedman 1975; Schwartz, 1954). Black proposes that "societies with higher degrees of stratification have more social control. Law and social control also vary directly with culture: simpler societies have less law and social control than more differentiated societies" (Deflem, 2007). Black (1976) claims that the quantity of law in any society is greatest where the relational distance between persons is great. Where people enjoy intimacy or close relationships, the amount of law will be relatively low. He says that the greater the relational distance between persons, the more likely they are to use law to settle the dispute.

Austin Turk (1972) used the term "legalization" to describe the process through which normative expectations about deviant behavior are transformed into official laws for the purpose of identification, detection, and control. This has also been called "criminalization." A good example is smoking, which was once seen as medicinal, then seen as a social stimulant, and in recent years has been banned in certain areas and subject to fines and other penalties. Conversely, when behavior is seen as less harmful, the crime is "decriminalized," with penalties being reduced or removed, as has happened with marijuana possession for use in some cities, such as Ann Arbor, Michigan, and some states, such as California and Colorado. In some cities, such as Oakland and Denver, enforcement of marijuana possession laws has been designated a low priority, with police using their discretion as to whether a case should be prosecuted. So it is important to understand the continuum of social control and how behavior can move from being subject merely to informal controls, and then to formal social control, and vice versa.

DEFINING SOCIAL CONTROL

Social control, in its broadest sense, is a means to encourage, persuade, or coerce individuals to conform to societal norms, rules, and laws. In his classic 1901 book *Social Control*, Edward A. Ross saw social control as being a way to mold an individual's desires and feelings to suit the needs of the group. He said this was partly achieved though "social influence" and partly through "social control," which he described as the purposeful and conscious ascendancy of the group over the aims and acts of the individual. Ross defined social control

as: "Social domination which is intended and which fulfills a function in the life of a society" (Ross, 1901, p. viii). Ross saw social control being exercised both formally by the instruments of government on behalf of society, and informally by spontaneous agencies that serve social interests (Ross, 1901). He saw society as a living organism and social control as one of the ways it maintains itself as alive and well.

In discussing the grounds for social control, Ross was the first to distinguish between internal controls exercised within the individual, which can produce a temporary natural order, and external controls producing an artificial social order. The social control mechanisms of this externally produced social order are designed to unremittingly socialize each new generation through disciplinary mechanisms embodied in the engines of social control operated by the state, and supplemented by belief (Hertzler, 1951: 604). Although Ross identified 33 different types of social control, he argued that belief was far more influential than more formal mechanisms. Yet he also considered law to be: "The most specialized and highly furnished engine of social control employed by society" (Ross, 1922: 106).

This same theme of the broad span and generalized reach of social control is found in later writing. For example, Joseph S. Roucek, in *Social Control* (1947: 3), defines it as: "Those processes, planned or unplanned, by which individuals are taught, persuaded to conform to the usages and life values of groups." Sociologist George C. Homans, in *The Human Group* (1950: 291), defined social control as: "the process by which, if a man departs from his existing degree of obedience to a norm, his behavior is brought back toward that degree or would be brought back if he did depart."

Black (1983) provided a good illustration of the broad scope of social control, which he says involves any process by which people respond to what they see as deviant behavior. This includes:

> such diverse phenomena as a frown or a scowl, a scolding or a reprimand, an expulsion from an organization, an arrest or lawsuit, a prison sentence, commitment to a mental hospital, a riot, or a military reprisal.

But this concept entails no assumptions or implications concerning the impact of social control upon conformity, social order, or anything else, nor does it address the subjective meanings of social control for those who exercise or experience it (Black, 1983: 39).

However, some have criticized this broad brush approach to the concept. For example, Stanley Cohen, (1985) in *Visions of Social Control*, describes social control as a "Mickey Mouse" concept used to include all social processes, ranging from infant socialization to public education and all social policies, whether called health, education, or welfare. His more focused definition of social control is: "all organized responses to crime, delinquency and allied forms of deviance—whether sponsored directly by the state or by institutions such as social work and psychiatry and whether designated as treatment, prevention, punishment or whatever" (Cohen, 1985: 102).

According to sociologist James J. Chriss, social control since the 1920s has been the "general concept for describing all manner of activities involving the coordination, integration, regulation or adjustment of individuals or groups to some ideal standard of conduct … synonymous with regulation" (2007: 16). He characterizes social control into three categories: informal, medical, and formal or legal control.

- Informal: Influencing interpersonal relationships;
- Medical: Changing human behavior using medicine, psychology, and psychiatry;
- Formal/Legal: Enforcing laws and punishing offenders.

Crime as Social Control

Interestingly, in "Crime as Social Control," Black (1983) argued that many of the behaviors we classify as crime are similar to the behavior of "self-help" conflict management, in which people act to control or punish others in an informal attempt to bring about "justice" or to correct what they see as a wrong. For example, when a Pakistani father kills his daughter for dishonoring the family by committing adultery, he is exercising social control. When a gang member shoots a rival gang member, it can be for disrespect, or to serve justice for a previous gang murder. When an abused spouse kills her husband, it can be to control or punish him for abuse. When a bullied kid shoots his fellow students, it can be to correct the injustice. So crime itself can be an illegitimate attempt at self-help social control, just as social control is an informal or formal attempt to control crime and deviance.

TYPES OF SOCIAL CONTROL

Systems of social control can be considered to operate along multiple dimensions. Two dimensions seem to be particularly germane. First, we have whether the system of social control is state run (public, as in formal criminal justice), or private, or a non-state system of social control (Henry, 1983). Stuart Henry (1983; 1987) argues that such "non-state systems of social control should be termed 'Private Justice,'" and suggested that they include the practices of such institutions as the disciplinary bodies, boards, and councils of industrial and commercial organizations, professional and trade associations and unions, to the peer sanctioning of relatively autonomous voluntary associations, like self-help and mutual aid groups. "Private Justice comprises those institutions of social control that maintain the normative order of institutions" (Henry, 1987: 89). From this perspective, social control denotes that all interaction is subject to a degree of control by others who are agents of the group, organization, community, and society, and it is social in that it is limited by these agents' use of sanctions, socialization, and the manipulation of symbols (adapted from K.H. Wolf, 1964: 650).

A second dimension of social control concerns whether the system is formal—as in organized, systematic, and written down—or alternatively, whether it is informal, unorganized, and spontaneous (Gurvitch, 1947). Gurvitch draws on Eugene Ehrlich's (1913) idea of "living law," which recognizes that there are multiple forms of "law" and that most are not part of the formal legal system. In order to comprehend the relationship between formal and informal law,

Gurvitch developed a framework for conceiving of forms of law as existing in two planes. On one plane are the range of different types of law based on the level of organizational complexity and scale on which they operate. Adapting Gurvitch, we can consider a vertical continuum ranging from the individual to group to societal to global, with a variety of intermediate levels, including community, organization, and in between. Within any one type or level of social structure, there are many different subtypes of organization and many subtypes of groups, each with its own kind of law. On a horizontal plane, and existing for each type of law at each level of organization, is the degree of formality, ranging from formal to informal.[1] For Gurvitch (1947), the formal is characterized by being organized, written, fixed, and planned in advance, whereas the informal is unorganized, flexible, spontaneous, and intuitive.

This schema shows that informal law is not the exclusive control mechanism of the group, but exists in a greater or lesser amount in any kind of law. Conversely, formal law is not the exclusive mechanism of the state or formal organization. Even characteristically formal systems of social control, such as criminal justice, have aspects that are informal. Policing is highly formalized, but police discretion involves informal negotiation; courts and trials are highly rule-governed and procedurally formal, yet plea bargaining and informal negotiations are how 95 percent of cases are settled. The reality is that both formal and informal systems of social control work together in any system—even in private systems, such as disciplinary justice in universities or corporations (Henry, 1983; 1994).

While their level of organizational development typically precludes small groups having highly formal law, they do develop a rudimentary formal law. This web of what Leopold Pospisil (1971) called "legal pluralism" may exist in harmony, symbiosis, and mutual reinforcement or in conflict, reinforcing or undermining the informal law of other subsystems and even the formal law of the state.

Table 1 is a synthesis based on typologies of systems of social control derived from Ellickson (1991: 131), Henry (2001: 8690), and Kokswijk (2010). The schema shows the level of social organization, from individual (micro) through organizational (meso) to societal/global (macro) in a vertical plane, but it also acknowledges the insights of Gurvitch, as it includes both the formal and the informal for each organizational level of social control.

The characterization of social control presented in Table 1 suggests that there are both informal and formal mechanisms of control both at the meso- and macro-levels. Criminal justice is predominantly a public formal system of social control operating at the macro-level, but with an informal underbelly that permeates through to the meso- and micro-levels. The following sections describe the continuum of social control, based on Chriss's (2007) three-part model that includes informal (predominant at the micro-meso-level), medical (predominant at the meso-level) and formal/legal social control (predominantly at the macro-global level), to provide more detail on each component.

INFORMAL SOCIAL CONTROL

Chriss (2007) describes the more traditional view of informal social control as the mechanisms and practices of everyday life that encourage us to follow the rules and traditions set forth by family, social groups, or the larger society. Sociologists use the term "socialization" to describe the process by which we learn the rules, norms, and expectations of the world around us. Socialization is our first introduction to social control. If you think about your social networks today, you can identify many ways in which your behavior is influenced by others. Your mother may send you an article on the dangers of smoking, your friend may advise you on how to dress for a party so you will fit in, or your employer may tell you that you shouldn't make personal calls at work. Consider college student Chuck Vincent, who was subject to social control from his peers for not drinking enough while out partying.

---

1 Gurvitch actually had different types of law as created by the social association along a horizontal plane and different levels of formality on a vertical plane, but for our purposes this is not important.

Table 1. Systems of Social Control

Control Agent	Norm/Rule/Law	Sanction/Response	System Type	
			Formal	Informal
Micro-level				
Rule violator/deviant (individual first party)	Personal ethics & values	Self-restraint		Self-control
Victim/person violated (individual second party)	Contracts/informal agreements	Individual self-help (can be punitive or nonpunitive)		Victim-enforced control
Meso-level				
Group social context/environment (third-party control)	Social norms	Group sanctions, shaming, exclusion		Informal social control; community justice
Collective victim (third-party control)	Conflict norms	Group self-help sanctions (collective aggression, crime as self-help, negotiation, settlement-directed talking)		Communal self-help; justice as social control
Organization/Communal (third-party control)	Organizational rules	Organizational discipline, sanctions	Private justice system: Organizational control/ professional association	Informal organizational controls
Organizational/Communal victim (third-party control)	Conflict norms	Professional standards/ Competitive shaming	Professional association guidelines	Organizational counter control/ public pressure
Macro-level				
Government/State (third-party control)	Law (state, statutory, common law)	State enforcement/ sanctions	Formal legal system	Informal discretion/ plea bargaining
Global/International (third-party control)	Treaty/International law	Cooperative enforcement	Formal legal system	Noncompliant resistance

When certain drinking norms are enforced it is not easy to resist them. For instance, it is not acceptable to fall behind in drinking. If you do so comments are received like: "Come on man. You are two shots behind. You've got some catching up to do." At this point everyone gets behind the "up man" and the "behind man" has to slam the two shots in order to stay even. If he doesn't catch up the person is reminded that he's "a lightweight" (Vincent, 1999: 98).

In some instances, the rules are set forth for you, such as policies and procedures guidelines at work. But in many cases, the norms, or social rules, are shared through interaction with others and are not as clearly defined. You may only find out that you violated a "rule" when you see the reaction of your friends or family. In the classroom, you have learned certain behaviors based on observation of others or instruction by teachers over the years. For example, many instructors would prefer that you raise your hand before speaking in class. But the rules are not the same in every classroom and in some classes, rules are more vigorously enforced.

Rules can be enforced for a variety of different forms of deviance. Most commonly, when we think of social control, we think of *behavior* that is deviant or offensive. However, social control can also be exercised over *physical appearance* (too obese, thin, pierced, tattooed, etc.), *ideas* (too extreme, illogical, racist, fundamentalist, eccentric, etc.) and even **lifestyle** (gay, vegan, loner). As a social actor in all these settings, the individual needs to understand the norms and values of each social group. Norms are rules for behavior or a guide for conduct (Chriss, 2007).

+ Norms need not be explicit or codified into polices or laws;
+ Many norms are passed on informally through socialization.

An overriding question with all types of social control, including socialization, is who determines what is normal? Who defines the norms of society? Who defines the norms of a group? Sociologist Howard Becker called those who mobilize others and whip up support to ban behavior "moral entrepreneurs."

So it is important to realize that the exercise of social control involves a set of norms agreed on—albeit often loosely—by a group, community, or society. Those who determine the norms are referred to as an "audience" that is made up of group members who engage in a three-step process. The audience (1) identifies behavior (appearance, ideas, or lifestyle) that is different from the group norm; (2) judges the difference to be significant; and (3) judges the behavior to be negative (Henry, 2009). If all three of these elements occur, then the audience may act to exercise social control over the individual social "actor" or over the group of actors exhibiting the deviant behavior.

It is worth noting that difference of ideas, style, or food preference is respected as a right and is "seen to contribute to the vitality and creativity of modern society." In contrast, what audiences define as deviance is "a culturally unacceptable level of difference" that is subject to suspicion, surveillance regulation, sanction, or penalty by society's social control agencies because it is seen as posing a "threat to the social fabric" (Sumner, 2006: 126).

As mentioned previously, the criminal justice system has both formal and informal control mechanisms. In the juvenile justice system, for example, young offenders were often treated informally for the first offense. Police departments in the 1970s developed diversion programs in lieu of referral to probation, in which the youth could write an essay, provide community service, or in some other way learn from their mistakes. The hope was that the program would avoid labeling the juveniles as delinquents and avoid escalation into more serious offenses. One could view these efforts as a form of socialization, similar to what occurs within families or in schools.

MEDICAL SOCIAL CONTROL

Medicine is becoming a major institution of social control, nudging aside, if not incorporating, the more traditional institutions of religion and law. It is becoming the new repository of truth; the place where absolute and often final judgments are made by supposedly morally neutral, objective experts in the name of health. And these judgments are made, not in the name of virtue or legitimacy, but in the name of health. Moreover, this is not occurring through the political power physicians hold or can influence, but is largely an insidious and often undramatic phenomenon accomplished by "medicalizing" much of daily living, by making medicine and the labels "healthy" and "ill" relevant to an ever increasing part of human existence. (Zola, 1972: 487)

Samuel Cartwright first coined the term "medicalization" in 1851 to describe the foundation for medical social control. According to Cartwright, medicalization is the process by which personal and social problems are redefined as psychiatric and medical problems and the ways "medicine functions ... to secure adherence to social norms—specifically, by using medical means to minimize eliminate or normalize, deviant behavior" (Cartwright, 1851, cited by Chriss, 2007: 64). More recently, Peter Conrad and Joseph Schneider (1992: 242) defined medical social control as "a variant of medical intervention that seeks to eliminate, modify, isolate, or regulate behavior defined as deviant with medical means, in the name of health." The corresponding medical social control mechanisms include medication, psychoanalysis, and treatment.

Psychiatry and treatment at the individual level promote pro-social adjustment, and public health operates at the group or societal level to prevent disease, prolong life, and promote health: "in modern or postmodern society, there are increasing numbers of legal, administrative or quasi-legal regulations pertaining to the reduction of accident, injury and death, but also an ever-expanding array of 'risky' behaviors, including gambling, aggression and violence, drug use, sexual promiscuity, stalking, using the Internet, watching television, and so forth ... the discourse of 'addiction' has attached itself to these and many other social activities" (Chriss, 2007: 72).

The case of hyperactivity serves as a good illustration. In a previous generation, aggressive behavior by young boys might have been described as "naughty," having a lot of "pizzazz," or overactive, which might have resulted in a variety of sanctions by parents; it would not have been diagnosed as a medical condition. However, beginning in the 1970s, children seen by their parents and teachers (primary social control agents) as overly aggressive were diagnosed as "hyperactive" by pediatricians, psychologists, and psychiatrists, and prescribed drugs (Ritalin in particular) to control their behavior. Take the case of Bud Bennett, whose mother describes him as "hyperactive":

> We'd go to the grocery store and I was afraid to turn my back for a second. If I did I was afraid he would start pulling everything off the shelves. It made me feel crazy (Bennett, 1990: 103).

From attempting to deal with the issue within the family and with teachers, the level of social control escalated to medical and drug intervention. Bud's sister Debbie explains:

> Bud's first grade teacher referred mom to a family therapist ... who specializes in hyperactivity ... the therapist had told her that Bud's learning disability is caused by "a lack of chemicals in the brain that helps him

retain information and this same deficiency is associated with "hyperactivity." ... When Dr. Marsden prescribed Ritalin to Bud he became a new person ..."The Ritalin helped Bud's word retrieval. It also helped him screen out other activity so as to increase his attention span." The use of Ritalin made great differences ... the calming effect of Ritalin has allowed Bud to better deal with these situations. In observing Bud recently I have noticed a change in his behavior in situations which used to produce conflict and aggression. (Bennett, 1990: 104–106)

The change in behavior with the administration of the drug Ritalin was perceived not only to have been a necessary intervention, but one that was valued by the family, as his sister attests, though she is not certain whether the drug was the cause. Importantly, the medicalization of the behavior problems helps to take away the moral culpability of both Bud and his parents:

> Although Bud's hyperactivity goes virtually unnoticed now ... he will continue to be labeled hyperactive. He will be labeled, not least because our parents may fear their own labeling as inadequate parents. Because hyperactivity is considered a medical disorder, our parents are not condemned but given sympathy. The label is comforting for us all. (Bennett, 1990: 107)

From the medical social control perspective, it is important to understand how deviant childhood behavior resulted in the acceptance by teachers, therapist, family members, friends, and even Bud himself that he has a biologically determined mental illness called "hyperactivity." This is confirmed by all parties and supported by the fact that administered drugs have suppressed the disruptive behavior and is even acknowledged by the child himself who stated, "he can't help it." A critical issue is the way the parties come together to arrive at a common definition and how this version of reality that treats his behavior as mental illness allows medical social control to be imposed on the child, such that science takes over from moral judgment. Indeed, the characteristic of medical social control is that it renders deviant behavior a nonmoral issue, and in doing so removes responsibility from those subject to the label.

The behaviors that are considered "illnesses," or psychiatric conditions, vary over time. Chriss (2007) notes that homosexuality has been characterized as follows in the American Psychiatric Association's *Diagnostic and Statistical Manual of Mental Disorders* (*DSM*), first as sexual deviance, then as mental illness, then subsequently dropped from the *DSM* altogether.

A concern with the medical model is that "experts" define what is "normal" within a medical context and treat individuals accordingly, when it may not be appropriate or in the best interests of the individual. While the criminal justice system provides due process rights to individuals, the public health model is proactive and is interested in the greater good, sometimes at the expense of individual rights. Chriss (2007) suggests that there is a potential dark side to medical social control, which includes the following:

+ Behavior is redefined as disease or a psychiatric problem and individuals may not take responsibility for behavior;
+ People may assume that medical providers are neutral when they have a vested interest in promoting or selling sickness (e.g., prescriptions, procedures, services);
+ There may be an over-reliance on "experts" without evaluating their qualifications and recommendations;
+ Social problems may be defined as individual problems without consideration of the effects of social policies and politics.

In many cases, a medical response is initiated by individuals or families to resolve a perceived problem (an intervention with a drug addict to encourage treatment or a prescription of a drug for attention deficit disorder). But there is some overlap between medical social control and legal/formal control under the criminal justice system. With legal control, agents of the state (i.e., police officers, courts) may use the medical model to address public safety problems,

ranging from a 72-hour commitment for psychiatric evaluation for someone who is behaving strangely in public to drug courts, which mandate treatment for offenders convicted of spousal abuse or drug offenses. The term used by some in the criminal justice system is "therapeutic jurisprudence," in which social and behavioral science is used to study the extent to which legal rules or practices promote the psychological well-being of participants in the criminal justice system. We'll see later that criminal justice systems that make heavy use of medicine and scientific experts are described as operating as a "medical model."

FORMAL / LEGAL SOCIAL CONTROL

Although most people are subject to informal social control mechanisms far more often than formal social control (Henry, 1994), legal control or government social control through the criminal justice system symbolizes the power of the state over social institutions. Formal social control consists of the following subsystems:

+ Law, courts, and the administration of justice;
+ Police;
+ Corrections.

In traditional societies, the emphasis of social control was on socialization—learning the norms, values, and traditions. The families, kin, and social groups enforced the rules. In the modern industrial world and the postmodern information society, there has been increasing formalization of social institutions. The norms and mores have been codified into laws enforced by police and the courts. And the number of acts defined as crimes has increased. For instance, technological advances have created new ways to commit crimes and new behaviors that may be offensive to others or present a high risk. Hacking into a computer to gain access to account information to steal someone's identity to commit theft is one example. Banning the use of handheld cell phones while driving is another.

Legal philosophers have long debated the essential components of a legal system. In H.L.A. Hart's (1961) classic work, *The Concept of Law*, he defines law as a union of primary and secondary rules. According to Hart, primary rules are informal rules of obligation through which the basic conditions of social existence are satisfied. They are what a society considers as right and wrong. It is possible to live by primary rules alone in extremely stable, close-knit, face-to-face communities. Under more complex and diversified societies, informal primary rules cannot cope with the changing conditions. In response, secondary rules develop.

Based on Hart's (1961) analysis, we can describe a legal system as having five elements:

1) Declarations of rules (Hart's legislation of primary rules);
2) Administration of rules (Hart's secondary rules, including rules for recognizing authoritative primary rules, rules of adjudication that empower individuals to make authoritative judgments about whether, on a particular occasion, a primary rule has been broken);
3) Methods of changing rules (Hart's secondary rules of change);
4) Enforcement of rules;
5) Sanctioning of rule breakers (rules authorizing the application of penalties where primary rules are violated).

Each of these elements is carried out in the formal criminal justice system by different government institutions. So rules that become laws are "declared" by **legislators**, though also sometimes by courts when they set precedent or by appeals courts and the U.S. Supreme Court. **Courts** at varying levels are responsible for administering the rules through a constitutionally governed set of procedures. Rules can be changed, by being repealed or reenacted through **legislative action** or can be interpreted by **superior courts** and by **appeal courts**, which make rulings that, in effect, change the law. In one sense, the whole system is responsible for enforcing the rules, but this function is exclusively the role of **the police**. Finally, although the courts sentence those convicted of violating the rules/laws, it is the system of **corrections** that implements the sanctions.

This is not the place to delve deeply into different types of formal law. However, just as we saw that there are different types of social control, so there are different types of law, and these are discussed in depth in law courses. Here, it is enough to know that legal theorists distinguish between 1) public and private law; 2) substantive and procedural law; 3) civil and criminal law; and 4) civil and common law. In looking at the formal criminal justice system, we are dealing with public law, specifically at the duties and powers of government officials and the relationship between individual and the state. Criminal law is one of several types of public law (which also includes constitutional law, administrative and regulatory law, executive orders, etc.). Criminal law and procedure address harms against individuals who are represented by the state, which acts against offenders to control their behavior through imposing a variety of sanctions as specified within the law.

LAW IN CONTEXT

Law Creation and the Origins of Law

Substantive law concerns what behavior is prohibited and what is allowed, whereas procedural law deals with the rules governing how substantive laws are to be administered, enforced, and changed. The definitions of right and wrong (embodied in substantive law) vary between individuals and across social and cultural groups. What is viewed as crime is a social construct—meaning that it is created by humans, based on ethics, customs, traditions, and sometimes consensus—even if not everyone within the group agrees with the definitions. At other times, what counts as crime is based on the influence of interest groups (Henry and Lanier, 2001; Canadian Law Commission, 2003). While the laws that define crime are enacted by elected officials, those legislators are open to pressure from lobbyists and others. As such, crimes that are defined by criminal laws are determined by the powerful. We said earlier that laws are enacted as part of a political process by legislators as part of a governmental process. But where do these definitions of crime embodied in law come from? Those who study the origins of law have developed different models, or theories, to answer this question.

Where Does Law Come From?

Until the modern era, there were two basic approaches to the study of the origins of law. One approach saw all laws as being **divine products**; law was essentially God's law. If not a specific god, then law was seen as emanating from a supernatural power. In either case, law was beyond the will of humans. A second, and equally essentialist approach, saw law as "natural," where it was a product of the continuous flow of life and represented universal essential moral values. **Natural law philosophers** such as Thomas Aquinas saw law as bound up with human nature and the general plan of life; if this plan was seen as governed by divine reason, then there was not much to distinguish between divine law and natural law (Halsall, 1996). Chief Justice Clarence Thomas of the Supreme Court adopts this position.

Thus, lawbreaking was seen as an offense against God and/or humanity, or at the very least, against the underlying idea of universal morality. A major difficulty with these theories is, how do we know what is god-given or what is natural, and secondly, who decides this?

With the Enlightenment, these supernatural beliefs were replaced with rational ideas about law by philosophical thinkers known collectively as "**legal formalists.**" These philosophers believed that all laws were logical and consistent with each other. One group of legal formalists was known as the "**legal positivists.**" John Austin (1832), for example, distinguished between law and other rules such as morals and customs. Austin saw law as an independent, isolated, logical, and self-consistent system of rules and believed that the ethics of right and wrong are irrelevant. Law, unlike customs and norms, was the only type of rules that was commanded on a subject by a sovereign ruler on pain of sanctions. This was known as the "**command theory**" of law. Hans Kelsen (1930, 1941, 1967), also a legal positivist, developed the theory of "**Pure Law.**" He argued that customs or norms only become laws

because they are formed by the state, through its systematic legislative procedures. He pointed out that these laws were based on, and consistent with, a broad basic, commonly shared norm—the **grundnorm** or grand norm. The grundnorm, says Kelsen, explains the systematic unity of law. It is the idea that people ought to behave in the manner stipulated by the constitution of a state and by laws authorized by its constitution.

Legal positivists such as Austin and Kelsen were criticized for: (1) ignoring the will of the people in shaping law; (2) failing to see that social and human factors affect the application of law; (3) not recognizing that judges, as well as legislators, make law; (4) failing to identify in whose interests the law is made or in whose interests is the basic norm; and (5) assuming that nonindustrial societies had no law (even though they clearly have mechanisms of social control). From our perspective, then, there is a tension between the systems of social control that all societies use, and the creation of formal law that serves a societal-level social control function, yet also has a degree of difference from informal mechanisms of social control. Indeed, the sociological perspective increasingly addresses not only this tension, but recognizes that both systems are interdependent on the wider system of social control.

The Emergence of a Socio-legal Perspective on the Origins of Law

In introducing the concept of social control earlier, we mentioned the concept of "**living law.**" In Eugene Ehrlich's view, it is neither god nor nature that is the source of law. Nor is it rules developed through government process that are found in law books. In contrast to legal positivists, Ehrlich says sanctions are not peculiar to law but a feature of group membership: "[The] center of gravity of legal development lies not in legislation, nor in juristic science, nor in juristic decision but in society itself" (Ehrlich, cited by Treviño, 2011: 124). Indeed, he states in his classic 1913 text, *Fundamental Principles of The Sociology of Law*:

> The social association is the source of the coercive power, the sanction, of all social norms, of law … Man therefore conducts

himself according to law, chiefly because this is made imperative by his social relations. In this respect the legal norm does not differ from the other norms. The state is not the only association that exercises coercion; there are an untold number of associations in society that exercise it much more forcefully than the state ... This then is the living law in contradistinction to that which is being enforced in the courts and other tribunals. The living law is the law which dominates life itself even though it has not been posited in legal propositions. (Ehrlich, 1936: 63–64)

Ehrlich's concept of law, with its origins in custom, also exists in tension with the custom from which it is derived because it takes time to change law, which lags behind the living law of custom. Ehrlich saw law as the surface crust of a series of layers which reached down from the abstract propositions of formal positive law to the spontaneous living law beneath in the group and association.

We saw earlier that Ehrlich's and Ross's ideas led to the emergence of *sociological jurisprudence*, which was a major challenge to the legal positivism of the formalists. Drawing in part on the work of legal formalists and in part on the work of Ehrlich and Ross, Roscoe Pound defined law as "a highly specialized form of social control carried on in accordance with a body of authoritative precepts applied in a juridical manner and administrative process" (Pound, 1942: 41). Pound says that law exerts pressure on a person "in order to constrain him to do his part in upholding civilized society and to deter him from anti-social conduct; that is conduct at variance with the postulates of social order" (1942: 18). Law is social control "through the systematic application of the force of politically organized society" (1942: 83).

Pound argued that it makes no sense to say the law is independent of any social context because individual actions are necessary for the law's day-to-day operation and in the actual working of the legal system in society. He argued that good law cannot be made without knowing the social context in which it will operate.

Pound went further than simply recognizing the relationship between law and its social context, suggesting that law should be an instrument of social change to adjust society to the new and changing societal patterns. Because of this, his approach was referred to as a social engineering view of law, or as he himself described it, "functional jurisprudence." Alan Hunt (1978), a critic of Pound, said that while Pound started off with the right idea, he ended up abandoning any search for the social foundation of law and eventually was concerned only with the effect of law on society. Hunt says despite Pound's continued writings, sociological jurisprudence diminished after 1918 because he didn't really break from legal formalism.

A third school of thought leading to a fully sociological view of law was known as **legal realism**. Their ideas were rooted in the ideas of Oliver Wendell Holmes (1897) and developed by Jerome Frank (1930; 1949) and Karl Llewellyn (1930; 1960), who were sympathetic to the message of sociological jurisprudence but complained that it needed to be more activist. The core ideas of legal realists are their concern with "**law in action**" rather than the "**law in the books.**" Holmes (1897: 461) defined law as "the prophecies of what the courts will do in fact." He criticized legal positivists for not paying attention to the actual decisions made by judges, arguing that if judges systematically ignored legal theory or specific written laws, then it made no sense to call their decisions law. **Real law**, according to Holmes, is what actually happens when law is applied, rather than what the law books say happens.

Similarly, Benjamin Nathan Cardozo (1924: 52) defined law as "a principle or rule of conduct so established as to justify a prediction with reasonable certainty that it will be enforced by the courts if its authority is challenged." For example, there are antidiscrimination laws, but if the actual operationalization of these laws shows a bias toward race or gender in their application in the courts, then the real laws allow discrimination. Realists criticized sociological jurisprudence, arguing that just because the content of laws was changed, this was insignificant if the actual practice of applying the laws in reality by the day-to-day decisions of judges and law enforcers was different from their content.

Legal realists' concern was to improve the way law operated and to minimize the gap between **law in action** and **law in the books**. From our social control perspective, this is very important because it suggests that informal practices are themselves law. If informal practices are the basis of legal outcomes, then they are, in effect, the law (not surprising that the Supreme Court recently set some rules to govern the informal practice of "plea bargaining"). Moreover, legal realists point out that law must have orderly, authorized use of force, but it must also be used regularly, since law that is ignored most of the time by enforcement agents is not law.

Realists, however, like sociological jurisprudence theorists, have been criticized for failing to see that the way judges and courts make decisions is not only dependent on their individual decisions but is part of a wider social context within which the judges operate. They failed to recognize that these informal practices and failures to enforce some laws but enforce others are part of a political process involving powerful groups.

In summary, then, whereas **legal positivists** were concerned with the logic and form that law took, **sociological jurisprudence theorists** focused on the content and social context of the law, while **legal realists** were concerned with the actual administration and application of the law.

Black's Sociology of Law

One of the most prominent of recent sociologists of law, who tries to draw these various ideas together, is Donald Black (1976), whose book, *The Behavior of Law*, we mentioned earlier. Black takes a position that is not dissimilar to that taken by both legal positivists and legal realists. But unlike these theorists, he also acknowledges anthropological and sociological ideas by accepting the existence of other forms of social control; though critics point out that he eventually rejects these as relevant to the study of law.

Consistent with several of those whose ideas we have examined, Black (1976: 2) defines law as "government social control ... the normative life of the state and its citizens, such as legislation, litigation, and adjudication." He sees law as one special type of social control which develops only with the development of nation states. Black says that law is different from other forms of social control, because it involves government, is formal and rational, and must be understood separately from these other forms of control.

Like legal realists, Black argues that law can be understood only by focusing on the behavior of legal officials and citizens. Black (1976) sees four styles of law, each corresponding to a style of social control. He identifies four styles of social control in law: (1) Penal: offender violates a prohibition—subject to condemnation and punishment; (2) Compensator: offender violates a contractual obligation—subject to giving victim restitution; (3) Therapeutic: deviant broke norms—needs help, treatment; and (4) Conciliator: the deviant represents one side of a conflict in a larger dispute and needs resolution or settlement.

While Black's theory of law is considered sociological, it really builds on the formalism and sociological jurisprudential approaches, rather than the classical sociology of law. Before examining the criminal justice system, we need to go back to the roots of sociology to look at the way the founders envisaged law and formal social control.

Durkheim, Weber, and Marx on Law

As Alan Hunt (1978) has argued, the shift from a social jurisprudential perspective on law to a fully sociological perspective draws on the classical sociological theorists Émile Durkheim, Max Weber, and Karl Marx. Each was writing at a time when society's structure had undertaken massive changes, from a feudal era to an industrial society. In different ways, each of these theorists locates law in the context of the social structure of a society. The major idea of these theorists is how social structure and organization of society shapes its system of law, and how systems and law, in turn, can shape the structure of society. This occurs because the whole society comprises relatively stable social institutions such as law, government, education, family, religion, etc., and each part is interrelated with the others, so that a change in one part produces a change in the others.

The Move from Status to Contract. One of the first to observe this relationship was sociologist Henry Sumner Maine (1863) in his book, *Ancient Society*, which he based on analysis of law in Greek, Roman, and Indian civilizations. As Hunt (1978) points out, Maine described this shift as the movement from law based upon status to that based upon contract. Maine saw law emerge in an evolutionary three-stage process. Law began as the commands of the head of each isolated household; it became the rule of the patriarchal sovereign, which became codified as the customs and texts of state rulers and latterly of administrative elites. Maine believed that progressive societies changed from laws based upon one's social position or status—such as family member, serf, slave—to a system based upon contracted rights and duties determined by free agreement and voluntary consent, but this progress was complex and not inevitable (Scala, 2011).

Durkheim's Division of Labor

One of the first sociologists to examine how forms of law are related to social structure was Émile Durkheim in *Division of Labor* (1893). Division of labor means the division of the work needed for a society to survive into separate tasks performed by separate individuals and groups. Once work is divided, it becomes more specialized; those who develop specialized skills are less able to perform other tasks. Durkheim considers two types of society corresponding to two historical periods, each having their own characteristic type of law.

Mechanical Solidarity and Repressive Law. The first of these periods analyzed by Durkheim was preindustrial society, which he saw as associated with repressive law. Ancient societies and preindustrial societies have a minimal division of labor, meaning that their members do similar work; most share tasks necessary for maintaining the society. As a result, members are replaceable. The social order, or the way members are held together in such a society, is by the "spirit of similarity" or collective sentiment, which produces a common bond. Durkheim described this kind of society as being held together through "mechanical solidarity." Under mechanical solidarity, members are bonded together by tradition, friendship, common understanding, and shared beliefs. In such small-scale societies, everyone knows everyone else, members exist in face-to-face relationships, and they are involved in multiplex (multistranded) relationships, where each member knows the rules, customs, and norms of the group. Violation of norms presents a threat to the society's conservative values, such that it shocks the collective sentiment, or "common consciousness." Durkheim said these societies would have a repressive or punitive law; blame and moral condemnation would be heaped on the offender in order to express the community's displeasure. This form of law is manifest as a collective reaction to the threat, and since it is the common conscience that is attacked, it must be the common collective reaction that resists. These small-scale societies have little tolerance for the rule breaker—they emphasize social order over the individual, and they deny a person a place outside of the social status they hold in the society. Justice is directed toward the person as a social status in a social context rather than an isolated individual. The repressive law serves the society by bringing together the community, by clarifying its rules, and by maintaining social order.

Organic Solidarity and Restitutive Law. The second period Durkheim identifies is that characterized as industrial society. Population growth resulted in scarcity of resources, which was overcome by dividing work tasks and using rational means to achieve goals. Here, people developed specialized skills which increased efficiency. As a result, people became dissimilar in contrast to those in the preindustrial communal era. The industrial society, says Durkheim, was no longer held together by similarity, common interests, and values. There was a lack of interest in, or understanding of, people doing other specialized tasks, and there was no common consciousness to be shocked. This kind of society, with a high division of labor, was held together by the principle of differentiation. Because their work functions were indispensable to each other and the groups or different skills were dependent on each other, they needed each other to sustain the whole society.

Durkheim said this kind of society was characterized by "organic solidarity."

Because of the mutual interdependence of its members, a society characterized by organic solidarity developed a restitutive law, which is rational and designed to protect the individuals as isolated, specialized, and separate. Since people are not replaceable, restitutive law is designed to return things to how they were before the norm or law violation. This retains their valuable skills and does not waste the society's valuable resources. As a result of these social system demands, the law of contract emerged as the main vehicle of restitutive law. So Durkheim, who is described as a structural functionalist, argues that as society develops in complexity, these legal institutions expand in order to serve the growing needs of the society.

Others have argued that in addition to the division of labor, there are several other social structure factors that shape law. These include: (1) population growth and the need for coordination; (2) interaction density that suggests the more interaction, the more conflict, and the more conflict, the more law; the more law, the less people solve problems through settlement-directed talking, which results in an even greater need for law; (3) move from multiplex to simplex relations (Gluckman, 1967; Black, 1976), implying that divisions of labor and specialization actually reduce the number of face-to-face contacts we have with others, but that this simultaneously reduces the number of occasions we have to control others' behavior, with the result that in simplex societies with their single-stranded relations, the more law is needed; and (4) inequality across class, race, and gender lines produces differential access to the law and those who are excluded are forced to use other mechanisms.

Max Weber, Ideal Types, and Legal Pluralism

Max Weber's view of law is defined through his conception of the "**normative order**." A norm is a standard pattern of behavior accepted as typical for a society or subset of society, and a normative order is a body of enforced norms. So for Weber, law is a normative order, but so too are custom and other collective units, such as the rules of an organization. Weber (1954: 5) says: "An

order will be called law if it is externally guaranteed by the likelihood that (physical or psychological) coercion aimed at bringing about conformity with the order, or at avenging its violation will be exercised by a staff of people especially holding themselves ready for this purpose." For example, a shopping mall, with rules about dress and behavior, policed by a staff of uniformed security guards, would be a normative order. However, formal law is distinguished from other normative orders in that: (1) pressures to conform must come externally in the form of actions or threats of action, regardless of whether a person wants to obey the law or not; (2) external actions or threats always involve coercion or force; and (3) those who administer coercion are a staff specialized in law who have the authority to enforce orders and who have official positions in organizations for enforcement (e.g., police). When these people are part of an agency of political authority, Weber calls the form of normative order "**state law**."

For Weber, customs are not law because there is no sense of duty to follow them. Conventions, while they do involve rules and a duty or obligation to conform, and sanctions in the form of expressions of disapproval, are not law, says Weber (1954: 27) because they "lack specialized personnel for the implementation of coercive power." Nor do stateless nonindustrial societies have law because they do not develop specialization or organization. While informal control without organization is not law, informal controls used by private associations, where these are carried out by a special group such as private police and a disciplinary board, are laws. Because Weber's definition of the normative order is at the root of his definition of law, it permits **legal pluralism**, which as we saw presents society's members with competing legal demands because of their involvement in multiple groups and associations, each having their own normative order.

Weber, whose book *On Law, Economy and Society* (1954), was, like Durkheim, trying to explain the emergence of law in terms of the development of industrial society. Weber saw several structural factors explaining the emergence and change in law, including economic, political, technical, religious, and social status or prestige. Weber presents two theories of law and legal development. The first is a theory of domination of why people obey the law and the second is an analysis of models of law and legal systems.

Weber's Theory of Domination. Weber calls the probability that commands will be obeyed "domination," and identifies two types of domination: (1) **coercive domination**; and (2) **legitimate domination**. *Coercive domination* exists when a person or group exercises monopolistic power.

Coercive domination can be the result of one or more kinds of **force**: (i) physical; (ii) economic; or (iii) psychological. *Legitimate domination* is different. It tries to explain why people obey the law irrespective of the consequences to themselves. Weber says conformity under legitimate domination is a result of "**authoritative power**," of which there are three types:

(i) *charismatic domination*, characterized by: (a) exceptional qualities of leader; and (b) allegiance to **person**;

(ii) *traditional domination*, characterized by: (a) customary to follow the position; and (b) allegiance to the **office**;

(iii) *legal domination*, characterized by: (a) following the rules or principle; (b) having allegiance to **rules** (independent of person or office).

Thus, legal domination is not related to other influences; we obey the law because it is the law—because of the principle it represents.

Weber's theory of legal development. Weber was concerned with the factors that lead to the growth of rational justice (or rationalization of law) in the process of modernization. Weber said rational law only occurs when four factors coincide: (i) trade and commerce resulting from capitalist interests; (ii) competition, the use of money, and the need for predictability; (iii) the rise of monarchical interests, the development of the nation-state and its associated bureaucratic administrative form of government; and (iv) development of a legal profession, legal procedures, and techniques.

The importance of rational justice is its reliance on impersonal rules rather than personal authority.

Weber's analysis of law. Weber distinguishes between two dimensions of law: (i) formality; and (ii) rationality. **Formality** refers to the extent to which lawmakers, and those who enact the law, use standards internal to the system. This dimension results in two types of law: (a) **formal**, in which all the rules and all procedures necessary for decision making are available internally, from within the system; and (b) **substantive**, in which there is reference to external criteria, such as ethical, ideological, emotional, political, etc. **Rationality** distinguishes between two types of legal processes: (a) **rational** law, in which all like cases are treated equally; and (b) **irrational law**, in which like cases are treated differently—i.e., the same case can result in different outcomes and low predictability.

Combining these two dimensions, the degree of formality and the degree of rationality gives four logical possibilities or ideal types of legal system.

Weber's Legal Pluralism and Modern Law. Weber's theory of law, therefore, sees several types of law existing simultaneously—i.e., he is a legal pluralist. His analysis is complex and multifaceted but is typically simplified to considering two types of law: (i) formal rational law; and (ii) substantive irrational law. **Formal rational law** is law which goes by the book on the basis of rules made in advance, similar to what we discussed under "legal formalism," i.e., written law. **Substantive-irrational law** is more flexible and is influenced by the particular circumstances and by the social relationships involved, which is similar to informal norms and sanctions of custom and that which we discussed earlier as a "realist view of law," i.e., what people do in practice.

In reality, formal rational law and informal substantive law coexist in any society. For example, when ordinary people use the law we see that law is open to both of these two basic interpretations. Sally Merry (1986) shows that until working-class Americans experience the actual practice of law they understand it primarily

Table 2. Weber's Ideal Types of Legal Systems

	FORMAL (Internally validated and based upon rules)	SUBSTANTIVE (Externally validated and situationally based)
IRRATIONAL (Like cases treated differently)	**Charismatic Justice** Unpredictable e.g., magic, oracle	**Kadi Justice which is** Unpredictable e.g., jury decisions
RATIONAL (Like cases treated similarly)	**Rational Justice** Predictable e.g., ideal of U.S. justice	**Empirical Justice** Partially Predictable e.g., English common law

in terms of its formal-rational sense. But she found that working-class Americans also believe that the law is awesome and powerful, capable of uncovering the truth, applying laws firmly, and providing justice. Merry calls this the **dominant legal ideology** of American society (the main ideas conveyed by elite groups and accepted by the majority of society). The central ideas of formal law and justice are that: (i) people have broad legal rights that shade into moral rights, such as property rights—the right to use and retain possessions—and personal rights to be free from insult, harassment, threats, or violence without provocation; (ii) these rights are equal for all persons; (iii) these rights are routinely enforced by the state through a system of police and courts that are accessible to all; and (iv) the state takes infractions of these rights seriously.

However, when working-class Americans experience dealing with the law in practice by taking cases to court, they discover that **an ideology of situational justice** prevails. In practice, not only does the legal realist position have some truth, but so too do the ideas of anthropologists about substantive law. Working-class Americans encountering law find that it is: (i) situationally based; (ii) lenient; (iii) personalistic; and (iv) produced within a local setting. The ideology of **situational justice** has a number of components: (i) rights are viewed as embedded in social relationships and situations, rather than being distributed equally; they depend on a person's history, character, rank, and social and ethnic identity; (ii) the enforcement of laws is not automatic; it must be triggered by complaints; (iii) all cases with the same label (e.g., harassment,

assault) are not all considered as equally serious; (iv) seriousness depends upon (a) who you are; whether you have money, a job, a reputation for being in trouble with the law; and (b) the situation or context in which the incident occurs, such as the relationship between the parties, the mutuality of the conflict, the intent of the offender, the extent of injury; generally, interpersonal cases are not considered worthy of a full trial and rarely are severe penalties incurred by the participants; and (v) behavior is judged by customary standards. Merry calls the dominant ideology of formal justice **top-down ideology** and the ideology of situational justice **bottom-up ideology**.

Conflict Theory, Marx, and Critical Approaches to Law

Karl Marx was a philosopher and sociologist who also provided the foundation for conflict and radical theories of law. Marx influenced a variety of critical theories, including critical legal studies, critical race theory, and feminist legal studies. While we cannot consider these developments within the scope of this volume, it is important to understand their foundations in Marxist theory.

Marx (1911), like Durkheim and Weber, was concerned with explaining capitalist society and how its economic "mode of production" shaped and influenced its institutions, one of which is law. An essential difference between Marx and other theorists was that he saw capitalist society based on the private ownership of property as the dominant driving interest, which generates vast inequalities of wealth for owners of capital, leading to an economic class struggle. Marx saw the fundamental division in society between owners of wealth (capitalists) and owners of labor (working class or proletariat). The former earn income from investments and capital, particularly companies and corporations that they own; the latter earn income by selling their labor to capitalists, so they are dependent on their ability to work in exchange for a wage. As a result of these different roles, the two classes exist in a relationship of conflict that produces both crime and the law needed to control it. As Friedrich Engels, Marx's collaborator, says:

> In capitalist societies the basic class struggle is between the capitalist class (bourgeoisie) and the working class (proletariat). The economic site of this particular struggle is the productive process; it occurs over the distribution of the fruits of this process. The capitalist class, on the one hand, strives to maximize profit from the unpaid labor of the working class. Its income lies in rent, interest, and industrial profit. The working class, on the other hand, strives to maximize wages. It attempts to do so by reducing the length of the working day, by compelling employers to pay higher wages, and by wresting such concessions from the capitalist class as health insurance, work-safety regulations, and job security. The goals of the capitalist class and the working class are thus mutually exclusive. Typically, the one maximizes its return from the productive process at the expense of the other. (Beirne and Messerschmidt, 1991: 340)

This basic economic relationship between capitalists and workers constitutes the **economic mode of production**, or the "**infrastructure**," which lays the basis for the rest of society's institutions, called the "**superstructure**." The infrastructure shapes the superstructure to serve its interests. As one of those institutions, law is seen to serve the interests of the capitalist class to maintain their position of power and

control in society over the workers. Steven Vago summarizes Marx's position on law into three assumptions: "(1) Law is a product of evolving economic forces; (2) law is a tool used by the ruling class to maintain its power over the lower classes; (3) in the communist society of the future, law, as an instrument of social control, will 'wither away' and finally disappear" (Vago 2009: 51).

As we will see, however, to maintain its legitimacy, law actually protects some of the interests of the lower classes, and so is seen as valuable to both dominant and subordinate classes. As such, law becomes one of the institutions through which, and over which, the conflict of interests is fought, as each class struggles to capture the resources of the law to further its interests. Different interpretations of the nature of interests, particularly how they see economic power divided between capital, the state, and labor, have led to a different emphasis in conflict theories of law.

Marxist Theorists of Law. There are two Marxist views of law that differ, based on who has power and how power is distributed: (i) *Instrumentalist Marxist*; and (ii) *Structural Marxists*.

Instrumentalist Marxists such as Richard Quinney (1973; 1975; Krisberg, 1975) have argued that law is an instrument of repression used by the state (government) directed, or heavily influenced by, a dominant, monolithic economic elite. Quinney (1973; 1975, 1977) argues that this ruling economic elite is divided into two major groups. At the top of the class structure is the more powerful "**monopoly capitalists**," who own major units of the economy, and who head the most powerful corporate, banking, and financial institutions (Quinney, 1973: 53). Monopoly capitalists, says Quinney, totally control the state and orchestrate its every action through the legal system. They also delegate power to a subclass of elite, which he calls "**lieutenant capitalists.**" These subordinate groups own or manage less powerful companies. Together, the lieutenant capitalists and the criminal justice apparatus of the state act to repress the subordinate classes on behalf of the ruling dominant elite. They use the state's law and criminal justice system as a coercive apparatus to criminalize those threatening their superior position in the social order.

Structural Marxists such as William Chambliss (Spitzer, 1975; Greenberg, 1981; Chambliss and Seidman, 1982) criticize this crude instrumentalism, arguing that if such a view of society were accurate, it would be unnecessary for powerful elites to legislate against their own interests; they would simply change the law to suit their interests. Further, they say that the instrumentalist view ignores conflicts between capitalists and cannot explain conflicts over legislation on noneconomic issues such as abortion, drugs, and so on. While the instrumentalist position may better apply to early capitalist production, coercion becomes less necessary as the mode of domination "becomes supplanted by the silent compulsion of the market" (Young, 1981: 296). Einstadter and Henry say, "The capitalist system of production serves as its own system of regulation and autonomous discipline in which the reality of having to compete in situations of exploitation in order to survive is accepted by subordinate classes as natural. As a result, the state can take a less coercive role, reserving its repressive apparatus for use in exceptional cases of riot and collective protest" (2006: 245). Instead of a dominant monolithic economic elite, structural Marxists argue that the state has some degree of independence from the owners of capital. The law provides a degree of real protections to the working class. If the laws did not have these protections, there would be a loss of governing legitimacy. Structural Marxists argue that the state (government) is "semiautonomous," meaning that it is influenced by economic power (e.g., through lobbyists, donations), but the state also exists independently of the economically powerful and is able to exercise some controls over their excesses (e.g., health and safety laws, consumer protection laws, food and drug laws). Einstadter and Henry summarize this dual power model of society comprising of two elites: an economic class and a governing class. This dual power model produces an appearance of neutrality that adds legitimacy to the system. "Through its mediating influence, the worst excesses of economic exploitation, and the crises these create, are controlled in the interests of legitimating the long-term maintenance of the system

of inequality" (Einstadter and Henry, 2006: 238). As a result, then, "the state, as an allegedly neutral element in the power structure, allows capitalist inequality to prevail without obvious challenge" (Einstadter and Henry, 2006: 238). While this system may result in short-term losses for capital in relation to labor, the concession is enough to serve the long-term interests of capitalism. From the structural Marxist perspective, it is the behavior of those threatening the overall system of capitalism that is criminalized. This threat can come as much from the very individuals and corporations that hold power (if their behavior threatens to expose the system) as it can from the resistance and protests of the economically powerless.

Law, then, does not just promote ruling-class interests, but contains the language of universal justice—i.e., consensus—the idea that law is for all the people. The idea that law serves everybody dampens the resistance of the poorer classes by obscuring its real imbalances. Stanley Diamond (1971) says law is more effective as a class domination tool than exercising simple force because it can incorporate custom into its rules, thereby deceiving people into thinking that law is in all people's interests.

By making law appear to contain customs, the ruling class can defuse any organized resistance. By focusing on rights, such as the freedom of the individual, the impression is created that law serves the population as a whole. Individual leaders of local groups who once had the power to gain support for resisting the class interests are stripped of that power. The flow of authority from the local group to the state destroys local social units, which could protect the individual from state domination. So by promoting the individual as the basic unit, people are separated from the mass of those in a similar class position and collective opposition is splintered.

Austin Turk's Law and Ideological Domination. Austin Turk adds a further dimension to this notion of a more subtle form of domination. Like Structural Marxists, he says law is more effective at producing ideological domination than it is as a coercive mechanism for domination. Turk (1969) summarized this argument into five kinds of power that legal systems can give those who control them. First, law transfers the use of physical force as an available means for getting what is wanted to those who control the law. Second, law gives economic power to those who control it because it creates rewards and punishments for economic activity, e.g., tax. Third, law gives political power to established political institutions. Fourth, law provides an ideological environment promoting compliance. And finally, law provides diversionary power. So by capturing law, dominant interests can create an ideological environment favoring their interests without the need for coercion, except when the legitimacy is challenged or undermined. Turk (1969; 1976; 1982) believes that under these social-structural arrangements, particular groups emerge as more powerful. These groups command an authority relationship over others, who in turn become subject to their control. Turk (1969) argues that people have to learn to deal with others having authority over them. This results in a permanent adjustment of the subordinate to those in authority. Over time, this authority–subject relationship becomes less coercive and more autonomous as new generations are born into the existing structural arrangements containing preexisting laws, rules, and definitions of reality.

In summary, whereas Durkheim took a functionalist view of law, indicating that as various social structures change, so law changes to fit the needs of the new order, Weber saw law tied to a variety of structural processes and that different types of law could exist simultaneously, depending on the characteristics of its generative normative order. In contrast, for Marx and Marxist conflict theorists, law emerged as an institution of both coercive, though ultimately ideological, control, serving the broad interests of maintaining the system of capitalism, mystifying its contradictions, and as part of the state apparatus, maintaining the system of class exploitation in favor of those who own the means of production.

Readings for a Sociological Perspective on Social Control

Stuart Henry in the reading, "Why People Ban Behavior," looks at the social process for defining behavior as unacceptable. This process can be informal but it can also be political, publicly identifying behavior or ideas that are deviant and developing rules for handling those who break the rules.

Henry introduces the concept of **moral panic** in his article on banning behavior. According to Erich Goode and Norman Ben-Yehuda (1994), moral panics are societal reactions to perceived threat that have certain characteristics. The moral panic, often fueled by media coverage, results in a reaction that may be based more on myth than fact. Sean P. Heir, *et al.*, in the reading "Beyond Folk Devil Resistance: Linking Moral Panic and Moral Regulation," apply the concept of moral panic to discuss claims of threats posed by youth who wear "hoodies" in public places in England.

In "Social Class and Crime," Michael T. Costelloe and Raymond J. Michalowski look at how social class, defined as economic resources, social resources, political resources, cultural authority, and lifestyle resources, shapes definitions of crime. They suggest that those who are most advantaged influence how we perceive and define crime in the United States.

Looking at social control from a broader global perspective, the International Council on Human Rights Policy in the article, "Modes and Patterns of Social Control," includes the formal aspects of control by the criminal justice system, the health system, the welfare system, and urban planning entities. Their focus is on the impact of social control on human rights. In the criminal justice system, there is a tension between public safety and due process rights of individuals, but it is also relevant to view formal legal and government actions from the perspective of human rights.

CRIMINAL JUSTICE: SYSTEMS, MODELS, AND ISSUES

Criminal Justice Systems

So far, we have discussed social control and the law, but not the formal criminal justice system. While from the outside it might seem that criminal justice is one large bureaucracy run by the state, it is actually a series of subsystems comprised of rules, procedures, and practices. Moreover, there is not so much one criminal justice system but several. By several, we mean that while the courts, the police, and corrections make up key institutions of the criminal justice system, they operate according to prevailing models of criminal justice, with different combinations of models and emphases, depending on the agency.

Models of Criminal Justice: The Tension Between Human Rights/Due Process and Social Control

As operated by the criminal justice system, formal social control is a framework of different subsystems that are shaped by the prevailing ideas about how social control should operate. At its simplest, we can see the existence of two contrasting ideologies of criminal justice. One is based on the idea that the most important role for the criminal justice system is to protect the public from harms caused by crime. This **public order model** of justice takes the view that a person is guilty until proven innocent. The opposing view, the **due process model**, on which the U.S. criminal justice system is based (as is the U.S. Constitution), is the view that a person's individual rights must be protected from the power of the state and others—thus, people are assumed innocent until proven guilty. The whole purpose of the due process system of justice is to protect the rights of individuals.

Herbert L. Packer (1968) describes these two models of the criminal process, a dichotomy that ranges from **due process** to **crime control**. According to Packer (1968), the due process model stresses the possibility of error in the system and insists on a formal, adversarial fact-finding process, with rules designed to protect the defendant's rights. The crime control model pays attention to efficiency and an early determination of the probability of innocence or guilt, with few restrictions on the fact-finding process, and the primary aim of crime suppression. These are the two extremes on a continuum of social control, and a tension often exists because of their very different goals.

King (1981) added four more models of criminal justice to Packer's original two, including the **Medical Model** (emphasizing individual or social pathology, diagnosing causes of crime, and prescribing treatments), the **Bureaucratic Model** (focusing on efficiency and

records), the **Status Passage Model** (concentrating on criminal justice as a system of shaming and redefining of a person into a different social status), and the **Power Model** (which sees criminal justice as a system used by the powerful to maintain the status quo by exercising social control over the lower social strata). King's (1981) six models of how the court functions are shown in Table 3.

The point here is not to detail each of these different approaches, but to indicate that even though we have one criminal justice system, it operates in different ways, depending upon which of these different ideological models prevail at which time.

Indeed, at different times in history, the emphasis of the formal social control system has changed, depending upon prevailing and emerging ideologies of criminal justice policy. The 1960s saw an emerging recognition of the idea that societies rather than individuals were pathological, leading to an emphasis on rehabilitation and community corrections, which is a social pathology version of the medical model. Starting in the 1970s and for the next 30 years, with an emerging concern for equal justice against an increasingly wide range of different sentences—often for the same crimes—there was an increasing emphasis on social control and punishment. In particular, we saw an increasing focus on crime control with the reinstatement of the death penalty in many states, the advent of career criminal programs targeting repeat offenders, and increases in length of prison sentences to incapacitate offenders (crime control model), with laws such as "three strikes" at the federal level and in many states. In 2004, there was a renewed interest in rehabilitation and reintegration because of the high cost of mass incarceration and the revolving prison door, which produced recidivism rates of 60 to 70 percent. This reached a high impetus in 2010 in California, when the courts ordered a reduction of the number of state prisoners under what was referred to as "realignment."

More recently, Peter Kraska (Kraska and Brent, 2011) has identified eight frameworks of criminal justice, noting that each has a different emphasis. Some of Kraska's models overlap with those of Packer and King, and other models, such as the Postmodern Industrial Complex, are new.

Table 3. King's Six Process Models of Criminal Justice: The Court

CRIMINAL JUSTICE PROCESS MODEL	SOCIAL FUNCTION	FEATURES OF COURT
Due Process Model	Justice	-Equality between parties -Rules protecting defendant against error -Restraint of arbitrary power -Presumption of innocence
Crime Control Model	Punishment	-Disregard of legal controls -Implicit presumption of guilt -High conviction rate -Unpleasant experience -Support for police
Medical Model	Rehabilitation	-Information-collecting procedures -Individualization -Treatment presumption -Discretion of decision makers -Expertise of decision makers or advisers -Relaxation of formal rules
Bureaucratic (Administrative) Model	Management of Crime and Criminals	-Independence from political considerations -Speed and efficiency -Acceptance of records -Minimization of conflict -Minimization of expense -Economical division of labor
Status Passage Model	Denunciation and Degradation (Shaming)	-Public shaming of defendant -Priority for community values -Agents' control over the process
Power (Radical) Model	Maintenance of class domination	-Reinforcement of class values -Alienation and suppression of defendant -Deflection from issues of class conflict -Differences between judges and judged -Contradictions between rhetoric and performance

(Adapted from King, 1981: 13).

It might seem problematic to have these various different and often conflicting philosophies circulating around the institutions of formal social control that we call criminal justice, until you realize that the very "informal" mechanisms that we described earlier underlie the formal policies and practices. They are the reality of law, as the realists would remind us. One manifestation of this is discretionary justice, where individual police officers, for example, decide whether an incident is serious enough to require formal action.

Discretion can lead to unequal, unfair treatment. For example, plea bargaining takes place between the prosecutor and defense attorneys over the charges brought against the defendant or the recommended sentence. This is a more informal adjudication of the criminal case which, in the past, was not well documented. Over time, more stringent guidelines have been established by prosecutors for plea bargaining and more complete documentation provided of the plea agreements to increase transparency in the process.

In the courts, judges' discretion has been limited by truth-in-sentencing and mandatory sentencing laws such as three strikes, a version of which currently exists in 26 states. One goal of these statutes was to ensure equal treatment of offenders for similar crimes. However, the effect of these laws has been a significant increase in length of stay in prison and prison crowding. Some experts in the field argue that sentences may be excessive when a judge is not allowed to take into consideration the circumstances of a case, such as the third-strike offense, which in California, until Proposition 36 passed in 2012, could be any felony such as petty theft with a prior petty theft. In the case of three strikes, the result of simply using the broad category of "felony" for the third strike was that it included such a diverse range of offenses that sentences of 25 years to life can be given for crimes as different as homicide and shoplifting, if one of these is the third felony offense. These contradictions led to reformers successfully campaigning to modify the law.

Readings on Adjudication and Sentencing

The most extreme punishment that a state can impose on an offender is capital punishment. A justification for the death penalty is its often perceived potential deterrent effects, but some, like John T. Whitehead and Michael C. Braswell, in their article, "To Die or Not to Die: Morality, Ethics, and the Death Penalty," think that the overriding question is whether the death penalty is moral and ethical.

Related to the ethics of capital punishment is the problem of executing the innocent. Thus, a key issue for courts and the criminal justice system is wrongful conviction. With the introduction of DNA evidence, investigators can now test evidence from prior cases to determine if a conviction was justified. Marvin Zalman's article, "Wrongful Convictions," discusses the rise of the innocence movement and what has been learned

about the reasons mistakes are made at all levels in the criminal justice system. He argues that understanding wrongful convictions will lead to reforms that increase fairness and professionalism.

Cassia Spohn, in an article entitled "American Courts", discusses changes in the structure and procedures of the courts related to adjudication and sentencing in criminal cases over the past 50 years and examines the policy implications. As part of her assessment, she looks at specialized or problem-solving courts that have expanded the role of criminal courts in recent years.

The criminal justice system, especially the courts, often must determine whether mentally ill suspects or offenders are responsible for their criminal acts. Melissa Thompson provides an overview of the extent of the problem and the issues. This article, "The Mental Health and Criminal Justice Systems as Agents of Social Control," is the introduction to Thompson's research study, designed to assess how criminal responsibility is assigned to defendants.

A recent development in adjudication of cases comes from a peacemaking philosophy that strives to achieve positive change outside the more formal adjudication process. Michael Brasswell, John Fuller, and Bo Lozoff, in their article, "Toward Restorative and Community Justice," provide an overview of the principles of restorative and community justice and explain why they believe this approach improves the current criminal justice system. The goal is to provide a bridge that recognizes the harms and fears of victims and offenders and a path to resolution and restoration.

POLICE AND THE ENFORCEMENT OF LAW

Trends in Policing

Police agencies in the United States evolved into formal institutions in the 1800s, beginning with the Boston Police Department in 1838. The model was based somewhat on Robert Peel's police force in England, which established a professional, paramilitary, bureaucratic force with powers of investigation and arrest and some degree of discretion. Several historians have identified three eras of policing, starting with the political spoils era, when police chiefs were appointed by—and beholden to—elected officials, leading to corruption (Chriss, 2007). In the 1930s, there was a move led by August Vollmer to develop a professional model of policing with more distance between city officials and chiefs, formal policies and procedures, specialization, and training. Officers patrolled in vehicles responding to radio calls, which created distance between citizens and police, who had previously walked a beat. This led to reactive policing, where police would drive their beats or precincts waiting for calls, rather than proactively engaging in the communities they served.

This distance between police and citizens that had been a part of 1950s-era policing, as well as social unrest in the 1960s, brought about a paradigm shift in policing to a model called Community-Oriented Policing (COP), in which police learned about the communities they served, developed closer ties to those communities, and became more proactive in responding to crime (Chriss, 2007). In this third era of policing, instead of reactively responding to public reports of incidents, police agencies began to develop a model of problem-oriented policing. The idea was to solve community-originated problems before they escalated into crime and violence. This is the current model in many areas, but budget shortfalls have limited the ability of police to be as proactive as they once were.

In 2006, Braga and Weisburd evaluated the effectiveness of some of these new police strategies. Despite the promises of community-oriented policing, they conclude that these programs did not reduce crime, but in some cases they improved citizen satisfaction with police, which was one of the goals. Problem-oriented policing focused on solving specific crime problems and in some cases reduced crime in a specific area. Examples of successes cited by Braga and Weisburd (2006) include reductions in burglaries in apartment complexes and convenience store robberies, and effectiveness of what is referred to as hot-spot policing that targets crime-prone areas based on data regarding crime patterns. Police agencies now employ "crime analysts" whose job it is to use GIS computer mapping systems to identify "crime hot spots," with a view to rapidly deploying police resources to high-crime areas before crimes can escalate into more serious problems.

As indicated in the previous discussion, the way that law enforcement agencies operate is shaped by the prevailing model of criminal justice. So it is not surprising that as a whole, police practices change over time. However, it is also the case that police agencies, as subsystems of the total criminal justice system, have a degree of autonomy (semi-autonomy) to operate according to their own model of criminal justice. Just like courts, these vary over time and between different jurisdictions. Some police agencies will operate consistently with the crime control model, yet others may operate with a rehabilitative and restorative justice approach (See Stamper, 2005).

One of the reasons that law enforcement agency practices vary is that they are not centrally controlled. Another is that they are managed by a police chief or sheriff whose personal views or policy priorities can make a major difference in the emphasis of a department. Third, the institution of "**police discretion**," or the informal practices of policing, can create a unique and specific set of agency practices.

Police Discretion Historically, discretion has been an issue in the criminal justice system because it can lead to disparate, unequal treatment of suspects and defendants. Joseph Goldstein (1960) describes law enforcement decisions regarding enforcement that lead to discretion that are not consistent with the intent of crime control statutes. He categorizes enforcement as follows:

- Total Enforcement—enforcement of all violations of the law, which is unrealistic in part because of resource limitations and due process restrictions;
- Full Enforcement—the offenses that police are expected to enforce based on limitations of resources, budgets, and community expectations;
- Actual enforcement—some offenders are not prosecuted and enforcement is not consistent with the intent of legislation.

Goldstein (1960) reviewed daily police logs to determine the level of discretion used for three offenses: drug enforcement, felonious assault, and gambling. One example of the impact of discretion is leniency for drug offenders or street dealers who provide information on higher-level suppliers or distributors. Goldstein states that in addition to being contrary to the law:

+ Offenders are not offered treatment;
+ The practice negates deterrent effects of the law;
+ The drug problem has not been significantly reduced.

In more recent years, there has been standardization of some law enforcement practices based on new laws or professional standards developed by organizations such as the International Association of Chiefs of Police or the Commission on Police Officer Standards and Training (POST) in California. For example, in California and other states, responses to domestic violence incidents were standardized with enactment of laws requiring arrest of suspects, rather than counseling and releasing suspects at the time of the incident, as had been the practice in many jurisdictions. In California, POST provided training to all law enforcement officers in the state to ensure compliance with the law.

Readings in Policing and Investigations

Law enforcement arrest decisions determine who will be subjected to formal social control in the criminal justice system, which can lead to disparate treatment. The article, "Police Discretion," by Larry K. Gaines and Victor E. Kappeler, provides a more extensive review of discretion in law enforcement, including the nature and types of discretion, factors influencing discretion used by officers, and policies and procedures departments implement to minimize abuses, such as excessive use of force.

Racial profiling is an issue in policing that is related to inappropriate use of discretion. Profiling has been used in law enforcement for years to develop profiles of offenders to help investigators identify perpetrators.

However, if that profile is based solely on race, the result is selective enforcement and discrimination. Michael E. Buerger, in "Racial Profiling," discusses the role of profiling in policing, the history of racial profiling, key legal cases, and research findings.

Racial profiling has been tied to the implementation of immigration policy. Immigration law and enforcement had previously been the responsibility of the federal government, but some states have enacted laws to control immigration at the state level, suggesting that the federal government has not been effective. Meghan G. McDowell and Nancy A. Wonders, in "Keeping Migrants in Their Place: Technologies of Control and Racialized Public Space in Arizona," look at the impact of immigration enforcement on migrants' use of and access to public space. In examining the impact of social control initiatives, we need to consider the policies from all perspectives, and McDowell and Wonders provide the perspective of those most affected by recent changes in Arizona's immigration laws.

PUNISHMENT, SANCTIONS, AND CORRECTIONS

Just as crime is a social construct, the sanctions for violations of laws are established by consensus of those in power. The sanctions employed are based on theories of social control that attempt to explain why individuals violated laws and what can be done to change or control their behavior.

As we saw in the earlier section discussing models of criminal justice, there are several philosophies that govern the response to law violators. Einstadter and Henry (2006) provide a summary of the rationale behind each approach Table 4 presents and philosophies of social control that have been employed, with the emphasis changing somewhat over time. Each philosophy justifies and shapes the ways those subject to criminal justice are dealt with in response to their offense.

Techniques of Crime Control

Einstadter and Henry (2006) point out that the techniques used to control crime, or the disposition that a court makes, are shaped by one or more of these

Table 4. Correctional Ideologies: Philosophies of Intervention and Their Policy Objectives

PHILOSOPHY OF SANCTIONING OR INTERVENTION	OVERALL POLICY OBJECTIVES
Prevention	Removing the conditions, motives, or incentive for crimes before they occur.
Incapacitation	Protection of the public by removing the offender's capability of committing further crimes.
Deterrence	Preventing crime either generally or specifically. General deterrence involves symbolic use of public punishment aimed at affecting the future actions of all potential offenders. Specific or individual deterrence is aimed at affecting the future behavior of particular individuals who have already offended or specific offenses that they might otherwise choose.
Retribution, Just Deserts	The idea that offenders deserve to be punished for their offenses based solely on the harm caused by the act, thus equating the balance of harm.
Conciliation	Resolving the conflict or dispute between offender and offended.
Restitution	Returning the situation to its pre-offense standing with regard to individual victims.
Reparation	Compensation for the offense to be paid to the state or community for the harm caused to collective victims.
Restoration	Reintegrating the offender back into the community by ensuring responsibility is taken for the offence and closure is brought to the victim.
Rehabilitation	Interventions designed to change or correct the offender's future behavior.
Treatment	Interventions designed to cure an individual of the cause of their offending.
Diversion	Providing alternatives to criminal justice system effects to avoid stigmatizing the offender.
Decriminalization	Removing offenses from the criminal code.
Celebration	Using the occasion of crime as an indication of the need for social, institutional, or structural change.

Source: Einstadter and Henry (2006: 25)

philosophies. However, any particular crime control technique does not have to be exclusively associated with one philosophy. We can identify several techniques of crime control, which are the actual practices administered to bring about compliance with the law. These include:

(a) death;
(b) transportation;
(c) prison;
(d) corporal punishment;
(e) fines;
(f) community service;
(g) work programs;
(h) civil commitment (hospitalization);
(i) drugs/surgery.

Prison is a good example to illustrate how one technique of crime control can serve multiple philosophies. Prison is an institution that houses offenders in confinement, but the prevailing philosophy could be depriving a person of their freedom as **retribution** or as **just deserts** for an offense. The offenders caused harm. They will have their liberty deprived as a counter-harm. The varying lengths of sentences can reflect the seriousness of the harm, and thus be adjusted to be proportionate to the offense. Of course, prison would then also serve as a **specific deterrence** for the person committing that crime, with the view that they would choose not to return, or it could serve as a **general deterrence**, in that others would see the consequences that happened to an offender, identify themselves as someone who could suffer that consequence, and decide not to commit the behavior. But prison could also be seen as serving the philosophy of **incapacitation**, in that while incarcerated, an offender cannot commit additional crimes—at least, that is the theory, though many commit crimes inside and outside while in prison. Now, if the prison was organized to have work facilities that trained people in job skills in manufacturing or auto repair, then it could be seen as meting the philosophy of **rehabilitation**, and if it had a medical and drug treatment center and provided psychological services such as cognitive behavioral therapy (CBT), then it could be seen as satisfying the medical model, specifically providing a **treatment** approach. Yet again, if the prison provided a caseworker who analyzed the needs of the offender and provided offender–victim mediation, it would serve the idea of **restorative justice**, though the extent to which that could be effective while all the other dimensions are in play is questionable. The point here is that one component of the criminal justice system—corrections, seen as typically associated with a few punitive philosophies of punishment—can and sometimes does at different times (depending on the prevailing correctional ideology) serve different correctional philosophies. This is also true for "fines" that can be to the state, or payment to victims (restitution), or as payment or work done to the community as in community service (reparation) or even as punishment (deterrence) to dissuade people from future law violation.

The types of sanctions or techniques of crime control that can be imposed for law violations have expanded since the 1970s and 1980s, when intermediate sanctions were added to provide a continuum of options from prison to probation. Intensive supervision and house arrest were developed to provide additional supervision for those who presented a higher "risk" to public safety and the community, with a view that they would serve a rehabilitative philosophy to transition a person from incarceration to life on the outside, in society. Other intermediate sanctions or crime control techniques include electronic monitoring, day reporting centers, restitution, fines, and community service.

With the increase in types of sanctions, and an ever increasing number of laws defining behavior as criminal, there has been the potential for net widening, or increasing the number of people under supervision or in custody.

> None of the goals of punishment/ sanctions/sentences which have been experimented with or pursued over the centuries—whether deterrence, incapacitation, rehabilitation, shaming or even retribution—have done much to reduce crime rates or reform deviants. As David Garland has argued, it is "only mainstream processes of socialization that are able to promote proper conduct on a consistent and regular basis." Formal punishment is at best a backup, a stopgap measure to be applied wherever and whenever the informal system fails to produce desired levels of control (Chriss, 2007: 105).

This raises the question of whether formal criminal justice should be left as this open, decentralized system that allows variations, diversions, and exceptions, or whether there should be one overall policy governing the system to provide consistency.

Readings on Correctional Policies and Issues

Several articles address correctional policies and issues related to the types of interventions listed in Table 3 and the techniques of crime. James Austin and colleagues, in "Unlocking America, Why and How to Reduce the American Prison Population," take an in-depth look at prisons in America to assess the current state of corrections, explore the accuracy of underlying assumptions about crime and punishment, and recommend changes that they argue would significantly reduce the prison population and save money without impacting public safety.

Barbara Owen and Alan Mobley, in an article entitled "Realignment in California: Policy and Research Implications," outline an attempt by one state to restructure corrections to deal with the increasing number of inmates, high return to custody rates, and budget constraints. The true effects of the realignment are not yet known, since the program has only been in effect since 2011.

As mentioned previously, there has been an increased interest in reintegration programs in recent years: a return to some of the principles of rehabilitation programs in the 1960s stressing community supervision and services. Michael Pinard, in his article, "Reflections and Perspectives on Reentry and Collateral Consequences," discusses what he calls a reentry crisis, with increasing numbers of prisoners released to the community at the end of their sentences, or because of programs to reduce the custody population due to budget shortfalls. He examines the collateral consequences of this significant change in corrections.

Barbara Bloom and her colleagues, in "Gender Responsive Strategies for Women Offenders," argue that male and female pathways to crime differ, and that taking these differences into account can lead to better outcomes during reentry from prisons. The authors discuss a number of factors that influence the path women take to criminal activity and present guiding principles for program development.

JUVENILE JUSTICE

The same social control intervention strategies discussed in previous sections can also apply to the juvenile justice system, but the emphasis is different because children are viewed as not having the same mental capacity and judgment as adults. It is important to know something about the history of juvenile justice to understand current-day philosophies of juvenile law and corrections to control delinquent behavior. Initially, youth 17-years-old and younger were considered juveniles, and their law violations were exclusively under the jurisdiction of the juvenile courts. Historically, the juvenile courts operated under the *parens patriae*, model, in which the court acted as the protector or as a parent and a delinquent youth became a ward of the court. The focus of the system was on prevention and rehabilitation.

Over the years, as the adult system became more focused on punishment, the juvenile justice response also changed. Juveniles were committing serious crimes such as homicide and robbery at a young age, and some felt they should be remanded to adult courts to receive the same punishments as adults for similar felony crimes. The state laws that authorize remand of juveniles to adult court are based on the type of crime committed and the age of the youth charged with the offense. The imposition of adult sentences for juveniles raises some interesting questions regarding where they serve their custody sentence as juveniles, and whether all adult sanctions apply. Some states had statutes authorizing the death penalty for juveniles, but this practice was overturned by the U.S. Supreme Court in *Roper v. Simmons* in 2005. And in 2012, the high court held that states could not impose a mandatory sentence of life without the possibility of parole for juveniles found guilty of certain crimes (*Miller v. Alabama*).

Research by Jeffrey Fagan (1996) assessed the impact of juvenile remands to adult court. "Results showed that incarceration rates were high for adolescents sentenced in criminal courts, but sentence lengths were comparable. However, recidivism rates were significantly lower for adolescents sentenced in the juvenile court, regardless of the sentence type or severity. Results suggest that efforts to criminalize adolescent offending may not produce desired results and may in fact be counterproductive" Fagan (1996: 1).

Readings on Juvenile Justice

With the move toward a more punitive response to juvenile law violators, some have expressed concerns about the response by more informal agents of social control, including the schools. Paul J. Hirschfield, in "Preparing for Prison? The Criminalization of School Discipline in the USA," raises concerns that the American school systems increasingly are considering school discipline within the context of social control. He assesses the impact of this trend, particularly for disadvantaged minority youth.

A related issue in the juvenile justice system, addressed by Franklin E. Zimring, is the harmful effects of disproportionate treatment of minority youth in the juvenile justice system. In his article, "Minimizing Harm from Minority Disproportion in American

Juvenile Justice," the author identifies key options to reduce injustice in the American juvenile courts.

Peter W. Greenwood and Franklin E. Zimring, in "Programming in the Modern Juvenile Court," discuss the need for effective programs for youth in today's juvenile court system. They see value in pursuing the goals of prevention, deterrence, and treatment and looking for treatment alternatives at all stages of the decision-making process in the juvenile justice system.

CONCLUSION: SOCIAL CONTROL POLICIES

The articles presented on the criminal justice system and formal social controls focus on current issues facing policy makers and potential policy options. To understand how to evaluate the effectiveness of the strategies, programs, and laws related to social control and positive change, one must understand the policy process.

A policy is an action to guide decision making by the government: "The term public policy always refers to the actions of government and the intentions that determine those actions. Making policy requires choosing among goals and alternatives, and choice always involves intention ... public policy is defined ... as an intentional course of action followed by a government institution or official for resolving an issue of public concern" (Cochran, *et al.*, 2009: 1–2). Government entities, including criminal justice agencies, develop policies and procedures to carry out the laws and their mandates. Public administration textbooks often describe the policy formulation process as an orderly sequence of events. For example, Marion and Oliver (2010) indicate that the following steps occur:

+ Problem Identification;
+ Agenda Setting;
+ Policy Formulation;
+ Policy Implementation;
+ Policy Evaluation.

A problem needs to capture the attention of major decision makers and be recognized as a significant issue. There are a number of ways this can happen. The problem can receive widespread attention and concern, or there may be a triggering event that brings the problem to the attention of policy makers (Marion and Oliver, 2010). There are generally alternative policy options that can be implemented and they can include widespread change, like the Patriot Act that created the Department of Homeland Security, or small/incremental changes to existing policies. An important issue is always the cost of the changes compared to the potential benefits received.

As part of policy formulation, one must determine how the policy will be formulated, define the intent, decide who will be responsible for the next steps, and plan for implementation (Marion and Oliver, 2010). In some cases, the policy or legislation provides specific guidelines (such as the three-strikes law for sentencing violent and serious offenders in California); in other cases, legislation is vague and those charged with implementation must provide more detail as to the processes and procedures required to achieve the goal (such as the medical marijuana statutes in several states).

Policy analysis can, or should be, a key element of policy implementation. A policy analysis is an unbiased, balanced assessment of alternatives that:

+ Defines the issue;
+ Documents current policy;
+ Identifies decision makers;
+ Presents alternative policies;
+ Analyzes alternatives in terms of pros, cons, and costs;
+ Identifies the issues in implementing policies; and
+ Recommends policy change based on analysis.

A number of actors in the political and criminal justice arena have the sole or joint responsibility for implementing policies. The decision makers vary, based on the issue or problem being addressed. Congress can pass legislation to be signed by the president of the United States to enact laws at the federal level, such as the Controlled Substance Act (CSA), which regulates the importation, manufacture, distribution, possession, and use of controlled substances such as marijuana, opiates, and methamphetamines. State legislatures can also pass bills to be signed by their governor to implement laws to define state crimes and provide sentencing guidelines, such as the addition of hate crimes as a designation and sentencing enhancement. Local governments, including cities and counties, can enact laws to regulate behavior with their jurisdictions.

The legal and formal regulations and policies provide an important foundation for social control in the criminal justice system, but are not the only policies that affect the way the system operates. Agency administrators can implement policies and procedures within their departments to define how legislative mandates will be carried out. For example, police chiefs and sheriffs allocate resources based on priorities and resources available. A police chief may reduce the number of officers assigned to enforcement of victimless crimes such as gambling and prostitution if resources are needed to address more serious crimes, such as homicide, rape, and robbery.

Citizens also play important roles in policy development and implementation. In some states, through an initiative process, citizens can propose new legislation that is approved by a vote in a general election. The medical marijuana statute in California, which allows possession and use of the drug by patients under specified circumstances, was enacted through the initiative process. Citizens and interested parties often serve on task forces to develop solutions to a problem or review the practices of criminal justice agencies. In the city of San Diego, a task force composed of experts, criminal justice professionals, practitioners, and citizens evaluated options for development of a citywide needle-exchange program. Citizens also have input through special interest groups, editorial comments or opinions in local media, and through the complaint processes that have been implemented in most criminal justice agencies.

There are many ways in which individuals and groups can influence policy decisions:

+ Campaign contributions;
+ Media articles;
+ Lobbying/lobbyists;
+ Research/policy analysis;
+ Citizen groups;
+ Protests.

At the end of the policy implementation process is an evaluation phase. Policy makers may want to determine if the program or statute is effective. There are often two phases of an evaluation:

+ Process—Determine if program was implemented as planned.
+ Impact or Outcome—Determine if the program had an effect on the problem.

Policy makers review the results of evaluation research and can decide to terminate a program or legislation, modify the program, or continue the program as implemented.

One example of a program that was terminated as a result of research findings showing it to be ineffective was the Scared Straight project, which provided youth with a view of the consequences of crime by taking them to prisons to talk firsthand to those who have been incarcerated. A study by Joan McCord found that not only did the program not have the desired impact of reducing crime among the youth exposed to prisons, but in some cases the program seemed to increase youth's involvement in crime (Sherman, et al., 1998).

The Drug Abuse Resistance Program (D.A.R.E.), which has been implemented in local schools across the country to provide drug education with the goal of reducing drug use among teens and young adults, has been evaluated at the local and national levels. The consensus among researchers is that the program has not achieved the goal of reducing drug use (Sherman, et al., 1998), but the program continues with the support of educators and special interest groups.

In recent years, a new approach to policy formulation and implementation that is often used by criminal justice agencies is evidence-based programming. Key decision makers review existing programs that show promising results based on evaluations that indicate effectiveness. The thinking is that proven programs will be more successful in achieving goals. However, this approach can limit innovation and new ideas for addressing social problems.

REFERENCES

Austin, John. (1832). *The Province of Jurisprudence Determined.* London: John Murray.

Becker, Howard. (1963). *Outsiders: Studies in the Sociology of Deviance.* New York: The Free Press. ISBN 978-0-684-83635-5.

Beirne, Piers, and James Messerschmidt. (1991). *Criminology.* New York: Harcourt, Brace, & Jovanovich.

Bennett, Debbie. (1990). Coping with Hyperactivity. In *Degrees of Deviance: Student Accounts of their Deviant Behavior,* edited by Stuart Henry (pp. 102–107). Salem, WI: Sheffield Publishing.

Black, Donald. (1976). *The Behavior of Law.* New York: Academic Press.

Black, Donald. (1983). Crime as Social Control. *American Sociological Review.* 48:34–45. www.csun.edu/~egodard/readings/Black-1983-CrimeasSC.pdf.

Braga, Anthony A., and David L. Weisburd. (2006). *Police Innovation and Crime Prevention: Lessons Learned from Police Research over the Past 20 Years.* Discussion paper presented at the U.S. National Institute of Justice Police Research Planning Workshop (November 28–29, 2006, Washington, DC).

Canadian Law Commission (2003). *What Is a Crime?* Ottawa, Canada: Canadian Law Commission.

Cardozo, Benjamin Nathan. (1924). *The Growth of the Law.* New Haven, CT: Yale University Press.

Chambliss, William, and Robert B. Seidman. (1971. 1982). *Law, Order and Power.* 2nd ed. Reading, MA: Addison-Wesley.

Chriss, James J. (2007). *Social Control: An Introduction.* Cambridge, UK: Polity Press.

Cochran, Clarke E., Lawrence C. Mayer, T.R. Carr, and N. Joseph Cayer. (2009). *American Public Policy: An Introduction.* 9th ed. Boston: Wadsworth/Cengage.

Cohen, Stanley. (1985). *Visions of Social Control: Crime Punishment and Classification.* Cambridge, UK: Polity Press.

Conrad, Peter, and Schneider, Joseph W. (1992). *Deviance and Medicalization: From Badness to Sickness.* Philadelphia: Temple University Press.

Deflem, Mathieu. (2007). "The Concept of Social Control: Theories and Applications." Paper presented at the International Conference on "Charities as Instruments of Social Control in Nineteenth-Century Britain," Université de Haute Bretagne (Rennes 2), Rennes, France, November 22–23. Available via: www.mathieudeflem.net.

Diamond, Stanley. (1971). "The Rule of Law versus the Order of Custom." *Social Research: An International Quarterly* 34(4): 42–72.

Durkheim, Émile (1893). *The Division of Labor in Society.* New York: Free Press, 1964.

Ehrlich, E. (1913, 1936). *Fundamental Principles of the Sociology of Law.* New Brunswick, NJ: Transaction Publishers, 2002.

Einstadter, Werner J., and Stuart Henry (2006). *Criminological Theory: An Analysis of Its Underlying Assumptions.* New York: Rowan & Littlefield.

Ellickson, Robert C. (1991). *Order without Law: How Neighbors Settle Disputes.* Cambridge, MA: Harvard University Press.

Ellickson, Robert C. (1998). *Law and Economics Discover Social Norms*. Faculty Scholarship Series. Paper 407. http://digitalcommons.law.yale.edu/fss_papers/407.

Fagan, Jeffrey. (1996). "The Comparative Advantage of Juvenile versus Criminal Court Sanctions on Recidivism Among Adolescent Felony Offenders." *Law and Policy*, 18 (1 & 2). Retrieved September 23, 2012. http://www.housedems.ct.gov/jjpic/Fagan_Comparative_Sanctions_in_Juv_and_Crim_Court_L%26P96.pdf.

Frank, Jerome. (1930). *Law and the Modern Mind*. New Brunswick, NJ: Transaction Publishers, 2009.

Frank, Jerome. (1949). *Courts on Trial: Myth and Reality in American Justice*. Princeton, NJ: Princeton University Press, 1973.

Friedman, Lawrence M. (1975). *The Legal System: A Social Science Perspective*. Englewood Cliffs, NJ: Prentice-Hall.

Gluckman, Max. (1967). *The Judicial Process among the Barotse of Northern Rhodesia*, 2nd ed. Manchester: Manchester University Press.

Goldstein, Joseph. (1960). "Police Discretion Not to Invoke the Criminal Process: Low Visibility Decisions." In George F. Cole, *et al.*, (eds.), *The Criminal Justice System: Politics and Policies*, ninth ed. Wadsworth, 2004.

Greenberg, David F. (1981). *Crime and Capitalism: Readings in Marxist Criminology*. Palo Alto, CA: Mayfield, 1993.

Gurvitch, Georges. (1947). *The Sociology of Law*. London: Routledge & Kegan Paul.

Halsall, Paul. (1996). *Aquinas on Law (Summa Theologica, I–II, Questions 90–97)*. Accessed September 30, 2012. www.fordham.edu/halsall/source/aquinas2.html.

Hart, H.L.A. (1961). *The Concept of Law*. Oxford, England: Clarendon Press.

Henry, Stuart. (1983). *Private Justice: Toward Integrated Theorising in the Sociology of Law*. London: Routledge & Kegan Paul.

Henry, Stuart (1987). "The Construction and Deconstruction of Social Control: Thoughts on the Discursive Production of State Law and Private Justice." In John Lowman, Robert Menzies, and Ted Palys (eds.) *Transcarceration: Essays in the Sociology of Social Control* (pp. 89–108). Aldershot, UK: Gower Press.

Henry, Stuart. (Ed.) (1994). *Social Control: Aspects of Non-State Justice*. Aldershot, UK: Dartmouth.

Henry, Stuart. (2009). *Social Deviance*. Cambridge, UK: Polity Press.

Henry, Stuart. (2001). Legal systems: Private. In N. J. Smelser and P.E. Baltes (eds.), *International Encyclopedia of the Social & Behavioral Sciences*, (pp. 8689–8693). New York: Elsevier.

Henry, Stuart, and Mark M. Lanier (eds.). (2001). *What Is Crime?* Boulder, CO: Rowan & Littlefield.

Hertzler. J.O. (1951) "Edward Alsworth Ross: Sociological Pioneer and Interpreter." *American Sociological Review* 16(5): 597–613.

Holmes, Oliver Wendell. (1897). "The Path of Law." *Harvard Law Review* 10: 457–78.

Homans, George C. (1950). *The Human Group*. New York: Harcourt, Brace, and World.

Hunt, Alan. (1978). *The Sociological Movement in Law*. London: Macmillan.

Kelsen, Hans. (1930). *Law and the Modern Mind*. New York: Coward-McCann, 1949.

Kelsen, Hans. (1941). "The Pure Theory of Law and Analytical Jurisprudence." 55 *Harvard Law Review*, 44.

Kelsen, Hans. (1967). *The Pure Theory of Law.* (Trans. M. Knight). Berkeley, CA: University of California Press.

King, Michael. (1981). *The Framework of Criminal Justice.* London: Croom Helm.

Kraska, Peter, and Brent, John J. (2011). *Theorizing Criminal Justice: Eight Essential Orientations.* 2nd ed. Long Grove: Waveland Press.

Krisberg, Barry. (1975). *Crime and Privilege: Towards a New Criminology.* Englewood Cliffs, NJ: Prentice-Hall.

Kokswijk, Jacob van. (2010). Social Control in Online Society—Advantages of Self-Regulation on the Internet (pp. 239–246), 2010 International Conference on Cyberworlds, 2010.

Llewellyn, Karl N. (1930, 1960). *The Bramble Bush: On Our Law and Its Study.* Dobbs Ferry, NY: Oceana Publications.

Maine, Henry Sumner. (1863). *Ancient Law.* London: Dent, 1917.

Marx, Karl (1911). *A Contribution to the Critique of Political Economy.* Trans. N. I. Stone. Chicago: Charles H. Kerr and Company.

Marion, Nancy E., and Willard M. Oliver. (2010). *The Public Policy of Crime and Criminal Justice.* New Jersey: Prentice-Hall.

Merry, Sally Engle. (1986) "Everyday Understandings of the Law in Working Class America." *American Ethnologist* 13(2): 253–270.

Packer, Herbert L. (1968). "Two Models of the Criminal Justice Process." In George F. Cole, Marc G. Gertz, and Amy Bunger (eds.). *The Criminal Justice System: Politics and Policies*, 9th ed. Belmont, CA: Wadsworth, 2004.

Pospisil, Leopold. (1971). *Anthropology of Law: A Comparative Theory.* New York: Harper and Row.

Pound, Roscoe. (1942; 1997). *Social Control through Law.* New Brunswick, NJ: Transaction Publishers.

Quinney, Richard. (1973). *Critique of the Legal Order.* Boston: Little, Brown, 1974.

Quinney, Richard. (1975). "Crime Control in a Capitalist Society." In Ian Taylor, Paul Walton, and Jock Young (eds.). *Critical Criminology* (pp. 181–201). London: Routledge & Kegan Paul.

Quinney, Richard. (1977). *Class, State, and Crime.* New York: David McKay.

Ross, Edward A. (1901). *Social Control: A Survey of the Foundations of Social Order.* New York: Macmillan, 1922.

Roucek, Joseph S. (1947). *Social Control.* New York: Van Nostrand.

Scala, Dante, J. (2011). "On Henry Sumner Maine Ancient Law." In A. Javier Treviño (ed.), *Classic Writings in Law and Society* (pp. 3–19). 2nd ed. New Brunswick, NJ: Transaction Publishers.

Schwartz, Richard D. (1954). "Social Factors in the Development of Legal Control." A Case Study of Two Israeli Settlements. *Yale Law Journal* 63:471–491.

Sherman, Lawrence W., Denise C. Gottfredson, Doris L. MacKenzie, John Eck, Peter Reuter, and Shawn D. Bushway. (1998, July). "Preventing Crime: What Works, What Doesn't, What's Promising." *National Institute of Justice Research Brief*, pp. 1–19. Washington, DC: U.S. Department of Justice, National Institute of Justice, Office of Justice Programs.

Spitzer, Steven. (1975). "Towards a Marxian Theory of Deviance." *Social Problems* 22: 638–51.

Stamper, Norm (2005). *Breaking Rank: A Top Cop's Exposé of the Dark Side of American Policing.* New York: Nation Books.

Sumner, Colin. (2006). "Deviance." In E. McLaughlin and J. Muncie (eds.), *The Sage Dictionary of Criminology.* 2nd ed. (pp. 126–127). London: Sage.

Treviño, A. Javier. (2011). *Classic Writings in Law and Society.* 2nd ed. New Brunswick, NJ: Transaction Publishers.

Turk, Austin T. (1969). *Criminality and the Legal Order.* Chicago: Rand McNally.

Turk, Austin. T. (1972). *Legal Sanctioning and Social Control. U.S. Department of Health, Education, and Welfare.* National Institute of Mental Health. Washington, DC: U.S. Government Printing Office.

Turk, Austin T. (1976). "Law as a Weapon in Social Conflict." *Social Problems* 23: 276–291.

Turk, Austin T. (1982). *Political Criminality: The Defiance and Defense of Authority.* Beverly Hills, CA: Sage.

Vincent, Chuck. (1999). In *Degrees of Deviance: Student Accounts of Their Deviant Behavior* (2nd ed.), edited by Stuart Henry and Roger Eaton (pp. 97–100). Salem, WI: Sheffield Publishing.

Weber, Max. (1954). *On Law, Economy and Society.* Cambridge, MA: Harvard University Press.

Wolf, Kurt H. (1964). "Social Control." In Julius Gould and William L. Kolb (eds.), *Dictionary of the Social Sciences* (p. 650). London: Tavistock Publications.

Young, Jock. (1981) "Thinking Seriously about Crime: Some Models of Criminology." In Mike Fitzgerald, Gregor McLennan, and Jennie Pawson (eds.). *Crime and Society: Readings in History and Society* (pp. 248–309). London: Routledge & Kegan Paul.

Zola, Irvine. (1972). "Medicine as an Institution of Social Control." *Sociological Review* 20(4): 487–504.

PART 1

Readings from a Sociological
Perspective on Social Control

Why People Ban Behavior

Stuart Henry

In the previous chapter we saw how deviance is variously defined and how the *audience* plays a significant role in the deviance construction process. In this chapter we consider the social process involved in defining certain behavior as deviant, a process that is nothing if not political:

> The creation of deviance … is part of a political process in which people's behavior (and/or condition) is publicly signified as different, negatively evaluated, and interpreted as violations deserving of condemnation and control. Rule-making also involves the process of defining rule violators as deviants liable to various actions allegedly designed to control them. These two features of rule-making are referred to as *banning* (Pfuhl and Henry, 1993: 85)

Perceived differences that are negatively evaluated are the source of much banning. The difference perceived may be in behavior, ideas or appearance. Identifying and defining a behavior draws it out from the vast array of possible behaviors as a special kind of behavior; one about which something needs to be done. Howard S. Becker, a jazz musician and sociologist whose book *Outsiders: Studies in the Sociology of Deviance* became one of the best selling sociology books of all time observed:

> *Social groups create deviance by making the rules whose infractions constitute deviance* and applying those rules to particular people and labeling them outsiders. From this point of view deviance is *not* a quality of the act a person commits but rather a consequence of the application by others of rules and sanctions to an offender. The deviant is one to whom that label has been successfully applied; deviant behavior is behavior that people so label. (Becker, 1963: 9).

Not only are behaviors seen as deviant, ideas judged to be too extreme are also banned. Communism and fascism are two obvious examples; Satanism and

37

cult worship are others. Paranormal beliefs are deviant according to society's dominant institutions even though widely accepted, because they challenge the view of science, and invoke a negative reaction from scientists (Goode, 2000). Indeed, "Beliefs are deviant if they fall outside the norms of acceptability and are deemed wrong, irrational, eccentric, or dangerous in a given society or by the members of a particular collectivity within a given society" (Perrin, 2007: 1140). Even within academic higher education, ideas that are deviant from an instructor's line of thinking are often subject to censure, and students have learned to be quiet in classes where they suspect the instructor is partial to either a strong left or right-wing ideology. Consider the case of Harley Quinn, a graduate student in a large Midwestern University studying for her Master's in Marriage and Family Therapy. Her program is considered one of the best in the country and so, having a bachelor's degree from a flagship campus of the University of California, Harley thought she was well suited to the challenges that a top professional program would offer. After all, being of Latino heritage, Harley had been schooled in critical social theory, particularly critical race and feminist theory and was well versed in the issues that confronted those marginalized by institutionalized racism. Soon into the program, however, Harley found that the faculty had a particular line of thought, particularly favoring multiculturalism and integration, and the program's students either reflected it or adopted it. In either case it was a far cry from the critical thinking of her UC undergraduate education. When Harley began to interject her comments into the discussion, and share her different ideas about what created the conditions for the problems that therapists had to deal with, other students reacted. Over the course of three semesters Harley became the outcast in her classes, and seemed to offend her fellow students simply by challenging their ideas. The collective opposition to her thought resulted in hostile and controlling e-mail from other students and complaints to the program director about Harley's offensive "behavior." This was a shock to her, but nothing like the shock she experienced when she was reprimanded and put on probation, not for poor work—she was a straight "A" student—but for saying

things about institutionalized racism embedded in practices and curriculum that intimidated other students. As part of the conditions for her continuation in the program she was told that anything she said in classes and via email that other students in the program found offensive would cause her to be thrown out of the program. And this went all the way to the Universities disciplinary officer who endorsed the decision. The result was extreme self-censure for fear that she would be "in trouble." Even her now minimal participation was objected to by other students who wanted her to participate in the discussions, so long as she did so in ways that affirmed their view of reality. It seems that what they really wanted was for Harley to "convert" to their way of thinking and show that she had "reformed." Not only does such treatment cause extreme stress and anxiety, and generate feelings of frustration and anger, but it also shows that even in the most mundane settings of a university educational program, "incorrect" thinking can be subject to banning and sanctioning through collective and authoritative social control.

Similarly appearances can be banned and stigmatized. Obvious examples are people with disabilities, such as the blind, crippled, the disfigured, like the Elephant Man, and those who wear outrageous clothes, hairstyles or tattoos. As Heitzig points out, "appearance is a form of non-verbal communication … Through our appearance we identify ourselves to others and allow them to identify us":

> Of course clothing itself is a major source of symbolic meaning. Particular items of clothing, as well as cut, fabric, color, and pattern are taken as clues to the identity of the wearer. Accessories such as shoes, purses/bags, gloves, and jewelry are also part of the symbolic communication of appearance. Physical characteristics such as height, weight, muscle development, breast size, and tans are imbued with meaning as well … the adherence to, or violation of these informal norms of appearance allows both the wearer and the observers to make

an identification of conformity or deviance. (Heitzig, 1996: 353).

Indeed, simple appearance can result in censure and attempts at control. Consider the following account of the "trouble" caused by a teen's Goth appearance:

> Most of them are dressed in black with dyed jet-black hair or a bouffant, pale skin and black make-up, regardless of sex. They go to great lengths to pick and choose their clothes. They mousse and gel their hair until it stands straight on the end and they stay out of the sun at all costs. They want to shock yet they want respect. Kelly was in McDonald's one night taking crap from a preppie university student. Her hair was a black and straggled mop. She had shocking black eyeliner and ripped black tights with some sort of black mini t-shirt. The cross hanging from her ear didn't help … The scene resulted in a fist fight outside the restaurant which brought the police and ended in arrest. How can someone's dress and appearance lead to so much trouble? (King, 1999: 160)

The interpretation of another's appearance as different and offensive can lead to a reaction that seeks to control or sanction the perceived offender. In this sense, appearance can be compared to behavior in that it has an effect on others. When that effect is seen as negative, and applied to children, it can be a powerful weapon in the banning process. For example, being obese in public might be disturbing to those worried about America's obesity problem. In this context writer Jacob Sullum proposed:

> Banning fat people from public parks, where they set a bad example for the kids … Ideally, though, we should be moving toward a world in which no child is exposed to potential role models who normalize obesity and cause overeating to be approved behavior. I'm not talking about a complete ban on

obesity. People would still be free to be fat in the privacy of their own homes (provided they have no children); they would just not be allowed to go out in public until they slimmed down. (Reasononline, 2001).

So, from this perspective appearance is seen to have behavioral effects; this is similar to banning children's access to the Internet or suppressing their ability to view mutilated bodies. The point is that we make meaning out of appearance, just as we do out of behavior or ideas, and if these are viewed negatively in their effects, then we seek to ban them. Clearly, what makes a behavior, idea or appearance stand out as different, or deviant, depends on the audience and their values. Whether a behavior is banned also depends on a social process.

While we are accustomed to think of banning as a formal process in which communities or whole societies are offended by the behavior or appearance, most banning starts out and continues as part of an informal process by groups of people with power and privilege; part of retaining their power and privilege involves them policing the boundaries that separate them from others. As an example, consider high school students in suburban and rural United States. They are typically organized into a social hierarchy of peers who rank themselves according to various "social types" that include: "jocks" (good looking athletes, football players, wrestlers); "preppies" (who wear the latest designer fashions, are seen as superficial yet believe they are superior to others, some of whom become "cheerleaders"); "geeks" (technical and computer minded, into sci fi, with hi IQ and no interest in sports, also known as "losers"); and "nerds" (who are thought to be super-smart, read books and are loners). Others include: dorks, dweebs, freaks, retards, gamers, goths, gangstas, and posers (for definitions and meanings of these and more see www. urbandictionary.com). The jocks and cheerleaders tend to top the high school social hierarchy in popularity and determine what behaviors are valued and what are not. The following account illustrates the social typing process at work in this former student's school which shows how deviance and "conformity" are inextricably linked through defining who is "in" and who is "out," or who is "hot" and who is not.

> When we were in junior high school my friend Rich and I made a map of the school lunch tables according to popularity. This was easy to do because kids only ate lunch with others of about the same popularity. We graded them from A to E. A tables were full of football players and cheerleaders and so on. E tables contained the kids with mild cases of Down's Syndrome, what in the language of the time we called "retards." We sat at a D table, as low as you could get without looking physically different. ... Everyone in the school knew exactly how popular everyone else was, including us ... I know a lot of people who were nerds in school, and they all tell the same story: there is a strong correlation between being smart and being a nerd, and an even stronger inverse correlation between being a nerd and being popular. ... teenagers are always on duty as conformists. For example, teenage kids pay a great deal of attention to clothes. They don't consciously dress to be popular. They dress to look good. But to who? To the other kids. *Other kids' opinions become their definition of right, not just for clothes, but for almost everything they do, right down to the way they walk.* And so every effort they make to do things "right" is also, consciously or not, an effort to be more popular. (Graham, 2003)

Those who are popular set the values that others should follow, which tend also to be shaped by prevailing socio-cultural norms about masculinity. So, in U.S. high schools, physical strength and attractiveness are valued, as is a certain kind of style and dress. Boys also value being able to succeed in attracting good-looking female students over whom they have power. Boys who don't possess these characteristics of manly success, or behave in ways that contradict them, such as being weak in physique, having acne, studying, being

obsessed with computers and technology, are excluded from the popular group's social interaction.

In later chapters we'll have more to say about the social construction of social types and stereotypes and the effects of exclusion on the excluded. Here it is important to recognize that powerful groups establish the norms and then police them by attacking, taunting and disparaging those whose behavior or appearance is different. So what is the process that leads groups, whether high school students or citizens to ban, and condemn others' behavior, ideas or appearance?

BANNING BEHAVIOR AS A SOCIAL PROCESS

Banning may be accomplished in the course of asserting a positive direction and intention, often to prevent health hazards and protect people from harmful consequences that might arise in the future. For example, banning may be done to protect us from human cloning or genetically altered foods, or to protect us from environmental hazards or food born contaminants. However, it is more common to think of banning as a reactive, rather than proactive process. Banning is action taken by audiences against some behavior, appearance or threat, real or imagined. Audiences are often made up of groups of informally unorganized people such as our high school student example. However, they can also be formed around ordinary citizens' interests or for the purpose of advocacy such as members of residence associations, community groups or self-help or mutual aid groups organized to lobby for their particular educational, moral, or political cause. Examples are ASH (Action on Smoking and Health), ACT UP (AIDS Coalition to Unleash Power), COYOTE (Cast Off Your Old Tired Ethics—a group organized to legalize prostitution, and NORML (National Organization for the Reform of Marijuana Laws). Such groups are no less social types than the social types their banning creates, as we saw with the high school example. They are people who perceive or feel threatened, powerless, offended or unsettled and see banning a behavior that they find unacceptable, as part of the solution to their problem. (It should be noted that for organizations like COYOTE and NORML their objective is *decriminalizing* a behavior they believe is acceptable since they believe the law criminalizes what they claim is victimless behavior).

The process of banning and rule-making may begin with fear but quickly moves to a shared sense of danger and a belief among the fearful that the behavior in question is not going to go away by itself. Moreover, the problematic behavior is seen as controllable, and its control can be implemented by creating new rules, or by strengthening existing ones through extra enforcement. It is not clear why people continue to believe that rules can directly control people's behavior, especially when much of the behavior that is reacted to is already breaking norms. We'll first look at who are the people who create rules and ban behavior called "moral entrepreneurs" and then at how they create "moral panics" in furtherance of the behavior they seek to ban. Then we'll look at the way the mass media serves as a partner in the rule-creating process.

Moral Entrepreneurs

Sociologist and jazz musician Howard Becker eloquently describes the rule making process used by audiences as being led by enterprising 'moral entrepreneurs':

> Before any act can be viewed as deviant, and before any class of people can be labeled and treated as outsiders for committing the act, someone must have made the rule which defines the act as deviant. Rules are not made automatically. Even though a practice may be harmful in an objective sense to the group in which it occurs, the harm needs to be discovered and pointed out. People must be made to feel that something ought to be done about it. Someone must call the public's attention to these matters, supply the push necessary to get things done, and direct such energies as are aroused in the proper direction to get the rule created. Deviance is a product of enterprise in the largest sense. (Becker, 1963: 161).

Moral entrepreneurs make rules by converting the meaning that activities have for their participants into new meanings, and by presenting these, with the help of pressure groups, through the mass media and the Internet in a way that gains the public's attention. This is usually by exaggerating an extreme form of the behavior in order to create fear and concern. An example is the banning of alcohol consumption on Southern California's (and particularly San Diego's), beaches. Known as the "Beach Booze Ban," 2008 saw the culmination of a campaign that had sought to ban drinking alcohol at the beach (San Diego Alcohol Policy Panel, 2009). As part of the social activity and beach culture in Southern California alcohol had been consumed in public for years. A growing concern by local residents, supported by restaurant and bar owners, responding to a series of what were argued to be rowdy incidents, including some folks publicly urinating in the neighborhoods surrounding the beaches, led to a campaign to ban alcohol from all beaches. The ban was supported by several prominent interests groups such as MADD (Mothers Against Drunk Driving), The San Diego County Policy Panel on Youth Access to Alcohol, the San Diego Police Officers' Association. They gave the following reasons for supporting "alcohol-free beaches." Using government statistics, they claimed, "Alcohol consumption is closely linked to violence." Using local police crime data they asserted that the Mission Beach and Pacific Beach areas had three times the rate of violent arrests than the rest of the city and a fifth of the entire city's alcohol-related arrests. They claimed that alcohol consumption on the beaches was undermining the community and drawing excessive police resources:

> Beach residents have complained of public urination, vandalism, noise, and other alcohol-related problems. Oceanside, Carlsbad, Imperial Beach, and La Jolla have banned alcohol consumption on public beaches with positive results. Law enforcement officials report a reduction in alcohol-related problems, as well as more diversity in the composition of beach crowds. (San Diego Alcohol Policy Panel, 2009).

They stated that teen parties using alcohol, presumably on the beach, are associated with a host of teen problems:

> Some consequences associated with youth alcohol problems are unwanted pregnancy, sexual assault, suicide, homicide, scholastic failure, and HIV and other STD transmission. Beaches provide appealing settings for underage drinking. The beach atmosphere is a major contributor to the drinking culture of San Diego. Allowing alcohol consumption on our beaches encourages a dangerous social norm of complacency towards underage and binge drinking. To make matters worse, police officers often cannot be certain which drinkers are and are not 21 and over. Research illustrates that *banning alcohol from beaches is an effective way to reduce alcohol-related problems, especially among youth* … making our local beaches alcohol-free is an example of good public policy based on a public health and safety necessity. Experience shows that once bans are in place, drunk and disorderly behavior is greatly diminished, and the beach becomes a serene and safe place where families and others can enjoy the ocean environment. *Please join law enforcement officials, community groups, and San Diego residents in making our beaches safer and healthier places to live in and visit for all!* (San Diego Alcohol Policy Panel, 2009).

In the Spring of 2008 advocates of the alcohol ban appeared in newspaper columns and on local TV and radio talk shows debating the issues, with drinking advocates pointing out that earlier bans had concentrated the problems into a few areas where bans did not exist so exaggerating them. They argued that there were already laws that governed problems associated with rowdy behavior, but to no avail. The moral entrepreneurs eventually succeeded in banning alcohol from all of San Diego's area by persuading local councils to vote in favor of the ban. As we have seen, similar campaigns have been waged against smoking in public places, against assisted suicide, abortion and drug use generally. The point here is not whether the arguments of those seeking to ban various behaviors are right or wrong, but how these interest groups marshal forces in a political campaign to bring off the resulting changes in public policy. These kinds of moral campaigns to create or change laws against certain behavior have both instrumental goals and symbolic goals. The instrumental goals are typically those stated explicitly in the campaigns, as well as some that are implicitly, including, in the case of the Beach-Booze-Ban increasing restaurant and bar trade because alcohol must be consumed on licensed premises. Less obvious are the symbolic motives (San Diego Alcohol Policy Panel, 2009).

The more symbolic motive underling rule-making activity often has to do with status conflicts between the respective supporters or defenders of the ban. Here the goal may be about establishing or underpinning a particular social group's position in the society, as Joseph Gusfield (1963) has forcefully demonstrated in the case of the early twentieth-century Prohibition laws. These laws were passed more as a status marker of middle-class Protestant America's demonstration of its continued dominance in the face of their fear that Irish Catholic immigrants would threaten their moral control. Small-town Protestant America feared that rapid urbanization and Catholic immigration would undermine its economic and social position. Through the Women's Christian Temperance Movement, they pushed to have alcohol banned throughout the United States. In these kinds of cases, a change in law, or implementing a new law, may symbolize which groups are in control of the moral order of a society: "Even though it may not be enforced, merely having a law on the books reflecting one's values and interests may be taken as a measure of a group's moral stature or social status" (Pfuhl and Henry 1993: 89). For example, analysis of the implementation of a smoking ban in Shasta County, California shows a similar pattern as the California Beach-Booze-Ban but as the account below reveals, the ban also reflects the different economic and social status of the competing groups in the social order:

Moral entrepreneurs crusading for the ban argued that secondhand smoke damages public health, implicitly grounding their argument in the principle that people have a right to a smoke-free environment. Status quo defenders countered that smokers have a constitutional right to indulge wherever and whenever they see fit ... The moral entrepreneurs who engineered the smoking ban campaign were representatives of the prestigious knowledge class, including among their members officials from the local chapters of respected organizations at the forefront of the national anti-smoking crusade. In contrast the small business owners, who were at the core of the opposing coalition of status quo defenders, represented the traditional middle-class. Clearly there was an instrumental quality to the restaurant and bar-owners' stance, because they saw the ban as potentially damaging to their business interests ... In many respects, the status conflicts involved in the Shasta County smoking ban were symbolic ... Ultimately, a lifestyle associated with the less educated, less affluent, lower occupational strata was stigmatized as a public health hazard and targeted for coercive reform. Its deviance status was codified in the ordinance banning smoking in public facilities, including restaurants and bars. The ban symbolized the deviant status of cigarette smokers, the prohibition visibly demonstrating the community's condemnation of their behavior. Further the smoking ban symbolically amplified the purported virtues of the abstinent lifestyle. (Tuggle and Holmes, 2006: 158).

Whether it is instrumental or symbolic, the conversion of some groups' private moralities into public issues is necessary if their concern is to gain sufficient legitimacy to warrant more formal rule-making. In this process, a principal partner is the media. They can act either as a forum for the display of concern or as an instrument for agitating it, as we shall see later in this chapter.

Clearly the range of strategies for mobilizing public moral support is as wide as that available to candidates in a political campaign. Moral entrepreneurs can promote their case for a behavioral ban by associating their proposed rules with positive values or benefits to society. Particularly popular are those bans claimed to increase health or freedom. A similarly powerful impact can be achieved by associating the continued existence of questioned behavior with negative values, pointing up its threat to the mental, physical or moral fabric of organized society. Groups of moral entrepreneurs can draw respectability from the public by establishing alliances with respected members of society or by recruiting these people's testimonies, if not their person. Any endorsement by public officials takes the rule-making case towards a complete ban. Any mythmaking, which can be employed to exaggerate aspects of the behavior or to help hang the activity on the backs of already recognized undesirable social types, will help their cause. The strategy of creating "moral panic" and of demonizing sections of the population is also used and can be based on fact or myth.

The Creation of Moral Panics

British sociologist Stanley Cohen (1972), in his *Folk Devils and Moral Panics* coined the term "moral panic." Cohen described the demonization through the mass media around the 1960s "Mods" and "Rockers," teen rebel groups whose behavior was claimed to threaten valued British cultural norms. In general, moral entrepreneurs promote the idea that particular groups in the population are "folk devils" doing evil regardless of whether any serious harm exists. According to Erich Goode and Norman Ben-Yehuda (1994) in *Moral Panics: The Social Construction of Deviance*, moral panics are societal reactions to perceived threat that have certain characteristics. They have volatility and a life cycle in which they suddenly appear in the media, rapidly spread among large sections of the population, and then just as rapidly decline in further instances of the problem. One example is the 1980s panic around U.S. private daycare providers who it was claimed were engaging in "satanic ritual child abuse" and who "were abusing their very young charges in satanic rituals that included such practices as blood-drinking, cannibalism, and human sacrifices" (deYoung, 2006: 163; 1997). These accusations began in 1983 and ended in 1991 and involved over one hundred daycare centers nationwide whose staff were investigated, charged, and in many cases convicted and given long prison sentences.

An important issue in considering the rule-creation process is how interest groups, moral entrepreneurs and social movements create claims about the behavior that they consider to be deviant. Criminologist Ray Surette describes how this "claims-making" works.

> Claims-makers are the promoters, activists, professional experts and spokespersons involved in forwarding specific claims about a phenomenon. Social problems emerge— become a focus for concern—through a process of claims-making. The process determines not only which phenomena come to be designated as social problems, but which characteristics are ascribed to those problems. Claims-makers do more than draw attention to a particular social condition, they shape our sense of what the problem is. Each social condition can be constructed as many different social problems ... and each construction implies different policy courses and solutions. The social roles and ideologies of claims-makers affect their characterization of problems; where moralists see sin, medical authorities detect disease, and criminal justice personnel see crime. (Surette, 1998: 8–9).

Claims-making, then, not only occurs at particular historical moments, but also involves a process of first assembling claims about behavior or conditions seen as morally problematic. Second, it involves presenting these claims as legitimate to significant audiences; not least through the news media. In this process claims-makers can gain more traction for the veracity of their claim if the questioned behavior is tied to other issues of concern. So, in the alleged daycare sexual abuse example, the linkage was made to Satanism. In the alcohol-free beach campaign the issue was tied to teenage suicide, sex and HIV-AIDS. Third, a key task in framing a moral problem involves the prognosis of how to address the problem in order to bring about a desired outcome by defining strategies, tactics and policy. Fourth claims-making involves contesting counter claims and mobilizing the support of key groups.

Erich Goode and Norman Ben-Yehuda say that moral panics also gain public legitimacy through the growth of experts who claim to be authorities in discerning cases of the said feared behavior. In the case of satanic ritual abuse this group of "experts" was comprised of social workers and mental health professionals, who claimed to be able to identify the satanic menace by reframing the words of children as young as two-years of age into accusations against their providers, as well as against others including business people, politicians and family members (de Young, 2006: 165). These professionals claim to expertise was bolstered by attorneys and law enforcement officials and was supported by a newly generated body of materials. Mary de Young describes the process:

> Professionals developed and widely disseminated a wholly synthetic diabolism out of materials haphazardly borrowed from eclectic sources on Satanism, the occult, mysticism, paganism and witchcraft ... They constructed "indicator lists" to assist other professionals ... in identifying child victims, and "symptom lists" to guide the course of their therapy ... a burgeoning critical literature was deeply dividing the professional field into claims-makers and counterclaims-makers, believers and skeptic. (de Young 2006: 166–67).

Following the initial revelations, a moral panic spreads by an increased identification of cases of the behavior that build into a "wave;" in the case of satanic ritual abuse, accusations began at one California preschool and spread to over a hundred child care facilities nationwide. The news was spread via local news media's sensational coverage of the latest "revelations," supported by the "experts" who appeared on television talk shows and news magazines and testified as expert witnesses at trials. Joining them were the parents of the allegedly victimized children, some of whom formed anti-child abuse interest groups such as Citizens Against Child Abuse, Believe the Children and CLOUT (which lobbied for children to be allowed to testify as witnesses in criminal trials).

Moral panics like this one produce an intense hostility towards the accused who are seen as enemies of society. As enemies they are then persecuted. In the alleged child abuse example this resulted in public vilification via the media and convictions by the courts resulting in long prison sentences. Moral panics also feature systems to assess the moral feeling of the public consensus about the seriousness of the threat. In moral panics there is typically a disproportional fear relative to actual harm caused. Indeed, Jeffrey Victor's study of this child abuse reported in *Satanic Panic* (1993; 1998) shows that moral panics need not be based in reality, but can be constructed on imaginary deviants whose existence gains credibility in the eyes of the public when authorities, and those who claim expert knowledge, particularly science or medicine, legitimize the accusations. Moreover, these panics are likely to occur when competing bureaucratic agencies are vying for jurisdiction of authority, when methods of detection result in errors, and when there is a symbolic resonance with a perceived threat identified in a prevailing demonology—which serves as a master cognitive frame that organizes problems, gives meaning to them, explains them, and offers solutions.

Finally, moral panics tend to unravel when a backlash against the persecution occurs; and when exposure of the flaws in identifying the problem begins to emerge. In the case of child abuse, the critics had exposed major flaws in the process and accounts that had silenced its most vocal advocates (Victor, 1993). Other factors contributed to the death of the panic including changes in the number of women in the workforce, changes in day care licensing, and changes in day care operations, including installing video cameras and making them more open and accessible (de Young 2006: 167–68; de Young 1997). In the end many of the charges against alleged offenders were dropped and previous convictions were overturned on appeal. Overall the phenomenon of moral entrepreneurs creating moral panics to establish rules and laws to control what they see as undesirable behavior depends on their ability to make credible claims and that too is a political process. The mass media plays a significant role in the process of moral conversion.

MASS MEDIA AND PUBLIC POLICY

Ray Surette has pointed out that the relationship between mass media and social culture is reciprocal, with each affecting the other:

> As the distributors of social knowledge, the media also legitimize people, social issues, and social policies for the general public. And though the media do not control the process of cultural change, the fact is that in large industrialized nations with hundreds of millions of people, cultural change without media involvement does not occur. The media simultaneously change, react to and reflect culture and society (Surette, 1998: 11).

Competing claims about a social issue or problematic behavior are played out in the mass media. Crime and deviance comprises a large part of television and popular culture where it is used not only to inform as in "news" but also as a source of entertainment (Altheide, 2007: 1107). Some of the most popular shows on television are crime, police or court dramas such as *The Sopranos, Law and Order, CSI, Boston Legal, Bones, and Criminal Minds* etc. This is the forum that claimsmakers compete for the public's attention. However, the media is itself a collection of competing interests groups, particularly the news media, each vying for the top stories and using the tried and tested formula that "if it bleeds it leads." Indeed, news media and television, especially local news media are interested in dramatic claims and sensational stories about problems and issues related to major cultural tropes. As a result not all news is covered; news editors filter out some news and promote other news. Without powerful or organized sponsors, and without journalistic ties, it is difficult to break into the media. Organizations that form around public issues must develop a public relations specialty that nurtures media relations and establishes channels for news releases and expert sources. Part of the job of these interest groups is to manage the quality of their media exposure, particularly including or excluding critical facts, and by a variety of strategies including presentational style:

> Of particular importance is how information is presented, e.g., the sequencing of contradictory positions, the amount of coverage each is given, and the orientations of those reporting the "facts." By altering these elements, the image and the desired definition (meaning) of an issue may be affected. Further, by varying visual and auditory stimuli it is possible to increase or decrease the likelihood that an audience will perceive a situation to be consistent with or contradictory to recognized standards or principles ... Legitimacy may also be generated by careful use of emotionally loaded words or images, and selectively linking a cause with (or disassociating it from) existing positive values ... In addition to aligning their own aims with positive values, moral entrepreneurs try to denigrate the opposition by linking it with negative values. (Pfhul and Henry 1993: 95)

This manipulation of the media by powerful interest groups supported by, and facilitated through, the media assisted by spin-doctors, is designed to shape public policy to reflect the views of these groups as Ray Surette notes:

> Policies and solutions sought are tied to the claims of the successful winning construction. The linking of claims to policies involves claims-makers who often describe a social problem in a simplified, dramatic,

worst-case scenario, launching media-based moral crusades and panics. The claims influence the formation of social policy and the solutions that are seen as "workable" (Surette, 1998: 11).

Indeed, in his comprehensive analysis of *Media, Crime and Criminal Justice*, Surette (1998) summarizes the key findings of the role that mass media play in creating public policy. He says that the news and entertainment media's effects on the public's conception of crime is difficult to predict and has uncertain effects on various claims-makers. However, more convincing evidence exists about "agenda building." Research supports the view that the most impact the media make is on raising the *fear* of crime among the population, and shaping criminal justice policy. Surette argues that models of the effects of mass media campaigns on the general public have shifted from the 1930s view that the media was a "Hypodermic needle-like mechanism that could be used to inject information and attitudes directly into the public" to a view in the 1950s and 60s that the media merely reinforced pre-existing views held by members of the public. By the 1970s the view emerged that the media's impact was affected by social factors and social demographics, including the notion that who viewed what kind of media had an effect on whether they were influenced by its messages. Although the media's effect was still strongest in reinforcing and strengthening existing attitudes, the new research also suggested that the mass media could: (1) form attitudes where the topic was new to the public; (2) change attitudes where attitudes were weakly held; (3) strengthen some attitudes relative to others; (4) change strongly-held attitudes with new facts; and (5) suggest new responses and policy directions. (Surette, 1998: 200).

The important point for our purposes in this chapter is that the mass media's impact is seen to be greatest in generating citizen awareness and attitudes about new problems, precisely the kind that moral entrepreneurs were intent on generating. Surette says there are three areas of importance. The first is the role of the media in raising the significance of crime as a public issue relative to other issues, which is called "agenda-setting." It appears that the linear model of the media influencing public policy is not supported by the research. In other words, it is not the case that the media creates a story on an issue, "the issue increases importance to the public, the public becomes alarmed, interest groups mobilize, and policy makers respond" (Surette, 1998: 202).

The second area of importance in shaping the public's beliefs and attitudes about crime called "agenda-building," resonates with the activities of moral entrepreneurs, and seems to have more research support. Here an interactive reciprocal effect occurs between the media and policy makers such that fear of crime victimization disproportionate with the real level of harm "encourages moral crusades against specific crime issues, heightens public anxiety about crime, and pushes or blocks other serious problems … from the public agenda" (Surette, 1998: 203).

The third significant area is the media's influence on criminal justice policy. Given the strong empirical connection between the fear of criminal victimization and mass media influences, moral entrepreneurs who emphasize and exaggerate the fear of crime have an obvious and clear strategy to bring about changes in policy. This is particularly the case in the criminalizing of new harms about which the public has little knowledge:

> Effects on policy are therefore the ultimate prize in the construction of crime and justice reality competition. Claims-makers forward their competing crime-and-justice claims in an effort to steer the social construction of crime-and-justice policy gaining power, resources, and credibility in the process … Recent research does suggest that the news media … significantly affect policy preferences among the public for general social issues. The content of television news broadcasts favoring or opposed to specific policies consequently shifts public opinion in the same direction as the news coverage … researchers generally interpret the association as part of a causal chain that results in real-world changes in public support for

policies that are reported favorably in the broadcast or print media. Recognizing this, claims-makers work diligently to garner media attention and favor. (Surette, 1998: 213).

The relationship between claims-makers, public opinion and public policy is conceived, therefore, not so much as a linear causal one but more as an ecological reciprocal one in which the mass media are themselves "claims-making actors in the politics of policy formation" (Surette, 1998: 214). In other words the media shape criminal justice policy "by establishing ongoing relationships with other local claims-makers including policy makers, lobbyists and public officials" (Surette 1998: 214). This process involves journalists collaborating with officials and policymakers, each of whom co-produce policy outcomes and can and do choose to draw on the cases that moral entrepreneurs bring before them and that resonate with their own policy aspirations.

It is important here to point out the changing form of news and entertainment which has increasingly become integrated around the Internet and hand-held phones such as Apple's iPhone and Blackberry. Some newspapers have moved from print to fully online (e.g., *The Christian Science Monitor*) and others have been launched only online (e.g., *The Voice of San Diego*). Regardless of the shift in form, these new organizations still rely on links through reporters to influential experts and the *process* of making the news to change ideas, views or policy toward banning behavior is as we have described it in this chapter. Ironically, the Internet itself has also become a subject for moral panic, as some moral entrepreneurs want it banned or controlled to stop children having access to pornography or extremist ideas.

FROM BANNING BEHAVIOR TO MAKING LAWS

Ultimately, of course, the goal of banning a behavior will be met if the powers of the state can be 'captured,' such that laws are passed criminalizing the behavior in question. This will empower the major law enforcement agencies to act, in the name of the whole society, on behalf of those groups with immediate concerns. At this point, the interest group can be said to have established an official ban against the behavior. To accomplish this, moral entrepreneurs need to use power. So far we have been largely using behavior as an example of the banning process, and it might seem too far-fetched to consider the banning of appearance. How can appearance be banned? Can laws be enacted to ban appearance? Well it is underway in Mississippi where the House Bill 282, sponsored by Representative Mayhall, a retired pharmaceutical salesman, made it to the Mississippi State House in January 2008. The proposed law would ban restaurants from serving people with a BMI (Body Mass Index) higher than 30 (For example, for a person of 5 ft 9 inches tall this would be anyone over 203lbs). Under the bill, restaurants would be monitored for compliance by the State Department of Health and those found in violation of the law would have their business permits revoked:

STATE OF MISSISSIPPI

HOUSE BILL NO. 282

An act to prohibit certain food establishments from serving food to any person who is obese, based on criteria prescribed by the state department of health; to direct the department to prepare written materials that describe and explain the criteria for determining whether a person is obese and to provide those materials to the food establishments; to direct the department to monitor the food establishments for compliance with the provisions of this act; and for related purposes. Be it enacted by the legislature of the state of Mississippi:

Section 1

(1) The provisions of this section shall apply to any food establishment that is required to obtain a permit from the State Department of Health under Section 41-3-15(4)(f), that operates primarily in an enclosed facility and that has five (5) or more seats for customers.

(2) Any food establishment to which this section applies shall not be allowed to serve food to any person who is obese, based on criteria prescribed by the State Department of Health after consultation with the Mississippi Council on Obesity Prevention and Management established under Section 41-101-1 or its successor. The State Department of Health shall prepare written materials that describe and explain the criteria for determining whether a person is obese, and shall provide those materials to all food establishments to which this section applies. A food establishment shall be entitled to rely on the criteria for obesity in those written materials when determining whether or not it is allowed to serve food to any person.

(3) The State Department of Health shall monitor the food establishments to which this section applies for compliance with the provisions of this section, and may revoke the permit of any food establishment that repeatedly violates the provisions of this section.

Section 2. This Act Shall Take Effect and Be In Force from and after July 1, 2008

If law is not the outcome of the banning process, "captured institutions" such as science, religion, education and public opinion, are a significant creative accomplishment in the social construction of deviance. But it must not be forgotten that all of these institutions and agencies are themselves groups with interests and they may divide on the issue depending whether these interests are advanced or threatened by the existence of a particular proposed ban. At the very least such groups are likely to graft their interests onto the proposed ban such that what emerges is some compromise position, not necessarily the one that the original advocates had in mind.

Not surprisingly, the chances of resisting the ban are considerably improved if those engaged in the behavior, or those who wish to see us remain free to choose it, engage in a counter political campaign. In this context, controversy, rather than consensus, can be claimed. In such circumstances the law becomes a weapon in the battle between competing interest groups and can actually create conflict by being a resource to be won.

In this chapter we have seen that rules are created to ban behavior based on an audiences selection of what it finds different and offensive. Audiences can be informally organized social cliques or more powerfully organized official interest/advocacy groups. In either case they enforce their view of what is acceptable or unacceptable. In the case of informal groups this can occur through a hierarchy of domination and exclusion. For more organized groups it involves a political process of escalation that moves a private problem to a public issue. Moral entrepreneurs mobilize the mass media and public officials to create public interest in their claim through moral panic and fear of harm with the objective of banning the behavior, preferably through enacting law. In the next chapter we will see what motivates people to behave in ways that others find offensive.

REFERENCES

Altheide, David L. 2007. "The media and Deviance," pp. 1107–10 in *The Blackwell Encyclopedia of Sociology*, vol. III. Ed. G. Ritzer. Oxford; Blackwell Publishing.

Becker, Howard. 1963. *Outsiders: Studies in the Sociology of Deviance*. New York: Free Press.

Cohen, Stanley. 1972. *Folk Devils and Moral Panics: The Creation of Mods and Rockers*. New York: St. Martin's Press.

de Young, Mary. 1997. "The Devil Goes to Day Care: McMartin and the Making of a Moral Panic." *Journal of American Culture*, 20: 19–26.

de Young, Mary. 2006. "Moral Panics: The Case of Satanic Day Care Centers," pp. 162–70 in *Constructions of Deviance: Social Power, Context and Interaction*. 5th edn. Ed. P. A. Adler and P. Adler. Belmont, CA: Thompson Wadsworth.

Goode, Erich, and Norman Ben-Yehuda. 1994. *Moral Panics: The Social Construction of Deviance*. Cambridge: Blackwell.

Goode, Erich. 2000. Paranormal Beliefs: A Sociological Introduction. Prospect Heights, IL: Waveland Press.

Graham, Paul. 2003. "Why Nerds are Unpopular." www.paulgraham.com/nerds.html (accessed July 15, 2008).

Gusfield, Joseph R. 1963. *Symbolic Crusade*. Urbana, IL: University of Illinois Press.

Heitzig, Nancy A. 1996. *Defiance: Rule Makers and Rule Breakers*. Minneapolis/St. Paul, MN: West Publishing.

King, Susan. 1999. "New "Wave Culture," pp. 158–61 in *Degrees of Deviance: Student Accounts of Their Deviant Behavior*. Ed. S. Henry and R. Eaton. Salem, WI: Sheffield Publishing Company.

Perrin, Robin D. 2007. "Deviant Beliefs / Cognitive Deviance," pp. 1140–1 in *The Blackwell Encyclopedia of Sociology*, vol. III. Ed. G. Ritzer. Oxford: Blackwell Publishing.

Pfuhl, Erdwin H., and Stuart Henry. 1993. *The Deviance Process*. 3rd edn. New York: Aldine de Gruyter.

Reasononline. 2001. "Lighten Up, America! Do Fat People Belong in Public Parks?" (December 25). www.reason.com/news/show/35948.html (accessed January 25, 2009).

San Diego Alcohol Policy Panel. 2009. "San Diego Beaches Alcohol Free". http://alcoholpolicypanel.org/sdcappblog/?p=41 (accessed April 11, 2009).

SmokeFree Illinois. 2008. "SmokeFree Illinois: Frequently Asked Questions," www.smokefreeillinois.org/impres/FAQ.pdf.

Sumner, Colin. 1994. *The Sociology of Deviance: An Obituary.* Buckingham: Open University Press.

Sumner, 2 Colin. 2006. "Deviance," pp. 126–7 in *The Sage Dictionary of Criminology.* 2nd edn. Ed, E. McLaughlin and J. Muncie. London: Sage.

Surette, Ray. 1998. Media, *Crime and Criminal Justice: Images and Realities.* 2nd edn. Belmont, CA: West/ Wadsworth.

Tuggle, Justin L., and Malcolm D. Holmes. 2006. "Blowing Smoke: Status Politics and the Smoking Ban," pp. 151–61 in *Constructions of Deviance: Social Power, Context and Interaction.* 5th edn. Ed. P. A. Adler and P. Adler. Belmont, CA: Thompson Wadsworth.

Victor, Jeffrey S. 1993. *Satanic Panic: The Creation of a Contemporary Legend.* Chicago: Open Court.

Victor, Jeffrey S. 1998. "Moral Panics and the Social Construction of Deviant Behavior: Theory and Application to the Case of Ritual Child Abuse." *Sociological Perspectives,* 41: 541–65.

Beyond Folk Devil Resistance

Linking Moral Panic and Moral Regulation

Sean P. Hier, Dan Lett, Kevin Walby, and André Smith

Introduction

Moral panic research traces to Jock Young's (1971) study of the social meaning of drug taking and to Stanley Cohen's (1972) canonical investigation of the construction of the mods and rockers. Moral panic research developed through the 1970s and 1980s, focusing primarily on the role that claims-makers, moral guardians, and the media play in the construction, amplification, and exaggeration of deviance. Significant contributions appeared in the 1990s that stimulated interest in moral panics (e.g., DeYoung, 1998; Goode and Ben-Yehuda, 1994; Hunt, 1997; McRobbie, 1994; McRobbie and Thornton, 1995; Thompson, 1998), and recent contributions have critically assessed moral panic in the context of broader theoretical formulations (e.g., Critcher, 2008, 2009; Garland, 2008; Hier, 2003, 2008; Rohloff, 2008; Rohloff and Wright 2010; Ungar, 2001).

Despite growing interest in moral panic analyses across sociology and criminology (see Hier, 2011), the full explanatory potential of moral panic studies has yet to be realized. Many scholars continue to conceptualize moral panics as exceptional rather than ordinary constructions of deviance to explain irrational and disproportionate reactions to exaggerated threats. One consequence of conceptualizing moral panic in this manner is that the explanatory power of moral panic studies has been minimized if not dismissed in wider investigations of routine moral regulation processes (Hunt, 1999; Moore and Valverde, 2000). A small number of contributions to moral panic studies has started to demonstrate how moral panics are rational, routine features of everyday life that contribute to ongoing processes of moral regulation within and beyond the State (e.g., Critcher, 2008; Hier, 2008; Rohloff, 2008). Nevertheless, efforts to 'widen the focus' (Critcher, 2009) of moral panic studies have only started to make an impact on the direction of research, analysis, and argumentation. Our aim in this article is to contribute to ongoing debates about widening the focus of moral panic studies by examining the relationship between the criminologies of moral panic and moral regulation. We argue that moral panic scholars have correctly emphasized tendencies for folk devils and their supporters to resist both typification and regulation (Hier, 2002a, 2002b; McRobbie, 1994; McRobbie and Thornton, 1995). We argue, however, that the scope of moral panic analyses must extend beyond the episodic nature of resisting primary definitions to assess the broader foundations that give rise to and sustain ongoing processes of moral regulation. Although folk devils and their supporters can and do fight back, their resistance to dominant claims can be subverted, particularly when primary claims are integral to the validation of (especially state-based) regulatory programs. In other words, moral panics represent episodes of contestation and negotiation that emerge from and contribute to or reinforce broader processes of moral regulation.

To substantiate these conceptual and theoretical arguments, we examine the emergence of 'hoodies' as an assumed indicator of moral decline among youth in contemporary Britain. Our specific focus is on claims-making activities in the British press after a shopping center in Kent placed a ban on hooded tops. On 11 May 2005, the Bluewater shopping center implemented a code of conduct forbidding attire that conceals customers' facial features from the gaze of nearly 400 closed-circuit television cameras distributed throughout the complex. The ban prevented anyone wearing a hooded top (aka 'a hoodie') from entering the mall. Given that the garment is a popular mode of attire for British youth, the ban functioned to exclude groups of young people from gathering in the mall. Our focus is not on the Bluewater ban *per se* but rather the extensive national newspaper and television media coverage that the ban incited.

Although moral regulation *vis-a-vis* the signification of hoodies garnered momentum from an established cultural impulse to moralize the activities of youth (Cohen, 1972; Coleman, 2005; Thornton, 1994), discourses opposing the ban appeared in the mass and alternative media. British government officials invoked the hoodies signifier to address assumed youth tendencies towards anti-social behavior, and to justify legislative attempts to impose regulatory measures on British youth. Media reports used the 'hoodies' signifier as a rhetorical device to ascribe blame for a range of crime and anti-social behaviors. These processes were indicative of what Hall *et al.*, (1978) conceptualized as a signification spiral: a mode of signifying events by the convergence of a newly identified concern with other social problems and issues, escalating the perceived threat of the emergent events beyond the thresholds of societal tolerance. However, diverse interest groups 'fought back' against the problematization of the hoodies in mainstream and alternative media counter claims. The struggle to define the problem of the hoodies occurred in the context of an established debate concerning the British government's Anti-Social Behavior Act of 2003 (ASBA) and the emergence of the Anti-Social Behavior Order (ASBO) as state-based techniques to enact forms of moral regulation.

Our purpose in this article is to neither quantify the regularity of ASBO deployment by authorities nor account for the legal technicalities of ASBOs; a burgeoning literature on youth and crime in the UK has already made these contributions (see Crawford, 2006, 2007, 2009; Millie, 2008; Pearson, 2006; Simester and Von Hirsch, 2006). Nor is our purpose to examine the origins of the Bluewater ban. Rather, our aim is to conceptualize the debate about hoodies as a volatile manifestation of long-term regulatory processes. Although several theorists of moral regulation have distanced regulatory projects from moral panic theory on the grounds that the latter imports a negative normative judgment, Hier (2002a, 2003, 2008; and see Critcher, 2009) has demonstrated that much can be made of a *convergence* of moral panic and moral regulation literatures. Whereas the moral panic literature has hitherto been concerned to show how contestation of primary definitions and dominant claims-making is possible, we demonstrate how resistance efforts are themselves undermined with reference to New Labour's 'Reform and Respect Agenda'. Our analysis is thus important in the context of Waiton's (2008) argument that the contemporary politics of anti-social behavior has ushered in the era of amoral panics, insofar as we demonstrate how seemingly 'amoral' politics of managing anti-social behavior is linked to both volatile and long-term forms of moralization.[1]

MORAL REGULATION AND THE VOLATILITY OF PANICS

Analyses of moral panic regularly begin with the arguments presented in Stan Cohen's (1972) *Folk Devils and Moral Panics*. For Cohen (1972: 41), every moral panic has its folk devil: the personification of evil who is (or that are) susceptible to recognition based on 'unambiguously unfavorable symbols'. The source of moral panic is not the folk devil itself; rather the folk devil serves as the ideological embodiment of the moral panic. When folk devils are revealed to the public in a stereotypical fashion through mainstream media reporting, they are constructed as threats to the social/moral fabric requiring immediate regulatory intervention (see Young, 2009). Often the symbolic folk devil correlates approximately to certain individuals and groups, but it is primarily a mode of representation that functions as a proxy for the harmful other in discourses about crime, law, and order.

Cohen's framework corresponds to what Goode and Ben-Yehuda (1994: 124–143) describe as the 'interest group' theory of moral panic—one of three traditional models of moral panic. In this model, moral panic is explained as the unintended outcome of moralizing projects undertaken by interest groups in an effort to draw public attention to a specific 'moral evil'. Goode and Ben-Yehuda distinguish the 'interest group' from the 'elite-engineered' model. The elite engineered model conceives of moral panic as the outcome of manufactured campaigns that are designed to divert attention away from real social crises. Hall *et al.*, (1978), for example, argue that moral panic is a mechanism utilized by the ruling class to mystify deeper crises in the capitalist system. In contrast to the interest group and elite-engineered models, Goode and Ben-Yehuda (1994) propose a third model: grassroots. The grassroots model stipulates that moral panic originates with the general public. In the grassroots model, moral panic is understood to provide release for a reservoir of social insecurity.

The three traditional models of moral panic continue to influence moral panic studies, but subsequent efforts to 'rethink' moral panic theory have called into question the assumptions of the three foundational

models. They have done so to develop alternative ways to explain moral panic. It has been argued that most contemporary political strategies are media strategies, and that the relationship between processes of claims-making and social control is less circumscribed than past formulations concede (McRobbie and Thornton, 1995). For example, DeYoung (1998) argues that the daycare providers who became the focal point of satanic daycare panics through the 1980s were well integrated into their communities, and that they lacked the social marginality of traditional folk devils. Thornton's (1994) study of British club cultures reveals that fanzines, pirate radio, websites, and email distribution lists are among the plethora of media outlets regularly used to counter moralizing discourses. And Hier's (2002b) study of attempts to ban raves in the City of Toronto highlights the role of heterogeneous media outlets involved in the construction and contestation of moral panic.

The Volatility of Moralization

Efforts to rethink (and move beyond) traditional models of moral panic provide many progressive insights into the nature of moralization, and they have partially influenced the direction of theorization and empirical study. One of the problems with efforts to rethink moral panic, however, is that they have led to the deconstruction of traditional models without a reconstruction of alternative modes of explanation. In most moral panic research, there is an assumption that the harm believed to be posed by folk devils is dis-proportional to the harm that actually exists, which speaks to a tendency in moral panic studies to impose a negative normative judgment on explanations of volatile moralizing discourses as 'irrational' evaluations of the threat(s) posed (see Hier, 2008). Even though revisionist efforts have problematized the empirical bases through which these analytic judgments are rendered, analysts are forced to rely on normative value judgments to render assessments pertaining to the 'irrationality' of public beliefs (see Doran, 2008).

To remedy these theoretical difficulties, Hier (2008) draws from the sociology of governance studies to conceptualize 'moralization' (i.e., moral regulation) in terms of dialectic constructions of self and other that are transmitted through everyday discourses of risk management and harm avoidance. Conceptualized in this way, moralization references a liberal conception of 'the moral' that values individual rights. The deployment of contemporary liberal rights functions as a proxy for moralization, and one central, shared liberal moral value in an age of apparent moral relativism is to ensure one's right to freedom from harm (Hier, no date). As everyday activities become moralized in the form of judgments pertaining to what is right and wrong in terms of the negative consequences for other people, moralization finds expression through the proxies of risk, harm, and personal responsibility. One common feature of moralization in everyday life is that people are called upon to engage in responsible forms of individual risk management that exist in tension with collective subject positions of 'harmful others' (also see Hunt, 2003). On a conceptual level this implies that moralization is dialectical: individualizing discourses calling upon people to take personal responsibility to manage risk (e.g., drinking responsibly) are situated against collectivizing discourses representing the subject position of harm (e.g., the drunk driver).

The volatility of moralization brings into play a different nexus of values and emotions (Hier, 2008; Walby and Spencer, 2011). Through the deployment of a set of sensational discourses that erupt suddenly, and subside quickly, the moral dialectic that situates individualized risk management against a collective dimension of harm is inverted. Discourses that call upon individuals to engage in responsible forms of self-conduct to manage risk are transposed into collectivizing discourses of risk management. The latter take the form of defensive group reactions against what is represented as an immediate dimension of harm posed by 'irresponsible' others: those who fail to engage in individual risk management. As a volatile disturbance in the course of moral governance, 'moral panics' are short-lived disturbances focused on limiting the agency of 'folk devils'. Where conventional moral panic studies are often concerned with the 'origins' of each 'episode' of moral panic in terms of a particular event, claim or other 'tipping point' with causal primacy, the conceptual model we employ focuses on the implications of volatile moralization for the development of different regulatory approaches.

ANTI-SOCIAL BEHAVIOR ORDERS AND REGULATING BRITISH YOUTH

Although moral regulation projects in Britain are attendant to the activities of a wide range of people, 'no age group is more associated with risk in the public imagination than that of "youth"' (Thompson, 1998: 43; also see Fionda, 2006). Not only are British youth represented as a social group 'at risk' from harms posed by child abusers and pedophiles (e.g., Critcher, 2002; Hay, 1995; Jenkins, 1992), but they are also identified as a *source* of risk (e.g., Cohen, 1972; Hay, 1995). The contemporary preoccupation with youth as particularly risky can be explained in relation to the primary mode of moralization—responsibilization. Responsibilization presupposes rational, liberal subjectivity, which is a developmental rather than inherent characteristic of human beings. Long-term efforts to regulate British youth over the past decade have manifested in moral-legal regulatory apparatuses institutionalized to counteract 'anti-social behavior'. We conceptualize these mechanisms of regulation in terms of governmental and extra-governmental attempts to responsibilize youth conduct in public spaces by encouraging certain modes of dress and behavior. By explicating the ways that moral regulation is currently enacted in relation to British youth, we conceptualize the events that followed the ban of hooded tops by representatives of the Bluewater shopping center.

British Youth, Law, and Order

In 2003, the Home Office introduced the Anti-Social Behavior Act (ASBA). Applicable to England and Wales, the ASBA facilitated the regulation of 'anti-social behaviors' through the deployment of Anti Social Behavior Orders (ASBOs) and Acceptable Behavior Contracts (ABCs). The Home Office defines ASBOs as:

civil orders that exist to protect the public from behaviour that causes or is likely to cause harassment, alarm or distress. An Order contains conditions prohibiting the offender from specific anti-social acts or entering defined areas and is effective for a minimum of two years. (Home Office, 2003: 9)

Whereas the purpose of ASBOs is to act on the conduct of moral transgressors after the fact, ABCs are pre-emptive, non-legally binding agreements between offenders and police. The Home Office defines ABCs as:

an intervention designed to engage the individual in recognising their behaviour and its negative effects on others … An ABC is a written agreement between an anti-social behaviour perpetrator and their local authority, Youth Inclusion Support Panel, landlord or the police … ABCs are not legally binding, but can be cited in court as evidence in ASBO applications or in eviction or possession proceedings (Home Office, 2003: 9).

Together, ASBOs and ABCs act as a two-step prohibition (Simester and Von Hirsch, 2006). Despite the fact that neither ASBOs nor ABCs are exclusively applicable to youth, their primary target is youth transgression, which Crawford (2009b) argues follows the logic of de-differentiation insofar as all youth are problematized as probable sources of harm. The ASBA is also designed to enable spatial regulation—Section 30 of the ASBA invokes the notion of dispersal zones and orders. Crawford and Lister (2007) describe how dispersal orders are used to target youth simply on the basis of their presence in particular urban spaces (e.g., shopping centers). Millie (2008) comments on how ASBOs are used to regulate disparate forms of activity, which means there is no clear-cut definition of anti-social behavior. The application of ASBOs, argues Millie, is often based on aesthetics.

When New Labour introduced the Crime and Disorder Act (CDA) of 1998, government rhetoric problematized simultaneously the behaviour of youth and the existing institutional measures to counteract youth irresponsibility.

An excuse culture has developed within the youth justice system. It excuses itself for its inefficiency, and too often excuses the young offenders before it, implying that they cannot help their behaviour because of their social circumstances. Rarely are they confronted with their behaviour and *helped to take more personal responsibility for their actions.* The system allows them to go on wrecking their own lives and disrupting their families and communities. (Home Office, 1997: Preface, *emphasis added*)

The institutionalization of the CDA signified a wider ideological shift in the regulation of British youth from a 'minimum intervention' approach that predominated in the 1990s to a preventative 'early intervention' approach (see Crawford, 2009a; Squires, 2008). As Bottoms and Dignan (2004) explain, the reason for this shift was the perceived failures of the Conservative Party's so-called 'new-orthodoxy' that prevailed among youth justice workers in the period 1985–1997. The 'new orthodoxy' adopted two discernable governing principles: first, a retreat from carceral strategies based on the belief that institutionalization and the 'official processing of juvenile delinquents' (Bottoms and Dignan, 2004: 33) was both harmful to youth and conducive to establishing more long-term criminal tendencies in young offenders; second, the endorsement of the 'age-crime curve' (see Rutherford, 2002)—an assertion that the majority of young offenders naturally 'grow out of crime' over time.

The CDA was facilitated by the Audit Commission's report on the youth justice system, which found that much of the £1bn spent annually on processing young offenders 'was wasted through lengthy and ineffective court procedures' (Muncie, 1999: 150). The Audit Commission (1996: 96) recommended a shift to preventative policy, concluding: 'the present arrangements are failing young people—who are not being guided away from offending to constructive activities'. Jones (2001) argues the 1996 audit influenced the rise to prominence of ASBOs as mechanism of legal regulation in Britain and Wales. For Coleman (2005: 133), ASBOs and ABCs converge under the auspices of 'entrepreneurial urbanism': hybrid public/private regulatory projects negotiated between businesses and state agencies that wield control over the 'normative-cultural dimensions' extending beyond criminality. When youth skateboarders dodge the gaze of cameras, or when working class youth gather outside malls, these actions are met with fines, bans, and curfews. It is at the antagonistic intersection of entrepreneurial urbanism and youth cultural expression that the problematization of hoodies is articulated (Burney, 2005; Crawford, 2008; Pearson, 2006; Walsh, 2002).

Even though ASBOs are mechanisms of legal regulation, they depend on extra-governmental partnerships to be applied. State agencies must extend themselves through public/private partnerships and spaces (Button, 2003; Crawford, 2006; Raco, 2003). Bluewater is an example of private regulation in a quasi-public space, which leads to post hoc forms of state agency regulation in the application of ASBOs (see Crawford, 2008; Wakefield, 2008).

PROBLEMATIZING HOODIES AND THE BLUEWATER BAN

In this section, we explain how volatile moralization emerged where long-term regulatory efforts aimed at youth were perceived to be in a state of breakdown. We draw from two data sources. The first data source consists of newspaper stories in the mainstream newspaper media. We sampled six of the most widely circulated national newspapers in Britain: *The Times*, the *Guardian*, the *Express*, the *Daily Mail*, the *Sun*, and the *Mirror*. These sources were sampled to include coverage in quality broadsheets, middle-of-the-road tabloids, and redtop tabloids (Critcher, 2003). We do not present a detailed content or discourse analysis. We illustrate how the dominant discourse in the

mainstream press and political debate was countered in the context of a web of media relations and social activism. Legislation was enacted even in the absence of consensus, which is important to analyses of moralization of youth because it demonstrates how folk devils and their supporters fight back, but also how these counter claims can be reversed.

Primary Definition

On 12 May 2005, the day following the Bluewater ban, the *Express* ran front-page coverage under a headline reading, 'Shopping centre bans hoody yobs: Britain's biggest mall has had enough of menacing gangs' (Fagge, 2005). The article frames the Bluewater ban in the wider context of a moral decline in youth behavior: 'prowling gangs of "hoody" hooligans who plague our high streets and malls'; 'yobs who deliberately strike fear by skulking behind hooded tops'; and 'gangs of thugs have plagued the venue … making shopping a terrifying experience'. The following day, the *Mirror* (13 May 2005) proclaimed that, 'the sight of youths kitted out in [hoodies] strikes fear in law-abiding citizens'; 'in their Grim Reaper-style headgear, "hoodies" have become the reviled and feared bogeymen of modern Britain' (Roberts and Allen, 2005). The *Daily Mail* (18 May 2005) invoked the imagery of 'The feral gangs who rule our streets' (Seamark, 2005) to characterize youth who don hooded tops in public space. And the 'hoodies' signifier was adopted to denote a range of deviance and crime: '"Hoody" thug mugs pregnant woman in front of shoppers' (Ginn, 2005), 'Evil hoody battered me black and blue' (Hamilton, 2005), 'Fond farewells … and then a vicious attack by hoodies' (Moriarty, 2005), and 'Hoodies' rampage on train' (*Sunday Mirror*, 2005).

Following the Bluewater ban, Prime Minister Tony Blair and his deputy, John Prescott, laid claim to the problematic nature of youth behavior. Speaking in support of the ban, Blair argued that 'People are rightly fed-up with street corner and shopping centre thugs' (Fagge and Chapman, 2005), and he openly supported the banning of hooded tops (*The Guardian*, 12 May 2005). Prescott, too, endorsed the ban, reinforcing his support by recollecting a personal encounter with a group of 'hoodies' when he was surrounded and 'menaced' at a motorway service station; he reported that it was 'very intimidating' to be confronted by 'ten people wearing hoods—you know, these covers with hoods on' (Fagge and Chapman, 2005). The claims made by Blair and Prescott were articulated in the context of an established governmental discourse concerning anti-social behavior invoked in government rhetoric since the introduction of the ASBA.

Deviance Amplification

Emerging from the initial problematization of hoodies, newspaper coverage amplified the severity of the problem by linking hoodies to a range of crimes. For instance, under a headline reading, 'Hunt for hoodies', the *News of the World* (10 July 2005) reported that, 'a teenager may be blinded in one eye after an unprovoked attack by hoodies'. When Phil Carroll, a building site engineer, was attacked outside his house and left 'fighting for his life' in a coma (Seamark, 2005), newspaper coverage identified a 'feral, drunken and abusive hoodie gang' as the culprit. Three days later, the *Daily Mail* ran a front-page story about Alan Irwing, a 72-year-old pensioner who was beaten to death on his doorstep, adding: 'the area had been plagued by gangs of youngsters wearing "hoodies"'. In the span of two months, the repertoire of deviance attributed to hoodies included the rape of an 11-year-old girl (Sulaiman, 2005), underage drinking and sex (Mackay, 16 May 2005), murder (Taylor, 2005), 'binge-drinking' (Fagge and Chapman, 2005), and, somewhat contradictory, a '"Hoodies" nude riot' (Express, 2005b).

The escalating coverage on hoodies exemplifies what Hall *et al.*, (1978) conceptualize as a signification spiral, which designates the symbolic escalation of harm posed by deviants through a process that inflates the volume and magnitude of deviance attributed to signifying categories. This signification spiral is demonstrated by the newspaper media's conflation of hoodies and 'happy slapping': an ambush-style physical attack—sometimes a slap, but variously a punch, stab, or attack with a weapon, possibly in conjunction with a robbery—which is recorded on a hand-held video device for the amusement of the attackers or distribution via the Internet and mobile telephony networks. Happy slapping entered the inventory of deviance through the claims-making activities of primary definers and 'experts'. The Deputy Prime Minister, recounting his confrontation with a gang of 'hoodies', proclaimed: 'not only did they come with these kinds of uniforms but they had a movie camera to take a film of any such incident' (Fagge and Chapman, 2005). The 'expert' opinions of crime-control officers were drawn upon in efforts to link happy slaps to hoodies:

> Police have now identified so-called 'hoody' culture as a major concern, as yobs lurk in our streets and shopping malls with their faces hidden behind hoods and baseball caps ... innocent members of the public are being targeted in the latest craze for 'happy slapping' in which children randomly attack complete strangers just for fun. (Knapp, 2005)

According to Hall *et al.*, (1978), signification spirals precipitate the symbolic amplification of deviance across certain 'thresholds' of societal tolerance. Primary indicators of threshold breach in the hoodies discourse came in the form of increasing calls for regulatory action *vis-a-vis* the growing perception of an 'out-of-control' situation. The repetition of nomenclature including 'feral', 'yob culture', 'running riot', and 'culture of disrespect' attests to the perception of a widespread breakdown in the behavioral code, summarized by Lord Stevens (2005), ex-chief of the Metropolitan Police:

> After terrorism, the biggest single crime crisis facing this country is juvenile yobbery. It is a raging social cancer tearing away at Britain—but currently we are treating this terrible sickness with the moral and social equivalent of a sticking plaster ... I've been a policeman for 43 years, and have never seen such fear and helplessness about juvenile crime in our communities.

Before long, news sources called for new regulatory responses. Demands such as 'hooded thugs and happy slappers should get longer sentences than other criminals, a former senior policeman said yesterday' (Roberts, 23 May 2005), calls for 'compulsory national community service' (*Express*, 2005a), and a 'nationwide ban' of hoodies (Fagge and Chapman, 2005) followed.

The amplification of the harm posed by hoodies involved numerous converging factors. While the Bluewater ban was not the first prohibition of hooded tops or baseball caps in a UK shopping precinct, previous actions in Essex, Hampshire, Cornwall, and Devon (Coleman, 2005) did not lead to the level of coverage and debate that followed the Bluewater ban. One feature that was absent from earlier clothing regulations was the lack of a concerted attempt by primary definers to articulate the ban in the context of wider social problems. Although governmental claims contributed to the intensification of concern—and indicated attempts to seek consent for their proposed expansion of regulatory measures under the auspices of the ASBA—the newspaper media further imbued the hoodies signifier with a dimension of risk. Although it is important not to deny the seriousness of the real crimes and acts of violence reported by the media— which the term 'amplification' may appear to do—it is nevertheless justified to use the term amplification because of the array of unrelated crimes and offenses that are attributed to a singular subject position with little evidence.'

'FIGHTING BACK' AGAINST PRIMARY DEFINITION

In this section, we examine forms of contestation that emerged in opposition to the dominant hoodies discourse to empirically demonstrate how folk devils and their supporters fight back (McRobbie, 1994). Sociologists of risk, such as O'Malley (2006), contend that problematization engenders contestation among targets of regulation. Such contestation often takes forms that appear unorganized (Moore, 2007), as is the case with many of the examples discussed below. Opportunities to participate in the production of media messages have increased, due in part to technological means such as the Internet and the proliferation of desktop publishing software (Downey and Fenton,

2003). The increasing array of 'interpretive agents who are constructing our view of the world' (Vattimo, 2004: 17) weaken media claims to objectivity, and authoritative versions of events give way to numerous interpretations.

Problematization shifted somewhat from youth socialization to the Government's youth regulation policies. We provide an illustration of a heterogeneous oppositional movement that emerged following the Bluewater ban and that gained the attention of mainstream journalists. We also draw on data from Internet news publications and forums to show how alternative media enabled marginalized communities to enter into the debate about hoodies. The influence of diverse claims in the mainstream media, oppositional claims-making outside the press, and alternative media messages combined to precipitate a re-articulation of the hoodies discourse. However, it was not enough to halt the continuation of attempts to regulate youth through legislative activity.

Problematizing State Typifications: Counter Claims and Alternative Frames

The *Daily Mail* has long been associated with moralization as a standard mode of reporting (Hill, 2002). Following the Bluewater ban, coverage in the *Daily Mail*, instead of individualizing moral culpability through the hoodies signifier, invoked youth transgression as a platform from which to criticize Tony Blair's government. Playing on the language of Blair's 'Reform and Respect' agenda, the *Mail on Sunday's* 'Respect? Surely you abolished it, Mr. Blair' (Hitchens, 2005) attributed causality for anti-social behavior to an ideological shortfall inherent to Left-liberal governance: 'The liberal Left have been on a long march through this country, destroying old-fashioned authority. They believe deference and respect are wrong and bad and repressive.' Under a headline reading, 'When will our politicians wake up to the fact that it's THEY who have done more than anyone to create this culture of yobbery?' (Stevens, 2005), it was argued, 'disorder and threatening behaviour are a modern plague, and whole communities are under siege from crime and yobbery'. The problematization of New Labour in the *Daily*

Mail was attributed to a retreat from authoritarianism on behalf of the liberal Left that is responsible for 'the destruction of the family' (ibid.). By holding the Government culpable for the erosion of 'traditional' family values, including responsibility toward others and the behavior of British youth, the dominant discourse was countered by retaining the hoodies signifier. The newspaper subverted primary definitions to implicate New Labour as morally misaligned with public opinion.

The *Guardian* attacked the initial framing of hoodies as an attempt to draw attention away from the failure of the State's education and social order policies: 'the new concern for boys' underachievement, hoodies and chavs parallel fears of a black rap culture ... like "gangstas", the "dumbed down" are turning away from learning' (Ainley, 2005). At the same time, the *Guardian* remained reflexive about the role of the media: 'the latest moral panic over hoodies echoes the last one over chavs ... Manufactured moral panic, or last stand of the lost tribe of the white working class?' (Ainley, 2005). As McRobbie and Thornton (1995) contend, since the early 1990s 'moral panic' has entered the lexicon of mainstream society and media. Hay (1995) commented that the standardization of moral panics as ordinary modes of news reporting has heralded in the age of the 'reflexive moral panic'. Media opposition to the dominant discourse was buttressed by enlisting 'experts' to counter the vilifying claims. Angela McRobbie was recruited as an expert sociologist by the *Guardian* in the interests of normalizing hoodies: 'nowadays it is the norm among young people to flag up their music and cultural preferences in this way, hence the adoption of the hoodie by boys across the boundaries of age, ethnicity and class' (McLean, 2005).

Perhaps sensing the opportunity to align with a growing tide of populist dissent against representations of youths, the leader of the UK Conservative Party, David Cameron delivered a 'hug a hoodie' speech to the Centre for Social Justice on 9 July 2006. Cameron's speech sought to undermine New Labour's approach to youth regulation and presented an alternative interpretation of hooded clothing:

Because the fact is that the hoodie is a response to a problem, not a problem in itself. We—the people in suits—often see hoodies as aggressive, the uniform of a rebel army of young gangsters. But, for young people, hoodies are often more defensive than offensive. They're a way to stay invisible in the street. In a dangerous environment the best thing to do is keep your head down, blend in, don't stand out ... For some, the hoodie represents all that's wrong about youth culture in Britain today. For me, adult society's response to the hoodie shows how far we are from finding the long-term answers to put things right.

Fighting Back for Folk Devils

McRobbie (1994: 111) acknowledges that—once the sole torch-bearer for the defense of 'moral minorities'—the academic is now bolstered and even surpassed by 'a new band of experts' in the form of skilled representatives from pressure groups and voluntary organizations. Below we focus on how the dominant framing of hoodies was countered by activist groups, making no claims about the success of these attempts at fighting back. In 2005, attempts to deflect a general demonization of youth were made by organizations such as the British Youth Council (*The Guardian*, 13 May 2005a), the Children's Society Charity (*The Mirror*, 20 May, 2005a), and the charity NCH (*Mirror*, 3 June 2005) who went on record to decry the ban. The British Youth Council commissioned a report that found youths increasingly alienated by negative portrayals, and they circulated a press release recommending fairer media coverage, and greater political involvement opportunities for youth. The Children's Rights Alliance for England (CRAE) also raised questions about human rights violations.

Among organized attempts to counter negative typifications of youth through the hoodies signifier, the renowned subversive artists Gilbert and George produced *Hooded*, a work of art depicting the artists standing alongside two hooded youth (Kennedy, 2005). Two headmasters introduced attire codes including hooded tops as official school uniform (Harper, 2005; 20 May 2005)—each was quoted opposing the government-endorsed clothing bans. The most direct example of successful contestation involved the Scottish Socialist Party (SSP) and the subsidiary Scottish Socialist Youth (SSY) (see 'Young hoodies fight ban with street protest', O'Kane, 2005). In response to plans by businesses of the Eastgate Centre in Inverness to follow suit with Bluewater, SSY volunteers canvassed stores in the mall and publicized a Saturday demonstration against the ban. On 2 June, the mall released a statement retracting their plans, a decision the SSY attribute to their pressure. The Lambeth and Southwark Respect Coalition—a London-based activist group—coordinated a similar action at the Elephant and Castle mall in London. Although they failed to prevent the ban, they attracted the support of local community groups and formed an allegiance with the civil-liberties organization ASBO Concern.

Contestation involved the use of alternative media. While 'mass' media are regularly conceptualized as a monolith in analyses of public policy formation, it is important to consider texts that fall on the periphery of customary conceptions of the 'mass' media. Dominant, state-sponsored claims may be countered, or bypassed by particular efforts originating in micro, niche, or alternative media (Couldry and Corran, 2002; McRobbie, 1994) or through an engagement with the 'mass' media by organized groups who seek to subvert dominant discourses.

Dedicated communicative networks condensed around hoodies. The libertarian community 'libcom', for example, opened a forum dedicated to hoodies that yielded a critical discourse negotiating the politics of negative youth depictions and was subject to over 5000 views. The popular 'flikr', an online photograph hosting site, featured a 'hoody moral panic' area where the public could upload positive photographs of hooded clothing to stimulate political discussion. The 'Grime' musician, Lady Sovereign, began an online 'save the hoodie' campaign, inviting viewers to sign a petition opposing the ban that Sovereign would present to the Prime Minister. Although this coincided with the imminent release of Sovereign's 'Hoodie' single, the petition received over 1500 signatures and attracted

attention in the mainstream and 'alternative' media. Collectively, these strategies of contestation managed to partially shift the onus of problematization from youth transgression to governmental regulation. However, while studies of moralization have hitherto been concerned to demonstrate how contestation may be enacted, scholars interested in moralization have not pressed further to explore state agency responses to counter claims-making.

THE REFORM AND RESPECT AGENDA

The response of state agencies can be understood in two forms: a symbolic alignment with wider sentiments to legitimate further regulatory legislation, and the deployment of existing regulatory measures to intervene directly in the behavior of those failing to self-regulate. On 17 May 2005, six days after the Bluewater ban went into effect, New Labour's 'Reform and Respect Agenda' was announced in the Queen's Address at the State Opening of Parliament. The Prime Minister legitimized the agenda with reference to anti-social behavior: 'It is time to reclaim the streets for the decent majority'; and later, cited in the 'Respect Action Plan': 'I am pleased that an ASBO is now a household expression—synonymous with tackling anti-social behaviour' (Home Office, 2006b). The agenda included 45 bills and five drafts that introduced new measures to regulate anti-social behavior. In January 2006, the agenda was expanded to include additional regulatory measures, including fines for the parents of 'anti-social children', a new mandate allowing the judiciary to ban people from their own dwelling places for recidivist anti-social activity, and the introduction of 'on the spot' fines levied by patrolling police. The 'Respect Task Force'—tasked with delivering the Respect Agenda—was launched in January 2006 by Home Secretary Charles Clarke with this address:

> Tackling disrespect in our society is an absolute priority for the Government and this new task force will play a vital role in improving our communities and the lives of people in them. From bad behaviour

in schools and poor parenting to binge drinking and noisy neighbours, disrespect for others can take many forms. ... We all have the right to live our lives free from harassment. But with those rights come responsibilities, and we all need to play a part in tackling disrespect and unacceptable behaviour.

Regardless of whether New Labour acted to stimulate the hoodies discourse, the agenda's political efficacy lay in its linkage with an established discourse of anti-social behavior, and stylized representations of declining behavioral standards among the polis—youths in particular. Language employed by state spokespersons to legitimize the new legislation drew on the typifications of youth behavior in the media following the Bluewater action. While the long-term project of morally regulating youth hinges upon a call for rational risk subjects to self-regulate, the hoodies discourse is indicative of a temporary breakdown of moral regulation, whereby the agency of youth came under scrutiny and subsequent regulation.[2] Claims-making by politicians and law and order officials ascribed blame to youth in terms of an 'irresponsible' retreat into a 'culture of disrespect'.

DISCUSSION AND CONCLUSION

The individualization of harm has thus far been conceptualized in moral panic theory through signification of 'folk devils'. The folk devil concept, as 'unambiguously unfavorable symbols' (Cohen, 1972: 41), fails to account for the contingency by which harm becomes attributed to individual bodies in urban spaces. The temporary inversion of the dialectic that operates in the moralization in everyday life involves a conceptual shift from individualized discourses governing responsible and ethical self-conduct against a collective dimension of harm to collectivizing discourses that individualize responsibility for harm (Hier, 2008). The Bluewater ban opened possibilities for the articulation of familiar, cultural artifacts and the very *mise-en-scene* of urban spaces with a symbolic dimension of harm.

The symbolic dimension of harm articulated with pre-existing discourses of risky behavior through media sensationalism, retaining as an element certain signifiers originating in representations of commonplace phenomena of the cultural realm (e.g., hooded clothing, groups of congregating youths). Problematization of youth behavior thus involved the inscription of a dimension of harm into established cultural texts, which came to represent a range of risks associated with contemporary urban spaces in Britain. The hoodie emerged as a dialectical articulation of risk and harm in the context of a series of highly recognizable cultural motifs to negotiate the management of risks in localized settings.

Arguments to the effect that folk devils can contest regulatory efforts owe much to a conception of political power as the aggregate of dispersed forces. Folk devils and their supporters can and do 'fight back'; the opportunities to participate in and subvert problematization are opening up to more variegated publics. Although the contestation we discussed above was subverted by New Labour's 'Reform and Respect Agenda', these efforts and their ramifications for understanding moral panic should not be discounted. We have also shown that the volatility of moralization hinges upon the amenability of cultural representations to link up with pre-existing, or emergent, themes of risk (also see Hier, 2008). Such representations are tied to long-term political and moral projects, and they are not simply irrational, isolated episodic articulations.

A critical insight we draw from the integration of the studies of moral panic and moral regulation is that episodes of moral panic involve a unique political dynamic of 'double problematization'. While moral panic scholars focus primarily on the reasons for and implications of sensationalized representations of folk devils, they pay less attention to the fact that moral panics also involve problematization of existing regulatory measures. Claims, counter-claims, and resistance represent struggles over the ascription of blame, but also simultaneous struggles over the proper regulatory responses to matters of crime and law-and-order.

NOTES

1. We conceptualize 'the moral' in terms of a flexible set of normative understandings about what is right and wrong that operates through interactive circuits. Circuits do not determine but rather exercise an interactive effectivity with other circuits including economics and politics. We are interested in examining the various ways that moral phenomena are inscribed in and modified through everyday ethical practices that intersect with political and governmental practices and processes of self-formation (see Hier, 2002b, no date). Waiton (2008), by contrast, works with an assumed moral domain that cannot account for shifting forms of moralization.

2. Existing measures, combined with those introduced under the auspices of the Reform and Respect Agenda, have been brought to bear on specific youth behavior problematized through the hoodies signifier. To enforce this increasing array of conditions, ASBOs and ABCs are supplemented by Individual Support Orders (ISOs), Parenting Orders, Dispersal Orders and Injunctions, which Crawford (2009a) argues target not only youth but also their support networks. The breaching of ASBOs and other orders results, in many cases, with immediate detention for youths. Common to each of the orders mentioned above are the imposition of restrictions on actions, movements through space, and even gestures (also see Millie, 2008).

REFERENCES

Ainley, P. (2005). Open your arms. *Guardian*, 14 June. Available at: http://www.guardian.co.uk/education/2005/jun/14/furthereducation.socialexclusion.

Audit Commission (1996). *Misspent Youth*. London: Audit Commission.

BBC News (2006, July 10). 'Cameron Hoodie speech in full' Available at http://news.bbc.co.uk/2/hi/uk_news/politics/5166498.stm (retrieved March 6, 2011).

Bottoms, A., and Dignan, J. (2004). Youth justice in Great Britain. *Crime and Justice* 31: 21–183.

Burney, E. (2005). *Making People Behave: Anti-Social Behavior, Politics and Policy*. Cullompton: Willan.

Button, M. (2003). Private security and the policing of quasi-public space. *International Journal of the Sociology of Law* 31(3): 227–237.

Cohen, S. (1972). *Folk Devils and Moral Panics*. London: MacGibbon & Kee.

Coleman, R. (2005). Surveillance in the city: Primary definition and urban spatial order. *Crime, Media, Culture* 1(2): 131–148.

Couldry, N., and Corran, J. (2002). *Contesting Media Power: Alternative Media in a Networked World*. Toronto: Rowman & Rowman.

Crawford, A. (2006). Networked governance and the post-regulatory state. *Theoretical Criminology* 10(4): 449–479.

Crawford, A. (2008). Dispersal powers and the symbolic role of anti-social behavior legislation. *Modern Law Review* 71(5): 753–784.

Crawford, A. (2009a). Governing through anti-social behavior: Regulatory challenges to criminal justice. *British Journal of Criminology* 49(6): 810–831.

Crawford, A. (2009b). Criminalizing sociability through anti-social behavior legislation: Dispersal powers, young people and the police. *Youth Justice* 9(1): 5–26.

Crawford, A., and Lister, S. (2007). *The Use and Impact of Dispersal Orders: Sticking Plasters and Wake-Up Calls*. Bristol: Policy Press.

Critcher, C. (2002). Media, government and moral panic: The politics of paedophilia in Britain 2000–1. *Journalism Studies* 3(4): 521–535.

Critcher, C. (2003). *Moral Panics and the Media*. London: Open University Press.

Critcher, C. (2008). Moral panic analysis: Past, present, future. *Social Compass* 2(4): 1127–1144.

Critcher, C. (2009). Widening the focus: Moral panics as moral regulation. *British Journal of Criminology* 49(1): 17–34.

DeYoung, M. (1998). Another look at moral panics: The case of satanic day care centres. *Deviant Behaviour* 19(3): 257–275.

Doran, N. (2008). Decoding 'encoding' moral panics, media practices and Marxist presuppositions. *Theoretical Criminology* 12(2): 191–221.

Downey, J., and Fenton, N. (2003). New media, counter publicity and the public sphere. *New Media & Society* 5(2): 185–202.

Express (2005a). Slapping craze must end. *Express*, 21 May, p. 12.

Express (2005b). 'Hoodies' nude riot. *Express*, 2 July, p. 31.

Fagge, N. (2005). Shopping centre bans hoody yobs: Britain's biggest mall has had enough of menacing gangs. *Express*, 12 May, pp. 1, 7.

Fagge, N., and Chapman, J. (2005). Ban hooded thugs from our streets. *Express*, 13 May, pp. 1, 4.

Fionda, J. (2006). *Devils and Angels: Youth Policy and Crime*. Oxford: Hart Publishing.

Gallagher, P. (2005a). Buys in the hood: Massive surge in business at shops mall that outlawed hoodies. *Mirror*, 20 May, pp. 8–9.

Garland, D. (2008). On the concept of moral panic. *Crime, Media and Culture* 4(1): 9–30.

Ginn, K. (2005). 'Hoody' thug mugs pregnant woman in front of shoppers. *Daily Mail*, 15 June, p. 13.

Goode, E., and Ben-Yehuda, B. (1994). *Moral Panics: The Social Construction of Deviance*. London: Blackwell.

Guardian (2005, May 12). 'Blair pledges crackdown on yobs'. Available at www.guardian.co.uk/uk/2005/may/12/politics.society (retrieved August 5, 2010).

Hall, S., Critcher, C., Jefferson, T., Clarke, J., and Robert, B. (1978). *Policing the Crisis: Mugging, the State, and Law and Order*. London: Macmillan.

Hamilton, M. (2005). Evil hoody battered me black and blue. *News of the World*, 15 May, p. 1.

Harper, J. (2005). Head: Hoodies for school uniform. *Sunday Mirror*, 15 May, p. 40.

Hay, C. (1995) Mobilization through interpellation: James Bulger, juvenile crime and the construction of a moral panic. *Social and Legal Studies* 4(3): 197–223.

Hier, S. (2002a). Conceptualizing moral panic through a moral economy of harm. *Critical Sociology* 28(3): 311–334.

Hier, S. (2002b). Raves, risks and the ecstasy panic: A case study in the subversive nature of moral regulation. *Canadian Journal of Sociology* 27(1): 33–57.

Hier, S. (2003). Risk and panic in late-modernity: Implications of the converging sites of social anxiety. *British Journal of Sociology* 54(1): 3–20.

Hier, S. (2008). Thinking beyond moral panic: Risk, responsibility and the politics of moralization. *Theoretical Criminology* 12(2): 173–190.

Hier, S. (ed.) (2011). *Moral Panic and the Politics of Anxiety*. London: Routledge.

Hier, S. (no date). Linking the sociologies of moral panic and moral regulation. Unpublished manuscript.

Hill, A. (2002). Acid house and Thatcherism: Noise, the mob, and the English countryside. *British Journal of Sociology* 53(1): 89–105.

Hitchens, P. (2005). Respect? Surely you abolished it, Mr. Blair. *Mail on Sunday*, 22 May, p. 2.

Home Office (1997). *No More Excuses: A New Approach to Tackling Youth Crime in England and Wales.* Cm. 3809. London: The Stationery Office.

Home Office (2003). *A Guide to Anti-Social Behaviour Orders and Acceptable Behaviour Contracts.* London: Home Office.

Home Office (2006a). *Tackling Anti-Social Behaviour: 2005 Survey Results.* London: Home Office.

Home Office (2006b). *Respect Action Plan.* Ref. 272299. London: Home Office.

Hunt, A. (1997). Moral panic and moral language in the media. *British Journal of Sociology* 48(4): 629–648.

Hunt, A. (1999). *Governing Morals: A Social History of Moral Regulation.* Cambridge: Cambridge University Press.

Hunt, A. (2003). *Risk and moralization in everyday life.* In: Ericson, R., Doyle, A. (eds.) *Risk and Morality.* Toronto: University of Toronto Press, 165–192.

Jenkins, P. (1992). *Intimate Enemies: Moral Panics in Contemporary Great Britain.* New York: Aldine de Gruyter.

Jones, D. (2001). 'Misjudged youth': A critique of the Audit Commission's report on youth justice. *British Journal of Criminology* 41(2): 362–380.

Kennedy, M. (2005). Hoodie art unveiled Gilbert and George's new fashion statement. *Guardian*, 23 May, Home Pages, p. 1.

Knapp, M. (2005). Living in fear of ferals. *Sunday Express*, 22 May, p. 31.

Lakeman, G. (2005b). Hoodie 2-shoes. *Mirror*, 20 May, p. 9.

Mackay, C. (2005). Battered to death: Thugs use planks in birthday beating. *Mirror*, Scottish Edition, 16 May, p. 24.

McLean, G. (2005). In the hood: On the meaning of the hoodie. *Guardian*, 13 May, G2, p. 2.

McRobbie, A. (1994). Folk devils fight back. *New Left Review* 203(January–February): 107–116.

McRobbie, A., and Thornton, S. (1995). Rethinking 'moral panic' for multi-mediated social worlds. *British Journal of Sociology* 46(4): 559–574.

Millie, A. (2008). Anti-social behavior, behavioral expectations and an urban aesthetic. *British Journal of Criminology* 48(3): 379–394.

Mirror (2005). Now head bans kids in hoodies. *Mirror*, 3 June, p. 7.

Moore, D. (2007). *Criminal Artefacts: Governing Drugs and Users.* Vancouver: University of British Columbia Press.

Moore, D., and Valverde, M. (2000). Maidens at risk: 'Date rape drugs' and the formation of hybrid risk knowledges. *Economy & Society* 29(4): 514–531.

Moriarty, R. (2005). Fond farewells … and then a vicious attack by hoodies. *Express*, 18 May, p. 2.

Muncie, J. (1999). Institutionalized intolerance: Youth justice and the 1998 Crime and Disorder Act. *Critical Social Policy* 19(2): 147–175.

News of the World (2005). Hunt for hoodies. *News of the World*, 10 July, p. 1.

O'Kane, R. (2005). Young hoodies fight ban with street protest. *Express*, 2 June, p. 32.

O'Malley, P. (2006). *Risk, Uncertainty and Government.* London: Glasshouse Press.

Pearson, G. (2006). Disturbing continuities: 'Peaky blinders' to 'hoodies'. *Criminal Justice Matters* 65(1): 6–7.

Raco, M. (2003). Remaking place and securitising space: Urban regeneration and the strategies, tactics and practices of policing in the UK. *Urban Studies* 40(9): 1869–1887.

Roberts, B. (2005). Reclaim our streets: Hoodies jail plea. *Mirror*, 23 May, p. 28.

Roberts, B., and Allen, V. (2005). Reclaim our streets: Hoodies and baddies. *Mirror*, 13 May, pp. 8–9.

Rohloff, A. (2008). Moral panics as decivilizing processes: Towards an Eliasian approach. *New Zealand Journal of Sociology* 23(1): 66–76.

Rohloff, A., and Wright, S. (2010). Moral panic and social theory: Beyond the heuristic. *Current Sociology* 58(3): 403–419.

Rutherford, A. (2002). *Growing Out of Crime: The New Era.* Winchester: Waterside.

Seamark, M. (2005). The feral gangs who rule our streets. *Daily Mail*, 18 May, p. 1.

Simester, A., and Von Hirsch, A. (2006). Regulating offensive conduct through two-step prohibitions. In: Von Hirsch, A., Simester, A. (eds.) *Incivilities: Regulating Offensive Behavior.* Oxford: Hart Publishing, 173–194.

Squires, P. (2008). The politics of anti-social behavior. *British Politics* 3(3): 300–323.

Stevens, L. (2005). Lord Stevens has the cure for yobs. *News of the World*, 22 May, Leader, p. 1.

Sulaiman, T. (2005). Girls' rape 'filmed by teenagers on mobile'. *The Times*, 18 June, p. 2.

Sunday Mirror (2005). 'Hoodies' rampage on train. *Sunday Mirror*, 12 June, p. 28.

Taylor, B. (2005, May 21). 'Beaten to death on his doorstep'. *Daily Mail*, p. 1.

Thompson, K. (1998). *Moral Panics.* London & New York: Routledge.

Thornton, S. (1994). Moral panic, the media and British rave culture. In: Ross, A., Rose, T. (eds.) *Microphone Fiends: Youth Music, Youth Culture.* London: Routledge, 176–192.

Ungar, S. (2001). Moral panic versus the risk society: The implications of the changing sites of social anxiety. *British Journal of Sociology* 52(2): 271–292.

Vattimo, G. (2004). *Nihilism & Emancipation: Ethics, Politics and Law.* New York: Columbia University Press.

Waiton, S. (2008). *The Politics of Antisocial Behavior: Amoral Panics.* London: Routledge.

Wakefield, A. (2008). Private policing: A view from the mall. *Public Administration* 86(3): 659–678.

Walby, K., and Spencer, D. (2011) How emotions matter to moral panics. In: Hier, S. (ed.) *Moral Panic and the Politics of Anxiety.* London: Routledge, Forthcoming.

Walsh, C. (2002). Curfews: No more hanging around. *Youth Justice* 2(2): 70–81.

White, M. (2005). PM attacks yob culture and pledges to help bring back respect. *Guardian*, 13 May. Available at: www.guardian.co.uk/politics/2005/may/13/ukcrime.immigrationpolicy.

Young, J. (1971). *The Drugtakers: The Social Meaning of Drug Use*. London: McGibbon & Kee.

Young, J. (2009). Moral panic: Its origins in resistance, ressentiment and the translation of fantasy into reality. *British Journal of Criminology* 49(1): 4–16.

SOCIAL CLASS AND CRIME

*Michael T. Costelloe and
Raymond J. Michalowski*

The relationship between social class and crime has been a long-standing source of debate in criminology. Specifically, there is considerable disagreement as to whether crime is largely a lower-class phenomenon or is more broadly and equally distributed. The significance of this debate, and thus its longevity, stems from the fact that most established criminological theories are predicated on the belief that there is something about a lower-class lifestyle that is inherently criminogenic. In fact, during the early and middle decades of the 20th century, most new criminological theories began with the assumption that crime was primarily a lower-class phenomenon (see, e.g., Cloward & Ohlin, 1960; Cohen, 1955; Miller, 1958, Shaw & McKay, 1942).

More recently, the assumption of lower-class exceptionalism has been challenged by empirical research that has attempted to determine the class-crime relationship instead of accepting it as the starting point for criminological inquiry. Unfortunately, because of disparate findings and inconclusive results, criminologists have yet to establish a conclusive answer regarding the class-crime relationship, a relationship that is further complicated when crimes of the powerful, which normally are excluded from criminological analyses of class and crime, are entered into the equation.

This chapter examines the possibility that differing conclusions about class and crime by researchers supposedly analyzing the same phenomenon may be rooted in methodological differences. It also considers the possibility that if the long-assumed causal relationship between lower social classes and criminality is incorrect, not only are many theories of nature and origins of crime based on an erroneous supposition, but the criminal justice policies based on these theories are also formulated on a fundamental misperception. Most crime control policies disproportionately target individuals from the lower classes while ignoring the harms caused by people in the upper classes. If crime and other harmful activities are, in fact, more widely distributed across social classes, these policies, then, may be ineffectual at best and, at worst, counter-productive or even harmful when it comes to combating crime and reducing the harm that it causes.

There are several notable aspects of the relationship between social class and crime: (a) how social class shapes the definition of crime, (b) how social class influences patterns of victimization and wrongful behavior, and (c) how the commonly held societal perception that crime comprises largely lower-class behaviors influences the way the criminal justice system deals with lower income populations. However, before examining these topics, we must begin by examining the definition of *social class*, why social classes exist, and why they are an important aspect of free market societies.

WHAT IS SOCIAL CLASS, AND WHY IS IT IMPORTANT?

When discussing social class, we frequently hear terms such as *upper class, middle class, lower class, working class,* and *underclass.* These terms attempt to differentiate social groups according to their access to economic, social, political, cultural, or lifestyle resources. Although such terms present an overly simplistic description that ignores the complexity and difficulties in defining social class, they do provide a starting point for discussing social stratification.

Economic resources consist of the wealth and/or income controlled by different social groups. The extent to which groups can exert political influence and/or cultural authority constitutes *social resources*, and the ability to directly shape the actions of governmental institutions such as political leaders or governmental functionaries, or indirectly through the exercise of power outside of government, constitute *political resources. Cultural capital* refers to the capacity of social classes to shape popular perception through access and control of mass media, education, and other platforms of public communication.

Finally, the phrase *lifestyle resources* refers to the degree to which group-based patterns of behavior and belief are valued or devalued within a society. These include such things as modes of speech, style of dress, attitudes and values, and preferred and/or available pleasures. As illustrated in studies of ghetto youth (see, e.g., Bourgois, 1995, and Wilson, 1987),

the less individuals can look, talk, dress, and act in the approved white, middle-class manner, the less likely they are to be hired, even when they have the necessary skills for a job.

Attempts to understand social class typically fall into one of two types: (1) those following a *Marxian model* of social class and (2) those following a *Weberian model* of social class. Marxian models are concerned with locating individuals within distinct groups with respect to their relationship to the means of products, for example, those who earn some or all of their income through the ownership of productive wealth versus those whose only source of income is their ability to work for a wage. Because the social structure of modern industrial societies involves many more class locations than the simple distinction between owners and workers would allow, some analysts have developed the notion of *class fractions;* that is, although many people work for wages, some, such as corporate managers, are more closely linked to ownership structures than others, such as low-income wage workers. Considerable effort has been devoted to creating more precise definitions of where one class fraction ends and another begins. This theoretically grounded approach to social class has been incorporated into sociological and economic research, but it has rarely been used within criminological research.

Criminological research typically treats social class from a Weberian perspective that views class as a matter of relative income levels. A more useful model for viewing social class is to understand it not simply as a matter of relative income but as the intersection of economic, cultural, and political resources that place social groups somewhere along a social class continuum ranging from the least to the most advantaged groups. At the highest level of this social class continuum in the United States are those groups that (a) earn large annual incomes; (b) control much of the country's wealth, in the form of real estate and material objects as well as in financial securities such as stocks, bonds, and hedge funds; (c) exert substantial influence over developing and implementing laws and governmental policy; (d) use wealth and power to shape the content of mass media; and (e) live the kinds of lifestyles that many people envy and would like to emulate. At the lower end are social groups that (a) earn relatively low annual incomes; (b) own little material property and almost no financial securities; (c) have minimal influence over government or media; and (d) have patterns of speech, dress, and behavior that are often viewed as disturbing or "dangerous" by better-off segments of the society. Between these two extremes are other groupings characterized by differing configurations of economic, social, and lifestyle resources that afford them fewer benefits than elites but more than the worst off.

The criminological significance of this differential distribution of resources is how it influences justice processes. Specifically, the social class system in America enables resource-advantaged groups to implement definitions of crime and justice that ensure elite-caused harms will rarely be treated as crime while harms more common among less advantaged groups—so-called street crimes—will be criminalized and vigorously punished.

Another important question to address is: Why do social classes exist? Like most of the world, the United States is based on a political-economic system organized around free-market competition. In these competitive market systems, some people win a larger share of the society's resources and assets than others. A number of reasons explain why some people may fare better in the competition for resources than others. A commonly held perception is that people obtain more because they work harder and sacrifice more; however, this is not always the case. Some people fare better than others because they are healthier or start life with more cultural and economic advantages than others. Others gain more because they have more hope and have not succumbed to the frustrations caused by the constant negotiation of the obstacles that society has placed in front of them. Although these represent some *individual* reasons for success or failure, they are not the cause of inequalities among large social groups.

For societies organized around economic competition, the division of society into social classes based on varying levels of material success is an inevitable, *structural* outcome. In the absence of measures that work to reduce social inequality, these differences tend to solidify into highly unequal class *systems*, in which people who are advantaged acquire more than

the disadvantaged. The division of society into social classes also has a cumulative effect on economic disparity, whereby the more resources individuals bring to the game, the more resources they can win, in particular because economic expansion does not produce equal benefits to all social classes.

Between 1979 and 2005, for instance, the United States experienced a period of substantial economic growth. By 2005, however, the after-tax income of the richest 5% of the U.S. population had grown by over 80%, while the income of the bottom 20% of the population had declined by 1%. Although the middle fifth of the population, which represents the heart of America's hard-working middle class, did experience a 15% increase in net income during this time, this was still only about one fifth of the growth experienced by the top 5% of income earners (U.S. Census Bureau, 2006). In other words, according to a number of sources, it was clear that, during one of the strongest periods of income growth, income inequality increased.

In addition to shaping the distribution of financial wealth, economic stratification ensures the continuation of social class distinctions by determining access to *social capital*, that is, the nonmonetary resources and skills that enable individuals to do well in competitive societies.

Children who grow up in financially advantaged homes in neighborhoods with high-quality schools, and who enjoy important developmental experiences such as early exposure to reading, writing, and analytic reasoning, will characteristically do better in school, pursue more advanced levels of education, obtain better careers, and earn more money over the course of their lives than people who grow up in households that could not provide these benefits. It is true that some individuals who are born poor succeed beyond expectations, while some who have every advantage fail; however, this is atypical. For most of the people, most of the time, their social class origins will shape much of their adult lives. The process of uneven competition ensures that wealth will concentrate within relatively small segments of the population, ensuring the continuation of social class differences.

Although an uneven distribution of wealth and cultural advantages is inevitable in any competitive market society, the degree of inequality is the result of political forces. Governmental policies can either intensify or lessen class inequalities. Progressive taxation of income and capital gains can finance programs and policies that improve the chances of the people who are less well off while reducing income and wealth inequality. Alternatively, governments can pursue policies that make the poor poorer and the rich richer, such as regressive sales taxes and reducing the amount of money spent on social programs that would close the wealth gap.

EXPLORING THE SOCIAL CLASS-CRIME LINK

Whereas the origin of social classes is relatively clear, the effect of social class divisions on crime is less so. Annual reports of the characteristics of people arrested in the United States provide insight concerning gender, age, race, and ethnicity but tell us little about social class characteristics such as income, occupation, or residence. Consequently, the best information we have regarding the social class characteristics of the individuals who inhabit U.S. prisons and jails derives from surveys of prison inmates and, interestingly, the government provides very little money to fund research into these characteristics. The last detailed survey of prisoners serving felony sentences in state penitentiaries, who make up the majority of those incarcerated in the United States in any given year, was conducted in 1993. Apparently, the federal government has little interest in regularly gathering information about the class and other social characteristics of prisoners.

An examination of the U.S. correctional population leaves little doubt that most of the people serving time for criminal offenses come from the lower end of society's socio-economic continuum. Government statistics show that criminal offenders in prison tend to be less well educated, more likely to be unemployed, and to earn far lower incomes than the general population. A 2002 survey conducted on inmates incarcerated in local jails revealed a similar pattern: Only about half of jail inmates were employed full-time at the time of their arrest, even though the national unemployment rate was below 5%, and over half of jail inmates earned

less than $15,000 a year (Bureau of Justice Statistics, U.S. Department of Justice, 2004).

Although these statistics may be somewhat skewed by the fact that better-off offenders who are charged with street crimes are more likely to avoid imprisonment, there is little reason to believe the degree of error is substantial. All one has to do is observe any urban police station or city court to know that very few middle- or upper-class citizens are arrested and prosecuted for common street crimes. Clearly, the criminal justice net hauls in the poorest of the poor. What this tells us about the link between social class and criminal behavior, however, remains controversial. Some scholars argue that the disproportionate representation of poor people in prison is indicative of their overinvolvement in crime, whereas others suggest this disparity is the result of a criminal justice system that unfairly targets the poor.

The contradictory perceptions about the relationship between social class and criminality are, in part, the product of disparate research findings. There is no shortage of research studies that have examined this relationship; however, there is little consensus because of inconsistent findings and inclusive results. For example, some studies have concluded that crime is more likely among people in higher social classes, whereas others have found criminality more prevalent among the lower classes. Some of these inconsistencies are traced to the different research methods used to study this relationship. These include different data collection methods; different measures of social class, crime, and criminality; different samples; and different methods of data analyses.

An examination of the past research reveals that the earliest of these studies (those conducted before the 1950s) tended to find more criminality among the lower classes than the upper classes. These findings in turn provided the foundation for numerous theories of crime and delinquency that attempted to explain why poverty was criminogenic, focusing on factors such as individual and cultural deficiencies, lack of opportunity, and differential (and harsher) treatment of individuals in poorer communities by the criminal justice system. Many of these theories, however, were only tenuously rooted in empirical research.

Although the social class-crime link was widely accepted, there were criminologists of the time who took issue with the methods that produced the correlation between social class and criminality. Most commonly, they argued that measuring crime through the use of official data (i.e., arrest data, prison statistics) presented a biased picture of crime. This measure of crime simply did not take into account the reality that many crimes go unnoticed or unreported, or for some other reason simply do not become known to those who wish to count them. This unknown and uncounted crime is referred to as *the dark figure of crime*. The problem, as they saw it, was that there was no way to determine whether accurately measuring the dark figure of crime would or would not show crime to be more broadly distributed. Some criminologists also argued that official measures of crime may actually better measure police practices than actual levels of crime; that is, in reality they may simply reflect, at least in part, the discretionary practices of police officers concerning whom to arrest and whom not to arrest, or a judge's propensity for sending particular offenders to prison while reserving alternative, community-based sanctions for others.

The development of self-report data in the 1950s intensified the ongoing debate. Researchers administered surveys to individuals randomly selected from the population and asked them to report their criminal behaviors. Although many of the earliest of these studies did not support the belief that lower social classes were more criminal, there was also enough research that found contradictory results to ensure that the issue would not be resolved. Furthermore, there were as many sociologists and criminologists who attacked the validity of self-report data as there were those who took issue with the validity of official measures of crime. Their argument was that there is no way to determine whether people in self-report studies are telling the truth about their criminal behavior. Doubters suggested that self-report surveys were better measures of a participant's willingness to tell the truth about his or her criminality. They also speculated that people from the lower classes were underreporting their deviant and criminal behavior while those in the upper classes were overreporting, thereby artificially reducing the magnitude of the correlation between lower-class status and criminality.

Tittle, Villemez, and Smith (1978) reviewed 35 research studies that had examined the social class-crime link and concluded that there was an extremely small relationship, with the members of the lower classes exhibiting slightly more criminality. They also noted that this relationship had become smaller over the past four decades.

This by no means settled the debate; instead, research became the impetus for even more extensive and complicated empirical efforts. Much of these later efforts attempted to discover the conditions under which social class influences criminality. One set of studies attempted to determine whether the manner in which social class and crime were measured affects the likelihood of discovering a link between social class and crime. In terms of social class, several studies suggested that this relationship may exist only among people in the lowest economic strata, the group sometimes referred to as the *underclass*. These studies then measured social class by dividing populations into dichotomous categories such as welfare recipients and nonrecipients or, for school-age children, those who receive free lunches and those who do not. Other studies used a composite measure of social class, which often included education, occupation, and income. Still other studies used Marxian classifications of social class, conceptualizing social class in terms of an individual's (or his or her parents') relationship to the means of production—specifically, whether they owned some means of production or sold their labor for a wage. Still others expanded this fairly simple classification to include other variables, such as whether one has *control* over the means of production and/or *control* over the labor of others. The emphasis on control helped to distinguish between wage workers who have managerial positions and those who do not, an increasingly prevalent distinction in modern society.

Crime was also measured in a number of different ways in an effort to determine whether it conditions the social class-criminality relationship. For example, a number of studies have examined whether the negative relationship between social class and delinquency existed only for the most serious criminal offenses or the most frequent offenders. Also, the source of crime data was thought to have an effect on whether a relationship between social class and crime was uncovered. Some criminologists held that crime would be shown to be more prevalent among the lower class if official police data or court records are used to determine criminality. As previously mentioned, they argued that people from lower classes are more likely to underreport their criminal behavior on self-report surveys.

A number of studies also sought to determine whether demographic and environmental variables had important conditioning effects on the class-crime relationship. For example, some studies examined whether the effect of social class on criminality was greater among blacks than it was for whites or among males than among females. Given the contradictory results of these research efforts, it would be difficult to suggest that the social class-criminality relationship was specific to a certain race or gender. Still another set of studies has examined whether this relationship was more likely in areas that were characterized as being more heterogeneous, more urban, or in higher status areas, and again produced mixed results.

Tittle and Meier (1990) reviewed the research literature that examined the relationship between socio-economic status and delinquency and that attempted to specify whether any of the aforementioned conditions mattered. They concluded that there was little evidence that the link between social class and criminality existed under any of the conditions examined.

More recent and sophisticated studies have generally arrived at similar conclusions, although some studies did help clarify the relationship. For example, Wright and his colleagues (B. R. E. Wright, Caspi, Moffitt, Miech, & Silva, 1999) found that people in lower social classes experienced lower educational and occupational goals and more financial strain, aggression, and alienation, which in turn increase delinquency. Delinquency in the higher social classes, on the other hand, was the result of high socio-economic status causing increased risk taking and social power, and diminished the commitment to conventional values, all of which then predispose these youth to delinquency. Dunaway, Cullen, Burton, and Evans (2000) examined the relationship between social class (measured in a variety of ways) and criminality (based on self-report surveys) and found that, among adults, the correlation was weak for less serious offenses. They did, however, find a class effect for violent offenses and among nonwhites. This study was distinctive in that it measured adult criminality, a surprisingly underresearched population. In the end, the best conclusion that can be drawn about the relationship between social class and the commission of street crimes is that it tends to be weak and present only under certain specified conditions, and criminology researchers must continue to attempt to specify other circumstances that may influence this relationship.

What many of these studies do have in common is that most approached the definition of crime as being non-problematic instead of acknowledging crime as a multifaceted concept that includes crimes of the disadvantaged as well as crimes of the powerful. Unfortunately, the latter were, and still are, less apt to be considered. This is important, because if studies included offenses that powerful individuals are more likely to commit (e.g., insider trading), and that those in lower classes are in no position to commit, then there would be little question as to whether criminality would appear more evenly distributed across social classes than has traditionally been thought. Moreover, it is only by including a wider variety of offenses that we can consider the social class-crime link as having been more completely and fairly tested.

So, although there has been little advancement toward settling the social class-street crime questions, the introduction of self-report studies has generally confirmed that criminality is more broadly and equally distributed across social classes than previously suspected. In fact, to date, these studies have consistently shown that nearly 90% of Americans have committed at least one crime for which they could have been sentenced to jail or prison. These findings may confirm that the use of official statistics means that we may not actually be measuring the level of crime or propensity for criminality but instead are measuring the decision-making practices of the criminal justice system (i.e., when to file an official police report, whom to arrest, whom to charge, and whom to send to prison).

EXPLAINING THE RELATIONSHIP BETWEEN SOCIAL CLASS AND CRIMINALITY

Although the relationship between social class and crime remains contested and unclear, it has not prevented the development of a number of theoretical explanations, which are formulated around the belief that poor people simply commit more serious crime. There are three types of explanations: (1) individualistic theories, (2) social interactionist theories, and (3) structural outcomes theories.

Currently, the most favored theories are those that suggest that higher rates of street crime among the poor are the product of family failings and personal morality. Collectively, these theories are considered *individualistic explanations* for crime. *Body Count* (Bennett, Dilulio, & Walters, 1996), an influential, conservative assessment of crime trends, argued that crime is the result of "moral poverty." The authors claimed that high crime rates occur when families fail to impose clear moral understandings of right and wrong on the next generation. By focusing on "street criminals," the authors make it clear that they are primarily concerned with the "moral poverty" of the poorer classes, not the moral poverty of the families that produce corporate and political criminals.

A second set of approaches suggests that if it were not for the discriminatory practices of the criminal justice system, the affluent would appear to be as equally criminal as the poor or put in more positive terms, the poor would appear to be just as law abiding as the affluent. These social interactionist explanations contend that the criminals who show up in official statistics are disproportionately poor because (a) the justice system focuses on controlling poor communities, and (b) this practice increases the likelihood of future criminality by labeling residents of these areas, particularly young men, as criminals at an early age. A typical example put forth is that the proportion of drug users among college students is no less than in that in poor communities, yet college students have a far lower risk of serving time as drug offenders than residents of poor communities because they are not the targets of "wars on drugs"— which are really wars on poor people. Although there is some merit to this approach, the question that remains

is: Why does the criminal justice system do this? Is it merely a reflection of the discriminatory attitudes of the people who work in the justice system, or are they, as good workers, simply pursuing the goals set out for them by a broader political and economic system?

Finally, there are scholars who argue that poor communities suffer from higher rates of crime, in the same way that they suffer from disproportionate levels of other problems, such as alcohol and drug abuse, medical ailments, stress and hopelessness, not because of individual failings but because of the physical and emotional pressures of poverty and inequality. These *structural outcome* perspectives focus on the structurally induced discrepancy between the material desires of people in the poorer classes and their access to legitimate opportunities for fulfilling them. As initially described by Robert Merton (1938), this concept of *structural strain* contends that although desires for the "good things" in life are equally distributed across all social classes, the poor have fewer resources to obtain them. Some individuals resolve this pressure by resorting to illegal means to fulfill their culturally learned desires. When it comes to nonutilitarian crimes, such as interpersonal violence or drug use, structural outcomes models shift their focus toward how the daily frustrations and sadness of living poor can increase tendencies toward aggression or to self-medication with illegal drugs and alcohol as an escape from the hardships of daily life.

Regardless of the future outcome of the ongoing debate as to whether social class determines criminality in terms of the incidence or even prevalence of crime, it seems likely that social class at least shapes the types of crimes one commits. As the populist folk singer of the 1930s, Woody Guthrie, wrote, "Some men rob you with a six-gun, some with a fountain pen." Whether one uses a six-gun or a fountain pen depends on the socio-economic status of the individual. Although it is clear that those who occupy the most privileged and powerful positions certainly can and do at times engage in private crimes of greed, lust, or insanity, it is rarely possible for those in lower classes to engage in many of the illegal behaviors of the rich. Offenses such as price-fixing, embezzlement, and wire and securities fraud require jobs and circumstances possessed by people who have been exposed to advanced education and other social and cultural privileges.

The criminal justice system, however, is designed almost exclusively to control people who "rob you with a six-gun." Those who commit corporate and political crime with a pen have little to fear from the justice system. In other words, social class not only shapes the type of crime one can commit but also influences the likelihood of apprehension and severity of punishment. Many of the crimes in which people, from the lower class participate, such as drug dealing, prostitution, and robbery, occur outside in the street, where detection is more probable. However, state-sponsored, corporate, and white-collar crime tends to occur behind the closed doors of offices and conference rooms, where detection is much more difficult. Also, when apprehension and threat of criminal prosecution do occur, individuals who possess economic social capital are more likely to avoid punishment. They are able to post bail; employ high-priced, experienced attorneys; participate in developing their defense; and use their status in the community to decrease likelihood of conviction and/or severe penalties. Individuals in the lower classes, however, may not be able to raise bail and are more likely to be represented by an overworked, underexperienced public defender. Economically disadvantaged offenders may not even meet their attorneys until minutes before the trial, and, when they do, they are often persuaded to plead guilty in return for a less severe punishment.

PERCEPTIONS OF CRIME AS A LOWER-CLASS PHENOMENON

Perceptually speaking, there appears to be a consensus among a large segment of the U.S. population that crime is largely the product of the behavior of lower-class populations.

If the relationship between social class and crime is not supported by research, why does the perception persist? In his seminal work concerning the *social reality* of crime, Richard Quinney (1970) noted that certain forms of crimes are embedded in the psyche of the American people; that is, when we think about crime, we tend to think of it in very narrow terms,

often omitting the most prevalent crimes and, often, the people who cause the most harm. We tend to envision street crimes, such as murder, robbery, burglary, and assault, while rarely conceiving of white-collar, corporate, and state-sponsored crimes. Because street crime is often more likely to be carried out by people in the lower classes, and crimes of the elite—which generally do not occupy the public consciousness—are committed almost universally by people with economic, political, and social power, the theory of the social reality of crime neatly associates criminality with those on the lower rungs of the economic and social ladder. This remains true even in the face of the well-documented data demonstrating that crimes committed by the powerful cost the U.S. population more, both in terms of monetary and physical costs. Quinney (1977) suggested that this is so because the definition of what constitutes a crime is developed by those with economic, political, and social power and according to their own interests, whereas individuals without such power are more likely to have their activities defined as criminal.

Explanations for why the American public tends to have such a limited conception of crime are plentiful. The way crime is measured sheds light on one way that people obtain a narrow definition. There are three general methods used to measure crime: (1) official statistics, (2) victimization surveys, and (3) self-report studies. The last two methods measure various aspects of victimization and self-reported criminal behavior, and the first usually involves the Uniform Crime Reports, which relies on crimes known to the police to provide us with estimated crime rates. A crime become known to the police either because an officer discovers it or, more likely, 'because someone reports it to the police. As long as the police make a report of the crime, it is available to be counted and used in calculating crime rates. The caveat to this is that, in creating an overall crime rate, the Uniform Crime Report measures only eight offenses: (1) murder and nonnegligent manslaughter, (2) forcible rape, (3) robbery, (4) aggravated assault, (5) burglary, larceny-theft, (6) motor vehicle theft, (7) simple assault, and (8) arson. The first four are violent offenses, and the second four are property offenses. Because these offenses deal mostly with street crime, which the poor are more likely to commit, and omit a large number of offenses, many of which those in the upper economic strata are likely to commit, crime rates provide a skewed picture of crime.

Of course, news and entertainment media have also worked to present a picture of crime and victimization that is not necessarily rooted in reality. Crime has become a prominent theme in media content. One of the most noticeable aspects of media coverage of crime is that it tends to focus on the rarest of crimes. Images of relatively high-profile rapes, murders, and robberies are displayed on television screens throughout the day, throughout the country. Local newspapers and news shows typically adhere to the adage "If it bleeds, it leads." News stories about the deviant and illegal practices of political, economic, and social elites receive no comparable attention unless they occur on a very large scale, as was the case with the collapse of companies such as Enron and WorldCom because of financial crimes.

However, media practices are not a complete explanation. As social actors, people play a role in, if not creating, then surely allowing the emergence and sustainability of a distorted image of crime. Stories about violent and gruesome crimes tend to capture public interest. This interest is part of the reason that the newspaper articles we read, and the news, movies, and TV shows we watch are dominated by crime stories. Indeed, some analysts argue that the media are simply responding to the desires of the public. They are a business and, like all businesses, their primary goal is to increase market share, advertising income, and profits. Therefore, if the public did not consume what the media presented, then the media would have to change what they offer or go out of business.

Public perceptions of crime are also a product of ideology. Many of our ideas about crime and criminality are rooted in socialization and personal circumstances. Shaped by social background, religious principles, and political preferences, many people develop strong ideas about the causes and cures of criminal behavior relatively early in life. The extent to which people accept the common view of crime as a lower-class phenomenon is due in part to the fact that these views coincide nicely with the dominant rhetoric of religious, economic, and political leaders about the relationships among sin, poverty, and crime.

Finally, criminologists are complicit in creating an inaccurate depiction of crime. Criminology has historically focused almost exclusively on street crime in theoretical development and empirical research; that is, criminologists have devoted far more attention to describing and explaining crimes such as murder, burglary, robbery, and drug use than to white-collar offenses such as securities fraud, illegal price fixing, or other forms of elite deviance. It is only recently that a significant number of criminologists have started to empirically examine crimes of the elite.

SOCIAL CLASS AND CRIMINAL VICTIMIZATION

Although there is some debate about the relationship between social class and criminality, the link between social class and criminal victimization is well-known and commonly accepted. Data provided by the National Crime Victimization Survey indicate that although the link between social class and victimization varies according to crime, overall, people who are less well-off tend to bear a greater burden as crime victims, particularly with respect to crimes of violence. The difference between rich and poor households as victims of property crime is less dramatic, although for the more serious crime of burglary, poor households face greater risks than rich ones.

The popular image of street crime is often that of the poor preying on the rich, but the reality of crime is that most people tend to commit crime within a relatively short distance of where they live. Thus, if the structural contradictions of poverty and inequality are more likely to result in individuals committing ordinary crimes, it means that the poor are also more likely to be the victims of street crimes.

SOCIAL CLASS, CRIME, AND POLICY

Most problematic about the apparent misconception of the criminogenic nature of economic and social disadvantage is that policies implemented on the basis of this assumption are more harmful to the lower classes. Government policies can increase or decrease the criminogenic consequences of income and wealth inequality by choosing to pursue preventive or punitive justice strategies. Preventive strategies, such as pre-school education of poor children, housing subsidies, and income support policies for poor families, will help reduce the negative effects of inequality, lessening the number of low-income children for whom hopelessness becomes a pathway to delinquency, drug use, and maybe even adult crime. Punitive strategies, which are far more prevalent today, attack crime through get-tough tactics such as determinate sentencing, "wars" on crime and drugs, and removal of rehabilitation programs from prisons. This results in an increase in the number of people, mostly poor, who will be victims of the crimes committed by those who have become enmeshed in the justice system in ways that leave little option but to return to crime once they return to their communities.

Social class divisions are characterized by the asymmetrical distribution of political power, cultural authority, and wealth. Individuals whose money comes principally from investments or high-paying occupations have more opportunities to influence the formal institutions of government—including the justice system—than ordinary wageworkers, the poor, the unemployed, the young, or the undereducated. If you doubt this, examine the U.S. Senate, the Congress, or your state legislature, and you will find that most of the members tend to be wealthy, employed in high-status professions, or business owners, or possess some combination of these characteristics. At the federal level, one third of all senators and over one quarter of all congressional representatives are millionaires (Santini, 2004). The non-elite social groups that together comprise the vast majority of the American social landscape are almost entirely absent from the law-making process. As a result, the laws and policies that shape how we define crime are more likely to reflect the values, life experiences, and interests of the upper echelons of society.

Of course, laws and policies do not reflect the interests only of the upper echelons of society. Across social classes, there are many areas of consensus over

the definition of crime. Both the rich and the poor agree that murder, rape, and burglary should be treated as crimes. It is where this consensus over the definition of crime breaks down that the greater power of the upper classes becomes apparent. For example, most Americans view deliberate acts of white-collar crime that lead to death or injury as being as serious as street crimes that lead to death or injury, and view corporate and political corruption as being as deserving of punishment as ordinary acts of theft. Lawmakers, however, come primarily from the strata of society that has the exclusive ability to commit white-collar crimes. As a result, the prosecution and punishment of white-collar, corporate, and political crimes has always been more lenient than the treatment of street crimes.

WHOSE CRIMES ARE MORE HARMFUL?

In addition to the conflict over who is more likely to commit crime, there is considerable disagreement about whose crimes cause the most harm. Past research fortunately has provided some fairly clear answers to this question, resulting in the following observation: Elite offenders pose a far greater risk to health, life, and economic well-being than street criminals.

There are approximately 20,000 homicides in the United States every year; however, approximately 100,000 people die every year because of work-related illnesses and accidents, and almost 40,000 deaths occur because of inadequate medical care and unnecessary surgeries. Jay Albanese (1995) estimated that annual economic losses due to street crime are about $10 billion, whereas the losses due to white-collar crime were nearly $200 billion. As Jeffrey Reiman (2004) notes in his book, *The Rich Get Richer and the Poor Get Prison*, the latter figure is undoubtedly an underestimate. Reiman's own calculations put the cost of white-collar crimes in the United States at over $400 billion a year. He suggested that this figure also underestimates the true cost of white-collar crime. In fact, other researchers have estimated that the material and physical losses from white-collar and corporate crime may actually exceed $600 billion.

If we ask, then, who is more likely to cause harm to society, it would appear that the upper and middle-class sectors pose the greatest danger to our health, life, and economic well-being. If we stick to the question of who commits the crimes targeted by the justice system, the picture remains unclear.

CONCLUSION

Social class has always been a critical component in the study of crime, criminality, and the criminal justice system's responses. Although research is unclear as to the exact nature of the relationship, it seems evident that social class matters. It matters in determining who decides which harmful behaviors are criminalized and which are not. It matters when determining the severity of sanctions. It matters in the kinds of offenses one can commit and the quality of defenses one can mount when apprehended. It matters when one is looking at arrest records and prison populations. It matters when one is determining victimization patterns, and it matters in calculating the harm caused by crime. Ironically, where it may not matter is in determining who is more likely to be a criminal. Nevertheless, it matters, and because it matters, criminological research will, we hope, continue to explore the effects of social class on crime and, more important, its effect on justice, the one place where social class should definitely not matter.

REFERENCES AND FURTHER READINGS

Albanese, J. (1995). *White-collar crime in America.* Englewood Cliffs, NJ: Prentice Hall.

Barak, G., Leighton, P., & Flavin, J. (2007). *Class, race, gender and crime: Social realities of justice in America* (2nd ed.). Lanham, MD: Rowman & Littlefield.

Bennett, W. J., Dilulio, J. J., & Walters, J. P. (1996). *Body count: Moral poverty—and how to win the war against crime and drugs.* New York: Simon & Schuster.

Bourgois, P. (1995). *In search of respect: Selling crack in el barrio.* New York: Cambridge University Press.

Braithwaite, J. (1981). The myth of social class and criminality reconsidered. *American Sociological Review, 46,* 36–57.

Bureau of Justice Statistics, U.S. Department of Justice. (2004). *Survey of inmates of state prisons.* Washington, DC: U.S. Government Printing Office.

Chambliss, W. (1964). A sociological analysis of the law of vagrancy. *Social Problems, 12,* 67–77.

Cloward, R., & Ohlin, L. (1960). *Delinquency and opportunity.* New York: Free Press.

Cohen, A. K. (1955). *Delinquent boys.* New York: Free Press.

Dunaway, R. G., Cullen, F. T., Burton, V. S., Jr., & Evans, T. D. (2000). The myth of social class and crime revisited: An examination of class and adult criminality. *Criminology, 38,* 589–632.

Elliot, D., & Huizinga, D. (1983). Social class and delinquent behavior in a national youth panel. *Criminology, 21,* 149–177.

Merton, R. K. (1938). Social structure and anomie. *American Sociological Review, 3,* 672–682.

Michalowski, R. (1985). *Order, law and crime.* New York: Random House.

Michalowski, R. (in press). Social class, crime, and justice. In L. M. Jones, M. O. Nielsen, & B. Perry (eds.), *Investigating difference: Human and cultural relations in criminal justice.* Boston: Allyn & Bacon.

Miller, W. B. (1958). Lower class culture as a generating milieu for gang delinquency. *Journal of Social Issues, 14,* 5–19.

Quinney, R. (1970). *The social reality of crime*. Boston: Little, Brown.

Quinney, R. (1977). Class, state and crime: *On the theory and practice of criminal justice*. New York: Longman.

Reinian, J. (2004). *The rich get richer and the poor get prison*. Boston: Allyn & Bacon.

Santini, J.-L. (2004). Millionaires fill U.S. Congress Halls. Retrieved from http://www.Informationclearinghouse.info/article6418.htm.

Shaw, C. R., & McKay, H. D. (1942). *Juvenile delinquency in urban areas*. Chicago: University of Chicago Press.

Tittle, C. (1983). Social class and criminal behavior: A critique of the theoretical foundation. *Social Forces, 62*, 334–358.

Tittle, C., & Meier, R. F. (1990). Specifying the SES/delinquency relationship. *Criminology, 28*, 183–206.

Tittle, C., Villemez, W., & Smith, D. (1978). The myth of social class and criminality: An empirical assessment of the empirical evidence. *American Sociological Review, 43*, 643–656.

U.S. Census Bureau. (2006). Historical income tables, F3. Retrieved from http://www.census.gov/hhes/www/income/histinc/h01ar.html.

Wilson, W. J. (1987). *The truly disadvantaged: The inner city, the underclass, and public policy*. Chicago: University of Chicago Press.

Wright, B. R. E., Caspi, A., Moffitt, T. E., Miech, R. A., & Silva, P. A. (1999). Reconsidering the relationship between SES and delinquency: A causation but not correlation. *Criminology, 37*, 175–194.

Wright, E. O. (1997). *Class counts*. New York: Cambridge University Press.

MODES AND PATTERNS OF SOCIAL CONTROL

Implications for Human Rights Policy

International Council on Human Rights Policy

ACRONYMS

CSMs	Community Sanctions and Measures
EU	European Union
ICCPR	International Covenant on Civil and Political Rights
ICESCR	International Covenant on Economic, Social and Cultural Rights
ICHRP	International Council on Human Rights Policy
IHR	International Health Regulations
IHRA	The International Harm Reduction Association
IOM	International Organisation for Migration
MSEHPA	Model State Emergency Health Powers Act
OHCHR	Office of the High Commissioner for Human Rights
OSI	Open Society Institute
UIDAI	Unique Identification Authority of India

UK   United Kingdom
UN   United Nations
UNODC   United Nations Office on
         Drugs and Crime
US   United States (of
         America)

EXECUTIVE SUMMARY

1. Introduction: The Research

This report is the outcome of an enquiry into the human rights implications of contemporary patterns of social control—how laws, policies and administrative regulations define, construct and respond to people, behaviour or status defined as "undesirable", "dangerous", criminal or socially problematic. Five policy areas reflecting a wide range of contemporary policy concerns were chosen for specific examination:

1.   Policing and surveillance;
2.   Punishment and incarceration;
3.   Urban spaces and the poor;
4.   Migrants and non-citizens;
5.   Public health and infectious disease control.

A case study of the Roma in Europe was also commissioned.

1.1. Approach and Focus

The report approaches the idea of social control in terms of its role in securing conformity with established norms by preventing, adjudicating, remedying and sanctioning non-compliance. It focuses on formal mechanisms of social control that deal with crime, dangerousness, delinquency and other social problems, including the criminal justice system, the health system, the welfare system and urban planning authorities. These are broadly state-centred or privatised functions and operate at national, regional and transnational levels.

A "social control perspective" is valuable to human rights practice insofar as it throws light on the logic underlying the policy and practice of relevant institutions

that impose controls and their cumulative impact on human rights. Using such a perspective, this report invites a human rights engagement with questions, such as the following:

+   How do changing ideas of crime, criminality and risk shape social policy?
+   What purposes do prisons serve in modern society, and why does incarceration continue to be a preferred sanction?
+   How are public health and urban planning becoming regimes of discipline and punitiveness?
+   How do surveillance and data-gathering technologies order and organise social relations?

Given their significant human rights implications, such questions demand serious attention from human rights advocates.

A social control perspective reviews how a behaviour or activity comes to be constructed as a "social problem" or a "crime". It involves consideration of how these categories are produced and how individuals or their behaviour come to be attributed to them and, ultimately, how methods of intervention are selected. It throws light on the dynamics of the forces that shape attitudes and policy and their relationship with larger socio-political processes and institutions.

Within the context of the policy areas chosen for this project, this perspective focuses attention on policies and patterns that are broadly social rather than narrowly political, including both "new" (such as new technologies of surveillance) and old (such as probation regimes or imprisonment) and the forces that drive changes in governance and social policy (e.g., managerialism, privatisation, transnational transfer, medicalisation).

The report also considers how human rights standards and principles such as equality, dignity, indivisibility and universality might be applied to test and evaluate contemporary social control policies. As a contribution to a continuing debate that involves many communities of practice, the report is written for all who are concerned with human rights, whether they view themselves as human rights advocates or as professionals with an interest in specific areas like public health, urban poverty, policing, penal sanctions, migration, etc.

2. Key Findings of the Report: Modes and Patterns of Social Control

2.1. Criminalisation and Sanctions

The influence of the "crime control" model on social policy and the diffusion of an increasingly reductionist view of the criminal justice system (which considers security to be its primary goal) deserve closer human rights scrutiny, especially because they push impoverished and vulnerable groups onto a slippery slope of management, control and criminalisation. In particular, constructing policy around fear of crime permits a dangerously wide range of state interventions and sanctions based on uncertain criteria and increasing the risk of enforcement being disproportionate, discriminatory and arbitrary. Increasingly, control measures embedded within civil or administrative law target persons, status or behaviour categorised as social problems (e.g., homelessness, drug use, irregular migration, infectious diseases). While the consequences of controls on individuals vary, the spectrum of behaviour and status subject to controls is widening. It is vital to determine how such controls are enforced and against whom, again, underlining that such policies have differential and significant influences on vulnerable groups. For instance, while the number of laws that explicitly criminalise vagrancy may be in decline, a set of new administrative measures or policies often produce the same effect of criminalising poverty.

There is an urgent need for a human rights-based narrative of crime and criminality and responses to crime. On the one hand, it is critical to monitor the impact of both criminal and non-criminal control measures and to assess them against relevant human rights principles, including tests of proportionality, non-discrimination, reasonableness, least restrictive or intrusive means and non-arbitrariness. At the same time, as those who are poor and disadvantaged are more likely to be criminalised, human rights analyses of crime and criminality must take full account of the way in which crimes, social problems, victims and offenders are socially constructed and their relationship with marginality and structural exclusion.

When it comes to the imposition of sanctions, while the traditional civil liberties approach of focusing on prison conditions remains important to defend, the principle enshrined in human rights law that prison systems should be rehabilitative needs more vigorous advocacy in the face of concerns about the exclusionary nature of contemporary prison and post-prison regimes. There are good human rights grounds to look beyond even rehabilitative treatment models and at a penal philosophy that distinguishes constructive from punitive measures and recognises the importance of social justice.

Non-custodial forms of punishment themselves merit close human rights monitoring, especially because imprisonment remains the norm against which other sanctions, such as Community Sanctions and Measures (CSMs), are assessed. Such practices must be monitored to ensure that access to them is not subject to questionable assessment of the risks involved and that they do not contain conditionalities that are so intrusive or onerous that there is a high likelihood of violating them for technical reasons leading to more penalties.

2.2 Segregation

Segregating those considered undesirable or dangerous includes the act of imprisonment, but modes of segregation are also embedded in urban planning, treatment of infectious diseases or responses to irregular migration. Societies are being re-segregated using private as well as public means and both judicial and administrative mechanisms. The adoption of risk models and the categorisation of people in terms of dangerousness has had a range of adverse human rights consequences in a number of contexts.

The report stresses that the premise that segregating or confining a significant portion of those presumed dangerous can, by itself, make our society safer is increasingly influencing social policy and criminal justice. Prisons are increasingly becoming warehouses to segregate "undesirable" populations rather than to enable rehabilitation and reintegration, thus rendering imprisonment not just a tool of repression or punishment but also a means to produce and manage marginality.

In a rapidly urbanising world, urban planning practices are promoting the institutionalisation of segregation, crippling social trust and inhibiting the construction of inclusive social network structures, not to mention undermining human rights of poorer populations.

2.3 Surveillance

Focusing on risk has created an insatiable appetite for information on which to base policy and to intensify surveillance. An increasing proportion of security-related activities are focused on non-crime related matters, especially in surveillance of persons and spaces, based on the assumption that the more data, the better.

Contemporary sociological studies of surveillance are valuable from a human rights perspective because they demonstrate a broad concern with surveillance as a means to order, control and manage social relations; as a means of social sorting. Gathering of personal data facilitates convergence and tracking while syndromic surveillance that compiles health information anonymously contributes to the construction of notions and ideals of normality, furthering control. The involvement of private entities also blurs the distinction between governmental and commercial surveillance.

Human rights monitoring of surveillance can be more effective when it highlights the broader range of concerns and analyses surveillance as a tool of control and social management. Privacy rights are critical, but the range of issues has broadened, and human rights advocacy should take account of this and consider issues such as the interests that public and private institutions, especially corporations, have in using such technologies, their accountability and the use of surveillance technologies in socio-economic contexts that are often very unequal.

3. KEY FINDINGS OF THE REPORT: UNDERLYING FORCES AND CONTEXTS

3.1 Political Economy

It is vital to situate social controls within the context of wider political, social and economic forces, state as well as non-state. The mechanisms that legitimate social control are tied to the "political cultures" that shape responses to social marginality. When economic and social policies tend towards exclusion over universal welfare and inclusion, they impose more controls on those at the margins. Polities with greater socio-economic inequalities tend to be more likely to look to the criminal justice system to solve social problems and failures of governance. In many contexts, the increasing privatisation of state functions (particularly the growth of the private security sector) closely tied to an emphasis on managerialism is also critical in determining the nature and consequences of control regimes. Given the overwhelming power and influence of private capital and industry, depending only on state regulation of private actors may be insufficient. The legitimacy of privatising certain criminal justice functions, for example, must be challenged on human rights grounds.

3.2 Transnational and International Regimes

• International and transnational regimes (formal and informal) facilitate the transfer of policies and technologies of control. International regimes involve formal co-operation amongst States, often accompanied by an international normative framework; transnational regimes include non-state actors like large global private corporations or even epistemic communities of experts, ferrying knowledge across different spaces.

The complexity and opacity of policy transfer raises serious concerns related to monitoring and accountability.

There are also problems of coherence. The human rights protection regimes in relation to migration or health, for example, have different foundations from those of the International Organisation for Migration (IOM) or the International Health Regulations (IHR), which typically take an approach that constructs their subjects as problems in need of management rather than protection. Despite its significant expansion, the human rights framework receives insufficient attention in global and regional policing and criminal justice regimes, including the United Nations Office on Drugs and Crime (UNODC).

If human rights advocates were to monitor and map regional and global regimes of policy transfer, they could make a significant contribution. This also includes monitoring and mapping of the technologies and know-how that are transferred and the State and non-state actors involved, including private corporations. Beyond seeking to ensure that such policies comply with international human rights standards in a procedural sense, advocates could play a vital role in highlighting the extent to which such regimes are premised on respect for human rights, calling on principles such as equality, universality and indivisibility.

3.3 Risk and Security

Ideas of risk and danger are a major influence on contemporary public discourse and policy at the national, regional and international level. Policing, for example, is increasingly concerned with the prediction and prevention of future criminal acts, which necessarily entails the identification of dangerous individuals via risk profiling. The adoption of risk models has also undermined rehabilitative approaches to punishment in the prison context. "Moral panics" favour the imposition of more liberty-depriving sanctions. They also encourage the erosion of procedural safeguards and the creation of suspect populations in a number of different contexts, from public health to migration policy. An understanding of such panics is important in understanding how ideas of security, protection and victim rights can themselves generate and perpetuate control mechanisms that undermine rights.

There is a need for a stronger human rights narrative to counter the argument that increasing controls are justified on grounds of security. Human rights advocacy needs to interrogate risk claims that are advanced to justify the imposition of restrictions and controls to ensure they do not mask a failure by the State to fulfil its wider human rights responsibilities. It is also important to recognise the danger that "securitising" rights (i.e., grouping a range of human rights under the rubric of security, as embodied in ideas like human security) presents.

4. Additional Conclusions

The report suggests that there are key areas in which the human rights movement could deepen its analysis of the underlying forces that shape controls. The way in which human rights abuses result in the imposition of controls and the way in which those controls themselves violate human rights warrant equal attention.

In seeking to limit the negative impact of controls and to strengthen the benefits they may bring, human rights advocacy can draw on principles governing limitations on the exercise of rights that exist in international human rights law (i.e., proportionality, non-discrimination, reasonableness, least restrictive or intrusive means, and non-arbitrariness) and apply these to the exercise of controls. With regard to the State's positive duty to protect and its negative duty to refrain from abuse, the principle of non-discrimination, in particular, can be applied to highlight the differential impact of policies of control on access to social and economic as well as civil and political rights. The principle of non-discrimination can also help signal policies disproportionately targeted at the socially and economically vulnerable. In the context of drug use and drug dependence, the harm reduction approach serves as an example of how the principle of the least restrictive or least intrusive means might be used in other contexts to prevent policies of control that restrict rights.

At the same time, the political and social forces that influence modes of control and how they are imposed could themselves be challenged with principles of universality, equality and indivisibility. The aim of this project is to encourage co-operation in this endeavour between human rights advocates, social scientists, social policy analysts, practitioners, political activists and others.

I. SOCIAL CONTROL AND HUMAN RIGHTS

1. What Is Social Control?

In sociological dictionaries, "social control" is defined to include all social processes, institutions and methods that produce (or attempt to produce) conformity or regulate the individual and collective conduct of its members.[1]

This report considers social control in terms of its role in securing conformity with established norms by preventing, adjudicating, remedying and sanctioning non-compliance. It focuses on intentional, planned and programmed responses by state authorities and corporations to activities, behaviours or status that are perceived to be criminal, problematic, undesirable, dangerous or troublesome. The anchors of this form of social control are institutions that deal with crime, dangerousness, delinquency and other social problems, including the criminal justice system, the health system, immigration and border control, the welfare system and urban planning authorities.

For purposes of human rights policy, this enquiry is concerned with:

+ Forms of social control that are state-centred: criminal justice (criminal law, policing, courts, prisons) and other systems of legal and administrative regulation (e.g., immigration controls, welfare, urban planning);

+ Privatised systems of formal social control and security, such as private prisons or policing;

+ National, regional and global regimes of control and regulation (e.g., IHR, the IOM, Europol);

+ Less explicit but significant social control dimensions of other state or non-state institutions, such as the media or institutions engaged in education, planning, and health and welfare.

The report gives little attention to forms of informal social control that are "outside" the State's purview (such as socialisation, shame, gossip, public ritual, peer pressure). The importance of such measures and of related non-state actors is undeniable, but it was beyond the scope of this research to look at them in any detail.

The report and the research on which it relies draw on an approach to social control that can be traced back to "critical" or "radical" sociology at the end of the 1960s.[2] It will be referred to as "social control theory" or as the "social control perspective".

The approach adopts a social constructionist analysis of social problems. It assumes that social problems consist of an "objective" condition (e.g., the existence of homeless people, undocumented migrants, sexual offenders) and also a "subjective" condition (i.e., the perception that certain behaviours are undesirable or threaten dominant values or interests). A social problem goes through stages of "claims-making" which run from the initial creation of a problem to its categorisation (e.g., as a crime, an illness, a human rights violation) to a method of intervention (punishment, treatment, or political action).

For example, consider the category of "anti-social behaviour" in the United Kingdom (UK). The Crime and Disorder Act (1998) declares that behaviour causing (or likely to cause) " ... harassment, alarm or distress to one or more persons ... " can be characterised legally as anti-social. The anti-social character of an act does not lie in the act itself but in the reaction of others to it. Parmet signals how important it is to understand the social construction of risk, and address it in policy, arguing that "public health theory and international law overlook the role that social factors play in determining the nature and extent of health risks, as well as how risks are perceived and what interventions are chosen".

A social control perspective questions how a behaviour or activity comes to be constructed as a social problem or crime and seeks to throw light on the forces that shape attitudes and policy formation, shifts in those forces, and

---

1 Such definitions are both too broad for the purposes of this report—they cover anything from infant socialisation to public execution—and too abstract. The report therefore does not use "social control" in this universal or anthropological sense.

---

2 For guides to this approach, see Cohen (1985) and Blumberg and Cohen (eds.) (2004). For a current introduction, see Innes (2003).

their relationship with larger socio-political processes and institutions.

"Naming" a category can be controversial. This is clear from discussions of prostitution, where the descriptors "women in sex work", "women in the sex trade", "sex workers", or "commercial sex workers" each imply different, often nuanced understandings that reflect distinct worldviews and political or moral positions. Use of the term "irregular migrant" rather than "illegal migrant", or "person who uses drugs" versus "drug abuser" can be significant in exactly the same way.

Once categories have been created, people and behaviours must then be attributed to them. An important aspect of subjective attribution is that at different times and in different places the same behaviour may be perceived and responded to in quite different ways. A psychologist working with sex offenders in the US, commenting on changes of attitude (that now a 17-year-old teenager who has sex with his 15-year-old girlfriend or a drunk who exposes himself in public may be categorised as "sexual predators", whereas a man exposing himself on a popular TV show was once considered funny) wonders how we come to "fear and hate what we once found pathetic or even humorous".[3]

Categorisation determines who is labelled as criminal or dangerous, and this judgment is then liable to be articulated in criminal law and governance practices.[4] A vast apparatus of procedures, personnel, expertise and organisations is now devoted to the selection and application of judicial and non-judicial controls to identify people and behaviours that fit categories ("rule enforcement"). Some agencies that do this work have long been the focus of human rights attention, including the police, immigration and border control authorities, and parts of the criminal justice system. Others (e.g., welfare agencies, the health service, urban planners) have been scrutinised far less. These institutions increasingly employ private agencies to whom States have devolved the delivery of certain services.

Individuals or groups may be regulated by or subject to social controls because their existence is perceived to be threatening or to lie outside the dominant norms of society: they are considered deviant or dangerous, not necessarily for what they have done, but because of who they are or the traits they possess. Non-compliant behaviour or status, or its consequences, may be considered criminal, deviant, or a social problem, or even a human rights violation[5] and may be subject to measures of social control as a result.

In Visions of Social Control (1985), Stanley Cohen traces four key changes in modes of social control that occurred in the course of the nineteenth and the mid-twentieth centuries:

+ The locus of social control moved from informal social institutions to the State;
+ Deviants were classified and differentiated in various categories, each meriting scientific examination and expertise;
+ Different types of custodial institutions emerged;
+ Policy focused on changing the hearts and minds of offenders rather than on infliction of physical suffering.

In the 1960s, a counter-discourse emerged, which, according to Cohen, called for decentralisation, deprofessionalisation, decarceration and decriminalisation. Such "destructuring" movements downplayed due process in favour of non-intervention, inclusionary controls and pursuit of alternative correctional justice mechanisms. Cohen and other scholars have documented that this movement had the unintended consequence of excluding targeted groups because the alternative measures of control they espoused did not replace but only complemented the criminal justice system. As a result, the range of controls to which people

---

3 A Letter to the Editor of the Reno Gazette-Journal in Nevada, USA, from Steven Ing, a psychologist. Available on file.

4 The research papers refer to this process in different contexts. Oberoi refers to the role that human rights law plays in categorising migrants, refugees and others, for example, while Leman-Langlois and Shearing refer to the enlargement of categories of people subject to surveillance.

5 As discussed later in this report, human rights violations and abuses are also socially constructed. The international human rights law framework defines human rights violations and abuses, but interpretations of these definitions constantly change and develop, reflecting socio-political, moral and other factors.

could be subject broadened. An upsurge of interest in the rights of people who became enmeshed in the criminal justice system (particularly in the penal context), apparent in the second half of the 20th century, was overtaken during the 1990s and early 21st century by a preoccupation with risk. Concern about the risks that crime poses to potential victims caused a significant shift in social control practices. Governments focused increasingly on finding effective forms of control and crime prevention and paid less attention to the causes of crime and deviance. Social control today is characterised by the following features:[6]

+ Continued expansion of exclusionary practices, especially detention (often referred to as "hard" measures), including imprisonment in a criminal context but also civil commitment for mental illness or drug dependence, detention for irregular migration, etc.;
+ Continued expansion of inclusionary practices ("soft" measures), such as CSMs, electronic tagging, home confinement, etc.;
+ Emergence of pre-emptive inclusionary controls, notably the use of surveillance;
+ Justification of the above policies in terms of protecting the public from crime, immigration and insecurity more generally (especially after the terrorist attacks in the US in September 2001).

Groups may be subject to social controls because they are perceived as a threat or abnormal, considered deviant or dangerous, not necessarily for what they have done, but because of who they are or the traits they possess.

2. HUMAN RIGHTS AND SOCIAL CONTROL: TENSIONS AND COMPLEMENTARITIES

The over-riding aim of the project (as reflected in the research papers) is to view contemporary modes and patterns of social control from a human rights perspective. The human rights edifice, however, can itself be viewed as a form of social control. It seeks to regulate the exercise of power, mainly by the State, but in so doing it creates new forms of deviance and crimes (e.g., human rights violations and abuses, crimes of the State, crimes against humanity) and new deviants and criminals (e.g., perpetrators, abusers, war criminals). Similar social processes are at work (rule creation, rule enforcement and state-approved punishment of rule breakers) in the regimes of both social control and human rights. In both cases, rule creation is a form of social construction.

The most concrete and best-known form of rule creation is criminalisation. There are a number of ways in which human rights relate to criminalisation:

+ It categorises behaviour that had previously been normalised or tolerated (e.g., domestic violence, torture) as a "human rights violation";
+ It advances values that can be used by others to support either criminalisation or decriminalisation;
+ It promotes both decriminalisation (e.g., of HIV status or homosexuality) and criminalisation of particular actions (e.g., abuse or discrimination);
+ It regulates and limits state authority to construct laws or enforce norms (e.g., it restrains surveillance by asserting the "right to privacy").

Positions have also changed over recent history. For instance, human rights advocates were originally wary of state intervention in general. This was loosely in line with the destructuring movements of the 1960s (as described above). Whole areas of life were variously declared as "private", "not the business of the State" or "crimes without victims" (e.g., homosexuality, drug-taking, alcohol abuse, abortion, pornography, gambling). The extension of criminal law into these areas was seen as ineffective, corrupting, expensive, criminogenic and abusive of civil liberties.

By the 1980s, however, the emphasis radically changed. The progressive impulse was towards the stronger enforcement of some existing laws or the creation of new laws. The early libertarian streak was denounced for its unwitting support for conservative

---

6 Blumberg and Hay (2007).

roll-back of the State; applying the concept of "victim-less crime" to such areas as pornography was criticised, and there were calls for widening the criminalisation of sexual abuse and domestic violence; and "new" victims were found (of state violence, corporate greed and environmental damage).

More generic terms like "abuses of power" or "crimes of the State" became common. Methods of social control became increasingly judged in terms of preventing harm and damage, achieving social justice and conformity to universal human rights standards. Human rights campaigns have raised the visibility of "gross violations" such as war crimes, genocide and torture and also (more recently) offences of discrimination and violence perpetrated by non-state entities, such as multi-national corporations.

The law came to be seen as the protector of the weak and vulnerable and the State as ultimately responsible for ensuring protection through law-making processes. Social movements have increasingly come to use successful criminalisation (i.e., rule creation) as a more general index of success.

The role of criminalisation is further discussed [later in the chapter] in the overall repertoire of social control; however, generic categories of "gross violations of human rights" or "crimes of the State" are not further discussed. The research focuses more on "ordinary crime" (i.e., offences primarily committed by individual citizens against each other, such as theft, violence, or sexual abuse, or against the government in an abstract sense, such as breach of immigration rules or regulations concerning movement) rather than "political crimes".

In its formative years, the international human rights movement concentrated primarily on abuses defined in the political context of the Cold War; it was primarily concerned with violations of civil and political rights and claimed neutrality about the contested political conflict itself. Human rights values were seen as somehow "transcending" political ideology and choices, and advocates identified specific abuses and campaigned to remedy them.

Human rights organisations today have widened their remit beyond civil and political rights to include social, economic and cultural rights. They have also engaged more with the root causes of human rights violations and the status of human rights as a social problem.

Many observers within and outside the human rights community welcome this widening of theory and practice.[7]

This report invites human rights advocates to deepen analysis of and engagement with policies and patterns that are broadly social rather than narrowly political. This includes both "new" ones (e.g., new technologies of surveillance) and old ones (e.g., probation regimes, imprisonment). It also includes the forces that drive changes in governance and social policy (e.g., managerialism, privatisation, transnational transfer, medicalisation).[8]

Conversely, theorists and practitioners of social control are invited to consider how human rights standards and principles such as equality, dignity, indivisibility and universality might be applied to test and evaluate contemporary social control policies.

BIBLIOGRAPHY

Blumberg, Thomas and Stanley Cohen (eds.), Punishment and Social Control, New York, Aldine de Gruyer, 2003.

Blumberg, Thomas and Carter Hay. "Visions of Social Control revisited", in Crime, Social Control and Human Rights: From Moral Panics to States of Denial, David Downes, Paul Rock, Christine Chinkin and Conor Gearty (eds.), Willan Publishing, 2007.

Cohen, Stanley. Visions of Social Control, Cambridge, Polity Press and Blackwell Publishers Ltd, 1985.

Innes, Martin. Understanding Social Control, Berkshire, Open University Press, 2003.

---

7   Gearty (2008) and Douzinas (2007).
8   The research papers (available at either www.ichrp.org or on the CD-ROM accompanying the printed report) discuss in detail many specific problems that merit closer human rights scrutiny.

PART II

Readings on Adjudication
and Sentencing

To Die or Not To Die

Morality, Ethics, and the Death Penalty

*John T. Whitehead
and Michael C. Braswell*

The death penalty fascinates: its merits are debated, producers make movies about the death penalty (*Dead Man Walking, The Life of David Gale, The Green Mile*), and politicians use it as a sign that they are serious about the crime issue.

The fascination with the ultimate sanction persists even though most murderers do not receive the death penalty, and of those who are sentenced to be executed, many get off death row in other ways, such as through court appeals.

In this chapter we will focus on the ethics of the death penalty.

First, to put the death penalty in perspective we will present some basic information. Then we will outline how the three ethical theories—deontology, utilitarianism, and peacemaking—approach the issue of the ethics of the death penalty.

Finally, we will consider the specific issues concerning the debate on the ethics of the death penalty.

The Death Penalty in Perspective: Facts about the Death Penalty

The latest information available indicates that states executed 53 individuals in 2006 and that 3,254 persons were on death row at year-end 2004 (Bureau of Justice Statistics, 2007). California led the nation with 660 offenders on death row, followed by Florida (397), Texas (393), and Pennsylvania (226) (Death Penalty Information, 2007). Persons sentenced to death in 2005 were 55 percent white, 42 percent black, and 2 percent all other races. Death row prisoners were overwhelmingly male (98.5%) (Bureau of Justice Statistics, 2007).

RATIONALE FOR THE DEATH PENALTY

There are two basic questions regarding the death penalty. The first addresses whether we should even have a death penalty. This question is essentially philosophical in nature. Such a question is often argued in terms of religious values and beliefs. For example, one can find both support and opposition for the death penalty among various Christian denominations, often based on scriptural passages from the Old and New Testaments. This aspect will be discussed in more detail later in the chapter. The second question is judicial in nature. Does the criminal justice system process and prosecute capital cases justly and equitably? Are the laws, procedures, and decisions about such cases administered fairly and consistently, or does discrimination occur against any group? Issues such as race, gender, and economic bias are often debated and discussed when attempting to answer this question.

Concerning the philosophical question, some argue that if an individual takes the life of another person, then that individual should have to forfeit his or her own life, while others might contend that two wrongs don't make a right—that the state also commits murder when they execute a convicted murderer. Persons who support this line of thinking would maintain that advanced or evolved societies do not include the death penalty as a punishment option. Individuals who do support the death penalty would counter by suggesting that the ultimate crime requires the ultimate penalty. Proponents of the death penalty might place their argument in a deontological frame of reference: it is society's duty to punish the most serious crime with the most severe penalty.

The late Ernest van den Haag perhaps put it most eloquently: "Can any crime be horrible enough to forfeit the life of the criminal? Can death ever be a deserved punishment. ... I am confident that the following excerpt may help answer this question." Van den Haag went on to describe a gruesome murder in which two males tortured and sexually abused a female victim, including pouring salt into her wounds before strangling her. Afterward, they broke her neck and arms so that they could fit her body into a trunk, and then dumped her body in a dumpster (for more details, see van den Haag, 2003:235–237).

Van den Haag thinks the answer is simple: a murder as horrendous as this deserves the death penalty—even cries out for the penalty of death. In fact, van den Haag is in favor of the death penalty for all murders that so qualify according to the laws and jury decisions in the death penalty states.

Capital punishment opponents counter that a severe penalty is appropriate for the crime of murder but it does not have to include the taking of a human life. Opponents argue that a severe punishment such as life without parole (LWOP), life with the possibility of parole, or a lengthy prison sentence short of life are serious enough penalties to serve as commensurate punishment for the crime of murder. Additionally, opponents argue that sentences short of capital punishment have the advantage that if any error is made in determining either guilt or sentence, the error can be corrected, to some extent, if the offender is serving a life sentence or a lengthy prison term. If the offender has been executed, however, any mistake that is discovered years after the conviction and sentencing cannot be corrected. So, in a deontological framework, opponents could argue that LWOP, life, or a lengthy prison term can both satisfy the societal duty to demand a severe penalty for a severe offense and also satisfy any societal duty to rectify mistakes to the fullest extent possible (mistakes will be a separate topic below).

Utilitarians go further than simply offering a philosophical justification that capital punishment offers a severe penalty for a severe offense. Utilitarians argue that the death penalty has additional positive consequences that justify or demand its use, such as deterrence and incapacitation. We will discuss each of these issues in turn.

DETERRENCE

One such additional consequence, according to utilitarians, is deterrence. Utilitarians who favor capital punishment argue that capital punishment is a general deterrent: it is so severe a penalty that it deters or frightens individuals who might be contemplating committing a murder out of committing one. Capital punishment proponents usually argue from personal experience or common sense. They argue that most of us can recall experiences where we were tempted to do something wrong, such as shoplift or speed, but saw a police officer or thought of being caught and decided not to steal or speed down the highway. Proponents also offer some empirical evidence. Studies by Ehrlich and by Cochran and Chamlin claim that capital punishment has a deterrent effect (e.g., Cochran & Chamlin, 2000).

Capital punishment opponents argue that there are several problems with the deterrence argument. First, relying on our own experiences or common sense about deterrence is misleading. Most of us are law-abiding; we are good citizens who have been appropriately socialized. Many of the people who murder may not be so law-abiding and thus may not think about possible penalties. Second, many murders are committed on the spur of the moment or in an unstable emotional state that does not readily allow for a calm assessment of the possible penalty. Many homicides occur in argument situations in which the offender is agitated. Others occur in robbery situations in which both the offender and the victim are under considerable stress. In both situations as well as others, the perpetrators are not thinking rationally about the penalty for murder or other tragic consequences that are likely to result from their actions. Instead, a robber is often quite nervous and might well interpret a normal fear response by a store clerk (for example, a twitch) as a sign that the clerk is going to reach for a gun or alarm button and end up fatally shooting him or her.

Social scientists have conducted some research on the death penalty and on other penalties that shed some light on how much deterrent impact the death penalty has or might have. One of the first studies on the deterrent impact of the death penalty was conducted by Thorsten Sellin. What he did was to compare homicide rates in contiguous states that did have or did not have the death penalty. He chose Ohio, Indiana, and Michigan. These three states are mid-western states that share similar climates and economies. All three have both manufacturing (auto, steel, and related industries) and agriculture (such as soybeans). All three are a mix of both urban, suburban, and rural areas. There are also cultural, political, and social similarities. Comparing homicide rates across these three states over decades, Sellin concluded that there is no discernible impact of the death penalty. States that have the death penalty do not have lower homicide rates than states without the death penalty (Sellin, 1980).

Peterson and Bailey conducted a review of studies on the deterrent impact of capital punishment. After looking at many different types of research studies, they concluded: "In short, the empirical evidence does not support the belief that capital punishment was an effective deterrent for murder in years past. Nor is there any indication that returning to our past execution practices would have any deterrent impact on the current homicide problem" (Peterson & Bailey, 2003:277).

Other studies of deterrence also show negligible impact. For example, in the late 1970s, Scared Straight programs surfaced as a popular way to supposedly prevent delinquency. Scared Straight was the name of a program in New Jersey in which prison inmates gave prison tours to pre-delinquents or delinquents and then literally tried to scare the youths out of committing any further crime. The inmates yelled at the kids and informed them of all the horrible events that could befall them if they wound up in prison, such as physical and sexual assaults, and even being killed and carried out in a body bag. Although the documentary that promoted the program claimed tremendous success, systematic scientific research studies on the effectiveness of Scared Straight-type programs indicate that there is no significant difference between youths who experience such a program and youths who do not (Lundman, 1993).

To be fair, some studies do show some deterrent effects for some punishments. Granted, many of us fear penalties enough to avoid crime. A point to be considered, however, is that opponents to the death penalty are not arguing for no penalties for murder. Rather, they are advocates for either LWOP, life with the possibility of parole, or lengthy prison sentences for murderers. What is at issue is: What is the true effect of the death penalty? This means that proponents for the death penalty need to demonstrate that the ultimate penalty has more impact than a penalty such as LWOP, which to date has not occurred.

Some proponents of the death penalty argue that a serious problem in looking at the deterrent impact of it is that it is not imposed in such a way that it can be a deterrent. Deterrence theory maintains that for any punishment or sanction to be an effective deterrent, the penalty in question must be severe, certain, and quick. The death penalty is clearly severe, but it is not always certain or quick. Concerning certainty, while most murderers are caught, not all are convicted and not all receive the death penalty. In fact, even those who receive the sentence of the death penalty do not necessarily get executed. Between 1977 and 2002, about 7,000 persons were sentenced to death, but more than one-third (36.7%; 2,535 offenders) received other dispositions. They had their sentences or convictions overturned, received commutations, or died a natural death before they could be executed (Bonczar & Snell, 2003). Quickness is also problematic. The average stay on death row is about 10 years. Death penalty proponents argue that such lack of certainty and lack of speed in imposing the death penalty detract from its effectiveness. They argue that improvements in certainty and quickness could result in findings that deterrence works. A more recent discussion of the research on deterrence, however, disagrees that improvements will result in new findings of effectiveness (Peterson & Bailey, 2003).

One problem with increasing the speed at which death row offenders proceed to execution is that a major reason for the lengthy time on death row is to allow time for appeals. States usually have a mandatory appeal of the case. Then offenders often pursue discretionary appeals in an effort to save their lives. Liebman and his colleagues have shown that many of the appeals show reversible error. They studied more than 4,500 appeals from 1973 and 1995 and found the overall rate of prejudicial error to be 68 percent. "In other words, courts found serious, reversible error in nearly 7 of every 10 of the thousands of capital sentences that were fully reviewed during the period" (Liebman, Fagan & West, 2000). Death penalty opponents argue that if states were to shorten the time between sentencing and

execution, that would cut short the time for appeals. This would reduce the number of errors that are found. So it would become more likely for states to execute individuals who either did not commit the murder [or] deserved a conviction and sentence for a noncapital offense such as manslaughter that does not involve the death penalty. The question ends up being one of efficiency versus effectiveness, shortening the appeal process versus guarding against error when execution is the penalty to be rendered.

INCAPACITATION

Death penalty proponents are right about one thing: the death penalty is perfect incapacitation. Executing an offender prevents him or her from ever killing again. Therefore, in a way, the death penalty does satisfy the utilitarian goal of incapacitation.

Opponents cannot deny the incapacitative impact of the death penalty but they can argue that other penalties can also achieve very high degrees of incapacitation. LWOP, for example, will ensure that a murderer cannot commit another homicide on the street. He or she may kill a fellow prisoner or a prison guard, but they will not kill another person on the outside. Moreover, the number of killings in prison is quite small. For example, the latest figures show that approximately one prisoner per state is murdered in prison every year, and about 20 prison staff members are killed every five years (Bedau, 1997:177). Any loss of life is tragic, but unfortunately, these statistics are incomplete and dated. These statistics also do not tell us if convicted murderers were in fact the perpetrators of these in-prison crimes.

There is also substantial evidence that if society punished murderers with 10 to 20 years of imprisonment and then released them on parole, the released murderers would have very low recidivism (new crime) rates. Parole statistics consistently show that murderers make good parolees. Paroled murderers have the lowest crime rates of all parolees. One of the best pieces of evidence about the safety of parole for murderers comes from the *Furman* cases. *Furman* was a Supreme Court case that ruled the death penalty, as then practiced, unconstitutional. As a result, death row inmates in affected states were switched to parole-eligible status and were in fact later (after serving years of their sentences) paroled. The so-called *Furman* parolees performed quite well in the community. In one study of 188 murderers who were released on parole and served an average time of 5.3 years on parole, only one committed a new murder. Twenty (10.6% of those released) committed a new felony (Marquart & Sorensen, 1997).

Why do paroled murderers do so well on parole? There are several reasons for the success. One is that parole boards are more careful in deciding if a murderer gets parole than in deciding, for example, whether a car thief gets parole. If the parole board makes a mistake about a car thief, the damage is just one more stolen car. If they make a mistake about a murderer, there is the possibility that another murder will take place. Parole board members are concerned about avoiding such serious mistakes. A second reason is that even if the parole board releases a murderer, they usually make him or her serve quite a few years (10 or more) in prison before release. Those years allow maturation to occur; the parolee is often not the impulsive and immature person who entered prison. Simple aging also occurs; the released murderer is not as young, energetic, and angry as he or she once was.

As stated previously, the death penalty achieves perfect incapacitation: no executed killer can kill again in society. However, Life Without Parole also prevents killers from killing again on the street. Parole statistics, especially the *Furman* cases, indicate that even parole for murder is not necessarily a costly choice in terms of outcomes. Very few paroled murderers kill again, but a minority (about 10%) do indeed commit a new felony. So if society wants perfect incapacitation, the death penalty delivers perfection in one specific dimension. If society is willing to tolerate some error (e.g., some new crimes but very few murders), then parole is available as an option.

PEACEMAKING PERSPECTIVE

[T]he peacemaking perspective focuses on caring, connectedness, and mindfulness. Peacemakers oppose the death penalty because they think that it does not promote caring, connectedness, and mindfulness whereas other penalties do.

A living example of peacemaking and the death penalty is Jarvis Masters. Jarvis is a death row inmate in California. His time on death row has been an opportunity for him to examine his life and turn from crime and violence to Buddhism and promoting peace. By becoming a Buddhist he has come to realize that we are connected so that what each one of us does indeed affects others and oneself as well. In his book *Finding Freedom* (1997), he gives two dramatic examples of connectedness and caring.

One Fourth of July two guards who normally worked another cellblock were assigned to death row. They were anticipating a holiday barbecue that evening, so they were in a hurry to get through the day. Consequently, they practically threw the food at the inmates that day and ignored simple requests for silverware or toilet paper. Their disdain for inmates was causing rage to rise in the prisoners. Masters saw what was happening and felt he should do something to calm the prisoners. He decided that if the inmates stuffed their toilets with towels and flooded the cellblock, the flood would be a way for the inmates to respond to the guards in a controlled way. It would be an expression of prisoner anger, and it would make the guards late for their barbecue that evening because they would have to clean up the cellblock before they could leave work. More importantly, this minor expression of prisoner anger would prevent the inmates' anger from building up to a point at which inmates might attack a guard.

Another incident involved the guards putting a new prisoner into the yard in such a way that they were basically setting him up for an attack. Apparently the new prisoner was gay and was dressed in some fashion to draw attention to his sexual orientation. At the time, says Masters, there was considerable hatred for homosexuals in San Quentin Prison. Masters saw the guards let this new prisoner onto the yard and, shortly thereafter, saw an inmate coming toward the new prisoner with a shiv (prison weapon). Masters intervened; he simply went up to the new prisoner and asked him for a cigarette. Seeing Masters stopped the inmate from attacking the new prisoner. Afterwards, Masters wondered why he had risked his own life for someone he really didn't know. He asked himself if he was the only Buddhist there.

The example of Jarvis Masters shows that offenders can change in prison and have a positive effect on other prisoners. Although Masters did receive a death sentence, his time on death row allowed him to question his former lifestyle and change to one of genuine spirituality. If he had been executed sooner, he would not have had the chance to change. Nor would he have had the chance to do some of the positive things he has done in prison, such as the two examples just noted. Parenthetically, a death penalty proponent might argue that the inmate on death row didn't give his or her victim a chance to mature or experience such personal transformation. Peacemaking criminologists might also be concerned about the effects of death row on the family members of the death row inmates. One mother of a death row inmate notes that a detective magazine came out with an article depicting her son's "killing spree." She was so distraught that she tried to buy every copy so that her friends and neighbors would not see the story (Lezin, 1999). A few years later, a brother noted his painful experiences when friends would talk about criminals and say that "They ought to hang the bastard"(Lezin, 1999:18).

Sending offenders to death row seems to foster seeing these criminals as outside the human family and permitting the rest of us to depict them as less than human. Unfortunately, those who are parents, spouses, or siblings of the offender have to listen to and live with such depictions. The relative knows the offender as a flawed human, with good and bad traits, but the media and careless citizens may describe a relative on death row as a cold-blooded killer, a monster, an animal, and so on. It is painful to see and hear someone you love depicted in extreme terms.

MISTAKES

Determining who is eligible for the death penalty is far from an error-free process. Juries and judges make mistakes in determining guilt and determining sentences. Mistakes about guilt result in an innocent person being placed on death row and experiencing the stress of anticipating an execution that he or she does not deserve. Mistakes about the penalty—the sentencing phase—mean that a person who perhaps deserves a lengthy prison sentence is instead anticipating death/execution and spends his or her time trying to appeal an incorrect sentence.

A major source of the mistakes in the death penalty decision-making process is the quality of defense representation that many offenders get. Many offenders are poor and cannot attract the best defense attorney available. Moreover, many states are willing or able to spend only a limited amount of money on indigent offender defense representation. Liebman and his associates found that defense lawyers "who didn't even look for—and demonstrably missed—important evidence that the defendant was innocent or did not deserve to die" was one of the most common errors causing a majority of the reversals at the state post-conviction stage (Liebman, Fagan & West, 2000:ii).

In one case in Georgia the state paid for an assigned defense attorney who was actually a talented lawyer. The problem was that he was a skilled divorce attorney who had never worked a death penalty case. To make things worse, the attorney thought that just because he had done the judge a favor before the case, the judge would return the favor in the totally unrelated death penalty case (Lezin, 1999). Some states, such as New York, do provide competitive pay to attorneys assigned to death penalty cases so that they can put forth an adequate defense. However, many other states provide very modest compensation so that it is often difficult if not impossible to attract qualified individuals to work death penalty cases.

Recent studies have shown that in the "death belt" (nine southern states that use the death penalty frequently) more than 10 percent of the attorneys who have represented indigent capital defendants have been disbarred, suspended, or disciplined at rates significantly higher than average, even in those states. In fact, most of the attorneys in the death belt had not handled a capital case before, and the death belt states did not have training programs for these attorneys (Mello & Perkins, 2003:369).

The result is that many death penalty defendants do not get adequate (much less, superior) representation. Less than adequate representation means that some unknown number of death row defendants receive the death penalty improperly. Adequate defense counsel would mean at least a lesser sentence, if not exoneration.

Apart from what O.J. Simpson, Kobe Bryant, or Michael Jackson actually did or did not do concerning their alleged criminal actions, it is clear that these celebrities were able to hire the best defense attorneys they could afford. Many of the persons who wind up on death row quite simply could not afford that level of defense representation. If they could afford such high-quality attorneys, they would probably not end up on death row. The question, then, is whether it is ethical for wealth or the lack of it to have such impact on who is sentenced to capital punishment. One could argue that the prosecution may be at a disadvantage if the person who is tried for first-degree murder is very wealthy, but the prosecuting attorney and state have a substantial advantage if the defendant is poor.

Opponents of the death penalty argue that mistakes stemming from factors such as inaccurate eyewitness testimony and inadequate defense representation occur too frequently and are reason enough to abolish the death penalty. As noted above, the Liebman (2000) study of appeals found the rate of prejudicial error to be 68 percent. Abolitionists maintain that an error rate this high is simply unacceptable.

The proponent response to the issue of mistakes in the administration of capital punishment is that mistakes happen in all walks of life. Ernest van den Haag still supports the death penalty, arguing that all human institutions are flawed. For example, he has argued that driving to school or work is a very accident-prone activity. Every time we get in our cars and drive somewhere, we are taking our lives in our hands. We trade off the danger of driving for the convenience of driving to work or classes. Even ambulances, notes van den Haag, kill some innocent pedestrians, but they save more innocent people than they kill (van den Haag, 2003:241). In sum, he thinks that the death penalty is justified, despite mistakes, as long as it deters and the mistakes are few.

As noted, the deterrent impact of the death penalty is not as certain as van den Haag contends. Most social scientists conclude that the deterrent impact is either unknown or nonexistent. Moreover, the frequency of mistakes appears to be much more prevalent than few. Former Governor Ryan of Illinois was so concerned about mistakes that he put in place a temporary moratorium on executions. (For a look at the personal impact of mistakes, see Box 12.1.)

DISCRIMINATION AND RACIAL BIAS

As noted at the beginning of this chapter, death row is disproportionately populated by blacks. Although

---

Box 12.1. The Personal Impact of Mistakes

One of the authors of this chapter likes to have his classes consider that because human beings aren't perfect, neither is our system of justice absolutely perfect. Given that reality, is it acceptable to you that there are some mistakes about who gets the death penalty (for instance, one innocent is executed for every 10,000 who are deserving of death)? After the students raise their hands in support of this statement, he says "OK now keep your hands raised if you can live with such a mistake about the death penalty if it is your brother, your son, your spouse, or yourself who is the innocent victim of the mistake?" Without exception, hands drop one by one.

What about you? Are mistakes in determining who goes to death row all right with you? Are they still acceptable if you or a loved one is the one experiencing the mistake? Are you so much in favor of the death penalty that you can still support it even if it means you or a loved one will be wrongfully executed?

African-Americans make up only about 12 percent of the U.S. population, they constitute about 42 percent of the prisoners on death row (Bureau of Justice Statistics, 2007).

The first ethical concern is whether discrimination in fact occurs. The high percentage of African-Americans on death row does not in itself prove discrimination. If blacks make up about 44 percent of the murderers in the United States, then they should make up about 44 percent of the persons on death row. More specifically, if blacks commit about 44 percent of the capital murders (the homicides that deserve capital punishment), then they should make up about 44 percent of the prisoners on death row.

A recent review of research on discrimination in the administration of the death penalty led to several conclusions. First, the race of the defendant is not a significant factor in the prosecutor's charging decision. Second, the data "document race-of-victim disparities reflecting more punitive treatment of white-victim cases among similarly aggravated cases, regardless of the race of the defendant" (Baldus & Woodworth, 2003:241). These disparities seem to stem more from the prosecutor's charging decision than from judge or jury decisions. Third, "in several jurisdictions for which data are available, cases involving black defendants and white victims are treated more punitively than cases with all other defendant/victim racial combinations" (Baldus & Woodworth, 2003:241). Fourth, a few studies do show negative impact on black defendants or on defendants who killed white victims; these disparate impacts "arise from disproportionately punitive charging practices in counties with either particularly large numbers of black-defendant cases or particularly large numbers of white-victim cases on their capital case dockets" (Baldus & Woodworth, 2003:242).

The Capital Jury Project has discovered some interesting findings about how jurors make their decisions. Project researchers have found that the number of white males or even the presence of one black juror on a jury can make a significant difference in the decisions made by juries. Specifically, the Capital Jury Project found a "white male dominance" effect in black defendant/white victim cases. That is, the jury voted for the death sentence in only 30 percent of the cases

when the jury had fewer than five white male jurors, but the jury voted for death in 71 percent of the cases when there were at least five white male jurors on the jury. The researchers also found a "black male presence" effect: "Having a black male on the jury reduced the probability of a death sentence from 71.9 percent to 37.5 percent in the B/W [black defendant/white victim] cases, and from 66.7 percent to 42.9 percent in the B/B [black defendant/black victim] cases" (Bowers & Foglia, 2003:77).

Discussions regarding the actual extent of discrimination in the death penalty are important and need to continue. It is imperative to eliminate discrimination. It is also important to end any appearance of discrimination. The high percentage of African-Americans who receive the death penalty implies to many that there is discrimination. Even if careful investigation shows that discrimination is not occurring, and that prosecutors and juries are perfectly unbiased in their decisions, many individuals interpret the high percentage of blacks on death row as apparent evidence of discrimination. Discrimination or the appearance of discrimination can influence minority members to have negative attitudes toward police, judges, and others in the criminal justice system. Such negative attitudes can affect the administration of justice.

ARBITRARINESS

Closely related to the issue of discrimination is the issue of arbitrary selection of individuals for the death penalty. Although approximately 20,000 murders are committed each year in the United States, fewer than 500 cases result in the death penalty.

Ideally, those 500 cases should be the most deserving of the death penalty. Practically, however, that is simply not the case. As noted above, race appears to play some factor in the selection of cases for the death penalty. For one thing, black defendant/white victim cases are more likely to result in the death penalty than black defendant/black victim cases.

Even apart from any instances of racial impact, other factors such as location, judge, prosecutor, and case notoriety can play a role in determining whether one murderer gets capital punishment while another gets a life sentence or even less.

The deontologist would be quick to argue that arbitrariness should play no role in such a critical decision. The principle of the categorical imperative calls for not making exceptions but treating similarly situated individuals in similar fashion. Given the demonstrated arbitrariness in the death penalty, a deontologist could oppose the death penalty for this reason alone.

Arbitrariness is hard to eliminate. The federal courts now use a guidelines system that is meant to reduce arbitrariness in all criminal sentencing. Problems persist. For one thing, the Federal Sentencing Guidelines allow for reductions based on providing information on other criminals. Therefore, offenders who either have no information to give, or refuse to give information, receive no reductions. One first offender, for example, refused to implicate her own mother and was given a 10-year sentence, while an offender caught with 20,000 kilos of cocaine served only four years in prison because he "cooperated," that is, gave information on other dealers (Schlosser, 2003:61). Another effort to reduce arbitrariness is proportionality review. This means that courts review death penalty cases in the jurisdiction (usually, one state) to attempt to ensure that only the most horrible murders get the death penalty and that all murders less serious than the least serious death penalty case get a sentence less severe than the death penalty. The basic problem is that such a proportionality review is difficult to do (Mandery, 2003). Measuring severity is not as simple as measuring blood pressure, especially in light of the fact that "the fundamental equality of each survivor's loss creates an inevitable emotional momentum to expand the categories for death penalty eligibility" (Turow, 2003:47).

Abolishing the death penalty will not eliminate arbitrariness. Some murderers will get LWOP, some life with the possibility of parole, some shorter prison sentences, and some even probation. However, abolishing the death penalty could end the arbitrariness of some murderers getting executed and others getting much less severe penalties.

CONDITIONS ON DEATH ROW

Because more than 3,500 prisoners are currently on death row, it is important to consider death row conditions. What are death row prisoners experiencing as they wait for execution?

There are two main types of death rows: unreformed and reformed (Johnson, 1998). Unreformed death rows involve a great deal of isolation. Prisoners are kept in solitary cells and are released from their cells only for short periods for exercise or showers. Such prisoners spend a considerable amount of time reading or watching television.

Reformed death rows, on the other hand, allow prisoners to spend much more time out of their cells for work and recreation. Prisoners might work at jobs such as making clothes or entering computer data. Both work and recreation allow for more socializing with other prisoners. One death row resident in Texas spent much of his time painting pictures, including pictures of Jesus and of how he imagined the execution room to look (Frontline: The Execution).

Many think that a reformed death row represents considerable improvement over an unreformed death row because the inmate on a reformed death row is out of his or her cell more often and has more opportunities to work and engage in recreation or socializing with other inmates.

Robert Johnson, a strong opponent of capital punishment, is not so positive about reformed death row environments. Johnson argues that even a reformed death row does not help a prisoner get ready for his or her own death. In fact, Johnson thinks that there will never be an appropriate environment that truly prepares an inmate for death. Such a death row would be too painful, says Johnson, for both inmates and guards:

> Officials would be unable to ignore the hurt and loss they, as persons, would inflict on their prisoners, whom they would know to be frill human beings. The prisoners, too, no longer dulled to their own feelings, might well suffer greatly. Executions would be traumatic events, the virtual antithesis of

---

BOX 12.2. DONALD CABANA: A FORMER EXECUTIONER SPEAKS OUT ON DEATH ROW

Former warden Donald Cabana came to have doubts about working in corrections after executing some prisoners that he became quite close to, but he had no doubts about not wanting to supervise any more executions. "Of one thing I was certain, whatever the future might hold, I had privately concluded that I would not supervise another execution" (Cabana, 1996:191).

Several factors had caused Cabana to change. One factor was executing a man that Cabana knew had changed dramatically during his years on Mississippi's death row. "I was absolutely convinced that Connie Ray Evans would never kill again, and that he would present no threat to other inmates if his sentence were commuted to life. … Evans had arrived on death row a streetwise drug abuser, bitter and scornfully contemptuous of authority. He had changed, and I personally had watched the change, especially over the past three years." Cabana pleaded for a commutation from the Governor, imploring the Governor that "Isn't that [change] what prisons are supposed to be about?" (Cabana, 1996:179). The Governor, however, refused to commute the sentence to life, and Cabana had to carry out Evans' execution.

If you are preparing for a career in criminal justice and you go to work in a capital punishment state, you too might secure a position like Don Cabana's. He wound up having to supervise executions. You could end up arresting and investigating capital case defendants, prosecuting capital cases, defending capital defendants, guarding death row inmates, or, like Cabana, actually supervising executions. What do you think about actually being involved in executions or death row or capital cases? Would it bother you to be involved in any stage of the process? Now that about 80 percent of the states have capital punishment, a considerable percentage of criminal justice workers may become involved in the process to some extent.

---

their current bureaucratic reality (Johnson, 1998:215).

Aside from Johnson, most inmates and guards as well as most critics would probably endorse the reformed death row over the unreformed one. With more opportunities for work and recreation, the reformed death row seems to be the best that prisons can offer for those condemned to death by the courts.

JURORS IN CAPITAL CASES

Something relatively new in the debate on capital punishment is the examination of juror behavior in capital cases. The Capital Jury Project in particular has brought forth considerable information about how jurors go about making the decision to vote for or against capital punishment. Unfortunately, much of this information is quite disturbing.

First, many jurors make the decision in favor of the death penalty too soon. Specifically, 30 percent of jurors in capital cases make the decision at the guilt stage, prior to the penalty stage. This means that three out of 10 capital jurors decide on the sentence before they have a chance to hear the evidence about sentencing (Bowers, Fleury-Steiner & Antonio, 2003).

Second, many jurors hold inaccurate beliefs about how many years a prisoner would have to serve in prison if he received a prison sentence instead of the death penalty. For example, in both Alabama and California, the mandatory minimum sentence that a prisoner would have to serve would be life without parole. However, jurors thought the mandatory minimum sentences in those two states were 15 years and 17 years, respectively. Therefore, jurors thought prisoners would be out in a decade and a half, whereas the statutes stipulated life without parole. Such erroneous beliefs about alternative prison terms can easily influence jurors to vote for the death penalty in order to prevent perceived heinous murderers from being released from prison.

Third, capital jurors are often confused about mitigating factors, which are a critical part of the decision to impose the death penalty. Many jurors mistakenly think that mitigating factors must be proven beyond a reasonable doubt or that all jurors must agree that a factor is a mitigator (Bowers, Fleury-Steiner & Antonio, 2003).

Finally, as we noted previously, the Capital Jury Project has thrown new light on the issue of the impact of race on the capital punishment decision. If there is no black juror on the jury, compared to the presence of at least one black male juror, a death sentence is twice as likely. In trials with no black juror, the death sentences resulted 71.9 percent of the time versus 37.5 percent of the cases with at least one black male juror (Bowers, Fleury-Steiner & Antonio, 2003). It appears that the presence of at least one black male juror can get the other jurors to consider the evidence more deliberately.

RELIGION AND CAPITAL PUNISHMENT

Many people use religion to justify their views on the death penalty. This is not the place for a thorough theological debate on the subject, but because the death penalty debate often includes religious arguments, we think it important to note some of the Judaeo-Christian-based religious arguments surrounding capital punishment.

Sister Helen Prejean is a powerful example of someone who sees the message of Christ and Christianity as condemning the death penalty. While she was a nun working with the poor in New Orleans, a friend asked her to become a spiritual advisor for a death row inmate. That led to being a spiritual advisor for additional inmates and a book and movie entitled *Dead Man Walking* (Prejean, 1994). In the book she outlines her opposition to the death penalty. For example, she once asked a warden the following question:

Do you really believe that Jesus, who taught us not to return hate for hate and evil for evil and whose dying words were, 'Father, forgive them,' would participate in these executions? Would Jesus pull the switch? (Prejean, 1994:122).

Yet many Christians apparently do not see a contradiction between Sister Prejean's merciful Jesus and a perceived duty to execute. Many Christians point to Paul's Letter to the Romans (13.4) as proof that God endorses the death penalty when used appropriately (see, e.g., the June 2000 Southern Baptist Convention Resolution on Capital Punishment at www.sbc.net/resolutions supporting "the fair and equitable use of capital punishment by civil magistrates as a legitimate form of punishment for those guilty of murder or treasonous acts that result in death").

Some see the story of Jesus and the woman caught in adultery as another indicator of Jesus' stance against the death penalty. In this incident, the religious leaders brought to Jesus a woman allegedly caught in the act of adultery. The typical penalty was capital punishment, but Jesus told the questioners that "he who is without sin should cast the first stone." Ashamed, they all walked away (John 8:1–11). Many see this as evidence of Jesus' rejection of the death penalty.

One scholar disagrees. H. Wayne House argues that in this incident Jesus is really concerned about the other party, the man who also committed adultery. House argues that under Mosaic Law both parties to adultery should be charged. Furthermore, the witnesses are guilty of a capital crime by charging only the woman. House argues that here Jesus is taking the procedural issues very seriously and thus is not condemning capital punishment but calling for correct process (House, 1997).

In their official statement on the death penalty, U.S. Catholic Bishops urged fellow Christians "to remember the teaching of Jesus who called us to be reconciled with those who have injured us (Matthew 5:43–45) and to pray for forgiveness for our sins "as we forgive those who have sinned against us." (Matthew 6:12) (U.S. Catholic Bishops' Statement on Capital Punishment, 1980:7).

While Biblical scholars and theologians can argue about these and other passages, Sister Prejean's comment that it seems incongruous that the Jesus who preaches love and forgiveness (e.g., "Love your neighbor as yourself," "Forgive seven times seventy") would favor capital punishment seems logical. Furthermore, societal conditions have changed considerably since the time of Jesus. Lengthy prison terms were not the norm (nor viable alternative to capital punishment) 2000 years ago when Jesus walked the earth, but they are quite possible today.

Several Christian churches have issued formal statements against capital punishment based on their interpretation of the teachings of Jesus. For example, both the Roman Catholic Church and the Presbyterian Church have issued formal statements opposing the death penalty (U.S. Catholic Bishops' Statement on Capital Punishment, 1980; Presbyterian Moratorium on Capital Punishment). On the other hand, as noted above, the Southern Baptist Convention has issued a statement in favor of the death penalty.

Theologian George Boyd has an interesting opinion about the death penalty. He opposes it because he thinks that a convicted murderer might think that his or her debt to society can be paid by accepting the death penalty. Boyd does not want any murderer to be able to feel that way: "Murderers should never be allowed the comfort of the illusion that they can 'pay' for their crime" (Boyd, 1988:163).

In conclusion, churches and theologians are not in agreement over the death penalty. Some religious persons such as Sister Helen Prejean are very active in trying to abolish it. Others, however, such as the Southern Baptist Convention, endorse capital punishment. It is somewhat perplexing that followers of the same religious leader, Jesus Christ, sincerely maintain dramatically different positions on such a fundamental issue as the death penalty. Perhaps this controversy indicates that believers must struggle with such basic issues and try to come up with a workable solution.

ALTERNATIVES TO THE DEATH PENALTY

If states were to abolish the death penalty, the most likely current alternative would be a sentence of life without any possibility of parole (LWOP). In the last five to 10 years, this has been mentioned most frequently as an alternative punishment.

For example, in a 2004 nationwide poll, 50 percent of the respondents favored the death penalty and 46 percent favored LWOP (life without parole), compared to 52 percent favoring the death penalty and 37 percent favoring life without parole in 2000 (Gallup Poll, adapted by Sourcebook of Criminal Justice Statistics Online, www.albany.edu/sourcebook).

Some utilitarians question LWOP in terms of costs. Assuming that it costs approximately $20,000 to keep an offender in prison for one year and assuming about 50 years of incarceration for a typical murderer, LWOP could easily cost the state about $1 million per inmate. That is a considerable expense. It is not uncommon to hear citizens question the expenditure of so much money on someone who has taken a human life! ("Why should I as a taxpayer have to pay to keep a murderer alive?")

Opponents of the death penalty contend that it is in fact more expensive to execute a murderer sentenced to capital punishment. This statement at first seems difficult to believe, but capital cases take extra time and money, states mandate at least one court appeal, defendants usually pursue additional discretionary appeals, and death rows can be expensive if the inmates are not working. When all the costs of capital punishment are added up, it can cost the state from $2.5 to $5 million to execute one individual (Bohm, 2003).

To be fair, if capital punishment were abolished and LWOP were the most serious penalty, it is likely that murderers would pursue many appeals of that sentence as well. It also seems reasonable, though, that trials and other costs of LWOP sentences would never come to equal the time and expense of capital punishment verdicts.

Many murderers would probably accept LWOP sentences instead of capital punishment. Most seem to want to stay alive even if it means endless years in prison. However, it is important to note that not every murderer would agree. One murderer on death row, for example, was very clear in insisting that he was not desirous of spending the rest of his natural life on death row. In his words, he did not want to be "locked in Hell for all of eternity" (Arriens, 1997:82).

The other alternative to the death penalty is a life sentence with the possibility of parole. This option is not very popular at present. Most of the research focuses on either the death penalty or LWOP. A major reason seems to be public sentiment; the public wants murderers either executed or locked up permanently.

An argument in favor of the possibility of parole for murderers is the fact that some murderers succeed quite favorably on parole. ABC did a fascinating documentary about 20 years ago that followed the lives of 40 death row inmates in California. A state appeals court overturned the death penalty in California, and the death row prisoners (108 of them at the time) became eligible for parole. Over the years, the parole board paroled 40.

Thirty-four of the individuals succeeded—got jobs, married, raised kids, and even did such things as speaking to high school students to try to encourage them to live positive lives and stay out of crime. Some failed, however; one committed a new murder and one committed a horrible rape.

Although the current climate is not favorable for the option of life with the possibility of parole, evidence that some parole murderers do so well in terms of jobs, relationships, and parenting, raises the issue that perhaps this should be an option for some. (See Box 12.3 for Scott Turow's comments on the death penalty.)

CONCLUSION

In this chapter we have tried to present some of the ethical questions about the death penalty. This chapter is not meant to provide complete coverage of the topic. For further coverage, see Bohm (2003) or Costanzo (1999).

Utilitarians would consider the consequences of the death penalty such as deterrence, incapacitation, mistakes, and discrimination. Deontologists would consider the duty to punish and whether the death penalty is the deserved penalty for murder or whether other penalties such as life without parole can be a sufficient punishment for the crime of murder. The peacemaking perspective focuses on the core principles of caring, connectedness, and mindfulness as they pertain to the death penalty. As we have noted, many people also bring religious arguments into the debate.

What each person must do is examine the reasons for his or her current position on the death penalty and ask if those reasons seem sufficient. If not, then the individual should investigate further and come to a new position that is in line with the information that

---

Box 12.3. Scott Turow's Comments on the Death Penalty

Scott Turow, the author of such best-selling novels as *Presumed Innocent* and *Reversible Errors*, was a prosecutor and recently served on a governor's commission in Illinois looking into the death penalty in that state.

On the one hand, he notes that he himself would be willing to inject the fatal poison if the murderer were a killer such as John Wayne Gacy, who tortured and killed 33 young men. Along these lines, he and the other members of the commission voted to limit capital punishment to five criteria: multiple murders, murder of a police officer or firefighter, a killing in prison, a murder impeding the criminal justice system, or a murder with torture.

On the other hand, Turow is painfully aware that "[n]ow and then, we will execute someone who is innocent ..." (Turow, 3003:47). Thus when the commission came to a final vote on whether Illinois should have the death penalty or not, Turow reports "I voted no" (Turow, 2003:47).

is currently available about the death penalty and its administration.

REFERENCES

Baldus, D.C., and G. Woodworth (2003). "Race Discrimination in the Administration of the Death Penalty: An Overview of the Empirical Evidence with Special Emphasis on the Post-1990 Research." *Criminal Law Bulletin,* 39:194–226.

Bedau, H.A. (1997). "Prison Homicides, Recidivist Murder, and Life Imprisonment." In H.A. Bedau (ed.), *The Death Penalty in America.* New York: Oxford University Press, pp. 176–182.

Bohm, R.M. (2003). *Deathquest II: An Introduction to the Theory and Practice of Capital Punishment in the United States.* Cincinnati: Anderson.

Bonczar, T.P., and T.L. Snell (2003). *Capital Punishment, 2002.* Washington, DC: U.S. Department of Justice.

Bowers, W.J., B.D. Fleury-Steiner, and M.E. Antonio (2003). "The Capital Sentencing Decision: Guided Discretion, Reasoned Moral Judgment, or Legal Fiction." In J.R. Acker, R.M. Bohm, and C.S. Lanier, *America's Experiment with Capital Punishment: Reflections on the Past, Present, and Future of the Ultimate Penal Sanction.* Durham, NC: Carolina Academic Press, pp. 413–467.

Bowers, W.J., and W.D. Foglia (2003). "Still Singularly Agonizing: Law's Failure to Purge Arbitrariness from Capital Sentencing." *Criminal Law Bulletin,* 39:51–86.

Boyd, G.N. (1988). "Capital Punishment: Deserved and Wrong." *Christian Century* (February 17, 1988): 162–165.

Bureau of Justice Statistics (2007). *Capital Punishment Statistics.* Found at http://bjs.ojp.usdoj.gov.

Cabana, D.A. (1996). *Death at Midnight: The Confession of an Executioner.* Boston: Northeastern University Press.

Costanzo, M. (1997). *Just Revenge: Costs and Consequences of the Death Penalty.* New York: St. Martin's Press.

Death Penalty Information Center (2007). *Death Row Inmates by State and Size of Death Row by Year.* Found at www.deathpenaltyinfo.org/article.php?did=188.

Feld, B.C. (2003). "The Politics of Race and Juvenile Justice: The 'Due Process Revolution' and the Conservative Reaction." *Justice Quarterly,* 20:765–900.

Gillespie, L.K. (2003). *Inside the Death Chamber: Exploring Executions.* Boston: Allyn & Bacon.

House, H.W. (1997). "The New Testament and Moral Arguments for Capital Punishment." In H.A. Bedau (ed.), *The Death Penalty in America: Current Controversies.* New York: Oxford University Press, pp. 415–428.

Johnson, R. (1998). *Death Work: A Study of the Modern Execution Process.* Belmont, CA: West/Wadsworth.

Liebman, J.S., J. Fagan, and V. West (2000). *A Broken System: Error Rates in Capital Cases.* Found at www.law.Columbia.edu/instructionalservices/liebman.

Lundman, R.J. (1993). *Prevention and Control of Juvenile Delinquency,* 2nd ed. New York: Oxford University Press.

Mandery, E.J. (2003). "The Principles of Proportionality Review," *Criminal Law Bulletin,* 39:157–193.

Masters, J.J. (1997). *Finding Freedom: Writings from Death Row.* Junction City, CA: Padma.

Mello, M., and P.J. Perkins (2003). "Closing the Circle: The Illusion of Lawyers for People Litigating for Their Lives at the *Fin de siecle.*" In J.R. Acker, R.M. Bohm, and C.S. Lanier, *America's Experiment with Capital*

Punishment: Reflections on the Past, Present, and Future of the Ultimate Penal Sanction (pp. 347–384). Durham, NC: Carolina Academic Press.

Peterson, R.D., and W.C. Bailey (2003). "Is Capital Punishment an Effective Deterrent for Murder? An Examination of Social Science Research." In J.R. Acker, R.M. Bohm, and C.S. Lanier, America's Experiment with Capital Punishment: Reflections on the Past, Present, and Future of the Ultimate Penal Sanction (pp. 251–282). Durham, NC: Carolina Academic Press.

Prejean, H. (1994). Dead Man Walking: An Eyewitness Account of the Death Penalty in the United States. New York: Vintage Books.

Schlosser, E. (2003). Reefer Madness: Sex, Drugs, and Cheap Labor in the American Black Market. Boston: Houghton Mifflin.

Sellin, T. (1980). The Penalty of Death. Beverly Hills, CA: Sage.

Turow, S. (2003, January 6th). "To Kill or Not to Kill: Coming to Terms with Capital Punishment." The New Yorker, 40–47.

van den Haag, E. (2003). "Justice, Deterrence and the Death Penalty." In J.R. Acker, R.M. Bohm, and C.S. Lanier, America's Experiment with Capital Punishment: Reflections on the Past, Present, and Future of the Ultimate Penal Sanction (pp. 223–249). Durham, NC: Carolina Academic Press.

DISCUSSION QUESTIONS

1. How serious an ethical issue is the problem of mistakes relating to the death penalty? Is the death penalty ethical if there is only one mistake a year? One every five years? Is perfection necessary? Why or why not?

2. Discuss the relative merits and problems of a sentence of life without parole versus the death penalty. Which seems more ethical? What are the problems of each?

3. Would death penalty opponents really be satisfied if life without parole became the most serious penalty? If the death penalty were abolished, would death penalty opponents then try to abolish life without parole, claiming it to be too harsh?

4. Discuss religious arguments for and against the death penalty. What do you think religion suggests we should do about the death penalty?

CASE STUDY 12.1 POLITICS OR ETHICS? A GOVERNOR'S PREROGATIVE

"Joe, get in here. It looks like trouble with that D.A. down in Blackshear County."

The Governor's middle-aged Chief of Staff sat down on the leather chair facing the Governor's desk, a fax in his hand.

"It looks pretty bad, Governor. Boscoe's the D.A. down there. It looks like a major political screw-up, not to mention a legal nightmare."

Roy Maden, the Governor of his great state, drummed his fingers impatiently on his desktop. "And of course, Boscoe just happens to be one of the most vocal and high-profile Republicans in our fine state. That will be just dandy with me running for election next year. The Democrats will have a field day."

Joe shifted in his chair as he looked solemnly at his friend of many years.

"No question about Boscoe's political ambition. He has a perfect batting average with capital cases. He's sent 'em all to death row. Fact is, he's sent a little over four times as many to the row as any other D.A. in the state. Most of the folks around here feel like he's setting himself up for a run at Governor after you finish your next term."

"Well, 'the best laid plans of mice and men ... '" Boscoe the Bozo wasn't counting that group of law students and their professor taking a closer look at his cases."

Governor Maden rubbed his forehead as he stared out of his office window.

"Joe, what's the bottom line?"

"According to the legal and forensics experts I've talked to, there's a pretty solid buzz that at least a quarter of his cases are bogus and there are questions about a number of others. Missing DNA that's supposed to be on file, withholding evidence from defense attorneys and even worse, the names of two detectives keep popping up in the most suspicious cases."

The Governor's eyes widened. "You don't mean … ?"

"Yes sir, it looks like a criminal conspiracy could be involved."

Roy Maden could feel a headache coming on.

"Give it to me straight, Joe. What are my options?"

Joe stroked his chin and considered the choices at hand before speaking.

"You could stall the investigation until after you are reelected, then go after Boscoe. The downside is that two of the inmates on death row are out of appeals and are scheduled to be executed before the election. I've checked their rap sheets, and they both have a long list of assaults. Some of our folks say that the world would be better off without them."

The Governor looked intently at his trusted friend. "What do you say, Joe?"

QUESTIONS:

1. Discuss the different choices the Governor could make from utilitarian, deontological, and peacemaking perspectives?
2. What would be the most moral and ethical course of action he could take? What would be the probable consequences for the Governor, district attorney, and death row inmates?

WRONGFUL CONVICTIONS

Marvin Zalman

Wrongful convictions occur when innocent defendants are found guilty in criminal trials, or when defendants feel compelled to plead guilty to crimes they did not commit in order to avoid the death penalty or extremely long prison sentences. The term *wrongful conviction* can also refer to cases in which a jury erroneously finds a person with a good defense guilty (e.g., self-defense), or where an appellate court reverses a conviction (regardless of the defendant's factual guilt) obtained in violation of the defendant's constitutional rights. This chapter deals with the first type of wrongful convictions, or *wrong person convictions*. Note also that the verdict of acquittal in American law is "not guilty" rather than "innocent," meaning that an acquitted person might not be factually innocent. For the sake of clarity, the term *actual or factual innocence* is used to refer to persons who did not commit the crime. *Miscarriage of justice* (a legal term in England) is also used to describe wrongful convictions.

A wrongful conviction is a terrible injustice that is magnified when an actually innocent person spends years in prison or on death row. This has always been recognized by the U.S. legal system. The rising number of exonerations, however, and growing awareness that such injustices occur every day in American courts, raises profound doubts about the accuracy and fairness of the criminal justice system. This understanding is supported by considerable recent research. This surge in awareness and budding research has motivated a growing number of innocence projects, which work to exonerate wrongly convicted prisoners, to also propose justice policy reforms designed to reduce the number of wrongful convictions or to alleviate their effects. This chapter explains why wrongful conviction has become a prominent issue, the scope of the problem, its causes, and reform proposals.

The injustice of being convicted and imprisoned for a crime one did not commit is intuitively apparent. Research and anecdotal evidence shows that a high proportion of wrongfully convicted prisoners suffer severe psychological consequences, including post-traumatic stress disorder and anxiety disorders, which is not typical among actually guilty prisoners in the absence of life-threatening experiences in prison. This complicates the ability of exonerated prisoners to return to a normal life after release.

More than half the states do not legally authorize financial compensation for persons who were victimized by the criminal justice system in this way, although the number of states with compensation laws has grown in recent years. Moreover, exonerated prisoners do not receive the services provided to prisoners released on parole. Newer compensation laws provide for health and restorative services, as well as financial compensation, to help exonerated prisoners. A person who has been exonerated does not have automatic grounds to sue and recover money damages against police or prosecutors. A number of such cases have been successful in recent years, but they are infrequent and successful only when specific wrongdoing by criminal justice agencies can be proven and immunity defenses overcome.

THE RISE OF THE INNOCENCE MOVEMENT

Prior to 1990, wrongful convictions generated only slight interest. The famous writer of the "Perry Mason" legal thrillers, Erie Stanley Gardner, created an informal "court of last resort" in the 1950s to investigate and correct miscarriages of justice. For the most part, however, the public, as well as most judges and criminal lawyers, was convinced that very few innocent people were ever convicted. When the Supreme Court expanded defendants' trial rights in the 1960s, for example, the reason given was not to make the criminal justice system more accurate in determining guilt and innocence but to prevent government oppression.

Some pre-1990 scholarship did raise issues of trial accuracy. First, a group of cognitive psychologists began to conduct eyewitness identification experiments in the 1970s. By 1990, they had amassed a wealth of information showing that eyewitnesses were often mistaken and that lineup and identification procedures could significantly increase or decrease eyewitness accuracy. Next, a survey of criminal justice officials by criminologists C. Ronald Huff, Arye Rattner, and Edward Sagarin in the 1980s estimated that thousands of wrongful convictions occurred every year (Huff, Rattner. & Sagarin, 1996). Finally, philosopher Hugo Adam Bedau and sociologist Michael Radelet published a survey in a prestigious law journal in 1988 asserting that 350 innocent persons were convicted of capital and potentially capital crimes in the 20th century and that 23 were executed. Although a handful of these 350 might have been factually guilty, the study's overall correctness raised awareness in the legal community that an innocent person could be executed. This scholarship did not, despite occasional news stories about wrongful convictions, create widespread concern about miscarriages of justice.

It was DNA testing, used to prove guilt with near certainty and to absolutely exclude suspects or defendants, that caused a sea change in attitudes about wrongful convictions. Previously, blood testing based on group types and other blood factors could not exclude suspects whose blood factors matched the crime sample; even though a large percentage of the population also shared those factors, prosecutors placed these "matches" in evidence. In forensic DNA testing, 13 loci (sites) in a suspect's DNA strand that vary among people are analyzed to create a distinct DNA profile (or *DNA fingerprint*). The profile is compared with that of the same 13 loci in the biological sample linked to the crime (e.g., semen or blood deposited during a rape or assault). If the profiles match, based on population genetics studies, the probability that the suspect was the source of the crime scene DNA is astronomically high. If only 1 of the loci does not match, the suspect is absolutely excluded.

The first DNA exoneration in the United States occurred in 1989 and showed how DNA transformed a confusing tale of innocence or guilt into one of absolute clarity. Gary Dotson was convicted of rape in Illinois on a teenage girl's eyewitness identification. In fact, she made up the rape story to cover her fear and shame after consensual sex with a boyfriend. Six years later she was married, got religion, and recanted her story. The police and a judge refused to believe that the recantation was true, despite her pastor supporting her truthful state of mind and the former boyfriend admitting to the consensual sex. Dotson was released on parole by the governor of Illinois in 1985, who inconsistently said that he did not believe the recantation. Dotson was reimprisoned for a parole violation in 1987. Finally, with the support of journalists and a determined defense lawyer, a DNA test was performed on the semen in the rape kit. Dotson was absolutely cleared and formally exonerated. His case became a template for tens and then hundreds of thousands of police rape investigations, which exonerated suspects in the early stages of crime investigations. By the early 1990s, the FBI laboratory reported that one quarter of all rape kit samples from police around the country were exclusions. This meant that in thousands of cases, accusations based on eyewitness identifications were wrong.

Soon, prisoners who knew they were innocent and serving time or sitting on death row for crimes that did not happen or were committed by someone else began to petition for DNA testing. Most were denied testing because of prosecutors' resistance based on legal technicalities. However, a sufficient number of exonerations occurred by the mid-1990s to generate significant happenings. Newspapers prominently reported DNA exonerations. In New York, two enterprising law school clinical professors, Barry Scheck and Peter Neufeld, started the first law school innocence project at Cardozo Law School to pursue cases of inmates claiming innocence. Janet Reno, then attorney general of the United States, commissioned a report highlighting the weakness of eyewitness identification. The report raised the profile of the wrongful convictions issue in criminal justice and legal circles. By the late 1990s, several powerful documentaries, such as Errol Morris's *Thin Blue Line*, brought the issue to moviegoers and television audiences.

In 2001, Scheck and Neufeld, together with reporter Jim Dwyer, published *Actual Innocence*, recounting several of their exoneration cases in gripping detail. Each case listed a specific way in which the criminal justice system had failed. This list, along with previous studies, created catalogues of what are considered causes of wrongful convictions. Although the book was well received, the major event in 2000 that did more to put wrongful convictions on the map was Illinois Governor George Ryan's moratorium on executions. Between 1990 and 2000, Illinois had executed 12 prisoners while 13 on death row had been exonerated and freed. This so shocked Ryan that he halted all executions and set up a commission to review capital punishment in Illinois. The commission recommended many reforms,

and several were enacted. Ryan's continuing concern with unreliable death sentences led him to commute the sentences of all 167 death row prisoners and pardon 4 on the grounds of actual innocence before he left office in 2003. This led other states to impose moratoria or to end the death penalty. Exonerations have weakened support for capital punishment and raised general public awareness about wrongful convictions.

SIZE AND SCOPE OF THE WRONGFUL CONVICTION PROBLEM

If wrongful convictions were rare, they could be downplayed as inevitable failings of a complex human system. If they are frequent and are linked to systemic problems, then they pose a challenge to the fairness and accuracy of the justice system that calls for a public response. The issue is controversial. Some prosecutors and judges believe the number of wrongful convictions to be vanishingly small and have offered an estimate of approximately 260 a year or an error rate of 0.027% (or 0.00027). This figure is a mistaken interpretation of a study conducted by Professor Samuel Gross and colleagues that counted 340 known exonerations between 1989 and 2003 (Gross, Jacoby, Matheson, Montgomery, & Patil, 2005). Critics fail to note that an *exoneration* is not the same as a *wrongful conviction* (although the terms are loosely used as equivalents). Gross et al. (2005) defined an exoneration as an official act declaring a previously convicted defendant not guilty, by means of (a) a governor's pardon on the basis of evidence of innocence; (b) a court dismissing criminal charges on the basis of new evidence of innocence (e.g., DNA); (c) a defendant being acquitted on retrial after an appeal, on evidence of factual innocence; or (d) a state's posthumous acknowledgment that a defendant who had died in prison was innocent. The study, however, demonstrated that the 340 exonerations it catalogued were the tip of an iceberg, with the number of wrongful convictions probably reaching into the thousands.

Most known exonerations have occurred in murder and rape cases rather than more numerous crimes, such as robbery, for which unreliable eyewitness identification is the only evidence. This is so partly because DNA evidence is available in most rape cases (although 60% of known exonerations were revealed by means other than DNA testing). High-stakes capital cases also generate greater assistance to avoid executions. It is likely that more errors occur in assault, robbery, and burglary convictions based on erroneous eyewitness identification and circumstantial evidence. Studies of wrongful convictions in death penalty cases since 1973 (when the modem era of capital punishment began), as to which careful statistics are kept by the government, have estimated "wrong person" wrongful convictions at 1% to 3.5%. In Illinois, of the 289 persons sentenced to death between 1973 and 2003, 17 (or 5.9%) were exonerated and released.

Surveys of state judges, prosecutors, defense lawyers, and police officials have provided an alternate estimate of wrongful convictions—of about 1%. Although police and prosecutors give lower estimates than judges and defense lawyers, in light of what is now known about wrongful convictions a 1% felony error rate is plausible. On the basis of slightly more than 1 million state court adult felony convictions in 2004, and prison and jail rates of 40% and 30%, respectively, this rate translates to an estimated 10,790 adults wrongly convicted, of whom 4,316 were sent to prison and 3,237 wrongly jailed in 2004.

The number of wrongly convicted persons cannot be known with certainty, because no federal or state agency keeps track of exonerations, let alone wrongful convictions. Many news stories, reports, and books fairly describe wrongful convictions in detail, although not all of these wrongful convictions resulted in formal exonerations. In some of these cases, prosecutors insisted that the original verdict was accurate despite strong new evidence of factual innocence, further clouding an understanding of wrongful convictions.

CAUSES OF WRONGFUL CONVICTIONS

Studies reveal several factors related to miscarriages of justice, labeled "causes," although they are not so in a scientific sense. Typically, more than one factor is found in each wrongful conviction. Although a few wrongful

convictions are caused only by honest witness error, most involve some level of negligence or malfeasance by criminal justice officers or defense lawyers. A troubling minority of cases involve perjury or knowingly dishonest action by forensic examiners, prosecutors, and police. Brief descriptions of the major factors related to wrongful convictions follow. Note that the list that follows is not comprehensive.

Eyewitness Identification

Mistaken eyewitness identification is the leading cause of wrongful convictions. It was involved in 79% of the first 200 DNA exonerations. Although an overall error rate for eyewitnesses is not well established, some experts place it at about 25%. This figure is the same as the proportion of DNA tests in rape cases conducted by the Federal Bureau of Investigation laboratory in which the DNA did not match the mistakenly identified suspect. The human memory does not record all information like a video recorder; it drops most information out of short-term memory and stores the central, but not peripheral, elements of those events in long-term memory. This makes facial recall somewhat uncertain. Events during a crime, such as extreme stress or focus on a weapon, decreases facial recall by victims and witnesses. In addition, *unconscious transference* can lead witnesses to superimpose the face of someone previously observed but not well-known onto the memory of the perpetrator. Memory is dynamic and can change during the recall stage from what was observed. Memory is also malleable and can change under the influence of suggestion. These and other factors show that eyewitness identification should be received with caution, and yet police, prosecutors, and especially jurors tend to rarely disbelieve eyewitness evidence.

Problems with eyewitness identification are made worse by flawed police procedures. Police have relied on "showups," which is showing the suspect or the suspect's photograph alone to the witness without a lineup. Courts rule that showups are suggestive and will exclude showup evidence unless one of several easy-to-produce factors is present. The showup exception factors are whether the witness paid attention, had a good opportunity to view the perpetrator, gave an accurate description, was certain, and viewed the showup shortly after the crime.

Even lineups are often flawed. Police are not always scrupulous in ensuring that the suspect does not stand out from the lineup fillers. Laboratory research shows that more errors occur when fillers are selected on the basis of their similarity to the suspect than on the basis of the victim's description of the perpetrator. Police or prosecutors have at times suppressed the uncertain identification or nonidentification by one lineup witness while promoting the testimony of another. These and other elements often make lineups a less-than-optimal method of an accurate identification.

Forensic Science Error or Misconduct

Problems with expert evidence presented by forensic scientists or forensic examiners is the second leading cause of wrongful convictions; erroneous forensic evidence supported the convictions of 57% of the first 200 DNA exonerations. Forensic error and misconduct take a variety of forms, including problems inherent in the method, incompetent or untruthful experts, and substandard forensic laboratories.

Some expert evidence is based not on scientific testing but on comparisons that rely ultimately on the experts' subjective evaluations. Some of these methods, such as fingerprints, bullet and tool mark examinations, and footprint and tire impressions, are relatively credible and accurate, but known errors have nevertheless occurred. If such expert evidence goes unchallenged by defense attorneys (by having other experts evaluate it), it is possible that honest but mistaken conclusions will lead to false convictions. Other kinds of expert comparison, such as handwriting analysis, are more subjective and require closer scrutiny. Even lower on the reliability scale are comparison methods that are so tentative that some label it "junk science." Two such methods, microscopic hair analysis and bite mark impressions on skin, have caused numerous wrongful convictions. Hair analysis has now been largely replaced by DNA analysis, and bite mark evidence, although accepted in courts, has been subject to strong criticism.

Examiners have been known to err even where evidence is based on forensic science, which includes blood analysis (serology, which has been replaced by DNA analysis), drug analysis, forensic toxicology (the science of poisons), and organic and inorganic analysis of crime scene trace evidence. Even worse, in a few notorious cases forensic examiners have been exposed as pathological liars who always testified to benefit the prosecution, even when no tests were conducted. In addition to outright falsification, forensic experts can mislead courts and juries by overstating the strength of their findings, reporting inconclusive reports as conclusive, failing to report conflicting results, and the like. When expert witness perjury has been exposed, state criminal justice systems have had to reopen hundreds of cases to ensure that they did not result in wrongful convictions. Some specialized arson investigators have relied on incorrect or outdated fire science to report that fire and burn patterns were evidence of arson when this was not true.

Finally, even the most reliable methods can produce incorrect results if the forensic laboratories are substandard. As DNA testing becomes more sensitive, the risks of contamination rises unless the laboratories are in pristine condition. Testing in some inferior laboratories has even led to several people being wrongly convicted on the basis of erroneous DNA analysis. Among the worst cases was the Houston, Texas, police laboratory. A few years ago conditions were so poor that the laboratory's roof leaked, contaminating samples with excess moisture.

False Confessions

Most people cannot understand why innocent persons confess, especially as the "third degree" (beating and torture to get confessions) has mostly disappeared from American law enforcement. Yet, false confessions were obtained in about 20% of exonerations, and at least 125 false confessions have been documented. What people do not know is that police interrogation is a "guilt presumptive" process designed to extract a confession from the guilty person who is reluctant to confess. As such, it uses powerful psychological techniques to get suspects, even innocent suspects, to talk and to confess.

When police interrogate a suspect, they are usually not trying to solve a crime because they are already convinced that the suspect is guilty, even if the investigation has not been completed. Police conduct preinterrogation interviews to ascertain whether a suspect is truthful, but the ability of police to detect lies is no better than chance. Despite Miranda warnings, most suspects waive their rights. Laboratory experiments and case studies have shown that innocent persons waive more frequently because they know they have nothing to hide.

The interrogation setting and process create psychological pressure designed to extract a confession. The suspect is isolated and confined in a small, uncomfortable space. The interrogator forcefully asserts the suspect's guilt and cuts off any denials or objections. In the United States police may lawfully lie to a suspect during interrogation, by, for example, falsely asserting that his or her fingerprint or DNA profile was found at the scene. The interrogation creates a sense of hopelessness in the suspect. The interrogator then develops themes, such as minimizing the seriousness of the crime, that make it psychologically easier for the suspect to admit guilt. Once an admission is made, the process moves on to generating detailed oral and written admissions or confessions.

Police interrogation produces incriminating statements or full confessions two thirds of the time. The techniques and subterfuges are so powerful that interrogation also induces innocent persons to confess. Research suggests that teens, mentally impaired individuals, and people with personality deficits are more likely to falsely confess than normal adults. *Compliant* false confessions are made in order to end the psychological pressure of interrogation. Some who confess naively believe that they will be released, led to that belief by subtle police statements that do not amount to the clear promises banned by the rule against coerced confessions. Others think that once they get out of the interrogation room they will be able to explain their case to a judge and have their case dismissed. Less frequently, cases of *internalized* false confessions occur, where the innocent suspect comes to doubt himself, after extensive and insistent police persuasion that includes false statements presented as fact, and admits that he "must have" committed the crime while in a blackout state. Even when such confessions are retracted, they play a strong role in convicting innocent suspects.

Perjury: Perpetrators, Informants, Jailhouse Snitches, and Criminal Justice Personnel

Perjury in various forms is common in wrongful convictions. Informant perjury was a factor in 49% of the first 111 death penalty exonerations. In capital cases the real perpetrator is often a suspect, and in several cases where police focused on an innocent person, the actual killers led investigators further astray with false testimony. Witnesses frequently lie to police for a number of reasons, and although police tend to believe that they are proficient at detecting witnesses' deception, scientific studies show that investigators do no better than chance at detecting liars. In laboratory studies, all groups (whether police or students) could identify falsehoods about half the time.

Miscarriages of justice happen often when police pay informants to supply incriminating information about suspects, which the informants then fabricate. Informants are often criminals and can be paid in many ways: money, dropped criminal charges, leniency when they are charged with serious crimes, or favors to friends or family. This gives the most untrustworthy people incentives to lie, and police handlers often fail to properly screen their stories. A pernicious type of informant is the jailhouse snitch. Numerous false convictions are obtained in part on the testimony of jailed snitches who claim that the innocent suspect confessed the crime to them or made incriminating statements. It is not all that difficult for a clever snitch to get enough information about a case to make up a plausible story for the prosecution to use. In some jails the use of snitches has become so routine as to suggest willful blindness on the part of police and prosecutors.

Unfortunately, there are several recent notorious cases in which rogue police officers have framed innocent people for drug and weapons possession. Although this kind of corruption is rare, when it happens it requires officials to reinvestigate hundreds of convictions. Police and prosecutors have great discretion in conducting investigations and trying cases. Although the overwhelming majority are honest, their opportunity to cover the truth requires internal vigilance on the part of these agencies.

Ineffective Defense Counsel

Most defendants are poor (indigent) and rely on government-paid assigned counsel or public defenders rather than retained lawyers. Indigent defense is chronically underfunded, making it difficult for competent attorneys to routinely provide adequate defense. Studies in several states have shown a higher proportion of defense lawyers in exoneration cases with poorer disciplinary records than average, offering proof that substandard lawyering is a cause of wrongful convictions. The U.S. Constitution requires effective assistance of counsel for defendants, but the Supreme Court's standards for determining ineffective assistance are weak and require proof that attorney negligence caused a verdict. Only 38 of the first 200 (29%) DNA exonerees raised ineffective-assistance claims on appeal, reflecting the difficulty of making this kind of challenge, and only 4 received a reversal on ineffective-assistance grounds.

Egregious cases of defense attorney misconduct in court have ranged from sleeping or total unpreparedness to drunkenness and being high on drugs. Even ordinarily competent defense lawyers have failed to prevent the conviction of innocent clients in ways too numerous to catalogue.

Among the most serious underlying problems are failures to adequately investigate case facts and failing to properly challenge prosecutors' witnesses, including forensic experts. Although the wrongful conviction literature does not list ineffective assistance as the highest cause, in a sense there is a failure by the defense in every wrongful conviction.

Prosecutorial Misconduct

Prosecutorial misconduct, whether or not it leads to wrongful convictions, is common. In-court misconduct includes making inflammatory comments or mischaracterizing evidence to the jury, allowing witness perjury (suborning perjury), or permitting snitches to lie about their payoffs for testifying. Prosecutors have even been known to destroy evidence. The suppression of exculpatory evidence (that which points to innocence), in violation of Supreme Court rules, appears in many wrongful conviction cases. Suppressing exculpatory evidence is a cloudy issue because it is up to the prosecutor to determine in the first instance whether the evidence is exculpatory.

When DNA testing became standard in the 1990s, a large proportion of prosecutors, all of whom welcomed DNA as an investigation tool, strongly resisted post-conviction, post-appeal petitions by prisoners seeking to test DNA crime scene samples in storage. Such resistance added to the frustration and tragedy of actually innocent prisoners, and it delayed justice. In a few cases, any chance of getting to the truth was terminated when existing DNA samples in evidence lockers were deliberately destroyed after prisoners petitioned for testing.

Prosecutorial misconduct is especially significant because prosecutors are the most powerful figures in the criminal justice process, with great discretion as to whether to charge suspects or to dismiss cases. Before prosecutions are formally initiated, prosecutors have a judge-like role. They dismiss one quarter of all cases filed by police, often because they believe that the suspect is innocent. Two theories guide prosecutors in their discretionary decisions and in the way they prosecute their cases: the (1) adversary role and (2) the minister of justice role. In the *adversary role* a prosecutor can go forward with a case in which the evidence is equivocal, on the theory that it is up to the jury to decide whether a defendant is guilty beyond a reasonable doubt. As a *minister of justice* a prosecutor must be personally convinced that the defendant is guilty beyond a reasonable doubt. A problem with the adversary role is that prosecutors holding that view will tend to have a win-at-any-cost attitude, likely resulting in fewer dismissed cases, more aggressive trial tactics, more instances of misconduct, and greater opportunities of generating wrongful convictions. The minister of justice role requires the difficult human and institutional ability to balance vigorous prosecution with fairness and decency. This balance was captured in a 1940 speech to federal prosecutors made by Attorney General Robert Jackson, later a U.S. Supreme Court justice:

> Your positions are of such independence and importance that while you are being diligent, strict, and vigorous in law enforcement you can also afford to be just. Although the government technically loses its case, it has really won if justice has been done.

Police Investigation

At its best, police investigation is the patient, systematic, and dispassionate search for, discovery of, and evaluation of all relevant facts of a suspected crime. The goal is to establish whether a crime was committed and to identify and apprehend the perpetrators. This complex and sensitive task requires solid understanding of criminal law, extensive knowledge about criminal behavior and crime patterns, complete familiarity with the methods of evidence collection and analysis of forensic evidence, skill in interviewing witnesses, and good analytic and writing abilities.

Although it is inevitable that some crimes will not be solved and some innocent suspects will be mistakenly identified, several factors increase the probability of error. One is *tunnel vision*, which in fact affects all people and all criminal justice system participants. This term encompasses well-established psychological cognitive mechanisms such as *confirmation bias*, or the human tendency to seek and interpret new information in ways that confirm preconceptions and avoid information and interpretations that contradict prior beliefs. When applied to police investigation, tunnel vision is the tendency to focus on the first suspect and then to select and filter evidence that builds a case for guilt, while ignoring or suppressing exculpatory evidence. Tunnel vision is an unconscious or "natural" and entirely nonmalicious process. However, its worst effects are amplified by aspects of police investigation such as the nature of interrogation, discussed earlier.

Another problem is the nature of the police investigation report. This document is tremendously important, because in most cases there is limited or no investigation by the defense (in large part because of severely limited funds) and so the police case, found in the report, becomes the official facts in the case. The police report is relied on heavily by the prosecutor in deciding whether and what crimes to charge, by the magistrate in setting bail and ordering detention for psychological evaluation, and even by defense attorneys who do not independently investigate their client's cases for plea bargaining and trial purposes. It is the basis on which an officer testifies at trial and can influence sentencing decisions.

In contrast to European countries, where police investigation is supervised by investigative magistrates who are well-trained judicial officers in national ministries (departments) of justice, American police investigation (aside from federal cases) is almost entirely under the control of local police departments. European police reports are highly detailed, part of the official dossier, and geared to ascertaining the truth; American reports are internal documents that serve functions other than informing the prosecution, such as evaluating personnel. Police are not specifically trained to include exculpatory information in reports, despite orders to include "all" information. Severe time pressure makes it difficult for police to write comprehensive reports, and police are trained to not report information that could lead to civil suits against themselves or their departments. Studies indicate that police reports do not normally contain exculpatory facts, and in fact are often deficient in reporting inculpatory facts, to the discomfit of prosecutors. A few cases have uncovered deliberate fabrication and the exclusion of exculpatory evidence in police reports that framed innocent suspects. It is not known how pervasive these behaviors are. What is probably more common is for overworked police officers to focus on the initial suspect and enter facts in their field notes and follow-up reports that confirm their initial suspicion. Once written, there is no regular procedure to incorporate contradictory or exculpatory evidence in police reports.

Other Causes, Root Causes

This list of wrongful conviction causes is not comprehensive. Race may play a part, either by blatant discrimination, subtle bias, or as a result of the weaknesses of cross-racial identification. This last results not from bias but from familiarity that allows people to see subtle facial features among people with whom they are familiar. A disproportionate number of wrongful convictions have occurred against African-American men convicted of raping white women.

The death penalty may also generate a higher proportion of wrongful convictions. Police, under extreme pressure to solve capital murders, rely on marginal evidence to fasten their attention on suspects. The American war on crime and its hyper-imprisonment (at five to eight times the levels found in other advanced democracies with comparable crime levels except for homicide) has created a pro-prosecution atmosphere, leading police, prosecutors, judges, juries, and appellate courts away from balanced decision making, probably resulting in more miscarriages of justice.

In addition, pervasive root causes of wrongful convictions exist. One, discussed earlier, is tunnel vision. Another is the lack of resources for all actors (police, prosecutors, and courts, as well as defense lawyers). This creates extreme pressure to investigate cases within limited time periods. Overlapping with pressure is the system's normal bureaucratic functioning and production demands, which channel the work of justice officials into routines that make it difficult to slow case processing for more careful examination where called for. These bureaucratic imperatives are aggravated by structural factors that may be impossible to change. The American governmental and criminal justice system is the most fragmented of any modern nation. There are substantial differences in quality among the 16,000 local police departments and 3,000 prosecutors' offices in the nation. The election of prosecutors and judges, virtually unheard of anywhere else in the world, injects a level of partisanship into criminal justice that often undermines rational action. These factors may in turn create a culture of impunity among investigators and prosecutors in which errors are seldom restrained and misconduct rarely punished. The adversary system

of trial, which imposes a large burden on the defense to counter the prosecution with its own evidence, is fatally flawed when criminal defendants almost never have the ability to independently gather evidence.

REFORMS: REDUCING THE NUMBER OF WRONGFUL CONVICTIONS

Research and systematic thinking about the proximate causes of wrongful convictions have suggested a number of feasible reforms likely to reduce miscarriages of justice. At this early stage in the innocence movement, no comparable thought has been given to dealing with the far more intractable root causes. The partial list and descriptions that follow do not explain the research bases for the proposed reforms, but there is good reason to believe that the widespread adoption and systematic application of these reforms will reduce the number of wrongful convictions.

Recommended lineup reforms are grounded in laboratory research findings that show they will reduce the number of false identifications without significantly reducing accurate identifications. Witnesses in all lineups (live and photo) should be instructed that the perpetrator may not be present, to reduce the tendency to pick anyone. All lineup fillers should be selected on the basis of the victim's verbal description, and not on similarity to the suspect. Lineups should contain only one suspect and should be fair in that there are similarities of race, height, general appearance, facial hair, photograph characteristics, and the like between the suspect and fillers. It is best that the lineup administrator not know who the suspect is (blind administration), to ensure that there is no unconscious influence on the witness (as is done for subjects in medical and pharmaceutical trials). If lineup administration is blind, the lineup participants (live or photo) should be presented one at a time (sequentially) rather than as a group (simultaneously). This helps to prevent the exercise of *relative judgment*, by which a witness picks a person out of the lineup who looks most like the memory of the perpetrator rather than recognizing the perpetrator. A witness should be asked for a confidence statement immediately after making an identification, to prevent his or her inflation of confidence as the case proceeds.

All crime laboratories should be accredited and their examiners certified and required to undergo periodic proficiency testing. Defense attorneys, as well as prosecutors and judges, should be educated in forensic testing techniques, and funding should be sufficient to have challenged forensic evidence retested. Defense attorneys should become aware that comparison testing methods, like fingerprinting, are not infallible. Where standards for comparison testing are weak or even suspect, as with bite mark evidence, special caution must be taken in allowing and weighing such evidence. Forensic science research is needed to ensure that methods and findings are valid. Substandard laboratories should be closed and not reopened until all problems are remedied.

The most widely recommended interrogation reform is to videotape entire interrogations, from initiation and before Miranda warnings to the conclusion, and not just the confessions. Videotaping allows pretrial judges to determine whether interrogation was coercive or likely to produce a false confession. Police benefit from videotaped interrogations, because confessions by guilty suspects provide powerful prosecution evidence. Interrogations should be time limited, especially for vulnerable suspects, such as teenagers, to 2 hours, because many false confessions are the product of protracted interrogation. Police in Canada and the United Kingdom are not allowed to use lies to get suspects to confess. This rule should be adopted even though the U.S. Supreme Court has held that lies do not violate a suspect's constitutional rights. Another valuable reform would require police to provide, before interrogating, stronger evidence of their belief that a suspect is guilty than is now the case. A judicial instruction that informs the jury about the risks associated with nonvideotaped station house confessions creates incentives for police and prosecutors to adopt electronic recording.

If the use of jailhouse snitches is to continue, prosecutors should carefully corroborate their stories and take into account snitches' characters and past experiences before using their claims that suspects confessed to them. Legal rules should allow defendants extensive discovery to explore the nature of deals made in return for their testimony. Judges should warn juries that jailhouse snitch evidence should be examined with greater care than that of other witnesses.

At present, many groups urge that compensation for indigent defense be raised to reasonable compensation, to allow competent assigned attorneys the time to better represent clients and bring public defenders' workloads into compliance with established standards. Changes in appellate rulings should allow findings of ineffective assistance without needing to prove that incompetence caused a verdict. Greater bar association scrutiny of appointed counsel and public defenders can enjoin attorneys to do their jobs properly. Defense attorneys should be expected to visit crime scenes and interview all prosecution and defense witnesses. Funding for investigators should increase.

Additional funding for prosecutors and their investigators, by reducing caseloads, will create better understanding of cases and may reduce wrongful convictions. Prosecutors should advise police and forensic laboratories to include exculpatory evidence in their reports. As the leading executive branch participants in the criminal justice system, prosecutors should promote laws and regulations to improve lineups and interrogations in accordance with best practices established by psychological research and should not resist reasonable post-conviction requests for reinvestigation of evidence.

Police investigators also need greater resources to make work pressures more manageable. Standards should be rewritten and training revised to educate investigators in wrongful conviction matters, to become aware of the effects of tunnel vision, and to include exculpatory evidence in their reports. This may be very hard to achieve, because it calls for a change in police culture away from pro-prosecution partisanship and more toward a neutral and scientific attitude toward cases.

CONCLUSION

In 20 years, wrongful conviction has gone from a little-noted phenomenon to an important topic within criminal justice. The number of innocence projects working to exonerate prisoners has grown from 1 or 2 in the early 1990s to about 50 today. Partly as a result of their policy advocacy, innocence reforms have been enacted. Congress passed the Innocence Protection Act in 2004, providing funding for state post-conviction DNA testing, encouraging states to pass post-conviction DNA testing laws, and raising the annual compensation for exonerated federal prisoners to $50,000 for each year of imprisonment. More than 40 states have passed post-conviction testing laws. Six states and hundreds of police departments have required videotaping of interrogations. Seven states and a growing number of police departments have established eyewitness identification reforms. North Carolina created the first innocence inquiry commission that reviews wrongful convictions claims and presents successful claims to a special court.

The investigation of wrongful convictions, which challenge the fairness and accuracy of the criminal justice system, are becoming a necessary feature of criminal justice analysis. The adoption of innocence reforms will not only reduce this kind of injustice but will also improve the quality and professionalism of criminal justice participants.

REFERENCES AND FURTHER READINGS

Baumgartner, F. R., DeBoef, S. L., & Boydstun, A. E. (2008). *The decline of the death penalty and the discovery of innocence.* Cambridge, UK: Cambridge University Press.

Bedau, H. A., & Radelet, M. L. (1988). The myth of infallibility: A reply to Markman and Cassell (Response to a critique ordered by Attorney General Edwin Meese). *Stanford Law Review, 41,* 161–170.

Cole, S. A. (2001). *Suspect identities: A history of fingerprinting and criminal identification.* Cambridge, MA: Harvard University Press.

Cutler, B. L., & Penrod, S. D. (1995). *Mistaken identification: The eyewitness, psychology, and the law.* New York: Cambridge University Press.

Doyle, J. M. (2005). *True witness: Cops, courts, science, and the battle against misidentification.* New York: Palgrave Macmillan.

Findley, K. A., & Scott, M. S. (2006). The multiple dimensions of tunnel vision in criminal cases. *Wisconsin Law Review, 2,* 291–397.

Fisher, S. Z. (1993). "Just the facts, ma'am": Lying and the omission of exculpatory evidence in police reports. *New England Law Review, 28,* 1–62.

Forst, B. (2004). *Errors of justice: Nature, sources, and remedies.* Cambridge, UK: Cambridge University Press.

Garrett, B. L. (2008). Judging innocence. *Columbia Law Review, 108,* 55–141.

Giannelli, P., & Raeder, M. (eds.). (2006). *Achieving justice: Freeing the innocent, convicting the guilty.* Washington, DC: American Bar Association.

Gould, J. B. (2008). *The innocence commission: Preventing wrongful convictions and restoring the criminal justice system.* New York: New York University Press.

Gross, S. R., Jacoby, E. J., Matheson, D. J., Montgomery, N., & Patil, S. (2005). Exonerations in the United States, 1989 through 2003. *Journal of Criminal Law and Criminology, 95,* 523–560.

Harmon, T. R. (2001). Predictors of miscarriages of justice in capital cases. *Justice Quarterly, 18,* 949–968.

Huff, C. R., Rattner, A., & Sagarin, E. (1996). *Convicted but innocent: Wrongful conviction and public policy.* Thousand Oaks, CA: Sage.

Leo, R. A. (2005). Rethinking the study of miscarriages of justice: Developing a criminology of wrongful conviction. *Journal of Contemporary Criminal Justice, 21,* 201–223.

Leo, R. A. (2008). *Police interrogation and American justice.* Cambridge, MA: Harvard University Press.

Loftus, E. (1979). *Eyewitness testimony.* Cambridge, MA: Harvard University Press.

Rabinowitz, D. (2003). *No crueler tyrannies: Accusation, false witness and other terrors of our times.* New York: Wall Street Journal Book.

Radelet, M. L., Bedau, H. A., & Putnam, C. (1992). *In spite of innocence.* Boston: Northeastern University Press.

Scheck, B., Neufeld, P., & Dwyer, J. (2001). *Actual innocence: When justice goes wrong and how to make it right.* New York: Penguin/New American Library.

Vollen, L., & Eggers, D. (eds.). (2005). *Surviving justice: America's wrongfully convicted and exonerated.* San Francisco: McSweeny's Books.

Weinberg, S., Gordon, N., & Williams, B. (2003). *Harmful error: Investigating America's local prosecutors.* Washington, DC: Center for Public Integrity.

Westervelt, S. D., & Humphrey, J. A. (eds.). (2001). *Wrongly convicted: Perspectives on failed justice.* New Brunswick, NJ: Rutgers University Press.

Zalman, M., Smith, B., & Kiger, A. (2008). Officials' estimates of the incidence of "actual innocence" convictions. *Justice Quarterly, 25,* 72–100.

American Courts

Cassia Spohn

The past 50 years have witnessed significant changes in the structure of the American court system and the procedures that courts use to adjudicate criminal cases and sentence convicted offenders. Some of these changes resulted from Supreme Court decisions that interpreted constitutional provisions regarding right to counsel, selection of the jury, cruel and unusual punishment, due process of law, and equal protection under the law. Other changes resulted from legislative attempts to toughen criminal sentences and reduce sentence disparity, to provide alternatives to prison and probation, or to handle certain types of cases, such as drug offenses or cases involving mentally ill offenders, more efficiently and effectively. Considered together, these changes have revolutionized the way American courts do business.

The purpose of this chapter is to examine these changes and explore their policy implications. The chapter begins with an overview of Supreme Court decisions regarding right to counsel, selection of the jury, capital punishment, and the role of the jury in the sentencing process. The next section focuses on the sentencing reform movement of the past 30 years. The chapter ends with an examination of specialized or problem-solving courts.

Supreme Court Decisions and American Courts

The United States Supreme Court has played an important role in the development of the American court system, particularly with respect to such issues as right to counsel, jury selection, and sentencing. The decisions handed down by the Court in these areas have altered policy and practice and have led to fairer and less discriminatory court processing decisions.

The Right to Counsel

A series of court decisions broadened the interpretation of the Sixth Amendment's guarantee of the right to counsel and led to significant changes in requirements for provision of counsel for indigent defendants. The process began in 1932, when the Court ruled in *Powell v. Alabama* (287 U.S. 45 [1932]) that states must provide attorneys for indigent defendants charged with capital crimes. The Court's decision in a 1938 case, *Johnson v. Zerbst* (304 U.S. 458 [1938]), required the appointment of counsel for all indigent defendants in federal criminal cases, but the requirement was not extended to the states until *Gideon v. Wainwright* (372 U.S. 335 [1963]) was handed down in 1963. In subsequent decisions, the Court ruled that "no person may be imprisoned, for any offense, whether classified as petty, misdemeanor, or felony, unless he was represented by counsel"[1] and that the right to counsel is not limited to trial, but applies to all "critical stages" in the criminal justice process.[2] As a result of these rulings, states must provide most indigent defendants with counsel, from arrest and interrogation through sentencing and the appellate process.

States moved quickly to implement the constitutional requirement articulated in Gideon and the subsequent cases, either by establishing public defender systems or by appropriating money for court-appointed attorneys. In 1951, there were only 7 public defender organizations in the United States; in 1964, there were 136; by 1973, the total had risen to 573 (McIntyre, 1987). A national survey of indigent defense services among all U.S. prosecutorial districts found that 21% used a public defender program, 19% used an assigned counsel system, and 7% used a contract attorney system; the remaining districts (43%) reported that a combination of methods was used (Bureau of Justice Statistics, 2006). Although some critics have questioned the quality of legal services afforded indigent defendants (Casper, 1971; *Harvard Law Review*, 2000), particularly in capital cases where the stakes are obviously very high (Bright, 1994), the findings of a number of methodologically sophisticated studies suggest that case outcomes for defendants represented by public defenders are not significantly different from those for defendants represented by private attorneys (Hanson & Ostrom, 2004; Williams, 2002). These results suggest that poor defendants are no longer "without a voice" (Myrdal, 1944, p. 547) in courts throughout the United States.

Jury Selection

Supreme Court decisions also have placed important restrictions on the jury selection process. The Court has consistently ruled against racial and ethnic bias in the selection of the jury pool and has made it more difficult for prosecutors and defense attorneys to use their peremptory challenges to exclude black and Hispanic jurors. As the Court has repeatedly emphasized, the jury serves as "the criminal defendant's fundamental 'protection of life and liberty against race or color prejudice.'"[3] Reflecting this in 1889 the Supreme Court ruled in the case of *Strauder v. West Virginia* (100 U.S. 303 [1880]) that a West Virginia statute limiting jury service to white males violated the equal protection clause of the Fourteenth Amendment and therefore was unconstitutional.

The Court's ruling in Strauder made it clear that states could not pass laws excluding blacks from jury service, but it did not prevent states, and particularly southern states, from developing techniques designed to preserve the all-white jury. In a series of decisions that began in the mid-1930s, the Supreme Court struck down these laws and practices, ruling, for example, that it was unconstitutional for a Georgia county to put the names of white potential jurors on white cards, the names of black potential jurors on yellow cards, and then "randomly" draw cards to determine who would be summoned for jury service (*Avery v. Georgia* 345 U.S. 559 [1953], at 562). As the Court stated in this case, "the State may not draw up its jury lists pursuant to neutral procedures but then resort to discrimination at other stages in the selection process."

Critics contend that the Court's decisions regarding the peremptory challenge do, in fact, open the door to discrimination in jury selection (Kennedy, 1997; Serr & Maney, 1988). The Supreme Court's insistence that the jury be drawn from a representative cross-section of the community and that race is not a valid qualification for jury service applies only to the selection of the jury pool. It does not apply to the selection of individual jurors for a particular case. As the Court has repeatedly stated, a defendant is *not* entitled to a jury "composed in whole or in part of persons of his own race."[4] Thus, prosecutors and defense attorneys can use their peremptory challenges—"challenges without cause, without explanation, and without judicial scrutiny"[5]—as they see fit. Critics of the process contend that decisions handed down by the Supreme Court notwithstanding, prosecutors and defense attorneys can use their peremptory challenges to produce juries that contain few, if any, racial minorities.

The Supreme Court's rulings regarding racial discrimination in the use of peremptory challenges have evolved over time. The Court initially ruled that, although the prosecutor's use of peremptory challenges to strike all of the black potential jurors in a jury pool did not violate the equal protection clause of the Constitution, a defendant could establish a *prima facie* case of purposeful racial discrimination by showing that the elimination of blacks from a particular jury was part of a *pattern of discrimination* in that jurisdiction (*Swain v. Alabama* 380 U.S. 202 [1965]). The problem, of course, was that the defendants in Swain, and in the cases that followed, could not meet this stringent test. As Wishman (1986, p. 115) observed, "A defense lawyer almost never has the statistics to prove a pattern of discrimination, and the state under the Swain decision is not required to keep them." The ruling, therefore, provided no protection to the individual black or Hispanic defendant deprived of a jury of his peers by the prosecutor's use of racially discriminatory strikes.

It was not until 1986 that the Court, in *Batson v. Kentucky* (476 U.S. 79 [1986], rejected Swain's systematic exclusion requirement and ruled "that a defendant may establish a *prima facie* case of purposeful discrimination in selection of the petit jury solely on evidence concerning the prosecutor's exercise of peremptory challenges at the defendant's trial." The justices added that once the defendant makes a *prima facie* case of racial discrimination, the burden shifts to the state to provide a racially neutral explanation for excluding black jurors.

Although Batson seemed to offer hope that the goal of a representative jury was attainable, an examination of cases decided since 1986 suggests otherwise. State and federal appellate courts have ruled, for example, that leaving one or two blacks on the jury precludes any inference of purposeful racial discrimination on the part of the prosecutor,[6] and that striking only one or two jurors of the defendant's race does not constitute a "pattern" of strikes.[7] Trial and appellate courts have also been willing to accept virtually any explanation offered by the prosecutor to rebut the defendant's inference of purposeful discrimination (Serr & Maney, 1988, pp. 44–47). Decisions such as these led Kennedy (1997, p. 214) to characterize the peremptory challenge as "a creature of unbridled discretion that, in the hands of white prosecutors and white defendants, has often been used to sustain racial subordination in the courthouse." The Supreme Court's decisions notwithstanding, the peremptory challenge continues to be an obstacle to the creation of a racially neutral jury selection process.

Capital and Noncapital Sentencing

A third area that has been significantly reshaped by Supreme Court decisions is sentencing. The Court has handed down a series of important decisions on the capital sentencing process. Although the Court has never ruled that the death penalty *per se* is cruel and unusual punishment, it has said that the death penalty cannot be imposed on an offender convicted of the rape of an adult woman (*Coker v. Georgia*, 433 U.S. 584 [1977]) or child (*Kennedy v. Louisiana*, 554 U.S. [2008]) and that the death penalty can be imposed on an offender convicted of felony murder if the offender played a major role in the crime and displayed "reckless indifference to the value of human life" (*Tison v. Arizona*, 107 S.Ct. 1676; 481 U.S. 137 [1987], at 157). The Court also has ruled that the execution of someone who is mentally handicapped is cruel and unusual punishment in violation of the Eighth Amendment (*Atkins v. Virginia*. 536 U.S. 304 [2002]), that the Eighth and Fourteenth Amendments forbid the imposition of the death penalty on offenders who were younger than age 18 when their crimes were committed (*Roper v. Simmons*, 543 U.S. 551 [2005]) and that the Constitution does not prohibit the use of lethal injection (*Baze v. Rees*, 553 U.S. [2008]). With the exception of the felony murder and lethal injection rulings, these decisions all restrict the use of the death penalty by state and federal courts.

The Supreme Court also has addressed the issue of the role played by the jury at sentencing. The first case, *Apprendi v. New Jersey* (530 U.S. 466 [2000]) involved an offender, Charles Apprendi Jr., who fired several shots into the home of a black family; he made a number of statements, which he later retracted, suggesting that he had fired into the home because he did not want the family living in his neighborhood. Apprendi pled guilty to possession of a weapon for an unlawful purpose, a crime that carried a term of imprisonment of 5 to 10 years. The prosecutor then filed a motion for an enhanced sentence under the New Jersey hate-crime statute. The judge in the case found by a preponderance of the evidence that the shooting was racially motivated and sentenced Apprendi to 12 years in prison. Apprendi appealed, claiming that the due process clause of the Constitution required the state to prove the allegation of bias to the jury beyond a reasonable doubt. The Supreme Court ruled in Apprendi's favor, stating that any fact that increases the penalty for a crime beyond the prescribed statutory maximum, other than the fact of a prior conviction, must be submitted to a jury and proved beyond a reasonable doubt,. In 2002, the Justices similarly ruled that a jury—not a judge—must find the aggravating circumstances necessary for imposition of the death penalty (Ring v. Arizona, 536 U.S. 584 [2002]).

The Court reiterated this position in subsequent decisions involving defendants who were challenging sentences imposed under state and federal sentencing guidelines. In 2004, for example, the Court ruled in *Blakely v. Washington* (542 U.S. 296 [2004]) that the judge's decision to impose a sentence more severe than the statutory maximum allowed under the Washington sentencing guidelines violated the defendant's Sixth Amendment right to trial by jury. The Court revisited this issue 6 months later. This time, the issue was the power of federal judges to impose sentences more severe than called for under the United States sentencing guidelines. In *United States v. Booker* (543 U.S. 220 [2005]), the Court ruled, consistent with its decisions in Apprendi and Blakely, that the jury must determine beyond a reasonable doubt any fact that increases the defendant's sentence beyond the maximum sentence allowed under the sentencing guidelines.[8] The facts in

this case were similar to those in Blakely. Booker was found guilty of a drug offense that, under the guidelines, carried a sentence of 210 to 262 mouths. At the sentencing hearing, however, the judge found additional facts that justified a harsher sentence; he sentenced Booker to 360 months in prison. The Court held that the 30-year sentence imposed by the judge violated the Sixth Amendment right to a jury trial and ordered the district court either to sentence Booker within the sentencing range supported by the jury's findings or to hold a separate sentencing hearing before a jury. The Court also ruled that the federal sentencing guidelines were advisory, not mandatory. In two cases decided in 2007,[9] the Court reiterated that the guidelines were advisory and ruled that the below-guidelines sentences imposed in each case were "reasonable" and that the judges who imposed the sentences had not abused their discretion. In the Gall decision, the Court noted that, although the guidelines are the starting point and initial benchmark, they are not the only factors to be taken into consideration.

The Supreme Court's decisions in these sentencing cases enhance the role played by the jury in both capital and noncapital cases. The decisions emphasize that the jury, not the judge, is to determine the facts in the case, that juries must determine the existence of aggravating factors that justify the imposition of the death penalty, and that sentences cannot exceed the maximum sentence based on the facts that were admitted in a guilty plea or found by the jury.

THE SENTENCING REFORM MOVEMENT

In 1972, Marvin Frankel, U.S. district judge for the Southern District of New York, issued an influential call for reform of the sentencing process (Frankel, 1972). The focus of Judge Frankel's critique was the indeterminate sentence, in which the judge imposed a minimum and maximum sentence, but the parole board determined the date of release based on its assessment of whether the offender had been rehabilitated or had served enough time for the particular offense. Judge Frankel characterized the indeterminate sentencing system as "a bizarre 'nonsystem' of extravagant powers confided to variable and essentially unregulated judges, keepers, and parole officials" (Frankel, 1972, p. 1). Frankel, who maintained that the degree of discretion given to judges led to "lawlessness" in sentencing, called for legislative reforms designed to regulate "the unchecked powers of the untutored judge" (p. 41).

Judge Frankel's calls for reform did not go unheeded. Reformers from both sides of the political spectrum joined in the attack on indeterminate sentencing and pushed for reforms designed to curtail judicial discretion and eliminate arbitrariness and disparity in sentencing. In response, state legislatures and Congress enacted a series of incremental structured sentencing reforms. A number of jurisdictions experimented with voluntary or advisory sentencing guidelines. Other states adopted determinate sentencing policies and abolished release on parole. Still other jurisdictions created sentencing commissions authorized to promulgate presumptive sentencing guidelines. Most states and the federal government also enacted mandatory minimum sentences for certain types of offenses (especially drug and weapons offenses), "three-strikes-and-you're-out" laws that mandated long prison sentences for repeat offenders, and truth-in-sentencing statutes that required offenders to serve a larger portion of the sentence before being released.

This process of experimentation and reform revolutionized sentencing in the United States. Thirty years ago, every state and the federal government had an indeterminate sentencing system, and "the word 'sentencing' generally signified a slightly mysterious process which ... involved individualized decisions that judges were uniquely qualified to make" (Tonry, 1996, p. 31). The situation today is much more complex. Sentencing policies and practices vary enormously on a number of dimensions, and there is no longer anything that can be described as the American approach.

A discussion of each of the major reforms enacted during the sentencing reform movement is beyond the scope of this chapter. Instead, the chapter focuses on the movement away from the indeterminate sentence and toward a more structured sentencing process.

Determinate Sentencing

In the mid- to late 1970s, several states abolished release on parole and replaced the indeterminate sentence with a fixed (i.e., determinate) sentence. Under this system, the state legislature established a presumptive range of confinement for various categories of offenses. The judge imposed a fixed number of years from within this range, and the offender would serve this term minus time off for good behavior. Determinate sentencing, which was first adopted in California, Illinois, Indiana, and Maine, was seen as a way to restrain judicial discretion and thus to reduce disparity and (at least in the minds of conservative reformers) preclude judges from imposing overly lenient sentences. However, the degree to which the reforms constrain discretion varies. The California Uniform Determinate Sentencing Law, which took effect on July 1, 1977, provides that judges are to choose one of three specified sentences for persons convicted of particular offense. The judge is to impose the middle term unless there are aggravating or mitigating circumstances that justify imposing the higher or lower term. Judges have considerably more discretion under the Illinois Determinate Sentencing Statute. Felonies are divided into six classifications, and the range of penalties is wide, especially for the more serious offenses. Murder and Class X offenses are nonprobationable, but judges can impose prison terms of 20 to 60 years or life for murder and 6 to 30 years for Class X offenses. If there are aggravating circumstances, the sentence range for Class X felonies increases to 30 to 60 years.

Although judges in jurisdictions with determinate sentencing retain control over the critical probation or prison decision, their overall discretion is reduced, particularly in states like California. Evaluations of the impact of the California law showed that judges complied with the law and imposed the middle term in a majority of the cases (Cohen & Tonry, 1983). Despite predictions that discretion would shift to the prosecutor and that plea bargaining would consequently increase, there were no changes in the rate or timing of guilty pleas that could be attributed to the determinate sentencing law. On the other hand, there was some evidence that prosecutors were increasingly likely to use provisions regarding sentence enhancements and probation ineligibility as bargaining chips. One study, for example, found that the sentence enhancement for use of a weapon was dropped in 40% of robbery cases and that the enhancement for serious bodily injury was struck in 65% to 70% of these cases (Casper, Brereton & Neal, 1982). As Walker (1993, p. 129) noted, "The net effect of the law seems to have been to narrow and focus the exercise of plea bargaining discretion. Given the very restricted options on sentence length, the importance of the various enhancements and disqualifiers increased."

Partly as a result of research showing that determinate sentencing laws did not significantly constrain the discretion of judges, the determinate sentencing movement lost steam and eventually sputtered out. With the exception of the District of Columbia, no jurisdiction has adopted determinate sentencing since 1983.

Presumptive Sentencing Guidelines

Since the late 1970s, presumptive sentencing guidelines developed by an independent sentencing commission have been the dominant approach to sentencing reform in the United States. About half of the states have adopted or are considering sentencing guidelines, and sentencing at the federal level has been structured by guidelines since 1987. In 1994, the American Bar Association (ABA) endorsed sentencing guidelines; it recommended that all jurisdictions create permanent sentencing commissions charged with drafting presumptive sentencing provisions that apply to both prison and nonprison sanctions and are tied to prison capacities (American Bar Association, 1994).

The guidelines systems adopted by Congress and by state legislatures have a number of common features (Stith & Cabranes, 1998). In each jurisdiction with presumptive guidelines, there is a permanent sentencing commission or committee composed of criminal justice officials and, sometimes, private citizens and legislators. The commission is charged with studying sentencing practices and formulating presumptive sentence recommendations. The commission is also authorized to monitor the implementation and impact of the guidelines and to recommend amendments.

A second common feature is that the presumptive sentence is based primarily on two factors: the severity of the offense and the seriousness of the offender's prior criminal record. Typically, these two factors are arrayed on a two-dimensional grid; their intersection determines whether the offender should be sentenced to prison and, if so, for how long.

Jurisdictions with presumptive sentencing guidelines, as opposed to voluntary or advisory guidelines, require judges to follow them or provide reasons for failing to do so. Judges are allowed to depart from the guidelines and impose harsher or more lenient sentences if there are specified aggravating or mitigating circumstances. Some jurisdictions also list factors that should not be used to increase or decrease the presumptive sentence. For example, both the federal guidelines and the Minnesota guidelines state that the offender's race, gender, and employment status are not legitimate grounds for departure. In North Carolina, on the other hand, judges are allowed to consider the fact that the offender "has a positive employment history or is gainfully employed" (Bureau of Justice Assistance, 1996, pp. 79–80). In most states and in the federal system, a departure from the guidelines can be appealed to state appellate courts by either party. If, for example, the judge sentences the defendant to probation when the guidelines call for prison, the prosecuting attorney can appeal. If the judge imposes 60 months when the guidelines call for 36, the defendant can appeal.

The Impact of Sentencing Guidelines

A detailed discussion of the impact of sentencing guidelines would consume many pages: there have been literally dozens of studies focusing on compliance with the guidelines and attempting to determine whether the guidelines (and mandatory minimum sentences) resulted in more punitive sentences and reduced disparity and discrimination in the sentencing process. Although the evidence is somewhat mixed, it does appear that sentences are more punitive today than in the past (Austin & Irwin, 2001; Engen & Steen, 2000; Frase, 1997; Kramer & Lubitz, 1985; Marvel & Moody, 1995; Moore & Miethe, 1986; Spohn, 2000; United States Sentencing Commission, 1991a, 1991b,

2004). The movement away from indeterminate sentencing and the rehabilitative ideal to determinate sentencing and an emphasis on just deserts—coupled with laws mandating long prison terms—have resulted in harsher sentences. As a result of these changes in sentencing policy, offenders convicted of felonies in state and federal courts face a greater likelihood of incarceration and longer prison sentences than they did in the prereform era. These changes, in turn, have led to dramatic increases in the nation's prison population.[10]

The evidence regarding the question of whether sentences today are fairer or more equitable in the past also is mixed. Critics of sentencing reform contend that members of the courtroom workgroup have been able to circumvent—or even sabotage—the reforms enacted during the past 30 years; they argue that this makes it difficult to assess the impact of the reforms. Nonetheless, most studies of sentences imposed under federal and state guidelines conclude that guideline sentences are more uniform and less disparate (Anderson, Kling & Stith, 1999; Ashford & Mosbaek. 1991; Hofer, Blackwell, & Ruback, 1999; Knapp, 1987; Kramer & Lubitz, 1985; Stolzenberg & D'Alessio, 1994; United States Sentencing Commission, 1991a; Washington State Sentencing Guidelines Commission, 1992; Wright, 1998). There is less interjudge disparity in jurisdictions with sentencing guidelines, and sentences are more tightly linked to the seriousness of the offense and the offender's prior criminal record.

The evidence regarding the effect of legally irrelevant offender characteristics—race, gender, age, education, and employment status—is less inconsistent and, unfortunately, more negative. There is a lack of longitudinal research comparing the effect of offender characteristics on sentence outcomes before and after the implementation of guidelines; this makes it difficult to assess the degree to which the guidelines have reduced unwarranted disparities in sentencing. Nonetheless, the studies of sentences imposed in federal and state jurisdictions operating under sentencing guidelines showed that racial minorities and women were sentenced differently from whites and men (Albonetti, 1997, 2002; Demuth & Steffensmeier, 2004; Everett & Wojtkiewicz, 2002; Kramer & Steffensmeier, 1993; Kramer & Ulmer, 1996; LaFrentz & Spohn, 2006;

Mustard, 2001; Spohn, 2000; Spohn & Sample, forthcoming; Stacey & Spohn, 2006; Steen, Engen, & Gainey, 2005; Steffensmeier & Demuth, 2000, 2006; Steffensmeier & Hebert, 1999; Steffensmeier, Kramer, & Streifel, 1993; Steffensmeier, Ulmer, & Kramer, 1998). This suggests that attempts to constrain judicial discretion have not eliminated unwarranted disparities in sentencing. The guidelines notwithstanding, judges mete out harsher sentences to black and Hispanic offenders than to similarly situated white offenders. They impose more lenient sentences on females than on males, and the unemployed and less educated receive harsher sentences than their counterparts.

These conclusions apply to sentences imposed under the more restrictive federal sentencing guidelines as well as the looser guidelines at the state level. They imply that judges and prosecutors are reluctant to place offenders into cells of sentencing grids defined only by crime seriousness and prior criminal record and, thus, that statutorily irrelevant factors such as race, gender, age, employment status, and social class may be factually relevant to criminal justice officials' assessments of dangerousness, threat, and culpability. In sum, these conclusions attest to the validity of Tonry's (1996, p. 180) assertion, "There is, unfortunately, no way around the dilemma that sentencing is inherently discretionary and that discretion leads to disparities."

SPECIALIZED OR PROBLEM-SOLVING COURTS: A FOCUS ON DRUG COURTS

The last three decades have witnessed another important change in the American court system: the development of specialized or problem-solving courts. These are limited-jurisdiction courts specializing in certain crime problems, such as drugs, guns, and domestic violence. These courts are like traffic courts in that they address a specific problem, but several factors set them apart (Berman & Feinblatt, 2001). The typical specialized court focuses on case outcomes—for example, getting offenders off drugs or protecting women from further intimate partner abuse—rather than case processing, and judges closely supervise offenders and monitor their progress. Specialized courts also are characterized by collaboration among criminal justice and social service agencies, nontraditional roles for participants, and a focus on systemic change.

The Drug Court Movement

The development of specialized courts is best illustrated by the drug court movement. Increases in the number of drug offenders appearing in state and federal courts—coupled with mounting evidence of both the linkages between drug use and crime and the efficacy of drug treatment programs—led a number of jurisdictions "to rethink their approach to handling defendants charged with drug and drug-related offenses." (Drug Court Clearinghouse and Technical Assistance Project, 1999, p. 3). Some jurisdictions, such as Cook County (Chicago], Illinois, established specialized dockets designed to manage the drug caseload more efficiently and to alleviate stress on the felony court system (Inciardi, McBride, & Rivers, 1996). Other jurisdictions, such as Dade County (Miami), Florida, created "drug treatment courts," which incorporated intensive judicial supervision of drug offenders, mandatory drug treatment, and rehabilitation programs providing vocational, education, family, and medical services.

The drug treatment court concept spread rapidly during the 1990s. As of June 1999, 377 drug courts were operating, and an additional 217 drug courts were in the planning stages in 49 of the 50 states, the District of Columbia, Puerto Rico, Guam, several Native American tribal courts, and two federal district courts (Drug Court Clearinghouse and Technical Assistance Project, 1999, p. 1). By December 2007, there were 1,786 adult and juvenile drug courts operating in jurisdictions throughout the United States; another 284 courts were in the planning stages (Bureau of Justice Assistance, n.d.). A 2005 report by the National Drug Court Institute (Huddleston, Freeman-Wilson, Marlowe, & Roussell, 2005) estimated that, at any one time, more than 70,000 drug offenders were participating in drug courts throughout the United States and its territories.

Although the nature and characteristics of drug courts throughout the United States vary widely, they share several key elements (National Association of Drug Court Professionals, 1997):

+ Integration of substance abuse treatment with justice system case processing;
+ Use of a nonadversarial approach;
+ Early identification and prompt placement of eligible participants;
+ Access to a continuum of treatment, rehabilitation, and related services;
+ Frequent testing for alcohol and illicit drugs;
+ A coordinated strategy among judge, prosecutor, defense, and treatment providers to govern offender compliance;
+ Ongoing judicial interaction with each participant.

In the typical preadjudication drug court, drug offenders who meet the eligibility criteria for the program are given a choice between participation in the drug court and traditional adjudication. Although the eligibility criteria vary, most programs exclude offenders who have prior convictions for violent offenses or whose current offense invoked violence or use of a weapon. They target offenders whose involvement with the criminal justice system is due primarily to their substance abuse. The program may last 12 months, 18 months, or longer. Offenders who are accepted and agree to abide by the requirements of the program are immediately referred to a substance abuse treatment program for counseling, therapy, and education. They also are subject to random urinalysis and are required to appear frequently before the drug court judge. Offenders who do not show up for treatment sessions or drug court or who fail drug tests are subject to sanctions. Repeated violations may result in termination from the program and in adjudication and sentencing on the original charges. The charges against the offender are dismissed upon completion of the program.

The Effectiveness of Drug Courts

There is mounting evidence that drug courts reduce offender recidivism and prevent drug relapse. A report by the U.S. General Accounting Office (1997) summarized the results of 20 evaluations of 16 drug courts that had been completed by early 1997. The GAO report indicated that these early evaluations generally concluded that drug courts were effective in reducing drug use and criminal behavior. A later review by Belenko (1998) summarized the results of 30 evaluations of 24 drug courts that had been completed by May 1998. Belenko (1998, p. 29) observed that most of these evaluations concluded "that criminal behavior was substantially reduced during participation in the program." For example, an evaluation of a Ventura County, California, drug court, which tracked recidivism over an 8-month period, found that only 12% of the drug court participants were rearrested, compared with 32% of those in a comparison group. A Jackson County, Missouri, evaluation similarly revealed 6-month rearrest rates of 4% for program participants and 13% for nonparticipants.

Belenko's review also included studies that assessed the impact of drug court participation on postprogram recidivism. Eight of the nine evaluations reported lower recidivism rates for the drug court group, compared with a group of similarly situated offenders who did not participate in the drug court program. An evaluation of the Multnomah County, Oregon, drug court, for example, found statistically significant differences between drug court participants (0.59 new arrests) and drug-court-eligible nonparticipants (1.53 new arrests) over a 24-month tracking period. Belenko (1998, p. 18) concluded that "drug use and criminal behavior are substantially reduced while clients are participating in drug court, [and] criminal behavior is lower after program participation."

More recent and methodologically sophisticated studies also provide evidence that drug courts are effective in preventing recidivism. An evaluation of the Baltimore City Drug Treatment Court, for example, used an experimental design in which eligible offenders were randomly assigned either to the drug court or to traditional adjudication (Gottfredson & Exum, 2002). The results of the evaluation revealed that offenders assigned to the drug court were less likely than offenders placed in the traditional adjudication group to be rearrested during the 12-month follow-up period. A follow-up study using 3 years of recidivism data found

similar results: this study also found that the positive effects of participation in the drug treatment court extended past the offenders' involvement in the drug court (Gottfredson, Najaka, Kearley, & Rocha, 2006).

POLICY IMPLICATIONS

The American court system has undergone significant changes over the past three decades. Criminal procedure has been reformed as a result of Supreme Court decisions that broadened the rights of criminal defendants, established rules for the selection of juries and the use of peremptory challenges, and placed restrictions on judges' sentencing discretion. Sentencing policies and practices in state and federal jurisdictions have undergone important modifications, and specialized or problem-solving courts have spread throughout the United States.

The question, of course, is whether these changes have produced a fairer and more equitable court system. It seems clear that the Supreme Court's decisions broadening the right to counsel and restricting the use of race in the jury selection process have resulted in fairer treatment of poor defendants and defendants who are racial minorities, and that the Court's decisions limiting the use of the death penalty has made it more likely that capital punishment will be reserved for particularly heinous crimes. Less clear are the effects of the Court's decisions enhancing the role of the jury in sentencing and making the federal sentencing guidelines voluntary. Although these decisions, which place significant restrictions on judicial discretion, may produce less disparity in sentencing, it also is possible that discretion will simply shift downstream to prosecutors. In other words, the source of disparity, including unwarranted disparity, in the new regime may be prosecutors' charging and plea bargaining decisions.

The impact of specialized or problem-solving courts is also less evident. Research evaluating these courts is limited, and the research that does exist suffers from a number of methodological problems (Belenko, 1998). Nonetheless, there is mounting evidence that drug courts, domestic violence courts, and other specialized courts do reduce recidivism rates, and there is some evidence that these courts also lead to improvements in offenders' education and employment status, physical and mental health, and cognitive functioning. As research on problem-solving courts accumulates, our conclusions regarding their effectiveness will become less tentative.

DISCUSSION QUESTIONS

1. How have the Supreme Court's decisions regarding the right to counsel changed the American court system? In your opinion, have these been positive or negative changes?

2. Why would critics of the public defender system argue that criminal defendants "get what they pay for"? What are the problems inherent in the public defender system?

3. Evidence suggesting that prosecutors continue to use their peremptory challenges to preserve all-white juries in cases involving African-American or Hispanic defendants has led some commentators to call for the elimination of the peremptory challenge. What do you think is the strongest argument in favor of eliminating the peremptory challenge? In favor of retaining it? How would elimination of the peremptory challenge change the criminal trial?

4. What will be the impact of the Supreme Court's decision making the federal sentencing guidelines voluntary/advisory rather than mandatory? Will these decisions lead to less uniformity and more disparity in sentencing, or will they enable judges to individualize justice in appropriate ways?

5. An important goal of sentencing guidelines was to eliminate unwarranted disparity in sentencing. Given this, how would you explain the fact that research reveals that both the offender's race/ethnicity and the offender's sex influence sentences imposed under state and federal sentencing guidelines?

6. How do specialized or problem-solving courts differ from traditional courts? Why have these courts become so popular in the United States?

NOTES

1. *Argersinger v. Hamlin*, 407 U.S. 25 (1972), at 37.

2. A defendant is entitled to counsel at every stage "where substantial rights of the accused may be affected" that require the "guiding hand of counsel" (*Mempa v. Rhay*, 389 U.S. 128 [1967], at 134). These critical stages include arraignment, preliminary hearing, entry of a plea, trial, sentencing, and the first appeal.

3. *McCleskey v. Kemp* (481 U.S. 279 [1987], at 310), quoting *Strauder v. West Virginia*, 100 U.S. 303 (1880).

4. *Strauder v. West Virginia*, 100 U.S. 303 (1880) at 305; *Batson v. Kentucky*, 476 U.S. 79 (1986) at 85.

5. *Swain v. Alabama*, 380 U.S. 202, 212 (1965) at 380.

6. *United States v. Montgomery*, 819 F.2d at 851. The Eleventh Circuit, however, rejected this line of reasoning in *Fleming v. Kemp* (794 F.2d 1478 [11th Cir. 1986]) and U*nited States v. David* (803 F.2d 1567 (11th Cir. 1986]).

7. *United States v. Vaccaro*, 816 F.2d 443, 457 (9th Cir. 1987); *Fields v. People*. 732 P.2d 1145, 1158 n.20 (Colo. 1987).

8. Also decided at the same time, and with the same result, was *United States v. Fanfan* (125 S. Cr. 12 [2004]).

9. *Gall v. United States*, No. 06-7949, decided December 10 2007. *Kimbrough v. United States*, No. 06-6330, decided December 10, 2007.

10. Most scholars contend that this punitiveness has not produced the predicted reduction in crime. Conservative advocates of harsh crime control policies claim that locking up increasingly large numbers of felony offenders for increasingly long periods of time has caused the crime rate to fall; however, conceptual and methodological flaws in the "prison 'works'" argument call this conclusion into question. Critics suggest that a more careful examination of the evidence leads to the conclusion that increasing incarceration rates have little, if any, effect on crime rates (see, for example, Austin & Irwin, 2001; Tonry, 1995).

REFERENCES

Albonetti, C.A. (1997). Sentencing under the federal sentencing guidelines: Effects of defendant characteristics, guilty pleas, and departures on sentence outcomes for drug offenses, 1991–1992. *Law & Society Review, 31*, 789–822.

Albonetti, C.A. (2002). The joint conditioning effect of defendant's gender and ethnicity on length of imprisonment under the federal sentencing guidelines for drug trafficking/manufacturing offenders. *Journal of Gender, Race, and Justice, 6*, 39–60.

American Bar Association. (1994). *Standards for criminal justice—sentencing alternatives and procedures* (3rd ed.). Boston: Little, Brown.

Anderson, J.M., Kling, J.R., & Stith, K. (1999). Measuring interjudge sentencing disparity: Before and after the federal sentencing guidelines. *Journal of Law and Economics, XLII*, 271–307.

Ashford, K., & Mosbaek, C. (1991). *First year report on implementation of sentencing guidelines, November 1989 to January 1991*. Portland: Oregon Criminal Justice Council.

Austin, J., & Irwin, J. (2001). *It's about time: America's imprisonment binge* (3rd ed.). Belmont, CA: Wadsworth.

Belenko, S. (1998). Research on drug courts: A critical review. *National Drug Court Institute Review, 1*, 1–42.

Berman, G., & Feinblatt, J. (2001). *Problem-solving courts: A brief primer*. New York: Center for Court Innovation.

Bright, S.B. (1994). Counsel for the poor: The death sentence not for the worst crime but for the worst lawyer. *The Yale Law Journal, 103*, 1835–1883.

Bureau of Justice Assistance. (1996). *National assessment of structured sentencing*. Washington, DC: U.S. Department of Justice, Bureau of Justice Assistance.

Bureau of Justice Assistance Drug Court Clearinghouse Project at American University. (n.d.). Retrieved on October 21, 2009, from http://spa.american.edu/justice/documents/2343.pdf.

Bureau of Justice Statistics. (2006). *State court organization, 2004*. Washington, DC: United States Department of Justice, Bureau of Justice Statistics.

Casper, J.D. (1971). Did you have a lawyer when you went to Court? No, I had a public defender. *Yale Review of Law and Social Action, 1*, 4–9.

Casper, J.D., Brereton, D., & Neal, D. (1982). *The implementation of the California determinate sentencing law: Executive summary*. Washington, DC: Government Printing Office.

Cohen, J., Tonry, M.H. (1983). Sentencing reforms and their impacts. In A. Blumstein, J. Cohen, S.E. Martin, & M.H. Tonry (eds.), *Research on sentencing: The search for reform, Vol. 1* (pp. 305–349). Washington, DC: National Academy Press.

Davis, K.C. (1969). *Discretionary justice: A preliminary inquiry*. Baton Rouge: Louisiana State University Press.

Demuth, S., & Steffensmeier, D. (2004). Ethnicity effects on sentencing outcomes in large urban courts: Comparisons among white, black, and Hispanic defendants. *Social Science Quarterly, 85*, 991–1011.

Drug Court Clearinghouse and Technical Assistance Project. (1999). *Looking at a decade of drug courts*. Washington, DC: U.S. Department of Justice.

Engen, R.L., & Steen, S. (2000). The power to punish: Discretion and sentencing reform in the war on drugs. *American Journal of Sociology, 105*, 1357–1395.

Everett, R.S., & Wojtkiewicz, R.A. (2002). Difference, disparity, and race/ethnic bias in federal sentencing. *Journal of Quantitative Criminology, 18*, 189–211.

Frankel, M. (1972). Lawlessness in sentencing. *University of Cincinnati Law Review, 41,* 1–54.

Frase, R. (1997). Prison population growing under Minnesota guidelines. In M. Tonry & K. Hatlestad (eds.), *Sentencing reform in overcrowded times.* New York; Oxford University Press.

Gottfredson, D.C., & Exum, M.L. (2002). Baltimore City Drug Treatment Court: One-year results from a randomized study. *Journal of Research in Crime and Delinquency, 39,* 337–356.

Gottfredson, D.C., Najaka, S.S., Kearley, B.W., & Rocha, C.M. (2006). Long-term effects of participation in the Baltimore City Drug Treatment Court: Results from an experimental study. *Journal of Experimental Criminology, 2,* 67–98.

Hanson, R.A., & Ostrom, B.J. (2004). Indigent defenders get the job done and done well. In. G.F. Cole, M.G. Gertz, & A. Bunger, A. (eds.), *The criminal justice system: Law and politics.* Belmont, CA: Wadsworth.

Harvard Law Review. (2000). Gideon's promise unfulfilled: The need for litigated reform of indigent defense. *Harvard Law Review, 113,* 2062–2079.

Hofer, P. J., Blackwell, K.R., & Ruback, B. (1999). The effect of the federal sentencing guidelines on interjudge sentencing disparity. *The Journal of Criminal Law & Criminology, 90,* 239–321.

Huddleston, C.W., III, Freeman-Wilson, K., Marlowe, D.B., & Roussell, A. (2005). *Painting the current picture: A national report card on drug courts and other problem solving court programs in the United States.* Washington, DC: National Drug Court Institute.

Inciardi, J.A., McBride, D., & Rivers, J.E. (1996). *Drug control and the courts.* Thousand Oaks, CA: Sage.

Kennedy, R. (1997) *Race, crime, and the law.* New York: Vintage Books.

Knapp, K.A. (1987). Implementation of the Minnesota guidelines: Can the innovative spirit be preserved? In A. von Hirsch, K.A. Knapp, & M. Tonry (eds.), *The sentencing commission and its guidelines* (pp. 127–141). Boston: Northeastern University Press.

Kramer, J.H., & Lubitz, R.L. (1985). Pennsylvania's sentencing reform: The impact of commission-established guidelines. *Crime & Delinquency, 31,* 481–500.

Kramer, J.H., & Steffensmeier, D. (1993). Race and imprisonment decisions. *The Sociological Quarterly, 34,* 357–376.

Kramer, J.H., & Ulmer, J.T. (1996). Sentencing disparity and departures from guidelines. *Justice Quarterly, 13,* 81–106.

LaFrentz, C., & Spohn, C. (2006). Who is punished more harshly? An examination of race/ethnicity, gender, age and employment status under the federal sentencing guidelines. *Justice Research & Policy, 8,* 25–56.

Martinson, R. (1974). What works? Questions and answers about prison reform. *Public Interest, 24,* 22–54.

Marvel, T.B., & Moody, C.E. (1995). The impact of enhanced prison terms for felonies committed with guns. *Criminology, 33,* 247–281.

McIntyre, L. (1987). *The public defender: The practice of law in the shadows of repute.* Chicago: University of Chicago Press.

Moore, C.A., & Miethe, T.D. (1986). Regulated and unregulated sentencing decisions: An analysis of first-year practices under Minnesota's felony sentencing guidelines. *Law & Society Review, 20,* 253–277.

Mustard, D. (2001), Racial, ethnic and gender disparities in sentencing: Evidence from the U.S. federal courts. *Journal of Law and Economics, 44,* 285–314.

Myrdal, G. (1944). *An American dilemma: The Negro problem and modern democracy*. New York: Harper.

National Association of Drug Court Professionals. (1997). *Defining drug courts: The key components*. Washington, DC: Bureau of Justice Assistance, U.S. Department of Justice.

Serr, B.J., & Maney, M. (1988). Racism, peremptory challenges and the democratic jury: The jurisprudence of a delicate balance. *Journal of Criminal Law & Criminology, 79*, 1–65.

Spohn, C. (2000). *Thirty years of sentencing reform: The quest for a racially neutral sentencing process*. Washington, DC: U.S. Department of Justice.

Spohn, C., & Sample, L. (forthcoming). The dangerous drug offender in federal court: Stereotyping blacks and crack cocaine. *Crime and Delinquency*.

Stacey, A.M., & Spohn, C. (2006). Gender and the social costs of sentencing: An analysis of sentences imposed on male and female offenders in three U.S. District Courts. *Berkeley Journal of Criminal Law, 11*, 43–76.

Steen, S., Engen, R.L., & Gainey, R.R. (2005). Images of danger and culpability: Racial stereotyping, case processing, and criminal sentencing. *Criminology, 43*, 435–468.

Steffensmeier, D., & Demuth, S. (2000). Ethnicity and sentencing outcomes in U.S. federal courts: Who is punished more harshly? *American Sociological Review, 65*, 705–729.

Steffensmeier, D., & Demuth, S. (2006). Does gender modify the effects of race-ethnicity on criminal sanctioning? Sentences for male and female white, black, and Hispanic defendants. *Journal of Quantitative Criminology, 22*, 241–261.

Steffensmeier, D., & Hebert, C. (1999). Women and men policymakers: Does the judge's gender affect the sentencing of criminal defendants? *Social Forces, 77*, 1163–1196.

Steffensmeier, D., Kramer, J., & Streifel, C. (1993). Gender and imprisonment decisions. *Criminology, 31*, 411–446.

Steffensmeier, D., Ulmer, J., & Kramer, J. (1998). The interaction of race, gender, and age in criminal sentencing: The punishment cost of being young, black, and male. *Criminology, 36*, 763–797.

Stith, K., & Cabranes, J.A. (1998). *Fear of judging: Sentencing guidelines in the federal courts*. Chicago: University of Chicago Press.

Stolzenberg, L., & D'Alessio, S.J. (1994). Sentencing and unwarranted disparity: An empirical assessment of the long-term impact of sentencing guidelines in Minnesota. *Criminology, 32*, 301–310.

Tonry, M. (1995). *Malign neglect: Race, crime, and punishment in America*. New York: Oxford University Press.

Tonry, M. (1996). *Sentencing matters*. New York: Oxford University Press.

United States General Accounting Office. (1997). *Drug courts: Overview of growth, characteristics, and results*. Washington, DC: U.S. General Accounting Office.

United States Sentencing Commission. (1991a). *The federal sentencing guidelines: A report on the operation of the guidelines system and short-term impacts on disparity in sentencing, use of incarceration, and prosecutorial discretion and plea bargaining*. Washington, DC: U.S. Sentencing Commission.

United States Sentencing Commission, (1991b). *Special report to Congress: Mandatory minimum penalties in the federal criminal justice system*. Washington, DC: U.S. Sentencing Commission.

United States Sentencing Commission. (2004). *Fifteen years of guidelines sentencing: An assessment of how well the federal criminal justice system is achieving the goals of sentencing reform.* Washington, DC: Author.

van den Haag, E. (1975). *Punishing criminals: Confronting a very old and painful question.* New York: Basic Books.

von Hirsch, A. (1976). *Doing justice; The choice of punishments.* New York: Hill and Wang.

Walker, S. (1993). *Taming the system: The control of discretion in criminal justice, 1950–1990.* New York: Oxford University Press.

Washington State Sentencing Guidelines Commission. (1992). *A decade of sentencing reform: Washington and its guidelines, 1981–1991.* Olympia: Washington State Sentencing Guidelines Commission.

Williams, M. (2002). A comparison of sentencing outcomes for defendants with public defenders versus retained counsel in a Florida circuit court. *Justice Systems Journal 23,* 249–257.

Wilson, J.Q. (1975). *Thinking about crime.* New York; Basic Books.

Wishman, S. (1986). *Anatomy of a jury: The system on trial.* New York: Penguin Books.

Wright, R.F. (1998). *Managing prison growth in North Carolina through structured sentencing.* National Institute of Justice, Program Focus Series. Washington, DC: U.S. Department of Justice, National Institute of Justice.

THE MENTAL HEALTH AND CRIMINAL JUSTICE SYSTEMS AS AGENTS OF SOCIAL CONTROL

Melissa Thompson

MENTAL ILLNESS OR CRIME?

+ In January 2008, a 37 year-old Asian-American man threw his four children off an Alabama bridge. According to news reports, Lam Luong was motivated by an argument with his wife, or perhaps by a crack cocaine habit.
+ In October 2005, a 23 year-old African-American woman threw her three children off the Golden Gate Bridge. According to news reports, LaShaun Harris was influenced by voices in her head telling her to commit this offense.
+ In June 2001, a 36 year-old white woman drowned her five children in a bathtub in Texas. According to news reports, Andrea Yates suffered from post-partum psychosis which, together with her extreme religious values, resulted in her belief that she was saving her children from hell by killing them.

In cases like these, the criminal justice system has the difficult task of determining whether potentially mentally ill offenders bear criminal responsibility for their actions. Because lawyers and judges cannot know with certainty the mindset of these individuals at the time of the offense, they must rely on various other factors, including the offender's self-report of his or her mental status. Beyond this, there are other clues that might be used to determine responsibility or sanity. For instance, some legal commentators have suggested that socially constructed factors—including gender and race—might be considered in these decisions. Since a mother killing her children elicits a very different social reaction from a father committing a similar offense, gender may be one clue used by criminal justice decision-makers to determine whether the offender is legally sane and therefore criminally responsible for his/her offense. Furthermore, because the media tends to suggest that people of color—particularly African-Americans—are more "typical" criminals, the social reaction to a white offender versus an African-American offender is also quite different. To test these expectations, this book seeks to provide evidence of the impact of gender, race, and social class on attributions of mental illness, and treatment for mental illness in the criminal justice system.

133

A staggering number of persons with mental illness are confined in U.S. prisons and jails, according to one estimate more than half of all prison and jail inmates have (or had in the past) a mental health problem (U.S. Department of Justice 2006). This means that approximately 705,600 state prison inmates, 78,800 Federal prisoners, and 479,900 inmates in local jails are mentally ill (U.S. Department of Justice 2006). When combined with an estimated 678,000 mentally ill individuals on probation (U.S. Department of Justice 1999; 2007), it is clear that the U.S. criminal justice system is the primary source of social control for almost two million mentally ill criminal offenders. Since the 1970s, the incarceration rate has grown by almost 600 percent (U.S. Department of Justice 2000; 2009); at the same time, the rate of persons in mental hospitals has significantly decreased. At its peak, the rate of persons hospitalized for a mental disorder was 339 for every 100,000 persons in the population in 1955 (Mechanic and Rochefort 1990). Since then, the rate of mental hospital admissions has declined dramatically: from a rate of 283 admissions in 1990, down to 89 in 2004 (National Center for Health Statistics 2008). Furthermore, the number of available non-correctional mental health beds in the United States has significantly decreased, with a 1986 rate of 112 mental health beds per 100,000 persons in the U.S. reduced to 71 per 100,000 only 18 years later in 2004 (National Center for Health Statistics 2008). Meanwhile, the number of prisons continues to grow. Regardless of the causes, the effect of these trends is a significant increase in the number and rate of individuals with mental illness being handled by the criminal justice system and a disproportionately high rate of mental illness in the U.S. correctional system compared to persons outside the justice system. What has been largely ignored to date is the role of social factors such as race, gender, and social class in affecting these numbers. Thus, this book asks: how do race, class and gender affect mental health treatment in the criminal justice system? Mentally ill criminal offenders are in a unique position at the intersection of both the mental health and legal systems (Freeman and Roesch 1989), often resulting in debates over which system should control them. Consequently, involuntary civil commitment laws have changed dramatically, with patients' rights emphasized from the 1960s through approximately 1980; since then, the law has emphasized community security (LaFond 1994).

The analysis of the criminal justice system and the role of legal and extralegal factors in processing decisions is an important and well-established area of study in the sociology of law and criminology. This literature suggests that official responses of the criminal justice system to offenders are based on many intersecting factors, such as evidence, individual biographies, situational factors, cultural expectations, and prior legal events (Farrell and Swigert 1986; Reskin and Visher 1986; Steffensmeier and Allen 1986; Wooldredge 1998). The research in this area has also suggested that decision-makers' expectations about criminal defendants and their typical crimes affect criminal justice outcomes (Sudnow 1965; Bridges and Steen 1998). This set of expectations is developed through social interaction and results in at least two socially constructed sets of assumptions: one based on gender and another based on race.

The first set of expectations held by the criminal justice system is based on gender, where assumptions about normative male and female behavior may influence criminal justice decision-making. Stereotypes of feminine behavior include passivity, dependence, and submissiveness, whereas masculine stereotypes include dominance, assertiveness, and independence (Baskin et al. 1989; Chesney-Lind and Shelden 1998). Criminal behavior may be interpreted in light of these gendered expectations so that women who engage in non-normative criminal behavior—particularly violent crimes—are thought to violate these stereotypes (Baskin et al. 1989). Because of this, feminists have asserted that the criminal justice system is more likely to label female criminal offenders as mentally ill while treating male offenders as "rational" and therefore more responsible for their actions (Smart 1995); this process is termed "the medicalization of female deviance" (Offen 1986). Supporters of the medicalization of female deviance hypothesis point out that 23 percent of female prisoners have been diagnosed as mentally ill compared to only 8 percent of the male prison population (U.S. Department of Justice 2006), suggesting that mental disorders are over-diagnosed in female prisoners. An alternative hypothesis, however, is that female offenders are labeled mentally ill at a higher rate due to greater levels of actual mental illness in the female inmate population (see U.S. Department of Justice 2006).

The second set of expectations criminal justice officials hold are related to the race of the defendant. While violent women might be considered incomprehensible or mentally ill, stereotypes of African-Americans frequently focus on criminality and violence (Smith 1991; Sniderman and Piazza 1993; Emerson, Yancey, and Chai 2001; Quillian and Pager 2001). This stereotype of African-Americans as criminal is deeply embedded in Americans' collective consciousness and may be used by decision-makers who must make choices based on incomplete information (Devine and Elliot 1995; Emerson et al. 2001; Quillian and Pager 2001; Pager 2004). This argument is postulated by economic theories of statistical discrimination. Statistical discrimination refers to the use of information concerning groups, rather than individuals, in decision-making. These uses of group norms in decision-making often occur in the absence of scientific data—and may in fact be contrary to these data—yet are used in the pursuit of expedience (Phelps 1972).

Sociologists have similarly argued that individuals use stereotypes about racial minorities in their perceptions of neighborhood crime rates and the stigma of incarceration (Emerson *et al.* 2001; Quillian and Pager 2001; Western 2002). Applying this perspective to the legal system, the use of group norms is efficient in screening cases to decide which types of punishment are fair and appropriate. Group variables such as race, age, or gender are therefore assumed to provide information regarding an individual's expected criminality or insanity[1] (Becker 1985; Kennedy 1997; Konrad and Cannings 1997). Therefore, it is expected that stereotypically "normal" offenders will be less likely

than other defendants to be referred for a psychiatric evaluation to determine criminal responsibility. The average criminal defendant, who is young, African-American, and male (Steffensmeier, Ulmer, and Kramer 1998; U.S. Department of Justice 2009), will be less likely to be psychiatrically evaluated since he is not viewed as an abnormal criminal defendant. In fact, some have argued that behavior indicating severe mental pathology in minority groups is often ignored or considered to reflect criminality rather than mental illness (Kutchins and Kirk 1997:225).

DEINSTITUTIONALIZATION OR TRANSINSTITUTIONALIZATION?

Since its peak in the 1950s, the rate of hospitalization (or beds available for hospitalization) for severely mentally ill individuals has declined dramatically, particularly since the 1980s. At the same time, the rate of incarceration in prisons and jail has dramatically increased. Although we cannot know whether these individuals moved from the mental health system directly into the criminal justice system, there does appear to be a relationship between the criminal justice and mental health systems. This relationship is complex but essentially reciprocal, with increased hospital admissions in times of fewer jail admissions and decreased hospital admissions when jail populations increase (Rothman 1980; Hochstedler 1986; Cirincione et al. 1992; Torrey et al. 1992; Miller 1993; Cirincione, Steadman, and Monahan 1994; Teplin and Voit 1996; Hiday 1999; Liska et al. 1999; National Center for Health Statistics 2008).

As a general rule, if prison populations are large, the asylum populations are relatively small; the reverse also tends to be true (Steadman et al. 1984; U.S. Department of Justice 1997a; Kupers 1999; Liska et al. 1999).

Today the majority of mental health care is on an outpatient basis, as opposed to inpatient services. This was not always the case; in the 1950s, emphasis was on inpatient care. Several factors in the U.S. led to this push toward the deinstitutionalization of mental hospitals, including the passage of the *National Mental Health Act of 1946*. This Act led to significant increases in community programs and in training mental health

---

1   The term "insanity" is used throughout this book to refer to the use of a defense of mental disease or defect. Although the actual term "insanity" is not typically used in the statutory language of mental illness defenses, this term is nevertheless used because of its ease of use—it is significantly simpler to refer to an insanity defense than to repeatedly say "defense of mental disease or defect" (which is the actual statutory language).

practitioners and workers. There was a corresponding increase in numbers of outpatient clinics, general hospital inpatient services, and nursing home beds for the mentally ill. The increasingly widespread use of psychoactive drugs to treat mental patients has widely been considered the primary factor leading to deinstitutionalization. In addition, the enactment of the *Mental Health Study Act in 1955*, establishing the Joint Commission on Mental Illness and Mental Health, whose purpose is to analyze and evaluate the needs of the mentally ill played an important role. The passage of the *Mental Retardation Facilities and Community Mental Health Centers Construction Act in 1963* stimulated programs designed to provide community mental health services (Mechanic and Rochefort 1990). Finally, the Supreme Court also entered the fray, with the "Willowbrook Consent Decree." In 1975 the Supreme Court decided that mental patients must be kept in the "least restrictive setting" necessary for their well-being. Despite these efforts at deinstitutionalization, critics have suggested that rather than deinstitutionalization, what currently exists is "transinstitutionalization" with mentally ill individuals who would have, in the past, been kept in a psychiatric hospital setting, instead being moved into other institutionalized settings, in particular the criminal justice system. Concerns regarding transinstitutionalization and mental illness include the difficulties mentally ill prisoners face coping in prisons, due largely to inadequate mental health treatment. One issue that has been raised focuses on medication as the sole treatment for prisoners. There have also been concerns regarding a tendency to treat mental illness in segregation, which has a negative impact on the socialization and adjustment of the mentally ill. There are apparent race, class, and gender differences in the definition of and access to treatment in prison. With respect to gender, according to a 2006 Bureau of Justice Statistics report (the most recent year available), 55 percent of male inmates in state prisons had suffered a mental health problem in the past as opposed to 73 percent of females. To some extent, these gender differences may reflect differences in labeling on the part of the criminal justice system. For example, Auerhahn and Leonard explain that, depending on the institution, female inmates are medicated

at two to ten times the rate of their male counterparts (2000). Women who engage in violent offenses are also disproportionately medicated (Auerhahn and Leonard 2000). Luskin (2001) explains that part of the gender difference in receipt of psychiatric treatment has to do with perceptions of dangerousness. Luskin notes that due to the larger physical size and strength of men, they are often seen as more dangerous and thus are less likely to get diverted into mental health programs (2001).

Race can also affect whether or not one receives a mental health label and possible treatment. According to 2006 data from the Bureau of Justice Statistics, 62 percent of white inmates, 55 percent of black inmates, and 46 percent of Hispanic inmates had suffered a mental health problem in the past. Although inconsistent, there is some evidence that race might play a role in the diversion of convicts into the mental health system in lieu of prison (Luskin 2001). In addition, social class may affect mental illness and the labeling and treatment of these disorders. According to 2006 data from the Bureau of Justice Statistics, in state prisons 13 percent of mentally ill inmates had been homeless in the past year compared to only 6 percent of non-mentally ill inmates. Furthermore, 70 percent of mentally ill inmates had been employed in the month before their arrest in comparison to 76 percent of non-mentally ill inmates.

This book seeks to provide additional information regarding the impact of race, class, and gender on the diagnosis of mental illness and receipt of treatment.

THEORIES OF GENDER, RACE, MENTAL ILLNESS, AND CRIMINAL LABELING

Both gender and race affect criminal justice processing. Racial minorities are disproportionately represented in the criminal justice system (U.S. Department of Justice 2006). This has often been attributed to systematic discrimination in each stage of justice processing (Spohn and Holleran 2000; Steffensmeier and DeMuth 2000; Bushway and Peichl 2001; Chiricos, et al. 2004; Steen et al. 2005). Many researchers also argue that when decision-makers are free to exercise discretion, they systematically favor female offenders over similarly situated male offenders (Farrell and Swigert 1986; Simon and Landis 1991; Boritch 1992; Nagel and Johnson 1994; Daly and Bordt 1995; Katz and Spohn 1995; Kruttschnitt 1996; Steffensmeier et al. 1998).

While most gender roles are unwritten, Schur (1984) contends that gender norms work as a "mechanism for the social control of women" (p. 52). He explains that women are doubly stigmatized, since behavioral extremes are not tolerated, and instead are labeled. For example, women who show too little emotion are labeled "cold," "calculating," or "masculine." Conversely, if they demonstrate too much emotion, they are "hysterical" (Schur 1984:53). Therefore, women suffer from a double bind in which they are always labeled unless they act within narrowly defined limits. Thus, the response to different criminal women on the part of the criminal justice system may vary considerably, dependent on whether the woman's behavior is considered to be a violation of typical gendered expectations.

Many gendered explanations are based on the chivalry or paternalism thesis; while paternalism is considered more pejorative than chivalry, these terms tend to be used interchangeably. This concept is not always precisely defined, but generally refers to a protective attitude toward women that is linked to gender stereotypes of women as (1) weaker and more passive than men, and therefore not proper subjects for imprisonment, and (2) more submissive and dependent than men, and therefore less responsible for their crimes. Judges might also regard women as more easily manipulated than men, and therefore more receptive to rehabilitative efforts (Nagal and Johnson 1994).

A corollary to the chivalry/paternalism thesis: the "evil woman" thesis. This thesis hypothesizes that women whose criminal behavior violates gendered assumptions are treated more harshly than their male counterparts. In other words, not only do certain types of female offenders fail to benefit from paternalistic treatment, they are actually subject to heightened social control for their choice of an "unladylike" offense (Crew 1991; Boritch 1992; Nagel and Johnson 1994). Thus, the criminal justice system may punish women harshly only when they fail to live up to their expected role

(Simpson 1989; Worrall 1990; Kruttschnitt 1996). When women are fulfilling their gender roles (by marrying and taking care of their children), they are treated in a paternalistic manner, with more lenient treatment. When women fail to fulfill prescribed gender roles, however, social control is increased—more so than for men—in an attempt to bring the behavior back into line with what is expected of women (see Schur 1984; Horwitz 1990:113–114).

While women might be expected to act in a "feminine" manner, expectations of African-Americans include criminality and violence (Smith 1991; Sniderman and Piazza 1993; Quillian and Pager 2001). This stereotype of African-Americans as criminal is deeply embedded in Americans' expectations (Devine and Elliot 1995; Emerson et al. 2001; Quillian and Pager 2001). For example, individuals have used stereotypes about racial minorities in their perceptions of neighborhood crime rates, in support for punitive crime policies, and the stigma of incarceration (Chiricos et al. 2001; Emerson et al. 2001; Quillian and Pager 2001; Western 2002; Chiricos, Welch, and Gertz 2004). This perception of racial minorities as criminal is so strong and so deeply embedded that some have argued that behavior that actually reflects severe mental pathology in minority groups is often ignored or considered to be criminal behavior rather than mental illness (Kutchins and Kirk 1997:225).

RESEARCH QUESTIONS

The primary focus of this research is criminal responsibility and how it is attributed to defendants. The question that is addressed is: What effects do racial and gendered expectations have on criminal justice processing? More specifically: Are women labeled "mad" while men are labeled "bad?" Are African-American defendants "criminal" while non-African-Americans are "ill?" The primary objectives in this project include determining: (1) What is the role of race, gender, and social class in predicting psychiatric treatment for felony defendants?; (2) Are female offenders medicalized by being more likely to receive psychiatric treatment than similar male offenders?; (3) Are African-American offenders less likely to be psychiatrically treated than are non-African-Americans?; and finally (4) How does socio-economic status affect the receipt of psychiatric treatment?

To meet these objectives, demographic, criminal, familial, and psychiatric data were gathered for felony defendants in Hennepin County, Minnesota. These data were obtained for a detailed analysis of the cases referred by the criminal justice system for psychiatric evaluation to determine mental status at the time of the offense. Additional data were also analyzed to present national data regarding that status of psychiatric treatment for jail and prison inmates, and for offenders on probation.

The following chapters focus on the predictors of psychiatric evaluations and other forms of psychiatric treatment for criminal defendants, and the effects of psychiatric evaluations on case outcomes. This book aims to contribute to the state of sociological and criminological knowledge by using a sampling strategy that isolates the effects of race and gender on attributions of mental illness, by testing feminist, labeling, and social control theories about attributions of mental illness, and by determining the effect mental illness attributions have on final case outcomes.

REVIEW QUESTIONS

1. Roughly how many mentally ill individuals fall under the jurisdiction of the U.S. criminal justice system, either on probation or confined in prisons or jails?

2. The relationship between the criminal justice and mental health systems in the U.S. is best described as_____?

3. What is the name of the process in which large numbers of mentally ill individuals are moved from mental health facilities into criminal justice institutions?

4. Karen Luskin has argued that part of the reason women receive psychiatric treatment disproportionately to men in the criminal justice system has to do with perceptions of dangerousness. What does she mean by this?

5. What does the average criminal defendant look like in America and how does this fact affect the likelihood of one being psychiatrically evaluated?

Toward Restorative and Community Justice

*Michael Brasswell,
John Fuller, and
Bo Lozoff*

Peacemaking criminology has the potential to be effective at many levels. We have already discussed how personal transformation and institutional change can be envisioned by peacemaking criminology. While each of these levels of change are important, there is another opportunity to implement peacemaking that is rapidly gaining momentum around the world as an effective and humane way to deal with offenders. Community justice is emerging as an alternative to the traditional criminal justice system. While there are many variations of the community justice theme, we will concentrate on a process termed *restorative justice* as a way to demonstrate how positive change can occur outside the criminal justice system.

Community justice as practiced by the restorative justice movement cannot be called a new phenomenon, but rather a return to the days when conflicts were resolved at the level of the family, clan, group, and community. The emphasis of community justice is not on the punishment of the offender, but on the restoring of the relationship between the offender and victim, as well as on maintaining order and social and moral balance in the community. Community justice therefore has a broader mandate than the traditional criminal justice system. It must satisfy the concerns of several constituents and produce a result that is viewed both as just and satisfying. In other words, the limited institutional goals of clearing a court docket or ensuring that an offender is punished are not enough for community justice. A more inclusive and healing result is the goal.

Before we discuss the underlying principles of restorative or community justice, we need to examine why the criminal justice system is so unsatisfying in giving people a sense that crime is being dealt with in an effective manner. At the heart of the dissatisfaction with the criminal justice system are two issues. The first issue of concern is the general feeling that the criminal justice system does not work very well, particularly in reflecting the interests of the victims of crime. When an offender commits a crime against an individual, the state takes the case away from the victim and prosecutes it as its own. In point of fact, the state replaces the victim as an aggrieved party and uses its own values and constraints to decide on a disposition. The Norwegian criminologist Nils Christie argues that the conflict between the offender and victim are property that the state takes away.[1] The offender and victim no longer have the opportunity to resolve the case in a mutually satisfying way, and hope of repairing the relationship is diminished.

A second issue of concern with the traditional criminal justice system is its failure to change the criminal behavior of the offender. The over-reliance on punishment that is the hallmark of the criminal justice system ignores some of society's other important goals.[2] The determination of guilt or innocence and the imposition of a punishment are inherently shortsighted activities. If offenders are consistently embittered by their interaction with the criminal justice system, and the issues that contributed to their deciding to violate the law are not addressed, then we should not be surprised that when they are released from prison that they recidivate. A mean-spirited or apathetic criminal justice system will produce a mean-spirited, former inmate who feels he's got nothing to lose. While it is true that an emphasis on punishment does try to achieve the goals of retribution, deterrence, and incapacitation, viewing of the offender as an enemy rather than a family member or neighbor facilitates a punishment mentality that inevitably becomes a self-fulfilling prophecy. The restorative justice movement seeks to reclaim the offender and repair the relationship with the victim and community. Ultimately, this form of justice can be healthier for all concerned.

UNDERLYING PRINCIPLES OF RESTORATIVE JUSTICE

Before we examine the process of restorative justice it is useful to look at the underlying principles. Ron Claassen, from the Center for Peacemaking and Conflict Studies at Fresno Pacific College, lists these principles that will guide our later discussion.[3]

1. Crime is primarily an offense against human relationships, and secondarily a violation of the law (since laws are written to protect public safety and fairness in human relationships).

2. Restorative Justice recognizes that crime (violations of persons and relationships) is wrong and should not occur, and also recognizes that after it does there are dangers and opportunities. The danger is that the community, victim(s), and/or offender emerge from the response further alienated, more damaged, disrespected, disempowered, feeling less safe and less cooperative with society. The opportunity is that injustice is recognized, the equity is restored (restitution and grace), and the future is clarified so that participants are safer, more respectful, and more empowered and cooperative with each other and society.

3. Restorative Justice is a process to "make things as right as possible" which includes: attending to needs created by the offense such as safety and repair of injuries to relationships and physical damage resulting from the offense; and attending to needs related to the cause of the offense (addictions, lack of social or employment skills or resources, lack of moral or ethical base, etc.).

4. The primary victim(s) of a crime is/are the one(s) most impacted by the offense. The secondary victims are others impacted by the crime and might include family members, friends, witnesses, criminal justice officials, community, etc.

5. As soon as immediate victim, community, and offender safety concerns are satisfied, Restorative Justice views the situation as a teachable moment for the offender; an opportunity to encourage the offender to learn new ways of acting and being in the community.

6. Restorative Justice prefers responding to the crime at the earliest point possible and with the maximum amount of voluntary cooperation and minimum coercion, since healing in relationships and new learning are voluntary and cooperative processes.

7. Restorative Justice prefers that most crimes are handled using a cooperative structure including those impacted by the offense as a community to provide support and accountability. This might include primary and secondary victims and family (or substitutes if they choose not to participate), the offender and family, community representatives,

government representatives, faith community representatives, and school representatives, etc.

8. Restorative Justice recognizes that not all offenders will choose to be cooperative. Therefore there is a need for outside authority to make decisions for the offender who is not cooperative. The actions of the authorities and the consequences imposed should be tested by whether they are reasonable, restorative, and respective (for victim(s), offender, and community).

9. Restorative Justice prefers that offenders who pose significant safety risks and are not yet cooperative be placed in settings where the emphasis is on safety, values, ethics, responsibility, accountability, and civility. They should be exposed to the impact of their crime(s) on victims, invited to learn empathy, and offered learning opportunities to become better equipped with skills to be a productive member of society. They should continually be invited (not coerced) to become cooperative with the community and be given the opportunity to demonstrate this in appropriate settings as soon as possible.

10. Restorative Justice requires follow-up and accountability structures utilizing the natural community as much as possible, since keeping agreements is the key to building a trusting community.

11. Restorative Justice recognizes and encourages the role of community institutions, including the religious/faith community, in teaching and establishing the moral and ethical standards which build up the community.

It is easy to see how restorative justice principles encompass the concerns of peacemaking criminology. Additionally, the idea of community justice is emphasized. While some of the issues that are embedded in restorative justice can be addressed by the traditional criminal justice system, it is clear that an alternative philosophy is needed. In other words, the restorative justice, community justice, and peacemaking criminology concepts all require the traditional criminal justice system to focus much more broadly on the welfare of the victim, community, and offender. The limited focus on guilt or innocence and punishment are insufficient

to achieve the type of healing result that is part of the community justice model.

Given the underlying principles of restorative justice, it becomes useful to ask some questions about the traditional criminal justice system. How did the criminal justice system get to the point where conflicts are taken away from individuals and made crimes where the state is considered the aggrieved party? Is justice concerned only with the punishment of offenders? Is it dysfunctional for society to keep insisting on more and more punishment when it seems not to be effective? Is there a point where the criminal justice industry begins to advocate policies that are more concerned with narrow vocational and economic interests rather than broader concerns of justice?

THE PROMISE OF COMMUNITY

We all live in communities. By this we mean something beyond living in a physical neighborhood. To live in a community means that the individual is connected by social and economic ties to a group of other individuals. The concept of community can become confusing in postmodern times when one knows someone thousands of miles away through the Internet much better than his/her next-door neighbor. Nevertheless, the person next door has the potential to be a friend or a real pain in the neck, depending on just how well you both fulfill the expectations of being neighbors. Those with whom we share this sense of community are partners in developing a physical and shared world. Whether we personally like our neighbors or not, we alternately cooperate with and oppose them in our daily lives. They have a tremendous potential to contribute to our quality of life depending on whether they help in times of need or break into our homes and steal our belongings.

This sense of community is what makes stable society possible. In traditional societies, the community did the work that the criminal justice system does in more complex societies. For example, anthropologist William Ury, a leading scholar on conflict resolution, explains how the Bushmen in Africa use the community to resolve conflicts:

When a serious problem comes up, everyone sits down, all the men and women, and they talk and talk—and talk. Each person has a chance to have his or her say. This open and inclusive process can take days—until the dispute is literally talked out. The community members work hard to discover what social rules have been broken to produce such discord and what needs to be done to restore social harmony. A *kgotla*, which is what they call their discussion, serves as a kind of people's court except that there is no vote by the jury or verdict by the judge; decisions are made by consensus. Unlike a typical court proceeding where one side wins and one side loses, the goal is a stable solution that both disputants and the community can support. As the group conversation proceeds, a consensus about the appropriate solution gradually crystallizes. After making sure that no opposition or ill will remains, the elders voice this emergent consensus.[4]

It can be argued that the differences between the traditional Bushmen society and modern industrial society are vast and that making any kind of comparison between social institutions is fraught with problems. However, the intent of describing the process the Bushmen use for resolving conflicts is to suggest the adversarial way that is used in our court system is not necessarily something that is part of the natural evolution of social institutions. The intent of demonstrating how the Bushmen settle differences is to argue that for the vast majority of the time we have had human social institutions, cooperation and consensus have been important ingredients of stable societies. The contemporary criminal justice system is a relatively recent method for deciding how conflicts get resolved and, as we have previously stated, the results are not particularly satisfying.

Can the community be effective in resolving conflicts in contemporary society? Ury argues that it can. The same processes that are effective in traditional societies can work today. In looking at the declining juvenile crime rate in Boston, Ury credits the community.

> The key, according to Boston Police Commissioner Paul Evans, was "collaboration." The entire community was mobilized. The police worked closely with teachers and parents to search out kids who had missed school or whose grades had dropped. Local government agencies and businesses provided troubled youth with counseling, educational programs, and after-school jobs. Social workers visited their homes. Ministers and pastors mentored them and offered a substitute family for kids who almost never had two and sometimes not even one parent at home. Community counselors, often ex-gang members, hung out with gang members and taught them to handle conflict with talk, not guns.[5]

What is unique about the contemporary attempts to use the community in resolving conflicts is the partnering of the community with the government. It is easy to forget that in the larger context, government officials and community members live in the same neighborhoods. In traditional societies, the community performed the functions of government. Today, the social institutions of government have encroached into many of the arenas of the family and community to the point where the influence of the community has lost much of its relevance. The goal of restorative justice programs is bringing the community back into the conflict-resolution process. This involves looking at criminal acts in a more comprehensive and inclusive way. It expands the scope of focus beyond the conflict between the offender and the government by including the victim, other interested parties such as the families of the victim and the offender, and the community itself.

Restorative justice also measures success in a way that is different from the traditional criminal justice system. Rather than worrying about clearing the court docket with plea bargains that leave all parties unsatisfied or even bitter, or keeping score by the number of years of incarceration meted out to an offender, restorative justice is concerned with the healing of relationships and of reclaiming stability in the community. These are, admittedly, more difficult goals to measure but real social justice is a more complex value than the more limited concerns of the contemporary criminal justice system. Real social justice represents a more long-term, rather than short-term, view, and promises to be longer lasting and less likely to see repeated problems.

Finally, restorative justice in the community is superior to the traditional criminal justice system because of the responsibility it places on the offender. Rather than having something done to him or her, the offender must actively participate in the healing process of the community, the victim, and ultimately him or herself. This healing process might be as simple as an apology to the victim, or it might mean paying restitution to recompense the victim's loss. The offender might be required to perform some type of community service to repay the damage done to public property or the social order. But, most importantly, from a restorative justice perspective, the offender must willingly and actively participate in his or her own healing. This might include traditional treatment methods such as drug and alcohol programs, or it could include having offenders publicly take responsibility for their actions and engage in community education programs designed to prevent others from making the same mistakes.

FORMS OF RESTORATIVE JUSTICE

The idea of restoring the damage done by crime is appealing in theory but requires well-thought-out programs to become effective. Simply putting the offender and the victim in the same room together without some guidance or structure is a recipe for disaster. The unresolved conflict could quickly escalate into harsh words and/or violence. There is a process designed to aid the victim and offender in resolving the conflict to their mutual satisfaction. This process is called Victim–Offender Reconciliation Programs.[6]

Victim–Offender Reconciliation Programs (VORP)

Victim–Offender Reconciliation Programs are designed to bring the victim and offender together to forge a resolution to their problem. With the help of a trained mediator, they take proactive roles in inventing creative options to the traditional criminal justice system sanctions. By empowering the victim and offender to suggest and agree upon solutions to their conflict, the VORP process helps resolve disputes in such a way that the outcomes are long-lasting. Victim–Offender Reconciliation Programs may not be appropriate for many cases, so the voluntary participation of the parties is essential. While the term reconciliation implies that both the victim and offender need to reconcile, many times the victim has no motivation to work toward a middle ground because he/she has done nothing wrong for which to recant. Therefore, the term mediation might be a better description of what happens in these programs.

There are three basic objectives to these programs:

1. To identify the injustice
2. To make things right
3. To consider future actions

In the traditional criminal justice system, it is often the case where the victim and offender never get to hear and understand the other's side. The conversation in the traditional criminal justice system is filtered through the police, prosecutor, defense attorney, and the judge. In this adversarial process, the victim and offender are often driven farther apart by positional bargaining. The VORP process gives them the opportunity to meet face-to-face and explain their injuries, motivations, and concerns. In the process of this mediation they often come to understand, sometimes for the very first time, exactly what the other side was thinking. They ask questions of each other. The victim can put a human face on the loss, and the offender has a chance to show remorse. This step of identifying what the injustice has resulted in is, therefore, useful to the victim who gets to tell his/her story and to the offender who gets to explain his/her actions.

Once the facts of the case are agreed upon, or at the least each side has had an opportunity to gain an understanding of the other side's behavior, the stage is set to develop an outcome that makes things right. For the offender this might include such things as an apology, restitution, return of valuables, or any number of other ways to repair the harm done to the victim. For the victim, the setting right of things may include receiving these reparations from the offender in exchange for forgiveness. In many conflicts, the disputants have ongoing relationships whereby the repair of that relationship is important to repair the harm caused by the crime. Simply becoming financially whole often is not enough to satisfy both parties, especially when they may be related. Forgiveness, if sincere, can be a powerful healer and a profound way to correct an injustice.

Once an agreement has been reached, it is written up and signed by both parties. This then becomes part of the court record and has the impact of a legal document. Depending on the jurisdiction, this agreement can be ratified by the criminal court and any violation can result in the offender having to appear before the judge. Alternatively, this agreement can become the basis for a civil suit by the victim against the offender for failure to comply with the conditions.

The agreement may specify the conditions of future actions that could include a payment schedule for restitution, agreement to enter into a treatment program for drug or alcohol abuse, or a pledge to stay away from the victim. In order to prevent the conflict from recurring, this dimension of agreements for future actions can specify how any ongoing relationship might be monitored by the Victim–Offender Reconciliation Program.

Family Group Conferencing

Family Group Conferencing is an extension of the Victim–Offender Reconciliation Program. It involves not only the victim and the offender, but also other parties including family members, the arresting police officer, representatives from the community and/or the government. A mediator coordinates the conference and allows each to have their chance for input. An outcome is agreed upon that accomplishes several goals. First, it resolves the conflict outside the traditional criminal justice system. Secondly, the victim and

offender have a chance to confront each other and have their side of the story heard. Thirdly, there is an opportunity for other affected parties to provide input and express their concerns. And finally, the agreements that are forged strengthen the ties of the parties and ultimately of the community. Family Group Conferencing is a process that began in New Zealand and was adopted in Australia and eventually in the United States. The Family Group Conferencing model is used most extensively in the juvenile court where the concern for the offender's welfare is considered as important as the victim's.[7]

Victim–Offender Panels (VOP)

It is not always feasible or appropriate for the victim and offender to meet and try to work out their conflicts. For example, in the case of rape, the victim may be so traumatized that any contact with the offender would be harmful. Also, there are many instances in which the offender is not known and therefore not available for conferencing or reconciliation. This does not mean, however, that some of the benefits of conflict resolution cannot be employed. In these instances Victim–Offender Panels are useful.[8]

Victim–Offenders Panels allow victims to address offenders who have committed the same types of crimes as the victims have experienced. The victims do not confront the individual who harmed them directly, but rather, they confront an offender who has harmed someone else. The idea behind these panels is to allow the victim to express the nature and depth of harm they have experienced to offenders. The victim, thus, plays an educative role in showing offenders the human damage that their crimes can cause. Offenders get to see that their actions have consequences for others and can reflect on the harm they may have caused to their own victims. The result, hopefully, is that offenders will change their anti-social attitudes and behaviors.

Victim–Offender Panels have been shown to be effective with carefully chosen victims of drunk drivers and with victims of burglary. The exact process that these panels provide may vary, but the idea is to give victims a chance to tell their story and to give offenders an opportunity to see how their crimes impact on other people. Again, there is no chance for reconciliation in Victim–Offender Panels because the victims never meet the actual offender, just someone who has committed the same type of crime.

These three types of restorative justice practices demonstrate a very different philosophy from the traditional criminal justice system. They all aim at helping both the victim and the offender and, to a broader extent, the community. Critics of these practices would point to the consequences for the offender, claiming any reconciliation that the offender agrees to cannot include enough punishment to satisfy the concerns of justice. This myopic view of justice, one concerned with the amount of punishment, is inconsistent with restorative justice principles. For the long-lasting resolution of the conflict, and the ultimate well-being of the community, punishment has proven to be ineffective.

Reintegrative Shaming

How can restorative and community justice programs effect real change in the offender? For many individuals, looking at restorative justice for the first time, the idea that punishment is not paramount is disturbing. It appears to these observers that the offender is "getting away" with the crime when there is not substantial punishment. For those who embrace the restorative justice concept, however, there is a more powerful process at work than punishment. John Braithwaite contrasts shaming and punishment by calling attention to the symbolic nature of each:[9]

> Shaming is more pregnant with symbolic content than punishment. Punishment is a denial of confidence in the morality of the offender by reducing norm compliance to a crude cost-benefit calculation; shaming can be a reaffirmation of the morality of the offender by expressing personal disappointment that the offender should do something so out of character, and, if the shaming is reintegrative, by expressing personal satisfaction in seeing the character of the offender restored. Punishment erects barriers between the offender and punisher through transforming the relationship into one of power assertion and injury; shaming produces a greater interconnectedness between the parties, albeit a painful one, an interconnectedness which can produce the repulsion of stigmatization or the establishment of a potentially more positive relationship following reintegration. Punishment is often shameful and shaming usually punishes. But whereas punishment gets its symbolic content only from its denunciatory association with shaming, shaming is pure symbolic content.

Reintegrative shaming casts a stark and powerful light on the offender in a way that is both positive and transforming. This type of shaming (as contrasted with disintegrative shaming or stigmatization) is designed to bring the offender back into the social net of the community. Currently our traditional criminal justice system does little in the way of reintegrative shaming. The way the process now works, it is more likely that the victim feels more shame than the offender. The trial and sentencing that is supposed to be what Goffman calls a "successful status degradation ceremony" has become a spectacle about which many offenders feel little shame. This lack of shame on the part of the offenders occurs because many offenders identify with the deviant label. Their offender identity becomes a Master Status whereby they feel pride and accomplishment from the rejection and stigmatization of society.

Critics of reintegrative shaming point out that it works best in tight-knit, homogeneous societies like Japan. Given the individualistic nature of Western nations like the United States, there is concern that the shaming would not be reintegrative. Many people in the United States are poorly integrated into society to begin with, so the idea that they can be reintegrated becomes problematic. There are vast differences between cultures, according to the critics of shaming, and to expect cultural bound bonds that work in one society to be equally effective in another requires a leap of faith that many are not willing to make.

Some Recent Developments

Gordon Bazemore and Mara Schiff have edited a volume based upon a recent conference focusing on restorative justice's evolution into a broader context of community justice. Kenneth Polk advocates that restorative justice be expanded into the larger arena of social justice, including shifting our emphasis on delinquent and deviant youth to proactively increasing developmental opportunities for youth in general. He suggests the restorative justice movement is at a crossroads; either expand the idea of restorative justice or allow the movement to become one more innovative social control option for the criminal justice system. Mary Achilles and Howard Zehr propose greater, more active inclusion of victims in the restorative justice process, while David Karp and Lynne Walther describe how community reparative boards in Vermont attempt to implement restorative and reintegrative processes within a community justice context. Barry Stuart describes some guiding principles for designing peacemaking circles in communities including accessibility, flexibility, being holistic as part of the empowerment process, incorporating a spiritual dimension, building consensus and being accountable.[10]

In defense of restorative justice, it is just this lack of tightly-knit community that restorative justice is trying to inject into the western style of justice. In our postmodern world, we have lost the sense of togetherness that makes meaningful communities possible. No matter how large our efforts or how many "keep out" signs we have posted in our yards, the reality is that we are connected—we are in this thing called life together. What a person does, good or bad, affects others. Rather than seeing this fragmentation as a reason to dismiss restorative justice, we should see as a challenge. Restorative and community justice principles can facilitate not only the healing of victims and offenders, but also many of the ways institutions interact with individuals in society.

Faith-Based Corrections

One interesting trend in community justice is the re-emergence of religion as a legitimate and recognized correctional institution. Pepinsky and Quinney identified religious and humanistic intellectual traditions being influential in the development of peacemaking criminology and in an earlier chapter (Chapter 2) we discussed how a variety of religious and wisdom traditions are important precursors. Faith-based programs can provide a spiritual dimension to the rehabilitation of the offender that is not available from other types of programs. For instance, because of the constitutional separation of church and state, government programs must be careful about imposing a religious component into the treatment plan for offenders.

> Government programs are limited in their ability to help victims and offenders with faith issues, but faith-based programs are free to explore such issues if the person desires it. By providing practical assistance and opportunities to discuss spiritual and emotional issues in a supportive context, programs can assist victims and offenders in moving beyond their alienation to greater emotional, physical, and spiritual health. Of course, offenders and victims come from diverse ethnic, religious, and cultural backgrounds. They may have varying cultural assumptions about managing anger, grief, and stress. They may be deeply involved in other religions or may be hostile to religion. Programs offering a spiritual component must be sensitive to this and be able to help the victim or offender gain the most from their own tradition and support network.[11]

Faith-based programs can encourage positive changes in offenders in both community-based and institutional environments. Even in prison—even on death row—faith-based experiences can transform lives. While on death row for almost 13 years, Willie Reddix described an inner peace he had found by referring to it as a "quiet light." Walter Correll, an inmate on death row in Virginia, wrote, "Right now I may be on death row, but with Jesus in my life it's life row." (see Chapters 4, 6, and 7 for other examples).

Community Justice and Peacemaking

The purpose of this chapter is to establish the connection between peacemaking criminology and community and restorative justice. Having a correctional system that accomplishes the goals of changing the offender's antisocial behavior and protecting the community requires something that the traditional criminal justice cannot provide. In fact, as we have previously pointed out, the reliance on punishment does little to change the offender's behavior and, in fact, often results in a community that is further threatened with new victims who are harmed. Something else is required to bridge the need for change in an offender's life and the need for the protection of the community. A bridge of compassion recognizes the harms and fear shared by offenders and victims, but also offers a way back into the community for each as well. Community justice is a context where much restoration can take place.

QUESTIONS

1. Describe the two issues concerning the traditional criminal justice system that people find unsatisfactory and thus propose a form of community justice. Are these problems ones that can be fixed within the context of the traditional criminal justice system?
2. Ron Claassen presents some underlying principles of restorative justice. Give a brief summary of these principles. Which of them are at odds with the traditional criminal justice system? Which of these principles do you think is most important for healing individuals and the criminal justice system? Explain how the community is integral to the idea of restorative justice. Is the way the term community is used in restorative justice the same as our everyday understanding? What would a restorative justice program that is integrated into the community look like?
3. What is reintegrative shaming? Speculate on how this principle might be misused in the criminal justice system. Is reintegrative shaming something

that can be adapted to the materialistic culture of the United States?
4. Are faith-based correctional programs likely to be effective within the peacemaking criminology context? How might the issues of separation of church and state be addressed within faith-based correctional programs?

NOTES

1. Christie, Nils (1977). "Conflicts as Property." *The British Journal of Criminology*, 17(1):1–15.
2. Irwin, John and James Austin (1994). *It's About Time: America's Imprisonment Binge*. Belmont, CA: Wadsworth.
3. These principles are taken from Ron Claassen's web site (www.fresnp.edu/pacs/rjprinc.html). The content has not been edited and they are printed with permission.
4. Ury, William (1999). *Getting to Peace: Transforming Conflicts at Home, at Work, and in the World*. New York, NY: Viking. 5.
5. Ury, ibid. p. 10–11.
6. Van Ness, Daniel and Karen Heetderks Strong (1997). *Restoring Justice*. Cincinnati, OH: Anderson, p. 69–72.
7. Van Ness and Strong. ibid. p. 73–74.
8. Van Ness and Strong. ibid. p. 74–76.
9. Van Ness and Strong. ibid. p. 117.
10. Van Ness and Strong. ibid. p. 128.
11. Bazemore, Gordon and Schiff, Mara (eds.) (2001). *Restorative Community Justice; Repairing Harm and Transforming Communities*. Cincinnati, OH: Anderson Publishing Co.
12. Arriens, Jan (ed.) (1997). *Welcome to Hell*. Boston, MA: Northeastern University Press, p. 25.

When we speak of restorative justice, we run the risk of saying more than we know. And if we are honest, we must admit that we know more than we live.

—Daniel Van Ness

I aint what I wanna be
I aint what I'm gonna be
but Oh Lord
I aint what I used to be.

—An Unknown Slave

PART III

Readings on Policing
and Investigations

POLICE DISCRET...

152 CRIME, JUSTICE, AND SOCIAL CONTROL

to prosecute or plea b...
generally dismiss...
feel that the...
a convi...
off...

...r E. Kappeler

One can pass on responsibility, but not the discretion that goes with it.

— Benvenuto Cellini

D iscretion is at the heart and soul of policing. In fact, it is the very foundation of our criminal justice system. It is an inescapable part of our justice
process. *Discretion* is when the effective limits on a public official's power leave
him or her free to make a choice among a number of possible courses of action. It
is virtually impossible to provide employees with rules and regulations governing
how every aspect of a job is to be performed except in the most mechanistic,
repetitive jobs. Workers on an automobile assembly line have few choices about
how to do their jobs, but police officers, prosecutors, and judges deal with human
behavior and constantly are encountering new, unique situations. It is impossible
to provide criminal justice practitioners with guidance in every situation because
there are so many different situations, and to even attempt to do so would result
in a set of rules that would be too voluminous to comprehend. Therefore, we must
depend on the police and other practitioners to use "good judgment" and exercise
discretion.

Indeed, everyone in the criminal justice system makes discretionary decisions.
The police make these decisions everyday. They must decide if a case is to be
investigated, whether a suspect should be arrested, or if a traffic violation is severe
enough to warrant a citation. Even though a police department can provide some
guidance through training, rules, and supervision, there are situations in which
the police officer does not have ample official guidance, and the officer must make
decisions or use discretion when proceeding.

The police are not the only participants within the criminal justice system
who exercise discretion. Prosecutors exercise immense discretion when they
decide how to proceed on individual criminal cases. They examine the evidence
collected by police officers, analyze the circumstances surrounding the offense,
victim, and suspect, and then decide whether to dismiss, plea bargain, or prosecute
the case. Historically, prosecutors have been severely criticized when they refuse

...argain a case. But, prosecutors ... plea bargain cases only when they ... evidence is not strong enough to obtain ... ...tion. A plea bargained guilty plea to a lesser ...nse is much better than a not guilty verdict. Here, prosecutors use discretion in the best interest of justice.

Judges also exert discretion. They decide on the applicability of various motions as to the admissibility of evidence. Judges exert substantial discretion as a trial progresses. Beyond the technical aspects of the trial, judges exercise discretion when they consider probation or incarceration. Even when a judge decides to incarcerate an offender, the judge must exercise discretion when deciding on the length of the sentence. Thus, criminal justice can be viewed as a series of discretionary decisions commencing when an officer ponders whether to make an arrest until a suspect is ultimately released from the criminal justice system.

Given the setting in which discretion is used, it appears that there are two aspects that should be considered: judgmental and contextual. The *judgmental context* refers to whether discretionary decisions should be made. Prior to the 1950s, it was assumed by almost everyone that discretion was nonexistent within the criminal justice system (Walker, 1993). Supposedly, when police officers observed violations of the law, they wrote a citation or made an arrest. Prosecutors would then prosecute the case to the letter of the law, and judges would hand down inflexible sentences that were the same for every offender regardless of station in life or circumstances.

Even though no one would admit to the existence of discretion, most, if not all, criminal justice practitioners exercised discretion. However, the practice of discretion was viewed as being improper and in some cases, illegal. Corruption within the criminal justice system, which was rampant at the time, was considered to be the result of officers straying away from the strict standards by which the criminal justice system supposedly operated. Indeed, any deviation from accepted standards for any reason whatsoever was viewed as inappropriate. Discretion was also viewed as being extralegal, insinuating that it had no constitutional or legal foundation and therefore was improper. Rather than recognizing its existence, some called for the abolishment of discretion in criminal justice (American Friends Service Committee, 1971).

By the 1960s, discretion came to be viewed as a necessary evil. Discretion is a way criminal justice practitioners can counteract some of the imprudent or unworkable laws passed by legislative bodies. That is, laws frequently are passed in a vacuum to address a narrow range of behaviors. Police officers encounter a wide range of behaviors in a variety of situations. They must use discretion when applying laws to different behaviors to make the laws work. In some instances they may apply a law strictly, while in other cases, the same law may be applied very loosely. Because there is not always an exact fit, police officers must consider the context in which laws are applied.

The *contextual framework* for applying discretion is best understood by examining Packer's (1968) two models of criminal justice. The *due process model* emphasizes due process and individual rights. Its goals revolve around the individual and ensuring that people receive some measure of fundamental fairness when they come into contact with the criminal justice system. The *crime control model*, on the other hand, focuses on the rights and protection of society as a whole and gives the police larger measures of discretionary power to maximally protect society. The apprehension and prosecution of criminals is far more important than due process within the framework of the crime control model. Typically, the police have been criticized for adhering to the crime control model, especially when they neglect or violate suspect rights. On the other hand, proponents of the crime control model have criticized the police for not taking stronger measures against crime and criminals. Thus, the police must constantly strike a balance between crime control and due process.

One way to better understand the concept of discretion is to explore how police use it. Guyot (1991) examined how officers use discretion and found that officers, in order to apply discretion correctly, should possess certain qualities. First, officers should be *curious*. They must have the will to inquire into situations, especially those that are unusual or suspicious. Second, officers must *be able to perceive danger*. The ability to evaluate a situation in terms of dangerousness is critical to the safety of police officers, but officers tend to view many nondangerous situations as dangerous, which often results in an overreaction on their part (Skolnick, 1994; Kappeler & Potter, 2005). Third, Guyot maintains that officers must have what Muir (1977) characterizes as a *tragic perspective*. In essence, officers must be empathetic and have a compassionate understanding of the people and situations they police. Bureaucratic responses do not always lead to just outcomes. Fourth, officers must be *decisive*. When confronted with a situation, officers must be able to readily identify a workable solution. Fifth, officers must exercise *self-control*. Officers must always be aware of their roles, responsibilities, and duties. Vigilantism has no place in law enforcement. Finally, officers must learn to use *varied approaches* to unique problems. Here, problem-solving rules the day. Officers must be able to analyze situations and solve them, rather than treating their symptoms. If officers possess these six qualities, they should be able to exercise discretion in a just, fair way.

In this chapter we review the nature of police discretion and the police decision-making process. The way in which police view their role guides how they focus their activities. The primary role adopted by a particular department results in different styles of policing which, in turn, affects the type and amount of discretion used by officers. While decision-making is required in almost every facet of policing, certain situations are thought to involve more discretion than others. These would include domestic violence, vice crimes, problems of disenfranchised populations, policing hate crimes, and drug enforcement. Having discussed the nature of police discretion and how it is exercised, we conclude with an examination of how abuses of discretion can controlled.

THE NATURE OF POLICE DISCRETION

Discretion can have both positive and negative connotations. [Difficulties are] faced by police departments that do not have sufficient resources to respond to every request for service. In effect, the department exercises discretion when it prioritizes calls for service or selects a patrol technique. It would be virtually impossible to arrest everyone who has committed a crime. Seldom are the police criticized by people who benefit from a discretionary decision not to arrest them. Under the same circumstances, officers may be criticized by the victim, bystanders, or by the public for their lack of action.

Discretion also holds the potential for abuse. Decisions to perform a duty or refrain from taking action can be based on inappropriate criteria, such as gender, age, race, religion, physical appearance, political preference, or other prejudices held by the officer (Kappeler, Sluder & Alpert, 1998).

It is not discretion that is harmful to a department and community; rather it is the inappropriate use of discretion. Because police officers often deal with circumstances in which the legal solution is not clear, their decisions must be guided by ethical considerations […].

While discretionary decisions can reflect consideration of factors that are appropriate in a given situation or are based on existing legal requirements, others may be inappropriately made on the basis of prejudice and may represent a discriminatory action. While researchers will disagree as to how prejudice is developed, most separate it conceptually from discrimination. *Prejudice* is a reflection of one's values and attitudes that develop through the socialization process. We prejudge an individual or their behavior on the basis of what we believe is normal or acceptable. While prejudice is most often spoken of in negative terms—when someone is "against" something—a person can also be prejudiced "in favor of" something. *Discrimination* results when an officer acts overtly on the basis of their prejudices, and this overt act results in negative consequences for the person who was the object of the prejudice.

An example may help to illustrate this distinction. Officers may prejudge a minority group, believing their members are all criminals or, that certain conduct typifies a particular race or ethnicity. When they come into contact with a member of the minority and make decisions on the basis of their prejudice, such as to always make an arrest or to ignore the conduct because it is "typical" behavior, their decisions are based on their prejudices, and reflect a discriminatory action. The same officers may make decisions using factors other than their prejudices, such as the seriousness of the offense or the absence of probable cause to make an arrest, and these actions would not reflect discrimination. This illustrates the difficulty in evaluating a police officer's behavior. The same decision may represent either an appropriate use of discretion, or may be the result of overt discrimination. If officers act on the basis of their prejudgments, it is discrimination. If they act upon other reasons that are appropriate under the circumstances, it is not discrimination.

ADMINISTRATIVE DISCRETION

It is possible to establish a conceptual distinction between discretion exercised by administrators and operational personnel. The existence of administrative discretion is implicit in the organizational structure of police agencies. Police departments typically reflect a bureaucratic structure with a well-defined hierarchy. The administrative function is designed to establish policies and procedures that guide the actions of operational personnel. That is, administrators are responsible for such activities as: planning, organizing, staffing, directing, coordinating, and budgeting. These activities are how administrators ensure that operational personnel perform their expected duties. As such administrators have substantial discretion in how they perform these activities and their final operational decisions and dictates. Administrative discretion is the vehicle through which uniform policies and procedures develop. Although administrators exercise a choice among options, street-level officers theoretically translate their decisions into uniform activities.

Administrative discretion is exercised in determining the role orientation of the agency. This should reflect the administrator's perception of the needs and expectations of the community as a whole and the various neighborhoods that exist within the larger community. Every agency operates under fiscal constraints and it is not possible to meet all the demands for services that are requested. Through the process of budgeting and controlling expenditures, administrators are able to prioritize the types of services offered, thereby establishing the primary role and focus of the agency.

Funding levels for programs reflect the degree to which personnel concentrate on different activities. In one department a decision was made to discontinue the practice of opening vehicles for people who had locked their keys inside. This was prompted by the cost of answering the high number of requests for this service and the number of lawsuits filed against the department for damage to the vehicles. While the decision was motivated primarily by fiscal constraints, it removed one of the primary service activities performed by patrol officers.

Allocation of officers to programs and geographic areas is another example of administrative discretionary decision-making. When administrators allocate officers, their primary resource, they in essence are utilizing discretion by deciding upon priorities. That is, the most important or critical problems receive greater resources than problems of a lesser magnitude.

If a department assigns the bulk of its officers to random patrol, a different enforcement pattern will evolve as compared to balancing the number of officers between random and directed patrol. The manner of assignment and attending directives will influence the amount of discretion available to the officers.

Administrators may also affect discretion by directing officers to focus on particular crimes, or by establishing an unofficial policy of not enforcing others. In the current political climate, officers are expected to make arrests for almost every drug offense. This is a dramatic change from 30 years ago when officers were permitted, often encouraged, to seize or dispose of small amounts of marijuana and release the offender with a warning. Agencies may encourage officers to use discretion for public-order crimes, such as disturbing the peace, by first issuing a warning and resorting to arrests only if the behavior persists.

Administrators not only attempt to control what officers do, they also attempt to control how they do it. For example, Alpert and Dunham (1990) found that nearly one-third of police pursuits result in traffic crashes, with a majority of the pursuits for minor traffic violations. Many of these crashes involve innocent third parties or police officers. Given the relative dangerousness and possibility of civil litigation, police administrators have established rules dictating when pursuits can occur and how they are to proceed. In some cases, departments have completely discouraged pursuits except only in felony situations where there is a threat to life. These rules have reduced the number of crashes associated with police pursuits—they have also reduced officer discretion.

Along these same lines, Fyfe (1979) studied the incidence of police shootings in New York City. He found that the City's restrictive policy governing police use of deadly force resulted in an almost 30 percent reduction in the number of instances where officers shot citizens. There were no negative consequences as a result of the policy. Crime did not increase, nor was there an increase in assaults on police officers. Administrators can successfully control officer discretion that, basically, is a critical component of administrative discretion.

Administrators must constantly use discretion to guide their agencies. Their decisions place parameters around what operational personnel can or cannot do. From this perspective, administrative discretion is exercised through policies and direction and by establishing goals and objectives for operational units.

ENFORCEMENT DISCRETION

Administrators attempt to control officers' discretion by establishing policies and providing direction through orders and supervision. Even so, officers still have substantial *enforcement discretion* in terms of how they enforce the law, provide services, and otherwise maintain order. Officers use discretion in making a variety of decisions, such as whether to enforce specific laws, to investigate crimes, to stop and search people, to arrest or detain an individual or whether to refer cases to the prosecuting attorney for the filing of formal charges. An officer can, in many cases, decide not to file an official report or conduct an investigation into a particular crime. Discretion is routinely exercised in deciding whether to stop and interrogate or search individuals. Suspicious circumstances can be ignored by officers who are essentially reactive or may be investigated by those who are proactive. While many circumstances would permit an arrest, officers may decide an alternative course of action is preferable.

Although discretion can be abused, when properly structured, it can be very positive. Recent experiments in law enforcement, such as community policing, require officers to be given discretion if they are to be responsive to needs of the community. Indeed, officers must learn how to use discretion more effectively. Community policing requires that officers consider and utilize a number of different responses to problems. The focus of their behavior is outcomes, not codified police procedures. Today's police environment requires officers who can exercise good judgment while making such decisions.

THE POLICE DECISION-MAKING PROCESS

The nature of police work requires officers to make decisions about whether the criminal justice process will be initiated. In effect, this power of discretion makes them the "gatekeepers" of the criminal justice system (Alpert, Dunham, & Stroshine, 2005). Officers have wide latitude to decide whether to act when they observe someone who appears to be violating the law. They may ignore the situation altogether or decide to investigate further. Their investigation may lead them to believe no crime has been committed, or that someone else has committed it. If they determine a person has committed a crime they may decide to make an arrest or may believe some other type of disposition is warranted. Even after the arrest, their power to influence the criminal justice process is considerable. Officers may decide not to seek formal charges or may request the filing of a less serious charge. In making these decisions officers effectively determine who is subject to the criminal justice process, hence their role as "gatekeepers."

THE DECISION TO INVOKE THE CRIMINAL JUSTICE PROCESS

While police work is a complex mix of different roles and functions, the arrest is perhaps the quintessence of police work. It is most frequently the objective sought by officers and detectives as they carry out their duties and responsibilities, and it is the activity that many citizens associate with the successful completion of a police endeavor. It is most certainly an important police function to the citizen subjected to it. As such, it is prudent to examine how police officers exercise discretion when making arrests. Numerous studies have examined the decision to arrest. While almost all research concludes the most significant factor affecting an officer's discretion is the seriousness of the offense, other elements influence the decision-making process. The various decision elements can be grouped in three broad categories: (1) offender variables, (2) situational variables, and (3) system variables. Offender variables include considerations of gender, age, race, socio-economic status, and demeanor. Situational variables affecting the decision may revolve around the seriousness of the offense, whether officers were summoned by someone else or the visibility of their actions. System variables would include such factors as the officer's perception of the law, peer group relationships, community attitudes, department philosophy, and the system's capacity to process legal violations.

Offender Variables

Offender variables are attributes of the offender that influence officers to take action. Research has identified several factors that affect officers' decision-making. These can be the decision to make an arrest or issue a traffic citation or to allow the offender to go free with a mere warning.

Age. Research conducted on the relationship between age and the decision to arrest indicates officers take adult's complaints more seriously than those made by juveniles. An arrest is more likely if the victim is older and the offender young (Dunham & Alpert, 1989). Other research suggests that younger suspects are more likely to be arrested (Sherman, 1980) while elderly offenders are more likely to be treated with leniency (Forsyth, 1993).

Research also indicates that juveniles with "previous police contacts" are more likely to be arrested (Carter, 2006; Terry, 1967; Black & Reiss, 1970; Cicourel, 1976). One can only speculate as to why age would affect an officer's decision. It seems that adults are

perceived to be more credible or that they are in a better position to cause problems for the officer when incorrect enforcement decisions are made. It may also be possible that age is related to the demeanor of those involved; adults may appear to be more cooperative with the police and therefore receive better service or more lenient treatment.

Race. Many studies have examined the effect of race on officers' behavior. While most studies find people of color are likely to be treated more harshly by police than whites (Powell, 1990; Brooks, 2001), one study found that race does not make a difference in the decision to arrest (Klinger, 1996). Despite this single study the vast majority of research indicates that race does influence a police officer's decision to search, ticket, or make an arrest. One recent study of police traffic enforcement decisions based on a review of over 10,000 traffic stops found that a, "drivers' race and gender had a significant effect on officers' decision to search a driver/vehicle and invoke a legal sanction. Africana male drivers were more likely than White drivers to be searched, but were less likely to receive a legal sanction" (Moon & Corley, 2007). This finding could indicate that police are more likely to stop Africana motorists to "fish" for evidence of criminality and, not finding any evidence, more likely to allow them to leave without taking enforcement action. Minorities are more likely to be stopped by the police based on less evidence of a violation than their white counterparts.

The explanations for greater police use of force and race vary. Some contend that disparity in treatment is due to discrimination directed at the individual because of their race (Piliavin & Briar, 1964). Others argue that while Africana citizens are more likely to be arrested or have force used against them, force is governed by factors other than race (Black & Reiss, 1970; Fyfe, 1980; Smith & Visher, 1981).

The racial composition of a community may affect officers' discretion by clouding their perception of acceptable behavior or the potential danger to officers. In predominantly white neighborhoods, officers are viewed as being more punitive toward Africana citizens. In predominantly Africana neighborhoods, they exercise greater discretion but are more punitive toward whites (Powell, 1981). Other research (Bayley

Figure 1.

Arrests, by Offense Charged and Gender
(7,911 agencies; 2005 estimated population 148,665,653)

Offense charged	Number of persons arrested					Percent distribution[1]		
	Total	Male	Female	Percent Male	Percent Female	Total	Male	Female
TOTAL	7,723,696	5,859,492	1,864,204	75.9	24.1	100.0	100.0	100.0
Murder and nonnegligent manslaughter	7,379	6,632	747	89.9	10.1	0.1	0.1	*
Forcible rape	13,193	13,031	162	98.8	1.2	0.2	0.2	*
Robbery	72,073	64,032	8,041	88.8	11.2	0.9	1.1	0.4
Aggravated assault	249,572	196,158	53,414	78.6	21.4	3.2	3.3	2.9
Burglary	159,661	135,844	23,817	85.1	14.9	2.1	2.3	1.3
Larceny-theft	712,539	431,647	280,892	60.6	39.4	9.2	7.4	15.1
Motor vehicle theft	83,941	69,238	14,703	82.5	17.5	1.1	1.2	0.8
Arson	8,358	6,935	1,423	83.0	17.0	0.1	0.1	0.1
Violent crime[2]	342,217	279,853	62,364	81.8	18.2	4.4	4.8	3.3
Property crime[2]	964,499	643,664	320,835	66.7	33.3	12.5	11.0	17.2
Other assaults	710,869	534,579	176,290	75.2	24.8	9.2	9.1	9.5
Forgery and counterfeiting	64,874	39,436	25,438	60.8	39.2	0.8	0.7	1.4
Fraud	120,631	69,497	51,134	57.6	42.4	1.6	1.2	2.7
Embezzlement	10,341	5,099	5,242	49.3	50.7	0.1	0.1	0.3
Stolen property; buying, receiving, possessing	75,620	60,376	15,244	79.8	20.2	1.0	1.0	0.8
Vandalism	160,608	132,695	27,913	82.6	17.4	2.1	2.3	1.5
Weapons; carrying, possessing, etc.	112,585	103,526	9,059	92.0	8.0	1.5	1.8	0.5
Prostitution and commercialized vice	59,411	19,463	39,948	32.8	67.2	0.8	0.3	2.1
Sex offenses (except forcible rape and prostitution)	47,261	42,669	4,592	90.3	9.7	0.6	0.7	0.2
Drug abuse violations	1,025,810	834,053	191,757	81.3	18.7	13.3	14.2	10.3
Gambling	6,969	6,516	453	93.5	6.5	0.1	0.1	*
Offenses against the family and children	42,192	28,338	13,854	67.2	32.8	0.5	0.5	0.7
Driving under the influence	629,620	504,372	125,248	80.1	19.9	8.2	8.6	6.7
Liquor laws	348,779	257,745	91,034	73.9	26.1	4.5	4.4	4.9
Drunkenness	349,468	296,973	52,495	85.0	15.0	4.5	5.1	2.8
Disorderly conduct	430,347	319,765	110,582	74.3	25.7	5.6	5.5	5.9
Vagrancy	20,815	16,674	4,141	80.1	19.9	0.3	0.3	0.2
All other offenses (except traffic)	2,038,271	1,568,194	470,077	76.9	23.1	26.4	26.8	25.2
Suspicion	1,208	944	264	78.1	21.9	*	*	*
Curfew and loitering law violations	99,936	69,720	30,216	69.8	30.2	1.3	1.2	1.6
Runaways	61,365	25,341	36,024	41.3	58.7	0.8	0.4	1.9

[1] Because of rounding, the percentages may not add to 100.0.
[2] Violent crimes are offenses of murder, forcible rape, robbery, and aggravated assault. Property crimes are offenses of burglary, larceny-theft, motor vehicle theft, and arson.
* Less than one-tenth of 1 percent.

& Mendelsohn, 1969) indicates that police officers generally feel they are in greater danger in a minority neighborhood; therefore, they view the residents with suspicion and are likely to react more forcefully to situations.

Regardless of the perceptions of individual officers, research suggests that the way in which police resources are used and deployed can ensure racial disparity in enforcement practices. Beckett, Nyrop, and Pfingst's (2006:129) research on drug enforcement in Seattle found that it is very difficult to explain the over-representation of minority arrests in race-neutral terms. They explain that, "the majority of those who deliver methamphetamine, ecstasy, powder cocaine, and heroin in Seattle are white; blacks are the majority of those who deliver only one drug: crack. Yet, 64 percent of those arrested for delivering one of these five drugs is black. This disparity appears to be the result of three main organizational factors. First, the focus on crack offenders is an important cause of racial disparity in drug arrests. Second, we find that the focus on outdoor drug activity does exacerbate racial disparity, but that blacks are also overrepresented among indoor arrestees. And, third, outdoor drug markets are not treated alike: Predominantly white outdoor drug markets receive far less attention than racially diverse markets located downtown. It thus appears that the geographic concentration of law enforcement resources is a significant cause of racial disparity."

Socio-economic Status. Socio-economic status has been shown to affect the manner in which police respond to requests for service (Black, 1980; Smith & Klein, 1984) and the probability of being arrested (Black, 1971; Reiss, 1971). Those in the middle- or upper-income brackets generally receive more attention from the police when they file a complaint and are less likely to be arrested. Those in the lower socio-economic strata are more likely to receive harsher treatment when encountering officers (Riksheim & Chermak, 1993).

Demeanor. Citizens and offenders who show deference to the police by cooperating are more likely to be treated fairly. When citizens are antagonistic toward officers, their complaints are not taken as seriously and the officer is less likely to initiate formal actions. Most research finds that suspects who are uncooperative are more likely to be arrested than those who are respectful (Piliavin & Briar, 1964; Black & Reiss, 1970; Ericson, 1982) while others claim that demeanor is not a significant factor in the decision to arrest (Klinger, 1994). Despite this later claim the vast majority of research over the past four decades as well as reexaminations of data from older studies finds that demeanor is a substantial factor in police arrest decisions.

Worden and Shepard (1996), for example, reexamined the Police Services Study (PSS) data that included observations of citizen–police encounters from 24 police departments in three metropolitan areas (Rochester, New York; St. Louis, Missouri; and Tampa-St. Petersburg, Florida). The PSS involved observation of citizen demeanor in terms of disrespectful or hostile behavior at several stages of the encounters. Worden and Shepard found that the likelihood of arrest increased when citizens showed disrespectful or hostile demeanors. Likewise Lundman's (1996) examination of previously unpublished data from the Midwest City Police–Citizen Encounters Study concluded that demeanor was an important factor in arrest decisions even when controlling for the type of crime a citizen was suspected of committing. Lundman also noted that although the effects of demeanor varied, other extralegal factors like race and class affected police arrest decisions. The finding of a recent study on police enforcement practices put the issue quite well, police tend "toward strict enforcement of the law when a violation occurred and the offender failed to show appropriate contrition, cooperation, and deference" (Schafer, 2005:270). In essence, the decades of research that finds "citizens who are disrespectful are more likely to be arrested" still holds accurate (Carter, 2006:605).

Gender. Intuitively, one would believe that gender would make a difference in how officers react to complainants and suspects. The research on this issue has achieved mixed results. Some early research indicates that gender has little or no effect on police discretion (Klinger, 1996; Smith & Visher, 1981) while other studies have found that females are less likely to be arrested than their male counterparts especially when they commit crime typically seen as "male" offenses (Sealock & Simpson, 1998). One study of police officers decisions to issue traffic tickets found that females are more likely to receive more lenient treatment by the police than are males (Liu & Cook, 2005).

Situation Variables

Situation variables are the nuances of the interaction between officers and citizens. Situational variables are the context in which officers perform police activities. Research has also examined situation variables that affect the officer's decision-making.

Seriousness of Offense. Almost every study ultimately reaches the conclusion that the single most important factor in officers' decision-making is the seriousness of the offense. "Arrest is more likely for serious offenses than for relatively minor ones. This is an established finding from four decades of research explaining the effect of situational variables on police officers' decisions to arrest" (Carter, 2006:596; Sherman, 1980; Riksheim & Chermak, 1993). Officers can more readily justify ignoring a relatively minor situation, while they feel compelled to take some type of action when a serious crime has been committed (LaFave, 1965; Wilson, 1968; Smith & Visher, 1981). Officers tend to associate importance and success on the job with arrests in serious crimes. Also, there is a general expectation by the public, government, and police officials that officers make arrests in serious crimes. Such expectations do not always exist for less serious crimes.

The decision may be further influenced by factors such as the presence of a weapon or the offender's prior criminal record. The presence of a weapon generally results in officers taking official action. Research indicates that police officers are more likely to initiate formal actions for property crimes than minor crimes against persons. This may result from their belief that property crimes will generate requests from insurance companies for a copy of the report (Ericson, 1982), or that interpersonal crimes are best handled through mediation (Bayley & Mendelsohn, 1969).

Visibility of the event and the presence of others is another consideration. The nature of police work affords officers the opportunity to make decisions that are often concealed from the general public's view. These decisions are often not known of or reviewed by their superiors. Decisions that are not likely to become known afford officers more discretion. The decision to arrest may be guided by the probability of a complaint being filed, the ability to control others at the scene, and the availability of assistance. Officers may be subjected to criticism for either arresting or not arresting someone. Their decision to arrest or release may be influenced by their belief that a particular course of action is the least likely to result in a citizen complaint. In the presence of larger crowds, the officer may feel it necessary to arrest the offender to prevent any further problems. Officers tend to take more official, bureaucratic responses when witnesses are present.

Officer Initiated Actions and Citizen Calls for Assistance. How officers become involved in an event affects their discretion. One would assume that officers have less discretion when summoned by a citizen because they must report the disposition of such complaints to the communications center, but research indicates the contrary. Activities initiated by the police are more likely to result in a formal report or arrest than those initiated by a citizen's complaint (Wilson, 1968; Black, 1971; Reiss, 1971). It seems that officers do not initiate actions unless they have already decided to make an arrest. Another explanation is that there is a large number of citizen calls in which no law has actually been violated.

System Variables

System variables are the idiosyncrasies of the criminal justice system that may influence officers to exercise their discretion for reasons other than those already discussed. Often mentioned as a justification for discretion is the lack of system capacity to arrest, prosecute, and incarcerate every individual who commits a crime. Even beyond the system's capacity is the officer's perception of inequities in the law and the justice system that stem from statutes that are overreaching, ambiguous, obsolete, or are contrary to the community's needs and expectations. For example, Florida increased the penalty for the failure to wear a safety belt and the volume of traffic citations immediately declined. It seems that officers believed that the penalty was too severe and subsequently refused to invoke the criminal justice process.

Community Expectations. The community's expectations and standards will influence an officer's interpretation and application of the law. Some laws are seldom or never enforced. Police officers typically make decisions to enforce the law based on their perceptions of community expectations. Police officers are more tolerant of minor offenses if they believe residents are tolerant. The department size and structure will affect the amount of discretion exercised by individual officers (Mastrofski, Ritti & Hoffmaster, 1987). Officers in large departments have more anonymity and fewer supervisors, and therefore the officers have more latitude in decision-making than do officers in smaller departments that are more tightly controlled. On the other side of the coin, officers who perceive the courts as being too lenient may stack or jack-up the charges against citizens in an effort to secure a more harsh punishment for the offender (Kappeler *et al.*, 1998). Officers have also been known to attempt to "flood" the criminal justice system with tickets or arrests when they are pressured to increase their productivity.

Community Support Agencies. The existence of alternatives to arrest that are departmentally approved will affect the officer's discretionary decisions. In communities that have sufficient social service resources such as mental health facilities or detoxication centers, officers are provided an alternative to arrest that fulfills their order-maintenance role. The existence of these resources may make the officers more willing to intervene in situations that do not warrant an arrest, but nevertheless require that some action be taken. If a detoxification center is readily available, officers are more likely to intervene, relative to those jurisdictions where detoxification centers are not available. The officer may avoid the situation and do nothing unless it escalates to the point at which a serious crime is committed

Departmental Culture. Police departments have unique cultures, creating norms that guide officers' decision-making. Both the formal and informal norms of the department affect an officer's actions. While the formal norms are taught in the police academy, the officer's peers convey informal norms. The peer group can influence subtly or bring direct pressure on an officer

to behave in a certain way (Westley, 1970; Lundman, 1979; Ericson, 1982). By granting or withholding their approval, peers indicate what actions are acceptable (Kappeler *et al.*, 1998). A department's culture, through the creation of norms, places limits on police discretion by identifying activities that are important and not important. Officers often consider these norms when deciding to make an arrest or intervene in a situation.

Community Policing. The philosophy of a police organization or a unit within a police department can affect officers' arrest decisions. An interesting study conducted by Novak, Frank, Smith, and Engel (2002:91) looked at the differences between traditional "beat officers" and "community-oriented policing" (COP) officers and their use of discretion. These researchers found that, "beat officers are more likely to use indicators such as minority status, gender, intoxication, and hostile demeanor when making their decision to arrest." Whereas, "COP officers are less likely to use discriminatory factors (such as race or gender) and signs of nonconformity (including intoxication and hostile demeanor) when making their decisions to arrest ... Furthermore, COP officers are more likely to act on the preferences of the victim or a witness, indicating they are more responsive to the community that they serve."

DISCRETIONARY SITUATIONS IN LAW ENFORCEMENT

While decision-making is required in almost every facet of law enforcement, certain situations are thought to involve more discretion than others. These include domestic violence, vice crimes, hate crimes, and problems encountered with disenfranchised populations. In this section, we will explore these areas and the types of discretionary decisions officers must make.

Domestic Violence

Domestic violence is crime that results in physical harm or threats of harm by one intimate partner against another. "An intimate partner is a current or former spouse, boyfriend, girlfriend or same-sex partner.

Figure 2.

Community-Related Written Policy Directives in Local Police Departments, by Size of Population Served

Population served	Agencies with a written policy directive pertaining to:					
	Citizen complaints	Discretionary arrest powers	Domestic disputes	Homeless persons	Juveniles	Mentally ill persons
All sizes	77%	58%	85%	25%	82%	57%
1,000,000 or more	100%	69%	94%	44%	100%	100%
500,000-999,999	100	92	100	46	100	96
250,000-499,999	100	82	100	42	100	94
100,000-249,999	95	75	95	36	97	83
50,000-99,999	98	70	98	32	97	83
25,000-49,999	96	74	96	33	94	76
10,000-24,999	92	64	96	30	95	72
2,500-9,999	83	64	90	26	87	62
Under 2,500	65	49	76	21	72	43

Violence between intimates includes homicides, rapes, robberies and assaults committed by partners" (BJS, 2006:1). The primary focus, however, has been on spouses because of the high levels of violence in these relationships. On average 30 percent of all women murdered in the United States are murdered by intimates (BJS, 2006; Catalano, 2006). Husbands or boyfriends commit these murders. Every year, about 475,900 women or 5 percent of females in the United States fall victim to violence by intimates (BJS, 2006).

In the past, arrest was the least-used alternative in domestic violence situations. Police officers viewed domestic "quarrels" as private affairs that would in all likelihood only be made worse by official intervention and by processing the parties through the criminal justice system. Victims were viewed as uncooperative, because they often were seen as being reluctant to sign complaints and unwilling to follow through with prosecution if an arrest was made. Many states followed the common law rule that prohibited officers from making a misdemeanor arrest unless they had actually witnessed the crime taking place. This substantially reduced the probability that police officers would take any action whatsoever.

There are a number of factors that influence police officers' decisions to arrest in domestic violence cases.

Buzawa and Buzawa (2003) note there are situational and incident characteristics, victim traits, and suspect traits, which intervene in officer decision-making. Situational and incident characteristics include whether the suspect was present when officers arrived, who called the police (victim or third party), presence of weapons, injuries, and children. Victim traits include victim–offender relationship, victim preference for arrest, drug or alcohol involvement by the victim, and victim's demeanor. Suspects are evaluated in terms of criminal history, relationship with victim, drug or alcohol usage, and demeanor. Police officers often weigh a number of factors when deciding type of intervention into a domestic disturbance.

> You can learn more about domestic violence by contacting the violence against women office of the department of justice at www.usdoj.gov/ovw.

In the late 1970s, citizen groups began a campaign to change the police response to domestic violence. Pointing to the dangers of the recurring cycle of violence that occurs in domestic situations, they sought to limit police discretion and force officers to make arrests. In a nationally publicized incident that resulted

Figure 3.

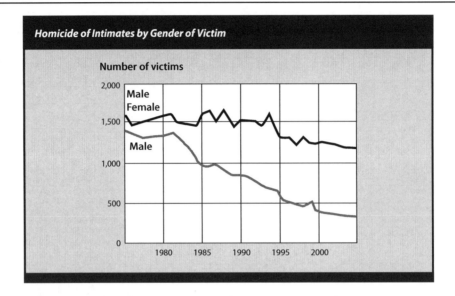

Figure 4.

Violence by Intimate Partners, by Type of Crime and Gender of Victim						
	Intimate partner violence					
	Total		Female		Male	
	Number	Rate per 100,000 persons	Number	Rate per 100,000 persons	Number	Rate per 100,000 persons
Overall violent crime	691,710	3.0	588,490	5.0	103,220	0.9
Rape/sexual assault	41,740	0.2	41,740	0.4	–	–
Robbery	60,630	0.3	44,060	0.4	16,570	0.1
Aggravated assault	117,480	0.5	81,140	0.7	36,350	0.3
Simple assault	471,860	2.1	421,550	3.6	50,310	0.5

Note: The difference in male and female intimate partner victimization rates is significant at the 95%-confidence level within each victimization category presented.
– Based on 10 or fewer sample cases.

in a television movie, Tracey Thurman successfully sued officers of the Torrington, Connecticut, Police Department for failing to protect her from her abusive husband. During a 1983 assault, Thurman received 13 stab wounds and was kicked in the head by her husband, whom she had reported to the police for abuse on several occasions. During the disturbance, police officers stood by and watched as Tracey Thurman was brutally beaten. Subsequently, many other victims have

filed suit against police departments when officers have failed to make an arrest or protect a victim from physical harm.

Support for mandatory intervention strategies was provided by the results of the Minneapolis Domestic Violence Study. For a period of 18 months, officers were required to randomly select one of three options to resolve misdemeanor-level family violence cases: arrest, mediation, or requiring the offender to leave the home for an eight-hour period. Interviews were then conducted with the victims during the six months following the incident to determine if any additional abuse occurred. Those who were not arrested committed almost two times as many subsequent assaults on their victims as did those who were arrested. The study concluded with the finding that arrest alone produced a deterrent effect (Sherman & Berk, 1984). Women's advocates welcomed these findings as vindication of their position (Sherman & Berk, 1989).

Under political pressure from citizens concerned with domestic violence and facing the ever-increasing threat of lawsuits, legislators were quick to enact presumptive or mandatory arrest laws. Relying on the proof of the well-publicized Minneapolis experiment, they legislatively limited officers' discretion in an attempt to reduce domestic violence. States required officers to make arrests when there was evidence of physical violence or abuse. Subsequent studies, which replicated the Minneapolis experiment, were conducted in Omaha, Charlotte, and Milwaukee. Using similar research designs, dramatically different results were reached: making an arrest did not result in fewer subsequent incidents of assault. The danger to the victim is not increased or decreased by an officer's choice to use mediation, to separate the parties, or to arrest the offender (Dunford, Huizinga & Elliott, 1986). Other studies have reached different conclusions.

Dugan (2003) examined the effects of mandatory arrests and found the laws reduced the incidence of domestic violence and reporting of such incidents to the police. Although the incidence of domestic violence declined, the decline may be the result of a decrease in reporting. Moreover, Dugan, Nagin, and Rosenfeld (2003) found that cities with mandatory arrest laws had a higher rate of spousal homicide as compared to cities without such laws. This suggests that mandatory arrest laws may, in some cases, lead to more violent spousal confrontations in the home. Buzawa and Buzawa (2003) note that mandatory arrest laws are flawed, but they are the most effective means of dealing with the problem.

It appears that only about half of the domestic violence cases are reported to the police (Dugan, 2003). Felson, Messner, and Hoskin (2002) have identified factors that encourage and discourage reporting. The factors discouraging reporting are fear of reprisal and a desire to protect the offender. If the police arrest a batterer there certainly will be court costs, fines, and possibly jail time. Victims have a vested interest in protecting their batterer, especially when the loss of time at work is involved. On the other hand, the factors motivating victims to report violence are desire for protection, belief that the violence is not a private matter, and belief that the incident is not trivial. Victims weigh these factors when deciding to call the police, and victims' experience with the batterer and the police will affect their ultimate decision.

While there is sufficient philosophical justification for treating domestic violence as seriously as officers would treat other forms of violence, evidence as to the effectiveness of mandatory arrests in reducing violence is at best uncertain (Felson, Ackerman & Gallagher, 2005). Research also suggests that despite changes in the laws on domestic violence and the political pressure brought on the police to effect arrests, police still have a tendency to differentially enforce domestic violence as compared to non-domestic assaults. Eigenberg, Scarborough, and Kappeler (1996) conducted a study of domestic violence enforcement in a medium-sized, Midwestern police department to determine whether police handled domestic assaults differently from other assaults and to determine what factors affect police decision-making in different kinds of assaults. The researchers examined a random sample of police reports. Results revealed, even when controlling for situational variables, that police officers are less likely to arrest in domestic violence cases than in non-domestic cases. In addition, injuries were about equally likely to be present in cases of arrest for domestic and non-domestic assault, although victims were more likely to experience minor injuries in domestic assaults. Thus, while victims of domestic violence cases are more frequently victims of minor violence, the level of injuries by itself has relatively little to do with arrest in either domestic or non-domestic assaults. It appeared that police officers were more willing to consider domestic assaults as real assaults only when weapons were used. Similar results have been achieved by other researchers who have examined the police handling of domestic violence cases (Fyfe, Klinger & Flavin, 1997).

Finally, there has been criticism of mandatory arrest policies as a result of a significant increase in the number of women being arrested for domestic violence (Chesney-Lind, 2002). Chesney-Lind examined the domestic violence arrests in a number of cities and found that sometimes females accounted for about one-quarter of the arrests. Mandatory arrest laws require officers to make an arrest when there is evidence of physical harm, regardless of gender. When officers had more discretion, they often did not arrest the female. More recent research into this issue examined the effect of expanding police power to make arrests for domestic violence. Simpson, Bouffard and Laura Hickman (2006:312) found that a "legislative initiative to expand police arrest powers positively affected the percent of reported cases that resulted in arrest ... arrest rates increased similarly and significantly for both male and female offenders as a result of the legislative change." Contrary to the researchers' expectations, it did "not appear that expanding police powers to arrest necessarily impacts women more than men. Nor are black women at a greater risk for arrest as a consequence of the legislation than are white women."

VICE CRIMES

Vice refers to criminal activity that is against the public order or public morality, but they are also enacted to curtail the economic benefits of these activities. Vice includes activities such as prostitution, gambling, pornography, the illegal sale of alcoholic beverages, and the trafficking in drugs and narcotics. Such crimes are "victimless," as parties involved in such activities participate willingly. Also, because the activities are consensual, there are no complaints, which substantially complicates their investigation. Vice activities consist of three types of activities: (1) illegal selling of goods or services, (2) illegal consumption of goods or services, or (3) illegal performance (McCaghy & Cernkovich, 1987).

Vice statutes generally are enacted to regulate or control morality. They are seen as instruments by which persons are protected from their own behavior. Sheley (1985) notes that some believe such activities result in spiritual and even bodily harm to those engaging in them. The legislation of vice laws is the result of group conflict in our society. Some groups are more tolerant or condone vice behavior, while others believe that it should be strictly regulated. Generally, the more conservative, religiously fundamental groups are less tolerant of vice activities. However, individuals opposed to vice laws are quick to point out that sin should not necessarily equate with crime (Geis, 1979). The enforcement of vice crimes often depends on which group comes to political power.

The enforcement of vice laws is controversial and problematic for the police. Because there is not a clear consensus in our society about such laws, the police frequently are placed in the untenable situation of enforcing unpopular or unenforceable laws. McCaghy and Cernkovich (1987) identify a number of problems associated with the enforcement of vice laws.

1. The laws are almost unenforceable. The police, when enforcing vice laws, must depend on peripheral individuals or persons who might have been a witness to such an act and were offended as a result of the act. This leads to a very small number of vice activities being reported to the police.
2. There is no uniformity in the manner in which vice laws are enforced. Police officers enforce them as opportunities avail themselves. Enforcement tends to be discriminatory, sporadic, and ineffective.
3. Vice laws encourage illegal activities by police officers. Illegal searches, planted evidence, and entrapment are some of the techniques that officers sometimes employ to enforce vice statutes.
4. Enforcement of vice laws is extremely time-consuming and expensive. Because there seldom are any witnesses or victims, enforcement tactics include undercover operations, payments to informants, and stakeouts. These tactics are labor-intensive relative to investigations of street crimes.
5. Vice laws encourage police corruption. The secrecy and large amounts of money associated with organized crime activities continuously lead to police corruption.

Figure 5.   Estimated Number of Arrests,a by Offense Charged, United States.

Offense Charged	Estimated Number of Arrests[a]
Total[b]	14,004,327
Murder and non-negligent manslaughter	14,004
Forcible rape	26,173
Robbery	109,528
Aggravated assault	440,553
Burglary	294,591
Larceny-theft	1,191,945
Motor vehicle theft	147,732
Arson	15,557
Violent crime[c]	590,258
Property crime[d]	1,649,825
Other assaults	1,285,501
Forgery and counterfeiting	119,410
Fraud	282,884
Embezzlement	17,386
Stolen property; buying, receiving, possessing	129,280
Vandalism	276,543
Weapons; carrying, possessing, etc.	177,330
Prostitution and commercialized vice	90,231
Sex offenses (except forcible rape and prostitution)	91,395
Drug abuse violations	1,745,712
Gambling	10,916
Offenses against family and children	125,955
Driving under the influence	1,432,524
Liquor laws	613,922
Drunkenness	550,795
Disorderly conduct	683,850
Vagrancy	36,082
All other offenses (except traffic)	3,836,877
Suspicion (not included in total)	3,554
Curfew and loitering law violations	138,685
Runaways	118,966

[a] Data are based on all reporting agencies and estimates for unreported areas.

[b] Because of rounding, figures may not add to total. Total does not include suspicion.

[c] Violent crimes are offenses of murder and non-negligent manslaughter, forcible rape, robbery, and aggravated assault.

[d] Property crimes are offenses of burglary, larceny-theft, motor vehicle theft, and arson.

Source: Sourcebook of criminal justice statistics, online at www.albany.edu/sourcebook/pdf/t412004.pdf.

6. Vice laws encourage organized crime. Organized crime groups ranging from the Mafia to rural criminal groups are involved extensively in vice activities because they are lucrative and difficult for the police to investigate.

Vice laws constitute only a small portion of police enforcement activities. For example, as shown in Table 1, vice violations accounted for only a small percent of all arrests, and most of those arrests were for drug violations.

Crimes of vice, prostitution, pornography, gambling, and narcotics have received different levels of attention by society, policymakers, and the police throughout history. Prostitution, often referred to as the "oldest profession," has always been subject to varying levels of interest and enforcement. These efforts are governed by community values and citizen condemnation. The "chicken ranch" of La Grange, Texas—made famous by the Broadway musical, and later the film, *Best Little Whorehouse in Texas*—was depicted as a benign enterprise that existed for decades until thrust into the limelight by an investigative reporter. The public attention generated by the media ultimately forced law enforcement officials to intervene and close its operations. On the other side of the coin, in 1998 investigators learned that at least a dozen New York Police Department officers were involved in protecting a brothel in exchange for free services. Nothing much has changed in the last decade. In 2006, two New York police officers were arrested for accepting sexual favors and free drinks from brothel owners in exchange for protecting their illicit business (Australian, 2006).

Most activities of law enforcement agencies aimed toward sexually-oriented business, however, are not initially based on a complaint from citizens or other governmental agencies and while it is commonly asserted that these types of businesses and activities generate additional crime, some research indicates the contrary. Ruiz (1996) reported findings from a survey of 18 Texas police agencies that regulate sexually-oriented businesses. This research found that sexually-oriented businesses in these jurisdictions ranged from nude dancing to prostitution and the sale of obscenity. None of the police agencies, however, reported that these businesses generated serious crime in the area or in the neighboring community. Likewise, while common sense suggests that police responded to these businesses because of citizens' complaints, the researcher found that the vast majority of law enforcement action was based on officer initiatives.

Prostitution and Human Trafficking

Prostitution, as stated earlier, is often referred to as the world's oldest profession. For example, the term "hooker," which is used to refer to prostitutes, dates back to the Civil War when Union General Joe Hooker employed prostitutes for himself and his army (Winick & Kinsie, 1971). Prostitution traditionally has been an enforcement and order-maintenance problem in most of America's major cities. For the most part, the police have two objectives when dealing with prostitution. First, the police enforce prostitution laws in an effort to control it. The police will never be able to eliminate prostitution, but through enforcement they can attempt to confine it to specific areas or make it less visible to the public. Second, the police are responsible for investigating and preventing crime associated with prostitution.

Traditionally, there are several different types of prostitution. *Streetwalkers* are commonly found in a city's vice or drug district. They work out of alleys, stairwells, cars, and cheap "hot sheet" hotels. They are vulnerable to problems such as diseases, arrests by the police, and physical abuse by customers and pimps. They receive little economic reward for their efforts, and generally are poverty-stricken women who are attempting to exist or support a drug habit. *Bar girls* (b-girls) work in bars, restaurants, and taverns most often with the consent of management. The b-girls attempt to sell patrons expensive, diluted drinks before offering or selling their sexual services. B-girl operations are often found adjacent to military bases and factories. Brothels, or houses of prostitution, are where clients can choose a specific type of sexual service and partner. Many brothels have been replaced by *escort services*, massage parlors, photographic studios, or tanning operations. Using the cover of a legitimate business makes

Figure 6.

Drug and Vice Enforcement Functions of Local Police Departments, by Size of Population Served		
	Percent of agencies with responsibility for the enforcement of:	
Population served	Drug laws	Vice laws
All sizes	88%	51%
1,000,000 or more	100%	100%
500,000-999,999	100	100
250,000-499,999	100	100
100,000-249,999	99	99
50,000-99,999	99	94
25,000-49,999	95	91
10,000-24,999	93	75
2,500-9,999	90	56
Under 2,500	82	33

it more difficult for the police to make arrests and for citizens to recognize that prostitution exists.

Prostitution is a compelling social problem because of the number of underage people engaged in prostitution. Some authors estimate the number of juvenile prostitutes in the U.S. to be between 100,000 and 300,000 (Flowers, 2001). Hagan (1986) estimated that in New York City alone there are 10,000 underage male prostitutes (chicken hawks). Many female prostitutes are underage, and there is a significant clientele that prefers underage prostitutes. Prostitutes often have long histories of sexual and physical abuse by family members often beginning at the age of 10 or 12 (Hotaling & Finkelhor, 1988).

The police have used a variety of tactics to deal with the prostitution problem. They sometimes use reverse stings to arrest clients, or johns. "Reverse prostitution stings, sometimes referred to as operations, crackdowns, John stings and roundups, have been conducted in many urban areas. In Savannah, Georgia a task force headed by Prostitution Czar, Juliette Tolbert began using female decoys and within one week 22 men had been arrested ... The city touted a conviction rate of

95 percent for men apprehended in these stings"(Dodge, Starr-Gimeno & Williams, 2005:3). Another way to control prostitutes is to eliminate their customers. In Aurora, Colorado the city council passed an ordinance allowing police to purchase advertising space in a local newspaper and publish the pictures of arrested johns. In a more controversial program the St. Paul Police Department created a web page that shows the pictures of people arrested for prostitution. Many of these people have yet to be convicted of a crime and the practice raises serious legal issues.

More recently public and police attention has turned toward the *international trafficking of human beings* to service the sex industry. The human trafficking as a social and legal problem in the U.S. can be traced as far back as passage of the *Mann Act* in 1911, which made it illegal to transport women across state lines for purposes of prostitution. Even though, historically local police knew little about human trafficking and paid little attention to it as a local police problem. "In the United States, until the passage of the *Trafficking Victims Protection Act* (TVPA) in 2000, human trafficking was approached as an immigration problem,

Figure 7.

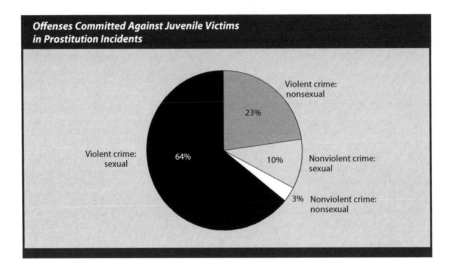

Figure 8.

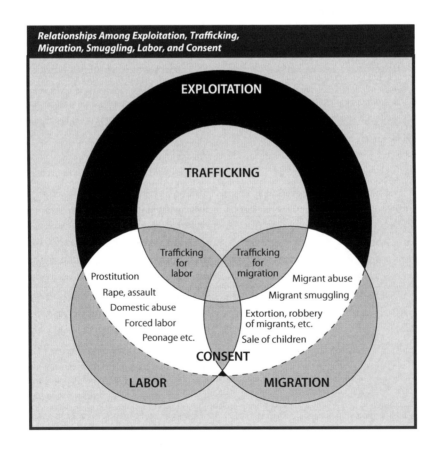

which meant that police viewed trafficking as a federal rather than a local responsibility" (Newman, 2006:1). The *Trafficking Victims Protection Act* defines human trafficking as:

1. Sex trafficking in which a commercial sex act is induced by force, fraud, or coercion, or in which the person induced to perform such an act has not attained 18 years of age.
2. The recruitment, harboring, transportation, provision, or obtaining of a person for labor or services, through the use of force, fraud, or coercion for the purpose of subjection to involuntary servitude, peonage, debt bondage, or slavery.

Wilson, Walsh, and Kleuber (2006:149–50) instruct that, "Trafficking in human beings is a modern form of slavery that is one of the fastest growing forms of crime throughout the world." Estimates are that "700,000–1 million women and children are trafficked each year across the globe, 50,000 of them are imported into the USA. The USA has become a major importer of sex slaves. However, these numbers are only estimates since human trafficking is a hidden transnational commerce that occurs in private homes or under the facade of legitimate businesses." Even though local police are more likely to confront both the victims of human trafficking and the perpetrators of these crimes than are federal law enforcement officials (De Baca & Tisi, 2002), they "are ill prepared to recognize human trafficking victims or investigate this emerging crime problem ... local police agencies view trafficking as a problem 'elsewhere' and for 'other' law enforcement agencies. Consistent with the attitudes that this was not really a local law enforcement problem, the majority of agencies believed that trafficking in human beings is 'best addressed by federal law enforcement'" (Wilson, Walsh & Kleuber, 2006:158). Human trafficking, unlike some views of prostitution, cannot be seem as a victimless crime since most of the workers involved in this trade are forced into the sex industry and many are children.

Pornography

Pornography is a complex law enforcement issue primarily because there are varying levels of public acceptance. In terms of public acceptance, the morals exhibited by the residents of Los Angeles, Las Vegas, or New York City are very likely to be quite different from those of the residents of the Bible belt or cities that have large concentrations of fundamentalist religious groups.

There is little agreement about pornography in most jurisdictions. For example, conservative, fundamentalist groups oppose pornography, while merchants and business people frequently do not oppose it because it attracts business to the community. A 1985 Gallup poll indicated that 60 percent of the people polled favored being able to go to an X-rated movie; 68 percent favored being able to rent X-rated movies; and 53 percent believed that magazines showing sexual relations should not be banned (Newsweek, 1985). The General Social Science Survey shows that less than 38 percent of the public would support making all pornography illegal to all people.

> You can learn more about the issues of free speech by going to the Thomas Jefferson Center for the Protection of Free Expression at http://www.tjcenter.org.

The United States Supreme Court attempted to provide legal guidelines for the regulation of pornography in the case of Miller v. California (1973). The Court opted to leave definitional problems to each local community, declining to even attempt to establish a national standard as to what is obscene. The standard used to enforce obscenity laws is, "that which violates the prevailing norms of the community," which results in substantial discretion and little consistency of enforcement. Specifically, the court established three standards:

1. The average person, applying contemporary community standards, would find the work, taken as a whole, appeals to prurient interests.

Figure 9.

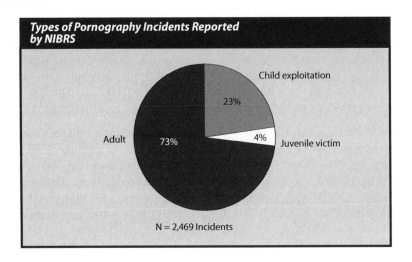

2. The work depicts or describes, in a patently offensive way, sexual conduct specifically defined by the applicable state law.
3. The work, taken as a whole, lacks serious literary, artistic, political, or scientific value.

There is also disagreement over the harmful effects of pornography. In 1970, the *National Commission on Obscenity and Pornography* concluded that exposure to pornography did not cause antisocial behavior and recommended that most anti-pornography laws be eliminated. However, the *Attorney General's Commission on Pornography* (Meese Report) (1986) recommended differently. Although the Commission could not find a direct link between pornography and violent sex offenses, it recommended strict enforcement of obscenity laws, especially in cases where the pornography depicts violence or is degrading to women. It should also be noted that many groups are particularly opposed to pornography because it: (1) subordinates and harms women through sex, (2) portrays women as objects to be controlled by men for their own pleasures, and (3) it not only promotes violence against women, but portrays it as pleasurable and gratifying by both men and women (MacKinnon, 1984).

Although there is general social acceptance of pornography, there is little acceptance of child pornography. Child pornography is the exploitation and abuse

of minors. Affording children legal protection from sexual exploitation is a relatively modern development. "As late as the 1880s in the United States, the age of consent for girls was just 10 years. In 1977, only two states had legislation specifically outlawing the use of children in obscene material. The first federal law concerning child pornography was passed in 1978, and the first laws that specifically referred to computers and child pornography were passed in 1988. Since that time, there has been a steady tightening of child pornography laws" (Wortley, 2006:4) but there has also been a growth in the industry. The kiddy porn industry is estimated at more than $1 billion annually. It is linked to pedophile rings that are involved in making children available for sexual relations with adults. These rings have extensive networks for recruiting young children and delivering a variety of sexual services.

Public attention was brought to the issue of pedophiles recently, when veteran San Francisco police Officer Donald Rene Ramirez was arrested in Phnom Penh for allegedly having sex with a 14-year-old girl. While in jail, the officer reportedly shot himself. According to Gary Delagnes, President of the Police Officers Association, "Everyone knew—absolutely— what he was going over there for … Nothing was ever written up, but they called him on the carpet and told him to knock it off," Delagnes said. "His response was basically, 'It's my time and I can do whatever the hell I want'" (*San Francisco Chronicle*, 2006:B1).

> You can review the Meese Commission Report by going to http://eserver.org/cultronix/califia/meese.

More attention is being paid to the issue of child exploitation especially because of the Internet. Police have also begun using reverse stings to catch would-be child pedophiles over the Internet. In Detroit three men were arrested for soliciting sex from people they thought were teens over the Internet. In one case the operation involved an undercover agent posing as a 13-year-old boy. The officer began talking with suspects on the Internet and when a suspect propositioned the agent to meet him for sex, he was arrested. In another case, a man was arrested for soliciting sex while chatting online with a sheriff's deputy who he thought was a 14-year-old girl. In still another case, a U.S. Secret Service agent, posing as a 13-year-old girl, assigned to the state's Internet Crimes against Children Task Force arrested a man when he solicited sex online and e-mailed adult pornography to the investigators (Angel, 2006).

In perhaps the most widely publicized case, Polk County undercover detectives created fictitious online profiles to catch would-be child pornographers and pedophiles. In the course of their investigations U.S. Department of Homeland Security deputy press secretary Brian J. Doyle was arrested on about two dozen felony charges for having sexually explicit conversations with a person he thought was a 14-year-old girl. "Detectives said Doyle had sexually explicit online and telephone conversations with the undercover detective, whom he contacted after reading the "girl's" profile on the Internet. Doyle sent the undercover detective sexually explicit digital movies and encouraged her to buy a Web camera so she could send graphic images of herself to him, officials said. The Federal Bureau of Investigation's Innocent Images Task Force, meanwhile, made more than 1,300 arrests nationwide in 2004 related to such crimes" (Edwards, 2006).

While the problem of pornography has traditionally been a local issue, federal and state officials aggressively investigate and prosecute those involved in making and distributing child pornography and attempting to sexually exploit children. For example, the United States Customs Service has several offices that attempt to intercept child pornography as it enters the United States, and the United States Postal Service attempts to monitor and prosecute individuals who use the mails to distribute pornography.

Gambling

Gambling includes a wide variety of activities, all of which include the element of chance. Bets or wagers are risked by a player who hopes to win by beating the odds. It is an ambiguous law enforcement issue because many forms of gambling have been legalized in recent years. State-supported gambling includes horse or dog racing, bingo, and lotteries. Nevada has had legalized gambling since 1931 and the first state-supported lottery began in New Hampshire in 1964. While Nevada and Atlantic City were the first to have casino gambling, it is now legal in many states, especially on the Mississippi and Ohio rivers where states have allowed riverboats to operate gambling casinos. Gambling has played an important role in our history. Lotteries helped finance the founding of the American Colonies—money generated from local lotteries was used to fund the Revolutionary War.

Scandals in the administration of state-run lotteries eventually led to their being outlawed, clearing the way for development of illegal number and policy games (Abadinsky, 2006). Although the exact figures are not known, there is a substantial amount of illegal wagering on sporting events and races in the United States (Reuter, 1983). Lower-level illegal gambling also exists, including such activities as craps games, card games, and wagering pools associated with sporting events. Many of these small operations are run out of the backs and basements of bars, barber shops, and restaurants.

Much of the literature on gambling focuses on large-scale operations and makes a connection between it and organized crime. This apparent control of gambling by organized crime—both legal and illegal—often forms the basis for enforcement policies

(Abadinsky, 2006) and legislation (Rose, 2006). "Since Prohibition, the main target of federal anti-gambling laws has been organized crime, which often seems to be beyond the power of state law enforcement" (Rose, 2006:1). The federal government's focus on organized crime was for many years directed at limiting the profits by these groups realized from gambling. Some scholars question whether there is sufficient evidence to believe illegal gambling is controlled by traditional organized crime groups like the Mafia (Reuter, 1983).

With the advent of the "war on drugs," priorities shifted to those groups that were involved in the manufacture, distribution, or sale of controlled substances. Today, even though there has been a renewed interest in gambling because of the Internet, it receives a low priority in most police departments, and no priority whatsoever in many departments. Even with, "thousands of websites taking billions of dollars in wagers each year, fewer than 25 people have ever been prosecuted in the United States for online gambling. Most were bookies who were also taking sports bets by telephone" (Rose, 2006:1). With some form of state-supported gambling existing in most states, few police officers or citizens view it as being harmful, especially in light of the many other problems facing society. Because most gambling offenses are misdemeanors and substantial effort is required to investigate gambling, police departments are not willing to devote the resources necessary to control it.

THE INVESTIGATION OF VICE

The basic investigative techniques required to enforce laws against prostitution, gambling, and narcotics are similar. Each of these crimes requires the use of undercover officers, informants, and wiretapping or surveillance. While the use of wiretaps and physical surveillance may produce some of the most convincing evidence of a crime, they are expensive to conduct and in the case of wiretapping are subject to strict legal requirements and controls. Officers may find themselves in a catch-22 situation. They cannot obtain a wiretap order from the court without sufficient evidence to convince the judge that a crime is being committed.

Without the wiretap, it is impossible to develop the evidence necessary to show that the crime is being committed. Moreover, a number of states do not allow state and local officers to conduct wiretaps, which further complicates the investigation of vice activities. Regardless, police departments frequently spend thousands of dollars to investigate crimes that result in fines of less than $500.

Undercover operations present many problems for the department. Officers are forced to assume a different lifestyle that thrusts them into the criminal subculture where they must do things that would otherwise be illegal. This extracts a heavy price from individual officers who must be separated from family, friends, and other department members for extended periods. They are required to participate in undesirable activities, and officers who remain in undercover positions for too long a period may begin to become corrupt. Even worse, the department can become involved in illegal activities. New York City undercover officers ran a pornographic bookstore as a part of an undercover sting operation. Officers, as a part of their undercover investigation, purchased 1,200 pornographic films and resold them for a considerable profit. After eight months, officers finally arrested several film distributors (*New York Times*, 1977). Furthermore, Langworthy (1989) postulates that some undercover operations cause or result in additional criminal activities. As a result of his analysis of a Birmingham undercover anti-fencing operation, he concluded that the operation caused a substantial amount of crime by creating a market for stolen goods. If the police operation had not existed, no market would have existed and criminals would have stolen less.

Any undercover operation is subject to claims of *entrapment*. While officers can do things that facilitate the commission of a crime, they may not induce someone to commit a crime. Because undercover operations generally may be initiated without prior judicial authorization, the results are subject to strict scrutiny by the court. Allowing police to make discretionary decisions to initiate undercover investigations based on a mere suspicion has been the subject of much criticism (Schoeman, 1986). Recognizing the magnitude of the problem, the FBI now requires that large-scale undercover operations first be reviewed by their *Criminal Undercover Operations Review Committee.*

Informants are particularly helpful and often necessary in the investigation of vice crimes. They are problematic because police must sometimes overlook illegal acts committed by informants in order to pursue their investigations.

Narcotics users or lower-level dealers may be allowed to continue violating the law in order to make cases against their suppliers. In order to move up the distribution network, officers may find it necessary to cooperate with dealers who are selling a significant amount of drugs.

Vice enforcement requires a number of discretionary decisions. Administrative discretion is exercised in determining what activities will be pursued. Operational discretion is exercised in determining who will be targeted for investigation. Because police do not have the resources to investigate every crime, they engage in selective enforcement; they enforce only particular types of violations or target specific types of offenders. The decision-making process for vice crimes is subject to the factors we have previously discussed. The most important criterion for officers is the seriousness of the offense. Most forms of vice, when considered alone, could be viewed as relatively minor crimes. However, under the current political climate, which emphasizes "zero tolerance," possession of even small amounts of drugs is viewed as serious. Officers are therefore much less likely to exercise discretion in their decision to arrest in drug cases.

With the exceptions of drugs and child pornography, officers may come to view enforcement of vice crimes as a waste of time. There is no evidence that their enforcement efforts will have any effect on limiting these activities, and the penalties received for conviction are relatively minor. Officers not specifically assigned to vice control units may be more likely to exercise discretion and not initiate any formal actions, preferring to resolve immediate problems through other means.

POLICING HATE CRIMES

The April 19, 1995 bombing of the federal courthouse in Oklahoma City and again with the terrorist September 11, 2001 attacks on the World Trade Center in New York, the nation was made acutely aware of the existence of hate groups and hate crimes. In the past, the police tended to dismiss the context within which hate crimes occurred. That is, an assault that was the result of a hate crime was viewed simply as an assault. However, in 1990, Congress passed the *Hate Crime Statistics Act,* which forced the police to collect statistics on crimes motivated because of a victim's race, religion, sexual orientation, ethnicity, or national origin. Crimes against persons with disabilities became an element of hate crime statistics with passage of the *Violent Crime and Law Enforcement Act of 1994.* In 1996, the *Church Arson Prevention Act* was signed into law extending data collection to the destruction of churches. Today, about 12,417 law enforcement agencies in 49 states provide information regarding hate crimes to the *Hate Crime Data Collection Program.* Hate crimes are crimes that manifest evidence of prejudice based on certain group characteristics. As such, "hate crimes are not separate, distinct crimes; instead, they are traditional offenses motivated by the offender's bias. An offender, for example, may damage or vandalize property because of his/her bias against the owner's (victim's) race, religion, sexual orientation, ethnicity/ national origin, or disability. ... Because motivation is subjective, it is difficult to know with certainty whether a crime was the result of the offender's bias. Law enforcement investigation is imperative in that it must reveal sufficient evidence as to whether the offender's actions were motivated, in whole or in part, by bias (FBI, 2006:1).

Clearly, Africanas, Jews, and homosexuals are the groups that are targeted most frequently. Many right-wing groups identify each of these groups as enemies. There more than likely will be an increase in the number of bias crimes directed toward Muslims and Arabs as a result of the war on terrorism and the wars in Iraq and Afghanistan.

There are currently more than 800 active hate groups in the United States (Southern Poverty Law

Figure 10.

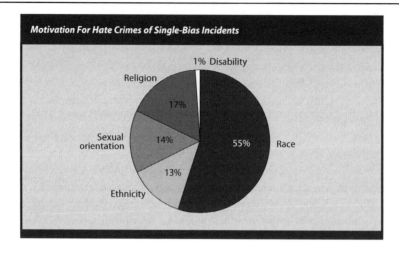

Center, 2007). They include: the American Nazi Party, Arizona Patriots, Aryan brotherhood, Aryan Nations, Christian Defense League,Christian Patriots Defense League, Identity Church Movement, Ku Klux Klan, Posse Comitatus, and skinheads to name a few. In addition, there are more than 200 militias operating in 39 states. Many of these militias have racist ties, while many have neo-Nazi ties (Southern Poverty Law Center, 2007). Almost all of the militias have anti-government tendencies. There are computer bulletin boards and other forms of sophisticated communications that link various groups together. Their goals range from the dissemination of "hate" materials to the coordination and commission of criminal acts against target groups and individuals. Some openly espouse the overthrow of the government.

The rationale for police involvement in hate crimes is that one of their primary roles is the enforcement or reinforcement of community values. Even though a particular hate crime may be relatively minor and unorganized (Martin, 1996), e.g., graffiti, simple assault, or disorderly conduct, it may attack the very fiber of a community. In reality, it may be a much graver offense because it may result in special or unusual effects on the victim or the community as a whole. Hate crimes have a compounding effect that touches a group of people, a neighborhood, or a whole community. They undercut our idea of justice, fairness, and constitutionalism that is the very foundation of our social order. As such, the police must react decisively to hate crimes to ensure that public confidence is maintained and that deterioration of the community does not occur.

The primary law enforcement activity relative to hate crimes is the reporting and documentation of such crimes. If these crimes are not properly reported and documented, authorities cannot successfully mount enforcement actions. The police must exhibit a commitment to eradicate such crimes by thoroughly investigating them. For example, Garofalo (1991) found that 90 percent of the bias crimes in New York City resulted in three or more investigative reports while 76 percent of the non-bias crimes resulted in no reports and only seven percent of the non-bias crimes resulted in three or more investigative reports. Indeed, the New York City Police Department was exerting extra effort in bias cases (Martin, 1996), which hopefully, communicated the department's commitment in such cases to the perpetrators, victims, and community. However, many jurisdictions fail to adequately report and investigate hate crimes (Nolan & Akiyama, 2002), which results in significant under-reporting of the problem. Martin (1995; 1996) investigated determinants of police responses to hate crimes including the types of bias and subjective judgments made by officers. Officers are more likely to make an arrest for crimes against persons than for property crimes, and they are more likely to make an arrest for hate crimes involving sexual orientation and race as compared to

Figure 11.

Bias Motivation in Hate Crimes Known to Police, United States				
Bias Motivation	Incidents	Offenses	Victims[a]	Known offenders[b]
Total	7,163	8,380	8,804	6,804
Race	3,919	4,691	4,895	3,913
Anti-white	828	935	975	963
Anti-black	2,630	3,200	3,322	2,581
Anti-American Indian/Alaskan Native	79	95	97	73
Anti-Asian/Pacific Islander	199	231	240	163
Anti-multi-racial group	183	230	261	133
Ethnicity	944	1,144	1,228	1,115
Anti-Hispanic	522	660	722	691
Anti-other ethnicity/national origin	422	484	506	424
Religion	1,227	1,314	1,405	580
Anti-Jewish	848	900	977	364
Anti-Catholic	58	61	61	22
Anti-Protestant	57	58	58	32
Anti-Islamic	128	146	151	89
Anti-other religious group	93	102	106	54
Anti-multi-religious group	39	42	47	18
Anti-atheism/agnosticism/etc.	4	5	5	1
Sexual orientation	1,017	1,171	1,213	1,138
Anti-male homosexual	621	713	743	715
Anti-female homosexual	155	180	186	146
Anti-homosexual	195	228	233	237
Anti-heterosexual	21	23	23	18
Anti-bisexual	25	27	28	22
Disability	53	53	54	54
Anti-physical	21	21	21	21
Anti-mental	32	32	33	33
Multiple-bias incidents[c]	3	7	9	4

[a] May include persons, businesses, institutions, or society as a whole.

[b] "Known offender" does not imply that the identity of the suspect is known, rather that an attribute of the suspect has been identified, distinguishing him/her from an unknown offender.

[c] A hate-crime incident in which two conditions must be met: more than one offense type must occur in the incident and at least two offense types must be motivated by different biases.

Figure 12.

Bias-Motivated (Hate) Crimes Known to Police, By Offense, United States			
	Offenses	Victims[a]	Known offenders[b]
Total	8,380	8,804	6,804[c]
Crimes against persons	5,317	5,344	5,646
Murder and nonnegligent manslaughter	6	6	17
Forcible rape	3	3	3
Robbery	127	154	289
Aggravated assault	1,062	1,062	1,381
Simple assault	1,566	1,566	1,957
Intimidation	2,539	2,539	1,974
Other[d]	14	14	25
Crimes against property	2,982	3,376	1,391
Burglary	136	165	88
Larceny-theft	221	232	146
Motor vehicle theft	18	19	14
Arson	39	48	32
Destruction/damage/vandalism	2,528	2,869	1,072
Other[d]	40	43	39
Other[d]	81	84	114

[a] May include persons, businesses, institutions, or society as a whole.

[b] "Known offender" does not imply that the identity of the suspect is known, rather that an attribute of the suspect has been identified, distinguishing him/her from an unknown offender.

[c] The actual number of known offenders is 6,804. Some offenders, however, committed more than one offense per incident and are counted more than once. Therefore subcategories will not add to total.

[d] Includes offenses other than those listed that are collected as part of the National Incident-Based Reporting System.

other types of bias. The police tend to exert greater efforts when the crimes are more severe (Wilson & Ruback, 2003).

DISENFRANCHISED POPULATIONS

A large segment of the American population has been disenfranchised from the rest of society because of our political economy and the stigma we attach to these people. This presents a special challenge for the police. *Disenfranchised people* include the mentally ill, public inebriates, drug abusers, and the homeless. Although many of the people in these categories experience homelessness, society tends to deal with them as the "homeless."

The Homeless

The best estimate of the number of homeless people was done by the *National Law Center on Homelessness and Poverty* which found that approximately 3.5 million people, 1.35 million of which are children, will experience homelessness in any given year (National Law

Center on Homelessness and Poverty, 2004; National Coalition for the Homeless, 1996). Estimates also indicated that about 1 percent of the U.S. population experience homelessness each year. The "homeless" are a diverse group of people and do not constitute a single group or a single social problem, treating them as such is an oversimplification. About 39 percent of the homeless are children, 17 percent are single women, and 33 percent are families with children. While almost all homeless people are poor, many are employed. Poverty and a lack of adequate shelter seem to be the only binding thread that unites the people we call homeless.

Lumping all disenfranchised people into a single group is ineffective, deceptive and results in the police having to deal with these problems rather than social service agencies and public programs. For the most part, homelessness, drug abuse, alcoholism, and mental illness are intermingled. The U.S. Conference of Mayors (2005) found that about 30 percent of the adult homeless had an alcohol disorder or drug problem, and 22 percent had severe mental disorders. This becomes a significant problem for the police considering that it is estimated that there are over three million homeless and only about 100,000 shelter beds available to the homeless in the United States (Orr, 1990) and their numbers are currently decreasing (USDHUD, 2004).

You can learn more about the issues associated with the homeless by going to the International Homeless Discussion List at http://homepages.dsu.edu/nelsonj/comp/homepages.htm. This site has more than 450 links on the topic.

Melekian (1990:2) identifies three areas of concern for the police when they encounter the homeless: "(1) conflict over the use of public facilities, (2) public demands for enforcement action against activities that are often only marginally criminal, and (3) the need to provide police service to an economically disenfranchised class of people." Citizens complain about the homeless because they feel threatened by their appearance or annoyed by their panhandling. Merchants request that the police remove them because shoppers refuse to frequent their stores while they are present. Other citizens, however, empathize with the plight of the homeless and demand that the police do not "harass or abuse" them. Regardless, the Santa Monica Police Department found that calls relating to the homeless accounted for 26.9 percent of all police calls. The homeless accounted for 35.4 percent of all bookings in the jail. Santa Monica is probably atypical, but the homeless remain a significant problem for police agencies.

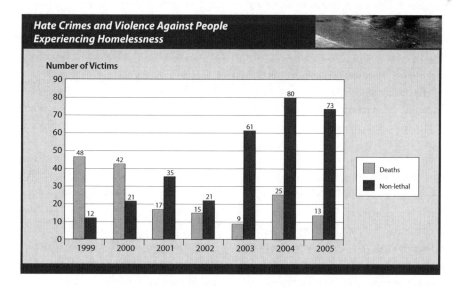

Figure 13.

The Mentally Ill

Persons who are mentally ill account for a significant number of the calls for police service. It has, however, been pointed out that, "mental illness is not, in and of itself, a police problem. Obviously, it is a medical and social services problem. However, a number of the problems caused by or associated with people with mental illness often do become police problems" (Cordner, 2006:1). The problem has grown larger due to the *deinstitutionalization policies* of the 1960s and 1970s, when thousands of mentally ill patients were released from state hospitals, and laws restricting the involuntary commitment of mentally ill people were enacted. Consequently, the police in many instances have become the agency responsible for handling the mentally ill. This is especially true in the lower socio-economic segments of our society. While all socio-economic groups experience mental illness, the poor are most affected by its consequences. These segments of the population do not have access to private care so they call the police to forcibly obtain health care for family members and people who cause them problems. The problem is significant for the police. LaGrange (2000) surveyed one large police department and found that 89 percent of the officers in the department had contact with mentally disoriented persons in the previous year. Cordner (2006:1) reports that seven "percent of police contacts in jurisdictions with 100,000 or more people involve the mentally ill. A three-city study found that 92 percent of patrol officers had at least one encounter with a mentally ill person in crisis in the previous month, and officers averaged six such encounters per month." Police in Lincoln, Nebraska "handled over 1,500 mental health investigation cases in 2002, and spent more time on these cases than on injury traffic accidents, burglaries, or felony assaults. The New York City Police Department responds to about 150,000 'emotionally disturbed persons' calls per year."

Similar difficulties exist with people who are chronic public inebriates. Decriminalization of public intoxication coupled with jail overcrowding has limited the ability of police to do anything with these individuals. In areas where public intoxication is still a crime, many jails do not have room to house them.

They either discourage police from arresting or refuse to admit them to the facility.

There is a general lack of adequate detoxification centers in this country, leaving police with few alternatives. In areas where public intoxication is no longer a crime, these centers are often the only alternative. If facilities are not available, the police generally must allow them to remain on the streets.

Handling disenfranchised persons, particularly those with mental illness, is problematic. For the most part, officers do not receive adequate training on recognizing and handling mentally disturbed citizens. One recent study found that only about half (53.2%) of the officers participating in the study believed they were qualified to handle mentally ill persons (Ruiz & Miller, 2004). Teplin (1988) found that the police tend to use informal dispositions such as calming the person down or taking them home in 72 percent of the cases, while making an arrest in 17 percent of the cases and using a civil commitment in 12 percent of the cases. King and Dunn (2004) identified instances where officers essentially transported disenfranchised persons to another jurisdiction and dumped them, which raises a number of legal and ethical issues. The use of informal dispositions often is the result of a lack of adequate training, inadequate departmental policies, or the absence of community programs and facilities to deal with these individuals.

CONTROLLING POLICE DISCRETION

There has been considerable discussion since the 1960s about use of police discretion and the extent to which it should be controlled. Even today, many departments do not provide formal guidelines to officers in important areas such as the decision to arrest, patrol and investigative procedures, or the use of force. It is impossible to eliminate discretion. Instead, administrators must examine the manner in which discretion can be regulated or controlled.

A number of objections to the unstructured use of discretion are commonly raised by those wishing to control or eliminate it. The police traditionally have been viewed as a ministerial agency responsible for implementing policies established by elected officials or the courts. Use of discretion effectively allows them to form policy or establish the boundaries of legal versus illegal conduct through their decisions. Discretion allows for arbitrary enforcement of the law, which in turn leads to discriminatory practices. The police have a tremendous amount of power that includes the authority to use deadly force. Critics are quick to show that the police have a history of exceeding their authority and abusing citizens (Kappeler et al., 1998).

Equally vocal are those who oppose attempts to restrict the use of discretion. Decision-making is an important and necessary function of the police. Attempts to reform the system should focus not on limiting discretion, but on improving officers' capacity for judgment and teaching them how to make decisions properly. Focusing on the control of police discretion ignores the relationship between the law-enforcement, order-maintenance, and service roles. These roles cannot be compartmentalized into separate activities. Of necessity, they are often performed simultaneously. Each requires some degree of discretion. The decision to approach a particular situation from the law-enforcement, order-maintenance, or service perspective is itself a discretionary decision that cannot be controlled without a great deal of regulation.

Leaving the philosophical arguments aside, it is not possible in a practical sense to eliminate discretion. The question becomes one of how to structure and control the police decision-making process. While both internal and external control mechanisms can be imposed, it is generally conceded that measures designed and implemented by the police are the most effective. Ultimately, the success of any attempt to control police discretion rests on the willingness of officers to comply.

UNDERSTANDING THE NEED FOR CONTROL MECHANISMS

Police officers become involved in situations ranging from where they use bad judgment or indiscretion to where they commit illegal acts. In some cases, the behavior is deliberate, while in other cases it is accidental or unintentional. Internally, supervisors may observe

or otherwise become aware of such activities and take immediate action to correct it. If the transgression is severe enough, a supervisor may initiate formal charges against the officer in question. In other cases, a citizen may observe the behavior, or a citizen may believe that officers treated him or her improperly. Citizens, in some of these cases, lodge formal complaints against the officer with the department. Once such complaints are made, some form of investigation or inquiry usually ensues. Police departments have an obligation to ensure that officer behavior, agency procedures, and actions are reasonable and effective. One aspect of meeting this obligation is allowing citizens a readily accessible process of lodging complaints against the department and its officers. This process must be conducted in a prompt and fair manner to create citizen confidence (USDJ, 2001).

The idea of citizen complaints came to the forefront in March 1991, when America witnessed Los Angeles police officers beat Rodney King on national television. The confrontation between King and police officers remained a top news story for several months. Only recently have departments begun to collect and report statistics regarding inappropriate police behavior. However, Whitaker (1982) found that 13.6 percent of the respondents in his survey felt the police had mistreated them. Only about 30 percent of these people filed complaints with the police department. The New York Civilian Review Board (1990) reported complaint rates ranging from a high of five per 10,000 residents to a low of one per 10,000, depending on the neighborhood. Fyfe and Kane (2005:67) report that in a single year, the Internal Affairs Bureau of the NYPD processed 25,091 complaints against officers, 1,203 of which involved allegations that could have led to criminal charges or terminations.

Internal Control Mechanisms

Police departments must actively establish policies and other guidelines to control officers' behavior. Civil liability and the national move toward departmental accreditation has resulted in many departments comprehensively examining their policies and operating procedures and taking action to ensure that they are consistent with real-world necessity. Policies and procedures not only control what officers do; they also provide guidance when officers are confronted with situations where they need assistance. In the absence of such policies, officers conceivably could do anything they wished to resolve a situation. Such a laissez-faire attitude has resulted in substantial civil liability in the past, especially in areas such as domestic violence, pursuit driving, false arrests, and use of force (Kappeler, 2006). Policies have been used to provide officers direction and reduce departments' liability.

Policies that directly affect the department's ability to detect and correct abuses of discretion or authority include requirements that officers and interested parties who witness abuses should report them. In order to encourage the reporting of police abuses, the U.S. Department of Justice (2001:7–8) recommends that:

1. Law enforcement officers should be required to report misconduct by other officers that they witness or of which they become aware. The failure to report misconduct should be subject to appropriate discipline.
2. Agencies should have in place appropriate protection against retaliation for officers who report misconduct.
3. Law enforcement officers should be required to report to their agency any instance in which they are: arrested or criminally charged for any conduct; named as a party in a civil suit regarding on-duty conduct; or named as a party in a civil suit regarding off-duty conduct where the allegations are related to the officer's ability to perform law enforcement duties (e.g., improper force, fraud, or discrimination).
4. Law enforcement agencies should seek to be notified whenever a court or a prosecutor concludes that an officer engaged in misconduct in the course of criminal investigations or proceedings (e.g., engaged in false testimony or dishonest conduct, or improperly charged an individual with resisting arrest, assault on an officer, or disorderly conduct in an attempt to justify inappropriate use of force).

Simply issuing policy directives is not enough. Departments must also train officers and provide supervisory mechanisms to ensure that the policies are properly communicated and implemented. While the training should begin with recruits in the academy, it is also necessary to continually retrain officers in the field. Agencies must be willing to supervise employees consistently. Many agencies are adopting the EWS (*Early Warning System*) approach to monitor officer's behavior (Alpert, Dunham & Stroshine, 2005; Kappeler et al., 1998). The department keeps track of all complaints, justified or not, to identify officer behavior patterns. When officers begin to accumulate a number of complaints, their entire record is reviewed in an attempt to identify problem areas and provide early assistance. In some cases, the complaints may be an unjustified attempt to have an officer removed from the department. Others may reflect early signs of substance abuse, marital problems, or emotional difficulties that can be addressed if identified early enough. Many EWS collect the following types of information about officers, supervisors, and managers:

1. Information on shootings and use of force;
2. Arrests, traffic stops, searches and seizures;
3. Citizen complaints and commendations;
4. Criminal charges and traffic violations;
5. Lawsuits against officers;
6. Misconduct allegations;
7. Disciplinary actions and remedial actions;
8. Training and job performance history;
9. On-duty traffic accidents; and,
10. Use and abuse of sick leave (U.S. Department of Justice, 2001).

Brandl, Stroshine, and Frank (2001) investigated the characteristics of officers who most frequently receive complaints and found that numbers of arrests, officer age, and officer gender differentiated officers with high numbers of complaints. Females receive fewer complaints, probably because they tend to use reason and dialog in confrontational situations. They often are less threatening to citizens. One explanation for why younger officers receive more complaints is that they generally are more active, making larger numbers of stops and arrests. They also are more likely to use force relative to older officers.

Perhaps the most effective *internal control* a police department can use to ensure that officers are not abusing their discretion or authority is the development of an adequate process for the investigation of citizens' complaints. McCluskey and Terrill's (2005:525) research into citizens' complaints and actual police behavior on the streets shed light on the importance of using complaints to predict behavior. Their research suggests "knowing that officers with a greater number of discourtesy complaints are also more inclined to use higher levels of force may change the dynamic of how these types of complaints are perceived by administrators. In other words, such complaints may offer a warning sign that simple verbal disrespect leads to coercion, and more severe forms of it." The investigation of citizens' complaints against the police is usually handled by the Internal Affairs Unit of the police department. In this process citizens should be provided the opportunity to have a full and fair investigation into their grievance against the officer or department. The U.S. Department of Justice (2001:7) recommends that:

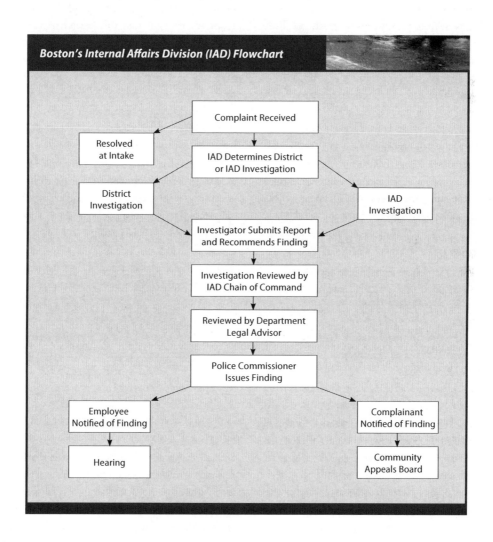

Figure 14.

1. Civilians should be allowed to file complaints in person, by mail, by telephone, by facsimile transmission, or, where possible, by e-mail. A complaint form should be offered, but completion of the form should not be required to initiate a complaint. Individuals should be able to obtain and file complaint forms at places other than law enforcement agencies.

2. Officers and other employees should be prohibited from refusing to accept complaints, or attempting to dissuade a civilian from filing a complaint. Civilians should not be required to meet with or speak with a supervisory officer as a requirement for filing a complaint.

3. Complaints should be accepted from all individuals, including those who request anonymity. Complaints should be accepted from third parties to ensure that witnesses of abuse or misconduct, as well as victims of such misconduct, can file complaints.

Through a process of policy formation, training, and adequate supervision, departments can begin to restrict and control discretionary decision-making. Although it is generally conceded that the most effective methods of controlling police behavior are those imposed by the police themselves, internal control alone is insufficient. It is necessary to utilize external methods of control as a way to ensure proper police conduct.

External Control Mechanisms

Unlike internal control mechanisms that reflect an attempt by the police to address inappropriate behavior, *external control* mechanisms are imposed on the department by other agencies or individuals who may or may not have an understanding of the police role and functions. This control can be achieved through civilian review boards, legislative oversight, or through the court system.

Control by the Citizens

External control of policing is usually associated with civilian review boards (CRBs). Many were created as

a result of community outrage over police misconduct in the 1960s. *Civilian review boards* were created to (1) maintain effective discipline of the police, (2) provide satisfactory resolution of citizen complaints against officers, (3) maintain citizen confidence in the police, and (4) influence police administrators by providing feedback from citizens (Maguire, 1991:186). In terms of functioning, they can assume several roles: oversight, rule making, investigative, and judicial. Walker and Bumphus (1992) have identified three distinct types of CRBs in their survey of the nation's 50 largest cities: (1) where fact finding is performed by civilians, (2) where fact finding is performed by sworn officers, but dispositional recommendations are made by civilians, and (3) where fact finding and dispositional recommendations are made by civilians to civilians who have ultimate authority over the final disposition. The most controversial CRBs are the ones that have a measure of judicial or dispositional power over police officer wrongdoing. Almost from their inception review boards were resented by the police, who viewed them as an unwarranted intrusion. Many officers believed that they reflected a lack of trust on the part of the public and did little to improve police-community relations. Police officers saw the majority of complaints as coming from citizens who were the recipients of police actions and feared that citizen review boards would be used as a method of retaliation against them (Goldstein, 1977). Research, however, indicates that CRBs are no more punitive than internal police boards when determining guilt or meting out sentences (Walker & Bumphus, 1992).

Many of the CRBs have been ineffective and have met with failure. They had no effective power. Many served in an advisory capacity with few resources.

The experience of the Oakland Police Department is illustrative of difficulties faced by these boards (Skolnick & Bayley, 1986). In response to widespread criticism of the police department, a citizen review board was formed. Although charged with investigating citizen complaints, the board was provided with almost no investigative resources. Officers could not be compelled to appear before the board, which substantially hampered the board's investigative powers. The police viewed the board as nothing more than a public relations tool that had to be tolerated. The city manager routinely failed to uphold findings of the board, citing a lack of evidence in the cases he reviewed. The board essentially could do little to control police behavior.

The number of cities utilizing CRBs is increasing, and today, more than two-thirds of the 50 largest cities have CRBs (Walker & Bumphus, 1992). It should be noted that not all of the CRBs have met with failure, and there are many that are performing effectively and the increase in their number is indicative that legislative bodies have found them to be effective.

Legislative Control

The legislative branch of government can affect the exercise of discretion in three ways: (1) enactment of laws, (2) allocation of funds, and (3) legislative oversight. Legislators can decrease an officer's discretion by writing laws clearly. When statutes are written in broad terms, they are subject to diverse interpretation, which creates more room for discretion. In recent years, legislators have enacted laws that restrict or eliminate an officer's discretion to arrest under certain circumstances. A number of states now require officers to make an arrest in domestic violence situations. Missouri's law governing protective orders issued by the court to prevent domestic violence (Mo. Rev. Stat., 1989) is illustrative of legislative attempts to control discretion. A court order may be issued to prevent an abuser from returning to the residence or engaging in further acts of abuse or harassment. When called to a disturbance, the law gives officers the authority to make arrests, even if they did not witness the offense. If they do not arrest the offending person, they must submit a written report that details their reasons. When a second call is received at the residence within 12 hours, the officers must make an arrest if there is probable cause and they can determine who is the "primary aggressor."

The law seeks to limit officers' discretion and to impose reporting requirements so that their actions can be reviewed. One of the difficulties with legislative attempts to limit discretion is the manner in which the law is written. In our example above, there is another paragraph in the law that stipulates that officers must

make arrests whenever an act of abuse occurs. Some argue that this completely removes an officer's discretion, while others maintain that they have limited discretion under the "12-hour rule." Determining whom the "primary aggressor" is, and whether there is probable cause are, in themselves, discretionary decisions.

Through the budgetary process, the legislature can control expenditure of funds, thereby establishing priorities for law enforcement. Specific instructions in the law as to which programs are to be initiated can effectively limit administrative discretion that would otherwise be permissible. Legislative oversight as a method to control discretion has not been the subject of much research. While it is common for the federal government to hold oversight hearings, some states also use this process. Legislative committees are given the authority to review the activities of government agencies. This review process is designed to ensure operational efficiency and integrity. The relative power of the committee to affect the overall operation of an agency will determine whether this method of oversight is effective.

Control by the Courts

The courts are perhaps the most visible bodies of external control over discretion exercised by the police. While appellate courts are responsible for determining the constitutionality of a law, they also have the authority to govern procedural aspects of the law and to limit the manner in which it is enforced by the police. One difficulty that arises in the court's attempt to control discretion is the manner in which cases are reviewed and in which the decisions are reported. Courts will normally take the narrowest approach possible when deciding an issue. The written decisions are often lengthy and difficult to understand, leaving room for various interpretations. Seldom does the court tell police specifically what they may or may not do. One notable exception is the now famous Miranda v. Arizona (1966) decision. In this case, the United States Supreme Court specifically set forth the steps that must be taken and the language that must be used to advise a suspect of his or her constitutional privilege against self-incrimination.

The criminal courts are generally restricted to dismissing cases or refusing to admit evidence as remedies for inappropriate exercise of discretion. Civil courts have the option of issuing a writ of mandamus to require agencies to do particular things, or issuing injunctions that prohibit them from committing certain acts. Officers and departments that make inappropriate decisions are subject to lawsuits, which can require the payment of enormous damage claims (Kappeler, 2006). With the proliferation of lawsuits against police, agencies are likely to take additional steps to define the boundaries of discretionary decisions in an attempt to limit their civil liability.

SUMMARY

Discretionary enforcement allows officers to make decisions as to what course of action will produce the most desirable outcome in a given situation. Properly used, discretion can be a positive aspect of the criminal justice system. When used improperly, it results in actions that are discriminatory, unethical, or illegal.

Use of discretion by administrators is implicit in the bureaucratic structure of police agencies. Through their discretionary function administrators are expected to develop policies and procedures that are translated into uniform activities by street-level officers. Operational personnel typically exercise more discretion. This is felt to be problematic because these are generally the officers with the least amount of training and experience. Many factors influence an officer's decision-making process. Research consistently shows the primary factor in the decision to formally process a case is the seriousness of the offense.

While decision-making is required in almost every area of law enforcement, certain situations more readily lend themselves to discretionary decisions—particularly domestic violence and vice crimes. In recent years, attempts have been made to structure and control the use of discretion by police. While no one seriously proposes eliminating discretion, most feel it should be structured so as to limit its harmful effects. Discretion can be controlled internally by the department through development of policies, procedures, training, and supervision. External controls may be imposed by citizen review boards, the legislature or the courts. Of these methods, internal controls are thought to be the most effective. In the final analysis, any attempt to control an officer's discretion rests on the willingness of the officer to comply. For most activities in law enforcement, there are no effective limits on officers' behavior other than those imposed by the officers themselves.

REFERENCES

Abadinsky, H. (2006). *Organized Crime*, Eighth Edition. New York, NY: Wadsworth/Thomson.

Alpert, G.P., Dunham, R.G., and M.S. Stroshine (2005). *Policing Continuity and Change*. Prospect Heights, IL: Waveland.

Alpert, G.P. and R.G. Dunham (1990). *Police Pursuit Driving: Controlling Responses to Emergency Situations*. Westport, CT: Greenwood Press.

American Friends Service Committee (1971). *Struggle for Justice*. New York, NY: Hill & Wang.

Angel, C. (2006). "3 men arrested in Web stings." *Detroit Free Press*, November 16, 2006.

Attorney General's Commission on Pornography (1986). *Task Force*. Washington, DC: U.S. Government Printing Office.

Australian (2006). "Cops' Free Sex for Shielding Brothels." *Australian*, March 11, 2006.

Bayley, D.H. and H. Mendelsohn (1969). *Minorities and the Police*. New York, NY: The Free Press.

Beckett, K., Nyrop, K. and L. Pfingst (2006). "Race, Drugs, and Policing: Understanding Disparities in Drug Delivery Arrests." *Criminology*, 44(1):105–137.

Black, D. (1980). *The Manners and Customs of the Police*. New York, NY: Academic Press.

Black, D. (1971). "The Social Organization of Arrest." *Stanford Law Review*, 23:1087–1111.

Black, D. and A. Reiss (1970). "Police Control of Juveniles." *American Sociological Review*, 35:63–77.

Brandl, S., M. Stroshine, and J. Frank (2001). "Who Are the Complaint-Prone Officers? An Examination of the Relationship between Police Officers' Attributes, Arrest Activity, and Assignment." *Journal of Criminal Justice*, 29(6):521–529.

Brooks, L. (2001). "Police Discretionary Behavior: A Study of Style." In R. Dunham & G. Alpert (ed.) *Critical Issues in Policing*, pp. 117–131. Prospect Heights, IL: Waveland.

Bureau of Justice Statistics (2006). *Intimate Partner Violence Declined Between 1993 and 2004*. Washington, DC: U.S. Department of Justice, Bureau of Justice Statistics.

Buzawa, E. and C. Buzawa (2003). *Domestic Violence*. Thousand Oaks, CA: Sage.

Carter, T. J. (2006). "Police Use of Discretion: A Participant Observation Study of Game Wardens." *Deviant Behavior*, 27:591–627.

Catalano, S. (2006). *Intimate Partner Violence in the United States*. Washington, DC: U.S. Department of Justice, Bureau of Justice Statistics.

Chesney-Lind, M. (2002). "Criminalizing Victimization: The Unintended Consequences of Pro-Arrest Policies for Girls and Women." *Criminology and Public Policy*, 2(1):81–90.

Cicourel, A. (1976). *The Social Organization of Juvenile Justice*. New York: John Wiley and Sons.

Cordner, G. (2006). "People with Mental Illness." *Problem-Oriented Guides for Police Problem-Specific Guides Series No. 40*. Washington, DC: U.S. Department of Justice, Office of Community Oriented Policing Services.

Davis, K.C. (1969). *Discretionary Justice: A Preliminary Inquiry*. Westport, CT: Greenwood Press.

De Baca, L. and A. Tisi (2002). "Working Together to Stop Modern-Day Slavery." *The Police Chief*, 78–80.

Dodge, M., D. Starr-Gimeno, and T. Williams (2005). "Puttin' on the Sting: Women Police Officers' Perspectives on Reverse Prostitution Assignments." *International Journal of Police Science and Management*, 7(2):71–85.

Dugan, L. (2003). "Domestic Violence Legislation: Exploring It's Impact on the Likelihood of Domestic Violence, Police Involvement and Arrest." *Criminology and Public Policy*, 2(2):283–312.

Dugan, L., D. Nagin, and R. Rosenfeld (2003). "Exposure Reduction or Retaliation? The Effects of Domestic Violence Resources on Intimate Partner Homicide." *Law and Society Review*.

Dunford, F.W., D. Huizinga, and D.S. Elliott (1986). "The Role of Arrest in Domestic Assault: The Omaha Police Experiment." *Criminology*, 28(2):183–206.

Dunham, R.G. and G.P. Alpert (1989). *Critical Issues in Policing: Contemporary Readings*, pp. 135–136. Prospect Heights, IL: Waveland Press.

Edwards, A.L. (2006). "Polk Takes Lead on Computer Crimes: Detectives Create Online Fictitious Profiles in a Search for Child Pornographers and Others Breaking the Law." *Orlando Sentinel*, April 9, 2006.

Eigenberg, H.M., K.E. Scarborough, and V.E. Kappeler (1996). "Contributory Factors Affecting Arrest in Domestic and Non-Domestic Assaults." *American Journal of Police*, 15(4):27–54.

Ericson, R. (1982). *Reproducing Order: A Study of Police Patrol Work*. Toronto, CN: University of Toronto Press.

Felson, R.B., Ackerman, J.M. and C.A. Gallagher (2005). "Police Intervention and the Repeat of Domestic Assault." *Criminology*, 43(3):563–588.

Felson, R., S. Messner, and A. Hoskin (2002). "Reasons for Reporting and Not Reporting Domestic Violence to the Police." *Criminology*, 40(3):617–648.

Flowers, R.B. (2001). *Runaway Kids and Teenage Prostitution: America's Lost, Abandoned and Sexually Exploited Children.* Westport, CT: Praeger/Greenwood.

Forsyth, C.J. (1993). "Factors Influencing Game Wardens in Their Interaction with Poachers: The Use of Discretion." *Free Inquiry in Creative Sociology*, 211:51.

Fyfe, J.J. (1980). "Geographic Correlates of Police Shootings: A Microanalysis." *Crime & Delinquency*, 17:101–113.

Fyfe, J.J. (1979). "Administrative Interventions on Police Shooting Discretion: An Empirical Examination." *Journal of Criminal Justice*, 7:309–324.

Fyfe, J.J., D.A. Klinger, and J.M. Flavin (1997). "Differential Police Treatment of Male-on-Female Spousal Violence." *Criminology*, 35(3):455–473.

Fyfe, J.J. and R. Kane (2005). *Bad Cops: A Study of Career-Ending Misconduct among New York City Police Officers.* Unpublished: Final Version Submitted to the United States Department of Justice, National Institute of Justice February 2005.

Garofalo, J. (1991). "Racially Motivated Crimes in New York City." In M. Lynch and E. Patterson (eds.) *Race and Criminal Justice.* New York, NY: Harrow and Heston.

Garofalo, J. and S. Martin (1991). "The Law Enforcement Response to Bias-Motivated Crimes." In R. Kelly (ed.) *Bias Crime: American Law Enforcement and Legal Responses.* Chicago, IL: University of Illinois at Chicago.

Geis, G. (1979). *Not the Law's Business.* New York, NY: Schocken Books.

Goldstein, H. (1977). *Policing a Free Society.* Cambridge, MA: Ballinger Publishing Company.

Guyot, D. (1991). *Policing as though People Matter.* Philadelphia, PA: Temple University Press.

Hagan, J. (1986). *Introduction to Criminology: Theories, Methods, and Criminal Behavior.* Chicago, IL: Nelson-Hall.

Hotaling, G. and D. Finkelhor (1988). *The Sexual Exploitation of Missing Children.* Washington, DC: U.S. Government Printing Office.

Hurst, J. (May 26, 1977). "Children–Big Profit Item for the Smut Peddlers." *Los Angeles Times.*

Kappeler, V.E. (2006). *Critical Issues in Police Civil Liability*, Fourth Edition. Prospect Heights, IL: Waveland Press.

Kappeler, V.E. and G.W. Potter (2005). *The Mythology of Crime and Criminal Justice*, Fourth Edition. Prospect Heights, IL: Waveland Press.

Kappeler, V.E., R. Sluder, and G.P. Alpert (1998). *Forces of Deviance: Understanding the Dark Side of Policing*, Second Edition. Prospect Heights, IL: Waveland Press.

King, W. and T. Dunn (2004). "Police-Initiated Transjurisdictional Transport of Troublesome People." *Police Quarterly*, 7(3):339–358.

Klinger, D.A. (1996). "Demeanor or Crime? Why 'Hostile' Citizens Are More Likely to Be Arrested." *Criminology*, 32:475–493.

LaFave, W. (1965). *The Decision to Take a Suspect into Custody.* Boston, MA: Little, Brown and Company.

LaGrange, T. (2000) "Distinguishing between the Criminal and the 'Crazy': Decisions to Arrest in Police Encounters with Mentally Disordered." *Paper presented at the American Society of Criminology,* San Francisco.

Langworthy, R. (1989). "Do Stings Control Crime? An Evaluation of a Police Fencing Operation." *Justice Quarterly,* 6:28–45.

Lehman, A.F. and D.S. Cordray (1993). "Prevalence of Alcohol, Drug, and Mental Disorders among the Homeless." *Contemporary Drug Problems,* 20(3):355–383.

Liu, P.W. and T.A. Cook (2005). "Speeding Violation Dispositions in Relation to Police Officers' Perception of the Offenders." *Policing & Society,* 15(1):83–88.

Lundman, R. (1979). "Organizational Norms and Police Discretion: An Observational Study of Police Work with Traffic Violators." *Criminology,* 17:159–171.

Lundman, R.J. (1996). "Demeanor and Arrest: Additional Evidence from Previously Unpublished Data." *Journal of Research in Crime and Delinquency,* 33(3):306–323.

MacKinnon, C.A. (1984). "Not a Moral Issue." *Yale Law and Policy Review,* 2:321–345.

Maguire, M. (1991). "Complaints against the Police: The British Experience." In A. Goldsmith (ed.) *Complaints Against the Police: The Trend to External Review.* Oxford, England: Clarendon Press.

Martin, S.E. (1996). "Investigating Hate Crimes: Case Characteristics and Law Enforcement Responses." *Justice Quarterly,* 13(3):27–49.

Martin, S.E. (1995). "A Cross-Burning Is Not Just an Arson: Police Social Construction of Hate Crimes in Baltimore County." *Criminology,* 33(3):303–326.

Mastrofski, S., R. Ritti, and D. Hoffmaster (1987). "Organizational Determinants of Police Discretion: The Case of Drinking and Driving." *Journal of Criminal Justice,* 15:387–401.

McCaghy, M.C. and S.A. Cernkovich (1987). *Crime in American Society.* New York, NY: Macmillan.

McCluskey, J.D. and W. Terrill (2005). "Departmental and citizen complaints as predictors of police coercion." *Policing: An International Journal of Police Strategies & Management,* 28(3):513–529.

Melekian, B. (1990). "Police and the Homeless." *FBI Law Enforcement Bulletin,* 59(7):1–7.

Miller v. California, 413 U.S. 15 (1973).

Miranda v. Arizona, 384 U.S. 436 (1966).

Missouri Revised Statute § 455.085 (1989).

Moon, B. and C. Corley (2007). "Driving across Campus: Assessing the Impact of Drivers' Race and Gender on Police Traffic Enforcement Actions." *Journal of Criminal Justice,* 35(1):29–37.

Muir, W. (1977). *Police: Streetcorner Politicians.* Chicago, IL: University of Chicago Press.

National Coalition for the Homeless (2006). *How Many People Experience Homelessness?* Washington, DC: National Coalition for the Homeless.

Nation Coalition for the Homeless (2006). *Hate, Violence, and Death on Main Street USA.* Washington, DC: National Coalition for the Homeless.

New York Civilian Complaint Review Board (1990). *Annual Report.* Author.

Newsweek (1985). "*The War against Pornography*." March 18, 58–67.

New York Times (Jan. 6, 1977). "*Police Sell Porn*." Author.

Newman, G.R. (2006). "The Exploitation of Trafficked Women." *Problem-Specific Guides Series Guide No. 38.* U.S. Department of Justice: Office of Community Oriented Policing Services.

Nolan, J. and Y. Akiyama (2002). "Assessing the Climate for Hate-Crime Reporting in Law Enforcement Organizations: A Force-Field Analysis." *Justice Professional*, 15(2):87–103.

Novak, K. J., James F., Smith, B. W. and R.S. Engel (2002). "Revisiting the Decision to Arrest: Comparing Beat and Community Officers." *Crime & Delinquency*, 48:70.

Orr, L. (1990). *The Homeless: Opposing Viewpoints*. San Diego, CA: Greenhaven Press.

Packer, H. (1968). *The Limits of the Criminal Sanction*. Stanford, CA: Stanford University Press.

Piliavin, I. and S. Briar (1964). "Police Encounters with Juveniles." *American Journal of Sociology*, 70:206–214.

Powell, D. (1990). "A Study of Police Discretion in Six Southern Cities." *Journal of Police Science and Administration*, 17:1–7.

Powell, D. (1981). "Race, Rank, and Police Discretion." *Journal of Police Science and Administration*, 9:383–389.

Reiss, A. (1971). *The Police and the Public*. New Haven, CT: Yale University Press.

Rennison, C. (2001). "Intimate Partner Violence and Age of Victim, 1993–1999." *Bureau of Justice Statistics Special Report*. Washington, DC: U.S. Department of Justice.

Reuter, P. (1983). *Disorganized Crime*. Cambridge, MA: The MIT Press.

Riksheim, E. and S. Chermak (1993). "Causes of Police Behavior Revisited." *Journal of Criminal Justice*, 21:353–382.

Rose, N. (2006). "Gambling and the Law: An Introduction to the Law of Internet Gambling." *UNLV Gaming Research & Review Journal*, 10(1):1–14.

Ruiz, J. (1996). "Regulation of Sexually Oriented Businesses." *TELEMASP Bulletin*, 3(4):1–11.

Ruiz, J. and C. Miller (2004). "An Exploratory Study of Pennsylvania Police Officers' Perceptions of Anger-ousness and Their Ability to Manage Persons with Mental Illness." *Police Quarterly*, 7(3):359–371.

San Francisco Chronicle (2006). "Within SFPD, little surprise over allegations that officer visited Asia for sex with children." *San Francisco Chronicle*, November 5, 2006, B1.

Schoeman, F. (1986). "Undercover Operations: Some Moral Questions." *Criminal Justice Ethics*, 5(2):16–22.

Sealock, M.D. and S.S. Simpson (1998). "Unraveling Bias in Arrest Decisions: The Role of Juvenile Offender Type-Scripts." *Justice Quarterly*, 15:427.

Schafer, J.A. (2005). "Negotiating Order in the Policing Of Youth Drinking." *Police Strategies & Management*, 28(2):279–300.

Sheley, J.F. (1985). *America's Crime Problem*. Belmont, CA: Wadsworth.

Sherman, L. (1980). "Causes of Police Behavior: The Current State of Quantitative Research." *Journal of Research in Crime and Delinquency*, 17:69–100.

Sherman, L.W. and R.A. Berk (1989). "The Impact of Research on Legal Policy: The Minneapolis Domestic Violence Experiment." *Law and Society Review*, 23:117–144.

Sherman, L.W. and R.A. Berk (1984). "The Specific Deterrent Effect of Arrest for Domestic Assault." *American Sociological Review*, 49(2):261–272.

Simpson, S.S., L.A. Bouffard, J. Garner, and L. Hickman (2006). "The Influence of Legal Reform on the Probability of Arrest in Domestic Violence Cases." *Justice Quarterly*, 23(3):297–316.

Skolnick, J.H. (1994). *Justice without Trial: Law Enforcement in a Democratic Society*, Third Edition. New York, NY: Macmillan.

Skolnick, J.H. and D.H. Bayley (1986). *The New Blue Line: Police Innovations in Six American Cities*. New York, NY: The Free Press.

Smith, D.A. and J. Klein (1984). "Police Control of Interpersonal Disputes." *Social Problems*, 31(4):468–481.

Smith, D.A. and C. Visher (1981). "Street Level Justice: Situational Determinants of Police Arrest Decisions." *Social Problems*, 29:167–178.

Southern Poverty Law Center (2007). "Active U.S. Hate Groups in 2005." *Intelligence Project*.

Southern Poverty Law Center (1995). "Over 200 Militias and Support Groups Operate Nationwide." *Klan Watch Intelligence Report*, #78.

Teplin, L.A. (1986). *Keeping the Peace: The Parameters of Police Discretion in Relation to the Mentally Disordered*. Washington, DC: National Institute of Justice.

Terry, R. (1967). "Discrimination in the Handling of Juvenile Offenders by Social Control Agencies." *Journal of Research in Crime and Delinquency*, 4:218.

Turque, B. and J. Stoffel (1989). "Fury over an Unholy Alliance: How Cleveland Cops Teamed Up with a Drug Dealer." *Newsweek*, 113(May 8):26.

U.S. Department of Housing and Urban Development (2004). *Strategies for Reducing Chronic Street Homelessness*. Washington, DC: Office of Policy Development and Research.

U.S. Department of Justice (2001). *Principles for Promoting Police Integrity: Examples of Promising Practices and Policies*. Washington, DC: U.S. Government Printing Office.

Walker, S. (1993). *Taming the System*. New York, NY: Oxford.

Walker, S. and V. Bumphus (1992). "The Effectiveness of Civilian Review: Observations on Recent Trends and New Issues Regarding the Civilian Review of the Police." *American Journal of Police*, 11:1–26.

Westley, W. (1970). *Violence and the Police: A Sociological Study of Law, Custom, and Morality*. Cambridge, MA: MIT Press.

Whitaker, G. (1982). *Basic Issues in Policing*. Washington, DC: U.S. Government Printing Office.

Wilson, D.G., Walsh, W. F. and S. Kleuber (2006). "Trafficking in Human Beings: Training and Services among US Law Enforcement Agencies." *Police Practice and Research*, 7(2):149–160.

Wilson, J.Q. (1968). *Varieties of Police Behavior*. Cambridge, MA: Harvard University Press.

Winick, C. and P.M. Kinsie (1971). *The Lively Commerce: Prostitution in the U.S.* Chicago, IL: Quadrangle Books.

Worden, R.E. and R.L. Shepard (1996). "Demeanor, Crime, and Police Behavior: A Reexamination of the Police Services Study Data." *Criminology*, 34(1):83–105.

Wortley, R. (2006). "Child Pornography on the Internet." *Problem-Oriented Guides for Police Problem-Specific Guides Series No. 41.* Washington, DC: U.S. Department of Justice, Office of Community Oriented Policing Services.

RACIAL PROFILING

Michael E. Buerger

R*acial profiling* is a disputed term, embodying either a pernicious police practice or an intelligent application of police investigative skills, depending upon ideological perspective. It is most commonly understood in the former context, a shorthand for unfair police targeting of persons of minority groups for greater scrutiny and intervention, based solely upon the belief that members of their ethnic group are more inclined to engage in criminal activity. The contemporary term has a specific history anchored in drug interdiction efforts (Buerger & Farrell, 2002), but its informal synonym, "driving while black" (or brown), predates drug interdiction, stemming from the racial and ethnic animus of earlier eras.

The debate is defined at one pole by a belief that racial prejudice leads to disparate treatment of minority citizens. At the other pole, the fundamental belief is that disparate attention by the authorities is fully justified by the different patterns of conduct by different groups, specifically documented rates of criminality. A third, complicated rationale lies between the two: a legacy of belief, embedded in police socialization and reinforced by selective perception, that minority groups are more prone to criminality. That middle ground ignores class distinctions that are masked by visible racial or ethnic identity.

More recently, the concept of racial profiling (as either allegation or practice) has expanded beyond its original framework to include anti-terror activities and immigration law enforcement, as well as scrutiny by private security in shopping malls and other venues. Scientific inquiry intended to confirm or refute the existence of bias has a wide range of methodological difficulties, and studies to date have produced mixed empirical evidence.

TWO PERSPECTIVES

Police and their supporters assert that profiling represents a legitimate practice grounded in criminal behavior, to which race is incidental. Profiles arose from patterns of observable behavior, verified and sustained by convictions in courts of law. Successful searches based upon the profiles validate the general application of profiles as an investigative tool. The police continue to make periodic seizures of large quantities of uncut, bulk drugs during motor vehicle stops, which in their eyes is proof that the profile technique is a valid law enforcement tool.

Opponents tend to regard the successful interdictions as little more than the blind squirrel stumbling across an acorn by chance. While not rejecting the importance of drug interdiction, critics hold that the greater danger lies in rampant, unjustified, and unrestricted government intrusion into the lives of citizens. They note that the verification of the profiles' accuracy has never been independently verified, and insist that the occasional triumphs must be judged in the context of the larger number of stops that yield no results whatsoever. Critics also point to a growing body of testimonial evidence that police stop vehicles with none of the attributes of the operational profile save that of the driver's race. A more critical figure, the number of incidents based upon closer matches to the profile and still yielding no drugs or contraband, has not yet been quantified.

DISPARITY OR DISCRIMINATION?

The central problem in racial profiling is whether disparity of treatment constitutes discrimination. In that respect, the issue mirrors many other debates in American life and jurisprudence.

Disparity can occur at multiple levels of police-initiated contact with citizens. The most basic level occurs in the act of being selected for police inquiry about a law violation. While motor vehicle stops are almost always supported legally by a threshold level of probable cause (a violation of the motor vehicle code, however minor), the greater issues hinge upon matters that occur after the stop.

Discrimination may be inferred from unequal numbers, but disparate treatment supports a stronger inference when persons of a minority class suffer a disproportionate burden than comparably situated majority citizens. In motor vehicle stops, requests for permission to search the vehicle in the absence of specific probable cause are the primary categories

examined. In the absence of a search, police may more often issue tickets instead of warnings; written warnings (which may influence future actions) instead of verbal warnings, which simply address the immediate infraction; or conduct lengthier detentions for investigative purposes, including ordering the occupants out of the vehicle. For pedestrian stops, the length and character of the detention, and being frisked for weapons, are major categories of disparate actions.

For any type of police-initiated contact, both verbal and nonverbal police behaviors can carry suggestions of bias as well (language choice, tone of voice, even body language that conveys feelings of contempt). These attributes are not recorded in official reports of the contact, and are observed only rarely by independent researchers, but they can leave a lasting negative impression in the minds of the citizens. Those feelings can shape citizens' interpretation of official statistics and explanations.

A comparable set of behavioral cues is embedded in the police evaluation of the people they stop, however. Evasive answers, disrespectful language or gestures, even body postures elevate the initial level of suspicion, and can both prolong a contact and lead to a harsher outcome than was originally contemplated. Though defenders of the police point to these behavioral cues as indicative of criminal behavior, a rival hypothesis centers negative reactions to the police in a longer history of mistrust based upon mistreatment by the police in earlier contact. That history may be both personal and vicarious.

PROFILING GENERALLY

Profiling compiles behavioral attributes linked to specific criminal activities, creating a rudimentary sketch of as-yet-unknown persons who might be more likely than others to commit the crime. The serial killer profiling developed by the FBI makes use of crime scene evidence that suggests the personality of the perpetrator, and helps narrow the scope of inquiry. It was based upon extensive interviews with 33 convicted killers, a factual grounding comparable to the drug courier profile of Operation Pipeline (below).

Racial profiling results when a complex set of factors (which can include race) comprising a specific criminal profile are stripped away in practice, transformed into an unjustified oversimplification: "Minorities are more likely to have drugs [or commit other crimes] than are whites." That stereotype overwhelms the elements of individualized facts required for probable cause. While it is the police who have borne the brunt of the criticism, the practice also exists in the operations of private sector security and asset protection (Meeks, 2000).

Since the attacks of September 11, 2001, "racial profiling" has been extended to persons of Middle Eastern origin or descent. A single factor shared with the 19 hijackers of 9/11—their region of origin, or physical features that appear to be of that region—casts suspicion of terrorism upon thousands of law-abiding citizens and visitors. They are more likely to be pulled aside for more extensive inquiries at airport security checkpoints and other sensitive areas. The historical antecedent most familiar to Americans is the internment of Japanese-Americans after the attack on Pearl Harbor, while members of the German Bund (a pro-Nazi organization) in America remained free and largely unmolested.

BASIC LEGAL FOUNDATIONS

The consent search is integral to the racial profiling controversy. The Fourth Amendment to the Constitution protects citizens from unreasonable search and seizure of their persons, property, and effects, but a large volume of case law continually refines the operational understanding of what constitutes an "unreasonable" search. As a result, a number of exceptions have been created, relaxing the general rule that the police must obtain a warrant before they search. Among them are searches incidental to a lawful arrest, exigent (emergency) circumstances, "hot pursuit," searches at ports of entry into the country, inventory searches of impounded vehicles, "inevitable discovery," and when the owner of a property gives voluntary consent to the search. Most challenges to consent searches center on whether the consent was in fact voluntary, or was influenced by coercive police tactics or deception.

American police have the power to detain citizens briefly, and to inquire of their actions, when the police have reasonable, articulable suspicion that something may be wrong. Most motor vehicle stops are supported by some violation of a motor vehicle law, and court cases allow for brief detention to make further inquiries, such as to identify passengers, if the "articulable suspicion" threshold is met.

Police have the power to arrest citizens—a lengthier and more intrusive detention—only when they have probable cause. *Probable cause* constitutes a set of facts and circumstances that would lead a reasonably prudent person to believe that a crime has been, is being, or is about to be committed. For certain crimes, including drug dealing, the courts have acknowledged that a "reasonably prudent and experienced police officer" can detect criminal activity that might escape the notice of a citizen. This recognition of training and experience underlies the police assertion that their "sixth sense" understanding of crime should be respected by the public as well.

Although citizens have more limited expectations of privacy in their vehicles than in their homes, police do not have the authority to search a car based upon whim or mere suspicion. The line that separates suspicion from probable cause is constantly tested in court proceedings. Though the racial profiling debate centers on searches for drugs, "contraband" includes other categories of items that are illegal to possess or transport: smuggled cigarettes, loaded firearms, explosives or other controlled ordnance, child pornography, even illegal aliens.

If the police have probable cause that a crime is being committed in their presence—such as the smell of marijuana, or the existence of drugs, paraphernalia, or weapons in plain sight—they can arrest the occupants of a car and conduct a full search incidental to that arrest. They may also impound the vehicle and conduct an inventory search of all contents, for the mutual protection of the vehicle owner and the officers. In the absence of those circumstances, however, a police officer may only request permission from the driver or owner to search the car for contraband.

Consent is a recognized exception to the Fourth Amendment warrant requirement: Police need not obtain a search warrant if the rightful owner of a property gives free and informed consent to the search. In the context of racial profiling, the central issue is whether any such consent is voluntary under the circumstances of the stop. Police assert that all adult citizens of the United States know that they have the right to decline to give such permission, and so all consent is voluntary. They offer no explanation of why so many people who are carrying contraband voluntarily consent to having their vehicle searched—a statement contrary to interest—except to note that "we don't catch the smart ones."

Opponents assert that the nature of the stop and the inherently coercive presence of the police effectively eviscerate the right of refusal. The implied threat of further detention, coupled with vague suggestions of "consequences" for refusal, coerce compliance. Opponents also point to instances where "probable cause" suddenly arose as soon as citizens declined to give consent; they consider such incidents further evidence that most "consent" claimed by the police is involuntary, a legal fiction.

Another objectionable category involves illegal police actions, searches conducted over the objections of the vehicle occupants. Though rare, such intrusions are insulated from sanction on two fronts. Searches that yield no evidence usually end with the release of the vehicle and driver. The ability of the aggrieved driver to seek redress is expensive, and often futile in the absence of independent evidence. When illegal searches are successful, the discovered contraband weights the case in favor of the police account of the incident (again in the absence of independent verification of the driver's version of the event). As more and more police agencies adopt in-vehicle recording devices for vehicle stops, such incidents are fewer and farther between, but suspicion remains in the eyes of many citizens.

GENERAL HISTORY

The overall history of race relations in the United States remains pertinent to discussions of racial profiling. The second-class citizenship of black Americans was enforced by white police officers throughout the Jim Crow era, and extralegal suppression of the rights of citizenship continued well beyond the *Brown v. Board of Education of Topeka, Kansas* (1954) decision. Passage of the 1964 Civil Rights Act coincided with the rise of black militancy, and continued conflict between blacks and whites continued well into the decade of the 1970s.

While mainstream American culture has changed dramatically since the "long, hot summers" of racial conflict in the 1960s, police culture changes slowly. There is a lingering suspicion that both police training and the police socialization process subtly perpetuate outmoded racial attitudes from that era. When racial profiling first emerged as a public issue, this view was reinforced by revelations in the high-profile cases discussed below. Though America's police forces are no longer a "white boys' club," that observation merely transfers animus—if any exists—from a white prejudice to a police prejudice.

CONTEMPORARY HISTORY

The U.S. Customs Service originally developed a profile of air travelers who had elevated probability of being a drug "mule." Like their equine namesake, drug mules were not drug lords, but beasts of burden: persons unconnected with a drug cartel's membership (and therefore relatively invisible to police narcotics intelligence) were paid on a one-time basis to carry drug packages in their luggage on international flights, and deliver it to cartel personnel soon after their arrival in the United States. Specific conditions and behaviors were tip-offs to Customs personnel to inquire and examine carry-on luggage more closely: Lone travelers with luggage inappropriate to their itinerary, flying with tickets purchased with cash, and several other elements were central to the original airline passenger profile.

In 1984, Operation Pipeline adapted the practice to police highway drug interdiction, which sought to intercept bulk drugs in transit from southern points of entry. Seizing bulk drugs before they could be delivered, cut, and distributed in northern drug markets would reduce supplies for the street markets, deprive the drug syndicates of profits, and perhaps drive more addicts into treatment.

Operation Pipeline arose from police awareness that vehicle stops yielding large quantities of drugs shared certain characteristics. The vehicles were northbound at high rates of speed, usually occupied by two black or Latino males in their late teens or early twenties. Vehicle interiors contained fast-food wrappers and pillows and blankets (both indicative of nonstop travel), and detergent or other strong-smelling substances to mask the odor of drugs. The trunk might be locked, with only a valet key for the drivers; there might be tool or burn marks or other indications that drugs had been secreted in hidden compartments. Road maps might indicate places and timetables to call the drivers' monitor (Buerger & Farrell, 2002).

The profile alone did not constitute probable cause for the police to conduct a warrantless search. It was only a prompt for officers to pay closer attention to the vehicle, to develop probable cause if possible, or to obtain consent to search the car in the absence of specific probable cause.

THE FLAGSHIP CASES

Three cases exposed the police application of the "drug courier profile" concept to scrutiny. In April 1998, two New Jersey State Troopers initiated a vehicle stop of a van on the New Jersey Turnpike that resulted in the shooting and wounding of three of four young minority men. The "profile" was cited as one reason for the stop, even though the vehicle was southbound. No drugs or other contraband were found in the van, and there were significant discrepancies between the official police report of the incident and other evidence.

The Turnpike shooting case revived scrutiny of New Jersey State Police practices that had languished since the 1996 case of State of New Jersey v. Pedro Soto *et al*. In that case, a New Jersey court overturned 17 drug possession cases brought by a state police drug interdiction team working another section of the New Jersey Turnpike. The defendants produced evidence that the team stopped and searched minorities,

particularly African-Americans, almost 5 times more frequently than they did white drivers.

Though black drivers were only 15% of the "violator" group (people driving at excessive speed, or committing other observable moving violations), vehicles driven by blacks comprised almost half of the stops made by the interdiction unit. By comparison, a state police unit doing speed enforcement in the same area of the New Jersey Turnpike stopped drivers at rates much closer to the observed proportion of highway use. The difference strongly suggested that the drug interdiction team equated racial identity with a greater likelihood of participation in illicit distribution of drugs.

A civil case, Wilkins v. Maryland State Police (2003), used the same analytical technique employed in the Soto case. Though whites comprised almost three quarters of drivers and speed violators, only 20% of the cars searched were driven by whites. Blacks made up 17% of the driving population, and slightly more of the violators, but were almost 73% of all persons searched. A total of 4 of every 5 drivers searched by the Maryland State Police interdiction team were of minority status.

If minority drivers were indeed more likely to have drugs than their white counterparts, a stronger argument might be made that the observed disparities were justified. However, the Maryland case revealed that the proportion of black and white drivers found to be carrying drugs was practically equal: 28.4% of blacks, and 28.8% of whites (other sources cite a slight difference: 34% of blacks and 32% of whites; the difference remains marginal). The New Jersey proportions were even lower: 13% of blacks, 10.5% of whites, and 8% of Latinos carried drugs. The New Jersey proportions are closer to the findings in other early studies; the Maryland hit rates are the highest in that first round of profiling inquiries.

More telling, none of the cases studied suggested that the drugs found in profile-based searches were pre-market bulk quantity (the quantum envisioned by the drug courier profile). New Jersey's post-Soto review explicitly noted that almost all seizures were of small amounts, consistent with post-market personal use (Verniero & Zoubeck, 1999); the conclusion is implicit in the absence of any discussion of the quantum of seizures in other studies. The inherent difference in the danger posed by market-quantity shipments, in contrast to personal-use quantities, is a potential limit on the latitude to be allowed government agents, and a fundamental problem with the game theory school of proof (discussed below).

Further inquiry into the New Jersey State Police practices in the wake of the April 1998 Turnpike shooting revealed that the state's training regimen included material that essentially equated minority citizens with greater criminality, effectively directing troopers to focus on minority motorists (Verniero & Zoubeck, 1999).

Both Maryland and New Jersey entered into consent decrees with the U.S. Department of Justice to amend their practices, monitor trooper performance, and revise training that had perpetuated the racial stereotype. Those findings established racial profiling as a "fact," but only in the two jurisdictions. In the public sphere, an ironic reversal of positions occurred. Where the police had tacitly assumed the actions of a small group of drug couriers were typical of the minority communities, the public now assumed that the practices of two agencies represented police practices everywhere. The distinction remains central to the debate over racial profiling in any guise: The generalizability of localized findings (or enterprise-specific profiles) to larger groups sharing only superficial aspects of the offending groups is limited.

The police insist that profiling is a legitimate tool of inquiry, well grounded in the experience of practice. The public points to the Maryland and New Jersey statistics, standing firm in their belief that it is merely a modern continuation of racial prejudice, now dressed up with pseudo-scientific prose. The scientific questions that have arisen in the wake of the Soto and *Wilkins* cases have examined a wider range of police activities and actions in numerous other venues. They embody an attempt to discern whether and where the "fact" of racial profiling by police exists beyond the specific milieu of the interstate highways in New Jersey and Maryland.

Overall, four issues are salient. The first is whether criminal propensity is more likely in one group than another, with a collateral question of what purported proofs should be considered valid. The second area involves the continuing refinement of methodology, and the factors to be considered when examining aggregate police data in vastly different locations for evidence of racial bias. A contemporary assertion, promulgated in different fashion by the police and by the econometric school of criminology, is that the "criminal propensity" point can be proven by a variation of game theory, based upon the results of consent searches without regard for any other considerations (including those of civil rights). The third is a legalistic consideration of whether elevated government intrusion justified against large-scale harm (proliferation of drug markets, or another 9/11-type attack) can be applied equally to smaller gains (seizure of personal-use drug amounts). A fourth operational issue rests upon the degree of precision with which the profile is applied by police officers and other agents of the state.

FOUR SALIENT ISSUES

I. The Legitimacy of Suspicion

For practitioners, the validity of the component of race rests upon personal experience and upon the evidence of aggregate crime statistics. The police arguments rest upon two separate but related features of police deployment. The first is accumulated personal and vicarious experience, in which minority offenders play major roles. The second is arrest statistics, the collective construct that is the cumulative result of individual decisions by police across the nation, over time.

Experience

Officers assert a claim for a "police intuition"—essentially an accumulated knowledge of subtle behavioral cues that operates below the conscious threshold—that properly targets criminals. In this view, the fact that those who draw police attention are members of one or another minority is incidental to their demeanor and behavior, and irrelevant to the police decision to focus on them.

A second component of the argument is essentially defensive, made by officers who work in districts heavily populated by minority groups. Their point—which is valid at the individual level—is that the vast majority of individuals with whom they have contact during the day are residents and visitors who are minorities. To apply the template used in the highway studies to local police work, they argue, unfairly paints officers as racist because the "disproportionate" number of minorities they stop reflects the area rather than police decision making. Such comparisons are valid only in areas where there are significant opportunities to choose between minority and nonminority persons to stop. The argument is particularly acute in minority-populated areas, because minority-status victims are frequently the complainants in the cases police investigate: The police are incensed by accusations of racism when they are in fact defending the interests of law-abiding minority citizens.

A variant objection by the police is the "hours of darkness" defense. This assertion denies that officers can have knowledge of a driver's race when they pull up behind a car during the nighttime. While intuitively logical, the defense has been countered on several levels. In the Soto case, a practice called "spotlighting" revealed the race of turnpike drivers: Parking a cruiser perpendicular to the road, with the high beams and spotlight on, created a zone of light that permitted the troopers to identify the race of the driver despite the brevity of illumination (the practice was independently examined by the New Jersey Attorney General's office and was confirmed). On city streets, vehicles passing through intersections provide a comparable opportunity.

In the context of local policing, vehicle models, vehicle condition, and personal adornments (bumper and window stickers, certain styles of air fresheners, and other ephemera) are correlated strongly enough with specific groups to provide proxy identifications in lieu of visual confirmation. They provide no probable cause, but serve to draw the attention of officers; probable cause for a pretext stop likely would soon follow, given the many possible infractions of the expansive motor vehicle code.

Different sets of proxy identifications exist for pedestrian stops at night, where slower speed and ambient light allow for the observation of race, bearing, and other factors. This is especially salient when the police are looking for a suspect who fits "The Description"—often an African-American male of medium build, undetermined age, and dressed in a style common to hundreds of residents of the area.

Crime Statistics

Supporters of police profiling efforts point to the disproportionate presence of African-American males in arrest, conviction, and imprisonment statistics. Those facts are presented as proof that the police properly focus their enforcement efforts on groups that demonstrate a greater propensity for crime. A corollary argument points to the racially homogeneous character of high-level drug gangs—from Jamaican posses to MS-13, from the Nicky Barnes organization to the Crips and Bloods—as a valid rationale for the police to focus on ethnicity or race in directing their drug-and crime-suppression efforts.

Opponents point to several flaws in the assertions that crime is a product of group characteristics. The history of racial prejudice created situations of real disadvantage: The arrest statistics and other perceptions of crime are more a reflection of class distinctions than group tendencies (see, e.g., Stark, 1987). Further, the fact that the upper echelons of a gang or criminal enterprise are of a common racial or ethnic heritage does not generalize their criminality to all who share their skin color or ethnicity.

In this view, both the police experiences and the criminal statistics reflect the impact of larger social forces rooted in America's sordid history of slavery, Jim Crow laws, and racial segregation. Despite the tremendous gains made by the civil rights movement, race-based isolation continues to be a factor for substantial numbers of African-Americans. Isolation by geography—whether based in Jim Crow segregation or the economic necessity of living in public housing—has had a negative influence on the employment and educational opportunities of the African-American and Hispanic immigrant communities.

Economic necessity compels residents of many urban neighborhoods to participate in their area's underground economy, even if they have a stable job and home life (Venkatesh, 2006); a large segment of that underground economy revolves around the drug trade. Street-level drug dealing has a relatively low capital entry threshold, and provides a reward structure far greater than comparable accessible legitimate employment. It is also a highly visible activity, more likely to come to police attention than corresponding drug trafficking in the suburbs.

2. Scientific Proof

Criminologists seek a scientific justification for police actions, in lieu of normative reliance upon unverifiable "sixth sense" justifications. The contemporary scholarly focus on racial profiling rests upon a debate regarding whether a variation on game theory can provide such a foundation.

One thrust of the early racial profiling research took up the question of whether disparity alone constituted *de facto* discrimination, or could occur innocuously. Various studies identified different uses of the highway for minority groups based on employment opportunities and recreational pursuits (Meehan & Ponder, 2002a). Another documented disproportionate representation of young minority males in the population of high-speed law violators on the New Jersey Turnpike, inferring the legitimacy of at least one assumption of the original profile (Lange, Johnson, & Voas, 2005).

The contemporary debate centers on a proposition by scholars drawing from the field of econometrics, asserting that the question of disparity or discrimination can be resolved by the application of a variation of game theory (Engel, 2008; Persico & Todd, 2008). This solution hinges on an examination of the "hit rate" (rate of discovery of contraband) of police searches, independent of any other concerns (Persico & Todd, 2008), treating the populations of white and non-white drivers as "urns" that can be sampled. This view posits that rational choice underlies the options of drivers to carry contraband (in the present discussion, drugs), and the choice of police officers to conduct investigations for drugs. Rational police officers would focus their efforts on groups most likely to carry drugs.

In essence, this econometric argument takes the side of the police, tacitly accepting the argument that group characteristics do exist, and can be inferred at the individual level. Furthermore, the acceptance of group-specific criminality (drug use, in this instance) assumes facts not in evidence. It is a hypothesis in the classic methodological sense, to be proved or disproved by scientific testing that cannot be conducted, and thus remains hypothetical.

Methodologically, the hit rate proposal encounters several difficulties. Police searches are conducted under a variety of situations, including searches incidental to arrest, inventory searches when a vehicle is towed, and in circumstances when probable cause is developed at the scene independent of the original reason for the stop. In addition, searches are conducted for a variety of motives, not just drugs (Engel & Tillyer, 2008). As a result, analyses based solely upon the hit rate for drugs must be able to discern those stops and searches motivated by an officer's desire to "maximize the probability of a 'hit'" (Persico & Todd, 2008). A further complication arises in the need to distinguish personal-use hits from the bulk drug seizures arising from the proper application of the drug courier profile, although the modern debate fails to pursue that distinction.

The proposition of hit-rate analysis has the advantage of being theoretical, unconnected from the larger concerns of the criminal justice system. The individuals who comprise the "urns" that police officers supposedly sample are not research subjects, but citizens of a country that presumes their innocence. They are defended by rules and expectations of conduct by agents of the state that do not allow random selection for the purposes of testing. Basic civil rights preclude the use of the motoring public (or the ambulatory public) as a laboratory.

3. Balance of Harms

American law is more tolerant of intrusive state action when the harm to be averted is great. Lower-level violations of the law are tolerated, if tacitly, by the rules of criminal procedure that erect barriers to their discovery. Though the Supreme Court has expanded police powers in the cases of *Atwater v. Lago*

Vista (2001) (permitting custodial arrest for conduct normally subject only to a citation) and *Whren et al. v. United States* (1996) (allowing the use of the pretext stop), the presumption of innocence remains a bedrock procedural right for American citizens.

Americans have a reduced expectation of privacy when driving a vehicle in public space, or when walking off their property. Nevertheless, a presumption of privacy remains, to be overcome only by an articulable danger to the public peace. Judicial tolerance of the consent search for drugs is one of the central questions in the racial profiling debate.

The original drug courier profile had a narrowly targeted objective: Intercept bulk shipments of illegal drugs in transit, before they could be cut and distributed to the public. That profile arose from a specific fact pattern, closely matching observable characteristics with searches that found bulk drugs.

Preventing illegal drugs from reaching the street has far more protective value to the public weal than a seizure of post-market, individual-use drugs. Post-market seizures occur only after the drugs have been distributed, and the profits returned to the middlepersons and the kingpins of the drug trade. The harm to the individual, and to society as a result of the individual's drug-induced actions, is much smaller than the aggregate of such harms embodied in the bulk shipment. They are also more hypothetical at the individual level, insofar as recreational drug use is not inevitably a cause of further criminality.

The contemporary debates embodying the "hit rate" hypothesis reflect an operational change from the bulk-drug courier profile to a broader "anyone carrying illegal drugs" foundation. That is a methodological convenience, in part: Many drivers and passengers carry small amounts of drugs for personal use; relatively few are involved in transporting pre-market bulk drugs. The numbers demanded by social science hypothesis testing can only be achieved by expanding the focus to personal-use quantities, at a sacrifice of the greater harms presented by drug couriers.

As profiling shifts to other areas of criminal conduct, the public interest in deterring harm also changes. Preventing mass casualty events like those of the September 11, 2001, attacks obviously meets the test of great social harm. However, when the harm remains hypothetical, unsupported by articulable facts and conditions, the "harm" argument alone is insufficient to justify governmental intrusion. Advances in technology will continue to test the proposition, particularly as data-mining techniques draw conclusions from the electronic traces of everyday activity.

4. Precision of Application

More important to the populations at risk is the degree of precision with which police employ the drug courier profile. The epithet "racial profiling" embodies a belief that the profile itself is merely a sham, providing faux legitimacy for decisions that are actually based upon racial prejudice.

Profiles are like fingerprints: They are composites of particular characteristics which, taken collectively, provide enhanced confidence of an identification. For fingerprints, that identification is of a known individual matched to an unknown sample (the latent print). In criminal profiles, it is identification of the behaviors or characteristics as indicative of probable criminal behaviors. In both cases, the greater the number of matches, the greater confidence can be had in the identification.

The public outcry against racial profiling is embodied in numerous testimonial cases, in which the only characteristic the individual stopped by the police shared with the drug courier profile was that of race. Such evidence is not collected on a scientific basis, but its cumulative weight creates a viable presumption. Though there have been inquiries into public perceptions of racial profiling, a viable study of persons stopped and released as a result of profiling activities has yet to be published.

At least one court case examined the profile itself: the 1993 Colorado case of *Whitfield v. Board of County Commissioners of Eagle County*. In a case involving a highway vehicle stop based solely upon a drug courier profile, the court dissected the profile point by point, finding no correlation to criminality of the various components (rental car, out-of-state plates in an area heavily dependent upon tourism, radar detector, tinted windows, and so forth). The court then concluded that the only remaining variable was the driver's race, which was inadmissible. Examining each individual variable in the profile, rather than the collective weight of all the components, is an unusual approach, but the evidence of the resulting search was nevertheless suppressed.

RESEARCH ON RACIAL PROFILING

In the wake of the 1998 New Jersey Turnpike shooting, a fairly broad scholarly effort ensued to establish whether or not police engaged in racial profiling in other jurisdictions. In major cities, "stop and frisk" questioning of pedestrians also fell under the racial profiling umbrella. Dozens of studies have been conducted, yielding mixed results. In the earliest round of inquiry, most reputable studies indicated that minorities were stopped in numbers disproportionately higher than their representation in population statistics (Engel, Calnon, & Bernard, 2002). Later studies have been mounted after the controversy spurred reform of practices and greater scrutiny; the results of emerging studies also document disparities, but generally are less inclined to conclude that discrimination drives them. However, the later studies also occur in a climate where police and civic officials are well aware of the racial profiling debate. Police agencies are more likely to have taken steps to minimize disparity, and are likely more politically astute in their interpretation of findings.

Whether such disparity represents police prejudice or is the by-product of patterns of civilian behavior has yet to be answered definitively. Because policing is locally based, practices differ by jurisdiction. One comprehensive study indicated wide diversity of practices across the 127 different jurisdictions in Massachusetts (Farrell, McDevitt, Bailey, Andresen, & Pierce, 2004). That study also uncovered evidence of a possible gender bias in some jurisdictions (i.e., the propensity of male officers to stop single, young, female drivers), an artifact not pursued in other studies.

Studying racial profiling has several methodological hurdles. First is establishing an appropriate population baseline against which to compare the proportion of minority stops. Second is the limited number of variables available in official records, the most common source of data for profiling studies. Because of these limitations, the most difficult task is determining whether any disparities are grounded in prejudice, or are a product of real (rather than presumed) criminal conduct.

The original New Jersey and Maryland turnpike cases were relatively easy: The proportions of drivers on the highway could be established by direct observation, as could the proportions of speeders and other motor vehicle code violators. Observable vehicle code violations constituted the sole basis for initiating a stop; the choice to request or initiate a search was less directly observable.

Away from limited-access highways, the question becomes more complex. Police officers working in neighborhoods populated by minorities rightly argue that most of the people they encounter will be of minority status, whether the officers are prejudiced or committed to equality. Furthermore, police investigative stops in cities and towns are often prompted by citizen complaints, providing specific descriptive information that is far more detailed than a profiling "hunch."

Studies note disparate patterns of highway use (both by time and route) by minority drivers, with differences linked to residential, employment, and recreational patterns (Meehan & Ponder, 2002a). Certain highways are transportation corridors from exurbs and suburbs into the core cities, and the commuting drivers may represent different ethnic proportions from the towns' resident populations. One post-shooting study in New Jersey suggested that young minority males comprised a much greater proportion of drivers using excessive speed (Lange et al., 2005).

It retroactively provided nominal support for the original profile, but remains untested against actual vehicle stop practices.

Another study found that even within a single jurisdiction, racial disparity in stops increased with distance from the city border. Minority drivers were far more likely to be stopped in homogeneous white suburban neighborhoods farthest from the city line, where black or brown faces stood out. Police activity was relatively race-neutral in areas abutting a core city, where a heterogeneous population mix was the norm (Meehan & Ponder, 2002b).

More critical to the interpretation of police stop data is the nature of formalized record keeping. Most police records systems were designed to facilitate case tracking and offender identification. Even in those jurisdictions that have adopted more rigorous tracking by race and ethnicity, either prospectively or in response to consent decrees or public criticism, few forms reveal the actual motivation of the officer. The Supreme Court decision of *Whren et al. v. United States* (1996) has legitimized the police use of the pretext stop, initiating action on the basis of a violation unrelated to the officers' real intent to conduct an investigation. Almost all vehicle stops meet the low threshold for probable cause (a moving violation or equipment defect), and are therefore legal.

Police records systems generally record only the fact of a stop, not its context. Computer analysis of aggregate stop data is insufficient to establish motivation because such information is not recorded. It remains difficult to determine whether disparate patterns represent overt bias, subtle bias, or a statistical artifact of police deployment based on crime and call patterns, or other localized phenomena.

Analyzing stop data at the aggregate level avoids any scrutiny of individual officers' work habits. Such techniques have political benefits, but if officers in small groups engage in prejudicial behaviors unrepresentative of the agency practices, the bias may be masked statistically in the larger agency patterns. The impact of their actions upon the minority citizens will remain vivid, however, and the gap between what is experienced by citizens and what can be demonstrated statistically will remain a cause of friction.

CONCLUSION

Central to the ongoing debate regarding racial profiling is the balance of the protection of public safety with the protection of individual liberty. In the original context, the potential gains in public safety to be realized by intercepting bulk drugs before they could be distributed might justify the tightly controlled use of an otherwise intrusive police tool. The contemporary focus of research ignores quantity, focusing instead on the appropriateness of a "hit rate" based on any quantity of drugs as a justification.

A decade after the New Jersey Turnpike shooting that revived the racial profiling controversy, the use of profiling continues, and continues to be problematic. Questions of the accuracy and precision of application remain unanswered: Given the local control of police agencies, the questions are revisited on a case-by-case basis. Moreover, it is likely that the police have become more astute, both politically and scientifically, in their ability to articulate the reasoning processes of individual officers, and the patterns of agency-wide actions. While that possibility invites the reaction that "the police have become better liars," it is equally possible that the police are becoming better at identifying and articulating the subtle behaviors that they observe, giving a more valid operational definition to the prized "sixth sense" of the street cop.

REFERENCES AND FURTHER READINGS

Atwater v. Lago Vista, 532 U.S. 318 (2001).

Brown v. Board of Education of Topeka, Kansas, 347 US 483.

Buerger, M.E., and Farrell, A. (2002). The evidence of racial profiling: Interpreting documented and unofficial sources. *Police Quarterly*, 5(1), 272–305.

Engel, R.S. (2008). A critique of the "outcome test" in racial profiling research. *Justice Quarterly*, 25(1), 1–36.

Engel, R.S., Calnon, J.M., and Bernard, T.J. (2002) Theory and racial profiling: Shortcomings and future directions in research. *Justice Quarterly*, 19(2), 249–273.

Engel, R.S., and Tillyer, R. (2008, March). Searching for equilibrium: The tenuous nature of the outcome test. *Justice Quarterly*, 25(1), 54–71.

Farrell, A., McDevitt, J., Bailey, L., Andresen, C., and Pierce, E. (2004, May). *Massachusetts Racial and*

Gender Profiling Project: Final report. Boston: Institute on Race and Justice, Northeastern University.

Harris, D.A. (2002). *Profiles in injustice: Why racial profiling cannot work.* New York: The New Press.

Lange, J.E., Johnson, M.B., and Voas, R.B. (2005). Testing the racial profiling hypothesis for seemingly disparate traffic stops. *Justice Quarterly,* 22(2), 193–223.

Meehan, A.J., & Ponder, M.C. (2002a). How roadway composition matters in analyzing police data on racial profiling. *Police Quarterly,* 5(3), 306–333.

Meehan, A.J., & Ponder, M.C. (2002b). Race and place: The ecology of racial profiling African-American motorists. *Justice Quarterly,* 19(3), 399–430.

Meeks, K. (2000). *Driving while black.* New York: Broadway Books.

Persico, N., and Todd, P.E. (2008). The hit rates test for racial bias in motor-vehicle searches. *Justice Quarterly,* 25(1), 37–53.

Schafer, J.A., Carter, D.L., Katz-Bannister, A.J., and Wells, W.M. (2006). Decision making in traffic stop encounters: A multivariate analysis of police behavior. *Police Quarterly,* 9(2), 184–209.

Stark, R. (1987). Deviant places: A theory of the ecology of crime. *Criminology,* 25(4), 893–909.

State of New Jersey v. Pedro Soto et al., 324 N.J.Super. 66, 734 A.2d 350 (1996).

Venkatesh, S.A. (2006). *Off the books: The underground economy of the urban poor.* Cambridge, MA: Harvard University Press.

Verniero, P., and Zoubeck, P. H. (1999). *Interim report of the State Police Review Team regarding allegations of racial profiling.* Trenton: New Jersey Attorney General's Office.

Whitfield v. Board of County Commissioners of Eagle County, Colo., 837 F.Supp. 338 (1993).

Whren et al. v. United States, 517 U.S. 806 (1996).

Wilkins v. Maryland State Police, Civil Action No. CB-93–483 (2003).

Withrow, B. (2004). Race-based policing: A descriptive analysis of the Wichita Stop Study. *Police Practice and Research,* 5, 223–240.

Keeping Migrants in Their Place

Technologies of Control and Racialized Public Space in Arizona

Meghan G. McDowell
and Nancy A. Wonders

International migration is an age-old phenomenon; however, economic globalization and responses of nation-states to this transformation have reframed migration in the contemporary era. We use the phrase *global disciplinary strategies* to characterize the interlocking policies and practices, both material and discursive, used by nation-states to criminalize and regulate the mobility of transnational migrants, typically by utilizing identity markers to engage in social sorting and exclusion. Drawing on contemporary scholarship, we have identified three global disciplinary strategies that operate to racialize and criminalize recent migrants: (1) anti-immigrant discourse; (2) immigration law and policy creation; and (3) surveillance tactics and policing rituals directed at migrants and performed by federal and local law enforcement, otherwise known as *"technologies of control"* (Pickering and Weber, 2006). Although our broader research project touches on each of these global disciplinary strategies, in this article we examine two closely related technologies of control—surveillance and "enforcement rituals" (De Genova, 2004; 2005)—two strategies designed to keep migrants "in their place" by keeping them out of public space. We use the category "migrant" to refer to any foreign national who has crossed a border with the intention of residing in that country, whether temporarily or permanently, with legal documentation or without.

As we establish below, although a relatively rich set of theoretical claims has been made about technologies of control, little empirical research has been conducted to investigate their impact on migrants' use of public space. It is this void that our research helps to fill. Utilizing the literature on neoliberal globalization, race and public space, as well as on policing and immigration enforcement, we explore the following research question: How do technologies of control shape migrants' use of, experience in, and access to public space in Arizona—a site deemed "ground zero" in the immigration debate?

TECHNOLOGIES OF CONTROL: SURVEILLANCE, ENFORCEMENT RITUALS, AND IMMOBILITY

The policies and practices associated with neoliberal globalization have stimulated mass migration across the globe; people migrate for many reasons, but frequently they are searching for economic and physical security (Sassen, 1998a, 1998b; Pickering and Weber, 2006). In the West, the development of global capitalism has been characterized by deindustrialization, a corresponding decline of welfare state provisions, a shift to consumption-based economies, and the casualization of the labor force (Schaeffer, 2009). The interplay of these global forces heightened the demand for an inexpensive flexible workforce, while simultaneously creating pressure to restrict access to the costly privileges of citizenship. Consequently, the plight of the "illegal migrant" has emerged as a significant manifestation of the contradictions embedded within globalization (Dauvergne, 2008; Calavita, 2005). Throughout the West, migrants are needed labor power, but unwanted citizens.

Since roughly the 1980s, many countries, including the United States, Australia, Great Britain, Spain, and Italy, have developed immigration policies, discourse, and enforcement strategies characterized "by a reversal of the image of migrants and asylum seekers in public space"; migrants and refugees who were welcomed into the labor force after World War II are now "demonized as criminals, economic and social defrauders, terrorists, drug traffickers, and so forth" (Ceyhan and Tsoukala, 2002: 22). As a result of this global dynamic, politicians offer up "illegal immigration as an explanation for internal and social ills, while promising to restore state sovereignty with new strategies to 'take control' of the nation's border" (Michalowski, 2007: 71).

In response, many Western nation-states are employing "highly technical, increasingly punitive and innovative methods of border control" and immigration enforcement strategies that Pickering and Weber (2006: 9) term "technologies of control." Broeders and Engbersen (2007) argue that the "technologies of control" deployed in the fight against "illegal" immigration follow two logics. First, technologies of control are used to locate, detain, or deport suspected "illegal" migrants.

Second, technologies of control are employed to "exclude [rather than locate, detain, or deport] irregular immigrants from key institutions of society, such as the labor market and the housing market, and even from informal networks of fellow countrymen and family" (p. 1595). Our research focuses on the rise of the surveillance state and enforcement rituals as two interlocking technologies of control that foster migrant identification and exclusion from public space.

THE SURVEILLANCE STATE AND SOCIAL SORTING

The literature on surveillance and social sorting as technologies of control argues that nation-states are (re)drawing moral boundaries, (re)fortifying "assumptions about national identity," and defending the body politic from the foreign Other, through practices of banishment and/or exclusion (Aas, 2007: 288). Aas suggests that the contemporary image of the disciplinary state is being transformed from a Panopticon to a "Banopticon" (p. 288). The "Banopticon" state continues to foster discipline in the classic Foucauldian sense by habituating migrants "to their status as excluded" (Engbersen, 2001: 242), but it also operates as a "factory of exclusion" for those marked as "undesirable," as well as one capable of selective inclusion of those same undesirables. The state uses technologies of control to engage in surveillance and "social sorting" (Lyon, 2003); a central strategic goal is to differentiate between legitimate and illegitimate mobilities in the global era (Amoore, 2006; Wonders, 2006). This state-sponsored commitment to surveillance and social sorting operates to discipline migrants and has fundamentally altered the character of the border and public space. The "idea" of the border has undergone a significant transformation due to globalization. No longer conceptualized as a fixed "line in the sand," the border is increasingly being understood through the lens of performativity (Wonders, 2006) and mobility (Amoore, 2006). Under pressure to curb "illegal" immigration, states have moved toward internal, mobile border-control policies that rely heavily on various forms of surveillance and exclusion by law enforcement officials and government workers. Weber (2006: 25) argues that "the state's arsenal of exclusionary devices increasingly involves preemptive measures to prevent and deter unauthorized arrival; efforts to increase the efficient sorting of desirable and undesirable passengers at the border; and punitive responses." Wonders (2006: 66) extends this point further by arguing that many "border performances occur in locations that may be far from the actual geographic border" and that day-to-day decisions by government agents, police officers, airport workers, employers, and others "play a critical role in determining where, how, and on whose body a border will be performed."

Some argue that these mobile border performances, along with the potential for 24-hour surveillance and the development of fortress-style architectures within urban and public spaces, have a subliminal impact, reinforcing a "culture of fear." As Davis (1992: 224) notes, "the social perception of threat becomes a function of the security mobilization itself [so that] fear proves itself." The result of the "secure the city crusade" in part has been the destruction of legitimate democratic public space and access to public space for society's "undesirables" (Mitchell, 2003). The ensuing proliferation of privatized and "defensible" public spaces has "become a means of constituting a public through relative inclusions and exclusions and the regulation of bodies within the space" (Peterson, 2006: 377).

A small, but growing body of literature discusses the impact of surveillance on the lives of undocumented migrants, as well as on migrants' access to, and use of, public space (see, for example, Inda, 2007; De Genova, 2005). It argues that the move toward internal controls of the border and 24-hour surveillance have pushed migrants further underground, intensifying the uncertainty of their lives and their condition as "illegal" and therefore disposable (Broeders and Engbersen, 2007).

In one of the few empirical studies to examine this theoretical claim, Stephen (2004) conducted interviews with migrant farm workers in the Pacific Northwest to determine how the "gaze of surveillance" affects their lives. Her discussions with workers reveal how migrants internalize, and are disciplined by, the fear of surveillance and their experience crossing the border:

for many confronted by racialized readings of all Latinos and Latin Americans as potential "illegals," the border is indefinitely elastic and can serve as a barrier and zone of violence anywhere they go in the United States. ... Surveillance and limited mobility are a major part of the experience of [migrant] workers (p. 99).

This research suggests that, for many migrants, the constant "gaze" of surveillance fosters self-discipline and ultimately produces, as Razack (2002: 11) argues, two kinds of bodies: "the normal and the abnormal, the former belonging to a homogenous social body, the latter exiled and spatially segregated." Commenting on the impact of surveillance and the mobile border, particularly the use of biometrics, Parenti (1999: 180) argues that "immigrants will fear the law more intensely knowing that [I.C.E.]/police intelligence systems are automatic, infallible, and instantaneous. The electronic dragnet will force internalization of the [I.C.E.] gaze, causing immigrants to keep to themselves, stay out of sight, and steer clear of politics." This work suggests that the act of surveillance *and* the resulting internalization of the security gaze work together to effectively regulate the mobility of migrants, restricting them from public space.

ENFORCEMENT RITUALS AND THE POLICING OF (IM)MIGRATION

Closely related to surveillance is a second technology of control, the daily "enforcement rituals" performed by local police and immigration officers. De Genova (2005: 246–248) theorizes that the objective of enforcement rituals is the everyday production of "migrant illegality," which serves as a disciplinary apparatus by exacerbating migrants' "sense of ever-present vulnerability" and by fetishizing "migrant illegality as a seemingly objective 'thing in itself.'" Enforcement rituals include racial profiling, immigration raids, neighborhood sweeps, detention, and the intimidation and harassment of communities of color. These rituals police the "illegalities of everyday life" and are expressed as "heightened [law enforcement] directed at the bodies, movements, and spaces of the poor, and especially those racialized as not-white" (De Genova, 2005: 246). As a result, migrants are disciplined by the threat of, and actual performance of, enforcement rituals in their communities. Because this threat is highly racialized, non-migrant members of particular racial groups are often disciplined as well.

A limited body of research has examined the relationship between "enforcement rituals" as disciplinary strategies and the exclusion of migrants from public space and public services (see, for example, Calavita, 2005). Most prominently, Mary Romero's case study of an immigration raid in Chandler, Arizona, argues that immigration raids serve several important disciplinary purposes beyond the netting of "illegal immigrants." Namely, they protect the "exclusionary use of public spaces" for white people, limit the freedom of movement of people of color, and promote ties between public space, citizenship (belonging), and skin color (Romero, 2006:453). Researchers Nelson and Hiemstra's (2008) comparative analysis of the politics of space and belonging in "small town America" powerfully demonstrates how discourses of "illegality" operate to normalize and/or mandate the enforcement of exclusion and the regulation of public space by the police, while disciplining the mobility of migrants. They explain:

> The social and political meaning given to migrants' legal status also operates to profoundly infiltrate and spatialize locale interactions. The racialized discourse of "illegality" constructing all immigrants (regardless of actual status) as criminal serves to deepen hierarchies of race and class. ... Furthermore, "illegality" instills a climate of fear among immigrants and naturalizes their spatial containment in trailer parks. Maria, an undocumented immigrant, spoke about how many women such as herself "shut themselves in" because they are afraid: "It felt like it said here on my forehead 'illegal'" (pp. 9–10).

Scholars have also highlighted the close relationship between the policing of space and the policing of race (Bass, 2001; Milovanovic and Russell, 2001). For example, researchers have demonstrated that the practice of racial profiling is "inextricably tied not only to race, but to officers' conceptions of place, of what should typically occur in an area and who belongs, as well as where they belong" (Meehan and Ponder, 2002:402). In his ground-breaking study on territoriality and police officers' conceptions of space, Herbert (1997) concludes:

> Simply put, many police strategies to create public order involve enacting boundaries and restricting access; police power rests upon a political geography. Social power relies fundamentally upon territoriality. It is certainly the case that the police would be largely impotent without the capacity to create and enforce boundaries, to restrict people's mobility in and around certain areas (p. 11).

This research suggests that the tactics police and immigration officers use are effective precisely because they *objectify* (predominately) people of color and visually *classify* them as dangerous outsiders, who are "out of place" (Mitchell, 2003; Cresswell, 2004). When local law enforcement officers heavily patrol the boundaries of Latino/a neighborhoods, or when ICE officers sit outside a local Food City known to be frequented by poor immigrants, they are policing space (impoverished, often segregated neighborhoods) *and* race (Brown skin as a proxy for illegality and criminality). Therefore, the presence of police and ICE officers in Latino/a communities serves as a constant reminder of migrant "illegality," and therefore, "deportability." They are disciplining the mobility of migrants and limiting their access to resources and social services.

As De Genova (2004: 178) eloquently argues, the "spectacle of enforcement" at the border and in interior sites within the United States is necessary "for the spatialized difference between the nation-states of the U.S. and Mexico to be enduringly inscribed upon migrants in their spatialized (and racialized) status as 'illegal aliens.'" When federal and local police and immigration officers perform the (often public) "spectacle of enforcement" on the bodies of undocumented migrants, they are in effect, if not intent, reifying connections between race, space, and "illegality."

In sum, the literature on technologies of control suggests that surveillance and enforcement rituals operate as disciplinary strategies frequently employed to monitor, detain, and/or exclude undocumented migrants. Scholars argue that these strategies have altered the character of public space and are often productive forces in the making of legitimate and illegitimate mobilities and identities. For people of color and undocumented migrants, the preemptive social control strategies of racial profiling, harassment, and sporadic immigration raids have become a means to facilitate their economic, political, and spatial subjugation. Although surveillance practices and enforcement rituals reflect different techniques for achieving social control, as a practical matter, they frequently work together to keep migrants in their place.

Despite the relatively rich scholarly literature on technologies of control, surprisingly few scholars have tested these broad claims via primary research within migrant communities. By adding the perspective of migrants to the debate, we seek to examine whether and how global disciplinary strategies, particularly technologies of control, are restructuring undocumented migrants' access to, use of, and experiences of public spaces in Arizona.

GROUND ZERO—ARIZONA

Arizona provides an important focal point for research on race, immigration, and public space. Deemed "ground zero" in the immigration debate, Arizona became the first state in the nation to pass legislation that penalizes employers for knowingly hiring undocumented immigrants (Archibold, 2008). In addition, Maricopa County Sheriff Joe Arpaio has gained international notoriety for his sweeping immigration raids in predominately Latino/a Phoenix-area neighborhoods (*Ibid.*) and his deployment of local police officers to enforce federal immigration laws (Gonzalez,

2009: A5). Significantly, the Tucson sector of the U.S.-Mexico border is "the busiest sector in the country" for "illegal alien" apprehensions (U.S. Customs and Border Protection, 2009), further heightening tensions concerning immigration within the state. Although many border crossers enter Arizona legally, the Department of Homeland Security estimates that there were 560,000 "unauthorized immigrants" living in Arizona in 2008 (Hoefer, Rytina, and Baker, 2009: 4). According to the Pew Hispanic Center (Passel and Cohn, 2009), undocumented immigrants comprised 4.0% of the U.S. population in 2008 and 5.4% of the labor force. In Arizona, the percentage is almost double, with unauthorized immigrants constituting about nine percent of the population and roughly 10% of the labor force. This is "the highest share of any state in the nation" (Gonzalez, 2009: A5).Consistent with much previous work on globalization, we view cities as important strategic sites for globalization, since global forces frequently find localized expression in cities (Sassen, 2006; Wonders and Michalowski, 2001). Phoenix, Arizona, is the fifth largest city in the United States, with roughly 1.5 million residents in 2007,30% of whom are of Hispanic or Latino origin (U.S. Census Bureau, 2009a). Tucson is the second largest city in Arizona, with just under 519,000 residents in 2007,40% of whom are of Hispanic or Latino origin (U.S. Census Bureau, 2009b). Although accurate city-level data on undocumented migrants are difficult to obtain, it is widely believed that most undocumented migrants in Arizona reside in these two cities, leading to their selection as our primary research sites.

RESEARCH STRATEGY

Our research strategy employed focus groups and interviews with staff at several agencies serving migrants in the state of Arizona. The use of focus groups as a research tool has a rich history in the social sciences (Hyden and Bulow, 2003). In particular, researchers have advocated for the use of focus groups when working with people of color, as well as vulnerable populations (Madriz, 2003; Pollack, 2003; Kamberelis and Dimitriadis, 2005).

We chose Arizona's two largest cities, Phoenix and Tucson, as research sites due to their very sizable migrant populations. Participants were recruited through local nongovernmental organizations and/or social service agencies that provide services to migrants. By partnering with agencies that work directly with migrants, we hoped to meet migrants in a safe space and, thus, to limit any risk that might otherwise be attached to our research project. Locating agencies willing to partner took many months because many agencies, although supportive of our project, feared that participation might increase the risk of detection for (undocumented) migrants they serve. Agencies that were willing to form a research partnership were asked to sign an agency cooperation consent form, which permitted us to work with agency staff to recruit participants from programs offered by the agencies, to host the focus groups at agency sites, and to conduct brief interviews with agency staff.

Following best practices, we encouraged agencies to recruit focus group participants who had some familiarity with one another, either through existing social or familial networks (Madriz, 2003). We gave all participants an informational flyer in Spanish and English to insure full comprehension of our project's goals. Throughout the recruitment and interview process, confidentiality and anonymity were stressed to potential participants. By design, focus groups were conducted in English. We wanted to speak with migrants who could "get by" in English so that their experiences could not be simply attributed to a lack of language proficiency. At the same time, some words, phrases, and ideas could best be articulated by participants in Spanish; for this reason, interaction was occasionally in Spanish to insure accurate communication of ideas and perspectives. With the participants' permission, all conversations were audio-recorded; detailed notes were also taken contemporaneously.

With their informed consent, after each focus group we conducted brief interviews with key agency staff. We asked staff to characterize the migrant population they serve and to describe the central issues faced by migrants in their respective communities. These interviews were useful for deepening our understanding of migrant experiences.

The Phoenix focus groups were held at two social service agencies. One provides educational opportunities to migrant women and the other a wide range of services to migrants and their families. As an incentive to participate, the latter agency supplied a $10 gift card to a local grocery store. No other incentives were provided to focus group participants. Participants were told that by participating in the research, they would be adding their voices to the national immigration debate, which has largely excluded the viewpoints of migrants. In our view, this proved to be an important incentive for participation. The Tucson focus group was held at an agency site that provides literacy classes to migrants. Thus, we conducted three focus groups with 23 migrants and interviewed five staff members.

The methodological literature on conducting focus groups with vulnerable populations suggests that homogenous groups can create solidarity among participants and enable them to validate one another's "everyday experiences of subjugation and survival" (Madriz, 2003; Kamberelis and Dimitriadis, 2005). Our focus groups were therefore conducted with migrant women. In a related project, we are more fully exploring the role of gender in shaping migrant experience. For this portion of the project, gender was not central to our analysis, but it is worth noting that the narratives analyzed below were provided by women. Since almost half of all migrants to the United States are women (Pew Hispanic Center, 2009), their perspectives are essential for exploring and understanding migrant experiences.

All but one of the focus group participants identified Mexico as their country of origin. The participants' ages ranged from 23 to 41. At a general level, these demographics reflect national immigration trends. Mexico is the country of origin for 59% of the undocumented population in the United States (Passel and Cohn, 2009); of Mexican migrants, 43% are women and the median age is 35 (Pew Hispanic Center, 2009). Half of the focus group participants had lived in the United States for less than five years; six participants had lived here from six to 10 years; and four participants reported living here for over 10 years. Most of those interviewed voluntarily self-disclosed within focus groups that they were undocumented, but a few had legal papers. This mix of long-term and recent residents, documented and undocumented migrants, was helpful for discerning the extent to which race operated as an independent force to shape migrant experiences.

Consistent with traditional techniques for analyzing focus group data, we worked together to identify common themes and patterns that emerged from participant narratives. We identified themes at the conclusion of each focus group and also after all focus groups had been completed. Perhaps more important, we sought to identify "critical stories" that captured significant majority or minority opinions (Krueger and Casey, 2009). Throughout this process, our goal was not to impose a structure on migrant narratives, but rather to listen to migrant voices in order to understand whether and how technologies of control affected their lives.

DISCIPLINING MOBILITY AND RACIAlIZING PUBLIC SPACE

In every focus group discussion, Maricopa County Sheriff Joe Arpaio emerged as one of the most powerful representations of the complex interplay between surveillance and enforcement rituals as a disciplinary force in the lives of migrants. Although we use Arpaio's name specifically, we are speaking more broadly about what his persona has come to embody, not simply the power he holds as an individual. In the lives of many of the participants, Arpaio represents global disciplinary strategies in their localized form. He is the "mobile, elastic border," the "gaze of surveillance," and the myriad enforcement rituals that (re)inforce migrants' "illegality" and vulnerability as a disposable source of labor.

One example of the broad impact Arpaio's image has in the community is that when participants were asked to give their first impressions about the words "border," "racial profiling," "freedom," and "immigration," Arpaio was associated with each word. As one participant argues, "I don't feel free here because of harassment; [because of] Sheriff Arpaio I am not free to visit Sedona or Flagstaff." In addition, some participants mentioned Arpaio to explain how their

access to, use of, and experience in public space has been restructured:

> What Arpaio is doing now, we cannot go somewhere like the State Fair. You don't go [out] feeling good. You do not go out of State. You cannot do a lot of things, like go places.

> I feel scared of Sheriff Arpaio. I feel scared to go places on the weekend.

The technologies of control deployed by Arpaio heightened the sense of fear and vulnerability experienced by migrants with whom we spoke. Identifying public places in which they felt safe came more easily to participants than did detailing the long list of areas in which they felt unsafe. As one individual said, "*there are just too many—it's the whole city.*" Other than their children's schools, safe spaces were the private spaces of home and church. Travel to public spaces is limited and done only when necessary: "We don't feel safe, but we must go, because we have to buy something to live [like] food and clothes." Prompted to address whether being women or migrants led to feeling unsafe in public spaces, the answer was definitively and consistently "*Being an immigrant.*"

The vulnerability felt in public space is so great that many participants said that they do not travel in areas where there is a known police presence for fear of detection. One participant told a story that powerfully captures how the threat of enforcement, rather than the enforcement itself, operates to discipline mobility:

> [I] heard on the T.V. that Arpaio is going for the libraries. My little boy needs to go the library for school, but I will not take him anymore [because I have no papers], so my husband takes him now.

An experience in our second focus group illustrates how the policing of public space disciplines the mobility of migrants. At an agency in Phoenix, we were awaiting the arrival of a vanload of seven migrants who had agreed to participate in our project. The staff member responsible for organizing their attendance was in touch with the driver via cell phone and assured us that they were on their way. Two participants had already arrived, but our informal conversation with them was interrupted by an urgent request from a staffer to join her in the hallway. Two police vehicles were stationed in the agency's parking lot, with their red lights blinking. Responding to a call next door, the officers had stopped in the agency's parking lot. Witnessing this, the vanload of participants feared they had been set up and sped away. The staff member immediately called them to convey that the police presence was a coincidence, but received a brief reply of "how could you" before being hung up on.

Such stories underscore De Genova's (2004 and 2005) argument that enforcement rituals serve a purpose beyond the netting of "illegal immigrants." These rituals exacerbate migrants' sense of vulnerability, by serving as a constant reminder of their "illegality," and therefore "deportability." One migrant narrative vividly illustrates this point:

> Someone broke into my sister's car and she was afraid to call the police because the guy was still in her car. When he left, she called the police, but they said there wasn't anything that they could do because he left the car. But she was really scared because the guy said he was going to come back. She said she was afraid and the police asked for her address, but she didn't give them her address because she was afraid ... she's not supposed to be here.

This story demonstrates how "illegality" deters individuals from seeking help even when they are the victims of a crime and/or their personal safety is at risk. In that narrative, the participant's sister had to restructure her use of space and access to social services to avoid detection from the authorities; her sense of vulnerability as an "illegal immigrant" disciplined her decision not to report her address to the police.

The pronounced sense of vulnerability in public space felt by many participants is illustrated by one person's preparations to leave the house and the daily fear she experiences for her husband:

> I drive every day to my job [and] to the school for my children. It is really stressful when you drive, because you see one patrol [car], "Oh my gosh," you are thinking—it's all you see. When I wake up in the morning, I check the car, the lights, because it is really hard. When my husband goes to work, it is really difficult, because you don't know if he will come back this day. ...

Agency conversations reinforced findings that enforcement tactics restructure migrants' access to, use of, and experiences in public space and highlighted counter-strategies migrants have developed in response to the disciplining of their mobility. For example, an immigration program manager at a long-standing community service organization in Phoenix characterized her client base as being "extremely fearful, stigmatized, and ashamed." She believes migrants practice a number of *"tactics of evasion"* to avoid detection by the authorities. These include "not driving, not leaving the house, not socializing in public, under-reporting crimes, and not seeking medical attention."

Further, this agency staffer believed that such tactics of evasion disrupt family networks because family members with legal status become hesitant to socialize or transport "illegal" family members, due to the "harsh" aiding and abetting laws passed in the state. Finally, she observed that many migrants simply "leave the state."

In other agency conversations, staff members characterized the migrant population they serve in terms of restricted mobility and fear, revealed in statements such as: "There are areas of town [migrants] just don't cross"; "I have heard [from migrants] that public spaces do not feel safe"; "[Migrants] no longer feel safe going to public parks"; "[Migrants] are afraid; they are staying in their homes ... many have just left the state"; and "[Migrants] are terrified—[fear] is the biggest issue they are facing right now." All of the agency staffers with whom we spoke believed that the various enforcement tactics performed by federal and local law enforcement officers in Arizona have heightened the fear and vulnerability of migrants and, as a result, have restructured migrants' use of public space.

Significantly, participants' narratives suggest that the surveillance and enforcement rituals employed in Arizona's two major cities are racialized. For example, some participants reported that if you "look Hispanic" or have "dark skin," you are at risk of being targeted by the police. "If you stand in the street and are Hispanic or Latin looking, [the police] stop you." Another participant mentioned the phrase "racial profiling," defining it as "What Arpaio is doing." Following this discussion, participants were asked whether they experience discrimination in Phoenix; many participants responded by nodding "yes." Asked why they feel they are discriminated against or treated differently, participants in one focus group looked around the room at one another and a few whispered, "color." This prompted one participant to relay this narrative:

> Two years ago, I came from Mexico to the U.S. I was in a truck at the border and they stopped us and made us all get off the truck very quickly. They saw me, because of my color, and asked me for my visa. I gave him my visa and he said, "Grab all your things. Who are you with?" I said my husband, my children, and my mother-in-law. He took me to the office. I was there for three hours. My husband was in an office upstairs for three hours, too. We didn't have any papers with us from the U.S. We were there for a very long time. They arrested my husband. I told them that my husband was working in the U.S. They kept us there for two days. They kept us all separate for two days, sleeping on the floor. They wouldn't let me be with my baby, and I didn't bring milk or diapers or anything. And my baby was crying from hunger. They took my husband's visa away for five years and mine and my children's for one year. I think it was because of my skin color, because everyone else on the truck was from here. And we all got off quickly—and the only [person] stopped [was] me.

Other participants discussed various forms of social sorting they had experienced; typically, they framed their experience of discrimination and racialization, in contrast to whiteness:

> I have crossed three times in my life, but each time I had papers. The police stopped me each time and there were three, four, five police in a little room asking the same question. My character was nice. I said, "see my visa, I need to go from Mexico to U.S.A." The police believed me because I had papers, but they stopped me three times. I think it is because of the color of my skin.

> I think it is more free for the white people than the Hispanic people, because even if we have citizenship they are mean. If they see white people, they say, "You can go." So that's why I think [white people] are freer to travel and the Hispanic people [are less free to travel].

These narratives highlight Mohanram's (1999: 8) argument that racialization "produces two types of bodies in space": whiteness has the ability to move, resulting in the unmarking of the body. The production of blackness, in contrast, is signified through marking and is static and immobilizing. In this instance, whiteness is a material force, in part, because it enables different forms of mobility.

Migrants with legal papers also reported experiencing differential treatment based on their race, providing further evidence that the immigration climate, at least in Arizona, is racialized and that technologies of control disproportionately target brown bodies. The story of one documented migrant illuminates this point:

> One time I was putting my kids in the car and a police arrived. He saw the color of my skin and he said that I didn't have documentation and that I had left my children in the car. I said, "No, I was right here, putting them in the car." A Mexican woman was there and she said that I didn't leave them in

the car alone; I was putting them in the car. And the police said, "Okay, someone is going to come and explain your rights to you." 1 told them that I have rights and papers and asked: "What is your motive for asking me for my papers?" The Border Patrol came and he checked [on the computer] and saw that I do have papers. He said that the police do this because they want to take people [deport them]. They asked all these questions because of the color of my skin.

Asked whether they thought that the climate toward migrants in Arizona is racialized, three staff members affirmed that it was. The first said, "it is racial, and if you notice on your tape, Joe Arpaio was mentioned several times as an issue that has come up a lot. People are wondering: Is it because of my skin color, it is because I am Latino, because I am Hispanic?" Moreover, her own family members had "been stopped several times without even having an excuse; they don't have a reason that they are being stopped, so, yes, definitely it is a racial issue." A second staffer agreed "completely [with her response], I think it is racial." The third added: "Absolutely [the climate is racialized] … I hear many stories of racism."

Most participants identified their race as the source of discrimination, but a few attributed their differential treatment primarily to language. In their view, speaking with a Spanish accent and/or not speaking perfect English marked them as "illegal" and therefore undeserving of social services, such as health care or protection from local law enforcement:

> All the time language is the barrier, and sometimes when they see you they say, "Oh, you cannot speak English, then we cannot see you" or something, but when you say you can speak English, they say, "O.K."

> [The police] say they don't know where [my] address is. I say "What?" I don't know why, because near to my house is a police station. You know why? Because they know I speak Spanish.

As noted, our conversations with migrants were in English. Despite their ability to communicate in basic English, some participants felt that officials, social service agencies, and store employees frequently used their lack of language proficiency to socially categorize them as "illegal immigrants" and, as a result, to deny them access to services and assistance. Thus, the enforcement of difference in this context is racialized, particularly given the discursive marking of brown Spanish-speaking bodies as "illegal" in the popular media and imagery. Ostensibly, it is not possible to determine from a person's appearance whether he or she is documented or a United States citizen. Yet the narratives here suggest that some law enforcement officers and social service employees use brown skin and Spanish as proxy for "illegality" and identity marker for being "out of place."

LISTENING TO MIGRANT VOICES

Migrant narratives in Arizona affirm the literature that suggests that law enforcement officers and government officials employ technologies of control to discipline and restructure migrants' use of, experience in, and access to public space. Narratives by staff at agencies serving migrants strongly support the perspective of migrants. In Arizona, some state actors combine surveillance and policing tactics, such as sporadic immigration raids and neighborhood "sweeps." These disciplinary strategies insure that migrants, Latina/os, and those with Spanish accents are less free to use public space than others are.

These migrant narratives affirm that the technologies of control employed in Phoenix and Tucson, Arizona, are racialized and are often indifferent to the legal status of those targeted. These findings illuminate Coutin's (2005) argument that the criminality of migrants has become individualized as a "condition of person," allowing law enforcement to regulate public space and, increasingly, civilians. This is physically performed on the racialized bodies of those identified as "illegal." Such strategies and tactics, which in Arizona target the bodies and spatial locations of those presumed to be Latina/o, significantly restructured the mobility of the migrants who spoke with us. Their narratives illustrate how global disciplinary strategies operate to reify connections between race, space, and "illegality," in part by normalizing the enforcement of policies and practices that regulate mobility and sanction exclusion, neglect, denial of social services, and access to public space. Racialization of public space insures that whiteness becomes valorized as an all access card, while people of color are made to feel out of place and suspect. For brown-skinned migrants in Arizona, movement in public spaces becomes marked and subject to technologies of control. Their experience of public space is profoundly shaped by their sense of "ever-present" vulnerability as a deportable/ disposable body (De Genova, 2004).

The surveillance and enforcement rituals used in Arizona's two largest cities fostered a sense of fear and vulnerability and, consequently, self-discipline among participants. This finding is consistent with Razack (2002) and Parenti's (1999) claims that surveillance is effective partly because it often becomes internalized. Virtually all participants regulated their mobility because of fear of surveillance and their perceived risk of being targeted by police. Undocumented and documented migrants raised the legitimate fear (given current enforcement practices) that they, or someone close to them, could be arrested and deported at any time. Arizona attorney Kara Hartzler reported seeing "40–50 jailings a month of people with potentially valid claims to citizenship"; in her words, "these cases are surprisingly, painfully common" (Gamboa, 2009: A1).

Migrants regulated their mobility and modified their daily activities to avoid the risk of detection by technologies of control within urban spaces in Arizona. Accommodation strategies employed by migrants reveal their power to resist *and* the oppression they experience within Arizona. Participants chose to self-segregate in the limited areas that they identified as safe: home, church, and their children's schools. Self-segregation is evidence that technologies of control, such as surveillance and policing, operate to cleanse or "purify" the body politic and to insure that public space—parks, libraries, streets, and hospitals—will be largely reserved for those privileged by citizenship,

wealth, and, more important, whiteness (Romero, 2006; Amster, 2008).

Although our primary research focuses only on Arizona, it is a site of strategic importance in the immigration and border debate within the United States. We do not claim that this research can be generalized to all cities, or that these findings can be generalized to other migrant groups. Yet we believe that listening to the voices of migrants has strong validity for exploring whether and how global disciplinary strategies come to ground in a particular locale to shape migrant lives.

By listening to the voices of migrants, researchers can begin to untangle the complex ways in which technologies of control shape their lived experience. Their narratives show that the disciplining of mobility is partly *physical*— it is about controlling or manipulating the body through arrest, detention, or deportation. Mobility is also restrained *spatially*, public spaces are either experienced as accessible or inaccessible, safe or unsafe. Perhaps most profoundly, mobility is restrained in the *imaginary*—the construction of what is possible in one's life. Migrants and Latina/os have had little influence over the political processes that have created the technologies of control that play a key role in self-disciplining their mobility through internalized fear and vulnerability. This dialectic between technologies of control and internalized social control guarantees that migrants will be kept intentionally outside public space and creates the opportunity for broader public discourse about borders, immigration, and citizenship.

We hope that our research will inspire others to explore how global disciplinary strategies and technologies of control are reshaping public life for recent migrants in other locales and countries. We urge researchers to promote the inclusion of migrant voices in the broader debate about who ought have access to public space and public life in the wealthy democratic societies of the West. Since the work performed by migrants in the United States and in many other nations has been pivotal to global and national economic growth, social justice demands no less.

REFERENCES

Aas, Katja Franko. (2007). "Analysing a World in Motion: Global Flows Meet 'Criminology of the Other.'" *Theoretical Criminology* 11, 2: 283–303.

Amoore, Louise. (2006). "Biometric Borders: Governing Mobilities in the War on Terror." *Political Geography* 25: 336–351.

Amster, Randall. (2008). *Lost in Space: The Criminalization, Globalization, and the Urban Ecology of Homelessness.* New York: LFB Scholarly Publishing LLC.

Archibold, Randal C. (2008). "Arizona Seeing Signs of Flight by Immigrants." *The New York Times* (February 12), at www.nytimes.com/2008/02/12/us/12arizona.html.

Bass, Sandra. (2001). "Out of Place: Petit Apartheid and the Police." Dragan Milovanovic and Katheryn K. Russell (eds.). *Petit Apartheid in the U.S. Criminal Justice System.* Durham, NC: Carolina Academic Press: 43–53.

Broeders, Dennis and Godfried Engbersen. (2007). "The Fight Against Illegal Migration: Identification Policies and Immigrants' Counterstrategies." *American Behavioral Scientist* 30,12: 1592–1609.

Calavita, Kitty. (2005). *Immigrants at the Margins: Law, Race, and Exclusion in Southern Europe.* NY: Cambridge University Press.

Ceyhan, Ayse and Anastassia Tsoukala. (2002). "The Secularization of Migration in Western Societies: Ambivalent Discourse and Policies." *Alternatives* 27: 21–39.

Coutin, Susan Bibler. (2005). "Contesting Criminology: Illegal Immigration and the Spatialization of Illegality." *Theoretical Criminology* 9, 1: 5–33.

Cresswell, Tim. (2004). *Place: A Short Introduction.* Maiden, MA: Blackwell Publishing.

Dauvergne, Catherine. (2008). *Making People Illegal: What Globalization Means for Migration and Law.* New York: Cambridge University Press.

Davis, Mike. (1992). *City of Quartz: Excavating the Future in Los Angeles.* New York: Vintage Books.

De Genova, Nicholas. (2005). *Working the Boundaries: Race, Space, and "Illegality" in Mexican Chicago.* Durham, NC: Duke University Press.

2004 "The Legal Production of Mexican/Migrant 'Illegality.'" *Latino Studies* 2: 165–185.

Engbersen, Gottfried. (2001). "The Unanticipated Consequences of Panopticon Europe: Residence Strategies of Illegal Immigrants." V. Guiraudon and C. Joppke (eds.), *Controlling a New Migration World.* London: Routledge Press: 222–246.

Gamboa, Suzanne. (2009). "Citizens Held as Illegals." *Arizona Daily Sun* (April): A1.

Gonzalez, Daniel. (2009). "Census Concern: Immigrants May Avoid the Count." *Arizona Republic* (April 13): A5.

Herbert, Steve. (1997). *Policing Space.* Minneapolis, MN: University of Minnesota Press.

Hiemstra, Nancy. (2008). "Spatial Disjunctures and Division in the New West: Latino Immigration to Leadville, Colorado." Richard C. Jones (ed.), *Immigrations Outside Megalopolis: Ethnic Transformation in the Heartland.* New York: Lexington Books.

Hoefer, Michael, Nancy Rytina, and Bryan C. Baker. (2009). "Estimates of the Unauthorized Population Residing in the United States: January 2008." Office of Immigration Statistics, Department of Homeland Security; at: www.dhs.gov/xlibrary/assets/statistics/publications/ois_ill_pe_2008.pdf.

Hyden, L.C. and Paul Bulow. (2003). "Who's Talking: Drawing Conclusions from Focus Groups: Some Methodological Considerations." *International Journal of Social Research Methodology* 6,4: 305–321.

Inda, Jonathan Xavier. (2007). "*The Value of Immigrant Life.*" Denise Segura and Patricia Zavella (eds.), Women and Migration in the U.S.-Mexico Borderlands. Durham, NC: Duke University Press: 134–157.

Kamberelis, George and Greg Dimitriadis. (2005). "Focus Groups: Strategic Articulations of Pedagogy, Politics, and Inquiry." Norman K. Denizin and Yvonna Lincoln (eds.), *The Sage Handbook of Qualitative Research.* Thousand Oaks, CA: Sage: 887–907.

Krueger, Richard A. and Mary Anne Casey. (2009). *Focus Groups: A Practical Guide for Applied Research.* Los Angeles: Sage.

Lyon, David. (2003). *Surveillance as Social Sorting.* New York: Routledge Press.

Madriz, Esther I. (2003). "*Focus Groups in Feminist Research.*" Norman Denizen and Yvonna Lincoln (eds.). The Sage Handbook of Qualitative Research. Thousand Oaks, CA: Sage: 835–850.

Meehan, Albert J. and Michael C. Ponder. (2002). "Race and Place: The Ecology of Racial Profiling African-American Motorists." *Justice Quarterly* 19,3: 400–430.

Michalowski, Raymond J. (2007). "Border Militarization and Migrant Suffering: A Case of Transnational Inquiry." *Social Justice,* 34,2: 60–72.

Milovanovic, Dragan and Katheryn K. Russell. (2001). *Petit Apartheid in the U.S. Criminal Justice System.* Durham, NC: Carolina Academic Press.

Mitchell, Don. (2003). *The Right to the City: Social Justice and the Fight for Public Space.* New York: Guilford Press.

Mohanram, Radhika. (1999). *Black Body: Women, Colonialism, and Space.* Minneapolis, MN: University of Minnesota Press.

Nelson, Lise and Nancy Hiemstra. (2008). "Latino Immigrants and the Renegotiation of Place and Belonging in Small Town America." *Social and Cultural Geography* 9,3: 319–342.

Parenti, Christian. (1999). *Lockdown America: Police and Prisons in the Age of Crisis.* New York: Verso.

Passel, Jeffery S. and D'Vera Cohn. (2009). "*A Portrait of Unauthorized Immigration in the United States.*" Pew Hispanic Center. At http://pewhispanic.org/files/reports/107.pdf.

Peterson, Marina. (2006). "Patrolling the Plaza: Privatized Public Space and the Neoliberal State in Down-town Los Angeles." *Urban Anthropology,* 35,4: 355–383.

Pew Hispanic Center. (2009). Arizona Population and Labor Force Characteristics, 2006–2008. Accessed January 12, 2009, at http://pewhispanic.org/files/factsheets/37.pdf.

Pickering, Sharon and Leanne Weber. (2006). *Borders, Mobility and Technologies of Control.* The Netherlands: Springer Press.

Pollack, Shoshana. (2003). "Focus-Group Methodology in Research with Incarcerated Women: Race, Power, and Collective Experience." *AFFILIA* 18,4: 461–472.

Razack, Sherene H. (2002). *Race, Space, and the Law: Unmapping a White Settler Society.* Toronto: Between the Lines Press.

Robinson, William I. (2007). "'Aqui estamos y no nos vamos!' Global Capital and Immigrant Rights." *Race and Class* 48,2: 77–91.

Romero, Mary. (2006). "Racial Profiling and Immigration Law Enforcement: Rounding up of the Usual

Suspects in the Latino Community." *Critical Sociology* 32: 448–472.

Sassen, Saskia. (2006). *Cities in a World Economy.* Third Edition. Pine Forge Press.

1998a "America's Immigration 'Problem.'" *World Policy Journal* 6,4: 811–832.

1998b *Globalization and Its Discontents: Essays on the New Mobility of People and Money.* New York: The New Press.

Schaeffer, Robert K. (2009). *Understanding Globalization: The Social Consequences of Political, Economic, and Environmental Change.* NY: Rowman & Littlefield.

Stephen, Lynn. (2004). "The Gaze of Surveillance in the Lives of Mexican Immigrant Workers." *Development* 47,1: 97–102.

United States Census Bureau. (2009a). "State and County QuickFacts, Phoenix, Arizona." Accessed April 14, 2009, at http://quickfacts.census.gov/qfd/states/04/0455000.html.

2009b "State and County QuickFacts, Tucson, Arizona." Accessed April 14, 2009, at http://quickfacts.census.gov/qfd/states/04/0477000.html.

United States Customs and Border Protection. (2009). "Welcome: Tucson Sector." At www.cbp.gov/xp/cgov/border_security/border_patrol/border_patrol_sectors/tucson_sector_az/tucson_index.xml.

Weber, Leanne. (2006). "The Shifting Frontiers of Migration Control." Sharon Pickering and Leanne Weber (eds.), *Borders, Mobility and Technologies of Control.* Dordrecht, The Netherlands: Springer: 21–44.

Wonders, Nancy A. (2008). "Globalization, Border Reconstruction Projects, and Transnational Crime." *Social Justice* 34,2: 33–46.

2006 "Global Flows, Semi-Permeable Borders and New Channels of Inequality." Sharon Pickering and Leanne Weber (eds.), *Borders, Mobility and Technologies of Control.* The Netherlands: Springer Press: 63–86.

Wonders, Nancy A. and Raymond J. Michalowski. (2001). "Bodies, Borders, and Sex Tourism in a Globalized World: A Tale of Two Cities—Amsterdam and Havana." *Social Problems* 48,4: 545–545.

PART IV

Readings on Correctional
Policies and Issues

UNLOCKING AMERICA

Why and How To Reduce America's Prison Population

The JFA Institute

James Austin, Todd Clear, Troy Duster, David F. Greenberg, John Irwin, Candace McCoy, Alan Mobley, Barbara Owen, and Joshua Page.

PROLOGUE

"Mr. Libby was sentenced to 30 months of prison, two years of probation and a $250,000 fine ... I respect the jury's verdict. But I have concluded that the prison sentence given to Mr. Libby is excessive."

—President George W. Bush. July 2, 2007.

President Bush was right. A prison sentence for Lewis "Scooter" Libby was excessive—so too was the long three year probation term. But while he was at it, President Bush should have commuted the sentences of hundreds of thousands of Americans who each year have also received prison sentences for crimes that pose little if any danger or harm to our society.

In the United States, every year since 1970, when only 196,429 persons were in state and federal prisons, the prison population has grown. Today there are over 1.5 million in state and federal prisons. Another 750,000 are in the nation's jails. The growth has been constant—in years of rising crime and falling crime, in good economic times and bad, during wartime and while we were at peace. A generation of growth has produced prison populations that are now eight times what they were in 1970.

And there is no end to the growth under current policies. The PEW Charitable Trust reports that under current sentencing policies the state and federal prison populations will grow by another 192,000 prisoners over the next five years. The incarceration rate will increase from 491 to 562 per 100,000 population. And the nation will have to spend an additional $27.5 billion in operational and construction costs over this five-year period on top of the over $60 billion now being spent on corrections each year.[1]

This generation-long growth of imprisonment has occurred not because of growing crime rates, but because of changes in sentencing policy that resulted in dramatic increases in the proportion of felony convictions resulting in prison sentences *and* in the length-of-stay in prison that those sentences required. Prison

"Punishment Does Not Fit the Crime"—Some Recent Examples

"Offenders"	Prior Record	Crime	Description	Prison Sentence
Elisa Kelly, George Robinson. *Mother and stepfather*[3]	None	Nine counts of contributing to the delinquency of a minor	Hosting drinking party for son's nine friends at parent's home	Original sentence of 8 years, later reduced to 27 months
Cecilia Ruiz. *Single parent—two children ages 6 and 8*[4]	None	Forgery	Deleting a DUI conviction from the county DUI data base	42 months
Jessica Hall. *Unemployed mother of three children with Marine husband serving in Iraq*[5]	None	Throwing a missile at an occupied vehicle	Threw a cup of McDonald's coffee at another car that cut her off while driving	24 months
Lewis "Scooter" Libby[6]	None	Perjury	Provided false testimony to U.S. Attorney (four counts)	30 months
Stephen May[7]	None	Child molestation	Inappropriately touched two girls and a boy—there was no sexual activity or penetration	75 years
Genarlow Wilson[8]	None	Aggravated child molestation	17-year-old male had consensual oral sex with a 15-year-old girl at a party that was video taped.	10 years

[1] Public Safety, Public Spending: Forecasting America's Prison Population 2007–2011. Phil, PA: Pew Charitable Trusts, 2007.

[2] In some cites the percentages are higher. For example, in Baltimore, one in five young black men between ages 20 and 30 is incarcerated, and 52% are under some form of correctional supervision. Jason Ziedenberg and Eric Lotke. *Tipping Point: Maryland's Overuse of Incarceration and the Impact on Public Safety*. Washington, DC: Justice Policy Institute, 2005.

[3] Washington Post, July 4, 2007, pages A1, A11, "Penalties for Teen Drinking Parties Vary Widely in Area".

[4] Washington Post, June 30, 2007, page B4, Ex-Aide Given 3 1/2-Year Sentence.

[5] www.washingtonpost.com/wp-dyn/content/article/2007/02/17/AR2007021701560.html

[6] Washington Post, July 4, 2007, page A4, "Bush Says He's Not Ruling Out Pardon for Libby".

[7] State of Arizona vs. Stephen May, Maricopa Superior Court, No. CR2006-030290-001 SE.

[8] abcnews.go.com/Primetime/LegalCenter/story?id=1693362&page=1.

populations have been growing steadily for a generation, although the crime rate is today about what it was in 1973 when the prison boom started. It is tempting to say that crime rates fell over the past dozen years because imprisonment worked to lower them, but a look at data about crime and imprisonment will show that prison populations continued to swell long after crime rates declined and stayed low. Today, whatever is driving imprisonment policies, it is not primarily crime.

Prisons are self-fueling systems. About two-thirds of the 650,000 prison admissions are persons who have failed probation or parole—approximately half of these people have been sent to prison for technical violations. Having served their sentences, roughly 650,000 people are released each year having served an average of 2–3 years. About 40% will ultimately be sent back to prison as "recidivists"—in many states, for petty drug and property crimes or violations of parole requirements that do not even constitute crimes. This high rate of recidivism is, in part, a result of a range of policies that increase surveillance over people released from prison, impose obstacles to their reentry into society, and eliminate support systems that ease their transition from prison to the streets.

Prison policy has exacerbated the festering national problem of social and racial inequality. Incarceration rates for blacks and Latinos are now more than six times higher than for whites; 60% of America's prison population is either African-American or Latino. A shocking eight percent of black men of working age are now behind bars, and 21% of those between the ages of 25 and 44 have served a sentence at some point in their lives. At current rates, one-third of all black males, one-sixth of Latino males, and one in 17 white males will go to prison during their lives. Incarceration rates this high are a national tragedy.[2]

Women now represent the fastest growing group of incarcerated persons. In 2001, they were more than three times as likely to end up in prison as in 1974, largely due to their low-level involvement in drug-related activity and the deeply punitive sentencing policies aimed at drugs. The massive incarceration of young males from mostly poor and working-class neighborhoods—and the taking of women from their families and jobs—has crippled their potential for forming healthy families and achieving economic gains.

The authors of this report have spent their careers studying crime and punishment. We are convinced that we need a different strategy. Our contemporary laws and justice system practices exacerbate the crime problem, unnecessarily damage the lives of millions of people, waste tens of billions of dollars each year, and create less than ideal social and economic conditions in many sections of our largest American cities.

This report focuses on how we can reduce the nation's prison population without adversely affecting public safety. For this to happen, we will need to reduce the number of people sent to prison and, for those who do go to prison, shorten the length of time they spend behind bars and under parole and probation surveillance. People who break the law must be held accountable, but many of those currently incarcerated should receive alternative forms of punishment, and those who are sent to prison must spend a shorter period incarcerated before coming home to our communities. Our recommendations would reestablish practices that were the norm in America for most of the previous century, when incarceration rates were a fraction of what they are today.

We first summarize the current problem, explaining how some of the most popular assumptions about crime and punishment are incorrect. In particular, we demonstrate that incarcerating large numbers of people has little impact on crime, and show how the improper use of probation and parole increases incarceration rates while doing little to control crime. We then turn to ideas about how to change this flawed system. We set out an organizing principle for analyzing sentencing reform, embracing a retributive sentencing philosophy that is mainstream among contemporary prison policy analysts and sentencing scholars.

Based on that analysis, we make a series of recommendations for changing current sentencing laws and correctional policies. Each recommendation is practical and cost-effective. As we show through examples of cases in which they have been tried, they can be adopted without jeopardizing public safety. If implemented on a national basis, our recommendations would gradually and safely reduce the nation's prison and jail populations to half their current size. This reduction would generate savings of an estimated $20 billion a year that could then be reinvested in far more promising crime prevention strategies. The result would be a system of justice and punishment that is far less costly, more effective, and more humane than what we have today.

I. CRIME AND INCARCERATION

By far the major reason for the increase in the prison populations at least since 1990 has been longer lengths of imprisonment.

Why The Prison Explosion?

America's incarceration rate is exploding. In 1970, there were fewer than 200,000 people in prison. By 2006, there were approximately 1.6 million state and federal prisoners (or nearly 500 per 100,000 population). Each year over 730,000 people are admitted to state and federal prisons, and a much larger number (over 10 million) go to local jails. If we add to the prison population the nearly 750,000 people incarcerated in local jails today—at the beginning of 2007—the total number imprisoned in the U.S. on any given day is 2.2 million.[1]

The United States is the world leader in imprisonment. China, with a much larger population, has the second largest incarcerated population, with 1.5 million imprisoned. With 737 people incarcerated per 100,000 persons, the U.S. also leads the world in rates of incarceration—well above Russia, which has the next highest rate of 581 per 100,000.[2] The other Western democratic countries manage with prison populations far smaller than ours.

By far the major reason for the increase in prison populations at least since 1990 has been longer lengths of imprisonment. The adoption of truth in sentencing provisions that require prisoners to serve most of their sentences in prison, a wide variety of mandatory minimum sentencing provisions that prevent judges from placing defendants on probation even when their involvement in the conduct that led to the conviction was minor, reductions in the amount of good time a prisoner can receive while imprisoned, and more conservative parole boards have significantly impacted the length of stay.

For example, in a special study by the U.S. Department of Justice on truth in sentencing, between 1990 and 1997, the numbers of prison admissions increased by only 17% (from 460,739 to 540,748), while the prison population increased by 60% (from 689,577 to 1,100,850). This larger increase in the prison population can only be caused by a longer length of stay.[3]

This is further confirmed in Table 1, which shows sentence lengths, time served, and period spent on parole supervision. These U.S. Department of Justice data are based on individuals released in 1993 and 2002. The 2002 data underestimate the average length of current prison sentences because they do not include time served by prisoners sentenced under recent punitive laws (such as "three strikes and you're out") who have not yet been released. Nevertheless, the average time served by those who were released still increased substantially—from 21 to 30 months. Similarly, the parole supervision period increased from 19 to 24 months, and the total average period of supervision increased from 40 to 56 months.

Table 1: Sentence Lengths, Time Served, and Length of Parole—Supervision, 1993 versus 2002

Length of Supervision	1993	2002
Average sentence	66 months	65 months
Average time served	21 months	30 months
Average parole supervision	19 months	26 months
Total time under supervision	40 months	56 months

Source: Prison Statistics. US Department of Justice, Office of Justice Programs, Bureau of Justice, 2006.

Not only are our lengths of imprisonment significantly longer than they were in earlier periods in our penal history, but they are considerably longer than in most Western nations. For the same crimes, American prisoners receive sentences twice as long as English prisoners, three times as long as Canadian prisoners, four times as long as Dutch prisoners, five to 10 times as long as French prisoners, and five times as long as Swedish prisoners.[4] Yet these countries' rates of violent

---

1   William J. Sabol, Todd D. Minton, and Paige M. Harrison. Prison and Jail Inmates at Midyear 2006. Bureau of Justice Statistics Bulletin, Washington, DC: US DOJ, Office of Justice Programs, 2007.

2   *Prison Brief—Highest to Lowest Rates*. International Centre for Prison Studies, King's College, London. 2006 www.kcl.ac.uk/depsta/rel/icps/world.

3   Paula M. Ditton and Doris James Wilson. "Truth in Sentencing in State Prisons." Washington, DC: US DOJ, Bureau of Justice Statistics, 1999.

4   David P. Farrington, Patrick A. Langan, and Michael Tonry, eds. *Cross-National Studies in Crime and Justice*.

crime are lower than ours, and their rates of property crime are comparable.[5]

Most prisoners are incarcerated for crimes that do not compare with the costs of their imprisonment. We spend over $200 billion each year to fund the criminal justice system.[6] In contrast, the total economic loss to victims of crime in 2002 was an estimated $15.6 billion, or about one-tenth of the total cost of the nation's criminal justice system.[7] The typical (median) costs per crime for each victim was $100, which includes losses from property theft or damage, cash losses, medical expenses, and lost pay. While the financial losses and physical and emotional injuries sustained by victims can be significant, they represent only a fraction of what it costs to incarcerate the offenders.

Table 2 illustrates the vast disparity between the

sentence for robbery in the United States is 94 months, or about eight years, of which the typical time served is 55 months. Together with the time spent in jail pre-trial, the average robbery offender is incarcerated for 60 months at a cost of approximately $113,000.

This historic rise in incarceration has often been attributed to the "fact" that in the early 1970s, the U.S. faced a steadily increasing crime problem, leaving no choice but to increase the use of incarceration mas-sively. But this explanation for the imprisonment binge is misleading and incomplete. Crime rates have grown in other countries and states within the U.S. without provoking a large growth in prison populations. There are various ways a country can respond to increased crime; more prisons is just one of them. Moreover, statistics show that it was not primarily a rise in crime

Table 2: Economic Loss to Victims and Costs of Incarceration

Type of Crime	Average Victim Loss	Prison Sentence	Pretrial Time	Time Served	Total Time	Incarceration Costs
Robbery	$1,258	94*	5	55	60	$113,000
Burglary	$1,545	52	5	29	34	$64,000
Larceny theft	$730	34	5	20	25	$47,000
Auto theft	$6,646	27	5	17	22	$41,000

*Times shown in months

Source: Matthew R. Durose and Patrick A. Langan. Felony Sentences in State Courts, 2000. Washington, DC: Bureau of Justice Statistics, 2003, and Callie M. Rennison and Michael Rand. Criminal Victimization, 2002. Washington, DC: Bureau of Justice Statistics, 2003.

economic losses associated with four common crimes and the amount expended to incarcerate the offender. For example, the average loss associated with a robbery reported to the police is $1,258. The typical prison

that fueled the increase in incarceration rates.

Figure 1 compares changes in the nation's crime rates—as measured by the FBI's Uniform Crime Reports (UCR) that are based on police records that primarily reflect victim reports to their local police departments—with changes in the rates of incarcera-tion from 1931 to 2004. After being relatively stable for decades, between 1964 and 1974 the UCR Crime Index—which measures murder, assault, rape, burglary, robbery, theft, auto theft, and arson—increased signifi-cantly even as the incarceration rate remained relatively

Washington, DC: US DOJ, Bureau of Justice Statistics, 2004.

5   Franklin E. Zimring and Gordon Hawkins, *Crime Is Not the Problem: Lethal Violence in America.* New York: Oxford UP, 1997.

6   www.ojp.usdoj.gov.

7   Callie M. Rennison and Michael Rand. *Criminal Victimization, 2002.* Washington, DC: Bureau of Justice Statistics, 2003.

Figure 1. Crime and Incarceration Rate Comparisons

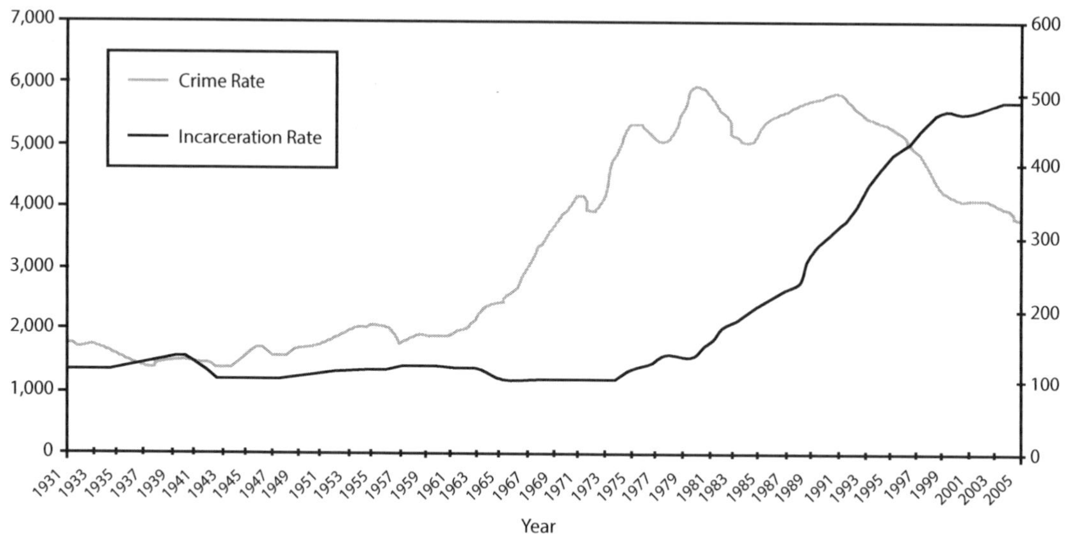

stable.[8] Thereafter, the UCR crime rate swung up and down until 1992 when it began a steady decline.

The UCR is one of two ways that the government tracks crime rates. The other, the National Crime Victimization Survey (NCVS), was established in 1973 in recognition of the fact that the UCR had major biases in the way it gauged crime. The NCVS is often considered a more accurate and complete picture of crime in the U.S., as it is based on interviews of household members.

As shown in Figure 2, NCVS shows no increases in property crimes from 1973 to 1980. Similarly, NCVS show no increase in violent crimes between 1973 and in 1993, unlike the UCR data which showed a steady increase over the same time period. There is contradictory evidence of a 1970s crime epidemic, which was a major rationale for expanding the use of imprisonment.[9] Regardless of which measuring method is used,

there was no large drop in the incarceration rate before crime rates began to increase after 1963. While a variety of theories exist as to why crime rates rose from 1964 to 1974, the cause was not a large drop in prison populations, which remained fairly stable until 1973.[10] Prison populations began increasing only *after* crime rates had already stabilized or, according to the crime victimization surveys, had already began to decline.

Beginning in the 1960s, law and order advocates declared a war on crime. Conservative politicians (starting with Barry Goldwater in the early 1960s), backed by religious groups (the Moral Majority of the 1970s)

---

8   Prison populations fell by about eight percent between 1960 and 1970. This small drop could not remotely have been a major cause of the 2.4-fold rise in UCR index offenses in that decade. *Sourcebook of Criminal Justice Statistics.* US DOJ, Bureau of Justice Statistics. 278, 500 www.albany.edu/sourcebook.

9   Criminologists debate the sources of the discrepancy between the growth in violent crime shown in UCR data and the decline shown by the NCVS. The U.S. Department of Justice has suggested that victims were more likely to

report crimes to the police, and law enforcement agencies improved their recording and reporting systems. If these explanations are correct, these changes in reporting created the illusion of a growing crime problem when there actually was none. Also note that the NCVS property rate is based on the number of households, which is lower than the number of persons.

10   As the NCVS was started in 1973, it cannot be used to determine if—or how much—crime rates increased between 1964 and 1973. Most criminologists agree, however, that there was an increase, and that some of the increase was due to demographics—the large numbers of baby boomers passing through their high crime-committing years. People aged 15 to 24 commit a substantial proportion of index crimes. The persons in the baby-boom cohorts started reaching 15 in 1964, and began turning 40 around 1990. But demographics cannot explain all of the increase.

Figure 2. UCR and NCVS Crime Rate Comparisons

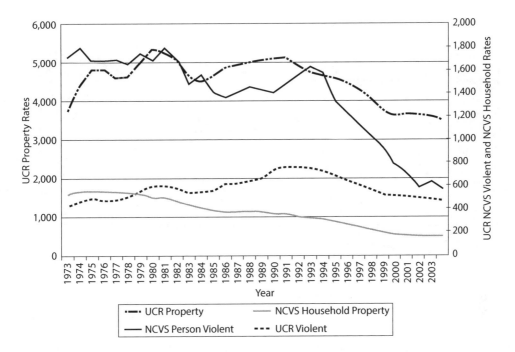

and right-wing media figures (such as talk-radio hosts of the 1980s), argued that crime was out of control largely because lenient judges gave lawbreakers too many chances before they were punished, predatory criminals avoided punishment because of technicalities in the law, and criminals returned to the streets after serving short sentences. These advocates of a war on crime suggested harsh mandatory punishments were needed that would both incapacitate people convicted of serious crimes and deter others from breaking the law.

The media contributed to the fervor over the "crime problem" through its unrelenting focus on crime—the more heinous and sensational, the better. Broadcast journalists discovered that sensational crimes drew large audiences. The media publicized horrific but rare crimes (the kidnapping and murder of Polly Klass, the sexual murder of Megan Kanka, and the attack perpetrated by Willie Horton while on work release). In so doing, it led Americans to believe wrongly that they were at high risk of being assaulted, raped, or murdered.

During this same period, a growing number of neo-conservative social scientists claimed that "law and order" ideas and policies rested on a sound scientific foundation. In 1975, political scientist James Q. Wilson published the widely read *Thinking About Crime*, in which he soberly admonished liberal/humanitarian social scientists to remember that " … *wicked people exist. Nothing avails except to set them apart from innocent people.*"[11]

For Wilson and those who initially shared his views, incapacitating what they believed was a growing and more menacing type of criminal was a necessary weapon in the war against crime. By insisting that *only* stepped-up criminal justice interventions could cope with crime, Wilson and others like John J. Dilulio and William Bennett were arguing against the strategies recommended by the riot commissions of the 1960s and by experts on poverty and racial problems: alleviating poverty, combating discrimination, and opening

---

11   James Q. Wilson. *Thinking About Crime*. New York: Random House, 1975. 235. See also by Wilson: "Lock 'Em Up." *New York Times Magazine* 9 March 1975: 11.

Figure 3. Incarceration Rates by Crime Category (1980–2003)

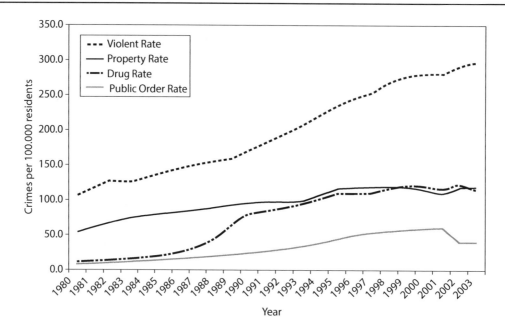

up opportunities that had previously been shut off by racial discrimination and class inequality.

Remedying social inequities, they maintained, was not the job of the government and would not reduce crime. Their solution—more people in prison—rested on the use of an institution that had become substantially discredited among penologists in the 1960s. Their views were enthusiastically supported by the federal government, which subsequently funded studies to identify the "career criminal."

Public receptivity to this hawkish perspective was enhanced by anxieties associated with the rapid rise in crime during the 1960s, the eruption of riots in a number of American cities, and the advent of the civil rights and feminist movements, challenging longstanding racial and gender hierarchies. These developments, exploited by well-funded conservative polemicists whose arguments were widely publicized in the media, helped to shape public response to the high-profile death of athlete Len Bias from a cocaine overdose in 1986. Along with the growing use of crack cocaine, his death sparked a rapid government response. All these factors converged, creating a "perfect storm" that drove the imprisonment binge.

Thus after 1975 many laws were passed, supported by politicians of both parties, designed to increase the probability of a prison sentence rather than jail or probation, dramatically increasing the length of prison sentences for certain crimes, and requiring prisoners to serve a greater proportion of their sentences—three results that we will discuss in greater detail below.

New legislation increasing the penalties for the sale and possession of cocaine, particularly crack cocaine, intensified the upward trend. As is evident in Figure 3, increased penalties for drug offenses strongly fueled much of the growth of state prison populations starting in the late 1980s. Since then most of the growth in prison systems has been due to the increased incarceration of persons for violent crimes (mostly robbery and assaults) and behavior related to "public order." Once begun, prison expansion has continued under its own momentum, oblivious to any obvious need and unrelated to any useful social function, at large social cost. Though penologists have called attention to the failures of mass imprisonment, the expansion has taken on a life of its own.

Along the way, Americans have become accustomed to demonizing certain people who break the law. This is somewhat odd, given the fact that breaking the law is neither a rare nor demonic act. Few citizens go through life without ever violating a law.

A significant number of Americans cheat on their taxes, steal from their employers, receive stolen goods, purchase illegal cable boxes, illegally download music, use illegal drugs, or participate in many other illegal acts. Hardly a day goes by without a newspaper story about corporate executives indicted for fraud, insider trading, or price fixing. Politicians are arrested and convicted for soliciting or accepting bribes. The most prestigious Wall Street firms have engaged in large-scale illegal trading practices. Some of our most successful and idolized entertainment figures are indicted for shoplifting, domestic violence, drunk driving, possessing drugs, and molesting children. Policemen are filmed using excessive force on citizens, make arrests based on racial stereotypes, deal in drugs, plant evidence on innocent people, and lie under oath. Sports figures are accused of rape, assault and taking steroids.

Priests are charged with child molestation. Doctors bill Medicare for procedures they did not perform. Each day thousands drive while drunk, with sometimes-fatal consequences.[12] Self-report surveys find that lawbreaking is widely distributed among the young, especially males. As many as one-third of all boys are arrested before reaching adulthood. A majority of males will be arrested for a non-traffic offense at some point in their lives.[13]

But given that most of us commit some type of crimes in our lifetimes, the most severe punishments are targeted toward lower class citizens. It is this class of people we are willing to punish disproportionately to their criminal acts.

This willingness to punish them is rooted in our culture of individualism, which holds that we are free-willed and fully responsible for our acts. This belief speaks to our tendency to assign personal blame for every disapproved act. The truth is that many factors, particularly race and economic status, affect our life situations and limit or expand our available choices.

Consider young people with college-educated parents. Middle and upper-class parents impart values of achievement through education to their children, arrange for their admission into better schools, help them get into good colleges, and support them after graduation while they attempt to start their "careers." Their children have a much higher chance of succeeding in America's economy than youth from poor, welfare dependent, and often broken families who are exposed to a much different life, including dangerous public housing buildings and dysfunctional public schools. For many of these youth, the expectation or norm is to drop out of high school and end up hanging out in neighborhoods filled with other under-educated, unemployed young people.[14] Rather than going to college they are headed toward prison.

Where lawbreakers differ culturally and socially, others are less able to empathize with their life circumstances. Middle- and upper-class people understand that they themselves, their families, and close associates are not defined entirely by their law violations.

---

12   In 2002, an estimated 1.5 million drivers were arrested for driving under the influence of alcohol or narcotics—surely more escaped arrest. In 2004, the National Center for Statistics and Analysis reported that just over 17,000 people died in alcohol-related crashes in 2003. This is slightly more than the 16,503 murdered or who died from non-negligent homicide in the same year.

13   In a study of a Philadelphia male birth cohort, 35 percent of the youths had at least one incident of contact with the police before age 18. These 3,475 boys with a contact were linked to 10,214 offenses, including 2,786 index crimes (Marvin E. Wolfgang, Robert M. Figlio, and Thorsten Sellin. *Delinquency in a Birth Cohort.* Chicago: University of Chicago Press, 1972. 65, 68–69. By age 30, 47% had at least one police contact for a non-traffic offense (James J. Collins. *Offender Careers and Restraint: Probabilities and Policy Implications.* Washington, DC: US DOJ, Law Enforcement Assistance Administration, 1977). In a

similar study carried out in Racine, Wisconsin, 59–69% had a non-traffic police confrontation by the same age. Joan Petersilia. "Criminal Career Research: A Review of Recent Evidence." *Crime and Justice: An Annual Review of Research* 2 (1980): 321–79.

14   See Pierre Bourdieu and Jean Claude Passeron. *Reproduction in Education, Society, and Culture.* London: Sage Publications, 1990, and, Jay MacLeod. *Ain't No Makin' It: Aspirations & Attainment in a Low-Income Neighborhood.* Boulder, CO: Westview. 1995. These books address the issues of transmission of cultural capital and success.

Table 3: If Black and Latino Prisoners Had the Same Jail and Prison Incarceration Rates as White Prisoners

Race	Current Prisoners	Male Incarceration Rates	Female Incarceration Rates	Prison Population if Same Incarceration Rates as Whites
Whites	731,200	681	75	731,200
Blacks	899,200	4,834	352	125,773
Latino	392,200	1,778	148	136,540
Total	**2,022,600**			**993,513**

But they often lack understanding for those whose life circumstances are different from their own.

The demonization of criminals has become a special burden for young black males, of whom nearly one-third will spend time in prison during their life.[15] The fear of black men and other factors fuel the racially disproportionate imprisonment and convinces many Americans that black males are an especially "dangerous" class of people, different from the rest of us, the so-called "law-abiding."[16] Today approximately 60% of those incarcerated are black or Hispanic.[17] In effect, the imprisonment binge created our own American apartheid.

To illustrate the significance of race in our incarceration policies, we estimated the size of today's prison and jail population assuming blacks and Latinos had the same incarceration rate as their white counterparts. The results are striking. *As shown in Table 3, if blacks and Latinos had the same rates of incarceration as whites, today's prison and jail populations would decline by approximately 50%.* While we may differ on the basis for racial differences in imprisonment, there can be no disagreement that this is not the sign of a healthy society.

Did Prison Expansion Cut Crime?

Proponents of prison expansion have heralded this growth as a smashing success.[18] But a large number of studies contradict that claim. Most scientific evidence suggests that there is little if any relationship between fluctuations in crime rates and incarceration rates. In many cases, crime rates have risen or declined independent of imprisonment rates. New York City, for example, has produced one of the largest declines in crime in the nation while significantly *reducing* its jail and prison populations.[19] Connecticut, New Jersey, Ohio, and Massachusetts have also reduced their prison populations during the same time that crime rates were declining.[20]

A study of crime and incarceration rates from 1980 to 1991 in all 50 states and the District of Columbia

---

15 *Prevalence of Imprisonment in the U.S. Population, 1974–2001.* Washington, DC: US DOJ, Bureau of Justice Statistics, 2003.

16 Controlling for crime rates, prison populations have grown faster in states with more black residents. Katherine Beckett and Bruce Western. "Governing Social Marginality: Welfare, Incarceration, and the Transformation of State Policy." *Punishment and Society* 3 (2001): 43–59; David F. Greenberg and Valerie West. "State Prison Populations and Their Growth, 1971–1991," and David F. Greenberg, "'Justice' and Criminal Justice." *Criminology* 39.3 (2001): 615–53. Darnell F. Hawkins, Samuel L. Myers Jr., and Randolph N. Stone, eds. *Crime Control and Social Justice: The Delicate Balance.* Westport, CT: Greenwood Press, 2003.

This is not to deny that for UCR crimes, rates of black involvement are higher than rates of white involvement. However, these disparities do not fully explain the racial disparities in prison populations, or their growth.

17 *Prisoners in 2004.* US DOJ. Washington, DC: Bureau of Justice Statistics, 2005.

18 John Dilulio. "Prisons Are a Bargain, by Any Measure." *New York Times* 26 Jan. 1996: A19.

19 Between 1993 and 2001, violent crime in New York decreased by 64%, and homicides by 69% while its jail population dropped by 25%, and the number of people sentenced to prison fell by 42%. Some analysts attribute the dramatic reductions in serious crime and felony arrests to the introduction of new methods of policing, particularly Compstat. However, San Diego, which also reduced its commitments to prison, experienced comparable declines in crime without using New York's methods (Michael Jacobson. *Downsizing Prisons: How to Reduce Crime and End Mass Incarceration.* New York: NYUP, 2005. 37, 113, 125–27).

20 Ibid., 128.

shows that incarceration rates exploded during this period. The states that increased incarceration rates the least were just as likely to experience decreases in crime as those that increased them the most.[21] The study's authors pointed out that although San Francisco and Alameda counties in California *reduced* the number of individuals sentenced to state prison, their crime rates dropped as much if not more than those California counties that *increased* their prison commitments.

Other studies reach similar conclusions, finding "no consistent relationship between incarceration rates and crime rates"[22] and "no support for the 'more prisoners, less crime' thesis."[23] One study discovered an initial decrease in crime related to increases in rates of incarceration, but no decrease from further increases in incarceration.[24]

Focusing on California, whose incarcerated population more than tripled during the 1980s, Franklin Zimring and Gordon Hawkins concluded that this remarkable expansion was paralleled by a reduction in crime of about 15%. Almost all this decrease was in burglary and larceny. For the other offenses the reduction was "weak to negligible." The role of the prison expansion in bringing about even that 15% was doubtful,

because arrest statistics showed that the drop occurred mainly for juveniles, who were less likely than adults to be locked up.[25] A contrary view has been offered by some analysts, such as William Spelman, who argues that the crime rate today would be 25% higher were it not for the large increases in imprisonment from 1970 to 1990.[26] Assuming for the sake of discussion that this figure is correct, it is not a large effect, considering the enormous increase in imprisonment needed to achieve it. However, Spelman's estimate is probably too large. His analysis is based on national trends and does not explain why some states and counties that lowered their incarceration rates experienced the same crime reductions as states that increased incarceration; and his estimates of crime reductions rely on controversial data in the form of prisoners' own claims about how much crime they had committed before incarceration. More significantly, Spelman agrees that further investment in expanding the prison population will have little if any impact on crime rates.

More recent estimates based on individual states and counties within states have estimated the crime-reduction impact of prison growth to be much smaller or nonexistent.[27] Research on crime and incarceration

21   Irwin and Austin, loc. cit., 154–56. For an updated version of this type of analysis, see: Jenni Gainsborough and Marc Mauer. *Diminishing Returns: Crime and Decarceration in the 1990s.* Washington, DC: The Sentencing Project, 2000.

22   Michael Lynch. "Beating a Dead Horse: Is There Any Basic Empirical Evidence of the Deterrent Effect of Imprisonment." *Crime, Law and Social Change* 31.4 (1999): 361. Lynch examined data on U.S. crime and imprisonment trends from 1972 through 1993.

23   Tomislav V. Kovandzic and Lynne M. Vieratis. "The Effect of Country-Level Prison Population Growth on Crime Rates." *Criminology & Public Policy* 5.2 (2006): 234. The authors examined the effect of incarceration on crime rates in different Florida counties.

24   Raymond Liedka, Anne Morrison Piehl, and Bert Useem. "The Crime-Control Effect of Incarceration: Does Scale Matter?" *Criminology & Public Policy* 5.2 (2006): 245–76. This study analyzed the data on crime rates and incarceration rates for all 50 states and the District of Columbia in the period from 1972 to 2000. The authors believe that whatever gains were achieved in the dramatic rise in imprisonment that began in the 1970s, there was a diminishing effect over time.

25   Franklin E. Zimring and Gordon Hawkins. *Incapacitation: Penal Confinement and the Restraint of Crime.* New York: Oxford UP, 1995. 101; Thomas B. Marvell and Carlisle E. Moody Jr. "Prison Population Growth and Crime Reduction." *Journal of Quantitative Criminology* 10.2 (1994): 109–40, similarly found just a small reduction in crime resulting from national prison expansion.

26   William Spelman. "The Limited Importance of Prison Expansion." The Crime Drop in America, Revised edition. Ed. Alfred Blumstein. New York: Cambridge UP, 2006. 97–129. Spelman based this estimate on the amount of crime recently incarcerated felons told interviewers they had committed the year before their arrest. Spelman then assumed that incarcerating and incapacitating those individuals averted the same amount of crime he assumed would be committed subsequently.

27   Bruce Western. *Punishment and Inequality in America.* New York: Russell Sage, 2006; James P. Lynch and William J. Sabol. "Did Getting Tough on Crime Pay?" *Crime Policy Report No. 1.* Washington, DC: Urban Institute, 1997. www.urban.org/publications/307337.html; Don Stemen. Reconsidering Incarceration: New Directions for Reducing Crime. New York: Vera Institute of Justice, 2007.

does not consistently indicate that the massive use of incarceration has reduced crime rates.

In sum, studies on the impact of incarceration on crime rates come to a range of conclusions that vary from "making crime worse" to "reducing crime a great deal." Though conclusive evidence is lacking, the bulk of the evidence points to three conclusions: 1) The effect of imprisonment on crime rates, if there is one, is small; 2) If there is an effect, it diminishes as prison populations expand; and 3) The overwhelming and undisputed negative side effects of incarceration far outweigh its potential, unproven benefits.

These studies have led former pro-incarceration advocates to change their positions. James Q. Wilson now concedes that we have reached a tipping point of "diminishing returns" on our investment in prisons.[28] According to Wilson, judges have always been tough on violent offenders and have incarcerated them for relatively long periods. However, as states expanded incarceration, they dipped "deeper into the bucket of persons eligible for prison, dredging up people with shorter and shorter criminal records."[29] Increasing the proportion of convicted criminals sent to prison, like lengthening time served beyond some point, has produced diminishing marginal returns in crime reductions. Similarly, former incarceration advocates such as John Dilulio and former U.S. Attorney General Edwin Meese are calling for a repeal of mandatory minimum sentencing and challenging the wisdom of a massive imprisonment policy.[30]

The Negative Side Effects of Incarceration

Incarceration may not have had much impact on crime, but it has had numerous unintended consequences, ranging from racial injustice and damage to families and children to worsening public health, civic disengagement, and even *increases* in crime.

Bruce Western demonstrates the extraordinarily disparate impact of imprisonment on young black males compared to any other subgroup of society. For example, he shows that nearly one half of all young black males who have not finished high school are behind bars, an incarceration rate that is six times higher than for white male dropouts. He then shows how incarceration damages the lifetime earnings, labor market participation, and marriage prospects for those who have been to prison and concludes that the U.S. prison system exacerbates and sustains racial inequality.[31]

British penologists Joseph Murray and David Farrington have analyzed data sets about child development from three nations and found that parental incarceration contributes to higher rates of delinquency, mental illness, and drug abuse, and reduces levels of school success and later employment among their children.

Their comparative analysis of data from high-imprisonment and low-imprisonment nations reveals that the negative effects of incarceration are most pronounced when a nation's incarceration rate is high, as it is in the United States.[32]

Epidemiologist James Thomas has analyzed incarceration rates in North Carolina, and shows that high rates of incarceration are associated with increased rates of teenage single-parent births and the risk of sexually-transmitted diseases among women. Other analyses have shown that the high rate of HIV among black women can be attributed to incarceration rates of black men.[33]

28 James Q. Wilson. "Crime and Public Policy." *Crime.* James Q. Wilson and Joan Petersilia. Oakland, CA: ICS Press, 1995: 489–507.

29 Wilson, op. cit., 501.

30 Jacob Sullum. "Prison Conversion: After studying non-violent drug offenders, a criminologist who once said, "Let 'Em Rot" now says "Let 'Em Go." *Reason* Aug./Sept. 1999.

31 Bruce Western, op. cit. See also, Raphael, op. cit.

32 Joseph Murray and David Farrington. "Effects of parental imprisonment on children." *Crime & Justice: A Review of Research.* Forthcoming; and Joseph Murray, Carl-Gunnar Janson, and David Farrington. "Crime in Adult Offspring of Prisoners: A Cross-National Comparison of Two Longitudinal Samples." *Criminal Justice & Behavior* 34 (2007): 133–49.

33 James Thomas and Elizabeth Torrone. "Incarceration as Forced Migration: Effects on Selected Community Health Outcomes." *American Journal of Public Health* 96 (2006): 17 62–65; Rucker C. Johnson and Steven Raphael. "The Effects of Male Incarceration on Dynamics of AIDS Infection Rates Among African-American Women and

There are an estimated five million Americans who are ineligible to vote because of felony convictions. About half of these are African-Americans; consequently, black communities have lost a significant amount of political power. Christopher Uggen and Jeffrey Manza have demonstrated that the loss of voting rights by felons has changed election outcomes across the nation, including in the two most recent presidential elections, weakened the political influence of minority communities, and detracted from civic participation by large classes of people of color.[34]

Clearly, prison terms have a residual impact on the families and communities of the imprisoned. Enduring years of separation from family and community—deprived of material possessions, subjected to high levels of noise and artificial light, crowded conditions and/or solitary confinement, devoid of privacy, with reduced options, arbitrary control, disrespect, and economic exploitation—is maddening and profoundly deleterious. Anger, frustration, and a burning sense of injustice, coupled with the crippling processes inherent in imprisonment, significantly reduce the likelihood that prisoners are able to pursue a viable, relatively conventional life after release.

II. THREE KEY MYTHS ABOUT CRIME AND INCARCERATION

Why has there been such a growth in imprisonment? The incarceration explosion has been based on a series of ideas that were widely accepted and broadly popular at the time, but have turned out to be erroneous.

The research summarized above shows that mass incarceration has a limited potential for reducing crime and has collateral consequences that outweigh its benefits. Why then has there been such a growth in

imprisonment? The incarceration explosion has been based on a series of ideas that were widely accepted once, but have turned out to be erroneous. The three main myths are:

1. There are "career criminals" we can identify and whose imprisonment will reduce crime;
2. Tougher penalties are needed to protect the public from "dangerous" criminals; and
3. Tougher penalties will deter criminals.

Because these ideas have been so central we discuss them in some detail.

Myth 1: There Are "Career Criminals" We Can Identify and Whose Imprisonment Will Reduce Crime

One of the primary justifications for lengthy sentences is that we can identify the "career criminals" or "violent predators" who commit most of the serious crime and who are not deterred or rehabilitated by short sentences or alternative punishments to incarceration. These people, it is argued, must be "incapacitated" for long periods of time to reduce crime significantly. However, scientific efforts to develop methods for identifying career criminals have failed.

In 1978, a National Academy of Science study by a panel of prestigious criminologists concluded that while most people have a relatively brief and modest criminal career, a small group persists in crime. However, the panel was unable to produce any valid methods for identifying the persistent criminals at the beginning of their criminal careers.[35]

Shortly thereafter, a group of RAND researchers thought they had found a way to identify persons who would eventually become repeat offenders. They discovered a group of "high-rate offenders" among samples of males imprisoned for robbery and burglary in three

Men." Unpublished paper presented to the incarceration study group of the Russell Sage Foundation (July 2006).

34 Christopher Uggen and Jeff Manza. *Locked Out: Felon Disenfranchisement and American Democracy.* New York: Oxford UP, 2006.

35 Jacqueline Cohen. "Research on Criminal Career: Individual Frequency Rates and Offense Seriousness." *Criminal Careers and "Career Criminals.* Alfred Blumstein et al., eds. Washington, DC: National Academy Press, 1986.

states (California, Texas and Michigan).[36] Significantly, the vast majority of the surveyed prisoners reported committing very few if any crimes the year before they were arrested (five or less). But the so-called "high-rate" offenders, who comprised 10% of the samples, claimed they had committed 4–5 robberies and burglaries per week in the preceding year. The researchers developed a profiling scale that distinguished the high-rate offenders, whom they labeled "violent career criminals"; from the others. Peter Greenwood claimed that if the people so identified were incarcerated for at least eight years, crime would decline by 20%. Because the lower-rate offenders could be released after serving reduced sentences, prison expansion could be avoided.

These claims were widely disseminated by the U.S. Department of Justice and used by elected officials to justify sentencing reforms such as mandatory minimums, truth in sentencing, and the abolition of parole boards. However, when Greenwood and his associate Susan Turner later followed a group of released prisoners identified as high-rate offenders by their profiles, they found that these individuals had not committed crimes of the type and at the rate expected.[37]

More recent research, nearly twenty years after the first studies on the topic, continues to discredit the claim that career criminals can be identified early by a profiling system. John Laub and Robert Sampson have re-examined data from Sheldon and Eleanor Glueck's 1950s seminal publication following the life careers of 500 Boston delinquents.[38] Although the vast majority

desisted from crime after the age of 25, a small minority persisted in committing crime into their later years. Using all available criteria, Laub and Samson could not distinguish these "persisters" at the beginning of their delinquent careers from the others who had followed the normal pattern of criminal involvement in adolescence and desistance after their early twenties.

Laub and Sampson were able to find a different set of predictive factors, none of which could be observed when the young people first committed crimes. Instead, they found there were major "turning points" in a person's life—such as getting and holding a good job, enlisting in the military, marrying, and establishing contacts with conventional institutions and groups—rather than personality characteristics or early childhood experiences that distinguished the careers of "desisters" from "persisters." Laub and Sampson also found that delinquents who had been incarcerated were more likely to commit crimes later in life than those who had been sentenced to probation or local jail time. The implication was that imprisonment itself can encourage criminality.

In a subsequent study, Michael E. Ezell and Lawrence E. Cohen published their analysis of the criminal careers of three cohorts of "serious chronic offenders" released from California youth prisons in the 1980s and 1990s. Although the offenders varied in the amount of crime they committed after their release from prison, all "aged out" of crime.[39] Similar to the other studies, Ezell and Cohen could not find any background characteristics that reliably distinguished those with different post-release criminal trajectories. Other researchers have employed mixes of psychological test scores and behavioral measures to predict serious violent recidivism or involvement in new sex

36   Peter Greenwood and Alan Abrahamse, op. cit.; Jan M. Chaiken and Marcia Chaiken. *Varieties of Criminal Behavior*. Santa Monica, CA: RAND, 1982.

37   Peter Greenwood and Susan Turner. *Selective Incapacitation Revisited: Why High-Rate Offenders Are Hard to Predict*. Santa Monica, CA: RAND, 1987. Christy A. Visher also found methodological weaknesses in the study; see "The Rand Inmate Survey: A Reanalysis." *Criminal Careers and "Career Criminals*," Vol. 2. Alfred Blumstein *et al.*, eds. Washington, DC: National Academy Press, 1986.

38   Sheldon and Eleanor T. Glueck. *Unraveling Juvenile Delinquency*. New York: The Commonwealth Fund, 1950. John Laub and Robert Sampson continued the follow up study of this cohort into the members' 70's. John Laub and Robert Sampson. *Shared Beginnings, Divergent Lives: Delinquent Boys to Age 70*. Cambridge, MA: Harvard UP, 2006.

39   Mike E. Ezell and Lawrence E. Cohen. *Desisting from Crime: Continuity and Change in Long-Term Crime Patterns of Serious Chronic Offenders*. New York: Oxford UP, 2005. 163. This "aging out" of crime is a consistent finding of most research on criminal careers. See, for example, David Greenberg. "Delinquency and the Age Structure of Society." *Contemporary Crises* 1.2 (1977): 189–224; David Farrington. "Age and Crime." *Crime and Justice: An Annual Review of Research*. Michael Tonry and Norval Morris, eds. Chicago: University of Chicago Press, 1986: 189–250.

crimes.[40] These methods predict recidivist crime better than random guessing, but they are also inaccurate.

Though improvements in statistical methods for predicting violent recidivism have produced modest gains in accuracy, they rely on data that would normally not be available in a typical criminal justice application.[41]

Criminologists have been unable to develop practical and reliable methods to select those who will become career criminals.[42] Attempts to incarcerate based on any predictive criteria will inevitably end up incarcerating a large number of people who do not persist in serious crime. As advocated later in the report, sentencing should not be based on what we think a person will do but rather on what they have done and in proportion to the seriousness of the crime.

Myth 2: Tougher Penalties Are Needed To Protect the Public from "Dangerous" Criminals

We can't seriously address our crime problem until repeat offenders learn that they will get no more breaks from the criminal justice system. ... When incarcerations increase, serious crimes go down.
—Andrew Thomas, County Attorney, Maricopa County, Arizona[43]

The failure of efforts to develop methods of accurately identifying the small number of offenders who do commit particularly horrendous crimes after serving their sentences fueled demands for longer sentences across the board.[44] The logic of this argument was that if we can't single out the truly dangerous, we will assume that anyone with two or three convictions for a relatively wide range of offenses is a dangerous habitual criminal, and keep them all in prison for an extremely long time. On the basis of this reasoning, a number of states adopted mandatory sentencing, truth in sentencing and in some states "three strikes" laws, all of which extend prison sentences.

These laws have done little to reduce crime. Few convicted persons have the requisite number of previous felony convictions to qualify for the enhanced sentences.[45] This is because rates of return to serious crime on the part of those released from prison are not high. Just 1.2% of those who served time for homicide and were released in 1994 were rearrested for a new homicide within three years of release, and just 2.5% of released rapists were arrested for another rape. Sex offenders were less likely than non-sex-offenders to be

40   Erica Beechner-Monas and Edgar Garica-Rill. "Genetic Predictions of Future Dangerousness: Is There a Blueprint for Violence?" *Law and Contemporary Problems* 69 (2006): 301–41; Richard Wollert. "Low Base Rates Limit Expert Certainty When Current Actuarials Are Used to Identify Sexually Violent Predators: An Application of Bayes' Theorem." *Psychology, Public Policy, and Law* 12 (2006): 56–85; Robert A. Prentky *et al.* "Sexually Violent Predators in the Courtroom: Science on Trial." *Psychology, Public Policy, and Law* 12 (2006): 357–93.

41   John Monahan. "The Future of Violence Risk Management." *The Future of Imprisonment.* Ed. Michael Tonry. New York: Oxford UP, 2004. 237–63.

42   Kathleen Auerhahn. "Selective Incapacitation and the Problem of Prediction." *Criminology* 37.4 (1999): 703–34; Jacqueline Cohen. "Incapacitation as a Strategy for Crime Control: Possibilities and Pitfalls." *Crime and Justice: An Annual Review of Research* 5 (1983): 1–84; Jacqueline Cohen and Jose A. Canela-Cacho. "Incarceration and Violent Crime, 1965–1988." *Understanding and Preventing Violence: Consequence and Control,* Vol. 4. Albert J. Reiss and Jeffrey A. Roth, eds. Washington, DC: National Academy Press, 1994; Rudy A. Haapanen. *Selective Incapacitation and the Serious Offender: A Longitudinal Study of Criminal Career Patterns.* New York: Springer-Verlag, 1990.

43   Christian Richardson. "Thomas: Probation Out in Major Felony Cases." *East Valley Tribune* 29 Nov. 2006.

44   Jonathan Simon. "Reversal of Fortune: The Resurgence of Individual Risk Assessment in Criminal Justice." *Annual Review of Law and Social Science* 1 (2005): 397–421; Bernard E. Harcourt. *Against Prediction: Profiling, Policing, and Punishing in an Actuarial Age.* Chicago: University of Chicago Press, 2007.

45   Franklin E. Zimring, Gordon Hawkins, and Sam Kamin. *Punishment and Democracy: Three Strikes and You're Out in California.* New York: Oxford UP, 2001.

rearrested for any offense.[46] Their rates of rearrest for a new sex offense were only 5.3%. A substantial percentage (over 60%) of released prisoners are eventually rearrested, but mostly for drug offenses or violations of parole regulations. Many of those eligible for sentence enhancements under these "habitual offender" statutes are at an age when they are reducing their involvement in crime, or abandoning it altogether.

The U.S. Department of Justice conducted a major study of criminal involvement of prisoners who had been released in 1994. It found that only 5% of the 3 million arrests made in seven states between 1994 and 1997 were of recently released prisoners (Table 4).[47] California's "three strikes" law has had a number of evaluations; almost all found that it failed to reduce crime.[48]

These studies make clear that, while many people who are released from prison end up back behind bars, they are but a fraction of the overall crime problem. Lengthening their sentences, as a means of dealing with crime will at best have only marginal impact.

---

46   A meta-analysis of 61 studies also concluded that sex offenders have low rates of recidivism. See R. Karl Hanson and Monique T. Bussiere. "Predicting Relapse: A Meta-Analysis of Sexual Offender Recidivism Studies." *Journal of Consulting and Clinical Psychology* 66 (1998): 348–62; and R. Karl Hanson *et al.* "Sex Offender Recidivism: What We Know and What We Need to Know." *Annals of the New York Academy of Science, Sexually Coercive Behavior: Understanding and Management.* Robert A. Prentky *et al.*, eds. (2003): 154.

47   *Recidivism of Prisoners Released in 1994.* US DOJ. Washington, DC: Bureau of Justice Statistics, 2002.

48   John L. Worrall. "The Effect of Three-Strikes Legislation on Serious Crime in California." *Journal of Criminal Justice* 32 (2004): 283–96.

Myth 3: Tougher Penalties Will Deter Criminals

The hope that the presence of brutal prisons will deter law violators is as old as the invention of the prison itself. Contemporary supporters of longer sentences argue that longer and harsher punishments are necessary to deter crime by making criminals think twice before committing another crime. This notion simplifies and distorts the dynamics of criminal behavior. When most people commit a crime, they correctly believe that they will not be caught. According to NCVS surveys, about 60% of all crimes are not reported to police. The FBI reports that 4.6 million arrests were made for property or violent crimes, a number representing only 19% of the reported victimizations. State and federal courts dealing with serious felony crimes produce about one million convictions—of which 68% result in a prison or jail sentence. Therefore, as illustrated in Table 5, the immediate chances of being arrested, convicted, and sentenced to jail or prison are quite small.

Further, different types of crimes vary markedly in their potential for being deterred and people differ in their susceptibility to being deterred by the threat of punishment. The population roughly divides into three groups: 1) those who, because of personal values and social commitments, would not knowingly commit crimes under any circumstances; 2) those who are deterred when they believe that there is some likelihood they will be caught and punished; and 3) those who are not deterred. The type of crime most likely to be reported and to result in arrest and conviction tends to be committed by those least likely to be deterred—generally young males excluded from the conventional pathways to success, many of whom already have been severely punished by the juvenile justice system early in

Table 4: Percent of Arrests Attributed to Released Prisoners

Arrests in 7 States	Number	Percent
Total arrests in 1994–97	2,994,868	100
Total arrests of prisoners released in 1994–97	140,543	5
Total arrests of released prisoners for violent crimes	36,000	1

Source: Recidivism of Prisoners Released in 1994. US DOJ. Washington, DC: Bureau of Justice Statistics, 2002

Table 5: Chances of Being Caught

Indicator	Number	% of Total
Victimizations	25,036,030	100
Reported to police	9,721,205	39
Arrests	13,699,254	55
Less drug, alcohol, and other victimless crimes	4,642,803	19
State and federal felony convictions	983,823	4
Convictions resulting in prison or jail	680,000	3

Source: U.S. Department of Justice, Office of Justice Programs, Bureau of Justice Statistics, Prison Statistics, 2006.

their lives and are unlikely to be deterred in the future. The vast majority of these youth desist from crime after their twenties for reasons unrelated to any penalties the state imposes on them. Ironically, those who are deterred when punishment is seen as likely—polluters, price fixers, slum lords, inside traders, stock swindlers, workplace safety violators, and other "white-collar" criminals—receive relatively lenient punishment when caught.

At the turn of the 19th century reformers realized that brutal prisons embitter prisoners rather than reform them. Yet this persistent faith that prisoners can be discouraged from returning to crime by subjecting them to harsh penalties, or that the population at large can be deterred more effectively with severe penalties than with milder ones, has never had empirical support. Decades of research on capital punishment have failed to produce compelling evidence that it prevents homicide more effectively than long prison sentences.[49] Community penalties, it has been shown, are at least as effective in discouraging return to crime as institutional penalties.[50] Rigorous prison conditions

substantially increase recidivism.[51] Evaluations show that boot camps and "scared straight" programs either have no effect on recidivism or increase it.[52]

"Tough" sanctions are popular, but they do not reduce crime.

III. THE LIMITS OF PRISON-BASED REHABILITATIVE AND TREATMENT PROGRAMS

> The danger of relying on treatment and programs to solve America's imprisonment crisis is that when recidivism isn't reduced, imprisonment will be regarded as the only viable answer to the crime problem.

There is a growing belief that prison populations can be reduced simply by expanding rehabilitative and

49   Sarah T. Dike. *Capital Punishment in the United States.* Hackensack, NJ: National Council on Crime and Delinquency, 1982; Richard A. Berk. "New Claims about Executions and General Deterrence: Deja Vu All Over Again?" *Journal of Empirical Legal Studies* 27 (1998): 209–19.

50   *Joan Petersilia and Susan Turner.* Prison versus Probation in California: Implications for Crime and Offender Recidivism. *Santa Monica, CA: RAND, 1986.*

51   M. Keith Chen and Jesse M. Shapiro. 4 Dec. 2006. "Does Prison Harden Inmates? A Discontinuity-Based Approach." Cowles Foundation, Harvard University http://home.uchicago.edu/c~jmshapir/prison120406.pdf.

52   Doris Layton MacKenzie and James O. Finckenauer. *Scared Straight: Delinquency and the Panacea Phenomenon.* Englewood Cliffs, NJ: Prentice Hall, 1982; Doris Layton MacKenzie. *What Works in Corrections; Reducing the Criminal Activities of Offenders and Delinquents.* New York: Cambridge UP, 2006; Mark W. Lipsey. "What Do We Learn from 400 Research Studies on the Effectiveness of Treatment with Juvenile Delinquents?" *What Works: Reducing Reoffending.* Ed. J. McGuri. New York: Wiley, 1995.

treatment programs within our prisons. This position is based largely on new studies showing that treatment or rehabilitation services can reduce recidivism and thus reduce the number of persons being re-admitted to prison after release. Increasingly, completion of rehabilitative or addiction treatment programs can and do result in a reduced period of confinement.

Our concern is that we delude ourselves that treatment programs hold the key to reducing the prison population. Prison populations did not increase in the 1970s because programs disappeared, causing crime and recidivism rates to increase. Rather—and it is important to be clear about this—prison populations increased because laws were passed that increased the number of people sent to prison and their length of stay.

Even if treatment programs were effective in reducing recidivism, recidivism is not the primary cause of the explosion in the prison population, as we have argued above. Evidence suggests, however, that such programs are in fact not particularly effective in reducing even the portion of prison overcrowding caused by recidivism. The most recent probation and parole success rates and the reasons for not completing probation or parole supervision have not changed since the U.S. Department of Justice began reporting them in 1995 (Table 6). The same holds true for recidivism rates of prisoners released from prison (Table 7). The Bureau of Justice Statistics national recidivism rates of prisoners after release have not changed between 1983 and 1994. Figure 4 shows recidivism rates for the states of Washington and New York, which have been recording their three-year return prison rates as early as 1985. Thus despite a number of reforms that have been designed to increase the availability of program services, recidivism rates have remained unchanged.[53]

A growing literature on "what works" in correctional programming has found that many programs have no impact on recidivism rates. A recent "meta-analysis" of treatment programs reviewed 291 evaluations of adult offender treatment programs, both in-prison and in-community, conducted in the United States and other English-speaking nations.[54] It reports that 42% of the evaluated programs, including jail diversion programs, domestic violence programs, faith-based, psychotherapy or behavior therapy for sex offenders, boot camps, electronic monitoring, and restorative justice programs *had no impact* on recidivism.

Of the 167 effective programs, only one-fourth were prison-based treatment programs. Of these programs, the reduction in recidivism rates generally ranged from 4% to 10%. These recidivism reduction results are similar to those found in other major evaluations of "what works" (or "doesn't work"). Notably, many other programs do not reduce recidivism and may actually increase rates of failure.[55]

Treatment and rehabilitative programs tend to be most effective when they are disassociated from government coercion.[56] Someone who doesn't want to be rehabilitated is not a promising candidate for being rehabilitated. Requiring someone to sit through a program designed to deal with dependence on alcohol or drugs may lead to resentment and shammed participation. It is not likely to bring about the inner transformation that will end involvement in crime. The association of help with punishment that occurs

53 See "State of New York Department of Correctional Services" (undated), 2001 Releases: Three Year Post-Release Follow-Up. Albany, New York; and the Washington State Department of Corrections Web site at: www.doc.wa.gov/BudgetAndResearch/ResearchData/Recidivism20.pdf.

54 Steve Aos, Marna Miller, and Elizabeth Drake. *Evidence-Based Adult Corrections Programs: What Works and What Does Not.* Olympia, WA: Washington State Institute for Public Policy, 2006. Only 20% of the evaluations used random assignment procedures to create treatment and control groups. The other studies used "matching techniques" to approximate the attributes of the "treatment" group, which is less rigorous.

55 Donald A. Andrews. "Principles of Effective Correctional Programs." *Compendium 2000 on Effective Correctional Programming.* Laurence L. Motiuk and Ralph C. Serin, eds. Ottawa: Correctional Service Canada, 2001; Larry Sherman *et al. Preventing Crime: What Works, What Doesn't, What's Promising.* Washington, DC: National Institute of Justice, 2006.

56 Ojmarrh Mitchell, David B. Wilson, and Doris L. MacKenzie, "The Effectiveness of Incarceration-Based Drug Treatment on Criminal Behavior," *Campbell Systematic Reviews* 2006: 11 DOI: 10.4073/csr.2006.11 which is a meta-analysis of in-prison treatment programs for drugs.

Table 6: Probation and Parole Success Rates—1995–2003		
Outcome Measures	Probation	Parole
Successful Completions		
1995	62%	45%
2000	60%	43%
2003	59%	47%
Reason for Failures		
Re-incarcerated	16%	38%
New conviction and sentence	5%	11%
Revocation	7%	26%
Other	4%	1%
Absconded	4%	9%
Other	22%	6%

Source: Probation and Parole in the United States, 2003. US DOJ. Washington, DC: Bureau of Justice Statistics, 2004.

when courts require treatment is likely to discourage those who could benefit from programs to seek them out on their own. The presence of substantial numbers of reluctant participants may undermine the quality of the programs, reducing their ability to help those who want to be helped. Those who administer programs are likely to become demoralized if they are forced to accept "clients" sent to them by a court, rather than working with those who seek help on their own.

Even under the most optimistic assumptions, the effect of in-prison rehabilitative programs is to reduce failure rates by 10% or so. If *all* correctional programs were to achieve this level of success, they would reduce failure rates for about one-third of those confined from about 40% to about 30%. A 10% reduction in return-to-prison rate for one third of the population translates to an overall system rate reduction in recidivism of 3%. This is not large enough to substantially reduce a prison population.

The inability of rehabilitation programs to stem prison expansion can be seen in several major states. The Florida Department of Corrections reported that it offered a wide array of treatment, education and vocational programs to over 6,500 prisoners released in 1995 and 1996. For those who completed the programs, a recidivism rate reduction of 6–10% was

Table 7: 1983 and 1994 Prisoner Three Year Follow-Up Recidivism Rates

Recidivism Measure	1983 Prison Releases	1994 Prison Releases
Re-arrested	63%	69%
Re-convicted	47%	47%
Re-imprisoned	41%	40–52%*

*52% readmission to prison with California prisoners and 40% without California prisoners included.

Sources: Recidivism of Prisoners Released in 1994. US DOJ. Washington, DC: Bureau of Justice Statistics, 2002; Recidivism of Prisoners Released in 1983. US DOJ. Washington, DC: Bureau of Justice Statistics, 1989.

achieved. But the estimated number of prisoners thus not returning to prison because of involvement in the programs was about 400 or two percent of the more than 18,000 persons admitted to prison in the same year. Indeed, while these programs operate, both prison

Figure 4. Three-Year Recidivism Rates

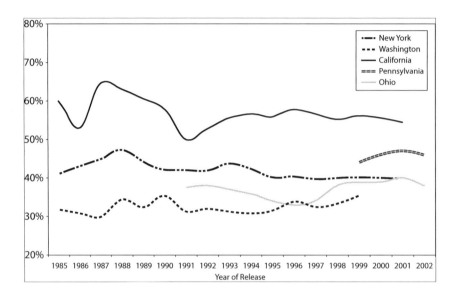

admissions and the prison population have continued to escalate.[57]

In California, a recent study by the state's Inspector General's Office concluded that California's $1 billion investment in drug treatment for prisoners since 1989 has been "a complete waste of money," and has failed to reduce recidivism rates. In fact a study by UCLA found that the state's two largest in-prison programs produced higher recidivism rates for inmates who participated in the programs as opposed to those who did not receive treatment.[58] Some of the reasons cited for the lack of impact are improper program design and operations.

With respect to treatment in lieu of incarceration, we agree that large numbers of persons charged with felony crimes should be sentenced to alternatives to state prison that also provide treatment services and education programs. But numerous studies of prison diversion programs show that these, too, may not reduce prison admissions. Too often, alternative programs have been reserved for people who would not otherwise have been sentenced to prison.[59] In some instances, diversion programs actually *increase* prison populations. This can occur when people who plead guilty to be eligible for treatment fail to complete the program and end up being sent to prison. In many of these cases, they would have had their charges dropped if they had not pled guilty or been given a county jail sentence or a shorter prison sentence than the one they received after failing the treatment program.[60]

Ultimately, the purpose of treatment and rehabilitation—and the criteria for assessing their usefulness and efficacy—should not be a major reduction in recidivism, much less reducing the size of the prison population. These are unreasonable burdens to place on programs that are, by their very nature, limited.

There is no question that providing meaningful work, education, and self-development programs to prisoners promotes more humane and safer prisons. And a growing body of research, as noted below, suggests that prisoners who seriously take advantage of

57   Analysis of the Impact of Inmate Programs on Recidivism. Tallahassee: Florida Department of Corrections, 2001 www.dc.state.fl.us/pub/recidivismproglindex.html.

58   Matthew L. Cate. "Special Review into In-Prison Substance Abuse Treatment Programs Managed by the California Department of Corrections and Rehabilitation." Sacramento: California Bureau of Audits and Investigations, 2007.

59   Larry Sherman *et al.*, op. cit.

60   Joan Petersilia. "A Decade of Experimenting with Intermediate Sanctions: What Have We Learned?" *Corrections Management Quarterly* 3.3 (1999): 19–27.

well-administered rehabilitative services and complete the programs are more likely to succeed in achieving satisfying conventional lives after prison than persons who do not receive these services. But expanding treatment services has not been shown to be an effective means of reducing prison populations. Indeed, relying on treatment and programs to solve America's imprisonment crisis carries the risk that, when they fail to reduce recidivism, imprisonment will be regarded as the only viable answer to the crime problem.[61] Treatment programs are necessary and humane, but they are not answers to the crisis of prison overpopulation.

IV. DECARCERATION, COST SAVINGS, AND PUBLIC SAFETY

The facts indicate that placing so many people in prison and jail or on probation and parole for long periods of time is not an effective crime control strategy.

The overuse of incarceration, along with the mistaken justifications that have supported this policy, have corrupted and compromised our criminal justice policies and paralyzed efforts to reform them. The net result is an expensive system that relies much too heavily on imprisonment, is increasingly ineffective, and diverts large sums of taxpayers' money from more effective crime control strategies. Even some of the leading criminologists who lobbied for putting more people in prison are now advocating that we invest some of the tens of billions we are now spending on imprisonment in more productive crime-reduction practices.

> The impact of a $1 million investment in … cash and other incentives to disadvantaged students to graduate from high school would result in a reduction of 258 crimes per year, and parent training therapy for families with young "acting out" children 160 crimes per year, compared to a reduction of 60 crimes a year through building and operating prisons.[62]

But to make such investments we must reduce the system that is draining our resources. The facts indicate that placing large numbers of people in prison and jail or on probation and parole for long periods of time is not an effective crime control strategy. One study found that after imprisonment exceeded a certain tipping point, it became counter-productive. When too many men are removed from a community, family and social life are destabilized, leading to higher crime rates.[63]

Making matters worse, we have squandered lean government budgets on corrections (responding to the symptom) instead of funding programs that shepherd dislocated young people onto conventional paths (responding to the cause). While we build prisons, we do not increase funding for academic and technical education, job training, healthcare, affordable housing, or other social services that assist people in getting a foot in the door to a better life.

The loss of manufacturing jobs in recent decades has reduced the opportunities for non-white, inner-city

---

61 In 1973, New York Governor Nelson Rockefeller proposed the infamous Rockefeller drug laws, imposing life sentences for possessing or selling drugs, after concluding that treatment programs for heroin users were not working. Other states followed suit with similarly long sentences for drug-law violators. These laws are widely seen as failures because they imprison low-level "mules" or street-level dealers for very long stretches, without capturing major operators or substantially reducing drug use. It is only because so much faith had been placed in rehabilitation that the publication of Robert Martinson's conclusion that most treatment programs had not been shown to be effective could have been construed, 30 years ago, as providing support for prison expansion. Robert Martinson. "What Works? Questions and Answers about Prison Reform." *The Public Interest* 35 (1974): 22–54.

62 Peter W. Greenwood *et al. Diverting Children from a Life of Crime*. Santa Monica, CA: RAND, 1998.

63 Dina R. Rose and Todd R. Clear. "The Problem with 'Addition by Subtraction': The Prison-Crime Relationship in Low-Income Communities." *Invisible Punishment: The Collateral Consequences of Mass Imprisonment*; Marc Mauer and Meda Chesney-Lind, eds. New York: The New Press, 2003. 181–94; Todd R. Clear. *Imprisoning Communities: How Mass Incarceration Makes Disadvantaged Places Worse*. New York: Oxford UP, 2007.

youth to get their feet in that door.[64] Prison expansion, by stigmatizing such a large number of black and Latino male youth, has placed an additional obstacle in their path. It interferes with family formation, strains existing family relationships, and disrupts careers.[65] Because employers commonly discriminate against minorities and also against ex-convicts, our current crime-control strategy dooms many people who start life with major disadvantages. The long-term association of minority status with crime in the public mind is strengthened when a highly disproportionate number of blacks and Latinos are locked up.

In the long run, these stereotypes reinforce discriminatory residential and employment patterns. Prospective employers, faced with a black male job applicant, are now more likely than in the past to suspect that the applicant has a criminal record, and decline to offer a job.[66] High rates of imprisonment may thus reduce legitimate stakes in conformity and eliminate lawful alternatives to crime, not just for those who are sent to prison but also for those who are not.

Careful analysis of variations in states' crime and incarceration rates reveals a consistent relationship: states with the *lowest* crime rates also have the *lowest* incarceration rates, and this is not primarily a result of incarceration reducing crime. Put differently, if incarceration were the key to a safer society, cities and states with exceptionally high incarceration rates (e.g., Baltimore, Washington, D.C., Louisiana, Texas, and Oklahoma) would be the safest—not the most dangerous—places to live. What makes a place safe are social and economic factors that deliver a high quality of life as measured by good education, strong families, informal social controls, viable networks, and opportunities for stable, meaningful, and well-paid work.[67]

While incarceration does not make us safer, decarceration, as recommended in this report, would free up the resources necessary to produce neighborhoods that are good places to live, work, and play, making people safe (and feel safe) from common forms of interpersonal violence and theft. It lies beyond the scope of this document to specify a program for doing this. There are, however, steps that government, business, and community organizations can take in preventing communities from deteriorating and in helping them improve when they are in trouble. The criminal justice system has a role to play in this process. Businesses will be reluctant to invest in communities where they will be at high risk for violence and theft. Neighbors will be reluctant to participate in and take responsibility for community affairs when the streets are unsafe. At the same time, it must be recognized that criminal justice agencies cannot do the job alone. We focus here on criminal justice, but insist that the contribution it makes must be informed by key facts we have spelled

64   John M. Hagedorn. *People and Folks: Gangs, Crime, and the Underclass in a Rustbelt City.* Chicago: Lake View Press, 1988; Loic Wacquant. "When Ghetto and Prison Meet and Mesh." *Punishment and Society* 3.1 (2001): 95–134; Steven Raphael, op. cit.; Bruce Western, op. cit.; Thomas J. Sugrue, *The Origins of the Urban Crisis: Race and Inequality in Postwar Detroit.* Princeton, NJ: Princeton UP, 1996.

65   John Hagan and Ronit Dinovitzer. "Collateral Consequences of Imprisonment for Children, Communities, and Prisoners." *Crime and Justice: A Review of Research* 26 (1999): 121–62; Bruce Western. *Punishment and Inequality in America.* New York: Russell Sage, 2006.

66   John R. Lott Jr. "The Effect of Conviction on the Legitimate Income of Criminals," *Economic Letters* 34 (1990): 381–85; Devah Pager. "The Mark of a Criminal Record." *American Journal of Sociology* 108 (2003): 937–75 and "Double Jeopardy: Race, Crime, and Getting a Job," *Wisconsin Law Review* (2005): 617–60; Robert J. Sampson and John H. Laub. *Crime in the Making: Pathways and Turning Points Throughout Life.* Cambridge, MA: Harvard UP, 1993; Joel Waldfogel. "The Effect of Criminal Conviction on Income and the Trust Reposed in the Workmen." *Journal of Human Resources* 29 (1994): 62–81 and "Does Conviction Have Permanent Effect on Income and Employment?" *International Review of Law and Economics* 18 (1998): 25–40; Jeffrey Grogger. "The Effect of Arrests on the Employment and Earnings of Young Men." *The Quarterly Journal of Economics* 11 (1995): 51–71; Marc Mauer. *Race to Incarcerate.* New York: New Press, 1999; Richard B. Freeman and Jeffrey Fagan. "Crime and Work." *Crime and*

Justice: A Review of Research 265 (1999): 225–90; Marc Mauer and Meda Chesney-Lind, eds. *Invisible Punishment: The Collateral Consequences of Mass Imprisonment.* New York: New Press, 2002; Michael Tonry. *Malign Neglect.* New York: Oxford UP, 1995; Bruce Western. *Punishment and Inequality in America.* New York: Russell Sage, 2006.

67   Arnold S. Linksy and Murray A. Straus. *Social Stress in the United States: Links to Regional Patterns in Crime and Illness.* Dover, MA: Auburn House, 1986.

out above if the result is to be progressive, humane, and effective.

V. RECOMMENDATIONS

Our Orienting Idea:
Punishment Should Fit the Crime.

Our resources are misspent, our punishments too severe, our sentences too long.

—Justice Anthony M. Kennedy[68]

We have argued that using imprisonment to reduce crime by deterring, incapacitating, or rehabilitating is of limited value, and is now yielding diminishing returns. What then should imprisonment be used for? The size of the literature addressing this subject is not matched by its success in forging a consensus on the matter, and we do not intend to settle all debates here. That said, we think it useful to be clear about our own guiding thoughts.

Imprisonment can legitimately satisfy a social and personal need for retribution toward those who violate society's laws. Most contemporary philosophies of punishment give a large role to retribution.

In addition to satisfying victims' needs, punishing lawbreakers according to what they deserve can perform important social functions. Punishment can promote social solidarity, while failure to respond to crime weakens commitment to social norms. At the same time, excessive punishment can exacerbate social tensions and widens divisions, reducing solidarity. It can corrode a nation's political culture, and obstruct efforts to deal constructively with social problems, including crime.

Retribution should not be used as an excuse for mindless punitiveness as is the case now. The essence of the retribution is to punish people proportionately to

what they deserve, based on the crime they have committed. Excessive leniency and undeserved harshness both violate the principle of proportionality. Failure to limit the severity of punishment to what is deserved is unjust. It alienates citizens from the government and undercuts the effectiveness of law enforcement. When those who are punished are disproportionately poor and members of minority groups, it is inevitable that they will believe that the law is being used to repress them, rather than holding them accountable for their crimes.

Public opinion polls have consistently shown that substantial numbers of people think that the courts are too lenient. These sentiments cannot be taken at face value, and should not be allowed to dictate sentencing policy unthinkingly. For example, the vast majority of crimes are neither as serious as the public believes them to be nor as heinous as the media portrays them. As shown in Table 8, very few (about 15%) of the crimes for which people are arrested are either violent or serious property crimes. Yet many of these arrests are resulting in prison terms. We have already noted that the costs of these crimes to the public are only a fraction of the costs of punishing those who are arrested and convicted. The volume of serious crime attributed to released prisoners is also much lower than is commonly believed.

In addition, many people do not fully appreciate how harsh and disruptive any form of imprisonment is because they have never experienced the total loss of agency and privacy that imprisonment entails. Most prisoners experience monotonous routines, medical neglect, physical danger, extreme isolation, and a myriad of deprivations—all of which worsen the trauma of imprisonment.

When people are presented a fuller picture of the facts of particular crime and the criminals' characteristics, they generally favor more moderate sanctions. Recent studies show that "when nonviolent offenders are involved, there is substantial support for intermediate sanctions and for restorative justice."[69]

68   Justice Anthony M. Kennedy. "Speech at the American Bar Association, Annual Meeting: An Address by Anthony M. Kennedy, Associate Justice, Supreme Court of the United States." American Bar Association. San Francisco, CA. 9 Aug. 2003.

69   Francis T. Cullen, Bonnie S. Fisher, and Brandon K. Applegate, "Public Opinion About Punishment and Corrections." From *Crime and Justice: A Review of Research*,

Table 8: Arrests by Type of Crime, 2005

Crime Type	Number	Percent
Total Arrests	14,094,186	100%
Total Serious Violent	**603,503**	**4%**
Murder and non-negligent manslaughter	14,062	0%
Forcible rape	25,528	0%
Robbery	114,616	1%
Aggravated assault	449,297	3%
Total Serious Property	**1,609,327**	**11%**
Burglary	298,835	2%
Larceny theft	1,146,696	8%
Motor vehicle theft	147,459	1%
Arson	16,337	0%
Drug Abuse Violations	**1,846,351**	**13%**
Alcohol/Liquor	2,525,924	18%
Driving under the influence	1,371,919	10%
Liquor laws	597,838	4%
Drunkenness	556,167	4%
All Other Crimes	**10,035,005**	**53%**
Other assaults	1,301,392	9%
Forgery and counterfeiting	118,455	1%
Fraud	321,521	2%
Embezzlement	18,970	0%
Stolen property, buying, receiving, possessing	133,856	1%
Vandalism	279,562	2%
Weapons	193,469	1%
Prostitution	84,891	1%
Non-rape sex offenses	91,625	1%
Gambling	11,180	0%
Offenses against the family	129,128	1%
Disorderly conduct	678,231	5%
Vagrancy	33,227	0%
All other offenses	3,863,785	27%
Suspicion	3,764	0%
Curfew/loitering	140,835	1%
Runaways	108,954	1%

*Percentages do not add up to 100% due to rounding.

Source: UCR 2005, Federal Bureau of Investigation.

We also note that problems can potentially arise when prosecutors, defense counsel and judges want to modify a sentence by taking into account other factors that are more related to the goals of deterrence, incapacitation and rehabilitation. For example, should we allow different prison sentences for two people who have committed the same crime but have different prior records or have been assessed to present a lower risk to public safety (male versus female, older versus younger, drug addiction versus none)? Similarly, one could argue that someone who has committed only a very minor crime but has been assessed as a "high risk" to commit a serious crime if released and hence in need of being deterred, incapacitated or rehabilitated should be incarcerated as opposed to someone convicted of a more serious crime but poses no such threat to public safety.

The prestigious American Law Institute's recently issued Model Penal Code endorses a concept of 'limited retribution,' which allows for the introduction of rehabilitative, deterrence and incapacitation factors which can influence sentences within minimum and maximum limits based on retributive considerations. This position has the merit of limiting the extent to which sentence lengths can be extended far beyond what a defendant deserves. Prosecutors and judges currently take such considerations into account as they negotiate pleas and set sentences.

Nevertheless we are concerned about the potential for injustice and discrimination associated with this practice. When decisions made as to whether someone should be imprisoned or for how long on the basis of what crimes one might commit if released, or on the basis of a person's needs for rehabilitation, they will often be incorrect. Subjecting people who will not commit serious new crimes to prison sentences (or to longer sentences) simply on the basis of predictions that are false is simply unfair.

We are also concerned that determinations—of dangerousness or whether people are in need of treatment—are likely to be skewed by racial and class biases. Racial stereotypes sometimes operate unconsciously and can influence perceptions of dangerousness even on the part of decision-makers who harbor no conscious prejudices.

Minority offenders' personal circumstances may make them appear to some judges as unlikely prospects for rehabilitation. Those who can pay for private drug or mental health treatment, provide restitution in large amounts to victims and communities, or attend educational and vocational programs often unavailable to the poor are likely to receive milder punishments than others who have committed exactly the same crimes.

This is especially so in the current political context, which increasingly relies on the private sector to provide correctional services. This means that middle-class criminals with drug or mental health problems get help because they can pay for it—and stay out of prison—while poor people who cannot do so go to jail. By reducing the magnitudes of sentences and restricting them within narrow limits, such disparities are likely to be reduced. But we remain concerned that poor and non-white people might be likely to receive harsher punishments within these limits.

For all of these reasons we oppose the practice of imposing prison sentences "so that the defendant can be rehabilitated," or "to protect society" from "a dangerous" person. On the other hand, retributivism does not require that everyone who violates a given statute receive exactly the same sentence. In determining the appropriate punishment in a particular case, some characteristics of the person and the crime committed can legitimately be considered. All violations of a particular criminal statute are not alike. A sentencing system should be "flexible enough to permit individualized sentences when warranted by mitigating or aggravating factors not taken into account in the establishment of general sentencing practices."

At the same time it should not be so unstructured as to create "unwarranted sentencing disparities among defendants with similar records who have been found guilty of similar criminal conduct." Flexibility and equity in sentencing can thus be achieved by considering the criminal's personal circumstances, the circumstances of the crime itself (e.g., was it spontaneous or premeditated?) and criminal record to influence the sentence.

Volume 27, Michael Tonry, ed, Chicago: University of Chicago Press, (2000): 1.

The implementation of these very general principles is a matter that deserves careful attention by state legislators. It lies beyond the scope of this report to specify the details of such a sentencing scheme. Nevertheless, we insist that the presumption against imprisonment should hold firm in all cases.

Given the excessive lengths of sentences now being imposed on many defendants, a reconsideration of sentencing structures should begin with the premise that sentence lengths should be reduced substantially. Furthermore, innovative methods of serving in-community sentences should be explored. Especially promising are programs of victim–offender restoration and community reparation such as are already operating in Europe, Australia and New Zealand.

Four Recommendations That Will Reduce Prison Population

To reduce the prison population, we propose four recommendations. If implemented, they would dramatically reduce current prison, parole, probation, and jail populations. All of these recommendations have been successfully implemented in some fashion in several jurisdictions *with no adverse impact on crime rates*.[70] By lowering the prison population, the associated costs—tens of billions of dollars now spent in an ineffective war on crime—could either be returned to tax payers or reinvested by the public and private sectors in those social, family, community, and economic institutions that have more direct influence on crime rates.

---

70 Reducing prison populations by shortening sentences and ceasing returning parole violators to prison could only occur over a span of several years and, therefore, there would be little or no impact on crime rates due to influx of released prisoners. In several instances, prison populations have been reduced in a short period of time and there was no resultant increase in crime rates. Similarly, decriminalization of drug crimes, even heroin and cocaine possession and use, has occurred with no increase in drug use or other crimes.

RECOMMENDATION I: Reduce Time Served in Prison

The fundamental and most powerful reform that must occur if we are to have any hope of reversing the imprisonment binge is to reduce the severity of the sentences that are given. For many prisoners now sent to prison, this would mean probation or a short jail sentence; for others, it would mean less time spent in prison, as well as less time on parole. An in-depth examination of sentence lengths and time conserved is called for, it might begin with the presumption that terms be cut back to what they were circa 1975 when the imprisonment binge began.

This central recommendation is grounded in three facts: 1) many prisoners are now serving longer prison terms; 2) the longer prison terms are not proportionate to the severity of the crimes they were convicted of; and 3) the extension of their length of incarceration has no major impact on their recidivism rate, or crime rates in general. As shown in Table 9 there is no association between length of stay and recidivism rates. Coupled with the previous research finding that released prisoners account for a small percentage of all arrests, one has to question the benefits of increasing the length of time served.

Table 9: Three Year Follow-Up **Rate of Re-Arrest of State Prisoners Released in 1994, By Time Served in Prison**

Time Served	Three Year Re-Arrest Rates
6 months or less	66.0%
7–12 months	64.8%
13–18 months	64.2%
19–24 months	65.4%
25–30 months	68.3%
31–36 months	62.6%
37–60 months	63.2%
61 months or more	54.0%

Source: Prison Statistics. US Department of Justice, Office of Justice Programs, 2006.

RECOMMENDATION 2: Eliminate the Use of Prison for Parole or Probation Technical Violators

Today anywhere from 50–65% of the 650,000 prisoners admitted to state prison are those who have failed to complete their terms of probation or parole. Of those who have failed probation or parole, about half are being sent to prison for what is known as technical violations. Such violations include such behavior as absconding from supervision, failure to pay supervision fees, restitution costs, or fines, failure to attend treatment, drug use as detected by urine-analysis, failure to maintain employment, or being arrested (but not convicted) for misdemeanor or felony level crimes.

While these behaviors are troublesome, they do not reach the level of seriousness of requiring incarceration for many months or years in state or federal prison. In many ways using the most severe form of punishment for behavior that only a probationer or parolee can be imprisoned for is a clear example of where the punishment does not fit the crime. For those that suggest that by incarcerating people for non-felony crimes or non-compliance with the terms of probation or parole we are preventing more serious crimes to occur, there is no scientific data to support such a claim. In fact as shown in recommendation No. 3, the evidence is that parole supervision is either ineffective or criminogenic with respect to public safety.

Parolees who are returned to prison because of technical violations often serve relatively long prison terms. The U.S. Department of Justice reports that parole violators returned to prison serve an average of 18 months before being re-released. In Louisiana, the state with the highest incarceration rate in the United States, the average length of stay for a technical violator is 20 months. Conversely, the state of Washington, by statute, does not allow technical violators to spend more than 60 days incarcerated for such violations and then only after a set number of violations.

These data clearly suggest that we are spending a great deal of money and wasting a large amount of prison space on people who fail to comply with parole and probation supervision rules and who have not committed new crimes. Prosecutors and correctional officials erroneously believe that unless individuals are re-incarcerated for technical violations, the individuals will commit serious crimes in the future. There is no scientific evidence to support this belief and attendant policy, yet it continues to be the primary rationale for re-incarcerating tens of thousands of people for criminal or non-criminal behavior for which ordinary citizens could not be incarcerated.

RECOMMENDATION 3: Reduce the Length of Parole and Probation Supervision Periods

Currently, persons placed on probation and parole remain in this status for extended periods of time (after three years or more). Violation of the rigorous rules imposed on probationers and parolees can result in return to prison. As we saw in Table 4, a substantial fraction of prison admissions are for these "technical" violations.

There is little evidence that lengthy parole and probation terms decrease crime. A number of studies in California discovered that there was no relationship between 1) the time on supervision and parole success, and 2) parole versus no parole supervision on recidivism rates.[71] Probation or parole supervision failure is most likely to occur within the first 12 months of supervision; thereafter, supervision is more of a nuisance than a means for assisting people after prison or preventing them from committing another crime.

Now, there is new research evidence indicating that parole supervision is largely ineffective with respect to reducing recidivism. Table 10 shows the recidivism rates by type of release for Kentucky, Texas, and Pennsylvania. Here one can see that people who complete their prison sentences without parole supervision have significantly lower recidivism rates than those placed on parole supervision. The obvious explanation

---

71 Dorothy R. Jaman, Lawrence A. Bennett, and John E. Berecochea. *Early Discharge from Parole: Policy, Practice and Outcome.* Sacramento: California Department of Sacramento Corrections, 1974; Deborah Star. *Summary Parole: A Six and Twelve Month Follow-Up Evaluation.* Sacramento: California Dept. of Corrections, Research Unit, 1979; Patrick G. Jackson. "Living Together Unmarried: Awareness Contexts and Social Interaction." *Journal of Family Issues* (1983), and Patrick G. Jackson. "Bay Area Parole Project." Mimeographed, 1978.

Table 10: Re-Incarceration Rates by Type of Release for Selected States

Release Type	Kentucky	Texas	Pennsylvania
Parole supervision	53%	26%	50%
Discharges	18%	11%	19%
Total	35%	25%	42%

Source: James Austin, Patricia Handyman, and John Irwin. "Exploring the Needs and Risks of the Returning Prisoner Population." (Presented to the From Prison to Home Conference, Jan. 30–31, 2002).

is that people who have no parole obligations when they leave prison ("max out") can only be returned to prison if they are convicted of a new felony crime. Conversely, those placed on parole and probation can be re-incarcerated for either non-criminal behavior or misdemeanor crimes. A 2005 Urban Institute study, among others, revealed that individuals released with no parole supervision return to prison at a significantly lower rate than those released on parole.[72]

RECOMMENDATION 4: Decriminalize "Victimless" Crimes, Particularly Those Related to Drug Use and Abuse

In recent years, behaviors have been criminalized that are not dangerous and pose little if any threat to others. A large group of people are currently serving time for behaviors that have been criminalized to protect people from themselves. Their offenses involved the consent of all immediate parties to the transaction. Common examples in American history have included abortion, gambling, illicit sexual conduct that does not involve coercion (e.g., prostitution and, until recently, homosexual activity), and the sale and possession of recreational drugs. According to the U.S. Department of Justice, approximately 30–40% of all current prison admissions involve crimes that have no direct or obvious victim other than the perpetrator (see Table 11).[73] The drug category constitutes the largest offense category, with 31% of all prison admissions resulting from such crimes.

In the late 19th and early 20th centuries, the United States government conducted a large-scale experiment regarding the social consequences of creating a new category of crimes by making it illegal to distribute alcohol. Prohibition aimed to stop people from drinking, and to an extent was successful. But the price of this success was ultimately considered too high. Revenues from selling alcohol illegally swelled the coffers of organized crime and magnified levels of corruption in local governments. Gangsters gunned one another down to gain control of the lucrative market for illegal liquor. Many died from drinking alcohol put on the market without quality control. Eventually, Americans realized that Prohibition was doing more harm than good and repealed it.

Politicians and the public have ignored the lessons of Prohibition in formulating drug policy. In an attempt to eliminate harms caused to individuals, their families and society from the abuse of heroin, cocaine, marijuana, and other drugs, legislatures have passed laws sending large numbers of users, abusers and low-level dealers to prison with very long sentences. This prohibition, like the earlier one, has led to violence as dealers have sought to eliminate rivals in the lucrative market. Like Prohibition, it has resulted in the distribution of adulterated drugs that have injured and killed users. The high profits of drug dealing are largely the consequence of legislation that eliminates competition from anyone unwilling to risk draconian penalties.

Every time a dealer is taken out of circulation by a prison sentence, a new dealer is drawn in by the lure of large profits. The prosecution and imprisonment

---

72   Amy L. Solomon, Vera Kachnowski, and Avinash Bhati. *Does Parole Work? Analyzing the Impact of Post-Prison Supervision on Re-Arrest Outcomes.* Washington, DC: The Urban Institute, 2005.

73   Criminological literature refers to these crimes as "victimless" (Edwin M. Schur. *Crime Without Victims: Deviant Behavior and Public Policy.* Englewood Cliffs, NJ: Prentice Hall, 1965), suggesting that they do no harm, which is not always the case. For that reason we call these crimes "consensual."

Table 11: Most Serious Offense for Sentenced Prisoners, 2002 Prison Admissions

Most Serious Offense	Percent
Number of admissions 508,955	
Violent offenses	27%
Property offenses	30%
Drug offenses	31%
Possession	10%
Trafficking	15%
Other/unspecified drug	7%
Public-order offenses	12%
Weapons	3%
Driving while intoxicated	3%
Other public-order	5%
Other offenses	1%

Source: Prison Statistics. US Department of Justice, Office of Justice Programs, 2006..

of low-level traffickers has increased racial disparities, and is the largest factor contributing to the rapid rise in imprisonment rates for women. Dealers' use of violence to eliminate competition helps to sustain the myth linking drug use to violence. Notwithstanding our extraordinary effort to discourage the use and sale of illegal drugs, they remain widely available and widely used.

Though other Western nations have not decriminalized commerce in illegal drugs, they give greater weight to medical and public health considerations in the formulation of drug policy. The violence that surrounds drug trafficking in the United States is largely absent in those countries, and governments are more receptive to needle exchange programs designed to limit the spread of AIDS.[74]

This does not mean that the government should simply walk away from the drug problem. It would be perfectly appropriate for governments to conduct educational campaigns about drugs, for example. Regulatory approaches, such as are now used for drugs that are not illegal should be given serious consideration. The success of recent referenda in several states allowing medical use of marijuana suggests that the public opinion may be changing.[75]

TWO ADDITIONAL RECOMMENDATIONS THAT BEAR ON HUMANE JUSTICE

In addition to the four recommendations to reduce the prison population, there are two other recommendations that need to be made that bear on the quality and fairness of our use of imprisonment.

RECOMMENDATION 5:
Improve Conditions of Imprisonment

Reducing the size of the prison population is not enough. We could not in good conscience recommend that anyone serve a prison sentence unless we ensure that those who do end up behind walls are treated in a humane manner. Prisons that systematically deny human dignity, basic human rights, and life necessities are creating festering sores that poison the entire society.

Unsafe, inhumane, and secretive prisons not only traumatize the incarcerated but also contaminate prison staff and their families, as well as townsfolk near the prison. More generally, support for an inhumane prison system requires that prison workers and the public embrace the simplistic concept that prisoners are unworthy beings that deserve their harsh punishment above and beyond the segregation from society and loss of freedom from incarceration itself.

---

74   Peter Reuter. "Why Can't We Make Prohibition Work Better? Some Consequences of Ignoring the Unattractive." *Perspectives on Crime and Justice: 1996–1997 Lecture Series, Vol. 1.* Washington, DC: National Institute of Justice, 1997. www.ncjrs.gov/pdffiles/166609.pdf.

75   Between 1995 and the present, a majority of voters in state initiatives held in Alaska, Arizona, Colorado, Maine, Nevada, Oregon, the state of Washington, and Washington D.C., voted to allow marijuana use in connection with medical treatment. In state and national polls, substantial majorities support legalizing marijuana for medical use. Details are available at www.medicalmarijuanaprocon.org.

The state can operate prisons efficiently and effectively while treating prisoners in a manner consistent with the minimum standards and rights for prisoners formulated by many private and public bodies in the 1960s and 1970s.[76] In the 1960s, the courts, particularly the U.S. Supreme Court, after virtually ignoring the plight of prisoners for decades, issued a number of decisions upholding prisoners' rights and due process, and banning cruel and unusual punishment. These decisions produced an array of mandated changes in prisons across the country. However, after the mid-1970s, the Supreme Court effectively returned to the "hands-off" policy.[77]

There are five fundamental features of prison administration that should be acceptable to anyone interested in accomplishing the prison's practicable purposes—punishment and deterrence—without engaging in unnecessary, counterproductive, and cruel practices.

1. Cruel and Unusual Punishment

Prison overcrowding, the adoption of excessively harsh and arbitrary control practices in reaction to prison violence, and the growing general punitive attitude toward prisoners have resulted in more punitive policies and practices. These include denial of adequate medical services, excessive use of physical force, and housing prisoners in exceptionally punitive arrangements, such as solitary confinement units and cells. The federal courts have ruled that all of these practices violate the Eighth Amendment of the United States Constitution.

2. Safety

Prisoners should be protected from assault, rape, murder, etc., by other prisoners and staff. Effective strategies such as adequate surveillance, voluntary access to safe living areas within the prison, housing prisoners in small units, and "single-celling" should be practiced to ensure prisoners' safety.

3. Health

Prisoners should have access to the resources and services required to maintain their physical and mental health. These include access to medical and psychiatric services, adequate diet, and recreation. Prisoners should not be subjected to physically and mentally deleterious incarceration regimens such as extended periods of isolation and, restricted mobility, and excessive noise.

4. Programs

Any rational and humane system of punishment should provide access to program opportunities that increase prison safety and improve prisoners' chances of making it in the community after prison. Such programs would include academic, technical and citizenship education, as well as a wide variety of treatment programs that help prisoners improve themselves and develop more conventional, law-abiding interests and pursuits. These types of programs should be provided regardless of whether they reduce recidivism.

5. Post-Release Assistance

Most prisoners receive little or no preparation for release from prison or assistance subsequent to their release. They face extraordinary difficulties in achieving stability, viability, and life fulfillment on the outside. States should develop and provide access to transitional and permanent housing, education, vocational training and placement, counseling, coaching, and mentoring.

---

76   In 1955, the United Nations Congress on the Prevention of Crime and the Treatment of Prisoners adopted a set of Standard Minimum Rules for the Treatment of Prisoners. See: Human Rights: A Compilation of International Instruments. New York: United Nations, 2002. Section G. In *The Struggle for Justice: A Report on Crime and Punishment in America*. American Friends Service Committee. New York: Hill and Wang, 1971. 168–69, the Working Party for the American Friends Service Committee, which consisted of individuals with a variety of prison-system experiences, produced one of the best-thought-out lists of humane conditions.

77   See: Jack E. Call. "The Supreme Court and Prisoners' Rights." *Federal Probation* (1995): 36–46, for a discussion of the Court's shift in prisoners' rights matters.

RECOMMENDATION 6:
Restore Ex-Prisoner Voting and Other Rights.

Prisoners face exceptional problems from their stigmatized and reduced social and civil status. They are automatically barred from most city, county, and state employment and from some housing such as federally subsidized housing and are systematically denied employment by many private employers. Their right to vote varies from state to state, even from county to county in some states.

It will be difficult to overcome private employers' restrictions on hiring ex-prisoners, but persistent efforts should be made toward this goal. Perhaps laws against discrimination against employment of ex-prisoners can be adopted in the future. Government agencies, however, could easily change their policies. In San Francisco, the city government has removed the question regarding prior arrests on job applications. Other government jurisdictions should follow this example. Opening up these relatively good-paying jobs to ex-prisoners greatly increases public safety by moving potential criminals into conventional pathways. Government subsidies for hiring ex-convicts could overcome some employers' hesitations. In addition, exclusion from welfare, public housing, and subsidies should be ended as should rules barring ex-convicts from living in certain neighborhoods. Licensing restrictions should be maintained only when they are demonstrably necessary to protect the public.

ESTIMATED IMPACT OF THESE RECOMMENDATIONS ON PRISON POPULATIONS

To illustrate what our recommendations can accomplish in reducing prison populations without impacting crime rates and at considerable savings to taxpayers, we have developed rough projections based on three of the four major recommendations for changing current sentencing and correctional practices:[78]

1. Time served in prison would be reduced.
2. Technical parole and probation violators would not serve time in prison for such behavior.
3. People convicted of "victimless" crimes would not be sentenced to state prison.

We discuss below the implementation of these three policy reforms briefly.

1. Time Served in Prison Would Be Reduced

Of the three recommendations, this one is clearly the most important and most powerful in terms of reducing the prison population. It also is the most acceptable to most politicians and the public as it does not eliminate incarceration but makes the amount of time served proportional to the sentence.

The length of imprisonment can be modestly reduced (3–5 months) by immediately increasing the amount of good time awarded to prisoners for good conduct and program completion. Within states with indeterminate sentencing, parole grant rates can be immediately increased especially for prisoners who pose little risk to public safety. But ultimately, legislation will be needed to remove many of the restrictions that have served to increase the period of confinement (e.g., mandatory minimums, truth in sentencing, etc.). Such reforms should be retroactive to the current prison population.

2. Technical Parole and Probation Violators Would Not Serve Time in Prison for Such Behavior

The imprisonment of technical parole violators is a clear example where the punishment does not fit the crime. Further, we also know that recidivism rates are lowest for persons who discharge from prison rather than facing a lengthy period of parole supervision.

This reform can be implemented administratively by not allowing revocations for such behavior. A number of states have administratively implemented such reforms including Michigan, Oregon, South Dakota, and Texas. As noted earlier, the state of Washington passed legislation more than 20 years ago that prohibits state imprisonment for technical parole violators with

---

78   We are unable to estimate the effect of reducing the length of parole and probation supervision.

no adverse impact on the state's crime rate. For those who are readmitted for a parole violation, the period of re-confinement would be far shorter than what it has been (no more than 90 days). This is consistent with recent legislation in Louisiana, which limits the period of confinement for first time violators to 90 days and in Washington where violators can serve no more than 60 days in a local jail. Similar to parole violators, few persons should be sent to state or federal prison for anything that does not constitute a conviction for a felony crime or for non-criminal behavior.

3. People Convicted of "Victimless" Crimes Would Not Be Sentenced to Prison

Large numbers of persons arrested and convicted of drug possession, disorderly conduct, public intoxication, drunk-driving, prostitution, curfew violation, vagrancy, loitering, gambling, and a wide variety of motor vehicle violations are being incarcerated in our jails and are being placed on years of probation. Once placed on probation, they are vulnerable to being sent to prison as probation violators for continuing such behavior, failing to pay their probation supervision fees, maintaining employment, attending treatment, or many other non-criminal acts.

Collectively, these three reforms, if implemented, would drop the prison population by over 50% and produce an incarceration rate of 222 per 100,000 people, which is what it was in 1986 and which is still well above the rates that existed for some 50 years

before that. The prison population would decline from 1.5 million to below 700,000 (see Table 12, and Figure 5). Persons convicted of serious and violent crimes would continue to be incarcerated. But large numbers of probation and parole violators and others now convicted of victimless crimes would be diverted from state prison. All of these reforms require no program funding—indeed the adoption of such reforms would more than pay for whatever prison and post-release programs that would be of benefit to released prisoners. All of this can be done without negatively impacting the crime rate.

To those who say that these three basic recommendations are neither feasible nor practical we would simply note that these practices and laws are now in place in many states and other countries. There are nine states with incarceration rates that are near or well below the 222 per 100,000 population rate. The state of Washington, by statute, does not allow parole violators to be sent to prison. Louisiana recently passed legislation that greatly restricts first time technical violators to be re-admitted to prison. Nevada recently passed legislation that reduced the period of parole supervision, which has increased the parole success rate and reduced the size and costs of the parole population.

In the area of decriminalization, 12 states (Alaska, California, Colorado, Maine, Minnesota, Mississippi, Nebraska, Nevada, New York, North Carolina, Ohio, and Oregon) and several European countries along with New Zealand and Australia have largely decriminalized or reduced the penalties for drug possession.[79] A number of local cities have also modified

Table 12: Current and Projected State Prison Systems Based on Recommendations

Prison Admissions	Current Practices			New Practices			
	Admits	Time Served (mos.)	Prisoners	Admits	Time Served (mos.)	Prisoners
Total	650,000	27	1,446,250	422,500	19	666,250
New Court Admissions	390,000	30	975,000	292,500	21	511,875
Probation Technical Violators	65,000	30	162,500	32,500	21	56,875
Parole Violators	195,000	19	308,750	97,500	12	97,500
Parole Technical Violators	97,500	19	154,375	0	0	0
Incarceration Rate	483 per 100,000			222 per 100,0000		

79   Robert J. MacCoun and Peter Reuter. *Drug War Heresies: Learning from Other Vices, Times, and Places.* New York: Cambridge UP, 2001.

Figure 5. Historical & Projected US Prison Population

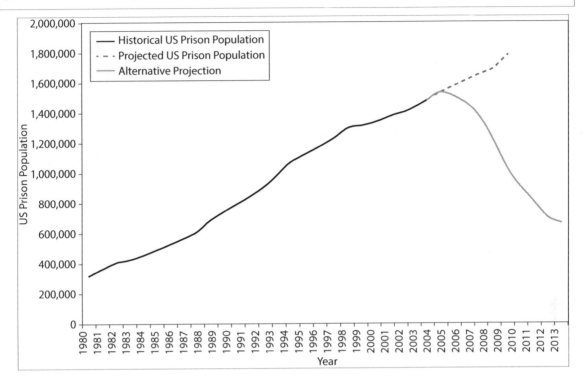

their local ordinances and criminal justice practices to decriminalize pot (Berkeley, Oakland, and San Francisco, California; Breckenridge, Colorado; Amherst, Massachusetts; Madison and Milwaukee, Wisconsin; Urbana and Carbondale, Illinois; and Colombia, Missouri). In all of these jurisdictions there has been no associated increase in crimes rates.

VI. CONCLUDING REMARKS

Reducing the number and length of prison terms will require changes in sentencing laws and parole and probation practices. This will not occur until the public passes referenda and successfully pressures legislators and executives, or enlightened political leaders better understand the realities and move on their own to make necessary changes. There are a variety of methods and strategies to achieve this goal. No particular political structure can guarantee or prevent the progress that is now needed. Sentencing commissions, for example, have been excellent devices for controlling over-incarceration in some states (Oregon, Minnesota), while in other jurisdictions, such as the federal, sentencing systems have been specifically designed to incapacitate as many people as possible, rather than focusing on what offenders deserve.

We also recognize that as the system of imprisonment has grown, so too has the investment and the vested interests that support its operations and growth. In order to reverse the current trends we will have to find a way to re-allocate the money, political influence, and jobs that the current system provides. This will not be easy and it will take many years to wean us off the excessive use of imprisonment.

Our first goal was to document the negative and ineffective consequences of mass incarceration in human, economic, and public safety terms. Our second was to offer one basic and simple recommendation that by itself would have a significant reduction in the prison population—shorter periods of imprisonment that are proportional to the harm inflicted upon society and individuals. We hope this report will stimulate a serious debate on the use of imprisonment and lead to a new policy of decarceration. If this would occur, we could re-invest some portion of the tens of billions of dollars we spend each year incarcerating millions of Americans into those communities and families that are now being unfairly devastated by imprisonment.

REALIGNMENT IN CALIFORNIA

Policy and Research Implications

Barbara Owen and Alan Mobley

INTRODUCTION

Corrections policy in California is undergoing an historic shift in response to a variety of pressures—budgetary, operational and judicial. In April, 2011, the California legislature passed the Public Safety Realignment Act (Assembly Bill 109). This law shifted responsibility for specific categories of low-level convicted felons from the behemoth California Department of Corrections and Rehabilitation (CDCR) to the 58 individual counties. Under this legislation, low-level drug and property offenders committing their crimes after October 1, 2011 will be sentenced to county facilities and programs. State prisoners in these same categories will be released to their county of commitment under a version of county probation called post-release community supervision (not state parole). This commentary will briefly outline the background of this historic legislation and detail selected consequences of the Act. A discussion of research and policy implications will follow, and an invitation to consider broader social justice concerns will conclude the essay.

This commentary will only summarize the complications of the Act and its implementation. Interested readers are referred to various publications and websites for more detail and discussion. The reports, *Public Safety Realignment: California at a Crossroads*, by the ACLU of California (aclunc.org), and *Rethinking the State-Local Relationship: Corrections* by Misczynski (2011) of the Public Policy Institute of California (ppic.org) are must-reads. The CDCR website contains basic information on the Act and various statistical reports that convey some of its impact (cdcr.ca.gov). The Center for Juvenile and Criminal Justice (cjcj.org); the Stanford Criminal Justice Center (stanford.law.org) and the Warren Institute on Law and Social Policy (warreninstitute.org) have developed several policy papers on the issue. The Partnership for Community Excellence (cafwd.org/pce) and the website for the Chief Probation Officers Organization (cpoc.org) act as repositories of documents related to Realignment. For a detailed overview of the legislation, Byers' (2011) statute review is instructive. Additionally, most counties have developed a section within their probation website to post Realignment information, including copies of their Country Plans and notice of related meetings.

BACKGROUND

Since the 1970s, the California prison system has expanded exponentially across several dimensions: population size, budget, staffing, and number of facilities. With some of the highest incarceration rates in the United States (which itself has some of the highest rates in the world), California has the dubious distinction of producing some of the highest recidivism rates as well. Overall, two-thirds of all inmates released from the CDCR returned to prison within three years, many of them for technical parole violations rather than new convictions (cdcr.ca.gov). Despite attempts at rehabilitation programs, and a name change in 2005 to highlight this new direction, recidivism rates remained high and few programs demonstrated any measurable result. At the same time, a shrinking California budget and decade-long lawsuits set the stage for significant policy change. While many observers see litigation as only one of many pressures, the lawsuit in question deserves some detail here. Following many challenges to state prison conditions of confinement in terms of medical, mental health and dental services, one lawsuit was ultimately decided by the US Supreme Court. Brown v. Plata found that overcrowding in California prisons did in fact constitute "cruel and unusual punishment."

As a consequence, the State was directed to reduce the state prison population by about one-third by May, 2013. At the time of this writing (mid-2012), CDCR has made progress toward this mandate. According to the Center for Juvenile and Criminal Justice (CJCJ), the first eight months of Realignment has seen a 41% reduction in new prison admissions and a drop of 28,300 inmates (Males, 2012, p. 1). The parole population has also been reduced by about half as well. More specifically, the CDCR Weekly Population Report from July 4, 2012 shows that the in-state[1] custody population was reduced by about 17% between July 2011 and July 2012. Like all criminal justice measures, there was a significant difference in the rates for women and men:

the male population was reduced by just over 16% while the female population has been reduced at 33%, double the rate for men. Note also that the incoming prison population has been reduced because parole violators—for the most part—are now sanctioned in the county rather than by return to state custody.

Krisberg and Taylor-Nicolson (2011) argue that three factors underlie the change: cutting state spending, reducing prison over-crowding, and improving the system. Critical to all three is the idea that local counties can be better equipped to develop innovations in rehabilitation and reentry. The budget matrix for realignment dollars is also specific but one thing remains clear: although county custody costs (county jail) may be somewhat lower than state prison costs, shifting the custody and supervision costs of selected offender groups to the county will only cut spending in state prisons, and may not reduce correctional costs for California overall. While state prison populations have been reduced and appear to be on track to meet the Court's mandated goal, this measure is shortsighted and somewhat deceiving. A corresponding rise in county jail populations will continue California's over-reliance on custody: it is possible that too many offenders will still be locked-up, regardless of the location. As will be discussed below, there are significant implications for conditions of confinement and rehabilitation in county jails ill-equipped to manage the influx of more prisoners, and for longer periods of time, as well as provide "evidence-based" rehabilitative programs. Finally, the goal of improving the system again assumes counties are willing and able to provide a wider range of rehabilitation and reentry options at the community level than that provided by CDCR. Joan Petersilia has recently stated, "So far, only 10 percent of that money is going to treatment programs, with the bulk going to sheriff's offices, local jails, probations staff, and court services. That bodes ill for keeping ex-inmates from returning to crime" (Cited in Gest 2012).

Public Safety Realignment[2], then, is based on the notion that overall, fewer offenders will be placed in lower-cost custody beds in the counties for shorter time periods. The assumption is that counties will develop a greater emphasis on "evidence-based" programs in local corrections, and importantly, in community supervision practices. AB 109 is specific on the kinds of "evidence-based correctional sanctions and programming other than jail incarceration alone or traditional routine supervision" that should be pursued at the local level. These include but are not limited to: day reporting centers, drug courts, residential multi-service centers, mental health treatment programs, electronic and GPS monitoring programs, victim restitution programs, counseling programs, community service programs, educational programs, and work training programs. "Risk assessment" is also implied in this process. The theory is that lower custody costs and better rehabilitation outcomes, including reducing recidivism, will both save money and improve public safety.

CONSEQUENCES OF AB 109

The legislation has multiple consequences for criminal justice operations at the local policy level. Sentencing, custody and supervision will be changed significantly. Most immediately, the Act increases the number and length of sanctions that result in county jail sentences and creates new categories of "post-release community supervision" (PRCS) for local probation departments. As of October 1, 2011, many felonies are "redefined" as punishable in jail for 16 months, 2 years, or 3 years instead of state prison as previously legislated. These felonies are informally known as "non-non-non"— felonies that are non-serious, non-violent, and non-sex offenses (defined as "not PC-290 Registerable"). Byers (2011) notes the presence of a fourth "non"—an offense that is not enhanced under Penal Code §186.11, but that this is rarely used. Enhancements are typically used to increase sentence length when the offense is seen as exceedingly violent, or when past offenses increase the penalty. Section 1170 (h) of the California Penal Code describes the sentencing options, with section (5) outlining the "county jail only" and the "split sentence" or "mandatory supervised release" options.

Judges have two general options for sentencing felons to county jail. A "county jail only" sentence means just that: an individual is sentenced to county jail and, after discharge, is not under any form of supervision. Mandatory supervised release (MSR) is a form of "split sentence," whereby an individual serves some portion of a sentence in county jail custody and is released to community supervision and/or programs. Byers' statute review also examines many unanswered questions about the Act and lists the "hundreds" of offenses that conceivably fall under this new sentencing structure.

The law also specifies certain offenses as "County Jail Ineligible" or "State Prison Eligible" which excludes defendants who must serve an executed felony sentence for a County Jail Felony in the state prison because of having a current or prior serious or violent felony, or some sex offenses (Byers 2011, p. 9).

This realignment of specific categories of felons to local sentencing is increasing local jail populations— and, equally important, the time served in local custody—as it decreases state prison populations. Prior to the Act, many jails in California were grappling with crowding, court-ordered caps on their populations, antiquated facilities and few programs. Budget cuts at the county level have also limited the ability of counties to respond to these problems. In 2007, AB 900 funded new jail construction in many counties, but financial responsibility for operating these facilities remains with local government.

The Act also has major consequences for state parole and county probation supervision. The assumption here is that county probation is better equipped to provide rehabilitative and reentry services than state parole for these released low-level offenders. Those state prisoners who fit the "non-non-non" definitions would have been released to state parole supervision prior to October 1, 2011. By creating "Post Release Community Supervision"(PRCS)", these individuals are now released to county probation supervision for a period not to exceed 3 years. Mirroring the metric of custody population, state parole populations are decreasing while county probation caseloads are increasing. CDCR provided estimates of the number of "non-non-nons" that the counties should expect, but in the first six months CDCR has under-estimated the number of individuals flowing into each county. County probation officers are now supervising former state prison inmates in ever larger numbers while the program and services designed to provide rehabilitation are being developed.

There are additional provisions under the Act that shift responsibilities from the state to the individual counties. Revocations for individuals on Post Release Community Supervision and state parole will change. The Courts will hear revocations of post-release community supervision while the Board of Parole Hearings will conduct parole violation hearings. If revoked, both types of offenders will serve their time in county custody. There will also be changes to custody credits ("good time"). Jail inmates will be able to earn four days of credit for every two days served. Time spent on home detention (i.e., electronic monitoring) is credited as time spent in jail custody.

Although there has been less attention to pretrial populations, there are also significant changes to how these populations will be managed. For example, Penal Code Section 1203.018 authorizes electronic monitoring for inmates being held in the county jail in lieu of bail. Eligible inmates must first be held in custody for 60 days post-arraignment, or 30 days for those charged with misdemeanor offenses.

WOMEN AND REALIGNMENT

There is a growing body of evidence that demonstrates that the majority of female offenders can be more effectively managed in community settings that provide gender-responsive services and programs to reduce recidivism. Addressing women's pathways to offending and structuring a safe and productive rehabilitative environment are critical to reducing recidivism and improving post-release outcomes. This approach emphasizes community placement where relationships and social support are prioritized. Confinement or other custodial settings are not the first choice in this model. When custody is necessary, it is invoked in the short term and as a step toward more community-based supervision and programming. Given the nonviolent nature of most women's crimes and their low level of risk to public safety, community-based and non-custodial placements should be the primary objective of realignment planning. Gender issues are seldom mentioned in the county Realignment plans, however, even though

women will be over-represented in the "non-non-non" population.

RACE AND REALIGNMENT

Advocates for the rights of racial minorities have been especially alarmed by mass incarceration in California and elsewhere. Many argue that prison overcrowding and racial segregation have worsened living conditions, both in prisons and in minority neighborhoods. The life chances of African-American and Latino males are severely diminished by their frequent interaction with the criminal justice system. Some critics of the prison industrial complex make the claim that mass incarceration is far from anomalous, but merely the latest punitive twist in America's hot and cold running fascination with race-based social engineering. Will Realignment change this? Racial issues are seldom mentioned in Realignment plans, in spite of their obvious importance.

IMPLEMENTATION OF THE ACT

The responsibility of realizing Realignment at the county level falls on the Community Corrections Partnership (CCP). Managed through an Executive Committee, the CCP typically includes the Chief Probation Officer as chair, the District Attorney, the Public Defender, a Judge, the Sheriff, the Police Chief, and the county directors of mental and behavioral health, and other social service programs. Most counties have established subcommittees that address the mechanics of realignment. The CCP is required to submit a Plan and a budget to the state each year that details their approach to Realignment. These county Realignment Plans have been analyzed by The Stanford Criminal Justice Center, the Partnership for Community Excellence, and the ACLU. Common to these analyses is the conclusion that most money is devoted to ramping up jail space, expanding probation to supervise the PRCS population, and further prosecution efforts, with lower funding for expanding programs and services. To be fair, such an enormous shift of responsibility demands improvements and enhancements to county criminal justice infrastructures. It is too soon in the process to conclude that treatment and services will continue to be lower priorities as reflected in the first year budgets and plans.

RESEARCH AND POLICY IMPLICATIONS OF PUBLIC SAFETY REALIGNMENT

The section above can only review the basic outline of Public Safety Realignment in California. While many critical questions remain about the Act and its implementation, this next section frames selected questions relating to consequences of this policy shift.

The State Prison System

As the California prison system shrinks, doing time in these facilities is undergoing a parallel change. As the previously sentenced lower-level offenders leave CDCR custody and new "non-non-nons" remain in the county criminal justice system, the composition of the state prison population will lean toward those serving longer prison terms and, in most cases, those convicted of more violent or serious offenses. The implications for managing these more distilled populations are varied. What kinds of programming and services can be designed for this population? Given that "evidence-based practice" recommends providing services nearer to release, what are the implications for longer-termed prisoners? CDCR has struggled with providing medical and mental health care in the past. Will the population reduction better equip the California prison system to provide services to these aging and long-term inmates? How does prison culture and "doing time" change under these conditions? What about staff: what will staffing patterns look like under this decreased population scenario? How will recidivism rates be changed by this modified prison system?

County Probation and Jails

As probation systems and county jails take on the responsibility for this influx of "non-non-nons," there are operational as well as outcome questions surrounding Realignment. How will counties plan and implement Realignment? How does the intention of the law play out in its actual implementation? How does managing a new type of released offender change local probation? Can local criminal justice systems develop and administer rehabilitative services that the state stumbled in trying to provide?

In terms of recidivism, can counties provide the necessary services and programs to improve outcomes? Will counties embrace the intent of the law: to provide reentry and related rehabilitation services necessary to improving outcomes? Or will counties continue the reliance on incarceration that has shaped criminal justice policy in California? What will this cost?

As offenders travel through the local criminal justice system and receive a county jail sentence, how do these overcrowded systems cope? In facilities that typically have held pre-trial populations, how will programming, staffing and services evolve to serve more sentenced prisoners who are likely to stay much longer than prior to AB 109? How will court mandated services, such as mental and physical health care, be provided?

Funding and Budgets

County officials and professional organizations have questioned the funding of realignment responsibilities from its inception. In general, how will counties modify the local criminal justice system with less money than CDCR was provided? Is the current funding system fair? Can counties "do better with less?" Does realignment shift the burden to counties without fair compensation?

Equity: 58 Counties, 58 Criminal Justice Systems?

There is also concern about fairness. California is politically diverse, with wide differences that play out in criminal justice philosophies. With variations in punishment philosophies and punitive sanctioning, will California fracture into 58 different systems? Will some counties develop alternatives to custody while others rely on jail time? What are the legal questions that underpin this potential inequity? How will the courts and the legislature respond to such potential unfairness?

Litigation

California and many other states have been subject to litigation for multiple issues related to conditions of confinement and provision of constitutionally-mandated services. How will this litigation translate into the 58 counties? Are the local jails equipped to follow these decisions and provide a constitutional environment? Will individual counties be sued and tie up even more funds in fighting lawsuits?

Research and Evaluation

So how will we know? Although the Public Safety Realignment Act stresses "evidence-based practice" with its core principle of measuring process and outcomes, there was no mention of fiscal support for the necessary evaluation. There are many questions related to this fundamental policy change. How will we know whether or not counties do a better job at incarceration or post-release supervision? If local strategies produce better outcomes than state prison? If recidivism rates change? Several counties are supporting data collection efforts from their local budgets, but, as of mid-July 2012, there is little evidence that the state is coordinating any common data collection. Most jail systems lack research staff. How will these outcomes be measured?

Various state agencies, professional organizations and other researchers are beginning to develop some common measures. While this is a step in the right direction, the question remains: how will we know if realignment is having the intended effect?

While most agree that community corrections should be grounded in non-custodial sanctions and alternatives to incarceration, how will we know if such programs as drug treatment, day reporting centers and the like do, in fact, produce better outcomes?

JUSTICE IN TRANSITION: TRANSITIONAL JUSTICE AND THE "BIG QUESTIONS"

The past 200 years and more have provided much evidence both for the harmful effects of prisons and for their utility to democratic societies. Few today, however, consider them to be much more than necessary evils. Is incarceration a *necessary* evil? We know that the penitentiary was birthed with great optimism. From Jeremy Bentham onward, adherents of a rehabilitative philosophy advocated for the prison and championed its redeeming potential. Indeed, the prison was designed to lead its inhabitants to salvation. Far from saving souls, however, the prison may have become a leading mechanism of social insecurity. As the era of mass incarceration begins its apparent decline, a key question might be to ask how we can make progress on achieving justice equitably.

In discussing the future, experience shows it is especially important to remember the past, and to acknowledge the harms and pains of people hurt by justice operations. In recent years, it has become common to hear residents in poor, minority communities in California speak of criminal justice as genocide. Whether or not you agree with this characterization, it is impossible to deny the devastating effects of crime and society's response to crime in these places. Many find it difficult to look forward with hope and empowerment without a deep recognition of the past, and its casualties and survivors.

Global examples of justice reformation have included, as integral elements, public hearings known as truth and reconciliation processes, where expressions of trauma and victimization have been offered as catharsis and as necessary to reconciliation. Criminologists have recently come to categorize the work of truth and reconciliation commissions as valuable tools of transitional justice, a framework most commonly applied to nation states seeking to recover from political revolution and civil war.

Transitional justice asks many questions, one of which is why the need for the transition? In penal policy the apparent answers may be insufficient. If overcrowding and onerous resource expenditures are the "triggers" for transition in California, we might ask what has brought about these conditions? Addressing questions of such complexity might lead us in many directions, but transitional justice suggests we keep our attention on the actions of the state, arguably the key actor in transition, but doing so without losing sight of the human beings most directly involved in state actions.

Restructuring state justice bureaucracies may lead to altered perceptions of justice, self, and other. Important policy choices might revolve around honest conversations that ask questions such as to what extent are the convicted of public concern? Do the families and communities of felons, for example, deserve more than simply serving as dumping grounds for "social junk" and "social dynamite"? Are felons deserving of our investment even when non-felons face cutbacks in social services? Do local community members care more than state-level bureaucrats?

Finally, along with justice systems, felons in California find themselves in transition also, from close custody to perhaps more open arrangements, and from operating within an environment of an ever active state shaping and responding to their conduct to one in which an ever shrinking state reduces its footprint on the pathways of their lives. Is this for the best? We especially invite the perspectives of restorative justice, community justice, convict criminology, and other scholars and practitioners of alternative justice strategies.

Conclusion

Many important questions surround the policy change. What does realignment say about our contemporary approach to crime and punishment? Will California continue to invest in a punitive criminal justice system, albeit at the local level, at the expense of needed social services? Will this touted reform change how offenders are treated and create rehabilitative and reentry services that do, in fact, reduce recidivism? Or, as many advocates fear, will this new system of punishment repeat the mistakes of the state prison system and continue the practice of "mass incarceration" that has affected mostly poor and minority communities? California, through its 58 local counties, has an opportunity to

do something different: to examine the purposes and rationale for punishment and address criminal offending in alternative ways, breaking the dependence on incarceration. We await answers to these questions—and many others—as Realignment and its consequences play out in the communities and people of California.

Notes

1. As of July 2012, about 9000 men were housed in out-of-state facilities in three other states (Arizona, Mississippi and Oklahoma). Most observers agree that these out-of-state placements will end in the near future.
2. Realignment has occurred in other public service sectors; health care is one example. The principle of realignment involves shifting responsibilities previously administered by the state to the counties.

References

Brown v. Plata, No. 09-1233 (2011)

Byers, Garrick. 2011. *Realignment.* Fresno, CA: Public Defenders Office.

Gest, Ted. 2012. "Can America Reduce its Prison Population?" *The Crime Report,* June 20. Accessed August 9, 2012.

www.thecrimereport.org/news/inside-criminal-justice/2012-06-petersilia-at-nij.

Hopper, Allen, Margaret Dooley-Sammuli, and Kelli Evans. 2012. *Public Safety Realignment: California at a Crossroads.* San Francisco: ACLU of California.

Krisberg, Barry and Eleanor Taylor-Nicholson. 2011. *Realignment: A Bold New Era in California Corrections.* Berkeley, CA: Warren Institute on Law and Public Policy.

Males, Mike. 2012. UPDATE: Eight Months into Realignment: Dramatic Reductions in California's

Prisoners. Research in Brief. *San Francisco, CA: Center on Juvenile and Criminal Justice. June 19.*

Misczynski, Dean. 2011. *Rethinking the State-Local Relationship: An Overview.* San Francisco: Public Policy Institute of California.

Williams Danielle and Mai Yang Vang. 2012. *County AB 109 Plans: Analysis & Summary.* Sacramento, CA: Partnership for Community Excellence.

Reflections and Perspectives on Reentry and Collateral Consequences

Michael Pinard

I. Introduction

The United States is in the midst of a prisoner reentry crisis. In 1980, fewer than 170,000 people were released from federal and state prisons in the United States.[1] By 2008, the number of individuals released skyrocketed to 735,454.[2] As a result, more individuals, families, and communities are impacted by reentry than at any point in history. This crisis will become more heightened in the immediate future, as the number of individuals completing their prison sentences will continue to climb and as states that can no longer afford to incarcerate at massive levels—and at staggering expense[3]—will be forced to release individuals early from their sentences or create other strategies to reduce criminal justice spending.[4]

---

1   Professor. University of Maryland School of Law. I am indebted to research librarian Maxine Grosshans and library research fellow Susan McCarty at the University of Maryland School of Law for tracking down various materials.
Jeremy Travis. U.S. Dep't of Justice. *But They All Come Back: Rethinking Prisoner Reentry,* 7 SENT'G & CORRS. 1, 1 (2000), available at www.nejrs.gov/pdffilesl/nij/81413.pdf.

2   William J. Sabol *et al.* U.S. Dep't of Justice. Prisoners in 2008, at 4 (2009), available at http://bjs.ojp.usdoj.gov/content/pub/pdf/p08.pdf. Additionally, approximately nine million individuals are released annually from local jails. Allen J. Beck. Chief. Corr. Statistics Program. U.S. Dep't of Justice. The Importance of Successful Reentry to Jail Population Growth (June 27, 2006), available at http://www.urban.org/projects/reentry-roundtable/upload/beck.ppt (noting that jail admissions/releases statistics of 12 million correlate to 9 million unique individuals each year).

3   According to the Pew Center, state spending on corrections eclipsed $49 billion in 2008. The Pew Center on the States, One in 100: Behind Bars in America 2008, at 11 (2008), available   at   www.pewcenteronthestates.org/uploadedFiles/8015PCTS_Prison08_ FINAL_2-1-1_FORWEB.pdf. These costs are estimated to increase $25 billion by 2011. *Id.*

4   See, e.g., David Crary. States' Budget Crises Prompting Urgent Prison Policy Reforms. Huffington Post. Jan. 10, 2009. www.huffingtonpost.com/2009/01/10/states-budget-crises-prom_n_156890.html, (describing several state reform measures); see also Jeffrey Rosen, Prisoners of Parole: Could Keeping Convicts from Violating Probation or Their

261

The reentry crisis follows three decades of exploding incarceration rates. "Tough on crime" measures that were implemented in the 1980s, most notably the War on Drugs, led to record numbers of incarcerated individuals[5] spending longer periods of time behind bars.[6] All individuals convicted of criminal offenses, regardless of their sentences, are forced to confront the various collateral consequences—additional legal penalties—that result from their convictions. These consequences, most of which attach to both felony and misdemeanor convictions,[7] can include ineligibility for federal welfare benefits, government-assisted housing, and jury service; various types of employment and employment-related licenses, and military service; as well as sex offender registration and voting disenfranchisement.[8]

Collateral consequences are nothing new. They are remnants of the "civil death"[9] that was imported from England and imposed on lawbreakers during the colonial period.[10] However, what is relatively new is the scope of collateral consequences that burden individuals long past the expiration of their sentences and which, individually and collectively, frustrate their ability to move past their criminal records. At no point in United States history have collateral consequences been as expansive and entrenched as they are today.[11] Indeed, the War on Drugs and other law and order policies have not only fostered an instinctive reliance on incarceration but also an intricate web of federal, state, and local post-sentence legal penalties that can burden individuals for the rest of their lives.

Collateral consequences impact not only those individuals upon whom they fall but also their families and communities.[12] For example, these consequences make it extraordinarily difficult and, in many instances impossible, for individuals with criminal records to find employment. As a result, they are unable to contribute financially to their family households. Moreover, just as mass incarceration has disproportionately impacted individuals and communities of color in urban centers in the United States, mass reentry is now doing the same.[13] Thus, these individuals are returning in large numbers to the relatively few communities where they lived prior to incarceration and are paralyzed by their criminal records for various reasons, including the col-

Terms of Release Be the Answer to Prison Overcrowding? N.Y. Times Mag. Jan. 10, 2010, at 38 ("[T]he U.S. prison population is increasingly seen as unsustainable for both budgetary and moral reasons … .").

5 E.g., Michelle Alexander, The New Jim Crow: Mass Incarceration in the Age of Colorblindness 59 (2010) ("Convictions for drug offenses are the single most important cause of the explosion in incarceration rates in the United States.").

6 See Mark Motivans. Bureau of Justice Statistics. U.S. Dep't of Justice. Federal Criminal Justice Trends, 2003, at 33 tbl. 25 (2006), available at http://bjs.ojp.usdoj.gov/content/pub/pdf/fcjt03.pdf.

7 In some instances, these consequences can attach even to non-criminal offenses. E.g., McGregor Smyth, Holistic Is Not a Bad Word: A Criminal Defense Attorney's Guide to Using Invisible Punishments as an Advocacy Strategy, 36 U. Tol. L. Riv. 479, 482 (2005) (explaining that a conviction for disorderly conduct, a non-criminal violation, "makes a person presumptively ineligible for New York City public housing for two years").

8 For a detailed overview of collateral consequences, see Margaret Colgate Love. Relief from the Collateral Consequences of Criminal Convictions: A State-by-State Resource Guide: (2006).

9 "Civil death" has been defined as "the condition in which a convicted offender loses all political, civil, and legal rights." Alec C. Ewald. "Civil Death": The Ideological Paradox of Criminal Disenfranchisement Law in the United States, 2002 Wis. L. Rev . 1045. 1049 n. 13 (2002).

10 Id. at 1061 ("English colonists in North America transplanted much of [England's] common law regarding the civil disabilities of convicts, and supplemented it with statutes regarding suffrage.").

11 See Joan Petersilia, When Prisoners Come Home 136 (2003) (noting that collateral consequences "are growing in number and kind, being applied to a larger percentage of the U.S. population and for longer periods of time than at any point in U.S. history"): J. McGregor Smyth, Jr., From Arrest to Reintegration: A Model for Mitigating Collateral Consequences of Criminal Proceedings, 24 Crim. Just. 42, 42 (2009) ("The collateral consequences of criminal proceedings inflict damage on a breadth and scale too shocking for most lawyers and policy makers to accept.").

12 E.g., Robert M.A. Johnson, Collateral Consequences. 16 Crim. Just. 32. 32 (2001) ("On a societal level, a problem arises when the degree of these collateral consequences reduces the possibility that [individuals] can return to be productive members of our society.").

13 Jeremy Travis & Joan Petersilia. Reentry Reconsidered: A New Look at an Old Question, 47 Crime & Delinq. 291. 299–301 (2001).

lection of collateral consequences that confront them during the reentry process and beyond.

Jeremy Travis has appropriately described these collateral consequences as "invisible punishment."[14] They are "invisible" because, despite their impact on individuals who cycle through the criminal justice system, they are not considered to be part of this system. They are civil, not criminal, penalties. As such, collateral consequences for the most part are ignored throughout the criminal process. Defense attorneys, prosecutors, and judges do not incorporate collateral consequences into their advocacy and sentence practices. As a result, defendants are generally not informed of—or warned about—collateral consequences as part of the plea bargaining or sentencing processes.[15]

This Article first provides a brief history of collateral consequences and reentry. It then describes the expansion of these consequences, particularly over the past few decades, and their impact on reentry. It concludes by highlighting some current efforts to better understand the scope of these consequences.

II. REFLECTIONS

Collateral consequences have always attached to criminal convictions in the United States.[16] They descend from the concept of "civil death," which continental European systems imposed upon individuals who committed criminal acts.[17] As Professor Nora Demleitner explains, "civil death," entailed, among other things, the permanent loss of the right to vote, to enter into contracts, and to inherit or bequeath property."[18] While the United States never fully embraced "civil death," it did, until the 1960s, impose collateral consequences that dissolved marriages automatically, disqualified individuals from various employment-related licenses, and barred individuals from entering contracts or engaging in civil litigation.[19]

For much of the twentieth century, rehabilitation was a central punishment goal in the United States.[20] The rehabilitative model sought to reform the offender, so that he or she would overcome his or her criminal record as well as the reasons that led to his or her involvement with the criminal justice system and eventually lead a productive, law-abiding life.

The rehabilitative ideal carried over to collateral consequences. In 1956, the National Conference on Parole (NCP), understanding that criminal records imposed significant legal burdens on individuals attempting to reintegrate, recommended that the "laws depriving convicted persons of civil and political rights" be abolished.[21] In addition, the NCP, in the 1950s,

---

14 Jeremy Travis, *Invisible Punishment: An Instrument of Social Exclusion, in* Invisible Punishment: The Collateral Consequences of Mass Imprisonment 16 (Marc Mauer & Meda Chesney-Lind eds., 2002) (explaining that these laws constitute "invisible punishment," because they "operate largely beyond public view, yet have very serious, adverse consequences for the individuals affected").

15 Gabriel J. Chin & Richard W. Holmes. Jr., *Effective Assistance of Counsel and the Consequences of Guilty Pleas.* 87 Cornell L. Rev. 697, 699 (2002) (explaining that most state and federal circuit courts have held that attorneys are not required to inform defendants about collateral consequences).

The one exception exists in the immigration context, as the United States Supreme Court has recently held that defendants in criminal proceedings must be informed of the possible deportation-related consequences of a guilty plea. Padilla v. Kentucky, 130 S. Ct. 1473, 1486–87 (2010).

16 E.g., Jeremy Travis, But They All Come Back: Facing the Challenges of Prisoner Reentry 252 (2005) ("Legislators

of the American colonies passed laws denying convicted offenders the right to enter into contracts, automatically dissolving their marriages, and barring them from a wide variety of jobs and benefits.") (citation omitted).

17 Travis, *supra* note 14. at 17.

18 Nora V. Demleitner. *Preventing Internal Exile: The Need for Restrictions on Collateral Sentencing Consequences*, 11 Stan. L & Pol'y Rev. 153, 154 (1999).

19 *Id.* at 154–55.

20 E.g., Michael Pinard. *Collateral Consequences of Criminal Convictions: Confronting Issues of Race and Dignity*, 85 N.Y.U. L. Rev. 457. 478 n.98 (2010) (citing Albert W. Alschuler, *The Changing Purposes of Criminal Punishment: A Retrospective on the Past Century and Some Thoughts About the Next*, 70 U. Chi. L. Rev. 1.6 (2003)).

21 Margaret Colgate Love. *Starting Over with a Clean Slate: In Praise of a Forgotten Section of the Model Penal Code*, 30 Fordham Urb. L.J. 1705. 1708 (2003). During this time, a felony conviction potentially led to several collateral consequences, including ineligibility for military service and public office, disenfranchisement, and the "den[ial] of access to such professions as law and medicine." Note, *The*

and the American Law Institute, in the early 1960s, proposed various reform measures to ease the stigma and legal burdens that fell on individuals with criminal records.[22] Among the proposals were expungement laws and laws granting courts discretionary authority to relieve individuals of the additional legal penalties that attached to criminal convictions.[23]

The Rehabilitation Era essentially ended in the 1970s.[24] During the next couple of decades, the federal government and many state governments turned to retributive and incapacitative models of punishment that were less forgiving of individuals engaged in criminal activity.[25] The demise of the Rehabilitative Era set the stage for the tough on crime movement of the 1980s and 1990s. As Professor Nora V. Demleitner explains, the "trend" to decrease "the number and restrictiveness of statutes imposing collateral consequences on offenders … during the 1960s and the early 1970s … was halted, if not reversed, in the late 1980s and the 1990s."[26]

The tough-on-crime movement led to an unprecedented increase in incarceration rates and length of prison sentences.[27] Between 1980 and 2005, the number of individuals incarcerated in U.S. prisons and jails for drug possession offenses increased more than 1,000%.[28] These movements also led to a significant expansion of collateral consequences in the 1980s and 1990s. Many of the consequences enacted during these decades—particularly those relating to various public benefits (including food stamps) and student loans—apply only to those convicted of drug offenses.[29] Other collateral consequences, such as public housing restrictions, were originally federal and attached mainly to drug-related activity but have been expanded by many local governments to attach to essentially all types of criminal conduct.[30] As a result, collateral consequences look drastically different today than they did at the beginning of the 1980s, as they now impact virtually all aspects of life for individuals with criminal records.

III. THE PRESENT FOCUS ON REENTRY ISSUES AND COLLATERAL CONSEQUENCES

The aftershocks of the tough-on-crime movement reverberate dramatically at present. Not only are more individuals serving prison and jail sentences in the United States than at any point in its history,[31] but

---

22 For a detailed discussion of these proposals, see Love, *supra* note 21, at 1708–12.

23 Id at 1710–11.

24 David Garland, The Culture or Control: Crime and Social Order in Contemporary Society, 61 (2001); see Francis A. Allen, The Decline or the Rehabilitative Ideal: Penal Policy and Social Purpose 10 (1981) ("[T]he rehabilitative ideal has declined in the United States: the decline has been substantial, and it has been precipitous."); Alschuler, *supra* note 20, at 9 (noting that from 1970 to 1985. "rehabilitation had gone from the top of most scholars' and reformers' lists of the purposes of punishment to the bottom").

25 Alschuler, *supra* note 20, at 9–14.

26 E.g., Demleitner, *supra* note 18, at 155.

27 E.g., John Irwin *et al.*, Justice Policy Inst. America's One million Nonviolent Prisoners 2 (1999), available at www.justicepolicy.org/images/upload/99-03 REP OneMillionNonviolentPrisoners AC.pdf ("Justice Department data released on March 15, 1999 show that the number of prisoners in America … more than tripled over the last two decades from 500.000 to 1.8 million …").

28 Don Stemen, Vera Inst, of Justice, Reconsidering Incarceration: New Directions for Reducing Crime 8 (2007), available at www.vera.org/content/reconsidering-incarceration-new-directions-reducing-crime.

29 Alexander, *supra* note 5, at 140; *Introduction* to Invisible Punishment: The Collateral. Consequences of Mass Imprisonment 6 (Marc Mauer & Meda Chesney-Lind eds., 2003) ("The drug war's influence on political decision making and conceptions of civil liberties has been profound. … , as legislators have increasingly adopted ever more punitive measures against those who have been convicted of a drug offense.").

30 As a result, housing-related collateral consequences attach to both felonies and misdemeanors. Some jurisdictions apply these consequences to non-criminal violations. Gwen Rubinstein & Debbie Mukamal, *Welfare and Housing—Denial of Benefits to Drug Offenders, in* invisible punishment: The Collateral Consequences of Mass Imprisonment, *supra* note 17, at 37, 43–49.

31 At the end of 2008, approximately 1 out of 198 individuals in the United Slates was incarcerated in a state or federal prison. Sabol *et al.*, *supra* note 2, at 1. The total incarcerated population—federal prisons, state prisons, and local jails—at this time was 2,304,115. *Id.* at 27 tbl. 8.

Need for Coram Nobis *in the Federal Courts.* 59 Yale: L.J. 786, 786–87 (1950).

record numbers of these individuals are being released from these prisons and jails each year.[32] In addition, approximately one in four adults in the United States has a criminal record.[33] Given the breadth and permanence of collateral consequences, these individuals are perhaps more burdened and marginalized by a criminal record today than at any point in U.S. history.

The reentry crisis over the last decade has brought significant attention to reentry issues. Federal legislation has been enacted recently that aims to, *inter alia*, expand and improve existing reentry programs, expand employment opportunities for reentering individuals, improve federal reentry programming, and reduce recidivism.[34] Federal, state, and local organizations have been formed or retooled to assist reentering individuals as they work through, or cope with, the various legal and non-legal issues they confront.[35] Within the criminal justice system, reentry courts exist in several jurisdictions.[36] These courts, established by the Department of Justice,[37] have "borrowed heavily" from the drug court model of seeking to coordinate services with

graduated sanctions imposed upon individuals who violate the conditions.[38] In addition, national criminal justice organizations, such as the National Legal Aid and Defender Association, are addressing these issues through practitioner-related trainings and advocating for expansive criminal justice services delivery models that account for the overlapping criminal and civil issues that converge during the reentry process.

Initially, the attention to reentry issues focused on services and programs for individuals with criminal records. More recently, the attention has increasingly focused on collateral consequences. This focus stems from greater recognition of the significant, and often insurmountable, challenges these legal barriers present.

The relative lack of attention to collateral consequences to this point stems in large measure from legal interpretations that these consequences are separate civil penalties that attach to criminal convictions rather than penalties that are part of the direct, criminal punishment.[39] Thus, these consequences technically reside outside of the criminal justice system. As a result, criminal justice actors are not fully cognizant of their existence and scope. Moreover, as several commentators have observed, it is difficult—essentially impossible—to fully grasp the scope of these consequences in a given jurisdiction, because they are dispersed throughout various federal and state statutes, federal and state regulations, and local policies.[40]

However, efforts are underway to increase awareness of both the existence and scope of collateral consequences. Two federal statutes, both of which were signed into law in 2008, call for these consequences,

---

32   E.g., Nancy G. La Vigne *et al.*, Office of Cmty. Oriented Policing Servs. U.S. Dep't of Justice, Prisoner Reentry and Community Policing: Strategies for Enhancing Public Safety 3 (2006), available at www.urban.org/publications/411061.html (noting the "historic volumes" of prisoners reentering society).

33   E.g., Madeline Neighly & Margaret (Peggy) Stevenson. Nat'l Employment Law Project, Criminal Records and Employment: Data on the Disproportionate Impact on Communities of Color (2009), available at www.nelp.org/page/-/SCLP/CriminalRecordsImpactCommunitiesofColor.pdf?nocdn=1.

34   See generally Second Chance Act of 2007, Pub. L. No. 110–199. 122 Stat. 657 (codified at 42 USC § 17501 *et seq.* (2006)).

35   E.g., Michael Pinard, *An Integrated Perspective on the Collateral Consequences of Criminal Convictions and Reentry Issues Faced by Formerly Incarcerated Individuals*, 86. B.U.L. Rev. 623, 651–52 (2006) (offering examples of various reentry programs).

36   The number of reentry courts will likely expand in the near future, as the Second Chance Act authorizes the Attorney General to award grants to agencies and municipalities to establish reentry courts. Second Chance Act of 2008. 42 U.S.C. § 3797(w)(2) (Supp. 2010).

37   Anthony C. Thompson, Releasing Prisoners, Redeeming Communities: Reentry. Race and Politics 163 (2008).

38   *Id.* at 165. For a discussion of reentry courts, including some of their shortcomings, see *Id.* at 164–65. See also Eric J. Miller, *The Therapeutic Effects of Managerial Reentry Courts*, 20 Fed. Sent'g Rep. 127 (2007).

39   E.g., Pinard, *supra* note 35, at 641–48 (citing appellate court rulings declaring that collateral consequences are civil rather than criminal penalties and therefore that defendants need not be informed of these consequences as part of the guilty plea or sentencing process).

40   E.g., Gabriel J. Chin, *Race, the War on Drugs, and the Collateral Consequences of Criminal Convictions*, 6 J. Gender, Race & Just. 253, 254 (2002) (explaining that collateral consequences arc "unstructured" and "[n]o one knows, really, what they are").

which are dispersed throughout various statutes, regulations, and policies, to be collected and analyzed. The Court Security Improvement Act of 2007[41] requires the National Institute of Justice to "conduct a study to determine and compile the collateral consequences of convictions for criminal offenses in the United States, each of the fifty states, each territory of the United States, and the District of Columbia."[42] Specifically, this agency is to "identify any provision in the Constitution, statutes, or administrative rules of each jurisdiction … that imposes collateral sanctions or authorizes the imposition of disqualifications … ,"[43] As a result, this Act requires an exhaustive review of the federal, state, and local consequences in each of these jurisdictions. Similarly, the Second Chance Act of 2007[44] requires that "[a] State, unit of local government, territory or Indian Tribe, or combination thereof," applying for a grant to reauthorize existing adult and juvenile offender programs must, *inter alia*, include "a plan [to] analy[ze] … the statutory, regulatory, rules-based, and practice-based hurdles to reintegration of offenders into the community … ,"[45]

Legal organizations are also taking steps to gain greater understanding of collateral consequences. The American Bar Association (ABA), recognizing that juvenile offenders also confront a wide range of consequences that impact their ability to, *inter alia*, secure employment, enlist in the military, and reside in public housing, has formed the Juvenile Collateral Consequences Project, which will collect the consequences that attach to juvenile adjudications in all fifty states and the U.S. territories.[46]

Some state bar organizations have also recognized the need to educate their members about collateral consequences. For instance, the State Bar of Michigan has created an initiative that will "consider problems in indigent representation, including the general ignorance of assigned counsel of the collateral consequences of a criminal conviction."[47] Also, the New York State Bar Association formed the Special Committee on Collateral Consequences of Criminal Proceedings. In 2006, this committee issued an exhaustive report that compiled and analyzed several collateral consequences in New York State, including consequences related to employment, housing, public benefits, education, civic participation, and immigration.[48] The committee recommended several measures, including compiling all collateral consequences of convictions in one section of New York law,[49] providing trainings to defense attorneys, prosecutors, and judges on these consequences,[50] requiring judges to inform defendants of these consequences prior to accepting guilty pleas or at sentencing,[51] developing referral programs to provide legal assistance to individuals confronting these consequences,[52] and facilitating the legal processes available in New York State to ease the burdens created by these consequences.[53]

Other efforts have taken the further step of recommending ways to minimize the impact of these

---

41 Court Security Improvement Act of 2007, Pub. L. No. 110–177, 121 Stat. 2534.

42 *Id.* at § 510(a).

43 *Id.* at § 510(b).

44 Second Chance Act of 2007. Pub. L. No. 110–199, 122 Stat. 657 (codified at 42 USC § 17501 *et seq.* (2006)).

45 *Id.* at § 101(d). (c)(4). In addition, the Judiciary Committee of the House of Representatives recently held a hearing to, in part, gather more information about collateral consequences, *Hearing on Collateral Consequences of Criminal Convictions: Barriers to Reentry for the Formerly Incarcerated Before the S. Comm on Crime, Terrorism, and Homeland Sec.*, 111th Cong. (2010), webcast available at http://judiciary.house.gov/hearings/hear_100609.html.

46 Hannah Geyer, ABA Juvenile Justice Collateral Consequences Proj., *An Open Letter to Legal Aid Attorneys & Juvenile Defenders*, http://njjn.org/media/resources/public/resource_1418.pdf (last visited Aug. 31, 2010).

47 Frank D. Eaman, *Public Defense in Michigan: From the Top to the Bottom*, 87 Mich. Bus. L.J. 40, 42 (2008).

48 N.Y. State Bar Ass'n, "Reentry and Reintegration: The Road to Public Safety": Report and Recommendations of the Special Committee on Collateral Consequences of Criminal Proceedings (2006), available at www.nysba.org/AM/Template.cfm?Section=Substantive_Reports&TEMPLATE=/CM/ContentDisplay.cfm&CONTENTID=11415.

49 *Id.* at 391.

50 *Id.*

51 *Id.* at 392.

52 *Id.*

53 *Id.* at 389.

consequences. Most prominently, in 2004, the ABA adopted standards for "[c]ollateral [s]anctions and [d]iscretionary [q]ualifications of [c]onvicted [p]ersons."[54] These standards are broad. They assert that consequences should not be imposed unless "the conduct constituting th[e] particular offense provides so substantial a basis for imposing the sanction that the legislature cannot reasonably contemplate any circumstances in which imposing the sanction would not be justified,"[55] that counsel or the trial court inform defendants about these consequences,[56] that judges consider these consequences when imposing sentences,[57] and that judges or "a specified administrative body" have the authority to "waiv[e], modify[], or grant[] timely and effective relief from any collateral sanction."[58]

Following the ABA's lead, the National Conference of Commissioners on Uniform State Laws authorized a project that has led to the Uniform Collateral Consequences of Conviction Act, which was approved in July 2009.[59] Similar to the ABA Standards on Collateral Sanctions, this Act urges that each state's collateral consequences be compiled in a single document,[60] that defendants be notified of these consequences during the pretrial stage,[61] at sentencing[62] as well as prior to release from incarceration,[63] and that processes be implemented that allow individuals to be relieved of disabilities related to "employment, education, housing, public benefits or occupational licensing."[64]

IV. THE FUTURE CHALLENGES OF REENTRY AND COLLATERAL CONSEQUENCES

Reentry has emerged as perhaps the most difficult and persistent criminal justice issue. It involves a complex and multi-layered mix of legal and non-legal issues that impact the record numbers of individuals released annually from U.S. prisons.[65] The issues are particularly thorny because of the broad impact mass reentry will continue to have on families and communities.

Scores of government programs and agencies are devoting significant resources to reentry issues at the federal, state, and local levels. Perhaps even more organizations—foundations, legal services organizations, policy organizations, and local organizations led or staffed by individuals with criminal records—are working tirelessly to assist individuals, families, and communities work through the myriad legal and non-legal reentry issues. Indeed, the exponential growth of these organizations over the past decade, as well as new or redirected funding streams that help to build and sustain them, exemplify the severity of the reentry crises that are confronting an ever-expanding number of reentering individuals.

The legal issues related to reentry (and specifically collateral consequences) are vast and significant. Such issues include housing, public benefits, employment, family, and broader civil rights issues. As illustrated above, there is a compelling need for legislators, legal actors, defendants, criminal justice personnel, various other decision-makers, and the general public to be aware of the collateral consequences that attach to convictions and that long outlast the direct punishment tied to those convictions. The efforts that have been undertaken to gather and compile these consequences will facilitate greater understanding of the true impact of criminal convictions.

---

54   ABA Standards for Criminal Justice: Collateral Sanctions and Discretionary Disqualification of Convicted Persons (3d ed. 2004).

55   *Id.* at 19-2.2.

56   *Id.* at 19-2.3.

57   *Id.* at 19-2.4(a).

58   *Id.* at std. 19-2.5(a).

59   Uniform Collateral Consequences of Conviction Act (2009), available at https://www.law.upenn.edu/library/archives/ulc/ucsada/2009_final.pdf.

60   *Id* at 10. The purpose of this compilation is to "make the law accessible to judges, lawyers, legislators and defendants who need to make decisions based on it." *Id.* at 5. The Act authorizes each state, in compiling these consequences, to rely upon the "collateral sanctions, disqualifications, and relief provisions prepared by the National Institute of Justice described in Section 510 of the Court Security Improvement Act of 2007, Pub. L. 110–177." *Id.* at 10.

61   *Id.* at 13.

62   *Id.* at 17.

63   *Id.*

---

64   *Id.*

65   See Beck, *supra* note 2 (documenting the number of individuals released from prison in 2008).

However, communities of lawyers are, and will continue to be, needed to help address—or, at the very least, to minimize—these legal issues. Specifically, co-ordinated legal services—services that breakdown the traditional divide between "criminal" and "civil" issues and recognize the complex, interconnected legal issues that stem from *any type* of conviction and regardless of the sentence imposed—are necessary to meet the vast legal challenges that await these individuals at the conclusion of their sentences.

Perhaps most significantly, collateral consequences must be restructured to minimize the legal hurdles imposed on individuals with criminal records. These consequences need to be tailored to individual criminal conduct and, as the ABA recommends, should be waived in instances where judges deem appropriate. In essence, the criminal justice system of the future has to be one that bends a little to afford individuals with criminal records the opportunities to move beyond their transgressions and lead productive post-punishment lives.

V. CONCLUSION

The emergent reentry crisis requires that the federal and state criminal justice systems in the United States be restructured to focus on reentry issues and needs, all of which impact the millions of individuals with criminal records, their families, and their communities. A criminal conviction in the United States is no longer the end point of the criminal process but rather the impetus for a collection of so-called civil penalties that will hamper the convicted individual long beyond the conclusion of his or her formal sentence. The criminal justice system of the future must recognize and account for the multitudinous effects of a criminal convic-tion—both the various civil penalties that immediately attach to the conviction and the impact these penalties have on the individuals, their families, and communi-ties. Thus, the overarching goal of the criminal justice system should be to allow individuals to maximize their chances of moving past their criminal records to lead productive post-punishment lives. This is the challenge moving forward.

Gender-Responsive Strategies for Women Offenders

A Summary of Research, Practice, and Guiding Principles for Women Offenders

Barbara Bloom,
Barbara Owen,
and Stephanie Covington

The Gender-Responsive Strategies Project: Approach and Findings

Women now represent a significant proportion of all offenders under criminal justice supervision in the United States. Numbering more than 1 million in 2001, women offenders make up 17 percent of all offenders under some form of correctional sanction.

To improve policy and practice regarding women offenders in corrections, the National Institute of Corrections undertook a 3-year project—titled Gender-Responsive Strategies: Research, Practice, and Guiding Principles for Women Offenders—to collect and summarize multidisciplinary research and practitioner expertise on gender-responsive strategies. The final report summarizes the following:

+ The characteristics of women in correctional settings.
+ The ways in which gender makes a difference in current criminal justice practice.
+ Multidisciplinary research and theory on women's lives that have significant implications for managing women in the criminal justice system.
+ Guiding principles and strategies for improving the system's responses to women offenders.

The National Institute of Corrections (NIC) is a center of correctional learning and experience. NIC advances and shapes effective correctional practice and public policy that respond to the needs of corrections through collaboration and leadership and by providing assistance, information, education, and training.

This bulletin summarizes the major findings of the report[1] and offers guidance to those throughout the criminal justice system who seek a more effective way to respond to the behavior and circumstances of women offenders. Policymakers from legislative, executive, and judicial branches of government and agency administrators should find this summary particularly useful. All are encouraged to obtain the full report for a more complete analysis of gender-responsive research and practice.

Approach

To construct a knowledge base that provides a foundation for gender-appropriate policy and practice, project staff reviewed multidisciplinary research literature in a broad range of areas, including health, family violence, substance abuse, mental health, trauma, employment, and education. This literature was analyzed to determine its application to gender responsiveness in criminal justice practices (see "Defining Gender Responsiveness" below).

Additional data pertinent to managing women offenders within the criminal justice framework were collected through national focus groups and interviews with experts representing various criminal justice agencies. Project staff conducted more than 40 individual and group interviews with policymakers, managers, line staff, and women offenders in all phases of the criminal justice system throughout the country. Written documents that included official and technical reports concerning women offenders, policies and procedures, and existing academic research were then collected and analyzed. Finally, the Practitioner Advisory Group, representing community corrections, jail, prison, and parole professionals, reviewed multiple drafts of these findings.

Potential Benefits of Gender-Responsive Practice

Study findings indicate that paying attention to the differences in male and female pathways into criminality and their differential responses to custody and supervision can lead to better outcomes for both men and women offenders in institutional and community settings. Policies, programs, and procedures that reflect empirical, gender-based differences can:

Defining Gender Responsiveness

Being gender-responsive in the criminal justice system requires an acknowledgment of the realities of women's lives, including the pathways they travel to criminal offending and the relationships that shape their lives. To assist those who work with women in effectively and appropriately responding to this information, Bloom and Covington developed the following definition:

Gender-responsive means creating an environment through site selection, staff selection, program development, content, and material that reflects an understanding of the realities of women's lives and addresses the issues of the participants. Gender-responsive approaches are multidimensional and are based on theoretical perspectives that acknowledge women's pathways into the criminal justice system. These approaches address social (e.g., poverty, race, class, and gender inequality) and cultural factors, as well as therapeutic interventions. These interventions address issues such as abuse, violence, family relationships, substance abuse, and co-occurring disorders. They provide a strength-based approach to treatment and skill building. The emphasis is on self-efficacy.[1]

---

1   Bloom, B., and Covington, S. (2000). Gendered justice: Programming for women in correctional settings. Paper presented to the American Society of Criminology, San Francisco, CA, p. 11.

- Make the management of women offenders more effective.
- Enable correctional facilities to be more suitably staffed and funded.
- Decrease staff turnover and sexual misconduct.
- Improve program and service delivery.
- Decrease the likelihood of litigation against the criminal justice system.
- Increase the gender appropriateness of services and programs.

The Foundation for the Principles

To develop guiding principles and strategies, the gender-responsive strategies project reviewed and integrated the characteristics of women offenders, the key elements of criminal justice practice, and theories related to women's lives.

Characteristics of Women in the Criminal Justice System

The significant increase in the number of women under criminal justice supervision has called attention to the status of women in the criminal justice system and to the particular circumstances they encounter. The increasing numbers have also made evident the lack of appropriate policies and procedures for managing women offenders. Women offenders typically have low incomes and are under-educated and unskilled. They have sporadic employment histories and are disproportionately women of color. They are less likely than men to have committed violent offenses and more likely to have been convicted of crimes involving drugs or property. Often, their property offenses are economically driven, motivated by poverty and by the abuse of alcohol and other drugs (see sidebar "National Profile of Women Offenders").

Women Offenders and Criminal Justice Practice

Two key findings emerge from an examination of the state of criminal justice practice regarding women. First, because of the overwhelming number of male offenders, the issues relevant to women are often overshadowed. Second, criminal justice agencies often have difficulty applying to women offenders the policies and procedures that have been designed largely for the male population. Most systems lack a written policy

---

National Profile of Women Offenders

A national profile of women offenders reveals they are:

- Disproportionately women of color.
- In their early- to mid-thirties.
- Most likely to have been convicted of a drug-related offense.
- Individuals with fragmented family histories; other family members also may be involved with the criminal justice system.
- Survivors of physical and/or sexual abuse as children and adults.
- Individuals with significant substance abuse problems.
- Individuals with multiple physical and mental health problems.
- Unmarried mothers of minor children.
- Individuals with a high school degree or GED but with limited vocational training and sporadic work histories.

on the management and supervision of women offenders. Further, in focus groups, a number of managers reported resistance to modifying policies to reflect more appropriate and effective responses to the behaviors and characteristics of women under supervision.

Gender differences in behavior, life circumstances, and parental responsibilities have broad implications for almost every aspect of criminal justice practice. The differences between men and women involved with the criminal justice system have been documented in terms of the levels of violence and threats to community safety in their offense patterns, responsibilities for children and other family members, interactions with staff, and relationships with other offenders while incarcerated or under community supervision.

Women are more vulnerable to staff misconduct and have different programming and service needs, especially in terms of physical and mental health, substance abuse, recovery from trauma, and economic/vocational skills. While all offenders must confront the problems of re-entry into the community, many of the obstacles faced by women offenders are specifically related to their status as women. The majority of women in correctional institutions are mothers, and a major consideration for these women is reunification with their children. The obstacles for these women are unique because their requirements for safe housing, economic support, medical services, and other needs must include the ability to take care of their children. These obstacles include system-level characteristics, such as the lack of programs and services designed and targeted for women, women's involvement with multiple human service agencies, and lack of community support for women in general.

In the full report, issues related to gender differences and their effects are described with regard to the following:

Criminal justice processing: Gender differences have been found in all stages of criminal justice processing, including crime definition, reporting, and counting; types of crime; levels of harm; arrest; bail; sentencing; community supervision; incarceration; and re-entry into the community.[2] For example, women as a group commit crimes that are less violent than the crimes committed by their male counterparts. The

Bureau of Justice Statistics reports that, according to victim accounts, only one of seven violent offenders is female. Drug offenses account for a greater proportion of the imprisonment of women than men, women have fewer acts of violence or major infractions in prison, and children play a more significant role in the lives of incarcerated women than those of men.

Classification and assessment procedures: Most of the classification and assessment instruments in use today were developed and validated for male offenders. Because these instruments were based on the behaviors of a male offender population, they are often unable to accurately assess either the risks or the needs of women offenders and tend to over-classify women, placing them at higher levels of custody or supervision than necessary. Moreover, most instruments do not assess the specific needs of women that are tied to their pathways to offending, specifically the interconnected problems of substance abuse, trauma and victimization, mental illness, relationship difficulties, and low self-efficacy.

Women's services and programs: Substance abuse, family violence, and their struggle to support themselves and their children are the main factors that drive women into crime. More often than their male counterparts, women need gender-specific services such as protection from abusive partners, childcare services, access to reliable transportation, and realistic employment opportunities that allow for self-support. In general, research shows an insufficient number of programs for women under any type of supervision that will help them prepare for career-oriented training and address issues common to women offenders such as sexual abuse, victimization through violence, and low self-esteem.

Staffing and training: In terms of staff training, standard training protocols often neglect or minimize information about woman offenders. There is a perception among correctional staff that women offenders are more difficult to work with than their male counterparts. Preparing staff to work with women offenders requires increased knowledge about women that will help staff members develop the constructive attitudes and the interpersonal skills necessary for working with women under correctional supervision.

Staff sexual misconduct: In the past decade, the problems of staff sexual misconduct have received significant attention from the media, the public, and many correctional systems. Most of the published work describes the problem in the institutional setting; however, the problem exists throughout the criminal justice system. Although the more publicized pattern of misconduct appears to involve male staff with female inmates, it is important to note that female officers have also been involved in serious misconduct. Sexual harassment may re-traumatize women with a history of abuse and diminish their ability to heal and engage in programming. Further, standard procedures in correctional settings (e.g., searches, restraints, and the use of isolation) can act as triggers to re-traumatize women who have histories of abuse.

Theoretical Perspectives Related to Women's Lives

Gender-responsive principles and strategies are grounded in three intersecting perspectives: the pathways perspective, relational theory and female development, and trauma and addiction theories.

The Pathways Perspective

Research on women's pathways into crime indicates that gender has a significant role in shaping criminality. Women and men enter the criminal justice system via different pathways. Among women, the most common pathways to crime are based on survival of abuse and poverty and substance abuse. Recent research establishes that, because of their gender, females are at greater risk of experiencing sexual abuse, sexual assault, domestic violence, and single-parent status. For example, girls and young women often experience sexual abuse in their homes; in adulthood, women experience abuse in their relationships with significant others.

Pathways research has identified key issues in producing and sustaining female criminality, such as histories of personal abuse, mental illness tied to early life experiences, substance abuse and addiction, economic and social marginality, homelessness, and dysfunctional relationships.

Relational Theory and Female Development

Theories that focus on female development, such as the relational model, posit that the primary motivation for women throughout life is the establishment of a strong sense of connection with others. Relational theory developed from an increased understanding of gender differences and, specifically, of the different ways in which women and men develop psychologically. According to relational theory, females develop a sense of self and self-worth when their actions arise out of, and lead back into, connections with others. Therefore, connection, not separation, is the guiding principle of growth for girls and women.

The importance of understanding relational theory is reflected in the recurring themes of relationship and family in the lives of women offenders. Disconnection and violation rather than growth-fostering relationships characterize the childhood experiences of most women in the criminal justice system. Women are far more likely than men to be motivated by relational concerns. For example, women offenders who cite drug abuse as self-medication often discuss personal relationships as the cause of their pain. The relational aspects of addiction are also evident in research indicating that women are more likely than men to turn to drugs in the context of relationships with drug-abusing partners to make themselves feel connected.

A relational context is critical to successfully address the reasons why women commit crimes, the motivations behind their behaviors, how they can change their behavior, and their reintegration into the community.

Trauma and Addiction Theories

Trauma and addiction are interrelated issues in the lives of women offenders. Although they are therapeutically linked, these issues historically have been treated separately. Trauma and addiction theories provide the integration and foundation for gender responsiveness in the criminal justice system. Trauma has been the focus of a number of studies, and various experts have written about the process of trauma recovery.[3] Because the traumatic syndromes have basic features in common, the recovery process also follows a common pathway. A generic definition of addiction as "the chronic neglect of self in favor of something or someone else" is helpful when working with women.[4] Some women use substances to numb the pain experienced in destructive relationships.[5] Women who abuse substances are also vulnerable targets for violence.

A New Vision: Guiding Principles for a Gender-Responsive Criminal Justice System

NIC's report on gender-responsive strategies documents the need for a new vision for the criminal justice system—one that recognizes the behavioral and social differences between men and women offenders that have specific implications for gender-responsive policy and practice.

Principles and Strategies

Empirically based evidence drawn from a variety of disciplines and effective practice suggests that addressing the realities of women's lives through gender-responsive policy and programs is fundamental to improved outcomes at all criminal justice phases. The following guiding principles are designed to address concerns about the management, supervision, and treatment of women offenders in the criminal justice system. Together with the general strategies (see sidebar "General Strategies for Implementing Guiding Principles"), the guiding principles provide a blueprint for a gender-responsive approach to the development of criminal justice policy.

Guiding Principle I: Acknowledge That Gender Makes a Difference

The foremost principle in responding appropriately to women is to acknowledge the implications of gender throughout the criminal justice system. The criminal justice field has been dominated by the rule of parity: Equal treatment is to be provided to everyone. However, this does not necessarily mean that the exact same treatment is appropriate for both women and men. The data are very clear concerning the distinguishing

aspects of men and women offenders. They come into the criminal justice system via different pathways; respond to supervision and custody differently; exhibit differences in terms of substance abuse, trauma, mental illness, parenting responsibilities, and employment histories; and represent different levels of risk within both the institution and the community. To successfully develop and deliver services, supervision, and treatment for women offenders, we must first acknowledge these gender differences.

The Evidence

The differences between women and men are well documented across a variety of disciplines and practices, and evidence increasingly shows that the majority of these differences are due to both social and environmental factors. Although certain basic issues related to health, such as reproduction, are influenced by physiological differences, many of the observed behavior disparities are the result of gender-related differences, such as socialization, gender roles, gender stratification, and gender inequality. The nature and extent of women's criminal behavior and the ways in which they respond to supervision reflect such gender differences, including the following:

- Women and men differ in levels of participation, motivation, and degree of harm caused by their criminal behavior.
- Women's crime rates, with few exceptions, are much lower than men's crime rates.
- Women's crimes tend to be less serious (i.e., less violence, more property- and drug-related offenses) than men's crimes. The gender differential is most pronounced in violent crime, where women's participation is profoundly lower.
- The interrelationship between victimization and offending appears to be more evident in women's lives. Family violence, trauma, and substance abuse contribute to women's criminality and shape their patterns of offending.
- Women respond to community supervision, incarceration, and treatment in ways that differ from those of their male counterparts. Women

are less violent while in custody but have higher rates of disciplinary infractions for less serious rule violations. They are influenced by their responsibilities and concerns for their children, by their relationships with staff, and by their relationships with other offenders.

Guiding Principle 2: Create an Environment Based on Safety, Respect, and Dignity

Research from a range of disciplines (e.g., physical health, mental health, and substance abuse) has shown that safety, respect, and dignity are fundamental to behavioral change. To improve behavioral outcomes for women, it is critical to provide a safe and supportive setting for supervision. A profile of women in the criminal justice system indicates that many have grown up in less-than-optimal family and community environments. In their interactions with women offenders, criminal justice professionals must be aware of the significant pattern of emotional, physical, and sexual abuse that many of these women have experienced. Every precaution must be taken to ensure that the criminal justice setting does not re-enact women offenders' patterns of earlier life experiences. A safe, consistent, and supportive environment is the cornerstone of an effective corrective process. Because of their lower levels of violent crime and their low risk to public safety, women offenders should be supervised with the minimal restrictions required to meet public safety interests.

The Evidence

Research from the field of psychology, particularly trauma studies, indicates that environment cues behavior. There is now an understanding of what an environment must reflect if it is to affect the biological, psychological, and social consequences of trauma. Because the corrections culture is influenced by punishment and control, it is often in conflict with the culture of treatment. The criminal justice system is based on a control model, whereas treatment is based on a model of behavioral change. These two models must be integrated so that women offenders can experience positive outcomes. This integration should acknowledge the following facts:

+ Substance abuse professionals and the literature report that women require a treatment environment that is safe and nurturing. They also require a therapeutic relationship that reflects mutual respect, empathy, and compassion.
+ A physically and psychologically safe environment contributes significantly to positive outcomes for women.
+ Safety is identified as a key factor in effectively addressing the needs of domestic violence and sexual assault victims.
+ Custodial misconduct has been documented in many forms, including verbal degradation, rape, and sexual assault.
+ Assessment and classification procedures often do not recognize the lower level of risk to public safety presented by women both in the nature of their offenses and in their behavior while under supervision. This can result in placement of women in higher levels of custody than necessary in correctional institutions and in inappropriate assessments of their risk to the community.
+ Women offenders' needs for personal safety and support suggest the importance of safe and sober housing.

Guiding Principle 3: Develop Policies, Practices, and Programs That Are Relational and Promote Healthy Connections to Children, Family, Significant Others, and the Community

Understanding the role of relationships in women's lives is fundamental because the theme of connections and relationships threads throughout the lives of women offenders. When the concept of relationship is incorporated into policies, practices, and programs, the effectiveness of the system or agency is enhanced. This concept is critical when addressing the following:

+ Reasons why women commit crimes.
+ Impact of interpersonal violence on women's lives.

+ Importance of children in the lives of women offenders.
+ Relationships between women in an institutional setting.
+ Process of women's psychological growth and development.
+ Environmental context needed for effective programming.
+ Challenges involved in re-entering the community.

The Evidence

Studies of women offenders highlight the importance of relationships and the fact that criminal involvement often develops through relationships with family members, significant others, or friends. This is qualitatively different from the concept of "peer associates," which is often cited as a criminogenic risk factor in assessment instruments. Interventions must acknowledge and reflect the impact of these relationships on women's current and future behavior. Important findings regarding relationships include the following:

+ Developing mutual relationships is fundamental to women's identity and sense of worth.
+ Women offenders frequently suffer from isolation and alienation created by discrimination, victimization, mental illness, and substance abuse.
+ Studies in the substance abuse field indicate that partners, in particular, are an integral part of women's initiation into substance abuse, continuing drug use, and relapse. Partners can also influence the retention of women in treatment programs.
+ The majority of women under criminal justice supervision are mothers of dependent children. Many women try to maintain their parenting responsibilities while under community supervision or while in custody, and many plan to reunite with one or more of their children on their release.
+ Studies have shown that relationships among women in prison are also important. Women

often develop close personal relationships and pseudo families as a way to adjust to prison life. Research on prison staff indicates that correctional personnel often are not prepared to provide appropriate responses to these relationships.

Guiding Principle 4: Address Substance Abuse, Trauma, and Mental Health Issues Through Comprehensive, Integrated, and Culturally Relevant Services and Appropriate Supervision

Substance abuse, trauma, and mental health are three critical, interrelated issues in the lives of women offenders. These issues have a major impact on a woman's experience of community correctional supervision, incarceration, and transition to the community in terms of both programming needs and successful re-entry. Although they are therapeutically linked, these issues historically have been treated separately. One of the most important developments in health care over the past several decades is the recognition that a substantial proportion of women have a history of serious traumatic experiences. These traumatic experiences play a vital and often unrecognized role in the evolution of a woman's physical and mental health problems.

The Evidence

The salient features that propel women into crime include family violence and battering, substance abuse, and mental health issues. Other considerations include the following:

+ Substance abuse studies indicate that trauma, particularly in the form of physical or sexual abuse, is closely associated with substance abuse disorders in women. According to various studies, a lifetime history of trauma is present in approximately 55 to 99 percent of female substance abusers.[6]
+ Research shows that women who have been sexually or physically abused as children or adults are more likely to abuse alcohol and other drugs and may suffer from depression, anxiety disorders, and post-traumatic stress disorder.

+ Co-occurring disorders complicate substance abuse treatment and recovery. An integrated program concurrently addresses both disorders through assessment, treatment, referral, and coordination.

+ Research conducted by the National Institutes of Health indicates that gender differences, as well as race and ethnicity, must be considered in determining appropriate diagnosis, treatment, and prevention of disease.

+ Experience in the substance abuse field has shown that treatment programs are better able to engage and retain women clients if programs are culturally targeted.

Guiding Principle 5: Provide Women with Opportunities To Improve their Socio-economic Conditions

Addressing both the social and material realities of women offenders is an important aspect of correctional intervention. The woman offender's life is shaped by her socio-economic status; her experience with trauma and substance abuse; and her relationships with partners, children, and family. Most women offenders are disadvantaged economically, and this reality is compounded by their trauma and substance abuse histories. Improving socio-economic outcomes for women requires providing opportunities through education and training that will enable them to support themselves and their children.

The Evidence

Most women offenders are poor, under-educated, and unskilled. Many have never worked, have sporadic work histories, or have depended on public assistance. Additional factors that affect their socio-economic conditions include the following:

+ Most women offenders are heads of their households. In 1997, nearly 32 percent of all female heads of households lived below the poverty line.

+ Research in the field of domestic violence has shown that availability of material and economic necessities—including housing, financial support, educational and vocational training, and job development—is essential to women's ability to establish lives apart from their abusive partners.

+ Research on the effectiveness of substance abuse treatment has noted that, without strong material support, women presented with economic demands are more likely to reoffend and discontinue treatment.

+ Recent changes in public assistance due to welfare reform (e.g., Temporary Assistance for Needy Families programs created under the Welfare Reform Law of 1996) affect women disproportionately. They negatively affect women's ability to support themselves and their children by making them ineligible for benefits. Even when eligible, women may not be able to apply for benefits until they have been released from custody or community supervision. They cannot gain access to treatment or medical care without Medicaid. Additionally, their convictions may make them ineligible for public housing or Section 8 housing subsidies.

Guiding Principle 6: Establish a System of Community Supervision and Re-entry With Comprehensive, Collaborative Services

Women offenders face specific challenges as they re-enter the community from jail or prison. Women on probation also face challenges in their communities. In addition to the stigma of being identified as an offender, they may carry additional burdens, such as single-parent status, decreased economic potential, lack of targeted services and programs, responsibilities to multiple agencies, and a general lack of community support.

Navigating through myriad systems that often provide fragmented services and have conflicting requirements can interfere with supervision and successful reintegration. There is a need for wraparound services—that is, a holistic and culturally sensitive plan for each woman that draws on a coordinated range of resources in her community. Types of organizations

---

General Strategies for Implementing Guiding Principles

The following general strategies can be applied to implementation of each guiding principle:

Adopt   Adopt each principle as policy on a system-wide and programmatic level.

Support   Provide full support of the administration for adoption and implementation of the gender-responsive principles.

Resources   Evaluate financial and human resources to ensure that implementation and allocation adjustments are adequate to accommodate any new policies and practices.

Training   Provide ongoing training as an essential element in implementing gender-responsive practices.

Oversight   Include oversight of the new policies and practices in management plan development.

Congruence   Conduct routine procedural review to ensure that procedures are adapted, deleted, or written for new policies.

Environment   Conduct ongoing assessment and review of the culture/environment to monitor the attitudes, skills, knowledge, and behavior of administrative, management, and line staff.

Evaluation   Develop an evaluation process to access management, supervision, and services.

---

that should work as partners to assist women who are re-entering the community include the following:

- Mental health providers.
- Alcohol and other drug treatment programs.
- Programs for survivors of physical and sexual violence.
- Family service agencies.
- Emergency shelter, food, and financial assistance programs.
- Educational organizations.
- Vocational training and employment services.
- Health care.
- The child welfare system, childcare, and other children's services.
- Transportation.
- Self-help groups.
- Consumer-advocacy groups.
- Organizations that provide leisure and recreation options.
- Faith-based organizations.
- Community service clubs.

The Evidence

Challenges to successful completion of community supervision and re-entry for women offenders have been documented in the research literature. These challenges can include housing, transportation, childcare, and employment needs; reunification with children and other family members; peer support; and fragmented community services. There is little coordination among community service systems linking substance abuse, criminal justice, public health, employment, housing, and child welfare. Other considerations for successful re-entry and community supervision include the following:

- Studies from such fields as substance abuse and mental health have found that collaborative, community-based programs offering a multidisciplinary approach foster successful outcomes among women. Research has shown that women offenders have a great need for comprehensive, community-based wraparound services. This coordinated or case management approach has been found to work effectively with women

---

Gender-Responsive Policy Elements

Create parity: Develop an understanding of parity or "equal treatment" that stresses the importance of equivalence (of purpose and effort) rather than sameness (in content).

Commit to women's programs: Create an executive-level position and provide appropriate resources, staffing, and training to ensure that women's issues are a priority.

Develop procedures that apply to women offenders: Review existing policies and procedures and develop operating procedures that address the needs of women offenders in such areas as clothing, personal property, hygiene, exercise, recreation, and contact with children and family.

Respond to women's pathways: Develop policies, programs, and services that respond specifically to women's pathways in and out of crime and to the contexts of their lives that support criminal behavior.

Consider community: Develop strong partnerships for community and transitional programs that include housing, training, education, employment, and family support services.

Include children and family: Facilitate the strengthening of family ties, particularly between mothers and their children.

---

because it addresses their multiple treatment needs.

+ Substance abuse research shows that an understanding of the interrelationships among the women, the program, and the community is critical to the success of a comprehensive approach.

+ Data from woman offender focus groups indicate that failure to meet the following needs puts women at risk for criminal justice involvement: housing, physical and psychological safety, education, job training and opportunities, community-based substance abuse treatment, and economic support. All of these factors—in addition to positive role models and a community response to violence against women—are critical components of a gender-responsive crime prevention program.

Policy Considerations

As agencies and systems examine the impact of their operations, policy-level changes are a primary consideration (see "Gender-Responsive Policy Elements" opposite).

Conclusion: Addressing the Realities of Women's Lives Is the Key to Improved Outcomes

This bulletin documents the importance of understanding and acknowledging differences between men and women offenders and the impact of those differences on the development of gender-responsive policies, practices, and programs in the criminal justice system. Analysis of available data indicates that addressing the realities of women's lives through gender-responsive policy and practice is fundamental to improved outcomes at all phases of the criminal justice system. This review maintains that consideration of women's and men's different pathways into criminality, their differential responses to custody and supervision, and their differing program requirements can result in a criminal justice system that is better equipped to respond to both men and women offenders.

The guiding principles and strategies outlined in the full report and this bulletin are intended to be a blueprint for the development of gender-responsive policy and practice. They can serve as the foundation for improving the ways in which criminal justice agencies manage and supervise women offenders in both institutional and community settings.

Ultimately, commitment and willingness on the part of policymakers and practitioners will be needed to actualize the vision and implement the principles and strategies of a gender-responsive criminal justice system. Reducing women's involvement in the criminal justice system will benefit the women themselves, their communities, and society. Such efforts will develop a more effective criminal justice system and generate positive effects for generations to come.

NOTES

1. See Bloom, B., Owen, B., and Covington, S. (2003). *Gender-Responsive Strategies: Research, Practice, and Guiding Principles for Women Offenders.* Washington, DC: National Institute of Corrections. NIC accession no. 018017.

2. Harris, K. (2001). "Women offenders in the community: Differential treatment in the justice process linked to gender." Information session on supervision of women offenders in the community. Lexington, KY: National Institute of Corrections, Community Corrections Division, Networking Conference.

3. Herman, J. (1992). *Trauma and Recovery.* New York, NY: Harper Collins.

4. Covington, S. (1998b). Women in prison: Approaches in the treatment of our most invisible population. *Women and Therapy Journal* 21(1): 141–155.

5. Covington, S., and Surrey, J. (1997). The relational model of women's psychological development: Implications for substance abuse. In S. Wilsnack and R. Wilsnack (eds.), *Gender and Alcohol: Individual and Social Perspectives* (pp. 335–351). New Brunswick, NJ: Rutgers University Press.

6. See Brown, V., Melchior, L., and Huba, G. (1999). Level of burden among women diagnosed with severe mental illness and substance abuse. *Journal of Psychoactive Drugs* 31(1): 31–40. Browne, A., Miller, B., and Maguin, E. (1999). Prevalence and severity of lifetime physical and sexual victimization among incarcerated women. *International Journal of Law and Psychiatry* 22(3–4): 301–322. Najavits, L.M., Weiss, R.D., and Shaw, S.R. (1997). The link between substance abuse and post-traumatic stress disorder in women: A research review. *American Journal on Addictions* 6(4): 273–283. Owen, B., and Bloom, B. (1995). Profiling women prisoners: Findings from national survey and California sample. *The Prison Journal* 75(2): 165–185. Teplin, L.A., Abram, K.M., and McClelland, G.M. (1996). Prevalence of psychiatric disorders among incarcerated women. *Archives of General Psychiatry* 53(6): 505–512.

PART V

Readings on Juvenile Justice

PREPARING FOR PRISON?

The Criminalization of School Discipline in the USA

Paul J. Hirschfield

That school was run more like a prison than a high school. It don't have to be nothing illegal about it. But you're getting arrested. No regard for if a college going to accept you with this record. No regard for none of that, because you're not expected to leave this school and go to college. You're not expected to do anything.

(JW—Former inner-city high school student, current maximum security prisoner[1])

Order and discipline have always been an animus of American public schools, especially those serving the children of the working class and the poor. Even comparisons of urban schools and prisons have become well established—even commonplace (Bowles and Gintis, 1976; Foucault, 1977; Parenti, 2000; Staples, 2000; Wacquant, 2001; Giroux, 2003; Fine *et al.*, 2004). The emphasis on the orderly movement of students and their obedience to strict codes of conduct is important both to schools' operational functioning and to their societal functions. Critical scholars have argued that strict disciplinary regimens in working class schools help to promote smooth and voluntary transitions into an industrial workplace that tightly regulates and subordinates laborers (Bowles and Gintis, 1976; Foucault, 1977). Commentators like Horace Mann and Emile Durkheim, both of whom saw mass education as the cornerstone of a cohesive, inclusive, and democratic society, also valued discipline for instilling moral and civic virtues (Durkheim, 1973; Bowles and Gintis, 1976).

Whether viewed as democratization or domination, the traditional disciplinary project of American mass education is slowly crumbling. The industrial economy and civil society have weakened considerably in recent decades, especially in cities. At the same time, the criminal justice system has ballooned in size and influence. These changes weakened the structural and ideological foundations of school disciplinary practice. The management of student deviance, divested of its broader social aims, is prone to redefinition and reappropriation for other ends. Especially in schools that face very real problems of gangs and violence (Devine,

1996), rule-breaking and trouble-making students are more likely to be defined as criminals—symbolically, if not legally—and treated as such in policy and practice. In short, the problems that once invoked the idea and apparatus of student discipline have increasingly become criminalized.

Studies of criminalization have a rich history (Jenness, 2004), so it is important to clarify and justify this article's usage of the term. Whereas the concept usually connotes the social and political process that culminates in behaviors like abortion or stalking becoming criminalized, only a small portion of the criminalization of school discipline fits this definition. Most legislative responses to school deviance do not codify new crimes or escalate penalties. Rather, legal reforms mandate that certain behaviors—already illegal—such as drug and weapons possession are referred to the police when they occur on school property. Other policies stipulate that students are treated like actual or suspected criminals, for instance by subjecting them to in-school suspension or scrutiny by armed police, dogs, or metal detectors.

Criminalization is conceived here even more broadly as the shift toward a crime control paradigm in the definition and management of the problem of student deviance. Criminalization encompasses the manner in which policy makers and school actors think and communicate about the problem of student rule-violation as well as myriad dimensions of school *praxis* including architecture, penal procedure, and security technologies and tactics. In *Governing through Crime*, Jonathan Simon (2006) analyzes the parameters of a crime control paradigm in the realm of school governance and elsewhere. He extends the concept of criminalization into the symbolic realm, arguing that non-crime problems such as school failure can become criminalized in political contexts through the use of crime metaphors in framing the problem and through embracing solutions that share the structure and logic of crime control.

I focus here on the most visible, clear-cut, and quantifiable manifestations of school criminalization in order to address the etiology of criminalization rather than its conceptualization and to lay the groundwork for empirical tests of my theoretical propositions.

However, even my proposed 'hard' indicators of criminalization are not necessarily or universally experienced as criminalization. Schools' practices, including the meting out of punishment and the provision of security, are widely variable both between and within jurisdictions. This corresponds to variation in state and local political conditions and to the unique professional and behavioral milieu of each semi-autonomous school (Bryk *et al.*, 1998). Still, an overall trend in school criminalization has accelerated since the early 1990s across the socio-economic and geographic spectrum. This article critiques extant accounts of school criminalization and introduces a new multilevel theoretical model that integrates structural and cultural approaches. Weaving together insights from extant theories, this account explains key patterns of divergence, as well as convergence.

The divergence pattern most fundamental and worthy of explanation is that criminalization is more prevalent and intense in schools that are heavily populated by disadvantaged urban minorities (Wacquant, 2001). The theory developed herein, which accounts for temporal, spatial, and demographic concentrations in criminalization, posits that schools' altered disciplinary and security regimes can be traced largely to deindustrialization, which shifted impacted schools and their disciplinary practices from productive ends toward a warehousing function, and the ensuing massive criminal justice expansion that deprived schools of potential resources. Aided by a crime-fixated and punitive political climate, these changes helped reorient school actors more toward the prevention and punishment of crime, and less toward the preparation of workers and citizens. The present account, unlike its predecessors, specifies the intermediary processes linking political-economic shifts to school practices, as well as subjective interpretations and other forces that condition these processes.

THREE DIMENSIONS OF SCHOOL CRIMINALIZATION

From the complex and variegated phenomena of school criminalization, I distill three distinct yet interlocking dimensions. To understand why schools have come to look, sound, and act more like criminal justice institutions, it is necessary to examine each of these developments. The first major trend is that school punishment has become more formal and actuarial. Mirroring developments in juvenile justice (Feld, 1999), school punishment is increasingly based on uniform procedural and disciplinary guidelines evolving around the nature of the offense rather than the discretion of teachers and other traditional disciplinary agents. This trend is most recognizable in the set of policies and practices dubbed 'zero tolerance'. Zero tolerance policies spread rapidly in the early 1990s in the midst of rising rates of school victimization and juvenile violence overall (Toby, 1998; Burns and Crawford, 1999). They were nationalized in 1994 with the passage of the Gun-Free Schools Act. Mandated to adopt zero tolerance for weapons, a large majority of school districts soon adopted 'zero tolerance' policies for alcohol, tobacco, drugs and violence (Simon, 2006). These policies resemble the determinate sentencing schemes that prevail in most states. But unlike mandatory criminal sentences, zero tolerance policies typically permit little consideration of mitigating circumstances (Schwartz and Rieser, 2001).

The transfer of disciplinary discretion from teachers and school authorities to disciplinary codes that stipulate exclusionary punishments has contributed to a second trend of more frequent suspensions and expulsions.[2] Expanded school exclusion is a symbolic form of criminalization, irrespective of whether it follows strict penal guidelines or the whims of authorities. Education agencies that increase their use of exclusionary punishments endorse the prevailing rationale of contemporary criminal justice practice—deterrence and incapacitation (Garland, 2001).[3]

Reflecting patterns in the criminal justice system, the intensification of school punishment is borne disproportionately by youth of color. Studies consistently document that minority students are more often subject to suspensions and expulsions and that these disparities do not closely reflect behavioral differences (Brooks et al., 1999; Skiba et al., 2002). Furthermore, suspensions for offenses that are not subject to automatic penalties, like disorder and insubordination, also appear to have increased, especially for disadvantaged minorities (Civil Rights Project, 2000).[4]

Declining teacher discretion and increased harshness in both defining and punishing school deviance can be properly understood only in relation to a third set of practices, namely, the importation of criminal justice into schools. This form of criminalization includes increased use of criminal justice technology, methodology, and personnel for disciplinary and security purposes. 'Zero tolerance' exemplifies this trend too, but it is merely the tip of the iceberg.

Criminal justice tools and personnel play an increasingly important role at nearly every stage of the disciplinary process. While police and security officers in schools are hardly novel, school policing is the fastest growing law enforcement field.[5] A 2004 national survey of teachers reports that 67 percent of teachers in majority-black or Hispanic middle and high schools report armed police stationed in their schools (Public Agenda, 2004). Suburban schools, where 60 percent of teachers work alongside armed police, are not far behind, however (Public Agenda, 2004).

Generally accompanying police and security guards are law enforcement methods like bag searches and video cameras. Among preventive practices, metal detectors and personal searches seem the clearest indications of criminalization since they define students as criminal suspects. Not surprisingly, the likelihood of metal detectors is positively related to the prevalence of minority students (DeVoe et al., 2005). Urban schools feature more gates, walls and barricades as well (Gottfredson et al., 2000). On the other hand, drug sniffing dogs are more commonplace in suburban, rural, and predominantly white schools (DeVoe et al., 2005).

To properly portray the extent and distribution of criminalization, one must dig deeper than national prevalence patterns. A reasonable proposition induced from journalistic and ethnographic accounts is that large, hyper-segregated school districts like New York

City (NYC) and Chicago, which have placed city or school district police departments in charge of school security, are the most criminalized. NYC's school police force is larger than the entire Boston Police Department (Devine, 1996). School resource officers (SROs) in these schools receive training specific to educational settings. However, as on the street, any violations of the law are subject to arrest, and school officers are not required to obtain permission from anyone to make an arrest (Devine, 1996; Hagan et al., 2002). Ethnographic research suggests that an influx of law enforcement erodes the traditional disciplinary role of teachers and other school authorities (Brotherton, 1996; Devine, 1996). In Miami-Dade, Florida, school arrests increased from 820 in 1999 to 2435 in 2001, and offenses that were once handled mostly internally—simple assaults and 'miscellaneous offenses'—comprised a staggering 57 percent (Fuentes, 2003).

The criminalization of school discipline extends into the juvenile court. Data from several jurisdictions including Toledo, Ohio, Miami-Dade (Rimer, 2004), and Katy, Texas (Graves, 2004), on the type of offenses that schools refer to the juvenile court show that the alleged misconduct leading to court referral is typically quite minor. This 'net-widening' effect reflects increased collaboration between schools and the juvenile justice system, which has eroded the traditional boundaries between the two institutions. As of 2000, 41 states mandated law enforcement referral for school crimes including drugs, violence, and weapons violations (Civil Rights Project, 2000). According to a recent news investigation, 'In Ohio, Virginia, Kentucky and Florida, juvenile court judges are complaining that their courtrooms are at risk of being overwhelmed by student misconduct cases that should be handled in the schools' (Rimer, 2004: A1). In addition, information-sharing agreements between education and justice agencies set the stage for laws that permit schools across diverse jurisdictions to expel students for outside legal entanglements (Bickerstaff et al., 1997; Spielman and Rossi, 1997; Brooks et al., 1999).

Although such hard indicators illustrate and quantify the problem of criminalization, they fail to convey its fluidity and complexity. Unidimensional descriptions tend to overstate the convergence in criminalization across contexts. It is true that some middle class suburban and rural schools have also instituted metal detectors and school police, along with tools at the less coercive end of the carceral continuum like video cameras (Kupchik and Monahan, 2006). However, homology of form does not dictate uniformity in substance, etiology, or function. While suburban schools are hardly immune from criminalization, criminalization in these contexts takes on more diluted or hybridized forms owing to the primacy of competing ideals like consumer choice and individual freedom (Casella, 2003). Casella (2003) views suburban schools' widespread adoption of security technologies as the result of concerted efforts on the part of private security companies to cash in on the fears of drugs and violence among educators and parents. Both the marketing of these products as well as their manner of implementation, however, are tailored to an audience that is wary of the prospect of criminalizing valued students. Surveillance technologies are most appealing to this audience if they embrace the logic and aesthetic of consumer freedom and individual productivity (i.e. self-discipline).[6]

At the same time, for reasons described in the next section, the imperatives of criminalization do weigh on suburban schools. These imperatives are often difficult to reconcile with the image and prevailing ethos of many of these schools. This distinction between the criminal justice mode of control and the softer, surveillance approaches embraced by the middle class is aptly described by Staples (2000). While contemporary criminal justice control is, for the most part, externally imposed, physically coercive, and exclusionary, post-modern 'everyday surveillance'—the logical culmination of the disciplinary power described by Foucault (1977)—is productive, relatively democratic, and inclusive (Staples, 2000). According to Staples, the latter forms of school control embody middle class parents' and education professionals' desires for greater order, efficiency, and predictability in an increasingly complex, scary, and fragmented social world.

Thus, school disciplinary and security planners in towns and suburbs, more so than in the inner-city, must pursue technologies and practices that are flexible enough to fit contradictory aims and discourses. Video cameras offer this flexibility, since they, on the one hand, expand disciplinary power through providing knowledge of students and promoting self-monitoring and, on the other hand, unobtrusively help to deter, detect, and prosecute potential crimes. In a similar fashion, I posit that SROs in these schools give more weight to their education and counseling functions and reserve coercive law enforcement methods for students identified as threats or trouble-makers. Metal detectors, in contrast, are less ambiguous and flexible in their purpose and symbolic associations. Accordingly, whereas a recent mass walkout among students in a NYC public school was unsuccessful in ending their use (Santos, 2005), these devices spark more effective and united resistance from students, parents, and educators in suburban schools, leading metal detectors to go unsold or unused (Cantor et al., 2002).

Thus, criminalization in middle class schools is less intense and more fluid than in the inner-city, where proximate or immediate crime threats are overriding concerns. Suburban security reforms are more likely to complement existing school disciplinary approaches rather than displace them (DeMitchell and Cobb, 2003). In short, the gated community may be a more apt metaphor to describe the security transformation of affluent schools, while the prison metaphor better suits that of inner-city schools.

Four Extant Interpretations of School Criminalization

Voluminous material has addressed the racial inequities and other harms associated with the criminalization of school security and discipline (Devine, 1996; Brooks et al., 1999; Beger, 2002), but detailed theoretical explanation of this multidimensional phenomenon is scarce (but see Kupchik and Monahan, 2006). This is surprising, given how vast are the separate literatures linking punitive criminal justice reforms and all key features of schooling, respectively, to the cultural, political, and economic order (Bowles and Gintis, 1976; Bourdieu and Passeron, 1977; Willis, 1977; Parenti, 2000; Garland, 2001). By contrast, etiological

discussion with respect to criminalization in the school sphere, as summarized below, tends to eschew deeper, structural underpinnings in favor of proximate influences within the socio-political milieu.

Most commonly, this discussion evokes the language and imagery of the 'moral panic' (Cohen, 1972), portraying the hardening of school discipline and security as a response to the upsurge of school crime and juvenile violence beginning in the late 1980s and several school 'rampages' in the 1990s (Brooks et al., 1999; Beger, 2002; DeMitchell and Cobb, 2003; Rimer, 2004). According to this perspective, jarring media constructions of the 'crisis' of school violence unite the public, stakeholders (e.g., teachers' unions), and public officials in a stance of righteous indignation toward a marginalized 'folk-devil' (Burns and Crawford, 1999). Often emerging from this emotional and political mobilization are quick-fix, punitive solutions (e.g., zero tolerance, metal detectors) that are disproportionate to actual threats of violence. Consistent with the moral panic perspective, school criminalization escalated throughout the USA in the 1990s, even though most schools reported no serious crimes, urban schools experienced no 'rampage' shootings, and overall rates of school violence dropped steadily from 1993 through 2000 (Brooks et al., 1999; Devoe et al., 2005: 11, Figure 2.1).

The moral panic framework suggests when a rigorous political response to an issue is required, but does not dictate a specific course of reform. Public and media outcries over school violence do not always result in a universal clamor for tighter security and more punishment, as evidenced by the school violence panic in the 1970s (Toby, 1998). At the same time, this framework does not explain why schools often maintain or intensify their punitive efforts long after public panics over school violence subside. Episodic moral panics help explain the initiation of criminalization but its institutionalization rests on political, organizational, and structural forces that fall outside of the scope of the theory.

A second account, which partially explains the sustainability of panic-inspired reforms, focuses not on the political management of periodic moral crises, but instead on the management of the neo-liberal push for school accountability. In brief, the school account-ability narrative suggests that teachers and principals from financially strapped schools can meet externally imposed demands to boost standardized test scores and attendance rates by excluding low-achievers and truants (Bryk *et al.*, 1998; Fuentes, 2003)—an outcome promoted by selective or frequent applica-tion of the exclusionary practices described thus far (Bowditch, 1993).[7]

The school accountability narrative is consistent with the spatio-temporal and demographic distribu-tion of criminalization. However, it is inconsistent with the character of some reforms like zero toler-ance. Criminalization for the purpose of excluding particular under-performing or disruptive students is best accomplished by strengthening school authori-ties' discretion rather than by transferring it to rigid guidelines and security agents that take little account of academic standing. It is certainly the case that zero tolerance and school police facilitate the exclusion of students accused of committing offenses, but the apparent willingness to sacrifice some promising stu-dents in the process begs explanation (Fuentes, 2003).

Both the moral panic and school accountability narratives give insufficient attention to the wider so-cial, legal, cultural, political, and economic contexts that frame schools' responses to moral panics about youth and to school accountability reforms. With respect to the legal context of disciplinary reform, sociologists offer a third, due process narrative. Toby (1998) and Arum (2003) both argue that a student rights movement occurred in the school disciplinary arena from the late 1960s through the mid-1970s as judicial rulings increasingly sought to curb the arbi-trary application of exclusionary school punishments and press for greater codification and standardiza-tion of disciplinary procedures. Both authors argue that these court rulings undermined the traditional moral authority of school authorities, and schools became more restrained in imposing exclusionary punishments (Arum, 2003). They further assert that these rulings emboldened students to openly defy teacher authority. Increasingly fearful of either being attacked or sued by their students and eager to focus on teaching instead of behavior management, teachers

generally desired clearer delineations of their disciplin-ary responsibilities, along with the delegation of some frontline responsibilities to other personnel. School principals, who levy exclusionary sanctions, were also wary of litigation. Accordingly, teachers unions and associations (e.g., American Federation of Teachers) and national school principals associations are the major stakeholder groups behind zero tolerance poli-cies (Boylan *et al.*, 2002). The due process narrative also helps explain the expanded role of police and the juvenile court in school discipline, since limiting the involvement of school professionals in the process re-duces their vulnerability to litigation. The reason why zero tolerance policies and SROs did not proliferate sooner may be that dual crises in school violence and school funding were necessary to garner the necessary political support for these initiatives.

Whereas the due process narrative illuminates the legal circumstances that hastened the formalization of school punishment, it fails to explain why harsh dis-ciplinary codes and an armed law enforcement pres-ence are especially pronounced in inner-city schools. Arum notes that, 'unlike middle class whites' many African-American and other non-white students and their families 'are not in a position to sustain serious legal challenges or pursue legal remedies related to the application of school disciplinary procedures without significant institutional support' (2003: 210). At the same time, judicial rulings since the 1980s—in keep-ing with 'get tough' sensibilities—have largely upheld harsh, exclusionary punishments in the sole interest of school safety (as long as no violations of due process are evident) (Arum, 2003). If concerns over liability are the primary impetus for the criminalization of school discipline, then one would wrongly predict greater criminalization in affluent suburban schools.

A fourth causal narrative, the 'governing-through-crime' thesis (Simon, 2006) also does not focus on the unique penal dynamics of inner-city schools. The proper backdrop of this meta-narrative, mapped extensively by David Garland (2001), features the decline of the industrial economy, the neo-liberal and conservative attacks on the social welfare apparatus and other 'non-market' institutions including public schools, the turbulent racial politics and rising youth crime beginning in the 1960s, and the decline of the rehabilitative ideal. Within this altered economic, cultural, and political context, Simon argues, fewer governmental entities pursue legitimacy through quality goods and services or through redistributive claims. Beginning with the Omnibus Crime Control Act of 1968, Simon traces the ascendancy of a new model of governance centered on the control and punishment of crime. In the school context, this mode of governance recasts disruptive students and failing schools as criminals, treats other students and their parents as potential victims, and elevates centralized education policy makers to the roles of prosecutor and judge. These role realignments temper and narrow both the obligations of government and the rights of citizenship with respect to education. Through instituting market competition, performance monitoring, and accountability, federal education reforms like the Safe and Drug Free Schools and Communities Act (SDFSCA) and No Child Left Behind, analogous to the criminal law itself (Reiman, 1979), place the onus of responsibility for school crime and the 'crime' of illiteracy on the under-performing students, teachers and schools, while exonerating the political and economic system and its leaders. Simon views federally sponsored or mandated responses to student misconduct such as zero tolerance, school police, metal detectors, and mandatory law enforcement referrals as instrumental to the shift toward a 'crime' model of school governance. At a rhetorical level, they aid in the attempt to imagine various school actors in the roles of criminal, victim, and law enforcers. At a political level, focusing on the crime issue is a safe and effective strategy for politicians vying for the moral high ground, as epitomized by Nixon in 1968 and Rudolph Giuliani and Clinton during the 1990s (Beckett, 1997). Finally, at a practical level, such reforms provide the 'techniques of knowledge and power' that form the actual apparatus of crime governance. They are the means through which schools are expected to document and manage their crime problem, or risk harsh judgment and sanctions.

The governing through crime meta-narrative provides a cogent account of governance at the upper-levels of school policy making, where criminalization initiatives often originate. However, a full explanatory account of criminalization must further scrutinize the consent and complicity of the governed. At the school level, criminalization is not merely accommodation to an altered set of government constraints, mandates, and incentives. Isomorphic institutional changes in schools also follow the diffusion of professional and broader cultural norms and related changes in the perceived needs, behaviors, and circumstances of their students (DiMaggio and Powell, 1983). Federal laws like SDFSCA afford states and localities considerable leeway in defining their own needs, goals, and objectives, leaving such issues as metal detectors, drug sweeps, specific zero tolerance provisions, and most other program-specific regulations up to local discretion. Compliance with key SDFSCA provisions is reportedly partial and haphazard within and across schools, and favored activities often stray from a crime control paradigm (e.g., counseling and recreation) (Gottfredson et al., 2000).

Collectively, the preceding accounts lend multiple layers and dimensions to our understanding of penal intensification within American schools. The remainder of this article adds some pieces to the theoretical puzzle. While integrating viable elements of all four narratives, I make two additional contributions. First, I affix these elements more securely onto the structural configurations of present-day America including the post-industrial economy and the expanded penal system. Second, whereas the extant interpretations imply that all schools or broad categories of schools sway in unison to prevailing political winds, the narrative developed here recognizes the limited agency that school actors possess in defining and pursuing ends and means other than those dictated by overseeing and regulating entities (Willis, 1977). One fundamental and enduring goal that school actors pursue, through diverse means and with variable success, whose critical relevance to school disciplinary reform has not been adequately theorized—until now—is the preparation and sorting of youth for future positions in the occupational and social order.

THE ROLE OF 'OBJECTIVE' STRUCTURAL CONDITIONS

The natural starting point for a narrative predicated on the interdependence between schools and the larger social order is an analysis of political-economic conditions. Various observers have described an economic contraction in the late 1960s that seriously threatened corporate profit margins by the 1970s (Parenti, 2000; Garland, 2001). In response, corporations reduced labor costs and increased profits through shifting industrial production offshore, automation, and mergers. The corresponding political agenda included deregulation and an ideological and policy assault on social welfare and worker protections. Public schools, which have provided a periodic locus for struggles for full citizenship and equal opportunity and a vision of the public good that counters the hegemony of the market (Katznelson and Weir, 1985), did not escape the conservative and neo-liberal offensive (Nolan and Anyon, 2004).

While the adverse consequences of these responses to the economic downturn trickled down through the social class structure, school criminalization is particularly bound up with the fate of two impacted groups. First, the accelerated deindustrialization in the USA's core urban manufacturing centers, coupled with the mass exodus of the middle classes and their property tax dollars to the suburbs, resulted in concentrations of unskilled inner-city minorities with little access to legitimate work—except in the expanding low-wage sectors (Wilson, 1996) and the military—as well as to opportunities afforded by an equitably funded public education.

While deindustrialization deprives overwhelming numbers of inner-city minorities of a productive role in the USA's economy and perpetuates cycles of drugs and violence, predominantly white cities and towns are also beset by huge job losses in industry, mining, and agriculture (Duncan, 2000). In earlier eras, the plight of these groups may have ushered in a second 'New Deal' or 'War on Poverty' including massive government outlays to rebuild the nation's infrastructure and train disadvantaged populations for the increasingly high-tech, flexible, global economy. But for reasons detailed elsewhere (Beckett, 1997; Simon, 2006), elected officials saw more advantage in fixating on urban crime and drug 'epidemics' and building a stable infrastructure around the control of crime.

While the rise of the 'criminal justice-industrial complex' may be, in large part, the long-term, unintended consequence of short-sighted 'get tough' campaigns, its staying power derives from its role in the post-industrial political economy. Penal expansion helped the State manage both rural and urban economic crises. With respect to urban economic devastation, a campaign of arrest and incapacitation of an unprecedented pace and scope kept a lid on unrest and opened the door to strategic urban redevelopment within designated 'safe zones' (Parenti, 2000).

The prison-industrial complex also curbed the decline of many white rural areas and, more broadly, pacified the white working class. Criminal justice expansion artificially tightens the labor market (Western and Beckett, 1999), stimulates the economy of ailing rural communities (Huling, 2002), and affords rural residents greater electoral representation and population-based federal appropriations (Huling, 2002). Accordingly, many rural politicians stake their political careers on the location of juvenile and adult prisons in their districts and the hundreds of stable, well-paying jobs that they promise to generate for their constituents.[8]

The twin developments of deindustrialization and mass incarceration, through shifting the political calculus of school policy decisions, have important direct implications for state-level education policy. The same state legislators with vested interests in building or expanding prisons in their districts are empowered to vote on state financing of urban education and state school security and penal initiatives necessitated by federal reforms. Politicians with largely rural and small town bases, who hold considerable sway over the legislatures in states with large prison populations like Texas, New York, and California, should benefit more politically from expansionist justice policies and exclusionary school policies—which help keep prisons full—than from generous urban school funding. Even urban mayors and school superintendents have little incentive to invest in genuine educational opportunities for unexceptional students trapped in under-performing schools. The post-industrial economy, relatively lucrative illicit opportunities, and limited social capital foster widespread inability and reluctance to take full advantage of these opportunities (Noguera, 2003). Political-economic transformations have resituated inner-city schools (and 'lockdown' environments therein) structurally alongside the aggressive policing and imprisonment of disadvantaged blacks and Latinos as a means to control and warehouse 'disposable' youth (Wacquant, 2001; Giroux, 2003; Nolan and Anyon, 2004).

Predictably, then, the criminal justice boom diverted public funds that could have been directed at public education (Western et al., 2003; Jacobson, 2005).[9] As criminal justice budgets have skyrocketed, lawsuits in more than 40 states have alleged that inequitable state financing of poor school districts is responsible for conditions in poor schools that run afoul of the states' own constitutions (*New York Times*, 2003). Extreme fiscal restraints coupled with pressure to lift sagging student performance and reduce school crime, leave school actors with a shrinking pool of ameliorative options. Part of the appeal of school accountability reforms, under which state and federal school disciplinary mandates can be subsumed, is that they are relatively inexpensive to implement. Forced inter-school competition, 'high-stakes' testing, and the removal of dangerous and disruptive students are cheap alternatives to renovating and modernizing schools and hiring more qualified teachers and counselors.

As mentioned, however, centralized mandates set only general parameters for district-level policy. They lack the necessary specificity, therefore, to explain convergent criminalization patterns such as increases in metal detectors, drug sweeps, and court referrals from schools. The diffusion of concordant practices across subsets of schools (e.g., inner-city) is rooted not only in state coercion and incentives and in similar triggering factors (e.g., overcrowded facilities and disengaged students) but, more fundamentally, in school organizations' shared quest for professional and political credibility. For schools to effectively interrelate across institutional domains—with government, employers, families, and the media—they must affirm

society's prevailing ideas and values, including the new 'political accord' (Gintis and Bowles, 1988) that has been reached on youth crime and punishment. One way that schools can openly endorse aspects of this accord such as incorrigibility, high rates of juvenile crime, the threat of youthful 'predators', and the necessity of expanded punishment and control (Garland, 2001; Giroux, 2003), is through the 'transportation of political practices', from the penal realm into the school (Gintis and Bowles, 1988).

The similarity of particular techniques, symbols, and rationales that schools borrow from the penal realm is also rooted in the shared pursuit of credibility. Schools can minimize political risks and maintain effective inter-institutional communication by adopting 'best practices' and relying on the advice of recognized school security professionals (DiMaggio and Powell, 1983). School security consultants are often rooted ideologically and professionally in the wider criminal justice profession (Trump and Lavarello, 2001) and have helped situate school misconduct within the purview of criminal justice (Simon, 2006). The independent contribution of criminal justice professionals to school penal trends is explored more fully later.

THE 'SUBJECTIVE' INFLUENCE OF SOCIAL STRUCTURE ON SCHOOL CRIMINALIZATION

Structural factors shape school penal trends, not merely through shifting the strategic calculus of lawmakers and policy makers, but also through exerting direct influence on individual actors operating at the levels of the school and the classroom. Most scholars who explore the relationship between structural realities, like social class hierarchies and individual subjectivities, follow in the path of Pierre Bourdieu. Bourdieu and Passeron describe how the parallel lines of social thought and actions entailed in group membership instill in group members a shared habitus or 'system of internalized structures, schemes of perceptions, conception, and action' (1977: 86).

The criminalization response, whether a teacher's decision to summon security guards to a minor classroom disturbance or a principal's pursuit of the arrest or removal of that student, is mediated by individual interpretations of social reality. While sociologists differ widely in how much autonomy they permit individuals in developing their own interpretations and acting upon them, few disagree that structural forces *condition* and *constrain* their thoughts and actions.

Two interrelated aspects of the habitus with profound implications for classroom and school disciplinary climate are perceptions of students' future prospects and the negotiated balance of power between teachers and students. While perceptions of the opportunity structure are an important mechanism linking social structure with student aspirations and effort (MacLeod, 1987), they also are an important component of the habitus of school staff, which should condition how these actors respond to errant students. Educators consciously and unconsciously aim to prepare youth to assume their rightful position in the social strata and hierarchical workplace (Bowles and Gintis, 1976; Katznelson and Weir, 1985; Ferguson, 2000). Accordingly, much school activity is organized around the tasks of classification and socialization. Even school punishment, which is generally depicted as a response to past and present behavior, also acts prospectively by sorting future 'dropouts' (Bowditch, 1993) and socializing students (Durkheim, 1973; Foucault, 1977). If schools' penal and surveillance practices are tools of classification and socialization, it follows that teachers' perceived changes in the occupational structure onto which these devices are mapped should prompt corresponding changes in these practices.[10]

This argument finds support in evidence suggesting that criminalization practices reflect increased perceptions of troublesome students as future criminals or prisoners. The needs of such students fall outside of the traditional school disciplinary paradigm, which is tied to images of students as future workers and citizens. Bleak prospects are so noticeable in poor communities and media constructions thereof, that they cannot have escaped the notice of urban school professionals. For instance, nearly 60 percent of black male high school dropouts experience imprisonment by age 30–4 (Pettit and Western, 2004).

Of course, many education professionals in distressed schools are dedicated to diverting as many students as possible from the 'criminal justice track'. On the other hand, recent examples abound of teachers and school administrators projecting criminal futures onto their students (Blum and Woodlee, 2001; Nolan and Anyon, 2004). Concordant research in California finds that many students in impoverished schools believe that educators perceive them as 'animals', 'inmates', or 'killers' (Fine et al., 2004) and that black males and females are less than half as likely as their white counterparts to believe that their teachers support them and care about their success (Noguera, 2003).

Ferguson (2000) offers deeper exploration into how objective penal realities are internalized by school staff and assimilated into the school disciplinary process, even for students as young as fifth and sixth graders. Through her inquiry into why African-American youth were disproportionately banished to the school's 'punishing room' and 'jailhouse', she discovered that young African-American children facing discipline, unlike white children, are written and cast into roles imagined for adults in the world outside the school. Owing to a dominant image of black males as criminals and prisoners, many school authorities view chronically disobedient black boys as 'bound for jail' and 'unsalvageable'.

Implicit in the designation of black students as unsalvageable is the recognition of two emergent structural realities discussed earlier: (1) that prison, which reifies criminality and tends to foreclose a productive future, looms over the future of African-American youth who fail in school; and (2) that schools lack the resources to reverse the downward trajectories of the most troublesome students without compromising the quality of teaching and services aimed at more deserving or promising students. It is likely that this dynamic is most conspicuous in the 'lowest tier' high schools where labels like 'bound for jail' are often legitimized through justice system interactions both inside and outside the school (Devine, 1996).

The anticipatory labeling of students as future prisoners in need of coercive control or exclusion can be a self-fulfilling prophecy as students frequently suspended from school face increased risks of juvenile and adult incarceration (Arum and Beattie, 1999; Skiba *et al.*, 2003). Just as the success of a 'College Prep' track can be gauged by the share of students in this track who attend college, the reliability of penal and exclusionary practices at weeding out those students on the 'fast track' to jail may, perversely, legitimate and reinforce these practices.

Focusing on perceptions of external opportunity structures is insufficient, however, since the attitudes and behaviors that confront school staff each day exert a much more decisive influence on their disciplinary responses. However, even those who believe that the complex, dynamic rituals of power and resistance within schools possess their own internal logic and autonomous sphere of influence (Willis, 1977) acknowledge that disciplinary regimes must assume new forms within a structural landscape of mass unemployment and incarceration (Willis, 2004). In *Learning to Labor*, Willis argues that most working class students cede to teachers' respect and obedience in exchange for their 'equivalents' in knowledge and credentials. For students who begin to see school knowledge and credentials as irrelevant, on the other hand, 'the teachers' authority becomes increasingly the random one of the prison guard, not the necessary one of the pedagogue' (Willis, 1977: 72). Pragmatic teachers often respond by offering freedom and fun instead of knowledge and expect, in return, that disaffected students not hinder the 'good students' or otherwise challenge the basic paradigm of power relations in the school. Both sets of terms may be more difficult to negotiate and maintain, however, with discontented students forcibly concentrated in today's inner-city schools. First, such an exchange system garners little faith from either teachers or students when unemployment and incarceration are objectively more plausible than college. Teachers are often bereft of not only sufficient resources but also a cogent narrative of opportunity that can help them gain voluntary compliance from students and couch their role in non-repressive terms. The second option of ceding more control to the disaffected students, while not uncommon, is also less viable where teachers are called to account for lax performance and behavioral standards. In this light, it is understandable that teachers and administrators often perceive little choice but to summon repressive means to swiftly remove disruptive students from the classroom and the school. Criminal justice offers a useful template and accessible tools for this purpose (Simon, 2006).

THE INDEPENDENT ROLE OF JUSTICE SYSTEM AGENTS

Teachers and other education professionals are not the only agents whose interests and subjectivities should figure prominently in a theory of school disciplinary transformation. It is also important to understand the role of security and criminal justice agents. As mentioned earlier, criminal justice professionals have assumed an enlarged role in the school disciplinary process, often usurping traditional responsibilities of teachers. The emergence of crime as a central pathway for governance (Arum, 2003 Simon, 2006) and the willingness of overwhelmed and fearful school actors to summon and to cede disciplinary authority to justice system agents help explain this trend. However, these explanations largely treat justice system actors as objects of reform rather than as agents of it.

While a passive characterization of justice system actors was appropriate when criminal justice fields were smaller and less professionalized, it is less tenable today. Criminal justice professionals, thanks to the vast expansion of the criminal justice system, are highly organized. Through professional associations, they seek to maintain or enhance their legitimacy, prestige, and working conditions (DiMaggio and Powell, 1983; Beckett, 1997; Simon, 2006).

Once justice system actors implicated in school criminalization are conceptualized as professional and political interest groups, one is compelled to ask how the flow of criminal justice personnel, technology, and expertise into schools serves these groups' interests and what role these groups play in school criminalization (Becker, 1984). For example, installing police to find and fight crime in schools can bring collective benefits to the policing profession by creating more jobs and funding opportunities, and, with the help of educational components like DARE, by promoting their image as a vital and benevolent institution.[11]

Similar explanations have been offered for the increased role of the juvenile court within the school disciplinary process. While many overburdened juvenile court judges resent the addition of school misconduct cases to their dockets (Rimer, 2004), others may welcome this change. Expanded procedural protections and moral panics about juvenile crime since the 1960s jointly led to the criminalization of juvenile courts (Feld, 1999). In the process, juvenile courts lost jurisdiction over tens of thousands of youth to criminal courts. Even more importantly, the increasingly adversarial and punitive thrust of juvenile justice reform threatens the professional status and survival of the large contingent of juvenile court professionals who retain a rehabilitative orientation (Leiber *et al.*, 2002). Expanding the juvenile court's jurisdiction over schools, which includes other popular initiatives like school-based probation, at once helps keep court dockets full (Becker, 1984; Schwartz and Rieser, 2001) and reclaims for the court a rehabilitative role within a marked rehabilitative space—the School (Muncie and Hughes, 2002).

While the involvement of police and juvenile courts in the regulation of student behavior obviously signals schools' incorporation of a crime control paradigm, it bears repeating that security guards, police, and judges, like students and teachers, are subjective actors, prone to accept, but capable of resisting, the imperatives of criminalization. For instance, Devine (1996) notes that school officers in the lowest tier schools of NYC build mentoring relationships with students. Likewise, a training model for school police officers developed by the Vera Institute of Justice that teaches adolescent development and positive reinforcement has been incorporated into the NYPD's training of 'all new school safety agents'.[12] The importation of criminal justice into schools thus involves a process of mutual accommodation. Whether some progressive schools are capable of co-opting criminal justice tools and agents to the extent that they no longer qualify as agents of criminalization is an open theoretical and empirical question.

CONCLUSION

The importation of symbols, tactics, and personnel from the realm of criminal justice into schools is neither an inevitable and universal trend nor an accident of social history. Schools, like all institutions, are sites of dynamic social interaction wherein functions are continuously negotiated, structural constraints subjectively interpreted, proper responses hotly contested and inconsistently implemented—and the results of this cacophony of conflicting forces never completely certain. Even in the most distressed urban schools, progressive visions of education—rooted in the values of liberty, equality, tolerance, citizenship, and personal growth—actively compete with penological imperatives in shaping personal and institutional agendas (Gintis and Bowles, 1988; Fine *et al.*, 2004). The extent to which students confront school environments that weigh penological imperatives and images more heavily than pedagogical ones is an empirical question that deserves more systematic attention. That said, sufficient evidence supports a provisional thesis of an overarching criminalization of school discipline, especially within urban schools.

At the same time, the criminalization of school discipline, however prevalent, should not be subsumed under a singular social project or process, whether it is the USA's moral panics about youth and school violence, school accountability reforms, the automation of school disciplinary procedures, or the ascendancy of crime as a narrative for governance. Rather, the present-day, multidimensional penal realities in the USA's schools are fully understandable only through tracing their multiple historical and social underpinnings (Garland, 2001). The increasingly bleak employment and imprisonment prospects of inner-city students and teachers' and administrators' perceptions of these realities should figure prominently in efforts to theorize criminalization in the school context and in strategies to reverse it.

NOTES

I thank the following people for helping guide this article's development: James Ainsworth-Darnell, Ira Cohen, Stephanie De Luca, Joseph Hirschfield, Monique Payne, Becky Pettit, Paul Reck, Pat Roos, Helene White, and three anonymous reviewers. Any and all errors and misconceptions are mine.

1. Personal interview with the author in May 2002.
2. The Department of Education's Office of Civil Rights estimates that from 1974 to 1997 the rate of suspensions increased steadily from 3.7 percent of all students to 6.8 percent (Brooks *et al.*, 1999). As states implemented zero tolerance policies during the 1990s, the number of expulsions mounted (Fuentes, 2003). In Chicago, officially recorded expulsions increased from 14 in 1992–3—before zero tolerance was enacted—to 737 in 1998–9 (Civil Rights Project, 2000).
3. It is true that virtually all the major stakeholders in education policy at the national level endorse alternative education programs for banished students (Boylan and Weiser, 2002). However, those who operate, staff, and fund such segregated school environments may come to define their purpose as the isolation and control (or even punishment) of a criminal population. Nolan and Anyon refer to urban forms of these settings as 'new intermediary institutions that manage the stages between school and prison' (2004: 142).
4. During the 1999–2000 school year, African-American students comprised 17 percent of San Diego's students and 50 percent of those suspended for 'disruption' or 'defiance' (Applied Research Center, 2002).
5. Thanks largely to federal funding begun under the COPS program, urban, rural, and suburban schools all vastly expanded the number of school resource officers. By 1997, public schools hosted 9400 school resource officers (Bureau of Justice Statistics, 2000). Their number mushroomed to 14,337 by 2003 (Bureau of Justice Statistics, 2006).
6. Even the West Paducah, KY high school that experienced one of the 'rampage' shootings of the 1990s has greeted criminalization with ambivalence. According to the school's principal, the main goal of the school's SRO is to be a 'positive role model' and 'build trusting relationships with students' (Pascopella, 2005). Likewise, the morning ritual in which teachers search book bags and pat down students is couched in a way that rejects the rhetoric of coercion and criminalization in favor of a consumerist discourse. The school principal asserts, 'We've tried to make it a Wal-mart greeter situation rather than, "I'm searching your book bag." We try to make it a positive experience' (Pascopella, 2005).
7. Many inner-city schools, in their zealous pursuit of performance standards, have adopted rigid drill-based instruction and 'proto-military' methods of classroom discipline (Duncan, 2000; Kozol, 2005). One may surmise that the importation of criminal justice tools and personnel helps to sustain this 'pedagogy of direct command and absolute control' (Kozol, 2005: 64).
8. Becoming a 'prison town' can sometimes be a mixed economic and social blessing (Huling, 2002).
9. Empirical research supports an inverse relationship between prison funding and school funding. For instance, Johnson (1996), in his study of 'transcarceration' across social control institutions in the USA, finds that states' prison admission rates negatively predicted states' high school population rates, and that they were the only significant predictor in multivariate models.
10. This interpretation of classification and socialization practices should not be confused with the correspondence principle, which posits a functional correspondence between the needs of the social structure, labor market, or corporate elite and the practices of schools and teachers (Bowles and Gintis, 1976). The correspondence thesis has been challenged by work showing that teachers' perceptions of the labor market are fuzzy, misguided, and contested, and that schools' sorting and preparatory practices often fail to produce their intended results (Weis, 1990). With respect to explaining criminalization, however, it is not important whether these perceptions perfectly mirror objective conditions of the labor market or are actualized in student outcomes. It is important only that they shift substantially and correspondingly in response to structural changes and that they influence disciplinary practices.
11. The criminalization of schools evolves new forms as terrorism becomes the major axis for new public safety initiatives. Facing progressive cuts in federal funding for SROs, the 9000-strong National Association of School

Resource Officers, along with school security consulting firms, have called for an Education Homeland Security Act to 'fund school terrorism training, improve security and crisis planning' (Porteus, 2003).

12. http://www.vera.org/section2/section2_4.asp.

REFERENCES

Applied Research Center (2002). *Profiled and Punished: How San Diego Schools Undermine Latino & African American Student Achievement*. Oakland, CA: Applied Research Center.

Arum, Richard (2003). *Judging School Discipline: The Crisis of Moral Authority*. Cambridge, MA: Harvard University Press.

Arum, Richard and Irenee R. Beattie (1999). 'High School Experience and the Risk of Adult Incarceration', *Criminology* 37(3): 515–40.

Becker, Howard S. (1984). 'Moral Entrepreneurs: The Creation and Enforcement of Deviant Categories', in Delos Kelly (ed.) *Deviant Behavior: A Text-Reader in the Sociology of Deviance*, pp. 21–8. New York: St Martin's Press.

Beckett, Katherine (1997). *Making Crime Pay: Law and Order in Contemporary American Politics*. Oxford: Oxford University Press.

Beger, Randall R. (2002). 'Expansion of Police Power in Public Schools and the Vanishing Rights of Students', *Social Justice* 29(1–2): 119–30.

Bickerstaff, Steve, Sara H. Leon and J. Greg Hudson (1997). 'Preserving the Opportunity for Education: Texas' Alternative Education Programs for Disruptive Youth', *Journal of Law and Education* 26(4): 1–39.

Blum, Justin and Yolanda Woodlee (2001). 'Tour Was for Youths "Beyond Control": Teacher Requested Prison "Experience"', *Washington Post*, 31 May, p. B1.

Bourdieu, Pierre and Jean-Claude Passeron (1977). *Reproduction in Education, Society, and Culture*. London: Sage Publications.

Bowditch, Christine (1993). 'Getting Rid of Troublemakers: High School Disciplinary Procedures and the Production of Dropouts', *Social Problems* 40(4): 493–509.

Bowles, Samuel and Herbert Gintis (1976). *Schooling in Capitalist America: Educational Reform and the Contradictions of Economic Life*. New York: Basic Books.

Boylan, Ellen M. and Jennifer Weiser (2002). *Survey of Key Education Stakeholders on Zero Tolerance Student Discipline Policies*. Newark, NJ: Education Law Center.

Brooks, Kim, Vincent Schiraldi and Jason Ziedenberg (1999). *School House Hype: Two Years Later*. San Francisco, CA: Center on Juvenile and Criminal Justice.

Brotherton, David C. (1996). 'The Contradictions of Suppression: Notes from a Study of Approaches to Gangs in Three Public High Schools', *Urban Review* 28(2): 95–117.

Bryk, Anthony, Penny Bender Sebring, David Kerbow, Sharon Rollow and John Q. Easton (1998). *Charting Chicago School Reform: Democratic Localism as a Lever for Social Change*. Boulder, CO: Westview Press.

Bureau of Justice Statistics (2000). *Local Police Departments 1997*. Washington, DC: Office of Justice Programs, US Department of Justice.

Bureau of Justice Statistics (2006). *Local Police Departments 2003*. Washington, DC: Office of Justice Programs, US Department of Justice.

Burns, Ronald and Charles Crawford (1999). 'School Shootings, the Media, and Public Fear: Ingredients for a Moral Panic', *Crime, Law and Social Change* 32(2): 147–68.

Cantor, David, Scott Crosse, Carol A. Hagen, Michael J. Mason, Amy J. Siler and Adrienne von Glatz (2002). *A Closer Look at Drug and Violence Prevention Efforts in American Schools: Report on the Study on School Violence and Prevention.* Washington, DC: US Department of Education, Planning and Evaluation Service.

Casella, Ronnie (2003). 'Security, Schooling, and the Consumer's Choice to Segregate', *The Urban Review* 35(2): 129–48.

Civil Rights Project (2000). *Opportunities Suspended: The Devastating Consequences of Zero Tolerance and School Discipline Policies.* Washington, DC: Civil Rights Project.

Cohen, Stanley (1972). *Folk Devils and Moral Panics: The Creation of the Mods and Rockers.* London: MacGibbon & Kee.

DeMitchell, Todd A. and Casey D. Cobb (2003). 'Policy Responses to Violence in Our Schools: An Exploration of Security as a Fundamental Value', *Education & Law Journal* 2: 459–84.

Devine, John (1996). *Maximum Security: The Culture of Violence in Inner-City Schools.* Chicago, IL: University of Chicago Press.

DeVoe, Jill F., Katharin Peter, Margaret Noonan, Thomas D. Snyder and Katrina Baum (2005). *Indicators of School Crime and Safety 2005.* Washington, DC: US Departments of Education and Justice.

DiMaggio, Paul J. and Walter Powell (1983). 'The Iron Cage Revisited: Institutional Isomorphism and Collective Rationality in Organizational Fields', *American Sociological Review* 48(2): 147–60.

Duncan, Garrett A. (2000). 'Urban Pedagogies and the Celling of Adolescents of Color', *Social Justice* 27(3): 29–42.

Durkheim, Emile (1973). *Moral Education: A Study in the Theory and Application of the Sociology of Education.* New York: Macmillan.

Feld, Barry C. (1999). *Bad Kids: Race and the Transformation of the Juvenile Court.* New York: Oxford.

Ferguson, Ann A. (2000). *Bad Boys: Public Schools in the Making of Black Masculinity.* Ann Arbor, MI: University of Michigan Press.

Fine, Michelle, April Burns, Yasser A. Payne and Maria E. Torre (2004). 'Civics Lessons: The Color and Class of Betrayal', *Teachers College Record* 106(11): 2193–223.

Foucault, Michel (1977). *Discipline and Punish: The Birth of the Prison.* New York: Pantheon Books.

Fuentes, Annette (2003). 'Discipline and Punish: Zero Tolerance Policies Have Created a "Lockdown Environment" in Schools', *The Nation* 277: 17–20.

Garland, David (2001). *Culture of Control: Crime and Social Order in Contemporary Society.* Chicago, IL: University of Chicago Press.

Gintis, Herbert and Samuel Bowles (1988). 'Contradiction and Reproduction in Educational Theory', in M. Cole (ed.) *Bowles and Gintis Revisited: Correspondence and Contradiction in Educational Theory,* pp. 16–32. London: The Falmer Press.

Giroux, Henry A. (2003). 'Racial Injustice and Disposable Youth in the Age of Zero Tolerance', *International Journal of Qualitative Studies in Education* 16(4): 553–65.

Gottfredson, Gary D., Denise C. Gottfredson, Ellen R. Czeh, David Cantor, Scott B. Crosse and Irene

Hantman (2000). *A National Study of Delinquency Prevention in School: Final Report*. Ellicott City, MD: Gottfredson Associates.

Graves, Rachel (2004). 'Zero Tolerance Raises Alarms: Parents Say Katy ISD Overdisciplining Students for Minor Offenses', *Houston Chronicle*, 18 April, p. A1.

Hagan, John, Paul J. Hirschfield and Carla Shedd (2002). 'Shooting at Tilden High: Causes and Consequences', in Mark H. Moore, Carol V. Petrie, Anthony A. Braga and Breanda L. McLaughlin (eds.) *Deadly Lessons: Understanding Lethal School Violence*, pp. 143–74. Washington, DC: National Research Council.

Huling, Tracy (2002). 'Building a Prison Economy in Rural America', in M. Mauer and M. Chesney-Lind (eds.) *Invisible Punishment: The Collateral Consequences of Mass Imprisonment*, pp. 197–213. New York: New Press.

Jacobson, Michael (2005). *Downsizing Prisons: How to Reduce Crime and End Mass Incarceration*. New York: New York University Press.

Jenness, Valerie (2004). 'Explaining Criminalization: From Demography and Status Politics to Globalization and Modernization', *Annual Review of Sociology* 30: 141–71.

Johnson, W. Wesley (1996). 'Transcarceration and Social Control Policy: The 1980s and Beyond', *Crime and Delinquency* 42(1): 114–26.

Katznelson, Ira and Margaret Weir (1985). *Schooling for All: Class, Race, and the Decline of the Democratic Ideal*. New York: Basic Books.

Kozol, Jonathan (2005). *The Shame of the Nation: The Restoration of Apartheid Schooling in America*. New York: Crown.

Kupchik, Aaron and Torin Monahan (2006). 'The New American School: Preparation for Post-industrial Discipline', *British Journal of Sociology of Education* 27(5): 617–31.

Leiber, Michael J., Kimberly Schwarze and Kristin Y. Mack (2002). 'The Effects of Occupation and Education on Punitive Orientations among Juvenile Justice Personnel', *Journal of Criminal Justice* 30(4): 303–16.

MacLeod, Jay (1987). *Ain't No Makin' It: Leveled Aspirations in a Low-Income Neighborhood*. Colorado: Westview Press.

Muncie, John and Gordon Hughes (2002). 'Modes of Youth Governance: Political Rationalities, Criminalization, and Resistance', in John Muncie, Gordon Hughes and Eugene McLaughlin (eds.) *Youth Justice: Critical Readings*, pp. 1–18. London: Sage Publications.

New York Times (2003). Editorial: *'Fighting for Fairness at School'*, New York Times, 27 June, p. A26.

Noguera, Pedro A. (2003). 'The Trouble with Black Boys: The Role and Influence of Environmental and Cultural Factors on the Academic Performance of African American Males', *Urban Education* 38(4): 431–59.

Nolan, Kathleen and Jean Anyon (2004). 'Learning to Do Time: Willis' Cultural Reproduction Model in an Era of Deindustrialization, Globalization, and the Mass Incarceration of People of Color', in Nadine Dolby, Greg Dimitriadis and Paul Willis (eds.) *Learning to Labor in New Times*, pp. 133–49. New York: Routledge.

Parenti, Christian (2000). *Lockdown America: Police and Prisons in the Age of Crisis*. London & New York: Verso.

Pascopella, Angela (2005). 'Money Makes Security Go Around', District Administration 41(7): 47–53. Available at http://www.districtadministration.com/viewarticle.aspx?articleid=414.

Pettit, Becky and Bruce Western (2004). 'Mass Imprisonment and the Life Course: Race and Class Inequality in U.S. Incarceration', American Sociological Review 69(2): 151–69.

Porteus, Liza (2003). 'Safety Experts: Schools Are Unprepared for Terror', Fox News on-line, 18 September. Available at www.foxnews.com/story/0,2933,97620,00.html.

Public Agenda (2004). Teaching Interrupted: Do Discipline Policies in Today's Public Schools Foster the Common Good? New York: Public Agenda.

Reiman, Jeffrey H. (1979). The Rich Get Richer and the Poor Get Prison: Ideology, Class and Criminal Justice. New York: Wiley.

Rimer, Sara (2004). 'Unruly Students Facing Arrest, Not Detention', New York Times, 4 January, p. A1.

Santos, Fernanda (2005). 'Protest over Metal Detectors Gains Legs: Students Walk Out', New York Times, 2 September, p. B1.

Schwartz, Robert and Len Rieser (2001). 'Zero Tolerance as Mandatory Sentencing', in W. Ayers, B. Dohrn and R. Ayers (eds.) Zero Tolerance: Resisting the Drive for Punishment in our Schools, pp. 126–35. New York: The New Press.

Simon, Jonathan (2006). Governing through Crime: How the War on Crime Transformed American Democracy and Created a Culture of Fear. New York: Oxford University Press.

Skiba, Russell J., Robert S. Michael, Abra Carroll Nardo and Reece L. Peterson (2002). 'The Color of Discipline: Sources of Racial and Gender Disproportionality in School Punishment', The Urban Review 34(4): 317–42.

Skiba, Russell, Ada Simmons, Lori Staudinger, Marcus Rausch, Gayle Dow and Renae Feggins (2003). 'Consistent Removal: Contributions of School

Discipline to the School-Prison Pipeline', paper presented at the School to Prison Pipeline Conference, Cambridge, MA, May.

Spielman, Fran and Rosalind Rossi (1997). 'Off-Campus Arrest Could Boot Kids: Expulsion Policy to Stiffen', Chicago Sun-Times, 11 March, p. 3.

Staples, William G. (2000). Everyday Surveillance: Vigilance and Visibility in Postmodern Life. Lanham, MD: Rowman & Littlefield.

Toby, Jackson (1998). 'Getting Serious about School Discipline', The Public Interest 133: 68–84.

Trump, Kenneth S. and Curtis Lavarello (2001). 'Buyer Beware: What to Look for When You Hire a School Security Consultant and to Arm or Not to Arm?', American School Board Journal 188(3): 30–4.

Wacquant, Loic (2001). 'Deadly Symbiosis: When Ghetto and Prison Meet and Mesh', in D. Garland (ed.) Mass Imprisonment: Social Causes and Consequences, pp. 82–120. London: Sage Publications.

Weis, Lois (1990). Working Class without Work: High-School Students in a De-industrializing Economy. New York: Routledge.

Western, Bruce and Katherine Beckett (1999). 'How Unregulated Is the U.S. Labor Market? The Penal System as a Labor Market Institution', American Journal of Sociology 104(4): 1030–60.

Western, Bruce, Vincent Schiraldi and Jason Zeidenberg (2003). *Education & Incarceration*. Washington, DC: Justice Policy Institute.

Willis, Paul (1977). *Learning to Labor: How Working Class Kids Get Working Class Jobs*. Lexington, MA: D.C. Heath.

Willis, Paul (2004). 'Twenty-Five Years On: Old Books, New Times', in Nadine Dolby, Greg Dimitriadis and Paul Willis (eds.) *Learning to Labor in New Times*, pp. 167–96. New York: Routledge.

Wilson, William. J. (1996). *When Work Disappears: The World of the New Urban Poor*. New York: Knopf.

Minimizing Harm from Minority Disproportion in American Juvenile Justice

Franklin E. Zimring

The issues we confront in trying to fix the damages of disproportion in juvenile justice are a mix of the obvious and the obscure. There can be no doubt that the handicaps imposed on youth by arrest, detention, adjudication, and incarceration fall disproportionately on males from disadvantaged minority groups in the United States. It is equally obvious that the hardships imposed on formally sanctioned youth are substantial by themselves and even worse when they aggravate the other by-products of social disadvantage. But this concluding note is about the not-so-obvious choices that we confront when attempting to reduce the harms that disproportionate minority concentration produces. There are a variety of different approaches that can be taken to reforming juvenile justice to protect minority youth, and not all of them are of equal effectiveness. How best to address the problems documented with passion and skill in previous chapters?

My ambition in these pages is to identify some of the key policy choices that must be made in reducing injustices found in American juvenile courts. A clear definition of goals and priorities is absolutely essential to intelligent policy planning. My argument is that reducing the hazards of juvenile court processing may be a better approach to protecting minority youth than just trying to reduce the proportion of juvenile court cases with minority defendants.

The essay is divided into two large segments and then subdivided into smaller units. Part 1 concerns the conceptual equipment necessary to assess the impact of legal policies on minority populations. A first section of part 1 discusses whether it is best to consider the minority concentrations in juvenile justice as a special problem in the juvenile-justice system or as part of the generally higher-risk exposures found in criminal justice and other state control systems. A second section proposes harm reduction as the principal criterion by which policies designed to respond to minority disproportion should be judged. A third section contrasts two competing measures of disadvantage to minorities—relative and aggregate disadvantage—as the appropriate goal of reforms. A fourth section compares two overall approaches to minimize harm—cutting back on the harms that juvenile-justice processing produces and cutting back on the number and proportion of minority youth who are pushed through the system.

Part 2 attempts to apply the apparatus developed in part 1 to discuss recent chapters in juvenile-justice law reform—changes in transfer policy, the deinstitutionalization of status offenders, and the embrace of diversion programs. A final subsection of part 2 contrasts the harm to minority youth from exposure to juvenile courts with the harm from criminal courts. If the proper standard for judging the impact of institutions on minority kids is reducing the harms these kids suffer, the current juvenile-justice system —warts and all—is vastly less dangerous to minorities than the machinery of criminal justice.

I. POLICY PERSPECTIVES ON THE PHENOMENON

A. Juvenile Justice in Context: A Special or General Case?

The first issue on my agenda is whether the kind and amount of minority overrepresentation is importantly different in the juvenile-justice system. How does the African-American and Hispanic overrepresentation we observe for delinquency cases in the juvenile system compare to the pattern of concentration of disadvantaged minorities found in the criminal justice system in the United States?

But why should a question about the generality of the pattern that produces minority disadvantage be a starting point for seeking remedial measures? The reason is that the data can be expected to reveal whether the special organizational and substantive provisions of juvenile justice should be regarded as the proximate causes of the problem, so that shifting the special provisions or procedures of juvenile courts could be expected to provide a remedy. If it does, the specific approaches of the juvenile court should be a high priority for reform. If, however, the extent of minority overrepresentation in juvenile justice is about the same as that found in criminal justice, it is less plausible that this pattern is the product of any special characteristics of the juvenile system.

One example of the usefulness of this type of analysis concerns the relative concentration of young girls in incarcerated populations in juvenile justice. Figure 1 turns back the clock to compare juvenile and adult incarcerations by gender for 1974, as a familiar example of looking for special patterns in juvenile justice. The 1974 vintage for these data is to summarize patterns

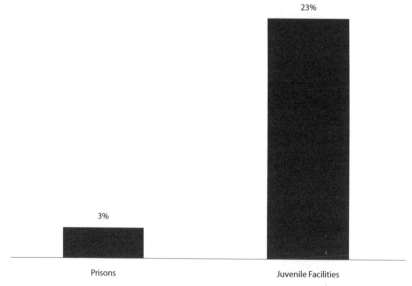

Figure 1. Percentage of incarcerated female persons in 1974.

(Source: Bureau of Justice Statistics [Prisoners]; U.S. Department of Justice, Children in Custody [Juveniles].)

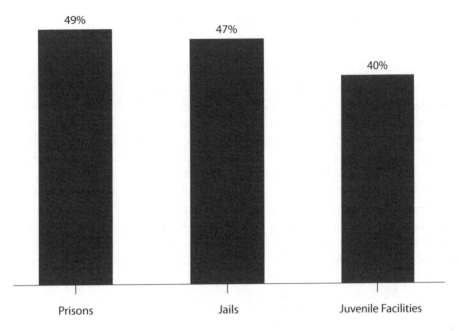

Figure 2. Percentage of incarcerated African-American persons in 1997.

at the time when federal legislation first mandated deinstitutionalizing status offenders.

The 23% of incarcerated juveniles who were female in 1974 constitute a proportion more than seven times that of females then found in prisons. The larger concentration of females in the juvenile distribution is an indication that different motives (including paternalism) and different substantive legal provisions (so-called status offenses) were producing different outcomes in juvenile justice. In such circumstances, reforming these special provisions should be an early priority of those concerned with the high traditional exposure of girls to juvenile incarceration. The juvenile system's rules and procedures have been clearly implicated in female incarceration.

Figure 2 contrasts the percentage of African-Americans in juvenile and adult incarceration facilities in 1997. I dichotomize populations in prisons, jails, and juvenile facilities into African-American and other groups to simplify the analysis. The other major minority group in criminal justice institutions—Hispanic populations—is more difficult to define and more uncertain in current measurements.

The 40% of incarcerated juveniles who are African-American are grossly out of proportion to the African-American percentage of the youth population (about 15%). Thus, overrepresentation is both obvious and substantial. But the concentration of African-Americans incarcerated in adult criminal justice populations is even greater, with close to half of jail and prison populations so classified. If we could add in other minority populations, the size of the total minority shares would increase but the contrast between systems would remain close to that portrayed in figure 2.

The importance of finding this general pattern is not to minimize the problem of juvenile minority overrepresentation, but to alert policy analysts that the pattern extends beyond juvenile justice and is therefore less likely to have been generated by the peculiar rules and procedures that the juvenile system uses. The lower concentration in the juvenile system might actually suggest that shifting juvenile system priorities and procedures to what the criminal justice system does to older offenders would make things worse for minorities. This is the opposite of the likely impact of using adult rules and procedures for young girls that can be inferred from figure 1. So it appears that minorities are at a disadvantage in the juvenile system, but no more so than minority persons are in the rest of the criminal process. What disadvantages minority kids in delinquency cases is part of a broader pattern that probably should be addressed by multiple system approaches.

B. Equalize Disadvantage or Minimize Harm?

My friend and teacher Hans Zeisel once published a note showing that a peculiar kind of disproportion was evident in the death sentences accumulating in the state of Florida. Zeisel found that 95% of the death sentences in that state were imposed on defendants who were charged with killing white victims (Zeisel 1981). Zeisel showed that some Florida prosecutors believed that the solution to this problem was to add more murder cases with African-American victims to Florida's burgeoning death row populations (Zeisel 1981, 464–466). The reason for Zeisel's anger at this tactic was that expanding a cruel and inhuman punishment was the last thing he wished to do, and moving closer to proportional representation by adding African-American-victim cases to death row was a cynical manipulation of the system that again established its arbitrary cruelty. For Zeisel, much more than proportional overrepresentation was wrong with the death penalty system in Florida.

I wonder whether this story has exemplary value for many of us who worry about the overrepresentation of minorities in dead-end detention centers and training schools in 2005. The test question is this: imagine a prosecutor who responds to a finding of imbalance not by releasing minority youth but by trying to lock up many more Anglo-Saxon whites. Would this brand of affirmative action please or trouble the social critic? Why?

Many persons who justly worry about the burden of disproportionate impact on minority youth believe that the deep end of the juvenile-justice system harms kids and they wish to minimize that harm. Expanding the number of kids harmed through an "affirmative action" plan that only adds nonminority targets is perverse from this perspective for two reasons. First, such an expansion of negative controls does not improve the life chances of any of the minority kids. They continue to suffer the same harms at the same rate. Second, the expansion of harms over a wider population hurts many new kids, placing them in positions of disadvantage close to those that troubled the critics about minority kids. Most of those active in addressing issues of minority overrepresentation care deeply about youth of all colors and backgrounds. This grisly form of affirmative action would be, in their view, a step backward.

My point here is that there are two problems that are rather different when addressing the impact of the system on minority kids: the disproportionate impact of sanctions on minorities and the negative effects that these sanctions have on the largely minority kids who are captured by the system. A critic of the system will have two goals—reducing the harm to kids and reducing the proportion of minority kids in the system. But which goal should have the larger priority?

In my view, the more pragmatic a system reformer becomes, the more she will choose measures that reduce the harms that minority kids suffer over programs of better proportional representation. If this is true, then harm reduction creates the opportunity to use concerns about the impact of the system on minority kids as a wedge to reduce the harmful impact of the system on all processed through it. The shift in emphasis from proportional concerns to harm reduction also means that there is no competition between minority and nonminority delinquents, but rather a natural community of interest across group boundaries to make the deep end of the juvenile system less hazardous.

There is also a dark side to the case for emphasizing harm reduction. The sharp edge of the blade in criminal justice almost always falls on disadvantaged minorities, and it is not clear that procedural reform can undo the damage. Some areas of criminal law (traffic and drugs) may respond to administrative controls that reduce the impact on minorities. Spreading traffic stops into nonminority areas can reduce the proportion of traffic arrests and fines that involve minorities. But other arenas, including violence, will remain problematic. Street crimes involve minority suspects more often than white kids for different reasons, and changes in law enforcement procedures will not end the overrepresentation of minority youth arrested for robbery and burglary. As long as minority crime victims are well served by city police, minority suspects will be a disproportionate segment of violence arrests in the United States.

C. Absolute versus Proportionate Standards of Harm in Choosing Reforms

The choice between harm reduction and proportional approaches to overrepresentation will lead to different judgments about which reforms work best. Assume that one reform will leave the proportion of incarcerated delinquents who are minorities the same but reduce the number of kids locked up by 10%. Another approach will lower the proportion of incarcerated minority kids by 10% but leave the number of minorities locked up the same. Which is better? The "least worst" outcome for minority kids in some settings will depend on what standard is selected as the most important measure of the problem. If a proportionate approach is most important, an observer will pick the outcome that results in the smallest percentage of total harm falling on the minority youth population. If a harm reduction standard is used, the observer will try to minimize the amount of harm the minority population suffers regardless of what share of total bad outcomes is absorbed by minority youth.

If highly selective styles of law enforcement concentrate bad outcomes on minorities, then the law enforcement approach that punishes minority kids in the highest percentage might still punish fewer minority kids than a system that spreads a much larger number of harmful outcomes somewhat more evenly across the youth population. The highly discretionary system may be more proportionally unjust than the system that spreads a larger level of punishment more evenly over the youth population, but the amount of harm the broader system does to vulnerable minorities is greater. A principled argument for preferring either outcome can be made. But more important than pointing to a particular preference is recognizing the potential conflict in standards.

My suspicion is that persons with backgrounds in child welfare will be more apt to choose the aggregate harm reduction standard and discount its distributive

implications, while persons with strong legal orientations may be more likely to select higher aggregate harm if it is more evenly distributed.

Whatever might separate those who prefer harm reduction to reducing disproportion when hard choices have to be made, I do not think that different choices can be explained as a liberal-versus-conservative distinction. Instead, I think the conflict highlights the difference between two competing strains of opinion on the left side of the political spectrum that point to different priorities in some circumstances. I will briefly revisit this problem when discussing rules-versus-discretion competitions in reforming the law of transfer of juveniles to criminal court.

D. Evening Out versus Softening Consequences in Delinquency Cases

If minimizing the harm that falls on minority youth becomes the dominant standard for choosing policy in this area, there are many different policy levers available to seek this end. One contrast is between trying to reduce the number of minority kids subjected to harmful results without attempting to alter the consequences of a delinquency finding and trying to lower the amount of aggregate harm suffered by minority kids by reducing the harm produced by juvenile-justice sanctions. The first approach tries to alter the distribution of sanctions but not the sanctions themselves. The second tries to take some of the sting out of the sanctions themselves.

Ultimately, which approach to take when choosing how to attempt reform is an empirical question that general statements cannot illuminate much. But there are some generalizations about such a choice that teach important lessons. The first point is that softening the bite of sanctions becomes a path to a priority reform only because harm reduction is selected as a priority. It is only when harm reduction is isolated as a goal that shifts in the content of sanctions rather than their distribution can compete with redistribution strategies on an equal footing in protecting minority kids.

A second point about taking some of the harm out of sanctions relates to its distributional advantage over reducing the number of minorities punished. The benefits of sanction reform reach all of those punished after the reform. All minorities who are sanctioned benefit, rather than just those who are spared the punishment as the result of a distributional reform. And all delinquents benefit, not merely the minority population. Further, since most youth held for serious acts of delinquency are at a social disadvantage, the nonminority beneficiaries of the process are not all that different from the minority kids who are its core concern.

There is one potential problem with sanction-softening approaches that carries no practical weight in current conditions. A strategy that pushes for reducing the harm in sanctions would generate conflict where the youth advocate feels there are strong social and justice benefits in severe sanctions. However, most youth advocates dislike severe juvenile sanctions, so it seems safe to discount the prospects that youth advocates would be reluctant to reduce the negative impact of recent levels of sanction in American juvenile justice.

A third contrast between proportional reduction strategies and harm reduction strategies concerns the inferences about overrepresentation that justify the approach. A focus on reducing the share of sanctions absorbed by minorities may not require the assumption that some form of discrimination has produced the overrepresentation, but it is certainly much easier to justify proportional remedies when discrimination is suspected. But what if the large percentage of delinquents incarcerated for robbery and homicide from minority backgrounds is matched by arrest rates of minorities for robbery and homicide? By contrast, the question of proving discrimination is not implicated by attempts to reduce the negative impacts on sanctions for all delinquents.

I will not speculate here on the political circumstances that favor emphasis on reducing the concentration of minorities as opposed to reducing the harmful content of sanctions. These two strategies can complement each other in a coordinated program to reduce harm. Here I suspect is the reason that one rarely encounters hard-line policies toward criminal offenders in those interest groups that serve disadvantaged minorities. Minority interest groups become penal reform advocates by structural necessity.

A further implication of the close connection between concern about proportional disadvantage and concern about the harms of juvenile sanctions is that often our worry about disproportion reflects concern about the justice of the harshness of a penal measure. One reason for special concern about the overrepresentation of minorities on American death rows is the feeling that capital punishment is too degrading a sanction for a civilized nation. Our prison populations are just as skewed racially as our death rows, but ambivalence toward the death penalty makes the concentration in death cases a larger concern.

This pattern of larger distrust of more severe sanctions would predict that the expansion of sanctions in blended-jurisdiction juvenile systems, and the legislative trends toward more frequent transfer to criminal court, would exacerbate fears about minority overrepresentation in juvenile justice. Just as lowering the punitive stakes may take some of the bite out of disproportionate minority representation, raising the punitive stakes in the juvenile system can be expected to increase concerns about the extent to which this heavier burden falls on members of disadvantaged minorities.

II. MINORITY DISPROPORTION AND MODERN JUVENILE-JUSTICE REFORMS

The first section of this chapter attempted to provide tools for policy analysis. The aim of this section is to apply the perspectives just outlined to consider the impact of three changes in juvenile-justice policy over the past generation: (1) the proliferation of legislative transfer standards to supplement discretionary waiver by juvenile court judges, (2) the attempt to protect status offenders from secure confinement by creating separate legal categories with restricted dispositional options for status cases, and (3) diversion programs to resolve minor delinquency charges without formal juvenile court charges or adjudications. None of these three reform programs was centrally concerned with minority overrepresentation in delinquency cases; but each set of changes has an impact on minority presence in juvenile and criminal justice. Further, evaluating the impact of such changes on minority prospects is a critical task in contemporary policy analysis. A final part of this section views the substitution of juvenile court for the criminal process as a law reform that has had a positive long-range impact on minority youth in the United States.

A. Automatic Transfer Rules and Minority Harm

Almost all juvenile-justice systems provide a method for transferring some accused delinquents close to aging out of the juvenile system who are charged with serious crimes into criminal court to face the much harsher sanctions than are available in the juvenile system (see Fagan and Zimring 2000). The traditional method of determining whether an older juvenile would be transferred was for a hearing to be held in the juvenile court and for the judge to decide whether he should "waive" the juvenile court's jurisdiction and therefore allow criminal prosecution (Dawson 2000). The issue before a juvenile judge in such a hearing is whether the youth is a fit subject for the juvenile court. This was always a discretionary decision, difficult to review and quite rarely reversed on appeal (Frost Clausel and Bonnie 2000).

This type of discretion would seem an ideal breeding ground for attitudes that prejudice the prospects of African-American and Hispanic juveniles. No precise studies have been done, but the track record of waiver for transferring high proportions of minority youth is not encouraging (Bortner, Zatz, and Hawkins 2000). At the same time, however, the signal virtue of traditional discretionary waiver was the low rate at which juveniles were transferred.

An almost universal addition to discretionary waiver provisions in recent years has been legislation that provides for automatic transfer of juveniles to criminal court if one from among a list of serious charges is brought against the juvenile. The charges frequently listed include murder, armed robbery, rape, and many other serious offenses (Feld 2000). The advantage of this legislative system is that it substitutes a clear rule for personal discretion. The disadvantage is that many more kids of all kinds, including many more minority kids, will be shipped to criminal court under mandatory transfer rules than under systems that transfer juveniles only after juvenile court waiver hearings. Even if the *proportion* of all kids transferred who are African-American or Hispanic goes down with automatic transfer rules, the *number* of minority kids disadvantaged will increase. The rules-versus-discretion choice looks at this first impression like a competition between proportional representation and harm reduction. When automatic transfer replaces discretionary waiver, the number of minority kids harmed will increase even if the share of transferred kids from minority backgrounds declines.

A second look, however, suggests that "automatic transfer" standards have nothing to offer minority kids, not even the certainty of the application of a uniform set of rules. The only discretion less reviewable than a juvenile court judge's is that of a prosecutor, and the adoption of automatic transfer standards really substitutes a prosecutor's discretion for that of a judge. A prosecutor can select the charge to bring against a juvenile, and that charging decision will determine whether the case goes to juvenile or criminal court. No review can force a prosecutor to file more serious charges than he wants to file, or indeed to file any charges at all.

My guess is that the proportion of minorities transferred might go down somewhat in regimes of prosecutorial rather than judicial discretion, but not because prosecutors are more sensitive to minorities. Instead, as the number of juveniles transferred increased substantially, the population transferred would tend to become somewhat more like the general population of accused delinquents. By disadvantaging a much larger fraction of the youth population, the proportional share of minorities hurt by prosecutorial discretion systems might decline, but this is nobody's definition of youth welfare. The number of minority youth at risk of criminal sanctions would be expanded, and it would be small comfort that they had been joined in this vulnerability by larger numbers of nonminority youth.

Further, there is no enforceable legal principle behind this change, only the substitution of prosecutorial for judicial discretion, a shift that moves the locus of authority from a legal actor with a formal commitment to consider the welfare of the accused to a legal actor under no such obligation.

B. Deinstitutionalization of Status Offenders

Since the original juvenile court was presumed to be taking power only for the welfare of its youthful clients, that court was given power to order institutional placements including detention and training schools for young people who were truant or disobedient but had not behaved in ways that harmed others. Since juvenile court sanctions were not regarded as punishment, it was said that there was no need for proportionality limits on power assumed over delinquents, and thus no need to differentiate between burglars and runaways when distributing the juvenile court's helpful interventions.

From the start, this theory suffered from two linked problems. First, the detentions and commitments of juvenile courts were punitive in effect and often in intent, so that imposing them on kids who did not deserve punishment, or imposing much more punishment than disobedience would merit, was manifestly unjust. Second, there was no evidence that the punitive treatment of delinquents in twentieth-century juvenile justice was effective either as therapy or social control (Titlebaum 2002). The legal realism about juvenile justice that produced decisions like *In re Gault* also demanded that proportional limits be placed on the power exercised by the state over runaways, truants, and adolescents in conflict with parents. The particular target of the Federal Juvenile Justice and Delinquency Prevention Act of 1974 was to discourage the states from the practice of putting status offenders in secure confinement. While the effort to break status offenders out of juvenile jails was neither an instant nor an unqualified success, its core judgment that unlimited detention is unjust and ineffective for noncriminal misbehavior has stood the test of time, even with shifting sentiments about many other aspects of juvenile justice.

The shift in status offender policy is rarely considered as an important aspect of policies relating to minority group overrepresentation. The paternalistic excesses of juvenile justice were concentrated on girls, but the status offenders pushed into state processes were no more concentrated among minorities than were delinquents.

But did the emphasis on this policy goal help minority kids? Considering this question again raises the contrast between aggregate and proportional measures of minority disadvantage. The number of African-American and Hispanic kids locked up in detention centers and training schools decreased as a direct result of successful deinstitutionalization. But the proportion of detained kids who were minorities may have increased as a result of the program. Although fewer African-American kids were locked up, a greater proportion of the kids locked up might have been African-American. Was this progress? I would suggest the answer to that question is yes.

But didn't the deinstitutionalization of status offenders strip the veneer of child welfare from the court and thus make harsher policy toward other classes of delinquency more acceptable (Empey 1979, 408–409)? After all, the intense pressure to crackdown on "juvenile superpredators" happened after the welfare facade of the court had been removed. So why not conclude that the latent function of status offender reforms was additional hardship for the largely minority residual of delinquents that stayed in juvenile court systems?

The first problem with such a spin on status offender reforms is that those who supported such reforms were skeptical about secure confinement for delinquents generally. There was no push to fill empty cells with burglars and joyriders from the policy analysts who had pushed the 1974 reforms on the public agenda. Nor did a juvenile court crime crackdown stem in any clearway from the status offender reforms. The get-tough rhetoric and punitive pressure that arrived in juvenile court policy debates in the 1980s were a spillover from crime policy changes in criminal justice that began in the late 1960s (Zimring, Hawkins, and Kamin 2001, chap. 9). The premises and the example of the status offender reforms probably worked against the push for punitive policy in juvenile justice and thus was consistent with the youth welfare interests of minority advocates. I will revisit this issue in the last section of this analysis.

C. Diversion and Minority Justice

What is the impact of reforms aiming to divert first-time and minor offenders from formal processing on the interests of minority offenders in juvenile justice? The policy thrust of diversion seems in harmony with lower levels of coercive controls and concern for youth welfare, but what are the results? Here again, the method of scorekeeping may determine the result. The aggregate impact of diversion on the number of minority youth in formal processing will be a benefit unless the diversion program is a complete sham. If substantial numbers of kids escape detention and adjudication, many of them will be African-American and Hispanic. But even if the number of minority youth benefiting is high, the proportion of those not diverted who are members of disadvantaged minorities will not go down, and it might increase. So a proportionate standard would not produce evidence that diversion had a positive impact on the problem of overrepresentation. Because I believe that harm reduction is the appropriate standard, my conclusion is that diversion programs benefit minority populations.

D. Juvenile versus Criminal Court

The last comparison that teaches us about harm reduction is between the current rate of minority incarceration from juvenile versus criminal courts. The comparison is instructive for two reasons. First, comparing the exposure to harm associated with these two systems is one way of forming a judgment about the aggregate impact of the juvenile court, itself a special reform in American law, on the welfare of minority populations. The second reason to compare aggregate juvenile and criminal court outcomes is to provide an indirect test of the effects that reforms like diversion and deinstitutionalization of status offenders have had on the welfare of minority youth. Comparing a system performing with these features against an alternative system for processing accused criminals might help us decide whether these major thrusts in juvenile justice over recent decades have made the system more or less sympathetic to the interests of minorities.

The juvenile versus adult data based on proportionate overrepresentation of African-Americans show that 40% of all juveniles incarcerated are African-American, a much higher proportion of the total incarcerated population than African-American youth are of the total youth population. Still, the proportion of inmates that are African-American is 20% higher for jails and prisons than for youth institutions.

But the important statistic for my argument is the rate of minority incarceration in juvenile and adult facilities. The incarceration rates for African-American kids in the age 13–17 bracket is 1,332 per 100,000. The rate for African-American males ages 18–24 is 3.5 times higher than for 13–17-year-olds. The adult system is not 20% more punitive than the juvenile system for African-American youth; it is 250% more punitive! I suspect that the same juvenile-versus-criminal-court pattern would hold for other discrete and overrepresented minority male populations. The big difference in incarceration rates suggests that the aggregate protective impact of juvenile-justice policy on minority youth is substantial when compared with criminal justice impact. To borrow a phrase from legal Latin, *res ipsa loquitur*.

CONCLUSIONS

The overrepresentation of disadvantaged minorities in the juvenile-justice system is part of a broader pattern observed throughout law enforcement in the United States and in most other places. The particular doctrines and processes of juvenile courts do not appear to exacerbate overrepresentation when compared to criminal courts. This analysis has contrasted two approaches to the problem of overrepresentation, a legalist view that emphasizes reducing disproportionate impact and a youth welfare view that attempts to reduce the harms suffered by minority youth.

The major positive reforms in juvenile justice over the past generation—deinstitutionalization of status offenders and diversion—have not had a dramatic impact on the disproportionate involvement of minority youth in the deep end of the juvenile system. But the lower levels of incarceration embraced by juvenile courts mean that the harms suffered within juvenile courts by all sorts of youth are much smaller than the harms imposed on young offenders in America's criminal courts. It turns out that the entire apparatus of juvenile justice is functioning as a substantial harm reduction program for minority delinquents.

What I have called a harm reduction perspective shows clearly that those concerned about the healthy development of minority youth must also be invested in the continued operation of the juvenile court as by far the lesser evil in modern crime control. That the institutions of juvenile justice need reform should not obscure the fact of their lesser harm or its policy implications.

REFERENCES

Bortner, M.A., Marjorie S. Zatz, and Darnell F. Hawkins. (2000). "Race and Transfer: Empirical Research and Social Context." In *The Changing Borders of Juvenile Justice*, ed. Jeffery Fagan and Franklin E. Zimring. Chicago: University of Chicago Press.

Dawson, Robert O. (2000). "Judicial Waiver in Theory and Practice." In *The Changing Borders of Juvenile Justice*, ed. Jeffery Fagan and Franklin E. Zimring. Chicago: University of Chicago Press.

Empey, LaMar T. (1979). *The Future of Childhood and Juvenile Justice*. Charlottesville, VA: University Press of Virginia.

Fagan, Jeffrey, and Franklin E. Zimring, eds. (2000). *The Changing Borders of Juvenile Justice*. Chicago: University of Chicago Press.

Feld, Barry C. (2000). "Legislative Exclusion of Offenses from Juvenile Court Jurisdiction: A History and Critique." In *The Changing Borders of Juvenile Justice*, ed. Jeffery Fagan and Franklin E. Zimring. Chicago: University of Chicago Press.

Frost Clausel, Lynda E., and Richard J. Bonnie. (2000). *Juvenile Justice on Appeal*. In *The Changing Borders of Juvenile Justice*, ed. Jeffery Fagan and Franklin E. Zimring. Chicago: University of Chicago Press.

Moone, Joseph. (1993). *Children in Custody 1991: Private Facilities: Prevention Fact Sheet 2, 5*. Washington, DC: Office of Juvenile Justice and Delinquency Prevention.

National Criminal Justice Information and Statistics Service. (1974). *Children in Custody*. Washington, DC: National Criminal Justice Information and Statistics Service.

Titlebaum, Lee. (2002). "Status Offenders." In *A Century of Juvenile Justice*, ed. Margaret Rosenheim, Franklin E. Zimring, David S. Tanenhaus, and Bernardine Dohrn. Chicago: University of Chicago Press.

U.S. Department of Justice, Bureau of the Census. (1997). *Current Population Reports: Estimates of the Population of the United States by Age, Sex, and Race*. Washington DC: U.S. Government Printing Office.

U.S. Department of Justice, Bureau of Justice Statistics. (1974). *Correctional Populations in the United States*. Washington DC: U.S. Government Printing Office.

1997a. *Correctional Populations in the United States*. Washington DC: U.S. Government Printing Office.

1997b. *Children in Custody*. Washington DC: U.S. Government Printing Office.

Zeisel, Hans. (1981). "Race Bias in the Administration of the Death Penalty: The Florida Experience." *Harvard Law Review* 95: 456.

Zimring, Franklin E., Gordon Hawkins, and Sam Kamin. (2001). *Punishment and Democracy: Three Strikes and You're Out in California*. New York: Oxford University Press. Washington, DC: National Criminal Justice Information and Statistics Service.

PROGRAMMING IN THE MODERN JUVENILE COURT

Peter W. Greenwood and Franklin E. Zimring

This final chapter addresses the current role of programming in the U.S. juvenile-court system. As the juvenile court enters its second century, philosophies of juvenile justice have changed markedly from those that were proclaimed with the optimistic rhetoric of intervention in the early years of the court. The modern court recognizes there are serious costs to intervening in the lives of young offenders and restricts its offices to cases of demonstrated seriousness. The modern juvenile court is also only one among many agencies that have evolved to serve youth and is not necessarily the agency of first resort for all children at risk. But the juvenile court of 2005 is still a powerful institution with a clear mandate to adjudicate and dispose of serious offenders in early and middle adolescence.

Earlier chapters have argued that health, education, and human-service agencies are better suited to deliver most prevention services than a court system confined to the already misbehaving and burdened with the stigma associated with delinquency and its control. Nevertheless, I argue in this chapter that extensive programming should be an important component in our society's responses to most serious delinquents—that is to say, that programming still has a central role to play within the juvenile-court system. The attempt to provide programmatic support to the juvenile courts' high-risk offenders is a critical part of the government's approach to providing services for the young.

MISSION AND MORALE IN MODERN JUVENILE JUSTICE

The political complaints about juvenile courts have been loud and effective since the early 1990s. The typical complaint is that the juvenile court is soft on young criminals. In the hyperbole of the *Wall Street Journal*, "the current system is essentially a license to kill. No matter how awful the crime, violent youngsters rarely get more than a suspension or a year or two in jail." (*Wall Street Journal*, 1998). Throughout the 1990s, this assertion of the undue leniency of juvenile courts primarily was based on a comparison between what juvenile courts did with their

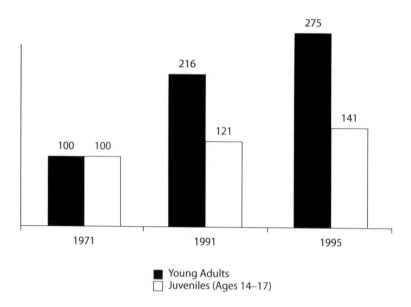

Figure 1. Trends in incarceration rates for juveniles and young adults (Zimring, 2002, fig. 5.2).

charges and the increasingly harsh sanctions of the criminal courts, which reflected major policy changes over the last three decades of the twentieth century.

Figure 1 shows trends in incarceration for juveniles (under eighteen) and young adults over the period 1971–95. It also illustrates a plausible explanation for legislative efforts to put more punitive bite in the policies of American juvenile courts during the 1990s. The first trend is the huge increase in rates of imprisonment in criminal courts for young adults after 1975. Incarceration rates more than doubled in twenty years and in twenty-five years they almost tripled. The second trend is relative stability in juvenile-court incarceration policy. Over twenty-five years, the gross incarceration rate increased by 40 percent, with half of that increase coming in the five years after 1991. That would be a significant increase when compared to most institutional trends, but it is less than a quarter of the growth rate in incarceration for young adults. So there has been a large and growing gap between criminal-court and juvenile-court punishment trends, which explains some of the hostility toward juvenile courts in the early 1990s. Given the wide gap in policy between juvenile and criminal courts, the minimal political damage to juvenile justice is quite remarkable.

There has certainly been some "mission creep" in juvenile courts owing to such innovations as sentencing guidelines and mandatory sentences (Feld, 1988). But the major story in juvenile justice is continuity rather than change, and consistency in mission and programmatic preferences. And business has been brisk. All fifty U.S. states have retained the juvenile court as the primary agency for adjudicating adolescent crime, and only one state lowered its maximum jurisdictional age (Wisconsin, from eighteenth to seventeenth birthday). Figure 2 provides some data on both the volume of juvenile arrests and the mix of offenses for which juveniles are arrested. The figure uses age eighteen as the cutoff point because that is the age threshold in two-thirds of the states; a minority of states use criminal courts to adjudicate seventeen-year-olds and in a few cases sixteen-year-old defendants.

The volume of youth arrests has been relatively stable while the volume of arrests for "index" offenses has declined since the mid-1990s. Figure 3 shows the approximate volume of juvenile justice cases in 1999 at every critical stage of relevance to the design of programs. Again, as in figure 2, there is a separate counting of index and non-index offense cases.

While the overall number of youth processed at each step of the American juvenile justice may seem

Figure 2. Trends in juvenile arrests (Snyder, 2000).

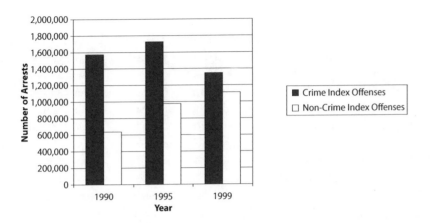

Figure 3. Disposition of juvenile arrests in 1999 (Puzzanchera et al., 2003).

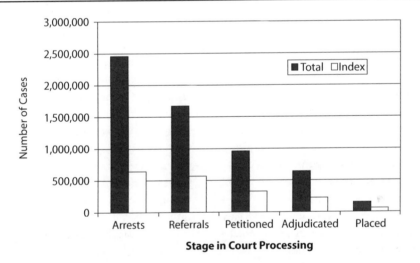

rather large, the most striking characteristic of the system is the steep drop from point to point along the way. The front door of the juvenile court receives about 1.5 million referrals each year, mainly from the police. But petitions beginning the formal adjudicatory process are filed in just over half of these cases. This rejection of hundreds of thousands of cases at what is called "intake screening" is based on a judgment that many cases do not require forceful interventions, that normal processes of maturity in community settings may be a preferable outcome. There is also, even amid the stricter climate characterizing juvenile courts of recent years,

no strong preference for formal over informal methods of disposing of cases.

Each of the major stages of decision-making in the juvenile court can be a basis for formal or informal linkage to treatment programs in community settings. Often juveniles are screened away from petitions because of explicit or implicit agreements to enter drug-, alcohol-, or psychological-counseling programs. Even after petitions are filed, charges are often suspended or dropped when the juvenile offers to enter treatment. And if a youth is adjudicated delinquent, treatment programs are frequently an element of the probationary supervision that is the disposition for a majority of formally processed youth.

The 10 percent or so of juveniles referred to court by arrest and subsequently placed in secure post-adjudication institutions cannot be involved in community-based programs while in secure confinement. For these youth, the choice is between programs that operate within the institution or no programming until the confinement period ends. The traditional preference in youth corrections is to tailor treatment programs to institutional environments, even if the setting compromised the efficacy of many treatment programs.

The danger of institution-based treatment is that the combination of poor quality, low visibility, and a coercive environment may cause a given program to be more harmful than nonintervention. Remember from chapter 4 that even proven programs delivered by incompetent therapists can be harmful, increasing recidivism. Incompetent staff are much more likely to be found in institutional programs than proven models because both expectations and accountability are lower in institutional settings.

Nevertheless, the failure to provide treatment to the most disadvantaged of all juvenile populations would undercut the legitimacy of the entire juvenile-justice system. Since institutional populations include heavy concentrations of disadvantaged minorities and also of the emotionally disturbed (Grisso, 2004), the system must remain committed to serving youth in secure confinement. But substantial resources must also be invested in quality control or the potential for positive program impacts will never really exist.

THE IMPACT OF SECURITY AND PUNISHMENT OBJECTIVES ON PROGRAMMING OPPORTUNITIES IN JUVENILE COURT

A new recruit at a monastery was surprised to see one of the regular members of the order smoking a cigarette while he was kneeling in prayer. "Are we allowed to smoke while we pray," he asked the brother when he got a chance. "I don't know," replied the brother, "but I asked the Monsignor if it was all right to pray while I smoked."

In the previous chapter, I argued that prevention programs should not be run by the same people who are responsible for enforcing sanctions. It is too easy to get the two functions mixed up. Prevention programs, by their very nature, are more effective when they are voluntary. They need to focus on positive reinforcement rather than the negative sanctions. However, just because a youth must be removed from his home and placed in stricter custodial settings because of the seriousness of his offense, there is no reason to give up on efforts to reduce the youth's future offending.

Secure confinement is never an optimal environment for multiphase programming, but any decent custodial setting can accommodate programming for a wide variety of goals such as drug and alcohol prevention, remedial education, anger management, social skills training, and the like. Meta-analyses of custodial programs for juvenile offenders have shown that some types of programs are more effective than others in reducing subsequent recidivism. General program characteristics were found to be more important than the specific type of treatment provided. The following characteristics were found to be associated with greater effectiveness (Lipsey & Wilson, 1998):

- The integrity with which the treatment model is implemented.
- Longer duration of treatment produces better results.
- Well-established programs perform better than brand new programs.
- Treatment administered by mental health professionals is more effective.
- Emphasis on interpersonal skills training.
- Use of the teaching family home methods.

A meta-analysis that looked at custodial programs for both juveniles and adults (Andrews et al., 1990) identified the following factors as being associated with the more effective programs:

- Focusing intervention efforts on higher-risk youth.
- Focusing on dynamic risk factors associated with criminal behavior.

+ Using treatment methods appropriate to the individual.
+ Using proven methods.

The research on custodial programs cited above has demonstrated that such programs can be effective in reducing recidivism, as well as in providing higher levels of public protection and accountability. Furthermore, the most effective of these programs have a number of characteristics in common.

The same meta-analysis that identified the characteristics of effective custodial programs also shows that programs implemented in community settings are more effective than similar programs in custodial settings (Lipsey & Wilson, 1998). Furthermore, participation in some community-based programs that are usually voluntary can be coerced by the juvenile court and still be effective. This finding holds true for compulsory education and drug treatment as well. There are limits, however, to the effectiveness of a coercive approach. Eventually, the targets of the intervention must choose whether to accept and act on the information and guidance provided by the intervention, or to just go through the motions without any real interest or intent of making the necessary changes in their behavior.

The juvenile court is situated in the overlap of societal interests for both preventive interventions and punishment. In many of its dispositions, the juvenile court must recognize the community's need for protection and accountability as well as the offender's need for therapeutic intervention. In fact, there is often a strong correlation between the requirements of punishment or accountability and intervention. A serious criminal act is both a threat to the community and a sign that some significant intervention may be required. Among youth aged six to eleven, participation in general offenses is the most important risk factor for serious delinquency (Lipsey & Derzon, 1998). It is the juvenile court's function to balance these two conflicting demands.

For much of its history, placement in a training school or other institution was seen as the most severe sanction the juvenile court could deliver. However, as reformers have attempted to improve the conditions and the quality of programs within these institutions, they may have lost some of their more punitive aspects.

In some states and communities the use of "balanced and restorative justice" (BARJ) incorporating restitution and community service have become the preferred modes of punishment, providing the offender an opportunity to repair the harm he or she may have caused to the community and the victim (Braithwaite, 1998).

None of the proven programs described in chapter 4 make satisfactory sanctions for those citizens or public officials who demand more punitive approaches. Home visitation, assistance in school, mentoring, having the assistance of a trained therapist to help solve family problems—none of these sound very punitive. Even placement in a therapeutic foster home is usually more benign than placement in a traditional group home.

In many ways, the improved scientific basis for identifying the characteristics of effective prevention programs has made it easier for the court to distinguish between sanctions and treatment—a situation with both positive and negative aspects. On the one hand, the court has less opportunity to place youth in programs that are supposed to be both punitive and preventive, because there aren't any. On the other hand, the court is denied the luxury of resolving a case with a single disposition, and playing up its punitive aspects to victims, while emphasizing its preventive aspects to the youth and his or her family. No more talking out of both sides of the judicial mouth.

For less serious cases, in terms of public safety, the balance should be more toward programming and less toward sanctions. For more serious cases, sanctions will play a bigger role. It is here that the BARJ approach can be used to ensure that the sanctions serve a productive purpose by repairing some of the harm done to the victim and community by the juvenile's offenses.

But even though security conditions and institutional contexts inhibit the effectiveness of treatment programs, the problems associated with treatment during custody are not a conclusive argument against programmatic effort. Effective programming is difficult in institutions, but the evidence in current literature does not demonstrate that it is impossible. The best combination for any youth is a community setting and an effective program. But an institutional setting with programming may still be superior to an institutional setting without it.

The question is not whether youths should be incarcerated while participating in a program; that is the equivalent to the question about smoking while praying in the opening to this chapter. Rather, the question is whether programs should also be available for those youth who must be subjected to secure confinement.

THREE LESSONS FOR JUVENILE COURTS

A number of lessons can be drawn from our review of delinquency-prevention efforts. Three have particular significance for treatment programs in juvenile courts. Two of these lessons identify problems for the court in its pursuit of delinquency-prevention goals. The third identifies a special opportunity. I first consider the problems.

The formal jurisdiction of the juvenile court is rarely a first strike for its subjects. The court stands at the end of a long series of possible interventions in the lives of most troubled youth. Pediatricians, preschools, parents, teachers, school counselors, coaches and other recreational specialists, clergy, and child and family therapists all usually have the chance to help a young person gain control of problem behaviors before resort is made to juvenile court. It is extremely rare for a youth who commits an offense that lands him or her in juvenile court not to have a history of problem behaviors. For so-called chronic or life-course persistent (Moffit et al., 2001) offenders, it will be a long history. For the "adolescent-limited offenders," who do not exhibit problem behaviors until after puberty, the history may be relatively short, but it will still be there. Delinquency begins with small acts of misbehavior and progresses to the more severe. The youth's appearance in juvenile court is a clear indication that the previous efforts at intervention failed, or at least did not accomplish all that was hoped. This is one of the problems the juvenile court must take account of.

It might be hoped that the impact of a sequence of intervention efforts would be cumulative, that each successive effort would add to the gains achieved by the previous efforts until the appropriate level was reached to prevent further recidivism. Unfortunately this is ordinarily not the case. Given the state of current practice, many of the interventions that may be tried may prove to be ineffective or inappropriate for the particular situation. Thus few if any positive impacts are achieved. In fact, the cumulative effect of previous efforts to intervene with troubled youth may be negative in that they exacerbate existing problems, reinforce negative labeling, and reduce expectations of help from additional intervention.

Failure to respond positively to an intervention that is touted as appropriate for a given situation produces negative expectations for the youth, their families, and the community in which they reside. The youth becomes more skeptical about the consequences of intervention, experienced in manipulating the interventionists or in avoiding the therapeutic thrust of their efforts, and more convinced of his or her own identity as a troubled youth. The family typically becomes more annoyed or angry at the youth or the intervening party, and more pessimistic about the potential for positive change. The system typically blames the failure of the intervention on the youth and not on the intervention program. The entry made in the juvenile's record is "failure to adjust."

So its relatively late position in the delinquency-prevention chain of interventions puts the juvenile court at a disadvantage. In addition to all of the other risks and problems that youths will face, by the time that they arrive in the juvenile court they will bear the additional stigma as one who does not respond positively to programs nor take advantage of help when it is offered.

This leads to the second problem facing juvenile courts: the negative labeling that any involvement in court-based programming involves. Youth involved with the juvenile court will be seen as more at risk than other adolescents. Being placed under the jurisdiction of the juvenile court only adds to the cumulative negative-labeling process that may have characterized all previous attempts at intervention. This process affects not only the youth involved but parents and interventionists as well. It is a significant disadvantage indeed, and one reason that diversion from formal processing has retained its attractiveness.

If the filtering-out of less serious cases has been done correctly, the juvenile court comes up to bat with two strikes against it: negative expectations on the part of youth and their families regarding attempts at successful intervention, and the potential that the youth will experience additional negative labeling from any intervention it attempts. But it also comes up to bat with the bases loaded. The juvenile court's unique advantage over every other potential venue for prevention programming is the high level of risk represented by its subjects. School-based or community-based programs for delinquency prevention may involve considerably less stigma, but they also must deal with youth from a much lower risk pool. Because they deal with youth in the highest risk categories, prevention programs sponsored by the juvenile court can afford to expend significantly more funding on each individual case, and still expect the potential benefits to exceed those costs. According to the cost-benefit analyses conducted by the Washington State Institute for Public Policy (Aos et al., 2001), this is clearly the case for such programs as Functional Family Therapy, Multisystemic Therapy, Multidimensional Treatment Foster Care, and Aggression Replacement Training.

FROM PREVENTION TO PROGRAMS: THE ROLE OF JUVENILE COURTS

Primary prevention addresses risk factors that apply to the population in general—for example, the use of alcohol, tobacco, or other illegal drugs. Secondary prevention addresses populations identified as being at a higher risk level than the general population, but not yet involved in delinquency.

From the description of the programs and the arguments presented in the previous chapters, it should be clear that operational responsibility for primary and secondary delinquency-prevention programs belongs outside the justice system in institutions dedicated to issues of education, health, and human services. These agencies are better suited to deliver the types of services these programs require, and are able to do so without the negative-labeling effects associated with the juvenile court.

But just because many programs should be carried out apart from justice-system involvement, it is an error to suppose that no prevention programming should be vested in juvenile courts. Programs can be cost effective even working with previous program failures.

Furthermore, a juvenile-justice system with a diversified portfolio of tertiary prevention programs is far superior to a court without treatment resources. Indeed, indications of program effectiveness in any domain should argue for more rather than less emphasis on programming throughout the system.

There is no level of custody that does not warrant some programming. The greater the level of custody probably the greater the need for programs. Even though the often-cited Lipsey and Wilson (1998) meta-analysis does show that community-based interventions are more effective, it also shows that custodial programs can also have positive impacts. If a custodial facility does not provide therapeutic programming, then that facility does not belong under the jurisdiction of the juvenile court.

The specific responsibilities that juvenile courts need to assume in order to ensure appropriate programs are deployed effectively include the following: awareness of the current evidence base; diversion of cases that can be handled informally outside the system; disposition of cases to appropriate programs; and quality control. I consider these responsibilities in turn.

Awareness of Current Evidence Base

Just because the juvenile courts are not responsible for every delinquency-prevention program does not mean they shouldn't stay abreast of the latest research and developments in the delinquency-prevention field. It is the court that in the end must hold the rest of the system accountable. Health and education institutions are likely to miss some new developments in delinquency prevention because their attention is directed mainly to new research in their own primary fields. The juvenile court has a role to play in ensuring that such information does not slip through the cracks.

Diversion

Intervention at the level of the juvenile court is an expensive proposition. Most programs are far from cheap, and the findings in regard to negative labeling and deviant peer contagion suggest that some can do more harm than good. The juvenile court is in the best position to distinguish between those cases that can be handled informally by diversion to appropriate services and those that require more formal proceedings.

Disposition

The juvenile court should consider programming needs as well as sanctions as part of the disposition of any case. It must do to develop an empirical basis for determining which programs work best for particular types of juvenile offenders, and for deciding when a youth needs to be removed from a particular program and placed in another. The availability of standardized assessment instruments (Grisso & Underwood, 2004) and more evidence-based programs can take some of the guesswork out of what has traditionally been a hit-or-miss process.

Quality Control

The juvenile court is in an excellent position to identify gaps in the current program mix and identify programs that are not performing up to their true potential. The court is in a good position from which it can observe the failures of other agencies. The records of individual cases that come before the court provide informative case studies of how well the system is currently performing and where there are screening, assessment, or programming gaps.

CREDITS

Modes and Patterns of Social Control: Implications for Human Rights Policy, pp. iii–ix, 5–11, 79–80, 83. Copyright © 2010 by International Council on Human Rights Policy. Reprinted with permission.

Stuart Henry, "Why People Ban Behavior," *Social Deviance*, pp. 25–43. Copyright © 2009 by Polity Press. Reprinted with permission.

Melissa Thompson, "The Mental Health and Criminal Justice Systems as Agents of Social Control," *Mad or Bad? Race, Gender, and Mental Disorder in the Criminial Justice System*, pp. 1–11. Copyright © 2010 by LFB Scholarly Publishing. Reprinted with permission.

Michael T. Costelloe and Raymond J. Michalowski, "Social Class and Crime," *21st Century Criminology: A Reference Handbook*, ed. J. Mitchell Miller, pp. 153–161. Copyright © 2009 by Sage Publications. Reprinted with permission.

Sean P. Hier, Dan Lett, Kevin Walby, and André Smith, "Beyond Folk Devil Resistance: Linking Moral Panic and Moral Regulation," *Criminology and Criminal Justice*, vol. 11, no. 3, pp. 259–276. Copyright © 2011 by Sage Publications. Reprinted with permission.

Meghan G. McDowell and Nancy A. Wonders, "Keeping Migrants in Their Place: Technologies of Control and Racialized Public Space in Arizona," *Social Justice*, vol. 36, no. 2, pp. 54–72. Copyright © 2009 by Social Justice. Reprinted with permission. Provided by ProQuest LLC. All rights reserved.

Larry K. Gaines and Victor E. Kappeler, "Police Discretion," *Policing in America*, pp. 231–280. Copyright © 2008 by Elsevier Science and Technology. Reprinted with permission.